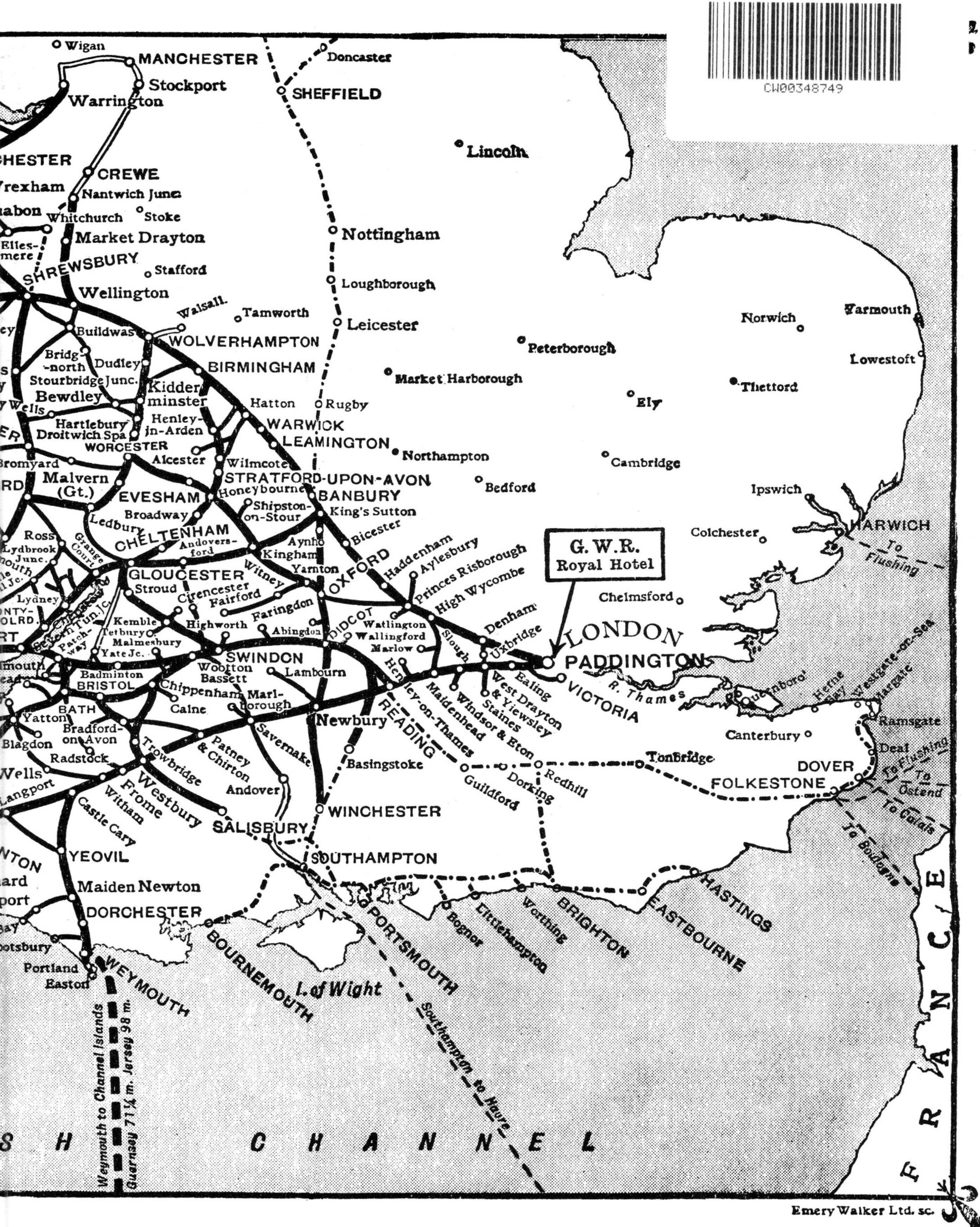

Emery Walker Ltd. sc.

Encyclopaedia of the

Great Western Railway

Patrick Stephens Limited, a member of the Haynes Publishing Group, has published authoritative, quality books for enthusiasts for a quarter of a century. During that time the company has established a reputation as one of the world's leading publishers of books on aviation, maritime, military, model-making, motor cycling, motoring, motor racing, railway and railway modelling subjects. Readers or authors with suggestions for books they would like to see published are invited to write to: The Editorial Director, Patrick Stephens Limited, Sparkford, Nr. Yeovil, Somerset, BA22 7JJ.

Encyclopaedia of the
Great Western Railway

Principal contributors
Christopher Awdry J. H. Russell
Michael H. C. Baker Peter Semmens
Geoffrey Body Adrian Vaughan

Edited by
William Adams

Patrick Stephens Limited

First published in 1993.

British Library Cataloguing in Publication Data.

A catalogue record for his book is available from the British Library.

ISBN 1 85260 329 1

Library of Congress Catalog Card No 92 75641.

Extracts from the *Great Western Railway Magazine* are reproduced by courtesy of InterCity Great Western.

Area maps drawn by Ian G. Body.

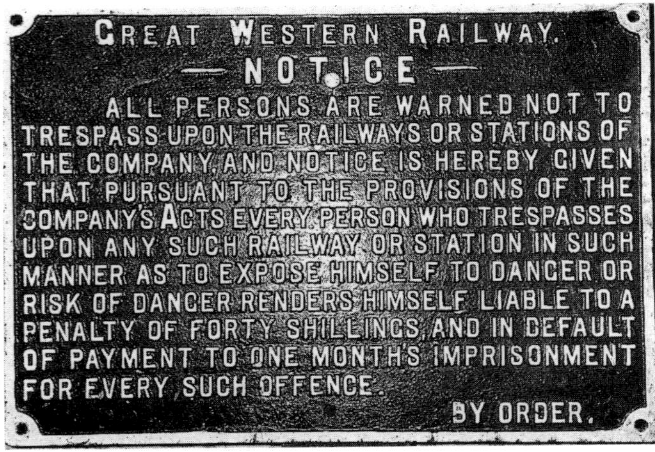

Patrick Stephens Limited is a member of the Haynes Publishing Group P.L.C., Sparkford, Nr Yeovil, Somerset BA22 7JJ.

Typeset by BPCC Techset Ltd, Marsh Barton, Exeter, Devon EX2 8RP.
Printed in Great Britain by Butler & Tanner Ltd, Frome and London.

10 9 8 7 6 5 4 3 2 1

Opposite *Ready for the off. A publicity photo advertising the new 'Sunshine' 3rds, March 1936.* (GW Society)

CONTENTS

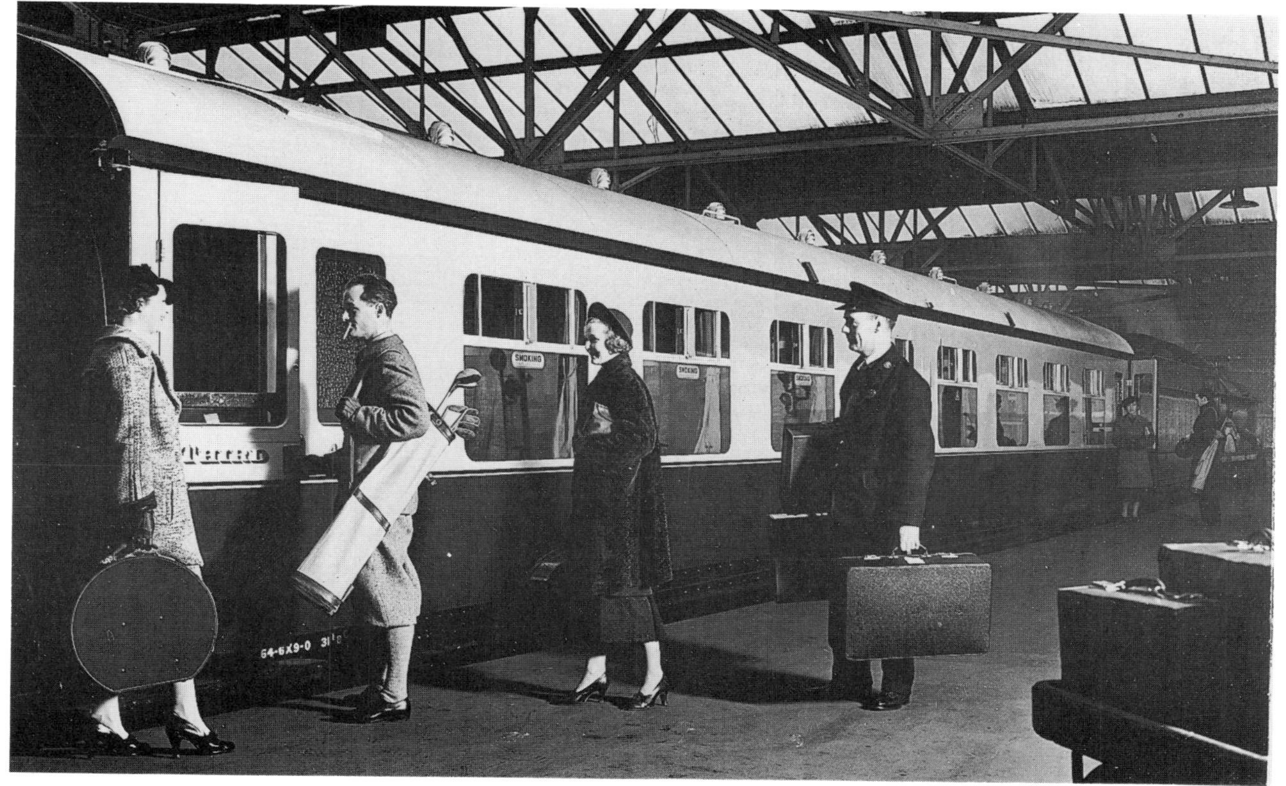

NOTES ON THE CONTRIBUTORS

Christopher Awdry
It was an attack of measles at the age of three that led to Christopher Awdry's father, the Rev Wilbert Awdry, to tell him the original 'Thomas the Tank Engine' stories; the family home was in Wiltshire, and Rev Awdry got the 'I can't do it, I can't do it' idea from listening to goods trains struggling up to Box tunnel, circa 1918. Christopher's other association with the GWR is that his great grandfather was a subscriber and first Director of the Wilts, Somerset & Weymouth Railway (taken over by the GWR in 1851).

Now a full-time writer, Christopher's previous books for PSL have been *Encyclopaedia of British Railway Companies* and *Brunel's Broad Gauge*.

Michael H. C. Baker
Before he was 1 year old Michael Baker had made his first GWR train journey, between Paddington and Shrewsbury, and has made the journey at least once a year ever since. A teacher at Swanage Middle School, he has been Editor of *Great Western Echo*, the quarterly journal of the Great Western Society, since 1978, and is also the author of some 15 books and numerous articles on the GWR and other railways, as well as buses, trams, places and people.

Geoffrey Body
Geoff Body joined the LNER just before Nationalisation, and was able to experience the traditional railway first-hand. He was thus able to relate easily to the former GWR area when the course of a 25-year railway career took him to the West of England Division which stretched from Swindon and Weymouth to Worcester and Penzance.

Author/editor of 25 railway and transport books, Geoff now uses his extensive research and records of the old GWR in his writing and publishing business. He has also worked in the container and road haulage fields and is a Member of the Chartered Institute of Transport.

Previous books for PSL include the 'Field Guide' series to the BR regions and, most recently, *Railway Stations of Britain*.

J. H. Russell
The GWR played a large part in Jim Russell's life. He worked for the company until 1945 on the locomotive side, as his father had done before him in the Traffic Department on the Birmingham Division. During the war he served with the Great Western 154 Railway Operating Corps, Royal Engineers, in France.

One of the original founders of the Talyllyn Preservation Society, he was an author for 20 years, writing extensively on the GWR in particular. This was his first work for PSL, but he was well-known for his authoritative books on GWR locomotives and rolling-stock published by OPC. Sadly, Jim died suddenly in February 1991.

Peter Semmens
Peter Semmens is a Cornishman, having been born at Saltash. After taking a degree in chemistry, he worked in that industry until becoming Assistant Keeper of the National Railway Museum from 1975 until his retirement in 1987.

He now devotes his time fully to writing, lecturing and broadcasting, and is author or part-author of 25 books, many on the GWR. He is also Chief Correspondent of *The Railway Magazine*, for whom he writes the 'Locomotive Practice & Performance' article, the longest-running railway column in the world.

His previous books for PSL deal with the modern developments on the former LNER main line, *Speed on the East Coast Main Line* and *Electrifying the East Coast Route*.

Adrian Vaughan
Adrian grew up with GWR trains in a family with Great Western connections going back to the days of the Broad Gauge. Introduced to the signal box at the age of seven, and to locomotives at 11, he joined the Western Region of BR in 1960 as a porter at Challow, still retaining its pre-Nationalization atmosphere. The following year he became a signalman there. His last box, in 1975, was Witham in Somerset.

Now a full-time writer, his first book, *Great Western Portrait*, was published in 1971, but he is perhaps best known for the highly acclaimed 'Signalman' trilogy published by John Murray. As well as many articles for railway magazines, he has written 17 books. His first for PSL, *Obstruction Danger*, dealt with railway accidents, and his latest work, again for John Murray, is a biography of Isambard Kingdom Brunel.

William Adams
A lifelong railway enthusiast who suffered a deprived childhood through being brought up in Coventry, an impregnable LNWR/LMS stronghold, 15 miles from the nearest Great Western line, he nonetheless survived to become Railway Books Editor for Patrick Stephens Limited between 1987 and 1990, and is now a freelance editor and Editorial Consultant to Silver Link Publishing Ltd.

INTRODUCTION

'Throughout its history,' wrote Hamilton Ellis in 1950, 'out of all its virtues and faults, there emerged a singular quality of the Great Western. It was a majestic railway.' *(Four Main Lines,* Allen and Unwin). He then went on to make 'some less reverent observations', concluding them by saying that 'Literary cadenzas must end, and business-like recording begin, but is is difficult to approach the more prosaic side of the Great Western because of the very reason that its history has been written and published so often.'

And that was in 1950 – the boom years of railway publishing had yet to come! One only has to glance at the Bibliography on page 308 to see a mere selection of upwards of 175 titles devoted to all aspects of the GWR. But for the student, author, historian and general enthusiast, there are very few opportunities to encapsulate all that knowledge in a manageable package—and one would need to be very much a devotee, and of considerable means, to justify the expense of even a proportion of the books listed.

It was this plethora of product that became the raison d'être of this Encyclopaedia, to attempt in as concise yet readable and 'dip-into-able' a manner as possible to 'approach the more prosaic side of the Great Western'. I would venture to say that nowhere is so much information and scholarship available in a single book on the GWR, for which as editor I should take very small credit, but rather express my thanks and appreciation to the contributors, whose book this is. In particular I would like to thank Geoff Body, whose help and sound advice lay the initial foundations on which the Encyclopaedia was built. (Incidentally, the reason why the GWR was chosen as the subject was not entirely because of its perennial popularity, but because uniquely the company retained its individual identity throughout and it was thus easier to marshall the facts logically, If, as is hoped, further volumes on the remaining three of the 'Big Four' are undertaken, the storyline will be less clear-cut!).

Basically, this Encyclopaedia was a book that I needed on my shelves, which is as good an impetus as any to creation. I'm interested in railways generally, and have a family and mortgage to support, so have only a modest collection of books on the GWR. Yet as a railway enthusiast and editor of railway books, I am constantly trying to find straightforward answers to various items of minutiae, spending hours poring over books that are inadequately indexed or simply don't, or don't need to, contain the crumb of information I need. The idea, then, was to present alphabetical entries on the places, companies, people, locomotives and rolling-stock, services and general lore of the Great Western Railway.

It must be stressed, however, that even in a fairly substantial book such as this, there is only space to present the bare bones of the information, albeit fleshed out with a little anecdote and trivia. Inevitably, the finer points, the minutiae, of a subject may have had to be generalized in order to convey an overall picture. And this is where the Bibliography comes in—as a signpost to far more detailed examinations of the topics than could ever be accommodated here.

As I said earlier, this is a contributed book, so inevitably the various aspects of the GWR are seen from varying perspectives, which I hope will add variety and humanity to the facts and figures. If, as reader, historian or researcher, you feel that, after all, there are a few significant stones that have been left unturned, do please write to me via the Publisher so we can tune what I hope may be future editions.

At the very least I hope the vast range of information contained herein will allow the GWR enthusiast for once to stand back from the individual cylinder diameter, Siphon livery variation, or branch line terminus signalling layout and view this quite remarkable organisation *as a whole*—not as a pageant created by Brunel, Dean, Churchward et al specifically for the entertainment of photographers and partisan enthusiasts for 113 years, but as a commercial enterprise, a body of men, a great machine striving more or less successfully to provide a service—and a profit—in the days when such things were not as totally incompatible as they are today.

William Adams
Denford
Northants

Acknowledgements

My debt to the principal contributors has already been mentioned, but many other individuals and organisations have given invaluable assistance, amongst them the staff of various libraries, Tim Bryan, Keeper of the Great Western Railway Museum at Swindon, and the staff of the National Railway Museum at York. In addition, many individuals provided information on specific specialist matters, and they are credited with the entry concerned.

The illustrations have been collected from many sources and, again, are credited individually. To all these sources my thanks for allowing me the free run of the various collections.

Finally, thanks to Patrick Stephens Limited, and their Editorial Director, Darryl Reach, for taking on this Leviathan and for giving me so free a hand in its preparation.

W.A.

Pre-First World War development of the Great Western: five maps showing the growth of the system between 1838 and 1913. (GWR Magazine)

NOTES AND ABBREVIATIONS

The main headings are, of course, alphabetically arranged, but since 'Swindon', for example, will appear in many more entries than simply under the main 'Swindon' heading, a full Index is also provided, which should be consulted if general information on a specific subject is required. In addition, there are certain places which are not sufficiently important to merit their own entry, but which are mentioned on numerous occasions in other entries, so again refer to the Index.

Cross references between entries are marked by '(qv)', indicating that further information can be found by referring to the entry under the word or words immediately preceding the 'qv', or under the different heading indicated.

'Location' headings are divided between specific companies, 'lines' in the geographical sense, and individual places. Full cross referencing between these categories is given as appropriate within each entry and, again, via the Index. In the main, Welsh spellings of station names etc have been anglicized to the form used by the GWR. Unless a period is quoted, descriptions of train services will be those applying at most periods (inter-war timetables have been used as references).

ABBREVIATIONS

The following are the most commonly used abbreviations—others are used, but are given in full where they first occur within an entry.

B&H	Berks & Hants (Railway)
B&M	Brecon & Merthyr (Railway)
CamR	Cambrian Railways
DN&S	Didcot, Newbury & Southampton (Railway)
GCR	Great Central Railway
GWR	Great Western Railway
GW&GCJ	Great Western & Great Central Joint (Railway)
LB&SCR	London, Brighton & South Coast Railway
LMS	London Midland & Scottish Railway
LNER	London & North Eastern Railway
LNWR	London & North Western Railway
LSWR	London & South Western Railway
MS&LR	Manchester, Sheffield & Lincolnshire Railway (later GCR)
MR	Midland Railway
M&SWJ	Midland & South Western Junction (Railway)
N&B	Neath & Brecon (Railway)
NER	North Eastern Railway
OW&WR	Oxford, Worcester & Wolverhampton Railway
RR	Rhymney Railway
SER	South Eastern Railway
SR	Southern Railway
TVR	Taff Vale Railway

KEY TO STATION LAYOUT PLANS

CP	Cattle pens
ES	Engine shed
GF	Ground frame
GS	Goods shed
LD	Loading dock
SB	Signal box
SO	Station offices
TT	Turntable
WT	Water tower or column

KEY TO AREA MAPS

GWR lines

Other companies' lines

Joint lines

Constituent lines

Closed or in tunnel

Siding, works or light railway

Station, halt or depot

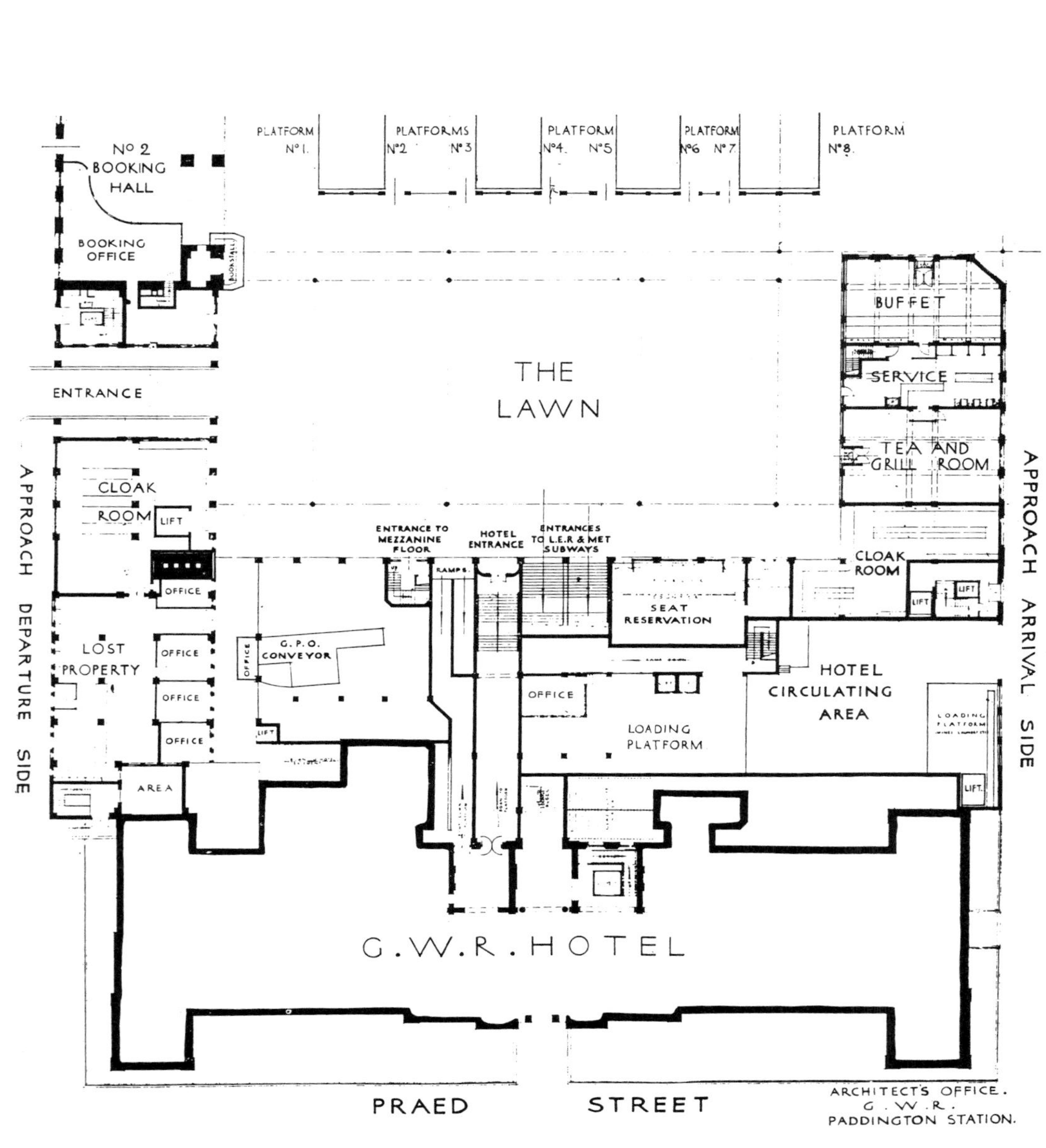

Starting point: plan of the new 'Lawn' at Paddington following the remodelling of 1934. (GWR Magazine)

ABBOTSBURY BRANCH

Stations: Upwey Junction (2¼ miles from Weymouth), Upwey (2¾ m), Portesham (6¾ m), Abbotsbury (8¼ m)

The 6 m 3 ch single line running west from the Dorchester–Weymouth line to the small town of Abbotsbury was a local enterprise, incorporated as the Abbotsbury Railway on 6 August 1877, opened on 9 November 1885 with the help of GWR capital, and taken over by the Great Western on 1 August 1896. The six weekday trains each way worked to and from Weymouth, took 24 minutes on their journey and called at two halts, Radipole and Coryates. Operation was by train staff and one engine in steam regulations, with the motive power usually 0-4-2 tanks. The station master at Upwey controlled the branch which had a ruling gradient of 1 in 44 and an upper speed limit of 40 mph.

GB

ABERAYRON BRANCH

Stations: Lampeter, Felin Fach (7¼ m), Ciliau–Aeron (9¾ m), Aberayron (13½ m)

Authorized by the Lampeter, Aberayron & New Quay Light Railway Order of 9 October 1906, this steeply graded independent line worked by the GWR ran from a junction north of Lampeter to a single platform terminus at Aberayron; it opened on 10 April 1911 for goods and 12 May for passengers. Its 12 m 10 ch course along the River Aeron had a passing loop at Felin Fach and five halts in addition to the main stations. The basic weekday service of four trains each way plus a school train between Aberayron and Felin Fach was worked by an auto shuttle, and the daily pick-up goods cleared the milk and agricultural traffic.

The line passed to the GWR at Grouping, its extension from Ciliau-Aeron to Newquay unbuilt.

GB

ABERBEEG

As the junction between the Newport–Brynmawr line and the branch to Ebbw Vale, Aberbeeg was constantly busy with passenger and freight trains. About 100 of the former called at either the two Brynmawr or two Ebbw Vale platforms each weekday, while the latter included the heavy ore trains up to the steelworks, slab and other products in the reverse direction, and a succession of coal trains from both routes.

Originating as early Monmouthshire Railway & Canal Company tramroads (qv), the two lines joined at the south end of Aberbeeg's pairs of platforms. To the north stood the goods depot, and on the Llanhilleth side the four-line engine shed with its allocation of tanks for train, shunting and banking duties.

GB

ABERDARE

The iron industry of the Aberdare Valley led to the incorporation of the Aberdare Railway on 31 July 1845 with opening between Abercynon and Aberdare Mill Street in the following year, and leasing to the Taff Vale Railway from 1 January 1849. The TVR company ran a passenger service from Pontypridd calling at Abercynon (3¼ m), Penrhiwceiber (6 m), Mountain Ash (7¼ m), Aberaman (9¾ m) and Aberdare Low Level (10¾ m). The route had links to the Aberdare Iron Co network, to Bwllfa Dare Colliery and to the GWR's Cwmaman branch and main line.

The GWR higher level line, part of the Neath–Pontypool Road route, was made up of the Vale of Neath line (qv) opened on 24 September 1851 and its extension to Middle Duffryn by the Aberdare Valley Railway five years later. The VofN line through Abernant and Merthyr Tunnel to Merthyr proper dates from 2 November 1853, the Nantmelyn Colliery Branch from 7 November 1854, that to Cwmaman Colliery from November 1856 and to Bwllfa Dare Colliery from 1 June 1857.

In addition to its two-platform station, goods depot and exchange sidings, Aberdare High Level was home to an allocation of some 60 locomotives.

GB

ABERGAVENNY

After all sorts of difficulties, the Newport, Abergavenny & Hereford Railway (qv) managed to open its line between Hereford and Pontypool on 6 December 1853 and gave Abergavenny its first station on 2 January 1854. The NA&H line was then joined by what was to become the LNWR's 'Heads of the Valleys' route, the connection being altered to north-facing and Abergavenny Junction station being opened just north of it from 20 June 1870.

Abergavenny proper had a local service to and from Newport, other slow services called at both stations and some longer distance trains on the 'North and West' route called at the GWR main station only. The service west from Abergavenny Junction included through trains from Hereford and Shrewsbury.

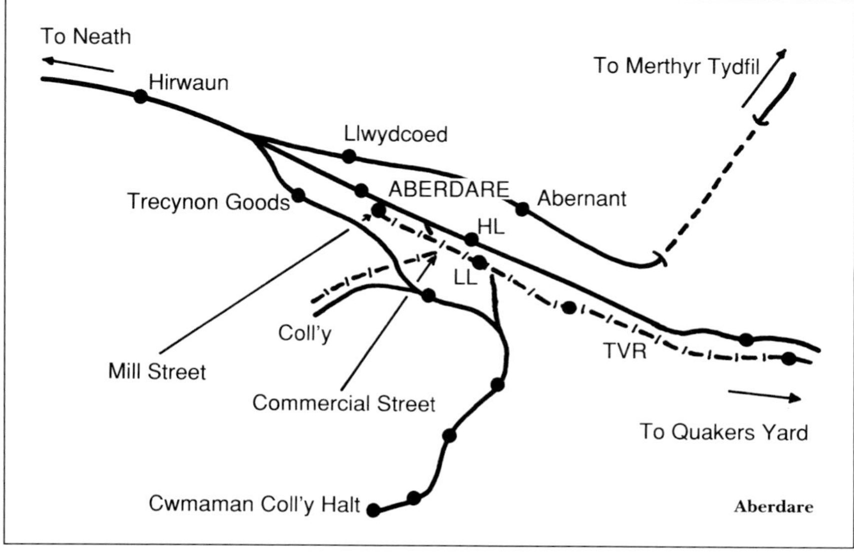

Aberdare

Both Abergavenny stations were joint locations with main and island platforms, Junction having an extra bay line and the LNWR/LMS engine and carriage sheds. The Great Western had its goods facilities at the Monmouth Road location and both companies served the coal wharf and Mental Hospital siding.

GB

ABERGWYNFI BRANCH

Stations: Bridgend, Tondu (3 m), Llangynwyd (6½ m), Troedyrhiew Garth (7 m), Maesteg Castle Street (8½ m), Nantyffyllon (9¼ m), Caerau (10¼ m), Cwmmer General (11½ m), Abergwynfi (14 m)

Pannier tanks and auto-train-fitted 2-6-2Ts worked most of the services on the three valley lines to the north of Tondu. That up the Llynvi Valley was the senior, dating back to the 4 ft 7 in gauge Duffryn Llynvi & Porthcawl Railway opened in 1829 and converted from horse to locomotive working on a new alignment by the Llynvi Railway in 1861. Under GWR management (an extension from Nantyffyllon was opened on 1 July 1878 (passengers 16 July 1880), this involving a 1 in 37 climb to Caerau and a long tunnel to Cwmmer. Abergwynfi was reached on 22 March 1886.

The route, which carried a Maesteg–Cwmmer service in addition to its through trains, was crossed by the Port Talbot Railway (qv) at Maesteg and connected with the Rhondda & Swansea Bay (qv) and South Wales Mineral lines at Cwmmer. It terminated at a single-platform hillside station, behind which ran the connection to Avon Colliery.

GB

ABERLLEFENNI BRANCH

Stations: Machynlleth, Fridd Gate (½ m), Llwyngwern (2½ m), Esgairgeiliog (3½ m), Corris (5 m), Garneddwen (6 m), Aberllefenni (6½ m)

Acquired by the GWR on 4 August 1930, this 2 ft 3 in gauge line through the Dulas Valley had started life as the Corris, Machynlleth & River Dovey Tramroad but is best known as the Corris Railway, the name it took in 1864. After securing its Act on 12 July 1858, the narrow gauge concern had opened to a wharf at Derwenlas on the River Dovey on 30 April 1859, but then abandoned the section beyond Machynlleth after the main line had been opened and slate traffic could be exchanged there.

The Corris company was acquired by Imperial Tramways of Bristol in 1878 and, after improvements, passenger services began between Machynlleth (qv) and Corris on 4 July 1883, with extension to Aberllefenni on 25 August 1887. Traffic was stimulated by horse bus services on to Cader Idris and Talyllyn Lake and a round trip facility with the Talyllyn and Cambrian railways. Slate traffic from the Corris main line and its Upper Corris and Ratgoed branches was brought down to a complex of wharves and exchange sidings at Machynlleth, where the two stations were within walking distance.

The GWR withdrew passenger services from 1 January 1931 but a daily freight train continued until 1943 when its frequency was reduced. Formal closure followed floods in August 1948.

GB

ABERYSTWYTH

The first Aberystwyth station was provided by the Aberystwyth & Welsh Coast Railway when its line from Machynlleth brought the first passenger trains to the town on 23 June 1864. Before the year was out there was a link with Euston, and on 12 August 1867 the Carmarthen line became operational. The two approaches became Cambrian and Great Western respectively and a major station remodelling followed their combination at the Grouping.

Aberystwyth station had a substantial frontage block leading to a glazed concourse area and five platform lines, all with engine release points to facilitate running round. The services from Paddington, Birmingham and the North West used platforms 1–3, and those from Carmarthen platforms 4 and 5. The station's goods depot lay on the north side and the engine shed alongside the down main, with sidings for holiday trains opposite.

The Great Western's 1 ft 11½ in gauge Vale of Rheidol Railway (qv Devil's Bridge branch), opened in 1902, used a separate Aberystwyth station in Smithfield Road.

GB

ABINGDON BRANCH

This 2¼-mile single-line branch paralleled the Oxford–Didcot line south from the down side island platform at Radley and then followed the Thames west to a pleasant, one-platform station and goods depot at Abingdon. Dropped from the original Oxford Railway (qv) proposals as a result of objections from the local MP, the line was then authorized to the Abingdon Railway on 15 June 1855 and opened to an exchange station where the main line bridged the Thames on 2 June 1856. Conversion from broad to standard gauge in 1872 was followed by the 61-chain extension north to a new station at Radley on 8 September 1873.

The GWR worked the branch, and took it over from the independent company in

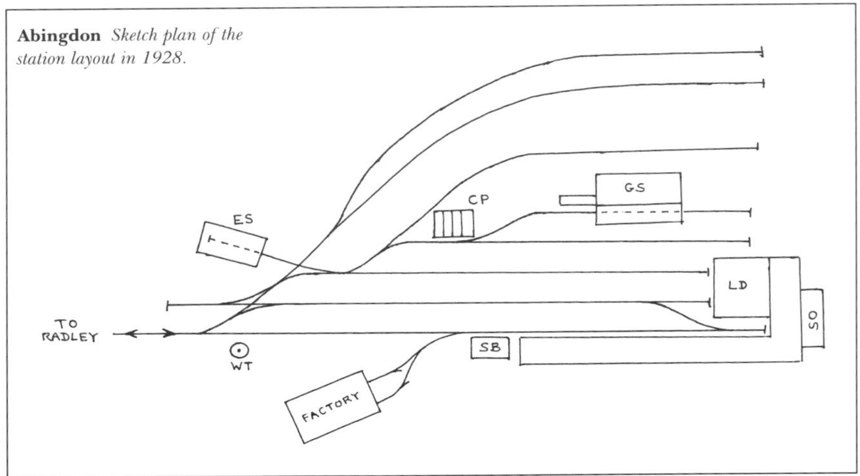

Abingdon *Sketch plan of the station layout in 1928.*

1904, subsequently providing an auto-train service of some 18 daily workings each way on weekdays.

GB

ACCIDENTS

There were innumerable small collisions and derailments on the GWR resulting in injuries and sometimes even fatalities. The following list is by no means complete, but gives a representative selection as well as all the major accidents.

Faringdon Road (later Challow) station, 25 October 1840
First recorded fatal train accident on GWR. Down goods train hauled by *Fire King* failed to stop at station, then temporary terminus of the GWR, and crashed through doors of engine shed. Driver was thought to have been asleep due to long hours on duty. 1 killed.

Sonning Cutting, 24 December 1841
Down goods train hauled by *Hecla* ran into landslide and was derailed. 8 killed.

Shrivenham station, 10 May 1848
12 noon Exeter train, hauled by *Sultan*, Driver Bob Roscoe, crashed into horse-box placed on up main line by porters without first consulting station policeman in charge of signals. 6 killed.

Aynho, 1 October 1852
Special train of GWR Directors and friends, drawn by *Lord of the Isles* with Brunel and Gooch on footplate, mistook disused signal, ran past actual signal at 'Danger' and crashed into rear of train stationary in Aynho station. No fatalities.

West London Crossing, end November 1855
GWR crossed West London Railway (Birmingham, Bristol & Thames Junction Railway) by right-angle level crossing at Wormwood Scrubs (Old Oak Common). Signalling system inadequate, and in darkness LNWR goods was propelled into side of GWR goods train. 1 killed. Resulted in erection of overbridge for BB&TJR.

Bruton station, 28 June 1865
Lack of interlocking allowed goods train to be signalled 'Main Line' although points set for goods shed siding. Train wrecked, 2 killed.

Shipton-on-Cherwell (1 m 300 yds north of Kidlington station), 24 December 1872
Tyre of four-wheel coach next to engine of double-headed 10 am Paddington–Birkenhead disintegrated. Coach continued to run—bumpily—until drivers noticed and braked violently. Coach pulverized between braking engine and 14 unbraked carriages running up behind. Next nine coaches overthrown, left and right, some over bridge into Oxford Canal. Remaining five remained upright, last two not derailed. 34 passengers killed, 65 others, including four railwaymen, injured—worst accident in GWR history.

Menheniot station, 3 December 1873
Crossing place on single track with up and down trains waiting to leave. Signal porter called 'Right away, Dick' to down train's guard, but up train's guard also called Dick. Latter started his train, and half-way to St Germans it collided head-on with down train. 1 driver killed, others seriously injured and locomotive *Lance* totally destroyed.

Norton Fitzwarren station, 11 November 1890
Down goods standing on up line to permit down express to pass was forgotten by signalman, who cleared signals for up Special express hauled by broad gauge saddle tank No 2051, resulting in head-on collision at high speed. 10 killed. Led to introduction of 'lever collars'.

Box Tunnel, 16 September 1893
Leading axle of 2-2-2 No 3021 *Wigmore Castle* broke inside tunnel; train derailed across up main line at 11.54 am. No 3240 on up main collided with locomotive, but no fatalities. Caused the rebuilding of the class as 4-2-2, possibly the most beautiful locomotives ever to run in Britain (qv, Locomotives).

Slough station, 16 June 1900
1.15 pm down Paddington behind No 3015 *Kennet*, Driver Woodman, driven past signals at 'Danger' to collide with rear of 1.5 pm Paddington. Resulted in improved vacuum brake (qv) for GWR, and may have inspired C. M. Jacobs (qv) to invent cab-mounted, audible distant signal.

Reading station, 17 June 1914
9 am up Worcester behind No 3816 *County of Leicester*, Driver Young, whilst passing on up main at full speed with signals cleared, collided with No 3387 *Reading*, emerging from up platform loop against 'Danger' signals. Driver Young killed.

Aller Junction, 29 May 1929
7.10 am Plymouth–Newton Abbot train, engine No 4909, crashed into rear of goods train on up main line through signalman's error. Guard of goods train killed.

Shrivenham (near), 15 January 1936
Signalman Head at Shrivenham failed to see tail lamp of an up coal train. Signalman Jefferies at next box, Ashbury Crossing, did not see tail lamp but gave 'Train out of Section' to Head. Head gave 'Line Clear' to Marston East for up express, 9 pm Penzance–Paddington. No 6007, Driver Starr, collided at 60 mph with detached portion of coal train standing in section. Driver Starr and one passenger killed.

Norton Fitzwarren station, 4 November 1940
9.50 pm Paddington–Penzance behind No 6028, Driver Stacey, left Taunton at 3.43 am on down relief line parallel to down main line. Signals on down main showed green for 12.50 am down Paddington, and Stacey obeyed them, forgetting he was on down relief. ATC (qv) warning siren for Norton Fitzwarren was cancelled and ignored. Train derailed at termination of relief line. 27 killed, including fireman of No 6028.

Slough, Dolphin Junction, 2 July 1941
Signalman Welch cleared signals on down relief line for freight train, but then replaced them to 'Danger' and sent passenger train across that line. Locomotive of freight, LMS 2-8-0 No 8293, struck passenger train engine, No 4091 *Dudley Castle*. 5 killed. Signalman Welch transferred to Burnham Beeches box where he earned a commendation on 14 January 1944 'for prompt and courageous action in stopping a runaway train in dense fog'.

AV

ACTON

There was a passenger station at Acton from 1868 but it was mainly important for the freight marshalling activity undertaken in the Up, Down and Transfer yards on the north side of the main line. The yards dealt with traffic to and from the GWR London depots and exchanges with other companies via the North London, Tottenham & Hampstead, North & South Western Junction and West London routes. In addition to sorting, making-up and dispatching dozens of freight trains each day, Acton Yard was involved in a host of ancillary operations such as Carriage & Wagon examination, feeding and watering livestock, segregating out-of-gauge and dangerous traffics, and so forth.

An area beyond Acton Yard was chosen as the site for Acton Garden Village Estate, 491 houses constructed by the GWR and made available to employees at weekly rents of 11s 3d (56p) for a non-parlour house and 13s 9d (69p) for a parlour type.

The link from Acton to the North & South Western Junction Railway's Kew–Willesden Junction line was opened on 1 January 1877 and carried a Southall–Willesden passenger service from 1888 to 1912.

GB

ADMINISTRATION AND MANAGEMENT

It was the Bristol Committee, a group made up of various citizens of that city, the Merchant Venturer's Society, the Dock Company and the Bristol & Gloucestershire Rail Road Company, which brought the GWR into being at a meeting in Bristol in July 1833, and a committee of four was set up to arrange a survey and estimates. A committee was also set up in London, and at a joint meeting on 19 August 1833 the title 'Great Western Railway' was adopted; from then on the company would be in the charge of a Board of Directors (qv).

Brunel (qv) had already been appointed Engineer, Charles Saunders (qv) was Secretary and the young Daniel Gooch (qv) became Locomotive Superintendent. Charles Russell (qv) became Chairman in 1839. The posts held by these four would have been key ones in anybody's hands, but such were the qualities of these almost legendary figures that they established the shape and character of the company for the rest of its existence. Gooch became Chairman in 1865 and held the post until his death 24 years later, three years before the end of the Broad Gauge (qv).

Throughout its existence, the GWR was continually absorbing smaller concerns, until eventually the company itself became part of British Railways; it administered its far-flung empire through a series of Divisions. At the turn of century there were, immediately beneath the General Manager (qv), three departments, the General Department, New Works and Government Enquiries, and Staff and Expenses. However, the General Manager then had no control over the Locomotive, Carriage & Wagon Superintendent (qv), who had the biggest budget of all. James Inglis (qv), on becoming General Manager in 1903, proposed a new, more tightly controlled structure, to which the Board of Directors agreed and which came into effect around the time of the Grouping. It worked well for the rest of the GWR's existence and played no little part in ensuring that the company remained profitable through the difficult 1930s.

On the operational side, the Superintendent of the Line (qv) was assisted by ten Divisional Superintendents based at London, Bristol, Exeter, Newport, Cardiff, Swansea, Gloucester, Worcester, Birmingham and Chester. The Goods Department was run on similar lines, with an additional District at Shrewsbury. Divisional Engineers were to be found at London, Bristol, Taunton, Plymouth, Newport, Cardiff, Neath, Gloucester, Wolverhampton, Shrewsbury and Oswestry; whilst Divisional Locomotive, Carriage & Wagon Superintendents, under the Chief Mechanical Engineer at Swindon, were at London, Bristol, Newton Abbot, Newport, Cardiff, Neath, Worcester, Wolverhampton and Oswestry. The furthest flung official was the Traffic Manager based across the Irish Sea at the North Wall, Dublin. There were also District Traffic Managers at Plymouth and Oswestry (it is curious to think that the grand offices at the latter are now a DIY emporium served by a disused freight-only branch line).

Docks (qv), greatly expanded after the absorption of the South Wales companies in 1922–3, were the responsibility of the Chief Docks Manager who had his office at Cardiff, and under him were various Divisional and Resident Dock Engineers.

Other departments looked after such administrative matters as Secretarial, Legal, and Financial, whilst there were also the Hotels and Catering, Surveyor and Estate Agent, Stores, and Road Motor Engineer's Departments.

MCHB

Administration and management *'Where the money goes': two 'pie charts' showing how the disposal of each £1 of revenue was distributed in 1913 and 1920. See also Dividends.* (GWR Magazine, May 1921)

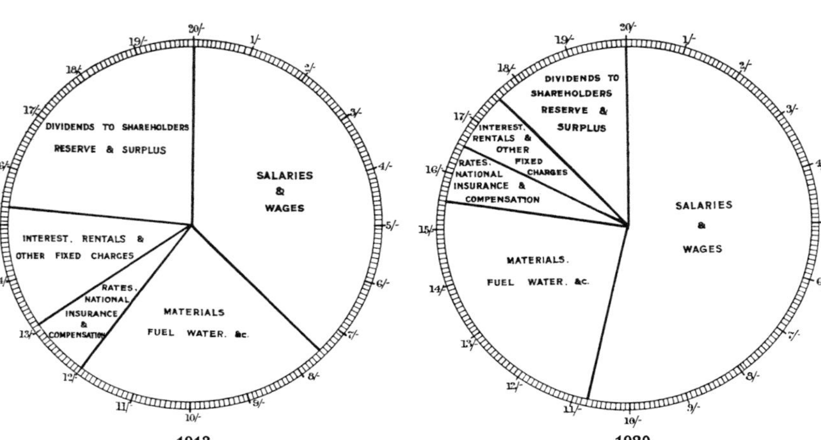

'AFGHAN'

This was one of the unofficial names applied to some of the GWR's expresses in the later days of the Broad Gauge. Although the names were widely used by the staff, in the case of the 'Afghan' there was an opportunity for some confusion. The train concerned was the 4.45 pm from Paddington to Wolverhampton, a 'narrow gauge' express, introduced on the same day as the fast 3 pm 'Zulu' (qv) broad gauge express from Paddington to Plymouth; there was clearly a need to differentiate between the two as far as Didcot, where their routes diverged. Beyond that point, however, the Wolverhampton express was known as the 'Zulu', or sometimes the 'Northern Zulu', but, for the purposes of this entry, the name 'Afghan', as it was known between London and Didcot, will be used. Its only stops between Paddington and Wolverhampton were at Oxford and Birmingham, although a slip carriage was dropped at Leamington. The up train thus had to call at this last-named station to balance the workings. Although speeds were not as high as those for the 'Zulu', the 'Afghan' averaged nearly 49 mph to Oxford, and slightly more on to Birmingham. Its popularity soon made it a heavy train, with five or six eight-wheelers for the north, including the Leamington slip, and a further three for Worcester, which were detached at Oxford. Motive power was provided by one of the 7-foot singles of the 'Queen' Class, built in the first half of the 1870s.

PWBS

ALCESTER BRANCH

Stations: Bearley, Aston Cantlow Halt (2 m), Great Alne (4¼ m), Alcester (7 m)

This east-west branch ran for 6 m 40 ch from a junction near the Stratford-on-Avon Canal aqueduct over the Birmingham & North Warwickshire line, along the River Alne, and then round the north side of Alcester to a junction with the Midland/LMS just west of the River Arrow. It was authorized as the Alcester Railway on 6 August 1872, opened on 4 September 1876, and then passed to the GWR and Stratford-on-Avon companies in 1878 after the former had taken over the maintenance from 4 September 1877.

The service on the line, 33 chains of which was used to form Bearley East Loop from 9 December 1907, consisted of six weekday trains to and from Stratford before closure on 25 September 1939. Services had previously been suspended between 1917 and 1922 but were reinstated briefly during the Second World War.

GB

ALDINGTON, CHARLES

Superintendent of the Line 1911–19, General Manager 1919–21. Aldington was born at Tanworth-in-Arden, Warks, in December 1862 and educated at Packwood School. Joining the GWR in 1876, he spent most of his early service in the Northern Division, moving to London in 1894 as Chief Clerk in the office of W. A. Hart (qv), the London Division Superintendent. He worked there for five years before resigning to become Traffic Superintendent of the Central London Tube. Back with the Great Western in 1902, however, he was appointed Assistant Superintendent of the Line in 1904, and succeeded Morris (qv) as Superintendent from 1 January 1911. After eight years in the post he became Assistant General Manager under Potter (qv) in 1919; Potter died in July of that year, and Aldington took over as General Manager.

It was a difficult time—railway rates had remained unchanged since 1913, but the Railway Unions were demanding an eight-hour day and extravagant wage increases. Material costs were rising too, as postwar inflation took its grip. Worry and overwork took its toll and led to a breakdown in Aldington's health: he was obliged to go away for rest early in 1921, and resigned in the following June, to be succeeded by his Assistant, Felix Pole (qv). He died on 10 October 1922, and was buried at Perranuthnoe, near Marazion.

CA

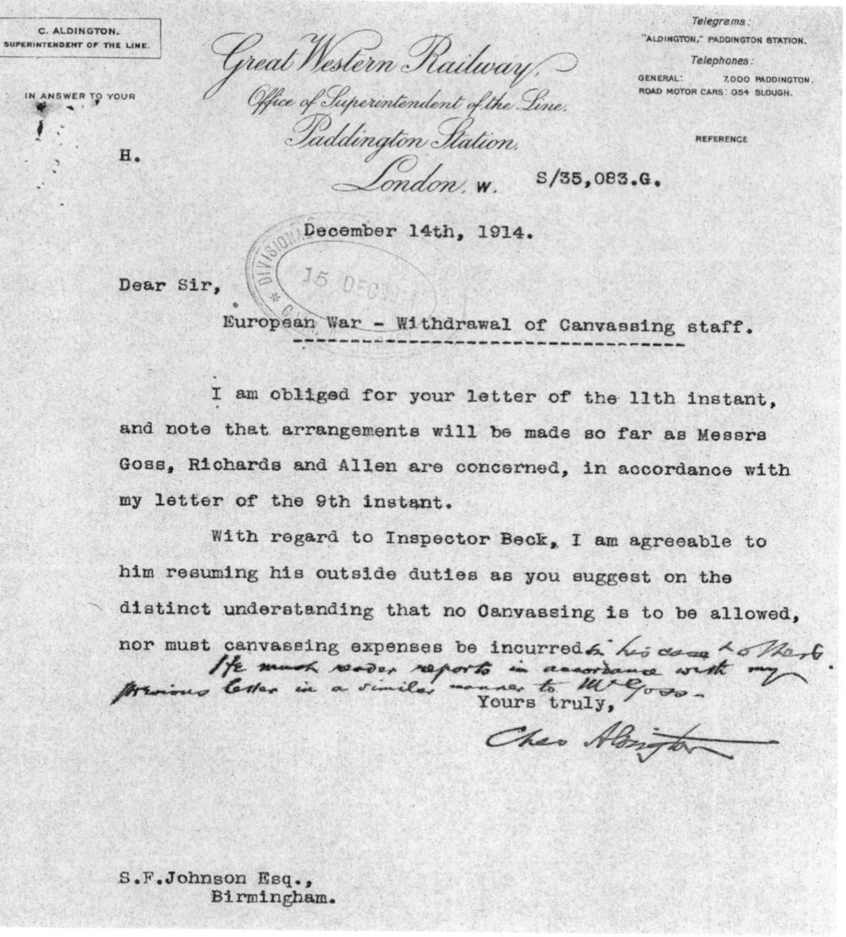

C. ALDINGTON.
SUPERINTENDENT OF THE LINE.

IN ANSWER TO YOUR

Great Western Railway.
Office of Superintendent of the Line.
Paddington Station,
London, W.

Telegrams: "ALDINGTON," PADDINGTON STATION.
Telephones: GENERAL: 7,000 PADDINGTON. ROAD MOTOR CARS: 054 SLOUGH.

REFERENCE

H.

S/35,083.G.

December 14th, 1914.

Dear Sir,

European War - Withdrawal of Canvassing staff.

I am obliged for your letter of the 11th instant, and note that arrangements will be made so far as Messrs Goss, Richards and Allen are concerned, in accordance with my letter of the 9th instant.

With regard to Inspector Beck, I am agreeable to him resuming his outside duties as you suggest on the distinct understanding that no Canvassing is to be allowed, nor must canvassing expenses be incurred in his case [illegible]. He must render reports in accordance with my previous letter in a similar manner to Mr Goss.

Yours truly,

Chas Aldington

S.F.Johnson Esq.,
Birmingham.

Charles Aldington *A letter signed by Aldington in 1914 when he was Superintendent of the Line.* (W. Adams Collection)

ALEXANDRA (NEWPORT & SOUTH WALES) DOCKS & RAILWAY

At the Grouping this undertaking contributed 136½ acres of deep water dock and a 19 m 8 ch rail route to the GWR system. The former was made up of the Alexandra and Town Docks at Newport and the latter of a route to Pontypridd—partly owned and partly using running powers over the Brecon & Merthyr (qv)—to tap the Glamorgan coalfields. The company owned 38 locomotives, 677 wagons and employed an average of 1,830 people.

The company obtained its first Act on 6 July 1865, opening North Dock ten years later, adopting the heading title in 1882 and taking over the 1835 Newport Dock Co in 1884. Between 1878 and 1887 it was involved, through the Pontypridd, Caerphilly & Newport Railway, in creating the route to Pontypridd which carried its first coal train on 7 July 1884. A passenger service was worked by the GWR from 1899 to 1907 when the AD&R's own Pontypridd–Caerphilly service was extended to Machen to connect with the Brecon & Merthyr trains.

The AD&R lines made east and west connection with the GWR at Alexandra Dock and Maesglas Junctions at Newport and with the B&M (for Pontypridd) at Bassaleg. Through these it received 5.9m tons of coal in 1913, handling this and its other movements with a varied stud of locomotives which owed more to the desire for a bargain than to any policy of standardization.

GB

ALLEN, T. I.

Superintendent of the Line, 1894–1903. He entered GWR service at the age of 15 in 1856, and by 1870 was in charge of the Newport Division, a post held (through a name change to the Cardiff Division in 1879) until 1888. He was then appointed Burlinson's (qv) Assistant, and, in 1891, Assistant General Manager, finally succeeding Burlinson as Superintendent in April 1894. An enterprising man, he continued his predecessor's improvements in revolutionizing the passenger service with new long-distance expresses, and himself inaugurated several cross-country services. The railmotor service (qv), introduced in the Stroud valley on 12 October 1903, was his brainchild. He retired at the end of 1903, and died on 20 December 1911. He is buried at Brighton.

CA

ARMSTRONG, JOSEPH

Locomotive & Carriage Superintendent, 1864–77. Armstrong, like so many of the early railway engineers, was born in the far north of England, at Bewcastle, Cumberland, in 1816. He began work under Robert Hawthorn, the engineer of a Tyneside colliery, and by 1836 was a driver on the Liverpool & Manchester Railway. He moved to the Hull & Selby Railway and then the LB&SCR before becoming Superintendent of the Shrewsbury & Chester Railway in 1852, and also of the Shrewsbury & Birmingham (the companies being run by a managing Joint Committee). Thus began his connection with the GWR, for in 1854 a further amalgamation saw the two companies absorbed into the Swindon empire.

Armstrong became Northern Division Superintendent, based at the Stafford Road Works at Wolverhampton, and assistant to Daniel Gooch (qv) throughout the system. The Broad Gauge had reached Wolverhampton in 1854, but the Wolverhampton works, modernized and enlarged by the GWR, concentrated on narrow gauge designs and, under Joseph Armstrong and his brother George, who succeeded him as Locomotive Superintendent, Northern Division (1864–97), tended to operate almost as an independent concern. The first narrow gauge engines to the GWR's own design came out of Wolverhampton works under Joseph Armstrong's direction. At its height the works employed 1,500 men and there was talk, as the Broad Gauge came to an end, of it taking over from Swindon entirely.

When Gooch announced his retirement there was, apparently, a move to appoint Sacre, of the Manchester, Sheffield & Lincolnshire Railway, as his successor at Swindon, but Gooch himself campaigned fiercely for his assistant and won the day. The Broad Gauge still had 28 years to go when Armstrong arrived at Swindon in 1864 and he produced a number of locomotives, chiefly convertibles, to run on it. But he is principally remembered for his standard gauge 2-2-2 and 2-4-0 passenger engines and 0-6-0 goods designs, some of the latter lasting into the 1930s (qv, Locomotives).

Armstrong took a great interest in the welfare of GWR employees and their families. He was Chairman of the Swindon Local Board, the predecessor of the Urban District Council. He also encouraged and often took part in the administration of the New Swindon Permanent Benefit Building & Investment Society, the Medical Fund, the Sick Fund Society, the Mechanics Institution, the Wesleyan Chapel, various schools, the New Swindon Park Committee, the swimming baths, and the cottage hospital.

Joseph Armstrong (GWR Museum, Swindon)

Swindon Works expanded enormously whilst Armstrong was in charge, the floor space being doubled. At the time of Armstrong's arrival at Swindon, only 44 narrow gauge locomotives had been built there, but within five years between 60 and 70 were being produced annually. In 1872 Armstrong had the celebrated works hooter installed, which could be heard up to 15 miles away and sounded out at regular intervals each morning from 5.20 to allow those employees living in the outlying Wiltshire villages to get up and walk to work on time.

Joseph Armstrong, like others before and after him, devoted his life to the GWR and in the end the strain was too much. He became ill at the beginning of 1877, was persuaded to take an extended holiday but died in the early summer of that year at Matlock, where he had gone to take the cure at the baths. His body was brought back to Swindon and almost the entire town turned out for his funeral, on Saturday 9 June. Special trains of mourners came from various parts of the GWR system and 1,500 Swindon employees and over 5,000 others followed the coffin to its burial in St Mark's Churchyard.

Instead of the usual statue or memorial hall, Joseph Armstrong's life and achievements were commemorated in a lifeboat named after him and stationed on the Lizard Peninsula in Cornwall. Armstrong had three sons, all of whom became locomotive engineers, and it seemed that one in particular, 'Young Joe', was destined to become as famous as his father. An innovator of brilliance, he was given the managership of Wolverhampton Works before he was 30, but his life ended tragically when he was killed on the line near the works at the age of 31.

See also Locomotives.

MCHB

ASHBURTON BRANCH

Stations: Totnes, Staverton ($3\frac{1}{4}$ m), Buckfastleigh (7 m), Ashburton ($9\frac{1}{2}$ m)

By Acts of 25 July 1864 and 26 May 1865 the Buckfastleigh, Totnes & South Devon

Ashburton branch *'48xx' (later '14xx') Class 0-4-2T No 4870 stands at the wooden-roofed terminus at Ashburton.* (H. C. Casserley)

Railway was authorized to build a line linking the stannary town of Ashburton with the head of the navigable portion of the River Dart at Totnes. Raising the necessary capital was a slow process but the line was finally opened on 1 May 1872 and a 62-chain horse-worked branch to the quay at Totnes was added on 10 November 1873. The South Devon Railway (qv) worked both lines, the local company being vested in the GWR from 1 July 1897.

The seven weekday trains each way on the branch followed the Dart to Buckfastleigh and then climbed at 1 in 60 along a tributary to the wooden-roofed terminus. The 9 m 37 ch single line was worked under normal block signalling with staff and ticket, and handled significant amounts of wool and livestock traffic in addition to its passenger business.

GB

ASSOCIATED BROAD GAUGE COMPANIES

In addition to their continuous broad gauge main line, the GWR, Bristol & Exeter and South Devon Railways (both qv) had many practical, financial and policy matters in common. Formal amalgamation between the GWR and B&E took place from 1 January 1876, with the SDR joining the GWR from 1 August 1878, but for many years before that the three had acted in concert in areas of mutual interest.

The Cornwall Railway (qv) provides an example, the Associated Companies providing £337,000 (in proportion to their proximity) of the authorized capital of £1,600,000 and having to pour in more funds before the line was completed. They eventually leased the Cornwall company and provided eight of the 12 Directors who made up a 'Joint Committee of Management'.

GB

ATMOSPHERIC PROPULSION

When the South Devon Railway (qv) projected a line from Exeter to Plymouth, its engineer, Brunel (qv), was concerned that the steam engines of the time would be unable to cope with an inevitably hilly and curving route. He therefore recommended atmospheric propulsion. It was not a new idea. The first suggestion that vehicles could be driven by air pressure was made by an 18th-century Frenchman named Papin, and from there the concept gradually developed.

In 1840 Samuel Clegg and Jacob Samuda leased ½ mile of the West London Railway near Wormwood Scrubs and carried out trials for two years. Many notable engineers came to see these, and the system was first adopted on the Dalkey extension of the Dublin & Kingstown Railway. Brunel visited Kingstown with South Devon Railway Directors, who subsequently decided to use the system.

A tube (of 15 inch diameter on the SDR) was placed between the rails. The first vehicle in each train had an arm projecting downwards: this passed along a continuous slot in the top of the tube, which was sealed by a flap of leather. This flap, raised by the arm as it passed, returned to its seating afterwards so that the seal of the tube was maintained. Inside the tube the downward-projecting arm was attached to a close-fitting piston. Pumping-houses, built at three-mile intervals along the route, exhausted air from the tube in front of the piston, which was thus forced along the tube by the atmospheric pressure behind it, so moving the train.

The South Devon line opened for passengers between Exeter and Teignmouth on 30 May 1846. There were problems, but things went reasonably well until increasing traffic showed that the pumping engines were sadly underpowered. The leather seal on the tube began to decay also, for various reasons, and on 1 August 1848 Brunel had to admit to the Board that the system should not be extended beyond Newton (Abbot). Locomotive working on the atmospheric section was resumed on 10 September.

There were many reasons for the system's failure: complication of arrangements at junctions and crossings, communication between pumphouses, and the condensation of water inside the tube all contributed. The main reasons though, so far as the SDR was concerned, were the underpowered pumps, compounded by the failure of the leather seal. Frost, heat and rats (which gnawed the leather) all took their toll, and in time it became difficult to create a vacuum in front of the piston.

George Stephenson, who had dismissed the idea as 'a lot of humbug', was thus proved right. Had the system appeared later, however, improved technology might have given it a better chance.

CA

AUTOMATIC TRAIN CONTROL

The original 'Audible Signal' was patented by C. M. Jacobs (qv) and R. V. Insell (qv) (No 12661) on 19 June 1905, and was an electro-mechanical device which repeated, by audible signal inside the cab, the visual aspect of the lineside Distant signal—a bell for 'All Right' and a steam whistle for 'Danger'. In the engine's cab a valve was held shut by an electro-magnet, maintained by current from a battery on the locomotive, the circuit of this current passing through a switch fixed to a 'shoe' projecting below the locomotive. Fixed between the rails, on the approach side of a Distant signal, was a 44 ft, 6 in timber ramp carrying a steel contact strip; 21 ft 10 in of the ramp rose at 1 in 90 to a level section 12 ft 5 in long, followed by a 10 ft tailing-off section.

The contact strip was connected to a lineside battery through a switch on the signal arm. When the shoe swept the ramp of a Distant signal at 'Danger', the contact strip was electrically 'dead'. The shoe was lifted 1 inch, interrupting the locomotive battery current to the electro-magnet which ceased to be magnetic and allowed the valve to fall open, admitting steam into a whistle. The driver could cancel the warning by lifting the valve up to the magnet which had by then become re-energized as the pick-up shoe had passed beyond the ramp.

If the lineside signal was showing 'All Right', the contact strip was electrically 'live' from the lineside battery through the switch on the signal arm. Current passed through the pick-up shoe to the electro-magnet in the cab and maintained it as a magnet when the locomotive battery current was cut off. The same current caused a loud bell to ring. The device did *not* apply the train's brakes. It was introduced on the double-track Henley branch in January 1906, installed on the quadruple tracks between Reading and Slough in November 1908, and extended to Paddington during 1910.

A modification for use on single lines was brought into use on the Fairford branch on 1 December 1906, when all 14 semaphore

Automatic Train Control *The cab equipment: bell on top of box, cancelling lever on the side.* (Adrian Vaughan)

Distant signals were removed and replaced by the 'Audible Signal' ramps. The Lambourn branch received the same treatment in September 1909.

The 'Audible Signal' system on single tracks had to differentiate between ramps. An up train required a signal from the 'up' direction ramp but required no signal from the 'down' direction ramp. For example, before an up train could leave Fairford, the signalman had to withdraw a staff from the electrically locked instrument. This was unlocked when he reversed his Interlocking lever which he could not move until it was released by a current sent from Lechlade box. Reversing the Interlocking lever energized Fairford's 'down' ramp on a positive polarity and cut off all current to the 'up' ramp on the approach to Lechlade. When the up train's locomotive passed over the Fairford 'down' ramp, the pick-up shoe took positive polarity current to maintain the magnet holding the steam whistle valve shut, but this current could not operate the 'All Right' bell.

Interlocking levers were used where the Webb-Thompson staff instruments were in use, Fairford–Lechlade–Bampton. The sections Bampton–Witney–Eynsham–Yarnton Junction, using Tyers No 7 tablet instruments (and later the key token), had their ramps switched by the action of removing the tablet/token from the instrument.

Where a level crossing intervened in a block section—such as Little Faringdon or South Leigh—a ground frame of 3 levers was provided. Lever 1 was the equivalent of the 'Up Distant' signal lever, lever 3 the 'Down Distant', and both were painted yellow. Lever 2 was painted blue, bolted the crossing gates and was interlocked with 1 and 3.

When an up train was signalled, the crossing keeper closed the gates across the road and pulled lever 1 which polarized the 'up' ramp negative and the 'down' ramp positive. The locomotive contact shoe thus picked up the correct current to operate its 'All Right' bell, which also maintained closed the steam whistle valve. If the Distant signal lever was not pulled, both ramps were 'dead' and the warning whistle would sound in the engine's cab.

The double and single track Audible Signal systems worked perfectly although they were somewhat unpopular owing to the steam whistle being so close to the driver's ear.

The 'Audible Signal' system was modified into the world's first 'Automatic Train Control' (ATC) in 1913. When the locomotive's pick-up shoe contacted a 'dead' ramp, the magnetic valve, which had previously opened to admit steam to a whistle, now admitted air to the vacuum brake pipe. As air rushed in to apply the brakes, it also operated a warning siren. The driver could cancel the warning by lifting the valve up to the magnet. If the driver ignored the warn-

Automatic Train Control *Proposed extension of the system in 1930.* (GWR Magazine)

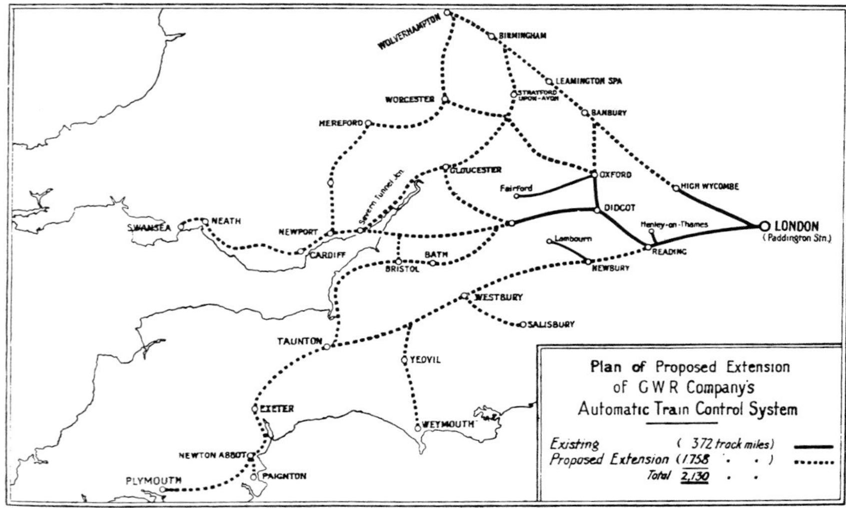

ing and kept steam on, the automatic brake application would bring the train to a stand before the first Stop signal. If the lineside signal was showing 'All Right', the system worked in the same way as in the double track 'Audible Signal' system. The ATC was not installed on any other single line and was removed from the Lambourn line on 20 March 1929 but the system remained in use on the Fairford line until 18 June 1962 when the passenger service was withdrawn.

In 1907 Jacobs and Insell patented a batteryless system using a Bowden cable from pick-up shoe to cab equipment. Amos Brooker, Telegraph Shop Foreman at Reading Signal Works, invented a similar system in 1930, and Swindon Drawing Office produced Bowden cable systems in 1938 and 1943 which were installed experimentally on at least one locomotive. There were problems with precise adjustments to the cable and the cable stretching, and the experiments came to nothing.

The locomotive battery maintained the electro-magnets continuously, and to prevent excessive use of batteries a vacuum-operated switch was provided in 1927 which automatically disconnected the battery after the engine had been standing for 1 hour.

The ATC was extended from Reading to Swindon and Oxford, and from Old Oak Common to High Wycombe, in 1929. Between March and September 1930, the main lines to Plymouth (via Bath and via Westbury), Wolverhampton (via Oxford and via Bicester), and Swansea (via Badminton and via Gloucester) were equipped, together with 2,500 engines. The system was not installed on all GWR double-track lines. It was not finally superceded until 1974 when the last ramps were replaced by the non-contact system using magnetic induction pioneered by A. E. Hudd on the Southern Railway in the 1930s.

The Hudd system was a better system than the ATC and was easily capable of audibly signalling the 'double yellow' signal found on four-aspect colour light signalling. However, it was very underdeveloped at Nationalization, so the GWR hoped that the Railway Executive would use ATC which the GWR's engineers cleverly modified to repeat a 'double yellow' light signal by giving a 'double hoot'. The newer technology of the 'non-contact' Hudd system was nonetheless accepted, and the BR standard was developed from it.

AV

AUTO-TRAINS

After the GWR's introduction of steam railmotors (qv) and specially designed auto-trailers in the 1900s, an alternative form of traction was devised to achieve the same economy of operation. This also involved auto-trailers, but they were worked by specially adapted tank locomotives. Up to two trailers could be coupled to each end of the locomotive, although it was common for just a single trailer to be used. In the early days, some of the locomotives were painted in coach colours, while others were fitted with casings to match the carriage contours.

Each auto-trailer had an end compartment for the driver, with controls to enable him to work certain controls on the locomotive when it was propelling. The regulator was connected mechanically by a rotating shaft running along the carriage underframe, with universal and sliding joints between vehicles. A wire at roof level enabled the driver to sound the locomotive's whistle, but a large foot-operated warning gong was subsequently also provided on the coach end. A brake valve was installed, and an electric bell provided communication between the driver, guard and fireman. In later years, Automatic Train Control (qv) was fitted in each cab, with a device to enable it to be isolated when not in use. Auto-train operation continued long after the last of the railmotors had been withdrawn in the mid-1930s, with more trailers and suitably fitted locomotives being built. In 1951, a batch of 35 new trailers were constructed by BR to a GWR design, while existing coaches were being similarly adapted as late as 1955.

PWBS

AVONMOUTH LINES

Stations: Bristol Temple Meads, Lawrence Hill (1 m), Stapleton Road (12 m), Montpelier (23 m), Redland (34 m), Clifton Down (4 m), Sea Mills (6 m), Shirehampton (72 m), Avonmouth Dock (9 m), St Andrew's Road (10 m), Severn Beach (132 m)

Bristol Temple Meads, Lawrence Hill (1 m), Stapleton Road ($1\frac{1}{2}$ m), Ashley Hill ($2\frac{1}{2}$ m), Filton Junction ($4\frac{3}{4}$ m), Henbury ($7\frac{3}{4}$ m), Avonmouth Docks ($12\frac{3}{4}$ m)

Auto-trains *Interior of an auto-trailer converted from a former steam railmotor, photographed in 1933. The driver's compartment can be glimpsed at the end.* (GW Society)

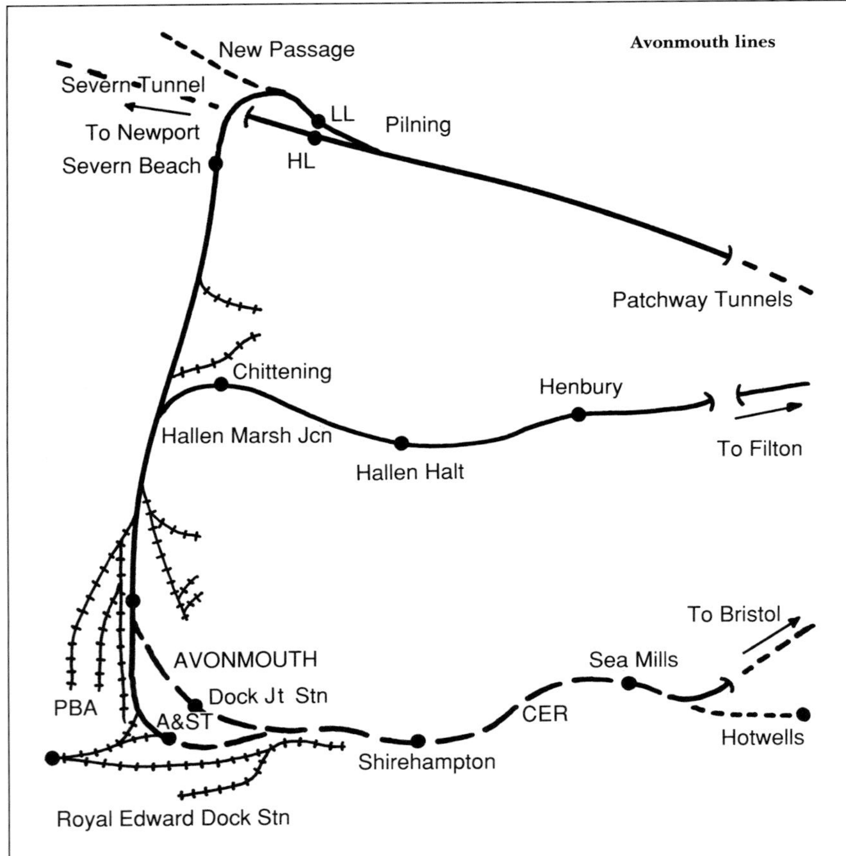

Size restrictions on ships using Bristol's city docks and the need to wait for tides on the journey through the Avon Gorge steadily made the case for new shipping facilities at the mouth of the Avon. The Bristol Port Railway & Pier Company arose from this need and was authorized to link its pier with Bristol by a railway along the north bank of the river on 17 July 1862. The line was opened on 6 March 1865 and two years later (on 15 August) the BPR obtained an Act for a link from its isolated route at Sneyd Park, under Bristol's Downs and on to join the Midland and GWR systems near Ashley Hill. By the end of the decade the cost of constructing the new line had put the BPR in Chancery and allowed the acquisition of its Clifton Extension Railway by the two main-line companies, which opened west through the 289 yd Montpelier Tunnel to Whiteladies Road in June 1874, on to Clifton Down on 1 October 1874 and through the 1,738 yd Clifton Down Tunnel to Sneyd Park (for freight) on 24 February 1877, coinciding with the opening of the new dock at Avonmouth.

Under MR/GWR control, passenger trains began running over the Clifton Extension Railway on 1 September 1885 linking St Philips (MR) and Temple Meads (GWR) with a new joint Avonmouth Dock station. They purchased the BPR's original Hotwells–Avonmouth line in 1890 and improved it, eventually selling the Hotwells–Sneyd Park section to Bristol Corporation in 1922 to permit the building of a new road.

At the Avonmouth end the docks continued to expand and the GWR's Avonmouth & Severn Tunnel Junction Railway (authorized 4 August 1890) was opened for goods between the dock sidings and Pilning on 5 February 1900. Banana traffic and boat trains started in 1901 followed by work on the Royal Edward Dock which necessitated the diversion inland of the A&STJ route and the abandonment of the original BPR Avonmouth station. Royal Edward Dock passenger station was opened on 29 April 1910, followed by the Avonmouth & Filton Railway (authorized 15 August 1904) on 9 May.

The wartime years saw the Avonmouth lines dedicated to hospital and troop trains plus countless wagons of foodstuffs and the materials of war. In 1928 a passenger service began on the Avonmouth–Pilning line to give Avonmouth three access routes, via Clifton Down, Henbury and Pilning, all carrying passenger services to Temple Meads, plus non-standard workings like the 'Monkey Specials' to Clifton Zoo. Other pleasure-seekers travelled to the estuary at Severn Beach, some of these trains being extended to create a circular route out via Clifton and back via Pilning. GWR freight, hotly disputed with the MR/LMS, was concentrated on the Henbury line and was exchanged with the Corporation's Port of Bristol Authority which had its own locomotive shed at Avonmouth.

GB

AYLESBURY BRANCH

Stations: Princes Risborough, Monks Risborough ($1\frac{1}{4}$ m), Little Kimble (3 m), Aylesbury ($7\frac{1}{4}$ m)

The single-line Great Western & Great Central (qv) Aylesbury branch had been opened on 1 October 1863 by the Wycombe Railway, using a joint station with the Aylesbury & Buckingham Railway. It passed to the GWR in 1867 and to the GW&GC Joint Committee in 1907, the junction with the Metropolitan line dating from 1 January 1894. A good weekday and Sunday passengers service operated from the up side bay at Princes Risborough to the up bay or down island at Aylesbury.

GB

BALA

The first of Bala's three stations was opened on 1 April 1868 as the terminus of the line from Corwen, but it was some way south of the town and closed in favour of a better situated station on the Bala & Festiniog Railway when the latter opened on 1 November 1882. Part of the site of the original terminus was later used for Bala Lake Halt which lasted from 1934 to 1939.

Bala Junction, the third station in the area, had started life in 1880 as the junction for construction trains on the Festiniog line and then developed as an exchange point, with no road access and with trains for Festiniog dealt with at the outer face of the up island.

In addition to originating and providing engines for the Blaenau Ffestiniog branch (qv) trains, Bala proper did the same for some Corwen line services and was connected to others by a shuttle to and from Bala Junction.

GB

BALDWIN, ALFRED

Chairman, 1905–08. Born in June 1841 at Stourport, and educated privately, he became head of the firm of Baldwins Ltd, and was Conservative MP for Bewdley for 16 years from 1892. He joined the GWR Board in place of F. G. Saunders (qv) in January 1901, at the age of 59, but his short period of office as Chairman ended suddenly when he died after a heart attack on 13 February 1908, the day before the Half-Yearly Meeting. He was buried at Wilden, Worcs, his successor in the GWR Chair being Viscount Churchill (qv).

CA

BALDWIN, STANLEY

The only son of Alfred Baldwin (qv), he was born at Bewdley on 3 August 1867 and educated at Harrow and Trinity College, Cambridge, where he gained an MA. He became a JP for the County of Worcester, and a member of Worcestershire County Council in 1900. He was returned unopposed for the Bewdley Seat (left vacant by the death of his father) in 1908, and was appointed a GWR Director the same year. In 1917 he resigned on being appointed Financial Secretary to the Treasury, eventually becoming Prime Minister from 1923–4, 1924–9 and 1934–7. He died on 14 December 1947.

CA

BANBURY

Banbury's first station was the Merton Street terminus of the Buckinghamshire Railway. This opened on 1 May 1850 but was quickly followed by a temporary and adjacent terminus for the single line of the southern section of the GWR's Oxford & Rugby Railway (qv). The route was doubled and extended on to Fenny Compton (for Birmingham) on 1 October 1852 and a two-platform station with overall roof provided, this being used for trains on the Banbury & Cheltenham route (qv) from 6 April 1887.

Banbury *Postcard view of Banbury, with its overall roof, after the improvements of 1903, looking south. The bay on the left was used for trains from the GCR.* (W. Adams Collection)

Station improvements in 1884 were followed by major alterations in 1903, partly as a result of the extra traffic from the 1900 GCR branch from Woodford which joined the GWR at Banbury North Junction. To the south of the station's twin islands with country-end bays lay the exchange line with the LNWR, a large down side loco depot and the hump yard, opened on 27 July 1931.

Banbury in GWR days was a busy location, initiating Cheltenham, Woodford and London services, handling the through Birmingham and South Wales–Newcastle trains, exchanging freight with the GCR/LNER and dealing with its own coal and goods yard wagons. It also dealt with tar, aluminium and ironstone from private sidings.

GB

Banbury *A luggage label demonstrating the opportunities for travel from the GWR to the East Midlands via the Banbury-Woodford link with the GCR.* (W. Adams Collection)

G.W.R.

Nottingham

G. C. R., via Banbury

BANBURY–BIRMINGHAM LINE

Stations: Banbury Bridge Street (86¼ miles from Paddington via Didcot), Cropredy (89¾ m), Fenny Compton (95 m), Southam Road & Harbury (100 m), Leamington Spa (106 m), Warwick Coventry Road (108 m), Hatton (112¼ m), Lapworth (116½ m), Knowle & Dorridge (119 m), Widney Manor (120¾ m), Solihull (122½ m), Olton (124¼ m), Acock's Green (125 m), Tyseley (126 m), Small Heath & Sparkbrook (127 m), Bordesley (128¼ m), Birmingham Moor Street (128¾ m), Birmingham Snow Hill (129¼ m)

Opened on 1 October 1852, the constituents of the GWR's first access to Birmingham were the 1845 Oxford & Rugby Railway (qv) and the 1846 Birmingham & Oxford Junction Railway (qv), both acquired before opening. Supplemented by trains on the 'New Line' via Bicester from 1910, the Banbury–Birmingham section came to carry prestige through trains (from the South Coast plus services from Paddington) which continued to Manchester, Birkenhead or the Cambrian Coast. Local services, sparse between Banbury and Leamington Spa, were numerous on the increasingly used portion thence to Snow Hill.

From Banbury the route followed the Oxford Canal to a brief meeting with the Stratford-on-Avon & Midland Junction line at Fenny Compton and then curved through Leamington Spa and Warwick to climb to a triangular junction with the Stratford and Honeybourne line at Hatton. On the section forward to Snow Hill commuter traffic increased steadily over the years, necessitating additional running lines beyond Tyseley where the later route via Henley-in-Arden joined.

GB

BANBURY–CHELTENHAM LINE

Stations: Banbury, Kings Sutton ($3\frac{1}{2}$ m), Adderbury ($5\frac{1}{4}$ m), Bloxham ($8\frac{1}{4}$ m), Hook Norton ($12\frac{1}{2}$ m), Chipping Norton (19 m), Kingham ($23\frac{1}{2}$ m), Stow-on-the-Wold (28 m), Bourton-on-the-Water (30 m), Notgrove (35 m), Andoversford ($39\frac{3}{4}$ m), Charlton Kings ($43\frac{1}{2}$ m), Cheltenham South ($44\frac{3}{4}$ m), Cheltenham Spa Malvern Road ($47\frac{1}{4}$ m), Cheltenham Spa St James ($47\frac{3}{4}$ m)

This line grew from two branches radiating from the old Oxford, Worcester & Wolverhampton Railway (qv) route at Chipping Norton Junction (later Kingham) into a significant cross-country route which carried a South Wales–Newcastle service for many years. From Cheltenham St James it ran via Lansdown and the southern suburbs of the town before taking up an easterly course through the 384 yd tunnel under Ladywell Park, Andoversford, and then looping north to Stow. The easterly course was resumed to the triangular layout at Kingham and then continued on to join the Oxford–Banbury line at Kings Sutton.

The route originated with the OW&W's branch (Act of 31 July 1854) to Chipping Norton which opened on 10 August 1855. The Bourton-on-Water (sic) Railway (Act of 14 June 1860) followed on 1 March 1862, with the GWR securing an Act for the Banbury & Cheltenham Direct Railway on 21 July 1873 and adding the extensions to Cheltenham (1 June 1881), Kings Sutton (6 April 1887) and the connecting link at Kingham (7 January 1906).

In addition to its through services to and from the GCR, the line carried local services, including a number of Road Motor Car workings. At one period a slipped coach at Kingham gave Cheltenham a better timing from London than that via Stroud, while the line's freight traffic included cattle to Banbury and iron ore to South Wales.

GB

BARMOUTH

The coastal route authorized to the Aberystwyth & Welsh Coast Railway on 22 July 1861 passed to the Cambrian Railways (qv) in 1865 and from 3 July of that year, when the line from Llwyngwril to Penmaenpool was opened, passengers could reach Barmouth by a hazardous ferry crossing of the Mawddach Estuary. Matters improved on 3 June 1867 when the line north from Barmouth was ready and Barmouth Junction was opened south of the waterway ready for the pending completion of the multi-span viaduct between the two.

The slow, mixed trains of the early years gave way to a good through service via the Ruabon line and locals from Machynlleth and Dolgelley, all bringing holidaymakers or day-trippers during the summer months. Barmouth's well-situated passing loop station acquired a separate up side platform for the excursion business, and the viaduct was renewed in 1899–1909.

GB

BARNSTAPLE BRANCH

Stations: Norton Fitzwarren (2 miles from Taunton), Milverton ($6\frac{1}{2}$ m), Wiveliscombe ($9\frac{1}{2}$ m), Venn Cross ($14\frac{1}{4}$ m), Morebath ($17\frac{3}{4}$ m), Morebath Junction Halt ($19\frac{1}{4}$ m), Dulverton (21 m), East Anstey ($24\frac{3}{4}$ m), Bishops Nympton & Molland (30 m), South Molton ($34\frac{1}{4}$ m), Filleigh ($37\frac{1}{2}$ m), Swimbridge ($40\frac{3}{4}$ m), Barnstaple ($44\frac{3}{4}$ m)

A line from Taunton to Barnstaple was proposed back in 1845 but it was 29 July 1864 before the Devon & Somerset Railway was incorporated, and 8 June 1871 before it managed to open the Norton Fitzwarren–Wiveliscombe section. Public services over the whole route, and worked by the Bristol & Exeter Railway (qv), began on 1 November 1873, but the local enterprise never really escaped its financial problems until the GWR acquired it in 1901 for £800,493.

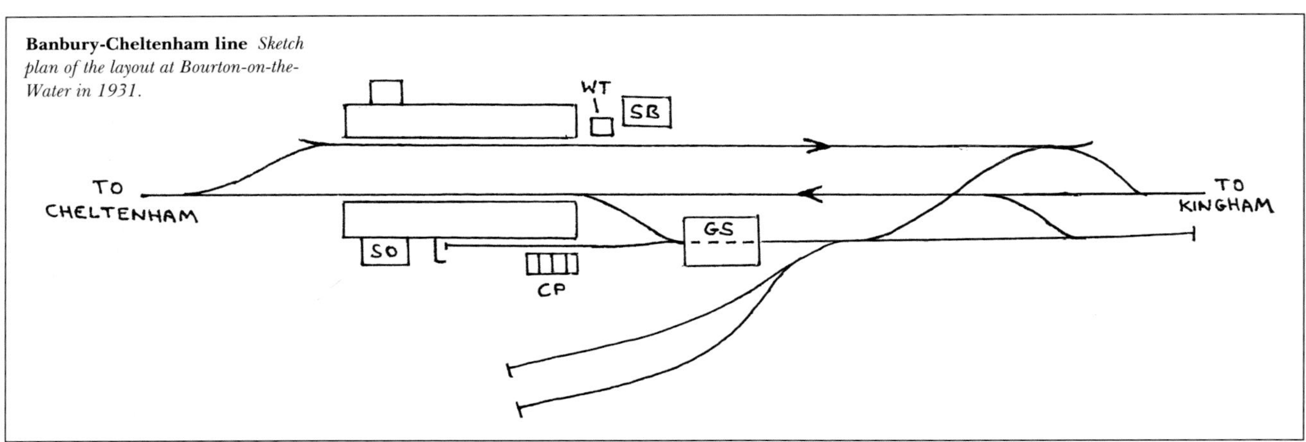

Banbury-Cheltenham line *Sketch plan of the layout at Bourton-on-the-Water in 1931.*

Barnstaple branch *Dulverton station, looking east, a Barnstaple-bound train having just arrived. Trains from the Tiverton line used the outer face of the down (right-hand) platform, which was later served by a continuous line, although buffer-stops are shown in this view.* (Steamchest Collection)

The line was single with passing loops at the main stations and had electric token working with auxiliary instruments to aid the movement of the summer holiday trains which supplemented the basic weekday service of six trains each way. There were steep gradients, several substantial viaducts and four tunnels (Bathealton, Venn Cross, Nightcott and Castle Hill). Tiverton line trains joined at Morebath Junction, but continued on to the outer face of the down island at Dulverton. A tramway from the Croborn and New Florence mines joined near South Molton.

The GWR station at Barnstaple Victoria Road had a long and a short platform face, a goods depot and an engine shed. A link to the LSWR's Ilfracombe line was opened on 1 June 1887 and a direct connection added on 1 July 1905. Most holiday trains went on to Ilfracombe via the latter, with any portion for the GWR station being detached at the junction.

Four gangs operated the motor trolley maintenance system.

GB

BARRINGTON, VISCOUNT WILLIAM KEPPEL

Chairman, 1856–57. He was born in London on 1 October 1793, and educated at Westminster School and Christ Church College, Oxford, where he gained a BA in 1813. He became the 6th Viscount on his father's death, 4 March 1829, and was elected Conservative MP for Berkshire in 1837. Two years later joined the GWR Board. At the February meeting of 1856, he was elected to the Chair as a stop-gap, having been Deputy Chairman under Walpole (qv) since 1843. He had agreed to take Office on Walpole's retirement, on the understanding that a successor would soon be found to replace him—this was to be the Hon F. G. B. Ponsonby (qv), who duly took over in 1857. Barrington died on 9 February 1867.

CA

BARRY

Barry was largely created by the Barry Railway (qv) which had its headquarters there along with two main docks covering 107 acres, 26,540 ft of quay and 108 miles of railway sidings. With its giant 20-ton hoists lifting coal wagons 60 ft above the ground, the complex could handle over 50,000 tons of coal a day and once loaded the SS *Knightsgarth* with 4,021 tons in 6½ hours.

Barry *A view of the steamer pontoon at Barry Pier station.* (Lens of Sutton)

The Barry Railway enterprise had been authorized in 1884 as a response to the congestion and high rates for export coal at Cardiff. A line from Cogan Junction reached Barry Dock on 20 December 1888 and was extended to Barry Town passenger station on 8 February 1889. By 18 July of that year the dock and the main line to Trehafod were operational. In the next decade the Barry company extended its empire, obtaining Acts for new inland lines, starting a Cardiff service (1893), extending to Barry Island (3 August 1896), working the Vale of Glamorgan line (1 December 1897), opening a second dock (1898), and adding a branch to Barry Pier (27 June 1899).

When amalgamated with the GWR at the Grouping, the Barry layout consisted of the main line in from Cadoxton and on as the Vale of Glamorgan route, a loop south serving the docks and goods depot, and the branch to Barry Island. The latter was 1 m 18 ch long with a 1 in 80 dip to Barry Island station and a 280 yd tunnel on the further descent to the Pier station and steamer pontoon used for the summer excursion part of the Bristol Channel pleasure steamer business.

Prior to the Grouping, the Barry Railway was carrying 3m passengers a year. The GWR maintained services on the Pontypridd/Porth, Llantwit Major/Bridgend and Cardiff routes and stimulated day trips to Barry Island for the steamers and other pleasure activities which grew up there. In addition to its passenger, docks and goods business, Barry had the full range of operational support facilities—loco, permanent way, signalling and wagon repairs.

GB

BARRY RAILWAY

Stations: Barry Island, Barry ($\frac{3}{4}$ m), Barry Docks (2 m), Cadoxton ($2\frac{3}{4}$ m), Dinas Powis ($4\frac{3}{4}$ m), Cogan ($6\frac{1}{2}$ m), Grangetown (8 m), Cardiff Riverside (9 m), Cardiff Clarence Road (10 m)
Barry Island, Barry ($\frac{3}{4}$m), Barry Docks (2 m), Cadoxton ($2\frac{3}{4}$ m), Wenvoe (5 m), Creigiau (11 m), Efail Isaf ($13\frac{1}{4}$ m), Treforest (16 m), Pontypridd (17 m), Trehafod (19 m), Porth ($20\frac{1}{4}$ m)

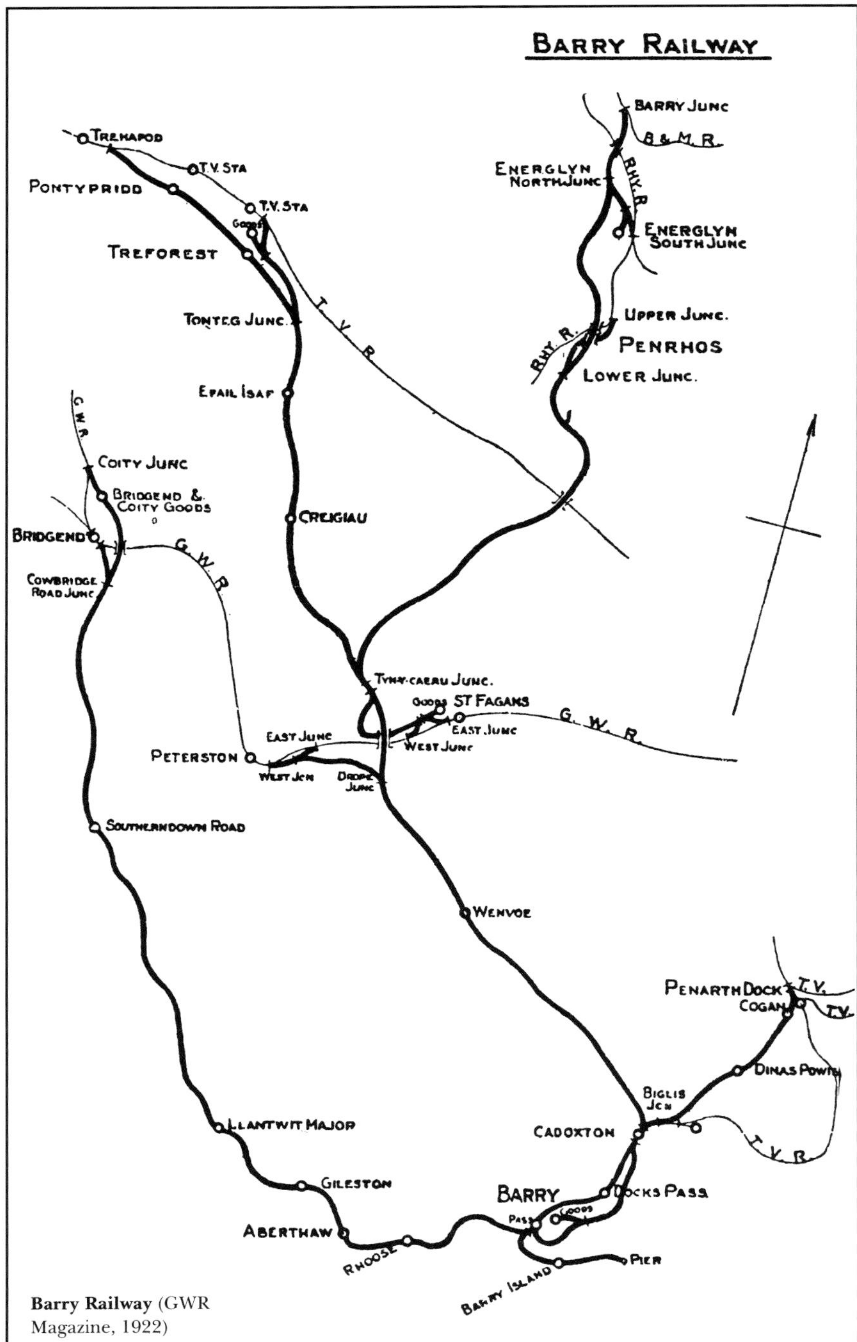

Barry Railway (GWR Magazine, 1922)

The Barry Railway passed to the GWR group under the 1921 Railways Act as a thriving concern whose docks at Barry and the associated $38\frac{1}{2}$ route miles of railway had consistently permitted dividends of 9% or more. In addition to the 26,540 ft of quays and 108 miles of sidings at Barry, the company operated an 18 m 65 ch main line to the Taff Vale at Treforest/Trehafod and branches to Cogan Junction (3 m 59 ch) for Cardiff, to Barry Junction B&M (9 m 64 ch) for the Rhymney, Brecon & Merthyr (both qv) and LNWR connections, to Peterston Junction (1 m 79 ch) and St Fagans Junction (1 m 9 ch) for the GWR main line, and to Barry Pier (1 m 18 ch) for the Bristol Channel steamers. It had also worked the Vale of Glamorgan line since opening.

Originally authorized by an Act of 14 August 1884 to provide an alternative to the cost and congestion at Cardiff docks, the Barry company opened its main docks in 1889 and 1898. The rail system built up gradually—Cogan Junction to Barry Dock, 20 December 1888; to Barry Town, 8 February 1889; to Peterston and St Fagans via Wenvoe Tunnel, 13 May 1889; and the main line to Trehafod, 18 July 1889; then by running powers over the TVR to Cardiff Riverside, 14 August 1893, and on to a new terminus at Clarence Road, 2 April 1894; to Barry Island, 3 August 1896; extension to the pier, 27 June 1899; and over the Vale of Glamorgan route from 1 December 1897.

Access to the eastern group of lines was obtained by Acts of 1896 and 1898 which produced the line from Tynycaeau to Penrhos via Walnut Tree Viaduct (1 August 1901) and the extension via the Aber and Rhymney viaducts to Barry Junction on the B&M route (2 January 1905). All this expansion produced massive conflict between the Barry Railway and its neighbours and, being last on the scene, its routes were frequently spectacular, the 125 ft high, 2,400 ft long Llanbradach Viaduct across the Rhymney River being a notable example.

Parts of the Barry system were pruned under the GWR's post-Grouping rationalization, notably the B&M Extension line between Penrhos Lower Junction and Barry Junction and the loco and marshalling facilities at Trehafod. The passenger services to Cardiff (via Cogan and St Fagans), to Bridgend and to Porth were all continued, although the latter used the TVR line from Treforest. Even more traffic passed to Barry Island and the steamers operating from there, but coal was never again to reach the 11m tons dealt with by the Barry system in 1913.

GB

BASINGSTOKE BRANCH

Stations: Reading, Reading West (¾ m), Mortimer (7¼ m), Bramley (10½ m), Basingstoke (15½ m)

In addition to its local trains, this double line carried important through services from Bournemouth and Portsmouth to Newcastle, Bradford, Wolverhampton and Birkenhead. The latter used a connection at the London end of Basingstoke LSWR/SR station, the GWR having its own station alongside from the opening from Southcot Junction on 1 November 1848 until 1 January 1932. This three-platform affair with wooden buildings lay on the up side of its LSWR/SR neighbour, and one of its platforms was retained when the services were transferred.

The use of the SR station by GWR trains from 1932 contrasts with the hostility which surrounded the original Berks & Hants Railway (qv) project. The LSWR even went as far as proposing rival lines to Didcot and Swindon before agreement was reached and the B&H obtained its Act on 30 June 1845.

GB

BATH

The Bristol Committee of the GWR had pretty grand ideas about the architectural standards of the line in its area. In Bath it was determined to match the city's elegance and provided not only a handsome stone station building but also some fine bridges (qv, Bridges and viaducts), tunnels and other features, including the walled approach through Sydney Gardens. These survived the enlargement works of 1897 (and 1942 bombing), although the overall roof was displaced in favour of extra lines between the platforms.

Bath station had an up bay and a down side signal box rising above the platform canopy. There was a large goods depot and a small engine shed to the west.

GB

BATHAMPTON–BRADFORD JUNCTIONS LINE

Stations: Bathampton (2¼ miles from Bath), Limpley Stoke (6½ m), Freshford (7¼ m), Bradford-on-Avon (9½ m), Trowbridge (12¾ m)

This pleasant rail route along the Avon valley required seven viaducts and a 159 yd tunnel east of Bradford-on-Avon. The Kennet & Avon Canal, acquired by the GWR from 1 July 1851 and then allowed to deteriorate, also chose a route beside the Avon and the railway twice passed beneath its rival. It carried Cardiff/Bristol–Salisbury trains, which joined the route east of Bathampton station, and had a form of crossroads at the southern end where Devizes–Bristol trains and those from Chippenham to Westbury/Weymouth used the Bradford Junctions triangle.

The Wilts, Somerset & Weymouth Railway (qv) had been forced into this link between its Thingley Junction–Weymouth line and the main line at Bathampton by a clause in its 1845 Act, but the initial branch to Bradford-on-Avon, although constructed by 1848, could not be opened for financial reasons and it was to be 2 February 1857 before the GWR began services on the whole route. The original single line was then doubled in 1885 with Avoncliff Halt being added in 1906, and Limpley Stoke gaining a branch to Camerton (qv) in 1910.

GB

BERKELEY ROAD–LYDBROOK JUNCTION LINE

Stations: Berkeley Road, Berkeley (2¼ m), Sharpness (4 m), Severn Bridge (5¼ m), Lydney Junction (8 m), Lydney Town (8¾ m), Whitecroft (11 m), Parkend (12¼ m), Speech House Road (14¾ m), Drybrook Road (17¼ m), Cinderford (18½ m)
Drybrook Road, Upper Lydbrook (18¾ m), Lydbrook Junction (20½ m)

The GWR and Midland companies acquired the ailing Severn & Wye system (qv) in 1894, running it through a joint management committee and each contributing stock and equipment. The one weekday through passenger train over the whole route provided a fascinating 92–93 minutes of travel, including a spectacular bridge crossing of the River Severn from Sharpness Docks to Purton.

The first section from the Bristol–Gloucester line was ex-MR although the GWR owned the southern curve at Berkeley. After its flat course, trains climbed past Sharpness Docks to cross first the steam swing bridge over the Gloucester & Sharpness Canal and then the main river and the Gloucester–Chepstow line beyond. From the connection with the latter at Lydney the route was broadly that of its 1813 tramway progenitor, with the 'Mineral Loop' taking its separate course between Tufts and Serridge junctions. During its climb and descent through the Forest of Dean, the single line had several colliery links and a 2¾-mile branch from Parkend to a station adjoining Coleford GWR. At Serridge Junction trains took the 1900 extension to Cinderford and returned to continue to Lydbrook Junction on the Ross–Monmouth line (qv).

Traffic to and from coastal vessels was exchanged with the line at Sharpness Docks and it also carried diverted services when the Severn Tunnel was closed for maintenance. Over the 21-span, 1,387 yd bridge, trains could only be headed by one engine drawn from the '2301', '2021', '7400' or '1400' Classes. The S&W system north of Lydney Town lost its passenger services on 8 July 1929 but coal traffic remained substantial.

GB

BERKS & HANTS LINE

Stations: Reading (36 miles from Paddington), Reading West (37 m), Theale (41¼ m), Aldermaston (44¾ m), Midgham (46¾ m), Thatcham (49½ m), Newbury (53 m), Kintbury (58½ m), Hungerford (61½ m), Bedwyn (66½ m), Savernake (70 m), Pewsey (75¼ m), Woodborough (78¾ m), Patney (81 m), Devizes (85¾ m)

Two railway projects created the line from Reading to Devizes and, in doing so, established a significant part of the future West of England main line. The first of the two

Berks & Hants line *Woodborough station* (GWR Museum, Swindon)

was the Berks & Hants Railway, a GWR subsidiary which had an easy passage through Parliament following a recent agreement with the London & South Western Railway and secured its enabling Act on 30 June 1845. The contractor made rapid progress and the line was opened from Reading to Hungerford on 21 December 1847.

Brunel provided a temporary terminus at Hungerford, clearly expecting extension westwards, but the LSWR saw this as a breach of the agreement between the two companies and the Berks & Hants Extension Railway was not authorized until 13 August 1859. Its course continued to follow that of the rival Kennet & Avon Canal, over whose tunnel it crossed near the Savernake summit, and it was brought into use with GWR working on 11 November 1862. Whereas the B&H proper was incorporated into the GWR before opening, the Extension remained independent until 1882 when its shareholders received £85 10s worth of GWR stock for every £100 of their own.

GB

BICESTER

Authorized in 1905, and part of the GWR's striving for a shorter route to Birmingham, the line from Ashendon on the GW&GC (qv) to Aynho, just south of Kings Sutton on the Banbury line, gave Bicester its second station, on the north side of the town. This was a simple, two-track affair with a small goods yard and receiving a modest Paddington–Bicester–Banbury service.

The Ashendon–Aynho line was opened in 1910, to goods on 4 April and to passengers on 1 July. It had flyover junctions at each end, two tunnels, several substantial cuttings, and intermediate stations at Brill & Ludgershall (47½ miles from Paddington), Blackthorn (50½ m), Bicester (53¾ m), Ardley (57¼ m), and Aynho Park (61½ m).

GB

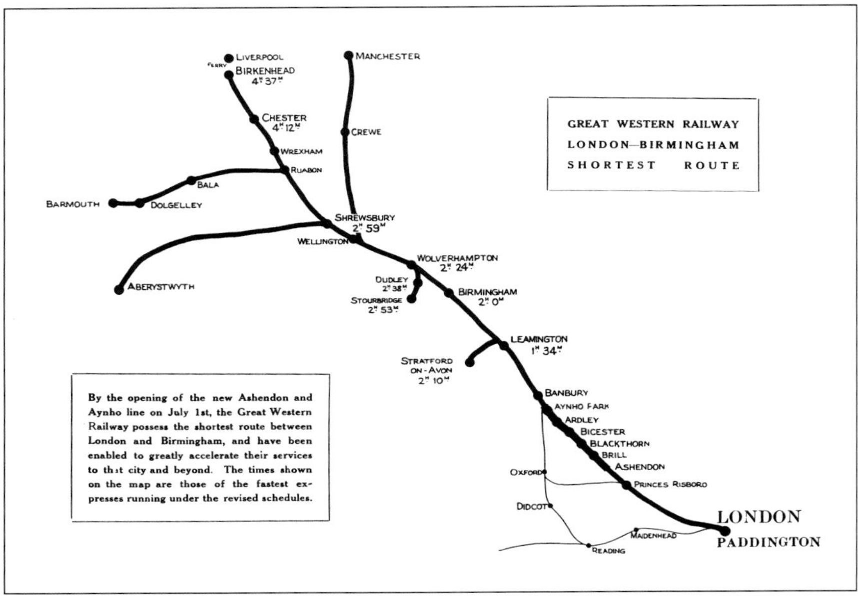

Bicester *The Ashendon-Aynho 'cut-off' line, opened in 1910, gave Bicester a second station and the GWR a shorter route to Birmingham.* (GWR Magazine, 1910)

BIRKENHEAD JOINT LINES

Stations: Chester General, Mollington (3 m), Capenhurst (5 m), Ledsham (6¾ m), Hooton (8 m), Bromborough (9¾ m), Spital (11 m), Port Sunlight (11½ m), Bebington & New Ferry (12¼ m), Rock Ferry (13¼ m), Birkenhead Town (14¾ m), Birkenhead Woodside (15¼ m)

The GWR gained access to the Mersey by its take-over, jointly with the LNWR, of the Birkenhead Railway on 20 November 1860. This move was to bring the company long-distance passenger business, commuters travelling on the steam railmotors and later auto-train services out from Birkenhead and Rock Ferry, and a steadily growing volume of freight business.

The Joint Lines network consisted of the main line from Chester to Birkenhead, the Chester–Warrington line, and the Helsby and West Kirby branches east and west from Hooton. It had originated with an Act of 12 July 1837 incorporating the Chester & Birkenhead Railway which opened a basic single line railway from Grange Lane, Birkenhead, on 23 September 1840, and added a branch to Monks Ferry on 23 October 1844. In 1847, after the opening of the Morpeth and Egerton docks at Birkenhead, and of an extension from Grange Lane to Cathcart Street Goods (5 April), the

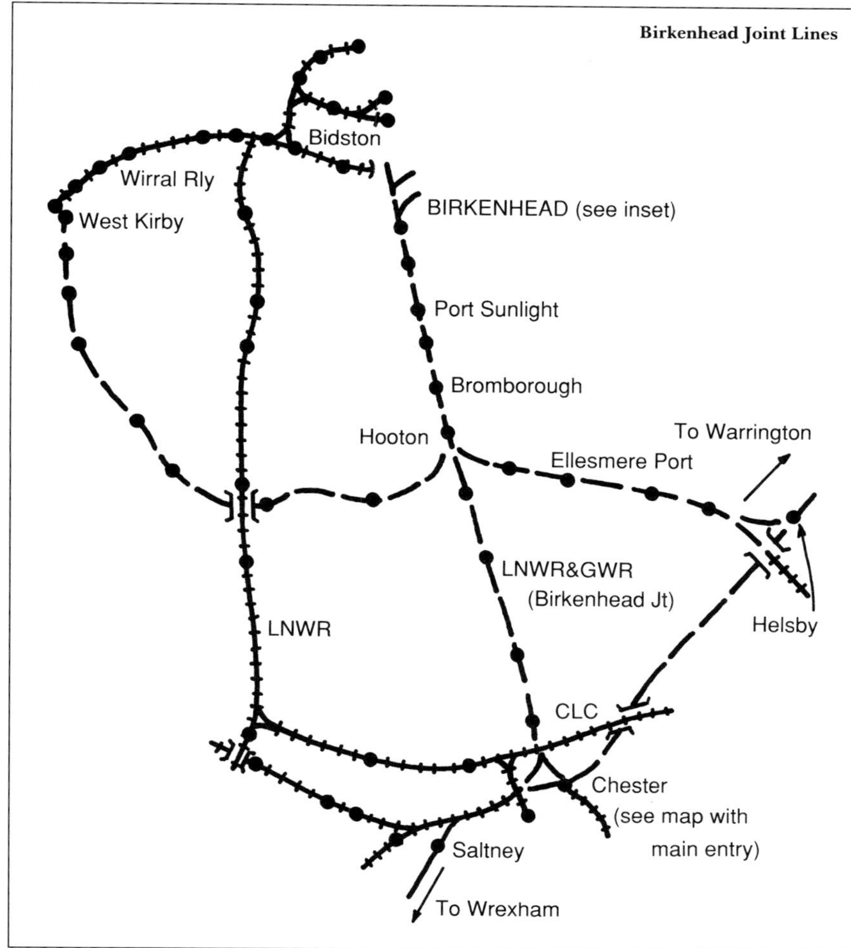

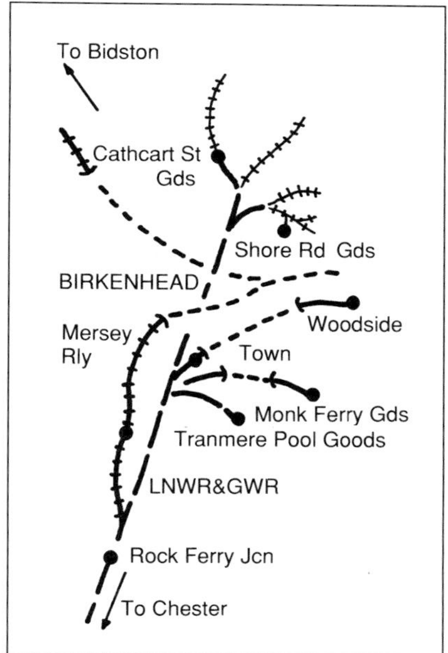

C&B was acquired by the Birkenhead, Lancashire & Cheshire Junction Railway on 22 July, that company becoming the Birkenhead Railway in 1859 and passing to the GWR and LNWR a year later.

Birkenhead continued to expand and the local railway network expanded with it. In addition to a new passenger line to a Woodside terminus adjoining the ferry (31 March 1878), the joint companies added lines to Tranmere Pool and Shore Reach Goods, a route over the docks lines to Morpeth Dock and a connection from Rock Ferry Junction to the Mersey Railway. At Morpeth Dock the GWR had lighterage facilities and sent cartage vehicles over on the ferries to Liverpool, where it had four more goods depots.

Goods traffic was very important in the Birkenhead area. In addition to ore imports and coal exports, the port handled large numbers of Irish cattle and the private sidings served businesses dealing with grain, flour, molasses, cement, oil, tar, timber, domestic coal, manure and guano. Surrounding areas like Port Sunlight added further traffics and the 3.35 pm for Smithfield ('The Meat') or the 6.5 pm 'Feeder' to Pontypool Road were quite as important as the 11.47 am 'Zulu' bound for Paddington.

GB

BIRMINGHAM

Stations: Tyseley (107¼ miles from Paddington via Bicester), Small Heath (108¾ m), Bordesley (109¾ m), Moor Street (110 m), Snow Hill (110½ m), Hockley (111½ m), Soho (112¼ m), Handsworth (113¾ m)

The GWR's route through Birmingham began at Tyseley, where the Banbury and North Warwickshire lines joined, and the GWR provided a new station and locomotive depot with the opening of the latter. The line continued north-west past Small Heath and its mileage depot to Bordesley, where the route was linked with the Midland/LMS Camp Hill–Saltley line. After Moor Street, GWR trains tunnelled to Snow Hill and again before Hockley and its sizeable goods complex, including canal basin, bonded store and 25-ton crane. Soho was then followed by Handsworth and the separation of the Stourbridge and Wolverhampton lines.

Part quadrupled as the GWR created its new route from Bristol in 1908, the line carried the company's express service from Paddington to Wolverhampton and beyond, plus North–South Coast trains, services to Weymouth, Cardiff, Bristol and the West and a host of local workings to Stratford, Stourbridge, Dudley and further. All these were dealt with either at Moor Street's three terminal platforms or at the 12 created at Snow Hill from the two long islands and country-end bays.

The original scheme for the Birmingham line had originated with the Birmingham & Oxford Junction Railway (qv), incorporated by an Act of 3 August 1846 and then granted extension powers for a separate access to the Midlands capital. After taking over the B&OJ and the Birmingham, Wolverhampton & Dudley Railway scheme, the GWR discussed with the newly formed LNWR the idea of a joint Birmingham station and the use of the latter's lines northwards, but this came to nought and the GWR line into Snow Hill from the south was opened on 1 October 1852. Extension to Priestfield followed on 14 November 1854 to give access to Wolverhampton.

The first Snow Hill station was replaced in 1871 by one with through lines, platform loops, bays and an overall roof, this being remodelled to the twin-island form in 1910–12. The GWR's Birmingham Hotel had been opened in 1863 and was incorporated in the remodelling. To the south, the route ran in tunnel to Moor Street and then became five tracks with an up goods line leading to that station's two hoists and low-level goods depot.

Moor Street itself opened on 1 July 1909 to deal with the increase in commuter traffic following the opening of the North Warwickshire line. It started life with a two-sided platform, gained its terminal block and the goods depot below Bordesley Viaduct in 1914, and a third platform in 1930.

GB

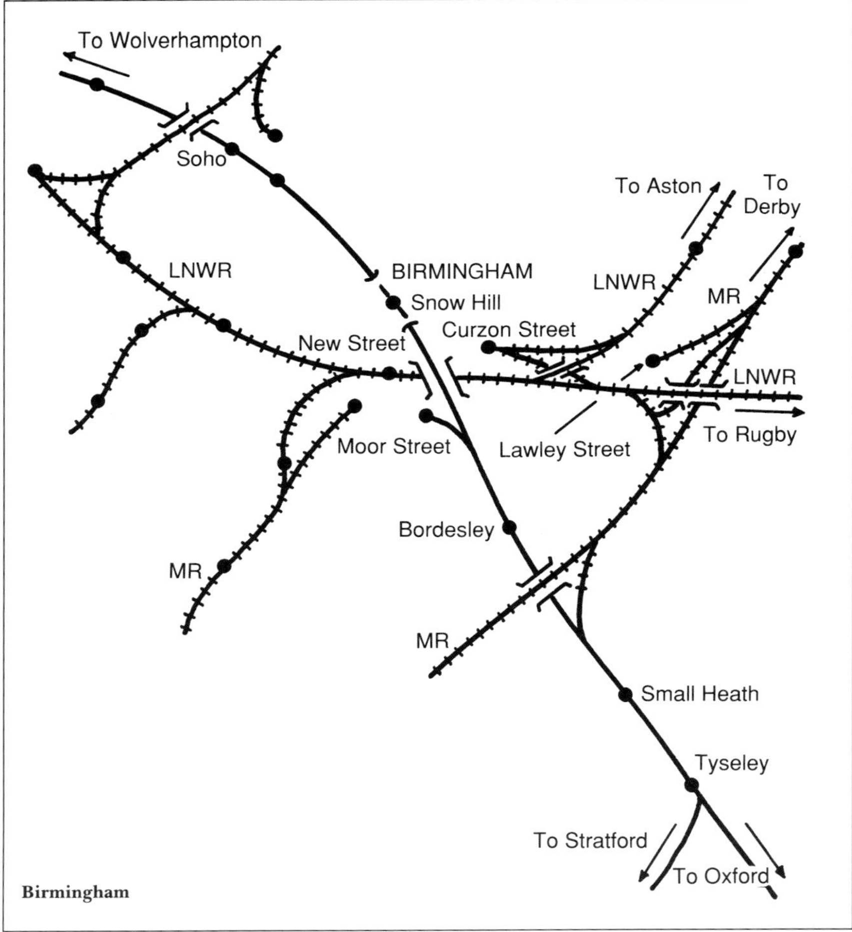

Birmingham

BIRMINGHAM & NORTH WARWICKSHIRE LINE

Stations: Birmingham Snow Hill, Moor Street ($\frac{1}{2}$ m), Bordesley ($1\frac{1}{4}$ m),

Birmingham *A magnificent view of the new Snow Hill of 1910–12.* (National Railway Museum, York)

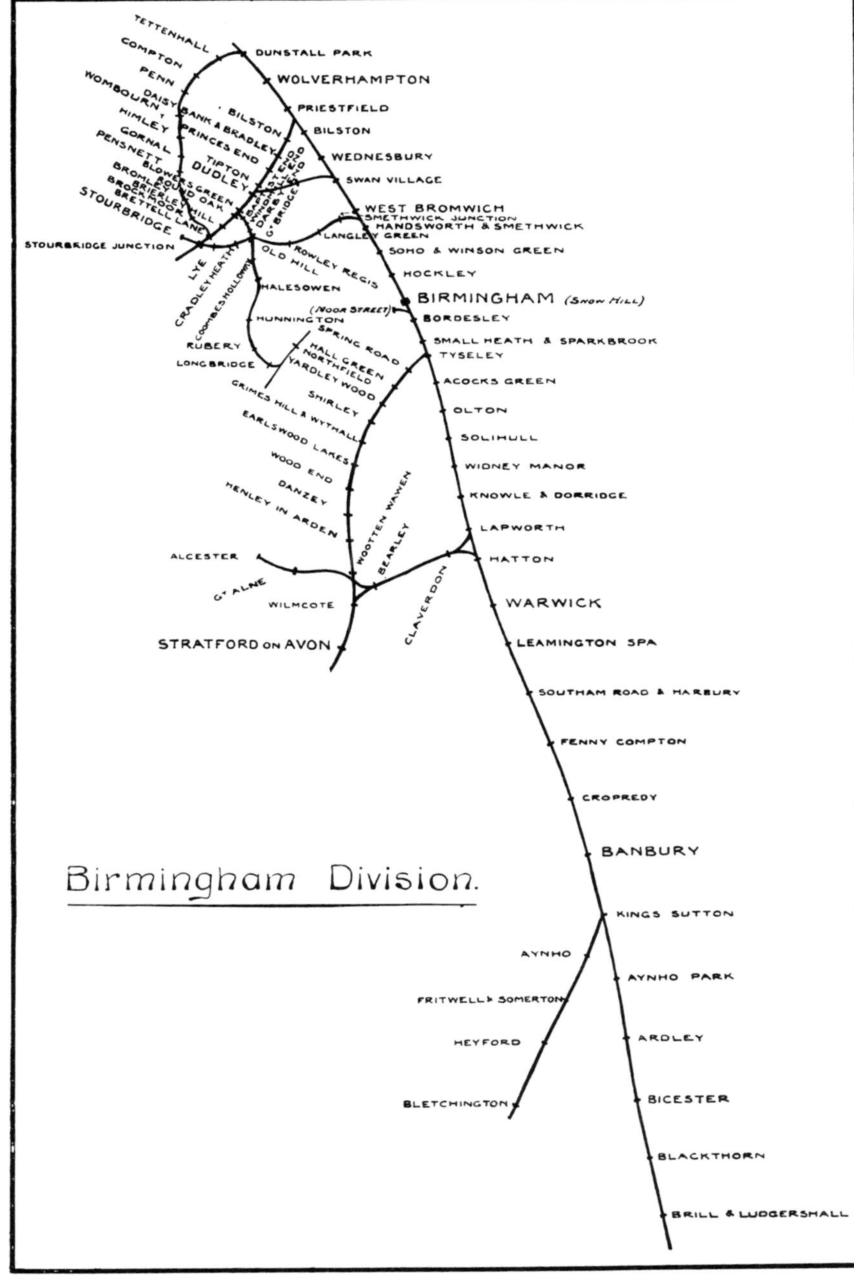

Birmingham *In 1929 the Birmingham Division led in the 'All-Line Passenger Train Competition'. 'This map shows the stations where credit is due for the best divisional time-keeping achievement.'* (GWR Magazine)

Small Heath (2¼ m), Tyseley (3¼ m), Spring Road (4¼ m), Hall Green (4¾ m), Yardley Wood (6 m), Shirley (7¼ m), Grimes Hill & Wythall (9¼ m), Earlswood Lakes (10¼ m), Wood End (12¼ m), Danzey (14 m), Henley-in-Arden (17 m), Wootton Wawen (18¾ m), Bearley (21¼ m)

This 17¾ miles of new railway, originally authorized as the Birmingham, North Warwickshire & Stratford-on-Avon Railway on 25 August 1894, was taken over by the GWR in 1900 and opened from Tyseley to Bearley on 9 December 1907 for goods and 1 July 1908 for passengers. Its completion gave the GWR a 95-mile route from Bristol to Birmingham compared with the 133 miles via Hereford and 141 via Didcot, and it was used for through services to South Wales, the West of England and Weston-super-Mare, as well as around 100 local trains on weekdays.

The new line required a 175-yard tunnel at Wood End to transfer its allegiance from the River Cole to the River Alne, and then continued to rise to a summit 500 ft above sea level at Earlswood Lakes. A 9-mile descent at 1 in 181/150 followed to pass below the Birmingham & Stratford Canal and use part of the Alcester branch (qv) to reach the loop at Bearley.

At Henley-in-Arden a new station was provided with a connection from the Rowington Junction branch (authorized 5 August 1873, opened 2 July 1894) and an island platform for its trains. The old station became a goods depot and the branch beyond it was closed on 1 January 1917 and lifted a few months later.

GB

BIRMINGHAM & OXFORD JUNCTION RAILWAY

Encouraged by the Grand Junction and GWR companies, the Birmingham & Oxford Junction Railway originated as a response to the London & Birmingham's cavalier attitude towards its customers. It obtained an Act for its line from Birmingham to join the Oxford & Rugby (qv) at Fenny Compton on 3 August 1846, but then became the subject of a boardroom battle between the GWR and LNWR companies before the former triumphed and acquired the enterprise on 31 August 1848. Its line from Snow Hill to Fenny Compton was opened on 1 October 1852.

GB

BIRMINGHAM–CHESTER LINE

Stations: Birmingham Snow Hill (110½ miles from Paddington), Hockley (111½ m), Soho & Winson Green (112¼ m), Handsworth (113¼ m),

Swan Village (116¼ m), Wednesbury (118 m), Bilston (120½ m), Priestfield (121½ m), Wolverhampton Low Level (123 m), Dunstall Park (124 m), Codsall (127¾ m), Albrighton (130¾ m), Shifnal (135½ m), Oakengates (139¾ m), Wellington (142½ m), Admaston (144¼ m), Walcot (146½ m), Upton Magna (149 m), Shrewsbury (152¾ m), Leaton (156½ m), Baschurch (160½ m), Rednal & West Felton (166 m), Whittington Low Level (169 m), Gobowen (170¾ m), Weston Rhyn (172¾ m), Chirk (174 m), Whitehurst Platform (175½ m), Cefn (176½ m), Ruabon (178¼ m), Johnstown & Hafod (179¾ m), Wrexham (183 m), Gresford (186¼ m), Rossett (187¾ m), Balderton (191¼ m), Saltney (193 m), Chester General (195¼ m)

Between Birmingham and Wolverhampton the route of the GWR main line was that of the Birmingham, Wolverhampton & Dudley Railway, incorporated on 3 August 1846 and vested in the GWR before opening from Snow Hill to Priestfield Junction on 14 November 1854. There was much industrial activity along its course, including the great goods yard at Hockley, the separate goods line to Soho & Winson Green, the Birmingham Railway Carriage & Wagon Works, Wednesbury's Tube siding and Basin connections, and Stewarts & Lloyds Works at Bilston. At Swan Village, a BW&D cut-off line to Dudley dated from 1866, the route then continuing through cuttings to the former Oxford, Worcester & Wolverhampton section from Priestfield Junction through Wolverhampton to Stafford Road Junction. Other junctions were at Handsworth for Stourbridge (see next entry) and at Wednesbury with the Dudley–Walsall line, and there were two tunnels.

On the next section the Shrewsbury & Birmingham Railway was the prime mover, receiving its Act on 3 August 1846, opening from Shrewsbury to Oakengates on 1 June 1849 and on to Wolverhampton on 12 November of that year. Several years of conflict with the LNWR was then followed by absorption into the GWR camp from 1 September 1854.

The local service extended beyond Wolverhampton to Wellington (qv), past Oxley yard and loco and the junction with the Kingswinford branch (qv), down at 1 in 100 towards Codsall and then up at 1 in 150 to Madeley Junction and the line to Buildwas. Down goods trains were banked up to Hollinswood after which came Oakengates Tunnel, the station, Ketley Junction and the second route to Buildwas, and then entry to Wellington along with the LNWR services from Stafford. The GW & LNW joint section on to Shrewsbury (qv) then began with the departure of the Crewe branch (qv) at Market Drayton Junction and a falling gradient for the next 4 miles.

Beyond Shrewsbury the route originated with the opening of the Shrewsbury & Chester Railway (qv) on 4 November 1846 and 16 October 1848, that concern becoming part of the GWR in 1854. It began with a steady climb after Crewe Junction and Coton marshalling yard, followed by several rises and falls, all modest except for the 4-mile descent at 1 in 82½ beyond Wrexham. After meeting the Oswestry branch (qv) at Gobowen (qv), the route crossed Chirk Viaduct over the River Ceiriog and came to Chirk station, interchange point for the Glyn Valley Tramway until 1935. The Cefn Viaduct then carried trains over the River Dee to the junction with the Dolgelley line (qv) at Ruabon (qv). The journey on to Wrexham (qv) saw the scenery change from rural to industrial with connections to collieries and steelworks, the risk of subsidence from the former imposing a 40 mph speed restriction on Gresford bank on the section to the junction with the LNWR at Saltney.

GB

BIRMINGHAM–STOURBRIDGE JUNCTION LINE

Stations: Birmingham Snow Hill, Hockley (1 m), Soho & Winson Green (1¾ m), Handsworth & Smethwick (2¾ m), Smethwick Junction (4 m), Oldbury & Langley Green (5¼ m), Rowley Regis & Blackheath (6¾ m), Old Hill (8 m), Cradley Heath & Cradley (9½ m), Lye (10¾ m), Stourbridge Junction (12¼ m)

The Stourbridge (qv) line carried a very useful commuter service made up of local trains and fast and semi-fast services which continued to Kidderminster, Worcester and beyond. There were also nearly 40 trains on Sundays and a considerable amount of goods activity, especially at Cradley Heath. In addition to the goods depot and private sidings there, the Congreaves branch (opened 1 April 1863) led below the main line to the Old Hill Goods branch (opened 1 August 1907). Other goods branches ran from Langley Green to Oldbury (1884) and from Lye to Hayes Lane (1863), and at Old Hill the station stood between the tunnel to the east and the 1878 branches to Dudley and Halesowen to the west (both qv).

The route derived from the Stourbridge Railway Act of 14 June 1860—for a line from Stourbridge Junction to Old Hill and a branch to Cradley Park Colliery—and the Stourbridge Railway Extension Act of 1 August 1861—for the Old Hill–Handsworth Junction section plus Old Hill Goods and Galton Junction branches. Worked by the GWR and vested therein from 1 February 1870, the line was opened from Stourbridge Junction to Cradley on 1 April 1863, to Old Hill on 1 January 1866 and through to the main line at Handsworth Junction on 1 April 1867.

GB

BLACKALL, THOMAS

Signal Engineer, 1885–93. He was appointed engineer in charge of new signalling installations on 13 March 1883, reporting to the Chief Civil Engineer. He retired in June 1893, and was succeeded by his son, Alfred Thomas Blackall, at Reading Signal Works, but now reporting to William Dean, Locomotive Superintendent. He became Chief Signal & Telegraph Engineer, reporting direct to the Board, on 27 July 1903, and retired in June 1923. A. T. Blackall directed the design and installation of signalling and communications throughout the great period of GWR expansion—1900–13—when over 400 route miles of new railway was built.

AV

BLAENAU FFESTINIOG BRANCH

Stations: Bala, Frongoch (2½ m), Arenig (7¾ m), Cwm Prysor (10½ m), Trawsfynydd (16¼ m),

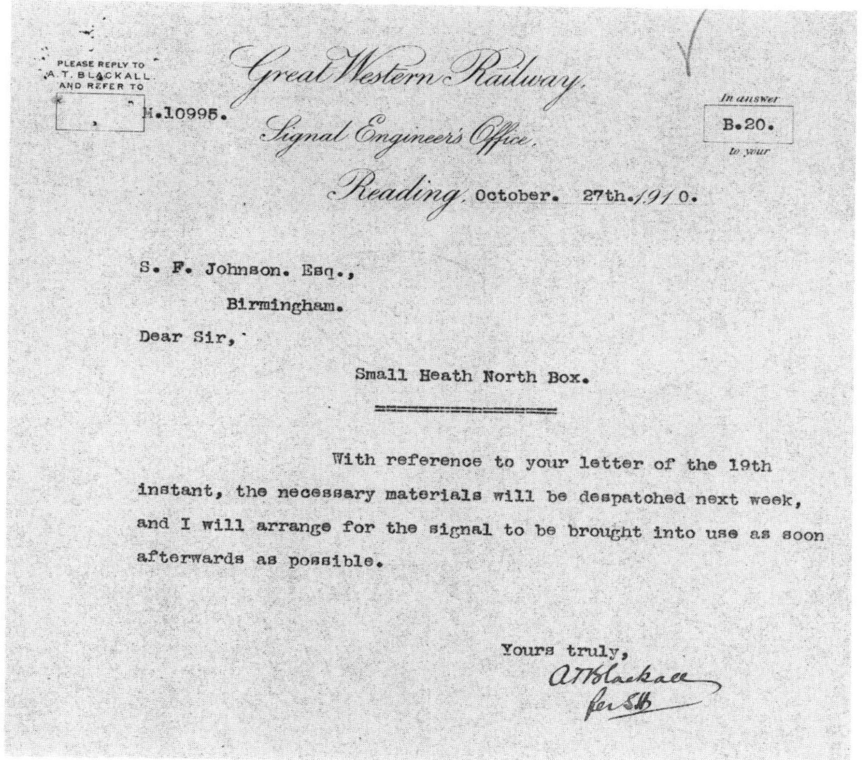

PLEASE REPLY TO
A. T. BLACKALL
AND REFER TO

M.10995.

Great Western Railway.
Signal Engineer's Office.
Reading, October. 27th. 1910.

In answer
B.20.
to your

S. F. Johnson. Esq.,
Birmingham.

Dear Sir,

Small Heath North Box.

With reference to your letter of the 19th instant, the necessary materials will be despatched next week, and I will arrange for the signal to be brought into use as soon afterwards as possible.

Yours truly,
A T Blackall
per SH

Thomas Blackall *A letter from the Signal Engineer's Office in Reading dated October 1910 during Blackall's time as Signal & Telegraph Engineer.* (W. Adams Collection)

Maentwrog Road ($19\frac{3}{4}$ m), Festiniog ($21\frac{1}{4}$ m), Manod ($23\frac{1}{2}$ m), Blaenau Festiniog ($24\frac{3}{4}$ m)

This lonely single line on the very edge of the GWR empire was conceived as a route for slate traffic to the West Midlands, but as that traffic dried up it came to depend on local people and summer tourists using the service of six weekday passenger trains in each direction. Those that made the 77-minute through journey climbed along the valley of the Afon Treweryn to Llyn Celyn and the 1,278 ft summit at Cwm Prysor before a curving descent to the lake at Trawsfynydd and another curving section northwards to the long, single-platform terminus at Blaenau. Festiniog Railway trains used the opposite face and slate was transhipped between the two railways in the adjacent goods yard.

The Bala & Festiniog Railway, incorporated on 28 July 1873, had been financed largely by the GWR and its associates, the former working the line and then absorbing it from 1 July 1910. The difficult construction task included the conversion to standard gauge of the 1868 1 ft $11\frac{1}{2}$ in gauge Festiniog & Blaenau Railway which the GWR had purchased. Eventually, however, the new railway was opened from Bala Junction, through Bala (qv) and on to Festiniog on 1 November 1882, with the section forward to Blaenau coming into use on 10 September of the following year.

There were five halts along this scenic route, small goods depots at most of the stations, private sidings at Arenig and Blaenau and, at one period, an army troop station at Trawsfynydd.

GB

BLAENAVON BRANCH

Stations: Newport High Street, Caerleon ($2\frac{3}{4}$ m), Ponthir ($4\frac{1}{4}$ m), Llantarnam ($5\frac{1}{2}$ m), Cwmbran ($6\frac{1}{2}$ m), Upper Pontnewydd ($7\frac{1}{2}$ m), Sebastopol ($8\frac{1}{2}$ m), Panteg & Griffithstown (9 m), Pontypool Crane Street ($10\frac{3}{4}$ m), Pontnewynydd ($11\frac{1}{2}$ m), Abersychan Low Level ($12\frac{3}{4}$ m), Cwmavon ($14\frac{1}{4}$ m), Blaenavon ($16\frac{1}{4}$ m)

The generous GWR passenger service on this route included trains from Newport to Pontypool Road, to Pontypool Crane Street and to Blaenavon, plus Cwmbran–Crane Street, Crane Street–Blaenavon and Panteg–Pontypool Road workings. Ascending services took about an hour for the journey, allowing for stops at four halts, and were usually worked by 0-6-0PT locomotives.

The route had originated on 1 July 1852 when the Monmouthshire Railway & Canal Co (qv) opened an $8\frac{1}{4}$-mile line from Newport (qv) to Pontypool (qv) along the eastern side of its canal. This was extended a further $5\frac{3}{4}$ miles to Blaenavon on 1 June 1854 (passengers 2 October), the whole enterprise being worked by the GWR from 1 August 1875 and amalgamated therewith on 1 August 1880. By that time the GWR-backed Pontypool, Caerleon & Newport Railway had been operating its alternative route, which joined the South Wales main line at Maindee Junction, since 17 September 1874 and passenger services were diverted to this via a Cwmbran–Llantarnam connection in 1879.

The lower section of the original MR&C route was fed by several colliery, brickworks, ironworks and quarry sidings and continued to handle their traffics after diversion of the passenger trains. North of Pontypool two steep colliery branches had been opened west from Pontnewynydd Junction (1870), and a branch north from Trevethin Junction to Abersychan & Talywain (18 September 1879) where it met the LNWR line down from Brynmawr. This carried a joint service to Newport, operated by the GWR from 1912 and ending on 5 May 1941. There was a short stretch of joint line at Abersychan & Talywain, a triangular connection to several collieries there, and connections from higher up both Blaenavon lines to Varteg Hill Colliery and Blaenavon Ironworks.

GB

BLAGDON BRANCH

Stations: Congresbury ($1\frac{1}{2}$ miles from Yatton), Wrington ($4\frac{1}{2}$ m), Langford ($5\frac{3}{4}$ m), Burrington ($6\frac{3}{4}$ m), Blagdon ($8\frac{1}{4}$ m)

The Wrington Vale Light Railway was conceived, with GWR support, as a line to serve

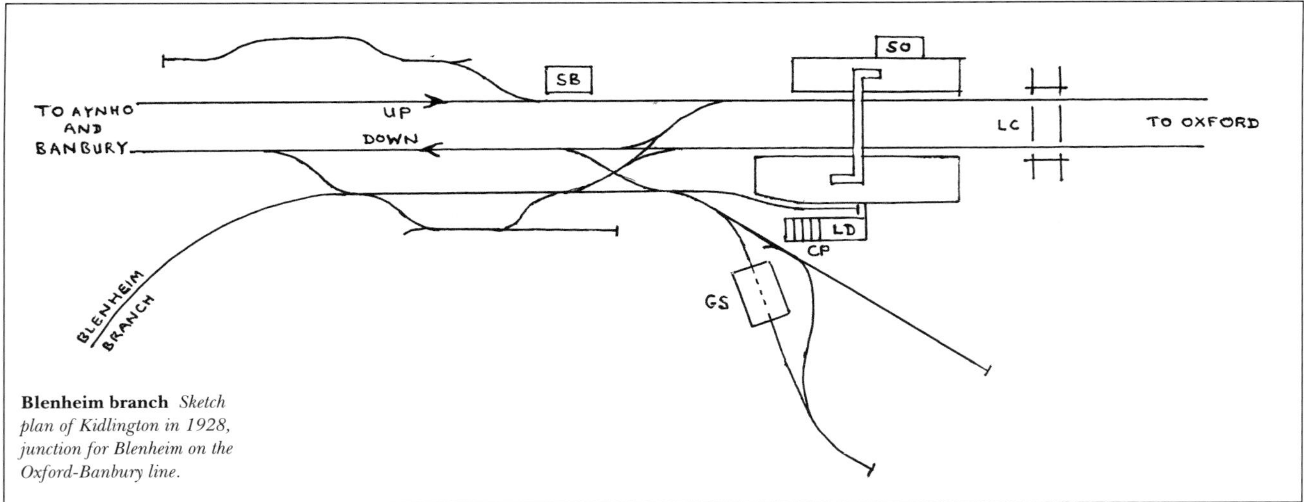

Blenheim branch *Sketch plan of Kidlington in 1928, junction for Blenheim on the Oxford-Banbury line.*

a new reservoir and pumping station at Blagdon and to cater for the travel needs of 14 parishes *en route*. After confirmation of its Light Railway Order on 18 March 1898, the venture was acquired by the GWR and its single line opened on 4 December 1901. It operated as a single section with a train staff and 'one engine in steam' regulations, but the five trains each way on weekdays (mostly to and from Yatton) declined to three, then to two, and finally ceased altogether on 14 September 1931, although freight traffic continued.

GB

BLENHEIM BRANCH

The 3 m 56 ch Woodstock Railway originated with an Act of 25 September 1886. Funded largely by the Duke of Marlborough, the single line was opened on 19 May 1890 and sold to the GWR for £15,000 seven years later.

The branch followed the main line from the down bay at Kidlington, past the scene of a bad accident in 1874, and over the River Cherwell and the Oxford Canal before turning west through the 1929 halt at Shipton-on-Cherwell to the single platform terminus at Blenheim & Woodstock. Revised signalling arrangements accompanied the introduction of auto-trains (qv) in 1926, three weekday services working to and from Oxford and six more from Kidlington.

GB

BODMIN

Although the Cornwall Railway's (qv) line reached Bodmin Road in 1859, the first railway service to Bodmin proper was provided by the pioneer Bodmin & Wadebridge Railway which had opened between those points on 4 July 1834. The B&W was purchased by the London & South Western Railway in 1846 but the town's first link with the outside world was via the GWR which opened from Bodmin Road to Bodmin on 27 May 1887 and on to a connection with the B&W line at Boscarne Junction on 3 September 1888.

From the outer face of the up island at Bodmin Road, the GWR single line branch took a winding 3 m 44 ch course to Bodmin General station. The trains continuing to Wadebridge then reversed direction on to the 2 m 46 ch link to Boscarne Junction where they met the LSWR/SR line from Wenford Bridge and its branch to Bodmin North station.

Bodmin Road had a goods depot and two clay sidings.

GB

BOOKS

The GWR, more than any other railway company, realized the publicity value of good quality publications and in all published 132 books, including new editions, for sale to the public.

The first GWR book was *The Cornish Riviera Express* by A. M. Broadley in 1904. It cost 3d, the first edition sold ¼m copies and it ran to five editions. The first of the enor-

Blenheim branch *The terminus at Blenheim & Woodstock.* (Steamchest Collection)

G.W.R. PUBLICATIONS.

ABBEYS.—By M. R. James, Litt.D., F.S.A., F.B.A., Provost of Eton, with a chapter on "Monastic Life and Buildings" by Professor A. Hamilton Thompson, M.A., D. Litt., F.S.A. 164 pages, 100 page plates, 56 line drawings, 13 plans, 7 coloured plates and a map.

CASTLES.—By Sir Charles Oman, K.B.E., F.S.A., F.B.A., etc., Chichele Professor of Modern History and M.P. for Oxford University. Containing 240 pages, 105 page plates, 65 line drawings, 5 plans, 2 coloured plates and a map.

Price **5s.** each Volume. *Bound in quarter cloth, Crown quarto.*

These companion volumes contain authoritative accounts of 78 Abbeys, and 76 Castles in the country served by the Great Western Railway. They are a triumph of artistic book production with well printed text, a wealth of beautiful photographic and other plates, and useful maps.

CORNISH RIVIERA
GLORIOUS DEVON — By S. P. B. Mais, the famous novelist and travel book writer. Two books that no visitor to the West Country can afford to miss. Both volumes profusely illustrated in photogravure, many sectional maps.

SOMERSET. By Maxwell Fraser, F.R.G.S. A book warmly commended to all visitors to Somerset. 300 pages delightfully illustrated in photogravure.

Price each volume **1s.** paper covers, **2/6** bound whole cloth.

THE G.W.R. ENGINE BOOK.—Names, numbers, classes and types of G.W.R. Locomotives. New and enlarged edition.

CHELTENHAM FLYER.—Story of Britain's Famous Record-breaking Train.

TRACK TOPICS.—A book of Railway Engineering. A companion to "Cheltenham Flyer."

LOCOS OF THE ROYAL ROAD.—The Book of a Century of Locomotive Construction.

Price **1s.** each Volume.

LOCOMOTIVE BROCHURE.—Photogravure Plates of 12 types of G.W.R. engines.

SOUTHERN IRELAND, by Maxwell Fraser; profusely illustrated in photogravure.

RAMBLES IN THE CHILTERN COUNTRY. By Hugh E. Page, describing 365 miles of rambles in the Western Chilterns, the Penn Country and the Thames Valley.

RAMBLES IN SOUTH DEVON. By Hugh E. Page. Describes 12 delightful rambles, embracing coast, river, and moorland scenery of Glorious South Devon.

RAMBLES IN SHAKESPEARELAND AND THE COTSWOLDS. By Hugh E. Page. 20 rambles through the heart of England.

RAMBLES AND WALKING TOURS IN SOMERSET.—By Hugh E. Page. Describing 20 rambles through a charming countryside.

RAMBLES AROUND THE CAMBRIAN COAST.—By Hugh E. Page. Details of 280 miles of Rambles, Embracing Hills, Valleys, and Coast.

NORTH PEMBROKESHIRE.—A Book for Hikers. By E. Roland Williams.

Price **6d.** each Volume.

These publications can be obtained from any G.W.R. Station, Office, Agency, Bookstall, your Bookseller, or from the Superintendent of the Line, G.W.R., Paddington Station, London, W.2.

Books *A list of GWR publications that appeared in the 1937* Holiday Haunts.

mously popular *Holiday Haunts* came out in 1906. The first engine book listing the names of all GWR engines was published in 1911. There were 16 variations of this in all, and the last, *GWR Engines, Names, Numbers, Types and Classes* by W. G. C. Chapman, came out in 1946.

Amongst many guide and ramblers' books on various parts of the GWR empire were *North Wales, the British Tyrol, The Cathedral Line of England, its Sacred Sites and Shrines, Rural London, The Chalfont Country and the Thames Valley, The Cornish Riviera* and *Glorious Devon* (both by S. P. B. Mais), *Pembrokeshire and South West Wales* by A. G. Bradley, and *Southern Ireland* by Maxwell Fraser. Two books were published to mark the 1935 Centenary (qv). One was a reprint of *The Times* special supplement, the other the amusing *Railway Ribaldry* by the famous cartoonist W. Heath Robinson.

Particularly popular were the 'Boys of All Ages' titles, among them *The 10.30 Limited* (1923), which at 1 shilling sold 71,000 copies in six months, *Cheltenham Flyer* (1934), *Track Topics*, (1935) and *Locos of the Royal Road* (1936). All were reprinted in the 1960s and '70s. After the Second World War the company published *Dunkirk and the Great Western* (1945), whilst the very last GWR book was *Next Station* (1947) by Christian Barman, which looked at some of the might-have-beens had not Nationalization intervened. The monthly *Great Western Railway Magazine* was launched in 1888 by the GWR Temperance Union and taken over by the company for £750 *circa* 1900. Unique was the sponsorship by the company of E. T. MacDermot's *History of the Great Western Railway* which came out in two volumes in 1927 and 1931. O. S. Nock brought the story up to 1948 with a third volume published after Nationalization.

MCHB

BOX TUNNEL

The section between Chippenham and Bath was the most difficult part of the GWR main line to construct. It involved tunnelling for nearly 2 miles through Box Hill plus a long, deep approach cutting before the 1 in 100 descent through the tunnel and a series of embankments afterwards. Essentially a manual task, it took some five years to complete and is said to have claimed nearly 100 lives.

After trial bores had been sunk in 1836, shaft contracts were let in the September and those for the tunnel proper just over a year later. There was no rush of applicants, but eventually the eastern end, which passed through the Bath stone layers, went to Lewis of Bath and Brewer of Box, with the remainder, which involved lining the bore, going to George Burge of Herne Bay. By August 1839 the work was two-fifths completed, but a wet winter then slowed things down and only a period of frantic activity achieved completion in time for public opening on 30 June 1841.

As completed, Box Tunnel was 3,212 yards long with six ventilation shafts 85–260 ft in height and 25 ft in diameter. Initially only a single line of rails was laid, Daniel Gooch himself acting as pilotman for the first 48 hours and narrowly averting a nasty collision. All up trains had assistance at first but this was later determined by weight.

The stone from Box Hill was used for the

Box Tunnel *The ornate western portal of the tunnel.* (Real Photos)

ornate western portal of the tunnel and for a number of local stations, later becoming a major freight traffic with a siding at the eastern portal (qv, Corsham). Beyond the main tunnel was the 198 yd Middle Hill Tunnel with Box station on one side and Box (Mill Lane) Halt on the other.

One of the two days in the year when the rising sun shines through the straight tunnel bore is close to Brunel's birthday, but does not coincide with it, despite the legend.

GB

BRECON

Nearly ringed by mountains, Brecon became the gathering point for railways as it had earlier been for roads. In less than a decade it became the focal point of four routes, those from Newport, Neath and Moat Lane Junction, eventually to become part of the GWR, and that from Hereford, a Midland/LMS tentacle with links on to Swansea. Before the Second World War, Free Street station's main, island and bay platforms handled around 50 trains a day, nearly half on the Mid-Wales line.

Brecon interests helped to promote the Brecon & Merthyr Railway (qv) which arrived at a temporary terminus at Brecon on 1 May 1863 via the route of the 1812 Hay Tramroad. The Mid-Wales and Hereford, Hay & Brecon trains joined in from the following September, with the Neath & Brecon (qv) reaching a temporary station in Mount Street from 3 June 1867. The B&M's Free Street station, opened on 1 March 1871, was also used by HH&B/MR trains, those of the Mid-Wales joining soon after and the N&B services in 1874.

Brecon's goods traffic was dealt with either at Free Street or at the original Watton terminus site.

GB

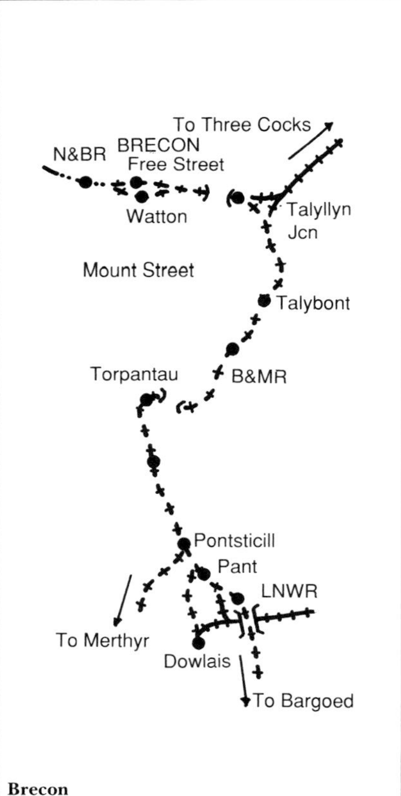

Brecon

BRECON & MERTHYR RAILWAY

Incorporated on 1 August 1859 as the Brecon & Merthyr Tydfil Junction Railway, this was a pugnacious little enterprise, ready to take on any rival, and eventually bringing to the GWR at the Grouping a 47-mile Brecon–Newport line with branches to Merthyr, Dowlais, Rhymney and Caerphilly (all qv).

After opening from Brecon to Dowlais on 1 May 1863, the B&M was seized with an ambition to reach Newport and acquired the 1825 Rumney Railway tramroad to further this aim. The RR lines from Bassaleg to Pengam and Caerphilly were upgraded and reopened and an extension to Rhymney brought into use on 1 May 1866. Despite a financial crisis, the Merthyr branch was opened on 1 August 1868, followed by the remainder of the link to the Rhymney Railway at Deri which finally permitted through B&M services between Brecon and Newport from 1 September.

This gutsy railway, with its 59 m 66 ch of track earning a 4% dividend, passed to the GWR on 1 January 1922.

GB

BRENTFORD BRANCH

Early supplies for the building of the GWR arrived via the Thames, Brentford and the Grand Junction Canal, but from 18 July 1859 there was a railway link with the river in the shape of a 3 m 77 ch branch from Southall (qv) to Brentford Dock. Authorized by the Great Western & Brentford Railway Act of 14 August 1855, the line was leased to the GWR in 1859 and vested therein from 1 July 1871. At one time a mixed gauge line was added to the original broad gauge one, but the two were worked as single lines until full conversion.

The Brentford branch ran east from Southall and passed beneath its 1789 canal rival before skirting Osterley Park, crossing the LSWR and reaching the twin platforms of Brentford Town. A final, mainly viaduct, section ran beside Syon Park to an irregularly shaped dock basin surrounded by three yards, eight warehouses and numerous sidings. Shipment traffic was handled by the GWR's own lighterage agent and the dock had a 40-ton capacity crane.

Passenger services began on 1 May 1860

and lasted until 4 May 1942. Latterly in the hands of auto-trains (qv), there had been seven trains each way morning and evening on weekdays. The intermediate Trumper's Crossing Halt closed on 1 February 1926.

GB

BRIDGEND

The South Wales Railway (qv) opened through Bridgend on 18 June 1850, but nearly 20 years earlier the town had been linked by a 4-mile, horse-worked tramway to Tondu (qv) and the pioneer line from Duffryn Colliery to Porthcawl Harbour (qv). This Bridgend Railway was taken over by the Llynvi Railway in 1854 and replaced by a broad gauge line on a new alignment which was carrying a Maesteg–Bridgend passenger service by 1864.

The separate Llynvi station on the up side of the main line was replaced by the main line one with gauge conversion in 1872, the latter then acquiring more work from 1 December 1897 when the Vale of Glamorgan line opened. From the latter's Cowbridge Road Junction, one track led to the main line while the other crossed to a separate goods depot on the up side and then on to Coity Junction on the Tondu line.

In later GWR years Bridgend consisted of a down main platform with a country end bay for the services via Tondu to Abergwynfi, Blaengarw and Nantymoel, plus an up island used by Barry (qv) trains as well as those on the main line. There was a down side goods depot and several private sidings including the War Department one at Tremains.

GB

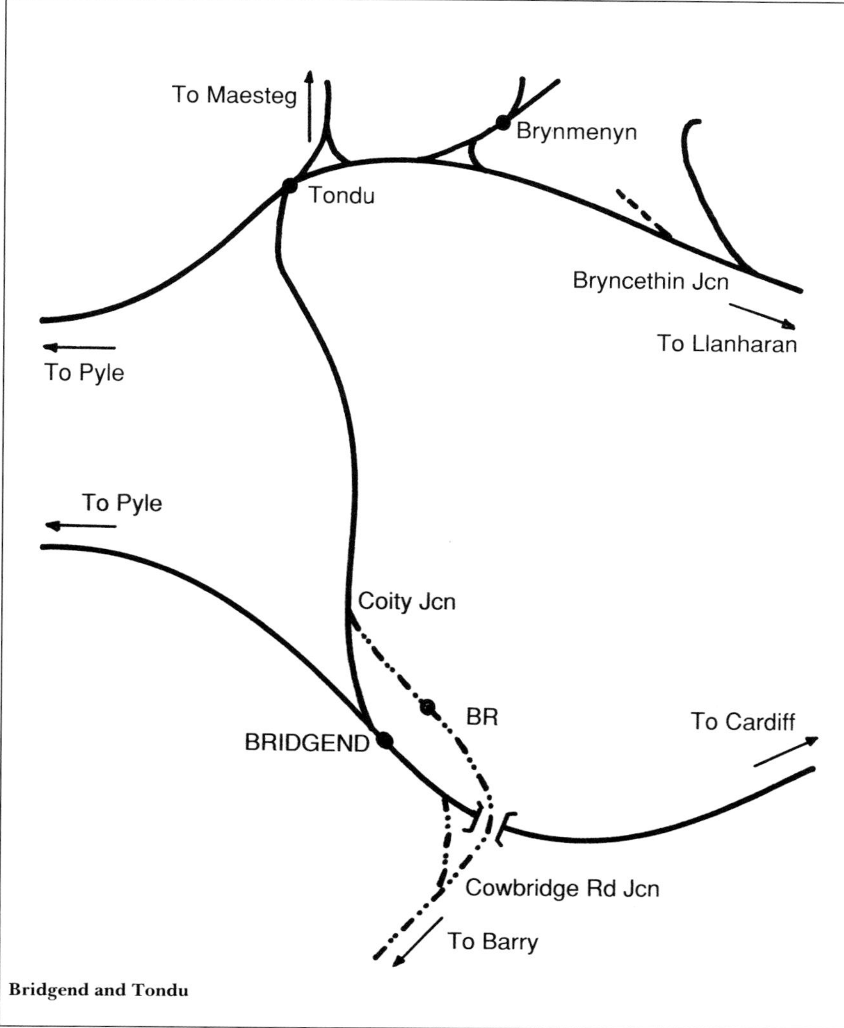

Bridgend and Tondu

BRIDGEND–BARRY LINE

Stations: Bridgend, Southerndown Road (4 m), Llantwit Major ($9\frac{1}{2}$ m), Gileston ($12\frac{1}{2}$ m), Aberthaw High Level (14 m), Rhoose ($15\frac{3}{4}$ m), Barry (19 m)

Although the Vale of Glamorgan Railway was nominally independent, its Directors were also Barry Railway (qv) Directors and the line was worked by its affluent neighbour for 66% of the receipts. The VoG had been incorporated on 26 August 1889 but needed a dividend guarantee by the Barry Railway before it could complete and open its line on 1 December 1897. It carried coal from the Ogmore, Llynfi and Garw valleys to Barry docks as planned, but had to share the traffic with other outlets and never quite realized its promoters' expectations. Other business developed during the GWR era and the line carried some 20 passenger trains on weekdays, about half operating between Barry and Llantwit Major.

After leaving Coity Junction and the South Wales main line, the Vale of Glamorgan route dropped at 1 in 100 to cross the River Ewenny and then rose at 1 in 140 to a long section with two summits before reaching Aberthaw and its cement works. A rise of $3\frac{1}{4}$ miles at 1 in 200/165 to cliff-top level was followed by a deep rock cutting and $2\frac{1}{4}$ miles of 1 in 87/81 down to Barry. On the latter section lay the 71 yd and 545 yd Porthkerry tunnels with the 18-arch Porthkerry masonry viaduct between.

GB

BRIDGEND–NANTYMOEL/ BLAENGARW LINE

Stations: Bridgend, Tondu (3 m), Brynmenyn ($3\frac{3}{4}$ m), Blackmill ($5\frac{3}{4}$ m), Ogmore Vale ($8\frac{3}{4}$ m), Nantymoel ($10\frac{1}{4}$ m)
Brynmenyn ($3\frac{3}{4}$ m), Llangeinor ($5\frac{3}{4}$ m), Pontyrhyll (7 m), Pontycymmer ($8\frac{1}{2}$ m), Blaengarw ($9\frac{1}{2}$ m)

Although primarily lines for coal and allied industrial traffics, these branches also carried passengers along the parallel Ogmore and Garw valleys. The main service followed a steeply graded course of up to 1 in 32 through the former, with connections from Brynmenyn over a line almost as steep to Blaengarw. The junction lay in advance of the four-platform station at Brynmenyn, with each route then continuing to a single platform plus wooden buildings and run-round loop of the end of the line. Both routes had colliery connections, Blaengarw including a 1 in 18 rise beyond the passenger station.

The Nantymoel line was the first to open, a product of the Ogmore Valley Railway Act of 13 July 1863 and hauling mineral traffic by 1865. A further Act of 23 July 1866 produced a link from Blackmill to the Ely Valley Extension Railway at Hendreforgan (1 September 1875) and the authority for the Garw branch, which was opened on 25 October 1876.

GB

BRIDGES AND VIADUCTS

Brunel's willingness to reach outside the limits of his period to solve engineering problems has often been remarked: perhaps because of this, much of his work remains to remind us of his 19th-century dominance. Mention of his major bridges at Maidenhead, Wharncliffe viaduct (Hanwell), Chepstow and the Royal Albert Bridge, Saltash appear under their individual headings.

To a great extent Brunel (qv) used local materials for his work, though a notable exception was the timber viaducts, built mainly but not exclusively in Cornwall. In fact, neither his first work in this medium nor the longest are actually in Cornwall—a prototype, long since replaced, spanned Sonning cutting (qv), and the longest trestle span (110 feet) was across the River Loughor near Swansea. In later years a characteristic of GWR bridges became the 'railway blue' brick, even in areas where there was, apparently, an abundance of building stone.

The first trestle viaduct Brunel built was on the Cheltenham & GW Union Railway (qv), and five on the South Devon Railway (qv) followed. The Cornwall Railway (qv), which had no fewer than 42, was opened in 1859. The main criterion in the West was cost, coupled with a need to begin a train service and earn quick revenue. Most of the viaducts had a fan-shaped spread of timber built on masonry columns to support the decking (Walkham Viaduct, near Tavistock, 132 ft high with 15 66-foot spans was one of these), but viaducts across estuaries were entirely of timber. The 'fans' consisted of four timbers on each side, locked to each other with cross-struts and strengthened with iron rods, the whole assembly supporting a deck about 35 feet overhead. All components were bolted together, so that renewal of the timbers was an easy matter.

Timber was cheap then, but the price of the yellow Memel pine from the Baltic, found to be the most durable, rose over the years and, by the time renewal of Brunel's work became necessary, it was prohibitively expensive. Between 1858 (the C&GWUR example) and 1934 (College Wood, on the Falmouth Branch, qv) the West Country viaducts were rebuilt in stone, sometimes incorporating the original pillars, but often on an easier alignment. The last Brunel timber viaducts, at Dare and Gamlyn, were demolished in 1947.

Brunel's skew bridge across the Avon at Bath was as much of a wonder in its day as Maidenhead had been. He had wanted to

Bridges and viaducts *Brunel's Coldrennick viaduct near Menheniot on the Cornwall Railway between Plymouth and Liskeard, clearly showing the four-strut timber 'fans' rising from each side of the masonry pillars. Photographed in 1895.* (GW Society)

use iron but, as he was to do in Cornwall, used timber for quickness. Each arch (there were two) was made up of six ribs about 5 feet apart, the ribs constructed of Memel timber in five layers, held together with bolts and iron straps. Cornice and parapet were also of timber, but the river's towpath was carried under the western arch on an iron platform. An iron girder structure replaced this in 1878. Other Brunel bridges at Windsor (qv), Moulsford and Goring are also notable.

In South Wales Brunel's influence is less strong. He had nothing to do with the viaducts at Crumlin (qv) and Walnut Tree, both now gone. Walnut Tree was opened by the Barry Railway (qv) on 1 August 1901, and was 1,548 feet long, of seven lattice-girder spans 120 feet above the valley at their highest. It closed on 18 December 1967. Henry Marc Brunel, IKB's son, was, however, involved in the design of Llanbradach viaduct, belonging to the same company, which was 2,400ft long and 125 feet high.

CA

BRIDGWATER

This Somerset town and port lies near the mouth of the River Parrett beside which a new dock was opened on 25 March 1841. The Bristol & Exeter Railway (qv) arrived soon after, on 14 June, and pushed on to Taunton in the following year. By 1845 railway and river were linked by a Corporation horse tramway which the B&E took over in 1863 and extended eight years later to the dock and (Bridgwater & Taunton) canal which they acquired. The B&E also produced rolling-stock at Bridgwater for a time, and the town had a second railway, a branch of the Somerset & Dorset from Edington Junction.

There were brickworks sidings between the River Parrett bridge and Bridgwater's two-platform station, with the cellophane works siding and goods yard at the London end. From the latter a 75-chain, 5 mph branch led first to the river wharves and then over a retracting bridge to the coal yards and two sides of the dock. The latter was kept clear by the Brunel dredger *Bertha*.

Just north of Bridgwater lay Dunball Wharf where the GWR had private sidings and a second connection to the River Parrett, inherited from an 1844 tramway reconstructed by the B&E in 1869.

GB

BRIDPORT BRANCH

Stations: Maiden Newton, Toller ($2\frac{1}{2}$ m), Powerstock ($5\frac{3}{4}$ m), Bridport ($9\frac{1}{4}$ m), East Street (10 m), West Bay ($11\frac{1}{4}$ m)

On 12 November 1857 the Bridport Railway opened a single broad gauge line from Maiden Newton to the small Dorset town of Bridport. The enabling Act of 5 May 1855 authorized GWR working and this was implemented by an agreement of 1 July 1858. An extension to Bridport's harbour was authorized on 21 July 1879 and opened on 31 March 1884, the new terminus being called West Bay to reflect its resort aspirations. However, traffic was never heavy and, after wartime closure (1 January 1916 to 1 June 1923), the Bridport–West Bay passenger service was replaced by a bus from 22 September 1930.

After leasing the Bridport line in 1882, the GWR rebuilt Bridport station and added a down island platform in 1894, then absorbing the local undertaking from 1 July 1901. In that era the section to Bridport had seven weekday trains each way, with three each way over the extension. Working in later years was by electric train staff.

GB

BRIGHT, ROBERT

Born in 1795, he presided over the original meeting to establish the GWR project, at Bristol on 30 July 1833 (qv Administration and Management), becoming a first Director of the company and Chairman of its Bristol Committee (Deputy-Chairman of the company) from 1835–43. He was succeeded by Viscount Barrington (qv). As a partner in Gibbs, Bright & Co he was a close associate of G. H. Gibbs (qv). Gibbs asked his advice on being offered the Chairmanship in 1837, a step favoured by Bright but not, in the end, by Gibbs. Bright's confidence in the undertaking appears to have waned slightly in the early years, but by 1837 had been restored again. He died at Abbots Leigh, near Bristol, on 19 September 1869.

CA

BRISTOL

This was the birthplace of the Great Western Railway and the original 1840 station survives together with the board room overlooking Temple Gate where decisions were taken that nurtured the enterprise during its vulnerable years. Prompted by the example of two local coal tramways,the GWR project became a reality in its home city when the first train left for Bath just after 8 am on 31 August 1840. By the following June the Bristol & Exeter line (qv) had been opened to Bridgwater (on the 14th) and the GWR main line to London completed (30th). Trains on both lines used the GWR station until a through line platform was added and the B&E eventually built a small terminus of its own. In that year, 1845, the GWR found a cuckoo in its nest when the Midland acquired the line opened by the Bristol & Gloucester Railway on 8 July 1844, this event beginning a joint presence in the heart of the GWR homeland.

The Bristol railway layout grew steadily with new lines being added to New Passage on the Severn (1863), Portishead (1867) (qv), Radstock (1873), and Avonmouth (1877) (qv). The GWR, B&E and Bristol Corporation were involved in the Bristol Harbour Railway (authorized 28 June 1866, opened 11 March 1872) line to the Floating Harbour, extended on 4 October 1906 (Bristol Harbour Extension Railway Act of 6 August 1897) from Wapping Wharf to Ashton with a branch to a goods depot at Canons Marsh and with a double-deck bridge. Coinciding with the 1886 opening of the Severn Tunnel (qv) a loop was opened to avoid Temple Meads, with a relief line south thereof being added six years later.

A new, joint MR/GWR passenger station at Temple Meads, a substantial affair by Digby-Wyatt and in a Gothic style, was brought into full use on 1 January 1878. Its dramatic main buildings led to roofed platforms which were extended and added to in a 1934–36 remodelling which also completed quadrupling between Filton Junction and Portishead Junction. New carriage sidings were provided at Malago, adding to the East and West marshalling depots, Kingsland Road full-load goods depot and the vast sundries depot at Temple Meads. The B&E loco depot at Bath Road and GWR one at South Wales Junction were concentrated on the former location after the 1876 amalgamation. By the 1930s about 100 passenger engines were based there, with freight locos at St Philips Marsh depot on the relief line.

Bristol was a focal point of the GWR's Centenary celebrations in 1935. *King George*

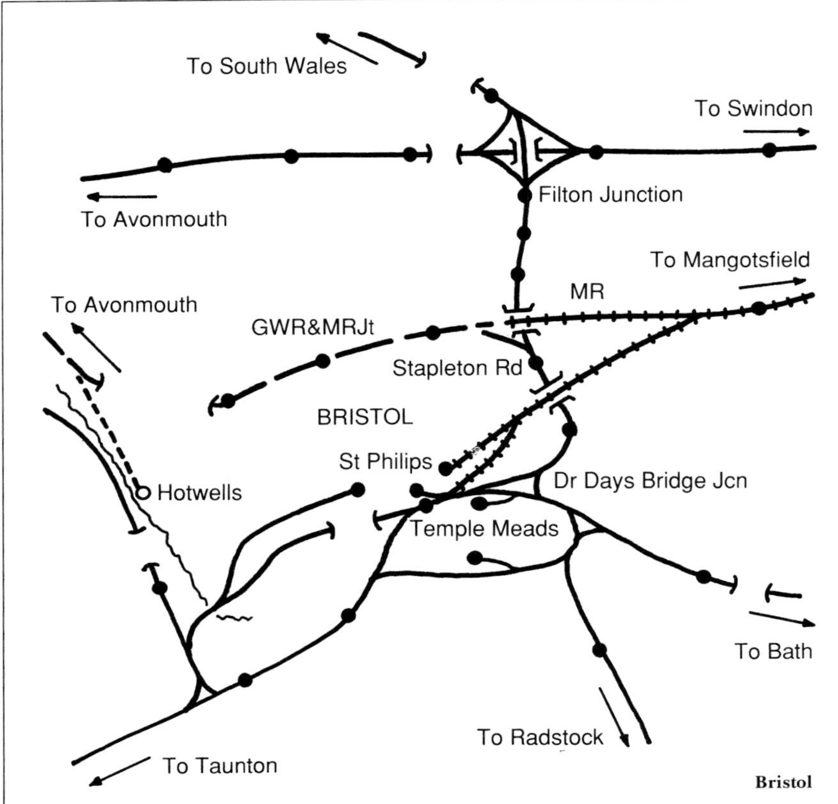

Bristol

V took the London party back from a special luncheon at the university on 31 August in what was to become, from 9 September, the 4.30 pm departure path of a new crack express, the 'Bristolian' (qv). This joined other long-distance trains on the London route, via Westerleigh Junction to Birmingham and via the Severn Tunnel to South Wales and the North West. A host of local services linked suburban stations at Parson Street, Bedminster, Clifton Bridge, Brislington, St Anne's Park, Lawrence Hill, Stapleton Road, Ashley Hill, Horfield, Filton, Montpelier, Redland and Clifton Down.

This complex and fascinating GWR location included many unusual features, like the tunnel beneath St Mary Redcliffe Church. Its range of activities was complete—from complex signalling to the operation of hundreds of cartage vehicles—and its area extended well beyond the city proper, especially in the Avonmouth direction where much of the industrial activity was located.

GB

THE Gentlemen deputed by the Corporation, the Society of Merchant Venturers, the Dock Company, the Chamber of Commerce, and the Bristol and Gloucestershire Rail Road Company, to take into consideration the expediency of promoting the formation of a RAIL ROAD from BRISTOL to LONDON, request you to favor them, in writing, with such information as you may be able to afford, respecting the expediency of the proposed Rail Road, addressed to the CHAIRMAN, in time to be laid before an adjourned Meeting of the said Deputies, to be held at the COUNCIL-HOUSE, on THURSDAY, the 31st Instant, at Twelve o'Clock.

I am, &c.

JOHN CAVE,

Chairman

BRISTOL, 21st Jan. 1833.

Bristol *The 'Birth Certificate' of the Great Western Railway?* (GWR Magazine)

BRISTOL & EXETER RAILWAY

Although conceived as an extension of the GWR main line, the Bristol & Exeter Railway was initially a totally independent project with different Directors and no GWR capital. It was incorporated on 19 May 1836, work started in 1837, and the first section of line was opened to Bridgwater (qv), with a branch to Weston-super-Mare (qv), on 14 June 1841. By that time, in order to avoid expenditure on locomotives and stock, the enterprise had been leased to the GWR at an annual rent of £30,000 plus a mileage toll. Relations between the two companies deteriorated subsequently and the lease was terminated from 1 May 1849, the B&E creating its own locomotive works at Bristol and a carriage and wagon works at Bridgwater.

After reaching Exeter on 1 May 1844, the B&E added branches to Clevedon (28 July 1847), Tiverton (12 June 1848) and Yeovil (1 October 1853) (all qv). It also built a branch to Dunball Wharf and one to Bridgwater Dock, acquired three canals, absorbed the Chard, Cheddar Valley and Exe Valley lines and worked those to

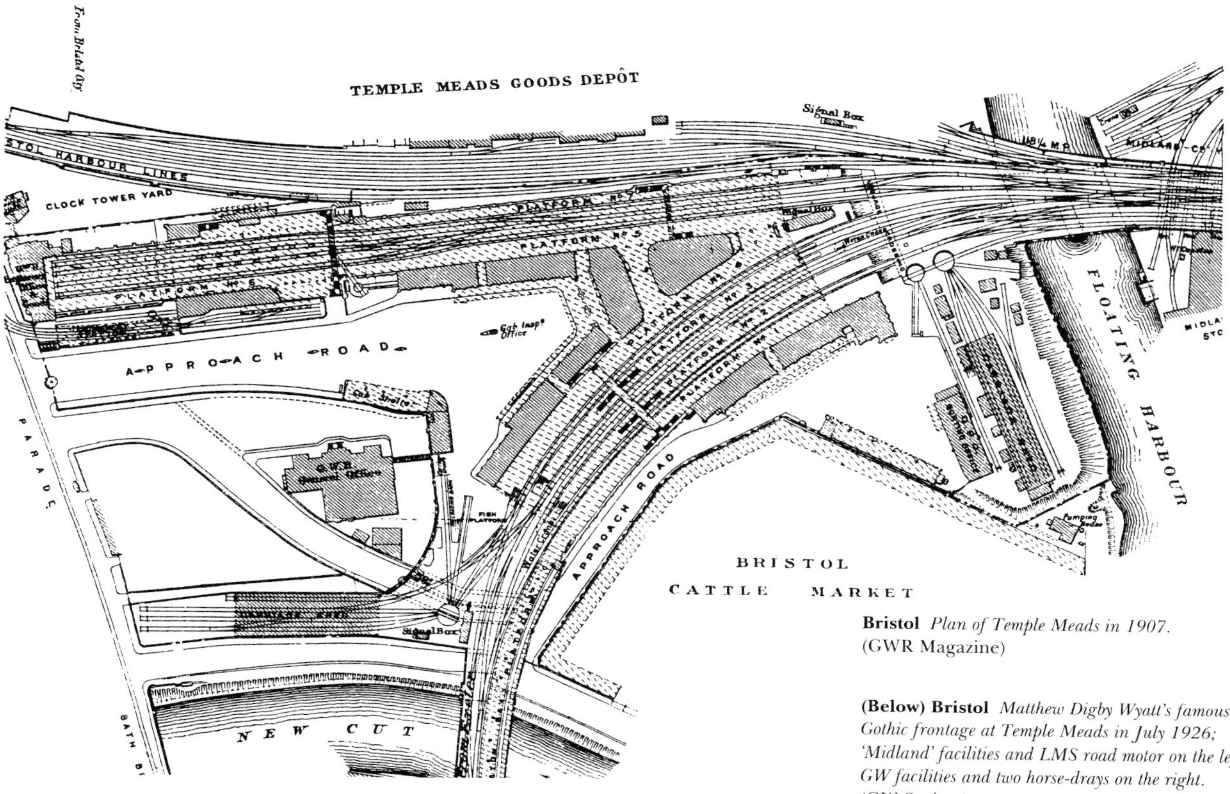

Bristol *Plan of Temple Meads in 1907.* (GWR Magazine)

(Below) Bristol *Matthew Digby Wyatt's famous Gothic frontage at Temple Meads in July 1926; 'Midland' facilities and LMS road motor on the left, GW facilities and two horse-drays on the right.* (GW Society)

Bristol *The approach to Temple Meads from the south with Bath Road bridge spanning the tracks and Bath Road loco depot beyond on the right.* (G. H. Soole, G. Body Collection)

Portishead, Barnstaple and Minehead (all qv). The result was a fair measure of prosperity, reflected in the provision for a 6½% dividend in the terms under which the GWR re-acquired the 138 miles of railway owned (and 75 miles worked) by its B&E neighbour in 1876 (qv, Associated Broad Gauge Companies).

GB

BRISTOL & NORTH SOMERSET LINE

Stations: Bristol Temple Meads, Brislington (2¾ m), Pensford (6¾ m), Clutton (10 m), Hallatrow (11½ m), Farrington Gurney (12½ m), Midsomer Norton (14½ m), Radstock (16 m), Mells Road (19 m), Frome (24¼ m)

Both the GWR and LSWR planned to link Bristol and Southampton via Radstock but had their Bills rejected. Later the Bristol & North Somerset Railway, a local enterprise seeking to cater for the development of the North Somerset coalfield, obtained an Act on 21 July 1863 and started work soon after. A series of financial problems and flirtations with other lines followed and opening between Bristol and Radstock did not come until 3 September 1873. Traffic receipts failed to resolve the company's near-insolvency and it was taken over by the GWR from 1 July 1884. By then the whole enterprise, including a branch to Camerton (qv) and the former mineral line south from Radstock to Frome (qv), had been converted to standard gauge.

The B&NS route involved a climb of 1 in 60/66 to Pensford and the high viaduct there. There were several colliery connections on the next section, including the Kilmersdon incline on the approach to Radstock which also served the Ludlows and Huish pits and had a sizeable repair works for coal wagons. The GWR and Somerset & Dorset stations stood side by side at Radstock, each with a level crossing over the main road. The line also had stone traffic sidings at Mells Road.

The branch passenger service varied between six and eight trains each way on weekdays. The route was single with passing loops and an unusual feature was the facility for booking tickets at the Miners Arms pub at Farrington Gurney.

GB

BRISTOL & SOUTH WALES UNION RAILWAY/LINE

Stations: Bristol Temple Meads, Lawrence Hill (1 m), Stapleton Road (1½ m), Ashley Hill (2½ m), Filton Junction (4¾ m), Patchway (6 m), Pilning High Level (9½ m)

From several schemes to improve communication between Bristol and South Wales emerged the Bristol & South Wales Union Railway which was incorporated on 27 July 1857 and opened its line north from Bristol and then west to the Severn on 8 September 1863. The GWR worked the line and provided the vessel which a contractor operated across the river from one pier and pontoon at New Passage to another at Portskewett. A short line connected the latter with the South Wales main line (qv).

With the opening of the Severn Tunnel (qv) the ferry service became redundant and the line from Pilning to New Passage Ferry closed on 1 December 1886. Doubling of the rest of the route gave Patchway a separate 1-mile New Tunnel on an easier gradient than the 1,246 yd Old Tunnel. Pilning then altered again when the line from Avonmouth (qv) opened along the east bank of the Severn estuary on 5 February 1900 using part of the 1863 line and joining the main line just east of Pilning station.

Seeing Severn Beach as a potential 'resort' for Bristol, the GWR provided it with summer services from 5 June 1922, making these regular on 26 May 1924 and extending them to Pilning Low Level via Cross Hands and New Passage halts in June 1928. There was also a branch off the Severn Beach line to the tunnel's pumping station at Sea Walls.

The B&SWU line carried main line services plus Bristol–Cardiff trains and those, including a 'circular' service, via Pilning to the Severn Beach line. Severn Tunnel emergency vehicles were kept at Pilning and a motor vehicle-carrying service (qv) ran from there to Severn Tunnel Junction.

GB

BRISTOL–EXETER LINE

Stations: Bristol Temple Meads, Bedminster (119¼ from Paddington), Parson Street (120 m), Long Ashton (122 m), Flax Bourton (124¼), Nailsea & Backwell (126 m), Yatton (130 m), Puxton & Worle (134 m), Bleadon & Uphill (138¾ m), Brent Knoll (142¾ m), Highbridge (145¼ m), Dunball

(149 m), Bridgwater (151½ m), Durston (157½ m), Taunton (163¾/143 m via Newbury), Norton Fitzwarren (145 m), Wellington (150 m), Burlescombe (154½ m), Sampford Peverell (157 m), Tiverton Junction (158¾ m), Cullompton (161 m), Hele & Bradninch (165¼ m), Silverton (166½ m), Stoke Canon (170½ m), Exeter St Davids (173¾ m)

The main line of the Bristol & Exeter Railway (qv) was opened to Bridgwater on 14 June 1841, to Taunton on 1 July 1842, to Beam Bridge on 1 May 1843 and to Exeter on 1 May 1844. Apart from the stretch near Flax Bourton Tunnel, the route followed a level course over the Somerset rivers before climbing to penetrate the Blackdown Hills by Whiteball Tunnel (qv) and descending to accompany the River Exe into Exeter.

In addition to the London and cross-country expresses, the route carried many semi-fast and local services to serve its intermediate centres and the branches to Clevedon, Weston-super-Mare, Yeovil, Chard, Minehead and Barnstaple and to Tiverton and Hemyock (all qv). It carried a significant volume of through freight and contributed its own agricultural, stone, livestock and general goods traffic plus shipment goods and to and from Dunball Wharf and Bridgwater Docks. To cope with all this traffic the GWR created several quadruple track sections, at the Bristol end, from Cogload Junction to Norton Fitzwarren, and through the main stations.

GB

BRISTOL MAIN LINE

Stations: Paddington, Westbourne Park (1¼ m), Acton (4¼ m), Ealing Broadway (5¾ m), West Ealing (6½ m), Hanwell & Elthorne (7¼ m), Southall (9 m), Hayes & Harlington (11 m), West Drayton (13¼ m), Iver (15 m), Langley (16¼ m), Slough (18½ m), Burnham (21 m), Taplow (22½ m), Maidenhead (24¼ m), Twyford (31 m), Reading (36 m), Tilehurst (38¾ m), Pangbourne (41½ m), Goring & Streatley (44¾ m), Cholsey & Moulsford (48½ m), Didcot (53¼ m), Steventon (56½ m), Wantage Road (60½ m), Challow (64 m), Uffington (66½ m), Shrivenham (71½ m), Swindon (77¼ m), Wootton Bassett (83 m), Dauntsey (87¾ m), Chippenham (94 m), Corsham (98¼ m), Box (101¾ m), Bathampton (104½ m), Bath (106¾ m), Saltford (111¼ m), Keynsham (113¾ m), St Anne's Park (116¾ m), Bristol Temple Meads (118¼ m)

This was the Great Western Railway's first tangible achievement. The opening of the section to the Thames at Maidenhead on 4 June 1838 represented the first benefit from over five years of endeavour and the £1,552 taken in that week was the first return on a vast capital outlay. Extensions followed—to Twyford on 1 July 1839, Reading on 30 March 1840, Steventon on 1 June 1840, Faringdon Road on 20 July, Bristol–Bath on 31 August and Faringdon Road to Wootton Bassett on 17 December 1840. Wootton Bassett to Chippenham was opened on 31 May 1841 and the final section through Box Tunnel to Bath on 30 June of that year.

Mistakes, or misjudgements, had been made, especially in the spheres of track and locomotives, but the route, without radical curvature and with no gradient steeper than 1 in 660 over much of its course, was to provide the GWR with a lifetime bonus in matters of speed, timekeeping and safety. Crack trains like the 'Bristolian' were later to take full advantage of this legacy.

Of course, the main line altered over the years, with changes to mixed (1861–75) and then standard gauge (1892), progressive quadrupling to Didcot (from 1874), resignalling, faster and heavier trains, and so on. But the essential character remained, the suburban section over Wharncliffe Viaduct and Maidenhead Bridge and on through Sonning Cutting to Reading, the company of the Thames into the Vale of the White Horse, the railway town at Swindon, the drama of Box Tunnel and its modest Middle Hill companion, with the Avon through Bath, and the further four tunnels (Twerton, Saltford and Fox's Wood 2 and 3) on the final stretch to Bristol. (Brunel's No 1 tunnel on the approach to the city had been converted to a widened cutting in 1888-9 to accommodate the shunting necks of Bristol East Depot.)

(See also entries for individual places and lines)

GB

'BRISTOLIAN'

The high-speed 'Bristolian' non-stop service between London and Bristol was introduced as part of the celebrations in 1935 to mark the Centenary (qv) of the GWR. The down departure from Paddington was at 10 am, and followed the original route through Bath, which gave it an average of 67.6 mph. In the afternoon the return working left at 4.30 pm, and operated over the slightly shorter 20th-century South Wales & Bristol Direct line (qv) through Badminton, in the same timing of 1¾ hours. The fastest train at the time of the introduction of the 'Bristolian' had taken 2 hours, so the new service represented a considerable acceleration, and put the train into second place after the 'Cheltenham Flyer' (qv) as far as start-to-stop averages on the GWR were concerned.

The formation was of seven coaches, approximately 220 tons, and included the latest type of buffet car, which had a full-length counter and pedestal seats for those wishing to sit down while they ate. To begin with, the train was worked by one of the 'King' Class 4-6-0s, but it was found to be more suited to the higher-speed capabilities of the 'Castles', which became the usual type of motive power until the train was withdrawn at the beginning of the Second World War. After Nationalization, in 1954, the train was restored to its old timings, and again the initial use of the 'Kings' gave way to the 'Castles'. By this time many of them had double chimneys, and maxima of 100 mph were not unknown. During steam's final fling before the take-over by the diesel-hydraulics, the train once completed the up journey in just under 94 minutes, at an average of 75.2 mph.

PWBS

BRITON FERRY

Although the South Wales Railway (qv) was forced round the top of the estuary at Neath, its advent provided a boost for the town's long established copper and iron industries and helped to create a need for improved shipping facilities. The result was a new dock and railway complex down the east bank of the estuary and authorized by the Briton Ferry Dock & Railway Act of 3 July 1851. The Vale of Neath (qv) worked the new railways from opening on 23 August 1861, subsequently transferring them to the GWR by two Acts of 1873.

The GWR and Rhondda & Swansea Bay lines ran parallel up the east side of the River Neath with Briton Ferry stations, goods and docks connection at the south end and the Court Sart complex, where the South Wales Mineral Railway joined, at the north.

GB

BRIXHAM BRANCH

The Torbay & Brixham Railway, authorized on 25 July 1864 and opened on 27 February 1868, was the project of a local man, who was brought to near ruin by the failure of the South Devon Railway (qv), which worked the line, to allocate his proper share of its earnings. After successful litigation the T&B worked its own line until it sold out to the GWR on 1 January 1883.

The 2 m 1 ch single line ran from the London end of Churston station (qv Kingswear branch), enlarged in 1912–13, to a curved site and single platform at Brixham, approached by a 1 in 78 descent. Electric train tokens were used, the fireman being responsible for these on auto-trains (qv) which had no guard, and the Brixham signalman making up the branch journals.

GB

BROAD GAUGE

On 15 September 1835 Brunel suggested to the GWR Board that a gauge of 7 feet be adopted for its railway, and thus was born the Broad Gauge. Brunel's 'baulk road' (qv, Permanent way) became famous—or notorious, depending on one's point of view—cleaving a way from London to Bristol, into South Wales, and ultimately to Penzance.

The fact that the gauge differed from most other lines, built to the Stephensons' preferred gauge of 4ft 8½ in, led to conflict. There were problems in particular at stations such as Gloucester (qv), where broad gauge met narrow: passengers had to change trains, and there were notable difficulties over the transfer of goods.

In 1846 a Gauge Commission was appointed to examine the matter. Its members, Sir Frederick Smith, George Biddell Airy and Peter Barlow, found that though the broad gauge was superior in terms of speed and steadiness, the narrow gauge suited the needs of an overall system better, with regard to goods in particular. It also made the point that 1,901 miles of railway out of a total of 2,175 was narrow at that time. The subsequent Gauge Act (Public General 9 & 10 Victoria c 57, 18 August 1846) watered down the findings, and, on grounds of expense, did not compel the GWR to convert its entire system. It also allowed broad gauge lines connecting with the GWR, or those already planned, to retain their gauge (qv, Associated Broad Gauge Companies).

The last broad gauge line authorized was the St Ives (Cornwall) branch, in 1873, part of which remained so to the end, but from 1846 more and more lines had a third (standard gauge) rail added. As finance allowed, the GWR began to convert lines to the narrower gauge: by 1872 the whole line between Swindon and South Wales had been changed.

Sir Daniel Gooch (qv) had always championed the Broad Gauge, and after his death it was decided to convert what was left of the broad system to conform with the rest of the country's lines. A massive operation (qv, Gauge conversion) was organized for the weekend of 21–22 May 1892. Final broad gauge trains to the West left Paddington on 20 May, and by the 23rd the Broad Gauge was no more.

CA

Broad Gauge *'The Break of Gauge at Gloucester': the pair of well-known engravings illustrating the chaos of transhipping GWR passengers and goods between narrow and broad gauge trains for the journey on to Birmingham.*
(GWR Museum, Swindon)

BROCCOLI TRAFFIC

The movement of broccoli from West Cornwall to London and the main provincial markets represented important business for the GWR. In 1907 an exceptional crop during the week ending 6 April resulted in 1,081 wagons being dispatched from Cornwall in 38 special trains. In the 1932–33 season 26,000 tons were carried, 16,000 tons in 230 special trains.

The activity involved the pre-season planning of train paths and the negotiation of rates with the major growers. Forwardings then gradually built up until cartage and loading activity became hectic at places like Ponsandane, Marazion, St Erth and the Helston branch, with a parallel operational need for adequate van supplies, a good run to the destination and early road delivery to obtain a good place in the market queue.

Some forwardings of broccoli went by passenger train but the whole business became increasingly vulnerable to road competition in the later GWR years.

(*See also Freight services*)

GB

BRUNEL, ISAMBARD KINGDOM

Born at Portsea on 9 April 1806, he was the third child and only son of French émigré engineer/inventor Marc Brunel and Sophia, née Kingdom, a Plymouth girl. He was educated at home until 1814 and then at Dr Morell's school, Hove. His technical education took place at Caen College and the Lyceé Henri-Quatre in Paris. He also spent periods in the workshops of Louis Breguet, learning instrument making.

He commenced work in his father's drawing office in April 1822 and gained experience in civil engineering design. He continued to learn manual skills at the workshops of Maudslay Son & Field. His father patented an engine powered by pressure of carbonic gas, the 'Gaz' engine, which Isambard built and attempted to perfect without success in 1823–33.

He was appointed Resident Engineer of the Thames Tunnel on 3 January 1828, but the roof collapsed on 12 January, seriously injuring him. He was ill until June, when he went to Clifton to convalesce.

He was elected a Fellow of the Royal Society on 10 June 1830, and his plan for a suspension bridge across the Avon gorge at Clifton was adopted on 16 March 1831. The foundations were laid on 21 June, but his plans were never realised, and the existing bridge was erected as a memorial to him, opening on 8 December 1864.

Brunel was appointed Engineer, Monkwearmouth dock, on 20 November 1831, then returned to Bristol in February 1833 to supervise dock improvements there. He became conditionally Engineer of the Bristol Railway (GWR) on 7 March 1833, and his appointment as Engineer of the GWR was confirmed on 27 August. Royal Assent for the GWR Bill was received on 31 August 1835, and Brunel introduced his idea of the 7-foot gauge on 15 September. The railway opened in stages commencing with Paddington–Maidenhead (old station east of Thames) on 4 June 1838, and finishing with Chippenham–Bath on 30 June 1841.

In addition, Brunel was Engineer to the following railways (the dates given are those of the final stage of openings, but he was engaged on the work for years prior to that): Bristol & Exeter Railway (1844), Taff Vale (1841), Cheltenham & Great Western Union (1847), South Devon (1848), Cornwall Railway (1859), West Cornwall Railway (1853), South Wales Railway 1858), Oxford & Rugby (1852, by which time its destination had changed to Birmingham), Wilts, Somerset & Weymouth Railway (1857), and Reading–Hungerford (1847). He was also engineer of the Oxford, Worcester & Wolverhampton from 1836 until 1850.

That brief list hides a multitude of enormous works from the Maidenhead bridge of 1838 and Box Tunnel, the wrought iron 'bow and string' bridge over the Thames at Windsor, the Wye bridge at Chepstow, the cast iron and glass Paddington station, and the Royal Albert Bridge of 1859.

Isambard's character was complicated and paradoxical. His father was a clever inventor and a competent engineer, but he was continuously under-rewarded for his efforts. Isambard grew up in an impecunious household, constantly under pressure from his father to be a success, to become the finest engineer in the world, achieve a household name, success and wealth, in that order. Although in charge of the driving of the Thames tunnel in 1828, aged 21, he did not at first have any title, let alone reward. After the collapse of the tunnel, due in a large part to his haste in pushing on the work, his illness was followed by five years of relative inactivity when he was subject to fits of black depression as he wondered when his day would come. He suffered, he privately confided to his diary, from 'blue devils'. This was a favourite phrase—sometimes he was 'driven by blue devils'.

On the one hand he was seeking to scale the dizziest heights of engineering, on the other hand the influences of his penniless early life at his father's home remained with him, making him insecure, always worried about failure—for the price of failure in those days was poverty, if not prison for debt. Isambard drove himself mercilessly, as if there would be no tomorrow, and he drove everyone around him equally hard. He created enormous works, none of which seemed to satisfy his ambition but were simply stepping stones to the next and even larger task. He forced the pace of progress in global steam navigation with his large ships, SS *Great Western*, SS *Great Britain* and SS *Great Eastern*.

Isambard had a few close friends who loved him very much, but many of his close assistants took him with the proverbial pinch of salt. 'In the name of fame and our Great Master's Name—press on the work', wrote his Resident Engineer of the London Division, John Hammond, to *his* assistant, Robert Archibald. Isambard was kind to everyone he met on the principle of getting the best out of them, but in a choice between a friend and The Work he had no friends. Isambard rarely, if ever, gave public acknowledgement of the debt he owed to the many men who helped him in his great works but always made sure he was well to the fore on public occasions. He was obsessed with his ideas and pursued them relentlessly without listening to any advice which conflicted with his own notions. The atmospheric railway was a classic example of this.

He suffered several long periods of illness over the years and from 1854 suffered increasingly from inflammation of the liver—Bright's or perhaps Weil's disease. He suffered a heart attack on the deck of his SS *Great Eastern* on 5 September 1859 and died on 15 September 1859. He was a stubborn man, a jealous man, a brave man, an insecure man, and a great civil engineering genius.

(*Refer to biographies listed in the Bibliography. See also entries for individual places and lines.*)

AV

BRYNAMMAN BRANCH

Stations: Pantyffynnon, Ammanford (1 m), Glanamman (4 m), Garnant ($4\frac{3}{4}$ m), Brynamman ($6\frac{1}{2}$ m)

The main passenger service to Brynamman was provided by the Midland/LMS trains over the former Swansea Vale line but the GWR operated a service up the Amman Valley from Pantyffynnon to a station adjoining its rival's terminus. The anthracite seams of the area had first attracted the Llanelly Railway with an 1840 line to Garnant, followed by an 1841 branch to Gwaun-Cae-Gurwen and a 1 in 63 Garnant–Brynamman extension a year later.

The GCG line, as it was generally known, got a new alignment from 4 November 1907 and a steam railmotor service (qv) from January 1908 to May 1926, with a total of seven trains covering the $1\frac{1}{4}$ miles from Garnant and calling at two halts on the way.

GB

BRYNMAWR BRANCH

Stations: Newport High Street, Bassaleg Junction ($2\frac{3}{4}$ m), Rogerstone (4 m), Risca ($6\frac{1}{4}$ m), Cross Keys ($7\frac{3}{4}$ m), Cwmcarn (9 m), Abercarn (10 m), Newbridge ($11\frac{1}{4}$ m), Crumlin Low Level ($12\frac{1}{4}$ m), Llanhilleth ($14\frac{1}{4}$ m), Aberbeeg (15 m), Abertillery (17 m), Blaina ($19\frac{1}{2}$ m), Nantyglo ($20\frac{3}{4}$ m), Brynmawr ($22\frac{1}{4}$ m)

This was the Western Valleys section of the Monmouthshire Railway & Canal (qv), authorized by an Act of Parliament on 3 June 1792, opened as a tramroad between Crumlin and Aberbeeg in 1798 and extended, first to Nantyglo Gate (1824) and then to Risca (1829) to meet the 1805 link between Newport and the Sirhowy Tramroad at Nine Mile Point. This latter section included the so-called 'Golden Mile' between Park Junction and Bassaleg, a six-track mile originally built by the landowner in return for toll rights which provided a phenomenal income until the GWR bought them out in 1923. At the other end of the route, Nantyglo was linked with Brynmawr over the Brynmawr & Western Valleys Railway, a local project incorporated on 13 July 1899 and opened as a joint GWR/ LNWR line for freight on 12 July 1905 (passengers 28 May 1906).

After the 'Golden Mile', or Park Mile Railway, the Western Valleys route began a four-track section through Rogerstone and past its adjacent marshalling yard to Risca, itself preceded by sidings at Pontymister for holding steelworks traffic. Beyond the four-platform Risca station the line to Nine Mile Point and the LNWR Sirhowy branch left via a diamond crossover, with Western Valleys trains continuing to Hall's Road Junction where the coal routes to Cwmcarn and Penar Junction departed. More colliery links followed as the route passed beneath Crumlin Viaduct (qv), received the 1855 connecting line just before the island platform at Llanhilleth and then came to the junction at Aberbeeg (qv). The Cwm Tillery Colliery branch departed ahead of Abertillery station and the connection for Blaina Works and Colliery and Coalbrookvale just after Blaina's curving platforms. Beyond Nantyglo the single line of the 1905–6 joint route, which had taken over from an earlier ironworks line, climbed at 1 in 47 towards its junction with the Merthyr–Abergavenny route and completion of the 75–89 minute journey.

GB

BUILTH CASTLE

In the early 1930s, doubts were expressed about the exact speed reached by *City of Truro* in 1904 (qv), but the ability of a GWR locomotive to reach 100 mph was confirmed just before the Second World War. No 4086 *Builth Castle*, one of the 'Castles' built in 1925 (qv), reached a speed of exactly 100 mph through Honeybourne in 1939 on the 12.45 Paddington–Worcester express. This was achieved at the foot of Campden Bank after the 4-mile descent at 1 in 100, the exploit being timed by R. E. Charlewood, a well-known recorder of train performance at that time.

(*See also Speed records*)

PWBS

Builth Castle *No 4086 passing through Campden with the 2 pm Worcester-Paddington express, near where, in the opposite direction, the locomotive attained 100 mph with a Worcester-bound express in 1939.* (G. H. Soole, G. Body Collection)

BURLINSON, NATHAN JAMES

Superintendent of the Line, 1888–94. He was born in London in April 1833 and entered the Accountant's Department of the GWR in December 1850. He was transferred to the Traffic Department five years later, becoming Goods Agent for Wolverhampton after three years' experience at Baschurch, Bilston and Oakengates. He then rejoined the Traffic Department in 1862 as District Superintendent at Slough, and was appointed Divisional Superintendent at Hereford, (1865) and Birmingham (1873), then Assistant Superintendent of the Line in 1879. He took Tyrrell's (qv) place as Superintendent in July 1888, aged 55, and began a programme of accelerated services and new expresses, introducing 3rd class travel on some of the expresses. In 1890 he was elected Chairman of the Superintendents' Meeting of the Railway Clearing House. He retired on 20 April 1894, was succeeded by Allen (qv), and died at Hampstead on 31 January 1916.

CA

BURNGULLOW

The first Burngullow station was replaced by one 11 chains to the west in 1901 but that, in turn, was closed from 14 September 1931 leaving the location important only as a main line summit with a local clay siding and a 4 m 46 ch mineral branch north to the Newquay line at St Dennis Junction.

The Newquay & Cornwall Junction Railway, authorized on 4 July 1864, was largely inert until acquired by the Cornwall Minerals Railway (qv) and opened on 1 June 1874. It came to serve six main groups of china clay (qv) sidings, including a sizeable complex at Drinnick Mill where there was a signal box and a passing loop. The New Carpella Siding, at 290 m 5½ ch from Paddington, was a reminder of the company that had succeeded in closing the line from 1909 to 1922 in exercise of its mineral rights.

GB

CAERPHILLY

The original 1858 route of the Rhymney Railway (qv) passed round the western side of Caerphilly, and although this was connected with the Brecon & Merthyr's Machen line seven years later, it was 1 April 1871 before the town got a better-placed station with the opening of the Rhymney's independent route to Cardiff. From these unpromising beginnings the location grew into one of the busiest railway centres in South Wales, gaining a locomotive works in 1901 and a station englargement in 1913. The four platforms and bay of the latter handled the passenger services to and from the Rhymney Valley, those from Newport and Cardiff to Merthyr, from Cardiff to Senghenydd and between Pontypridd and Machen (qv) via the old Pontypridd, Caerphilly & Newport route.

A loop and triangle west of Caerphilly linked the RR main line with the Barry, Taff Vale and Senghenydd lines (all qv) while east of the station the Cardiff and Machen routes separated, with the locomotive works access between them. After the Grouping, the GWR rationalized the lines from Penrhos Junction northwards but built up the works activity with a new erecting and carriage shop and the transfer of heavy loco repairs from Ebbw Junction, Newport.

GB

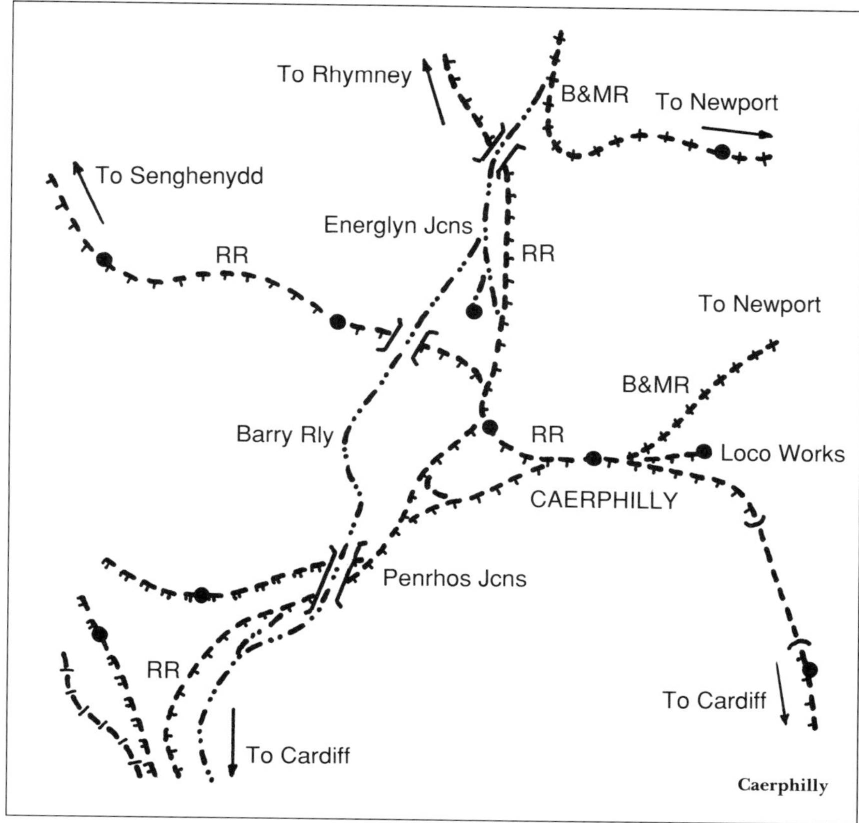

Caerphilly

CAERPHILLY CASTLE

When C. B. Collett (qv) introduced his new 4-6-0s in 1923, the first, No 4073, was named *Caerphilly Castle*, which became the prototype of the 'Castle' Class (qv). The new locomotive attracted a lot of interest, and in the following year it was displayed at the British Empire Exhibition alongside *Flying Scotsman* from the LNER. The label on the smaller GWR locomotive, proclaiming it as the 'Most powerful express passenger locomotive in Britain' (on the strength of its superior tractive effort), was to lead to the famous locomotive exchanges in 1925 between the two classes (qv). When withdrawn in 1960, the locomotive was preserved, and is on display in the National Museum of Science & Industry at South Kensington.

(*See also* Pendennis Castle)

PWBS

Caerphilly Castle *Proclaimed 'the most powerful express passenger locomotive in Britain' in 1925.* (Steamchest Collection)

CALNE BRANCH

The 5 m 24 ch branch south from Chippenham to the small Wiltshire town of Calne depended fairly heavily on the traffic of C. & T. Harris (Calne) Ltd. The Harris family had supported the original Calne Railway which had been incorporated on 15 May 1860, opened for goods on 29 October 1863 (passengers 3 November) and amalgamated with the GWR from 1 July 1892. They used the line for inwards coal, salt and livestock and outwards meat to and from their siding-connected premises at the small terminal station.

The single-line, electric train token branch had intermediate halts at Stanley Bridge and Black Dog, the latter for the Marquis of Lansdowne although its public use was also permitted. The basic service of 23 trains on weekdays was supplemented by a Calne Cattle Market working on the third Monday of each month.

GB

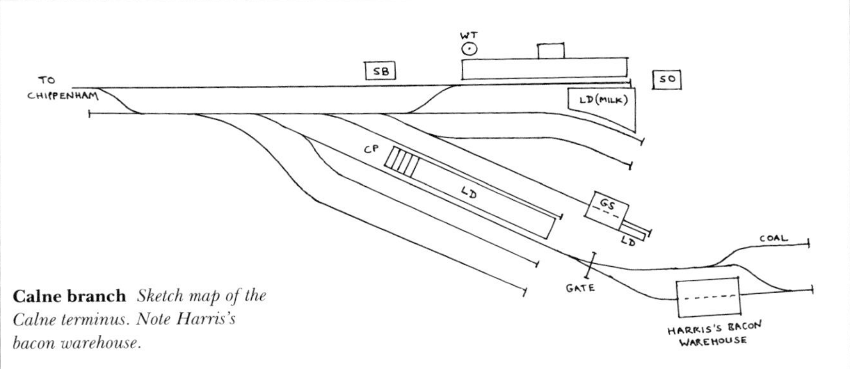

Calne branch *Sketch map of the Calne terminus. Note Harris's bacon warehouse.*

CAMBORNE

Like Redruth, Camborne was a key town in Cornwall's tin and copper mining area. The output of the latter prompted the Hayle Railway (qv) to provide branches to Roskear and Crofty and these survived as sidings, along with others for Holmans and at Dolcoath, into the GWR era. The line to Holmans and Roskear departed from a junction at the London end of Camborne's two-platform passenger station, with the Crofty line junction further east.

GB

'CAMBRIAN COAST EXPRESS'

The services over the mid-Wales lines of the Cambrian Railways (qv) were revitalized after the Grouping, and in 1927 the 'Cambrian Coast Express' was introduced, although an unnamed predecessor can be traced back to the summer of 1921. Unlike some other named trains, its schedules were altered frequently during the inter-war years, and for convenience we will look at the down train in the summer of 1927, which ran on Fridays and Saturdays only.

Travelling from Paddington to Birmingham via Bicester, the locomotive was then changed at Wolverhampton, so the train could miss Shrewsbury by taking the Abbey Foregate curve. With calls at Moat Lane, Machynlleth, and Dovey Junction, Aberystwyth was reached in just over 6 hours from Paddington. During this period, nothing larger than a 4-4-0 was permitted over most of the lines west of Shrewsbury. From 1936 the former Cambrian locomotives with this wheel arrangement began to be replaced by the 'Dukedogs', which Swindon produced by putting a 'Duke' boiler on the frames of a 'Bulldog' (qv, Locomotives). During the Second World War, however, the 'Manors' (qv) appeared on the line, and their association with the 'Cambrian Coast Express' continued to the end of steam. A pair of them double-heading a train of BR standard coaches in chocolate and cream made one believe the GWR was still in business.

PWBS

CAMBRIAN RAILWAYS

On 1 January 1922 the GWR absorbed the Cambrian Railways system which, over its 58 years of independent existence, had grown into a major railway undertaking as full of character as the Welsh landscape it served. Cambrian trains crossed Wales from Whitchurch to Cardigan Bay, extended from this main line to Aberystwyth, Pwllheli and Brecon, and fed it by a motley collection of branches and worked or absorbed lines. From its headquarters and works at Oswestry (qv), the Cambrian controlled and serviced 300 miles of railway, but much of it ran through remote and sparsely populated areas. As a consequence, the surpluses of 1917–20 failed to exceed £148,182, yet the authorized capital was over £7 million.

The first section of the system was opened for goods by the Llanidloes & Newtown Railway (incorporated 4 August 1853) on 30 April 1859 and for passengers on 31 August 1859. Next came the Oswestry & Newtown Railway whose Act of 26 June 1855 produced lines from Oswestry to Pool Quay on 1 May 1860 and on to meet the L&N 13 months later. Two more of the original Cambrian constituents were by now nearing completion. The Newtown & Machynlleth Railway, which had been incorporated on 27 July 1857, opened on 3 January 1863, and the Oswestry, Ellesmere & Whitchurch Railway (incorporated 1 August 1861) opened from Whitchurch to Ellesmere on 4 May 1863 and on to Oswestry on 27 July 1864.

All these local concerns became part of the Cambrian by the Cambrian Railways Act of 25 July 1864, later Acts covering amalgamation with the Aberystwyth & Welsh Coast Railway from 5 August 1865 (Act of 5 July 1865), the operation of steamers (9 July 1889) and the working, and then absorption, of the Mid-Wales Railway (24 June 1904).

GB

CAMERTON BRANCH

Stations: Hallatrow, Camerton ($3\frac{1}{2}$ m), Dunkerton (6 m), Monkton Combe ($10\frac{1}{4}$ m), Limpley Stoke ($11\frac{1}{2}$ m)

A debt judgement in favour of the Earl of Warwick put the Bristol & North Somerset Railway (qv) into the hands of the Court of Chancery in 1882, but an item of good news for the Directors was the opening on 1 March of the long-awaited branch from Hallatrow to Camerton. Primarily a coal line, passenger services were added a month later. Under GWR ownership the branch was extended to Dunkerton Colliery

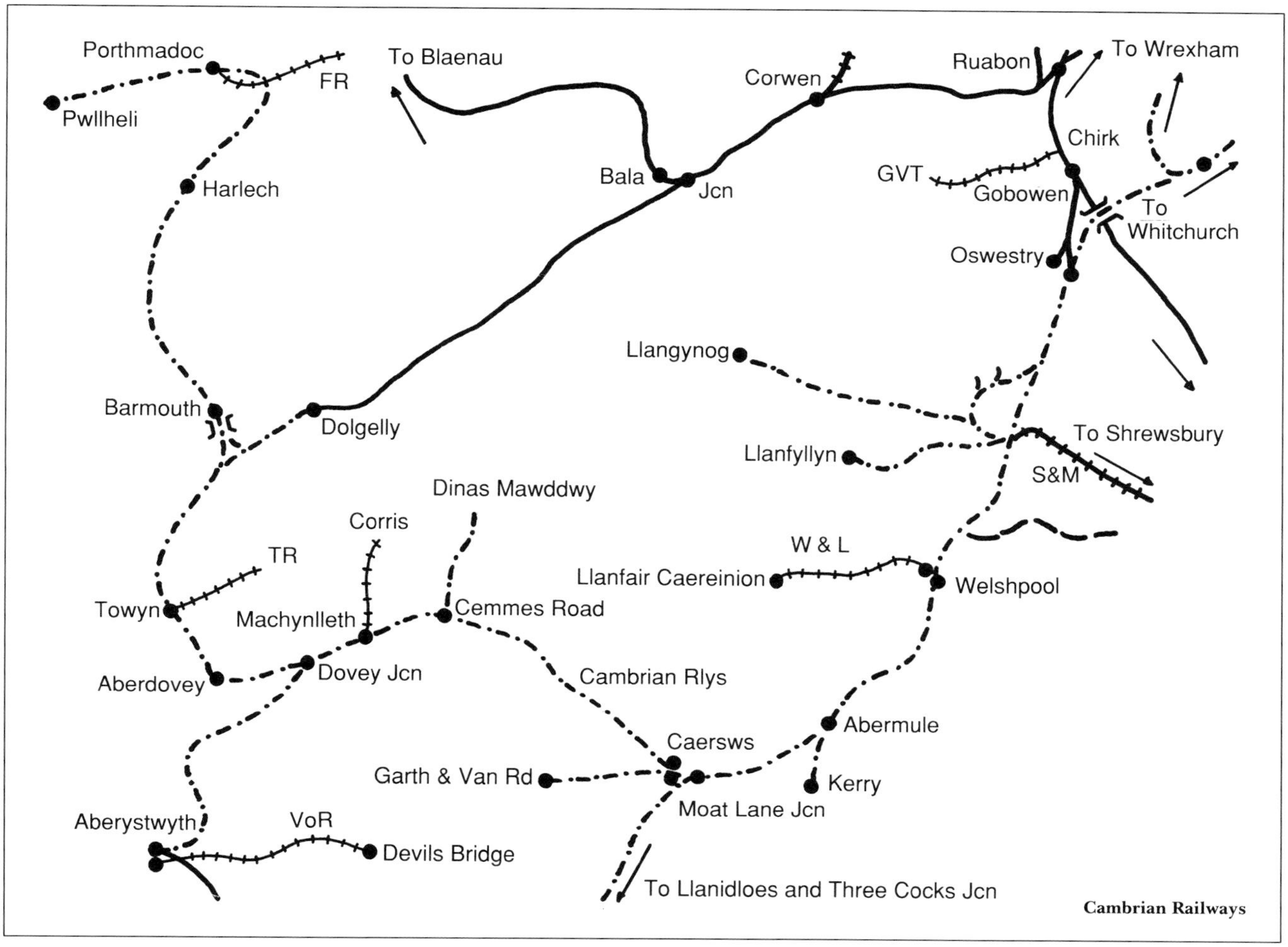
Porthmadoc
FR
Pwllheli
To Blaenau
Corwen
Ruabon
To Wrexham
Chirk
Harlech
Bala
Jcn
GVT
Gobowen
To
Whitchurch
Oswestry
Llangynog
Barmouth
Dolgelly
Llanfyllyn
To Shrewsbury
S&M
Dinas Mawddwy
Corris
TR
W & L
Llanfair Caereinion
Welshpool
Towyn
Machynlleth
Cemmes Road
Aberdovey
Dovey Jcn
Cambrian Rlys
Abermule
Caersws
Garth & Van Rd
Kerry
Moat Lane Jcn
Aberystwyth
VoR
Devils Bridge
To Llanidloes and Three Cocks Jcn

Cambrian Railways

RADFORD AND TIMSBURY
HALT

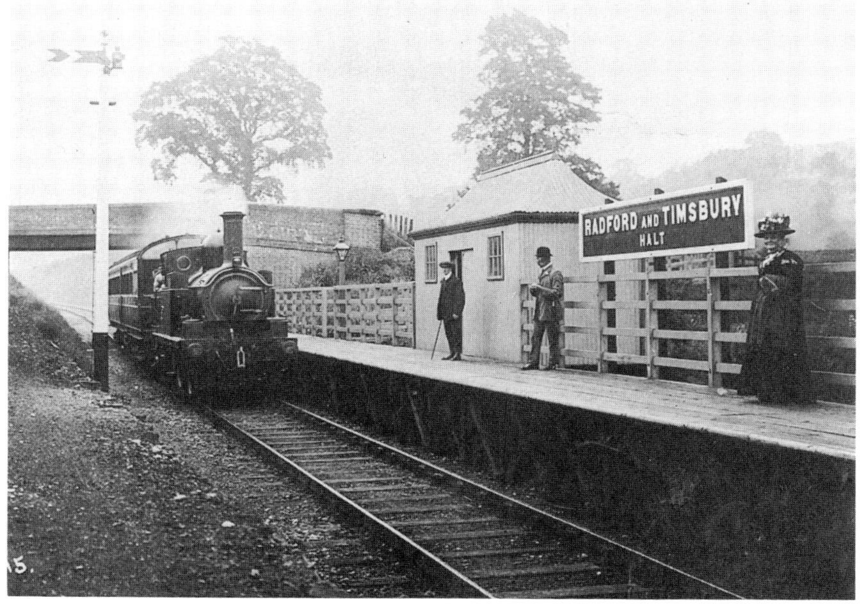

Camerton branch *Radford & Timsbury Halt, newly added between Hallatrow and Camerton.* (Steamchest Collection)

on 26 August 1907 and on to Limpley Stoke on 9 May 1910, using part of the route of the old Somerset Coal Canal and its 66 yd tunnel.

The branch lost its passenger trains for eight years from 1915, and again on 21 September 1925 when the 1882 section of the line was closed completely. Coal traffic supported the east end of the route for a while but diminished as pit rationalization began.

The Ghost Train (Gainsborough, 1931) was filmed at Camerton and *The Titfield Thunderbolt* (Ealing, 1953) at Monkton Combe.

GB

CAMPING COACHES

Camp Coaches were introduced by the LNER in 1933 and the GWR followed a year later, siting them at various places on the railway, usually close to the sea, where visitors might be enticed to spend a week or a fortnight's holiday. Converted from 18 four- and six-wheelers and one bogie clerestory vehicle, they were of six-berth layout, except for the bogie coach which could accommodate ten people. They proved instantly popular and more, both bogie and non-bogie, were added in subsequent seasons until by 1939 there were 65. Numbered 9935–9999, they were provided with oil for heating and lighting, but most had no toilets, this facility being available at the adjacent station.

Eleanor Fox and her family booked a week in camp coach No 9988, formerly No 6794, a six-wheeler built in 1884, at Tintern in August 1937 and received the following from the Station Master: 'I shall have the coach properly prepared after departure of previous tenants, kettle boiling, plenty of fresh (spring) water in readiness, an adequate supply of paraffin and methylated spirits, and I shall ask the Dairyman to leave about ½ or a dozen eggs . . . wishing you a cosy and comfortable journey when travelling down next Saturday.'

The war brought an end to camp coaches and the carriages were put into departmental use. It was not until the summer of 1952 that Camping (as they were now called) Coaches were again advertised to the public. New vehicles were required and as the last clerestory carriages had just been withdrawn from main-line work, 11 of them were converted to camping coaches, Nos 9900–10. As in pre-war years they found great favour with the public and more, all Churchward 'Toplights', Nos 9875–99 and 9911–34, were added until by 1958 the total stood at 60. At first painted green, the post-war carriages received chocolate and cream livery from 1958. All had toilets, and latterly propane gas replaced oil. In the early 1960s a number of Pullmans were converted to Camping Coaches and their arrival saw the withdrawal of almost all the clerestory vehicles.

Closure in the 1960s of many of the branch lines beside which Camping Coaches were sited, along with the economic reality of their being non-revenue-earning for most of the year, despite their popularity in the summer months, brought about their demise, although some survive for the use

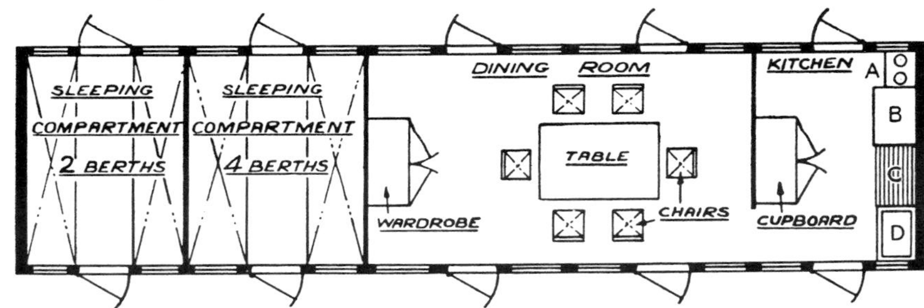

Camping coaches *'An Attractive Innovation – the Camp-Coach Holiday' announced the* GWR Magazine *in 1934, appending this plan of a six-berth vehicle. A – stove, with oven; B – table, with cupboard below; C – draining board; D – sink.* (GWR Magazine)

of BR staff at Dawlish (which had seen the largest group of such vehicles, nine in all).

A number of former camping 'Toplights' have been preserved, notably on the West Somerset Railway, where they provide sleeping accommodation for volunteers. A line of former Pullman Camping Coaches is still *in situ* beside the Penzance main line at Marazion on the edge of Mounts Bay, now the property of a local publican.

MCHB

CARDIFF

When the South Wales Railway (qv) opened through Cardiff on 18 June 1850, the capital city of Wales had just completed its first half-century of industrial growth and much more was yet to come. To the 1798 basin, canal and tramroads of the Glamorganshire Canal enterprise had been added the Bute West Dock (1839) and then the first section of the Taff Vale Railway (1840) (qv) with a line to and lease of the dock from the Marquis of Bute. From this beginning four more docks were to be added—Bute East Dock (1855–59), Roath Basin (1874), Roath Dock (1887) and Queen Alexandra Dock (1907)—with a total water area of 165 acres and coal exports of some 10 million tons a year. Over the same period came four more rail approaches bringing in their wake a level of traffic congestion that was to be a major factor in the establishment of rival docks and coal routes.

The GWR main line arrived in Cardiff along the flat estuarial plain to the east, crossed the Rhymney, Taff and Ely rivers and departed westwards along the Ely Valley. The Taff Vale line came through Walnut Tree Gap (9 October 1840) and

Camping coaches *Tea-time in a GWR camping coach.* (GW Society)

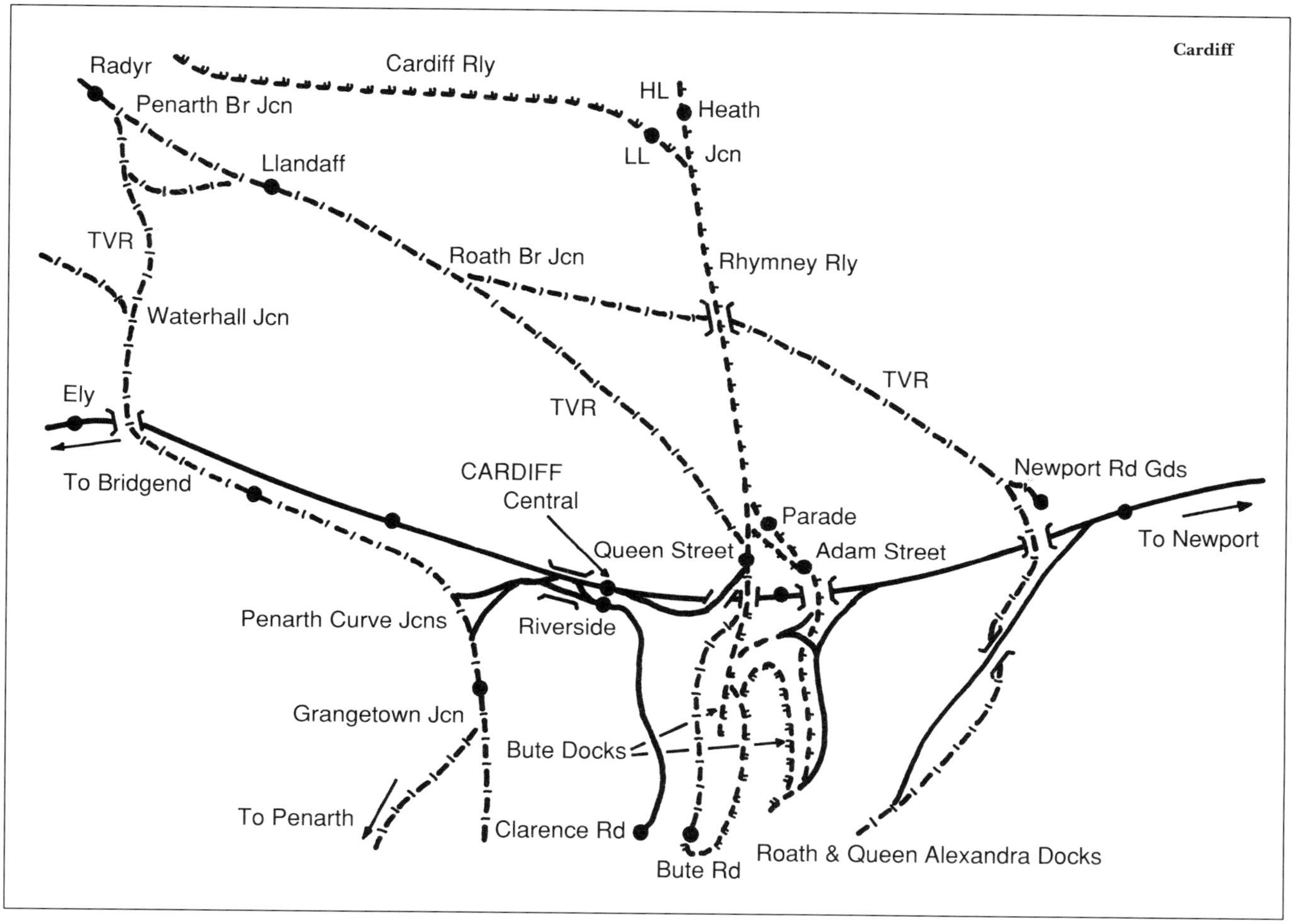

Cardiff

Cardiff *A plan of General station after the rebuilding of 1930-34.* (GWR Magazine)

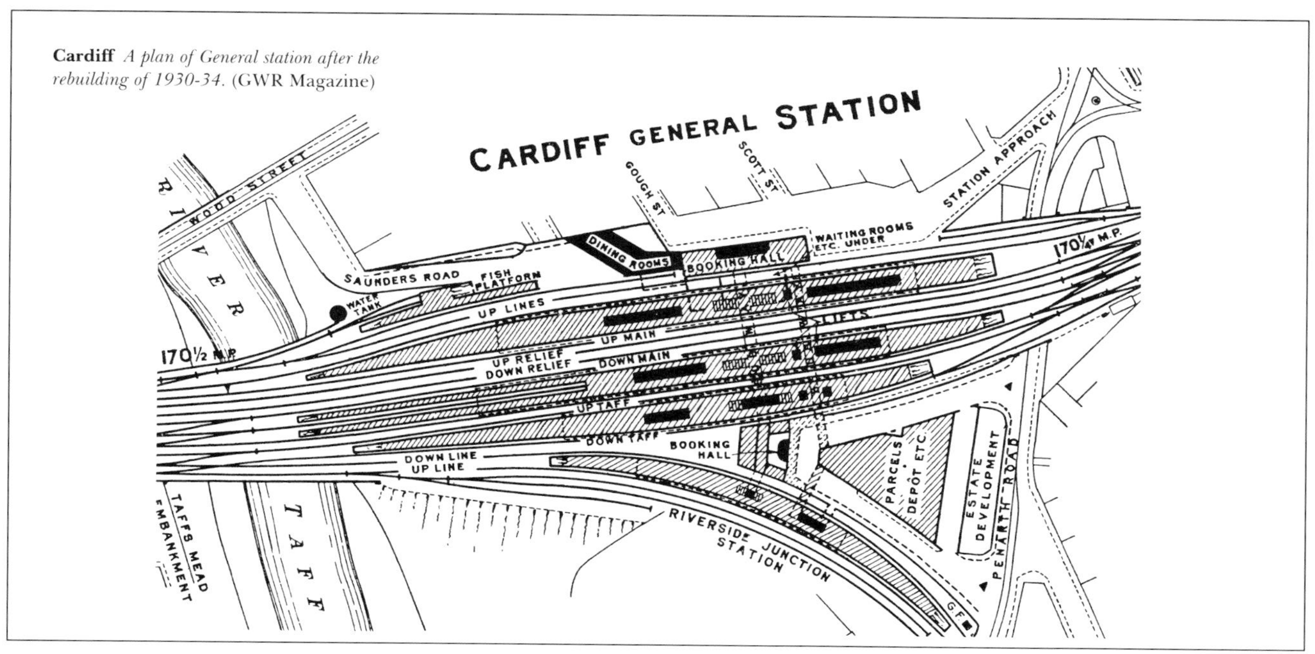

later added avoiding lines from Radyr to Penarth (July 1859) and round to Roath (23 April 1888). The Rhymney Railway (qv) used TVR metals until forced to open its own line from Caerphilly (1 April 1871), and Barry (qv) trains used the GWR approach from the west and the Riverside freight branch, carrying passengers to Riverside from 14 August 1893 and to a new terminus at Clarence Road from 2 April 1894. The less than successful Cardiff Railway (qv) entered the capital on Rhymney metals, as did the LNWR services.

The 1840 TVR passenger station near Bute Road was later overshadowed by Queen Street and the Rhymney's 1858 Adam Street gave way in 1871 to Parade, which the GWR closed in favour of an enlarged Queen Street from 15 April 1928. The main-line Cardiff General was completely remodelled between 1930 and 1934 with new buildings in Carrara blocks, four 1,000 ft main-line platforms, two 800 ft Taff Vale platforms and two 600 ft at Riverside plus a bay, fish dock and parcels area. Services along the main line used the two long islands while trains for the valleys ran via the Taff Vale island, Taff West Branch viaduct and Queen Street. At the latter they were joined by the Treherbert services from Bute Road while the originating services for Barry, Penarth and Pontypridd started at Clarence Road and called at Riverside.

The 1930s remodelling by the GWR embraced the great triangle west of General station which housed the huge Canton loco depot. It received a new 810 ft carriage shed, a 65 ft Mundt turntable and a new coaling stage, and Ninian Park got an extra platform. In addition to the principal goods depots at Canton and Newtown, 70-ton cranage was available at Roath Dock and 125 tons at Bute. Cardiff also embraced Cathays Works and over 100 private sidings, including those of the huge GKN plant at East Moors.

GB

CARDIFF–MERTHYR LINE

Stations: Cardiff Queen Street, Llandaff ($3\frac{1}{4}$ m), Radyr ($4\frac{1}{2}$ m), Taffs Well ($6\frac{1}{4}$ m), Treforest (11 m), Pontypridd (12 m), Abercynon ($15\frac{1}{4}$ m), Quaker's Yard (17 m), Merthyr Vale (19 m), Troedyrhiw ($20\frac{3}{4}$ m), Pentrebach (22 m), Merthyr ($22\frac{3}{4}$ m)

This was the busy former main line of the Taff Vale Railway (qv), authorized by an Act of 21 June 1836 to bring coal down from Merthyr Tydfil (qv) for shipment at a new dock at Cogan Pill. It opened from Cardiff to Abercynon on 9 October 1840 and on to Merthyr on 12 April 1841, subsequently acquiring a host of important branches and connections to add to its coal movements to Cardiff and Penarth or feed in passengers at the Merthyr, Quaker's Yard, Abercynon, Pontypridd and Treforest interchange points.

South of Llandaff the route was joined by the line from Roath Dock and at Radyr those from Penarth and Cardiff East Dock united. Junction with the Rhymney Railway (qv) was made at Taffs Well before the Merthyr line reached the Treforest/Pontypridd complex and there shed the Rhondda, Nelson and Ynysybwl branches (all qv).

The steeper top section of the Merthyr line commenced at Abercynon, junction for the Taff Vale's Aberdare branch (qv) and once the starting point for the 4 ft 4 in gauge Merthyr Tramroad on which Trevithick's *Penydarren* locomotive made its historic run on 21 February 1804. Originally cable-worked, the section to Quaker's Yard was eased to 1 in 38/44 for locomotive working, trains then running into the Low Level station there and exchanging traffic with the adjacent High Level station on the GWR Neath-Pontypool Road line. On the rest of the journey up the River Taff the TVR line was accompanied by the later GWR/RR Merthyr & Quaker's Yard line and crossed the course of the Merthyr Tramroad at Black Lion.

GB

Cardiff-Merthyr line *Panoramic view of Taffs Well looking north: the Taff Vale line straight ahead, with the Rhymney Railway to the right.* (Steamchest Collection)

CARDIFF RAILWAY

The Cardiff Railway represented the Bute Dock Company's attempt to emulate the Barry (qv) enterprise and build an independent line to bring coal to its quays. Amid much opposition it secured an Act of 6 August 1897 authorizing a link from the Rhymney Railway (qv) at Heath to the Taff Vale (qv) at Treforest and opened this on 15 May 1909, only to have the TVR deny the use of the junction for coal.

The Cardiff Railway had to settle for local goods traffic and a Queen Street–Rhydyfelin passenger service, the latter commencing on 1 March 1911 with two railmotors (qv) and then growing sufficiently to need locomotive and trailer coach sets. The whole dock and railway enterprise passed to the GWR on 1 January 1922.

GB

CARDIGAN BRANCH

Stations: Whitland, Llanfalteg ($3\frac{3}{4}$ m), Login (6 m), Llanglydwen ($8\frac{3}{4}$ m), Rhydowen ($10\frac{1}{4}$ m), Llanfrynach ($12\frac{3}{4}$ m), Glogue (14 m), Crymmych Arms ($16\frac{1}{2}$ m), Boncath (21 m), Kilgerran ($24\frac{1}{2}$ m), Cardigan ($27\frac{1}{2}$ m).

Cardigan branch *Cardigan station.* (Steamchest Collection)

Cardigan expected its first railway from the east, but the high hopes of the 1854 Carmarthen & Cardigan Railway petered out at Newcastle Emlyn and the eventual rail link was south to a junction $2\frac{1}{4}$ miles west of Whitland on the South Wales main line (qv). The first section of this was opened between Whitland Junction and Llanfyrnach by the Whitland & Taf Vale Railway and began carrying slate and lead traffic from 24 March 1873. By October 1874 the line was open to Crymmych and passenger trains were operating. As the Whitland & Cardigan Railway the route was completed to Cardigan, with GWR working, on 1 September 1886, the whole undertaking passing formally to the GWR from 1 July 1890.

The branch was single with passing loops at Llanglydwen, Crymmych Arms and Boncath, and goods loops at the other stations. As it followed the Taf valley the gradient steepened and the curves got tighter, the line then needing more curves, ledges, cuttings and a stretch of 1 in 35 to round the Prescelly foothills and descend to the single platform terminus beside the River Teifi. It was a typical rural GWR branch, the four daily trains each way rarely full except on market days and easy work for the '2021' Class pannier tanks. Goods traffic was limited in later years, but rabbits contributed to the parcels receipts.

GB

CARMARTHEN

Brunel's plans for the South Wales Railway (qv) avoided an awkward deviation into Carmarthen proper by crossing the River Towy south of the town, which received a temporary station on the east bank of the river on 11 October 1852. From there the Carmarthen & Cardigan Railway took a line through the town in 1860 and built a station which was also used by Pembroke & Tenby and LNWR trains. The GWR took over the troubled C&C from 1 July 1881 and replaced its Town station with a new one 18 chains to the south on 1 July 1902.

In 1902 the western leg of the triangular junction with the main line was reinstated, main-line services from either direction running into the station's down side platform or to the up island. The local services to and from Aberystwyth and Llandilo used the down bay or the up back platform which led via a level crossing to the C&C route bridge.

The old bridge at Carmarthen Junction was replaced by a new 385 ft structure with a 50 ft bascule lifting span in 1908, the station there closing to passengers on 27 September 1926.

GB

CARMARTHEN–ABERYSTWYTH LINE

Stations: Carmarthen, Bronwydd Arms ($3\frac{1}{2}$ m), Conwil ($6\frac{1}{2}$ m), Llanpumpsaint ($9\frac{1}{2}$ m), Pencader ($14\frac{3}{4}$ m), Bryn Teify ($16\frac{3}{4}$ m), Maesycrugiau ($18\frac{1}{2}$ m), Llanybyther ($22\frac{1}{2}$ m), Lampeter ($27\frac{1}{2}$ m), Derry Ormond ($29\frac{3}{4}$ m), Llangybi ($30\frac{3}{4}$ m), Pont Llanio ($34\frac{3}{4}$ m), Tregaron ($37\frac{1}{2}$ m), Strata Florida ($42\frac{1}{4}$ m), Trawscoed ($47\frac{1}{4}$ m), Llanilar ($50\frac{1}{4}$ m), Llanrhystyd Road ($53\frac{1}{2}$ m), Aberystwyth (56 m)

Carmarthen-Aberystwyth line *Map of the ambitious Manchester & Milford Railway.* (GWR Magazine, 1907)

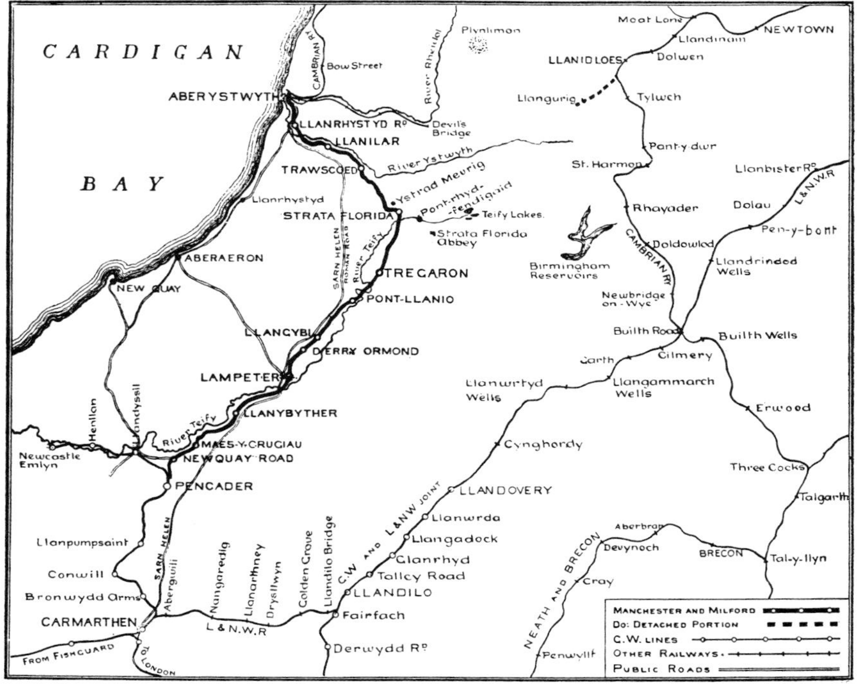

Carmarthen-Aberystwyth line *Llanpumpsaint station.* (Steamchest Collection)

Two independent railway companies created this route, the Carmarthen & Cardigan Railway building the southern portion and the Manchester & Milford Railway the section north of Pencader. Neither achieved the objectives in their title and both needed rescue, first by a Receiver and then by the GWR.

The C&C opened from the South Wales main line (qv) at Carmarthen Junction to Conwil around 1 July 1860 and to Pencader in March 1864. After all sorts of difficulties the GWR acquired the ailing company cheaply on 1 July 1881. It then had to exchange traffic with the M&M which had opened from Pencader to Lampeter on 1 January 1866, to Strata Florida on 1 September and to a junction with the Cambrian at Aberystwyth on 12 August 1867. The GWR leased the M&M from 1 July 1906 and took it over from 1 July 1911.

This picturesque, single-line route followed the Gwili and Teifi rivers for much of its course, but then had to climb via a short tunnel from the valley of the latter and descend that of the Afon Ystwyth. There was a basic service of five trains each way daily, taking some 2½ hours and with connections to and from the Newcastle Emlyn branch (qv) at Pencader and the Aberayron line (qv) at Lampeter. There were five halts in addition to the main stations.

GB

CARN BREA

Also known as Pool, Carn Brea consisted of a West Cornwall station, sidings for the local mine and water companies, and a sizeable yard for amalgamating potato and broccoli loadings. The yard had earlier been used for coal and ore traffic exchanged with the Portreath branch which closed on the 1 January 1936 joining the Tresavean branch to the Gwennap area mines, both of which involved a rope-worked incline.

GB

CASTLE CARY

The Wilts, Somerset & Weymouth Railway (qv) had only managed to reach Frome when the GWR acquired it and pushed the project forward through Castle Cary to Yeovil on 1 September 1856 and on to Weymouth on 20 January 1857. The modest country station at Castle Cary became a junction from 1 July 1905 when the first section of the new West of England main line was opened westwards.

The two routes parted company just beyond Castle Cary's two-platform station which was served primarily by Weymouth line trains, although some Plymouth stopping services originated there.

GB

'CASTLE' CLASS

C. B. Collett (qv) took over from Church-

'Castle' Class *A cab view.* (GWR Museum, Swindon)

ward as Chief Mechanical Engineer in 1922 and started to design his first locomotives, the 'Castles'. By and large they were a '10 per cent' job, the vital dimensions being scaled up by a constant factor from the last similar design, in this case the 'Stars' (qv). Elsewhere this technique was not always successful, with less skillful designers or a less satisfactory starting-point. The 'Castles', were, however, to become the GWR's most successful express passenger design, being built in batches for more than a quarter of a century.

Aesthetically they were an improvement on their predecessors, with a side-window cab, the whole being set off by the return to pre-war lining-out and brightwork. In 1925 they took part in the celebrated locomotive exchanges with the LNER Pacifics (qv), achieving superior coal and water consumptions, as well as better timings. After the Second World War larger superheaters were provided on the new locomotives being built, and in the last decade of steam on the former GWR many other changes were made to the boilers, with a number of locomotives receiving double chimneys. Better performance was obtained, but at some detriment to their appearance.

The 'Castles' had a wider route availability than the 'Kings' (qv), and operated over virtually all the GWR main lines. Five 'Stars'—and *The Great Bear* (qv)—were rebuilt as 'Castles', but the newly constructed ones were all named after British castles until a noble lord objected to the use of his name on one of the 'Dukedogs' in 1937, whereupon 21 'Castles' were renamed as 'Earls'. Another wholesale renaming took place in the early days of the Second World War, when the names of RAF aircraft were applied to a dozen of the class. There are a few others which did not have 'Castle' names, many of them commemorating personalities, such as *Isambard Kingdom Brunel*, associated with the railway. The name *Great Western* was applied to No 7007 because it was the last locomotive built by the GWR, and the final 'Castle' (No 7037) was named *Swindon* by Princess Elizabeth in 1950, to mark the borough's jubilee.

(See also Locomotives)

PWBS

CENTENARY

The GWR was the only main-line company in Britain to reach its centenary. This occurred in 1935, at a time when competition between the 'Big Four' and with the motor coach and the private car was intense, and was thus a heaven-sent opportunity for the GWR to sound its own praises. *The Times* newspaper published a special number on 31 August (the GW Society has a letter from C. B. Collett, the CME, to Sir James Milne, the General Manager, asking if Milne had any objection to publicizing the special edition amongst the company's employees at Swindon and elsewhere—presumably few of them would have been regular *Times* readers).

It appears that the Centenary passed largely unnoticed by the general public, not

Centenary *A scene from the GWR's centenary film, supposedly depicting the arrival of (replica)* North Star *with the first train at Maidenhead. In fact the set was constructed at Swindon. The GW Operatic Society supplied the cast, and a shunting engine, glimpsed at the rear, the motive power.*
(GWR Museum, Swindon)

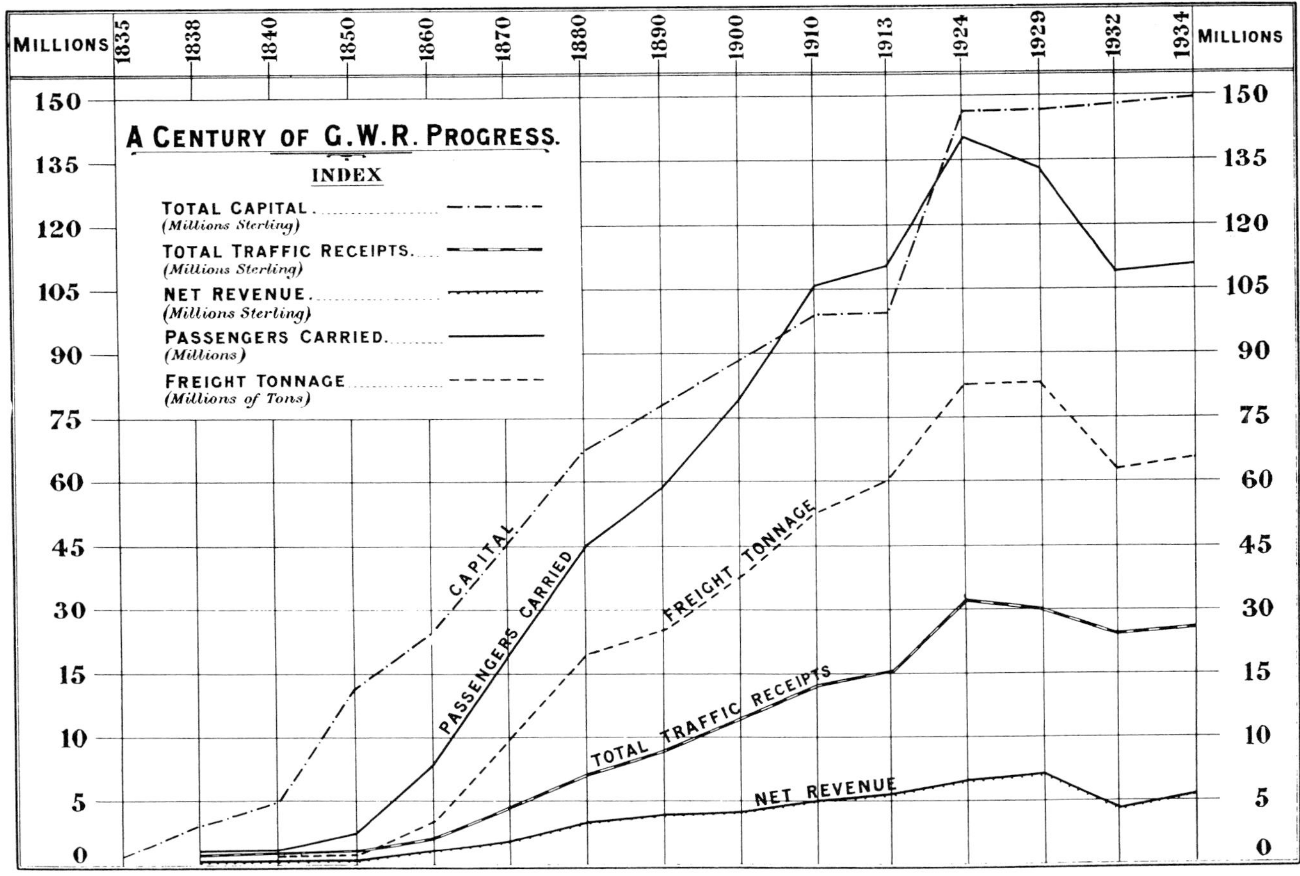

Centenary (GWR Magazine, 1935)

least because Britain had by no means recovered from the Depression and plans to spend some £15,000 marking the event proved to be far too ambitious. The initial plans included a 'procession of rolling-stock from the railways of Great Britain and Ireland', it was hoped 'American and Continental companies would send specimens in a like manner when *King George V* and *North Star* were sent to the Baltimore and Ohio exhibition', and 'temporary buildings for railway films, moving panoramas, model railways . . . music and refreshments and public conveniences to be considered essential'.

Sadly, none of this happened, although the Prince of Wales did attend a grand dinner in Bristol—but of course none of the general public would have been invited. Those who did notice the Centenary were probably locospotters of the day and patrons of the 'Cornish Riviera' express. The former would have been aware of the 'streamlining' (qv) applied to a Castle, No 5005 *Manorbier Castle*, and a 'King', No 6014 *King Henry VII*, whilst the famous Paddington to Penzance express was equipped with two magnificent rakes of carriages. Known as the 'Centenary' stock, the carriages were built to the generous proportions made possible by the GWR's Broad Gauge legacy, and although painted in traditional livery they were certainly the equal of the streamliners of the LNER. But like them, the 'Centenary' sets had a short life, being split up into individual carriages in 1941 (one, restaurant car No 9635, is preserved at Didcot) (qv, Rolling-stock, passenger). A sign of the hard financial times was that there was no money for special stock for the equally prestigious 'Bristolian' and 'Cheltenham Flyer' trains (both qv).

Amongst other events was a film commissioned by the company, but whilst not exactly a non-event, the Centenary was celebrated in a far less spectacular manner than might have been expected.

(See also Bristol)

MCHB

CHACEWATER

Although Chacewater's copper mines were served by the 1825 Redruth & Chasewater line, Chacewater had to wait for its first main-line trains until the West Cornwall Railway (qv) opened on 26 August 1852. The Perranporth and Newquay line then opened from Blackwater Junction, ½ mile to the west, in 1903–5, and Chacewater gained a Truro–Newquay service to add to the main-line trains which called. From 9 November 1924 the triangular branch junction was altered in favour of extending the single line to the outer face of Chacewater's up island platform.

GB

CHAIRMEN

Sixteen Chairmen in 113 years seems a high turn-over, particularly since two (Gooch and Churchill, both qv) spanned 50 years between them. Yet on the whole the GWR was lucky with its Chairmen—weaker ones seldom lasted long, and times of difficulty seemed usually to produce an officer capable of dealing with them. Two early Chairmen committed suicide, and Gooch had the task of keeping things together during a time of severe financial restraint after 1865. Viscount Churchill, succeeding after the tragically early death of Baldwin (qv), was in charge in 1922–3, when the GWR suddenly became a much bigger concern, took on a new shape and had to adopt a point of view to suit—or at least not to alienate—its new acquisitions under the Grouping.

The Chairmen were:

Benjamin Shaw	1835–37
William Sims	1837–39
Charles Russell	1839–55
Rt Hon Spencer Walpole	1855–56
Viscount Barrington	1856–57
Hon Frederick Ponsonby	1857–59
Lord Shelburne	1859–63
Richard Potter	1863–65
Sir Daniel Gooch	1865–89
Frederick Saunders	1889–95
Viscount Emlyn	1895–1905
Alfred Baldwin	1905–08
Viscount Churchill	1908–34
Viscount Horne	1934–40
Sir Charles Hambro	1940–45
Lord Portal	1945–48

(See also individual entries)

CA

CHANNEL ISLANDS TRAFFIC

The GWR's own involvement with the Channel Islands shipping traffic started in 1889, although as early as 1857 it had worked with a separate company to provide through services to Jersey and Guernsey from Weymouth. The Harbour Tramway there (qv) was opened in 1865, and until the late 1980s boat trains used this to make their way to the quay through the streets at walking pace. The GWR's first steamers grossed less than 600 tons, but the last one delivered for the service in 1947 had nearly six times the capacity, at almost 3,500 tons. As well as passengers, the GWR ships handled much freight on this route, the most notable being the vast quantities of spring flowers, early potatoes and tomatoes for which the islands are famous. In September 1926, for example, more than 94,000 packages of tomatoes were landed at Weymouth, while, after the Second World War, special passenger sailings brought workers from South Wales to help pick and handle the crop.

PWBS

CHARD BRANCH

Stations: Taunton, Thornfalcon ($3\frac{1}{2}$ m), Hatch ($6\frac{1}{2}$ m), Ilton Halt ($7\frac{1}{2}$ m), Donyatt Halt (12 m), Ilminster ($11\frac{1}{4}$ m), Chard ($15\frac{1}{4}$ m)

The LSWR opened a branch to Chard Town on 8 May 1863, the year in which the Bristol & Exeter Railway (qv) acquired the project authorized by the Chard & Taunton Railway Act of 6 August 1861. A single line from Creech Junction, along the route of the Taunton Canal, was then opened to a new, joint station on 11 September 1866, all passenger trains being concentrated there from 1 January 1917.

The GWR branch was divided into four block sections using electric train staff and token, and with electric tablet applying over the link to the LSWR/SR. The summer service consisted of six weekday trains each way, plus an extra on Saturdays, an afternoon Chard–Ilminster and return and one service to Taunton which called only at Ilminster. There was a service out from Taunton and back on summer Sunday afternoons. Freight traffic was dealt with at Chard, Thornfalcon, Hatch and Ilminster, the latter having a 12-ton crane.

GB

CHELTENHAM

Cheltenham had been linked with Gloucester and the River Severn in 1811 by the Gloucester & Cheltenham Tramroad, and a portion of this horse-worked line was incorporated in the standard gauge railway opened between the two towns by the Birmingham & Gloucester Railway on 4 November 1840. A line from Lansdown Road, Cheltenham, to Swindon had earlier been authorized to the Cheltenham & Great Western Union Railway (qv) whose acquisition by the GWR was the basis of the latter's part-ownership of the access to Cheltenham from the south. The C&GWU Act also authorized a purely GWR extension to a terminus in St James Square.

Cheltenham Spa (St James) was opened on Saturday 23 October 1847 with a service

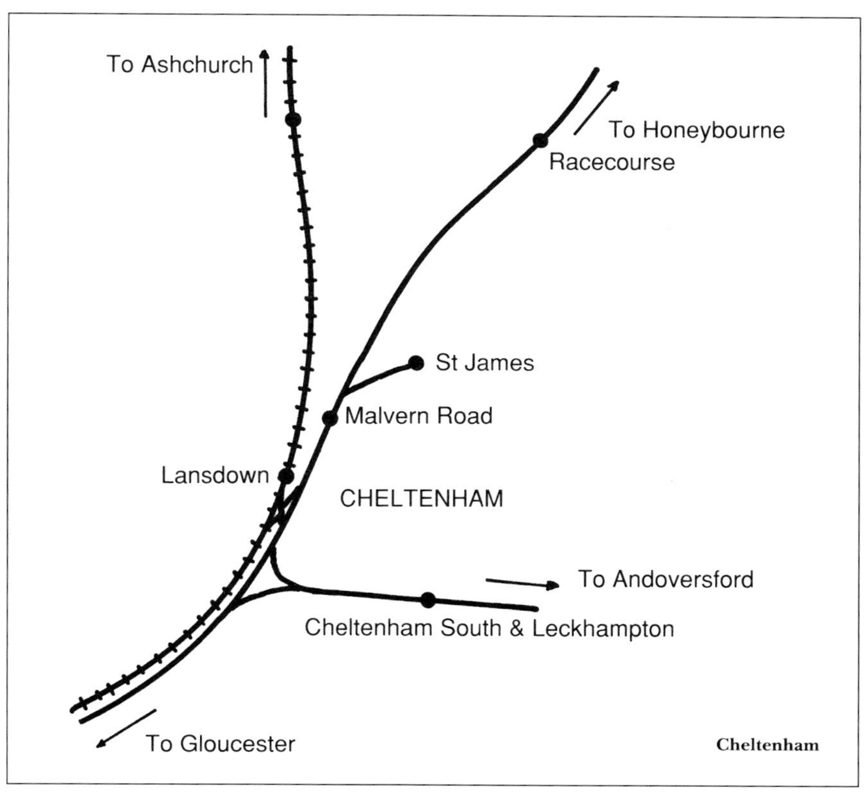

Cheltenham

of 10 up and 11 down trains. The 'Morning Express' to London took 3 hours 10 minutes and cost £2 1st class. A 3rd class ticket was only 10 shillings but the 'Parliamentary Train' took from 11.15 am to 6.13 pm for the same journey. In later years the 'Cheltenham Spa Express' was to reach Paddington in just $2\frac{1}{2}$ hours.

Over the years Cheltenham gained additional routes to Banbury, Andover and Honeybourne and additional stations at Cheltenham South on the Midland & South Western Junction route (qv), Cheltenham Racecourse on the Honeybourne line and at Malvern Road, just south of St James. The latter was a four-platform terminus while Malvern Road, which opened on 30 March 1908, consisted of a 700 ft island with footbridge access.

GB

CHELTENHAM & GREAT WESTERN UNION RAILWAY

Despite plans for a rival route to join the London & Birmingham Railway and opposition from the Thames & Severn Canal, the C&GWU obtained an Act to link Cheltenham and Gloucester with the GWR at Swindon as early as 21 June 1836. After opening the section from Swindon to Kemble (qv) and Cirencester on 31 May 1841 and leasing it to the GWR, the smaller company encountered increasing difficulty in raising capital and sold its undertaking to the GWR in 1843 for £230,000. The Cheltenham–Gloucester section, already opened by the Birmingham & Gloucester Railway on 4 November 1840, was extended to Standish on 8 July 1844 and the difficult section through the Cotswold ridge to Kemble came into use on 12 May of the following year.

GB

CHELTENHAM–ANDOVER LINE

Stations: Cheltenham Spa Lansdown, Cheltenham South & Leckhampton (2 m), Charlton Kings ($3\frac{1}{4}$ m), Andoversford Junction (7 m), Withington ($9\frac{3}{4}$ m), Chedworth ($13\frac{1}{2}$ m), Foss Cross ($14\frac{1}{2}$ m), Cirencester Watermoor ($20\frac{3}{4}$ m), South Cerney ($23\frac{3}{4}$ m), Cricklade ($27\frac{1}{4}$ m), Swindon Town ($35\frac{3}{4}$ m), Chiseldon (39 m), Ogbourne ($42\frac{1}{2}$ m), Marlborough ($47\frac{1}{4}$ m), Savernake Low Level ($52\frac{1}{4}$ m), Grafton & Burbage ($54\frac{1}{2}$ m), Collingbourne ($58\frac{1}{2}$ m), Ludgershall (61 m), Weyhill (65 m), Andover ($68\frac{1}{2}$ m)

Under the 1923 Grouping the Midland & South Western Junction Railway (qv) became part of the GWR, adding to the latter's system the 60 m 55 ch line from Andoversford Junction to Red Post Junction, Andover, and the 2 m 32 ch branch to Tidworth which was worked for the War Department. The route's through services included one between Liverpool and Southampton and its locals several permutations on the Cirencester–Marlborough section and trains to and from Tidworth. Freight services were generally handled by 0-6-0 locomotives and passenger workings by 4-4-0 types.

The ex-M&SWJR main line was double to Cirencester (singled 1928), again from Marlborough to Weyhill and then single (doubled 1943) to Red Post Junction and alongside the LSWR/SR main line to Andover Junction. The northern section involved gradients of 1 in 78/80 to Chedworth Tunnel and then an easy run through pastoral countryside to the junction with the GWR main line at Rushey Platt and round into Swindon Town. Another summit near Marlborough Tunnel led on to the connections at Savernake (qv), the lavish station and accommodation at Ludgershall and then a racing stretch to end the journey.

The M&SWJR route was brought up to higher engineering standards in the GWR era but its traffic levels tended to decline except during the wartime years when Marlborough, Savernake and the Tidworth line were all involved in the traffic preparations for D-Day.

GB

CHELTENHAM–BIRMINGHAM LINE

Stations: Cheltenham Spa St James, Cheltenham Spa Malvern Road ($\frac{1}{4}$ m), Bishops Cleeve ($4\frac{1}{4}$ m), Gotherington ($5\frac{3}{4}$ m), Winchcombe ($9\frac{1}{4}$ m), Toddington ($11\frac{3}{4}$ m), Broadway ($16\frac{1}{4}$ m), Weston-sub-Edge ($19\frac{1}{4}$ m), Honeybourne ($21\frac{3}{4}$ m), Long Marston ($22\frac{1}{4}$ m), Milcote ($27\frac{3}{4}$ m), Stratford-on-Avon ($30\frac{3}{4}$ m), Wilmcote ($33\frac{1}{2}$ m), Bearley (35 m), then via Birmingham & North Warwickshire Line (qv)

In 1908 the GWR began running expresses over a new route from Bristol to Birmingham and at last recovered from the loss of the Bristol & Gloucester Railway to the

Cheltenham-Birmingham line *An early view of Winchcombe station, opened in 1905 and apparently still being finished off in this view which also shows an early steam railmotor at the southbound platform.* (Steamchest Collection)

Midland in 1845. The new trains, which took 2¼–2½ hours, used the South Wales line as far as Filton, the new Bristol & South Wales Direct line (qv) to Westerleigh Junction (qv), then running powers over the Midland to Gloucester, the reinstated Avoiding Line there and on over the joint section to Cheltenham. There Malvern Road through station had been opened on 30 March 1908 and a new line to Honeybourne (qv) (GWR Act of 1 August 1899) completed on 1 August 1906, linked up with the branch opened to Stratford by the Oxford, Worcester & Wolverhampton (qv) on 11 July 1859. The Stratford-on-Avon Railway of 10 October 1860 took the new services on to Bearley and the Birmingham & North Warwickshire line opened to Tyseley on 1 July 1908.

The Cheltenham–Honeybourne section involved a steady but modest rise to Winchcombe with Hunting Butts Tunnel preceding the station provided for Cheltenham Racecourse, and Greet Tunnel at the summit itself. The long, undulating descent, over the 15 36-foot spans of Toddington Viaduct, to Stratford's Racecourse Platform was then followed by a 1 in 175 climb to Wilmcote and more climbing on the new line beyond. In addition to through services from the West to Birmingham and Wolverhampton, the line had a good Cheltenham–Broadway–Honeybourne local service, another on from Honeybourne–Stratford–Hatton–Leamington Spa, and further trains from Stratford and Henley-in-Arden to Birmingham.

The Cheltenham–Honeybourne line was opened in stages: Honeybourne–Toddington, 1 August 1904; to Winchcombe, 1 February 1905; to Bishops Cleeve, 1 June 1906; and on to Cheltenham on 1 August. It was well engineered and provided with generous station accommodation, including four halts.

GB

'Cheltenham Flyer' *H. M. Bateman's delightful cartoon, 'The man who pulled the communication cord of the "Cheltenham Flyer"'.* (GWR Magazine, 1933, but originally published in The Tatler)

'CHELTENHAM FLYER'

Although the name 'Cheltenham Flyer' was unofficial, for many years the train had the fastest start-to-stop schedule in Britain and the world. The acceleration started in 1923, when an afternoon train from Cheltenham was given a 75-minute booking over the 77.3 miles from Swindon to Paddington, which made it the fastest in Britain. The schedule was not a difficult one, even for a 'Saint' (qv), let alone a 'Castle' (qv); the latter had already started to appear and were later to monopolize the workings.

In 1929, 5 minutes were cut from the timing, to lift the start-to-stop average to 66.2 mph, enabling the GWR to claim it was the fastest train in the world. Not content with that, on the inaugural run they cut 2 minutes off the booking. The GWR's world supremacy was subsequently challenged by the Canadian Pacific, but in 1931 the 'Cheltenham Flyer' struck back. Five months after the record had crossed the Atlantic, the deletion of 3 minutes from the schedule of the 'Flyer' put it in front once more. To rub it in, on the first day they cut the actual time to under an hour, pushing the average to 77.8, with a maximum of 89 being achieved between Mileposts 5 and 3.

A year later a further 2 minutes were eliminated, which gave a start-to-stop average of 71.4 mph, beating the 70-mark for the first time. There was no doubt about such a schedule, as in June 1932, with *Tregenna Castle* (qv) in charge, the train reached Paddington in under 57 minutes, to achieve an average of no less than 81.7—another world record. Although the train often ran with a load of no more than six bogies, time could be kept with as many as ten. The train's British record average was marginally beaten in 1937 by the 'Coronation' on the LNER, but, by the Second World War, it had been well eclipsed by steam in North America, not to mention diesels and electrics in Europe.

PWBS

CHEPSTOW

The South Wales Railway (qv) opened from Chepstow to Swansea on 18 June 1850 with the line from the Gloucester direction then reaching a temporary station on the east bank of the River Wye on 19 September 1851. A horse bus service linked the two until the completion of Brunel's bridge over the Wye on 19 July 1852.

The bridge involved a cutting on the east bank of the river and three approach spans over the soft ground of the west. They were linked by a 300 ft main span, 50 ft above the river and carrying the main deck by means of twin tubular girders raised high above the end piers and four sets of suspension chains. The Wye Bridge, which used 2,340 tons of iron and cost £65,500, was used as a model for the bridge at Saltash. It was rebuilt in 1962.

Chepstow, with its small, chalet-style booking office, was served by Paddington/Cheltenham–Cardiff trains and those on the scenic Wye Valley line (qv). It got a new platform for race traffic in 1926 and its goods activities included a line down to shipbuilding premises on the river bank below.

(See also Bridges and viaducts)

GB

Chepstow *A view of Brunel's Wye Bridge from the east bank showing the twin-tubular-girder main span.* (GWR Museum, Swindon)

CHESTER

The GWR main line from Shrewsbury joined the LNWR/LMS Holyhead line at Saltney Junction for the final section to Chester General station, having just previously sent off a short branch to Saltney Carriage Works and a wharf on the Dee. The joint GWR and LNWR territory then began with the triangle linking the Shrewsbury and Birkenhead routes with the station, and continued beyond the latter towards Warrington. The line from Shrewsbury had come to the GWR from the Shrewsbury & Chester Railway (qv), which had opened a section south from Saltney Junction on 4 November 1846, and the other routes (Birkenhead, 23 September 1840, and Warrington, 18 December 1850) by the 1860 joint takeover of the Birkenhead Railway (qv).

The impressive station at Chester had originated in 1848 as a result of a commission from the four using railways to Francis Thompson who designed the Italianate main block with its turreted end sections and Venetian windows. Extension in 1890 added an extra outer island to the original combination of a single platform and bays. The GWR had a Divisional Superintendent here and operated its local trains from two down side bays. Through expresses used the main platforms except in the case of trains not booked to stop, like the Isle of Man Boat Trains and the Grand National specials, which used the direct spur of the triangle.

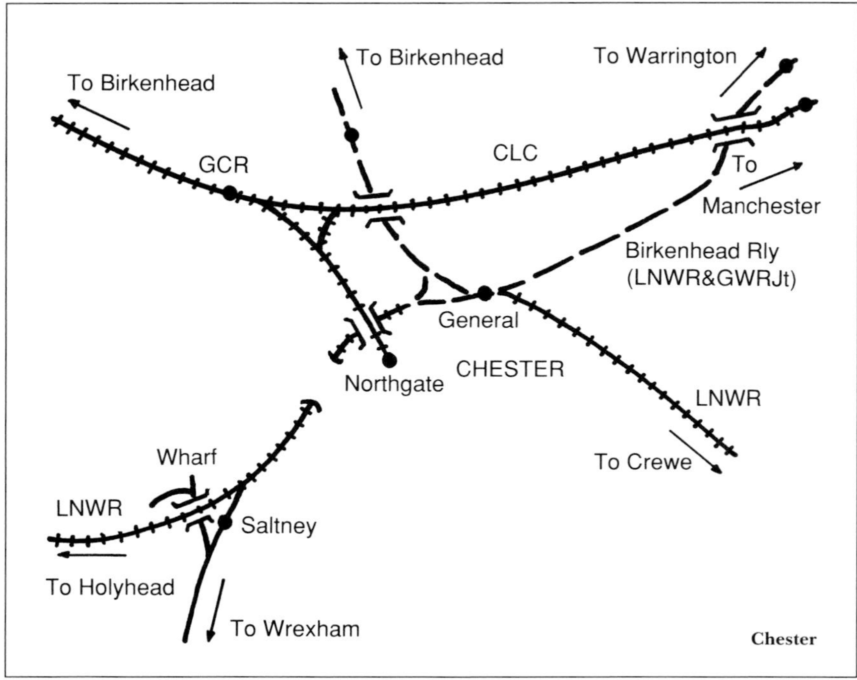

Chester

The GWR had a full range of facilities at Chester, including its own goods depot. It also had two engine sheds but mainly used the larger of the two which had once been a Chester & Birkenhead Railway building.

GB

CHESTER–WARRINGTON LINE

Stations: Chester General, Mickle Trafford ($2\frac{3}{4}$ m), Dunham Hill ($5\frac{1}{4}$ m), Helsby ($7\frac{1}{2}$ m), Frodsham ($9\frac{3}{4}$ m), Halton ($11\frac{1}{2}$ m), Norton ($13\frac{1}{4}$ m), Daresbury ($15\frac{1}{4}$ m), Warrington Bank Quay (18 m)

With the take-over of the Birkenhead Railway in 1860, the GWR became part owners, along with the LNWR, of the 18-mile line authorized to the Birkenhead, Lancashire & Cheshire Junction Railway on 26 June 1846 and opened on 18th December 1850. The GWR participated in the local service between Chester and Warrington, ran its Barmouth/Pwllheli–Manchester Exchange service this way, and also used the route for access to its Manchester depots at Cross Lane, Duncan Street, Exchange and Seedley.

GB

CHIEF CIVIL ENGINEERS

Known simply as 'Engineer' then 'Principal Engineer' until July 1916, and 'Chief Engineer' thereafter, the holders of the office on the GWR were:

I. K. Brunel (qv)	Mar 1835–Sept 1859
T. H. Bertram	Sept 1859–April 1860
Michael Lane (qv)	April 1860–Mar 1868
W. G. Owen	Mar1868–Mar 1885
L. Trench	Mar 1891–Sept 1892
J. C. Inglis (qv)	Oct 1892–June 1904
W. W. Grierson	Jan 1904–Dec 1923
J. C. Lloyd / W. Waddell (joint)	Jan 1924–Dec 1925
J. C. Lloyd	Jan 1926–Jan 1929
R. Carpmael	Jan 1929–Dec 1939
A. S. Quartermaine	Jan 1940–Dec 1947

MCHB

CHIEF MECHANICAL ENGINEERS

The holders of this post, with its various changes of title, were:

Sir Daniel Gooch
(Locomotive Superintendent)
August 1837–October 1864

Joseph Armstrong
(Locomotive & Carriage Superintendent)
January 1864– June 1877

William Dean
(Locomotive & Carriage Superintendent) June 1877–June 1902

George Jackson Churchward
June 1902– December 1921
(Title became Chief Mechanical Engineer in 1916)

Charles B. Collett
January 1922–July 1941

Frederick W. Hawksworth
July 1941– December 1947

(See also individual entries)

MCHB

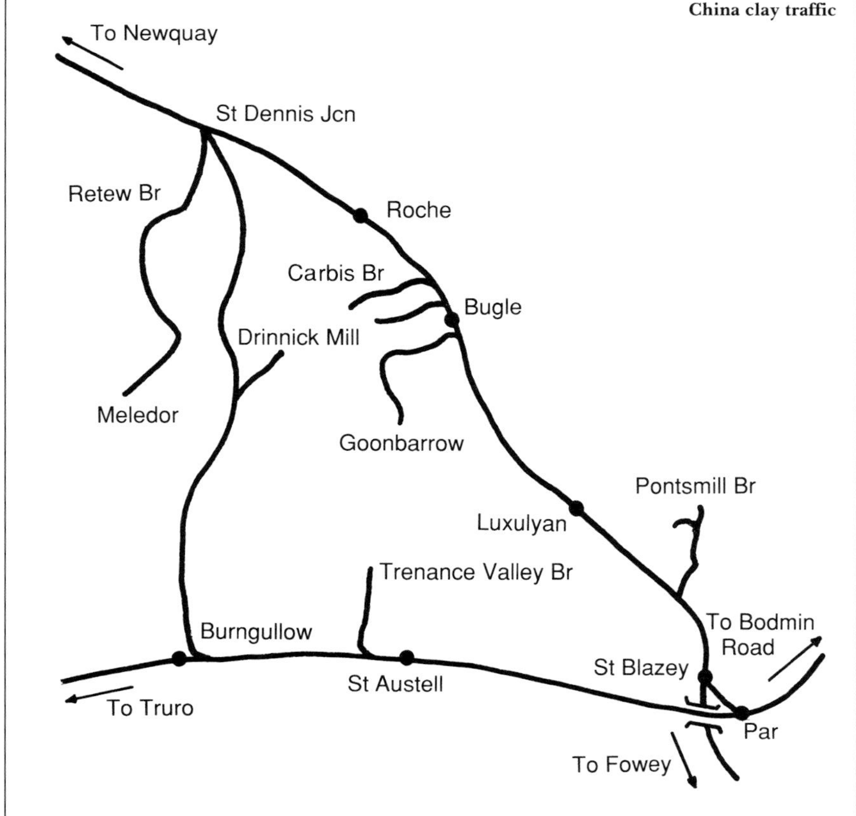

China clay traffic

CHINA CLAY TRAFFIC

Happily for Cornwall, the decline of metal mining in the county was followed by growth in the china clay industry. Extensive deposits in the area north-west of St Austell (qv) stimulated early tramways, a conventional rail network consolidated by the Cornwall Minerals Railway (qv) in 1874 and an expanded rail activity in the GWR era. The initial movements to smaller ports were replaced by a concentration of shipment traffic on Par Harbour and the Port of Fowey (qv).

Individual mineral lines are described in separate entries but the main network came to consist of:

- a 4 m 2 ch line south from the Newquay branch at St Dennis Junction to Melangoose Depot, extended to Meledor Sidings by the GWR on 1 July 1912 and known as the Retew Branch;
- a 4 m 46 ch line south from St Dennis Junction via Drinnick Mill to the main line at Burngullow;
- the short Carbis and Wheal Rose branches west from the Newquay line at Bugle;
- the 1 m 60 ch Goonbarrow branch south from Bugle to Caudledown/ Carbean;
- the 1 m $35\frac{1}{2}$ ch Trenance Valley branch north from St Austell.

Traffic from dozens of sidings within this network passed to the St Blazey complex near Par to be re-marshalled and re-engined for onward movement to inland destinations or for shipment. For the latter traffic through Fowey, the GWR provided eight jetties with cranes and shutes for wagon discharge, converting No 4 Jetty to conveyor belt operation in 1909 and No 8 to electric conveyor and movable shute in 1923.

GB

CHIPPENHAM

The extensive earthworks of the infant GWR's approach from Hay Lane were completed in time for the route to be extended to an incomplete station at Chippenham on 31 May 1841. By 30 June the even harder section on through Box Tunnel to Bath had been finished to allow the first through trains between London and Bristol. From Thingley Junction, 24 miles west of Chippenham, the Wilts, Somerset & Weymouth Railway (qv) was opened as far as Westbury on 5 September 1848, and Chippenham gained a short branch to Calne (qv) on 29 October 1863.

Following the completion of the WS&W route to Salisbury in 1856 and Weymouth in 1857, Chippenham was provided with an enlarged station with engine and goods sheds. Comprising a main down side platform, with Calne bay, and an up island, one side of which was used as a down bay, Chippenham was well served by Bristol and Weymouth line trains and had private sidings for Saxby & Farmer's (Westinghouse) signal works and for stone and bacon traffic.

GB

CHURCHILL, VISCOUNT

Chairman, 1908–34. Victor Albert Charles Francis Spencer, Viscount Churchill, was born in London on 23 October 1864, the only son of Baron Churchill of Whichwood. Educated at Eton, he went on to Sandhurst, and later became a Lieutenant in the Coldstream Guards. On 11 July 1902 he was created the 1st Viscount Churchill, and joined the GWR Board in place of Lord Cawdor in 1905.

An early task was to counter charges of wasteful competition raised by some newspapers and shareholders as a result of the company's declining an offer from the LSWR for the pooling of West of England traffic. With the cut-offs (qv) to the West open—which would have made nonsense of such a scheme—he guided the company ably through the years up to the Great War. Those immediately after the war were difficult: settlement of a strike in 1919 added £5.5m to the wages bill, and road transport began to compete with the railways when the Government of the day forced up rates.

Lord Churchill, a champion of railway interests, was closely involved in the negotiations which resulted in the Grouping (qv) under the Railways Act of 1921. He died of pneumonia on 3 January 1934, the longest-serving GWR Chairman, to be succeeded by Lord Horne (qv).

CA

CHURCHWARD, GEORGE JACKSON

Chief Mechanical Engineer, 1902–21. George Jackson Churchward was, without doubt, the greatest of all the GWR's Chief Mechanical Engineers, perhaps the greatest to serve any British railway. He was born at Stoke Gabriel in Devon in 1857 and went to work on the South Devon Railway (qv) at the age of 16. With the take-over of the SDR by the GWR, Churchward went to Swindon as a draughtsman and soon gained promotion as assistant to 'Young Joe' Armstrong. In 1885 he was appointed by William Dean (qv) as Manager of the Carriage Works; ten years later he moved to the locomotive works as Assistant Manager and in 1896 was put in charge.

Churchward became Chief Assistant Locomotive Carriage & Wagon Superintendent in July 1897. Almost immediately his theories on boiler design were put into practice on a remarkably ugly 4-6-0 freight locomotive, No 2601, which led to the scarcely beautiful but at least presentable and hard working 'Aberdare' Class 2-6-0s. These latter were both powerful and long-lived, many surviving beyond the second World War. Related to No 2601 was 4-6-0 No 100. It is easy to make extravagant claims for a particular locomotive design, but there can be no doubt that this Churchward outside-cylinder engine is one of the most significant milestones in the story of the British steam locomotive.

The essential characteristics of No 100 formed the foundations of most main-line passenger and mixed traffic locomotives built from around the First World War until the end of steam. Although Dean was nominally still in charge when No 100 entered service, he can have had virtually nothing to do with its design; shortly afterwards Churchward bestowed the name *William Dean* upon it (qv). From No 100 evolved all the standard GWR classes (and those of the LSWR in the Urie era and their Southern Railway successors, the LMS from the accession of Stanier, the later LNER mixed traffic locomotives, the small but important band of Irish 4-6-0s, and all the British Railways standard designs).

Under Churchward, Swindon Works was expanded and modernized. The best-known feature of the works, the celebrated 'A' Shop, was begun in 1900. Electricity was introduced in 1902 and had to be generated by the GWR as the town did not, as yet, have its own supply.

Churchward's post was the most important within the company and he earned something in the order of £150,000 pa in present-day terms. Although, like all GWR locomotive chiefs, Churchward was a GWR man through and through, he was fully aware of the newest innovations world-wide and was particularly impressed by what was happening in the USA and France. He imported some Bousquet-de Glehn compound 4-4-2s from France in order to compare them with his own 'Atlantics' and 4-6-0s. Although he concluded that compounding had no future on the GWR, there was much about the French design which did impress him and it led to his four-cylinder 4-6-0 No 40 of 1906, which became the prototype of those classic express engines, the 'Stars', 'Castles' and 'Kings' (all qv).

George Jackson Churchward (GWR Museum, Swindon)

In carriage design, Churchward abolished the familiar clerestory roof and in 1904 brought out the first of his massive, 70-foot long elliptical roof carriages. Dining cars were now the norm on all the best services and sleeping cars could be found on the night trains between Paddington and the West of England and Birkenhead, although 3rd class sleeping accommodation did not appear on the GWR until around 1930.

In 1905 Churchward authorized the cutting up of the preserved Broad Gauge locomotives *North Star* (qv) and *Lord of the Isles*. The destruction of such historically significant artefacts seems inexplicable to a generation which is prepared to find thousands of pounds to preserve a rusting hulk, and it is indeed difficult to understand Churchward's motives. It was claimed that space was at a premium, but in a site as vast as Swindon surely no one believed that even in 1905. In any event, the Board of Directors approved and the deed was done. Regrets were expressed shortly afterwards, rather too late, and when a replica of *North Star* was made for the 1925 Stockton & Darlington Centenary a fair number of parts of the original magically reappeared.

Throughout the Edwardian era and into the 1920s Churchward's locomotives eclipsed those of all other companies. But the patriarchal relationship which he, like his predecessors, thought natural, was increasingly resented by the men, and the unions were becoming a force to be reckoned with. Amalgamation was looming, and Churchward was coming up to his 65th birthday. He retired at the end of 1921, and became the first Honorary Freeman of the Borough of Swindon. Like nearly all senior GWR men, Churchward took a great interest in the welfare of the town and had become its first mayor in 1900. Despite changing times he was still greatly respected and liked and nearly everyone at Swindon contributed generously to his retirement present, most of it being put into the Churchward Memorial Fund which provided annual prizes for the students at the Swindon Technical School.

Churchward died on 19 December 1933. He was knocked down by a Paddington to Fishguard express on the main line beside the Works, where he was still a familiar and much respected figure. He was buried at Christ Church, Swindon.

(See also Locomotives, Rolling-stock, passenger, Swindon and Swindon Works)

MCHB

Cinderford branch

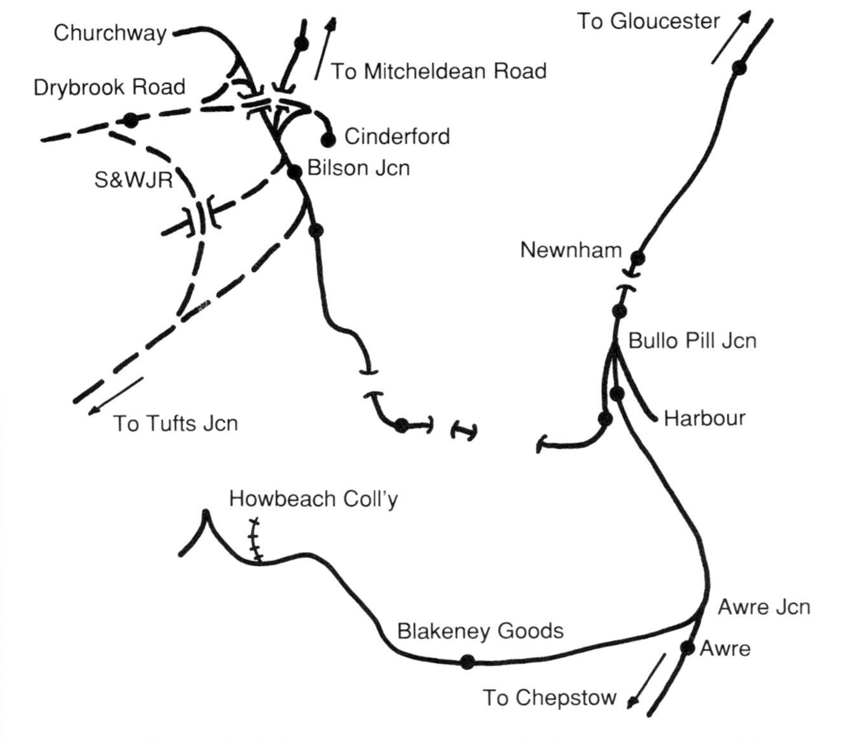

CINDERFORD BRANCH

Stations: Newnham, Cinderford ($5\frac{3}{4}$ m), Whimsey Halt ($6\frac{3}{4}$ m), Drybrook Halt ($8\frac{1}{4}$ m)

On 3 August 1907 the GWR introduced a passenger service on its Forest of Dean branch, using an 'Auto-Engine and Trailer' and offering a 30-minute journey over the 7 m 7 ch single line between Newnham and Steam Mills Crossing Halt, with calls at seven halts *en route*. From 4 November the service was extended a further 56 chains to Drybrook, but from 7 July 1930 was cut back to Cinderford.

The branch began life as a tramroad down to the River Severn at Bullo Pill, passed to the Forest of Dean Railway in 1826 and was then, with South Wales Railway (qv) backing, converted to a conventional railway from 24 July 1854. It then consisted of 7 m 20 ch inland from the junction at Bullo Pill and 53 chains down to the modest basin there. The section north from Bilson was authorized to the Mitcheldean Road & Forest of Dean Junction Railway on 13 July 1871 but that enterprise had to be rescued by the GWR in 1880, the latter eventually completing the line, including the 638 yd Euroclydon Tunnel, but never using it north of Drybrook.

From the up side bay at Newnham branch trains followed the main line to Bullo Pill Junction and then climbed at 1 in 50–71 and via three tunnels to Cinderford. There a triple junction separated the original route to Churchway, that to Cinderford (qv, Severn & Wye) and the MR&FoDJ section, which climbed at 1 in 43–52 to its summit before a steep drop to a junction in the Mitcheldean Road goods yard.

The 15 mph branch was worked by electric train staff to the passing loop at Bilson and then by train staff/one engine in steam.

GB

CIRENCESTER BRANCH

Authorized by the Cheltenham & Great Western Union Railway (qv) Act of 21 June 1836, this straight, easily graded, 4 m 17 ch broad gauge single line was opened on 31 May 1841 and became part of the GWR system two years later. Most timetables showed a service of 8–11 trains each way on weekdays to and from the single platform of 'Sheep Street Station', later Cirencester

Town. The terminus had an attractive Tudor-style building and a full range of goods facilities, including pig dock, cattle pens and 12-ton crane.

GB

'CITY' CLASS

The early 1900s were a period of great change on the GWR, as Churchward (qv) took over from Dean (qv) and started to develop his ideas for new motive power, which were to take the company into its pre-eminent position. The line of development was, however, by no means straightforward, as the history of the famous 'City' Class of 4-4-0s illustrates.

In 1902, the first 'modern' 4-6-0, No 100 *William Dean* (qv), had appeared, but in the following year Swindon built ten outside-framed 4-4-0s, which, admittedly, saw this late-Victorian type of locomotive reach its peak. Maybe Churchward was still waiting to assess the performance of his radical new design, but another possibility was that the facilities at Swindon were not yet capable of mass-producing the larger new designs. The 'Cities' (initially Nos 3433–3442, but later renumbered 3710–3719) were certainly an instant success, and, within a year of being out-shopped, *City of Bath* (qv) and *City of Truro* (qv) had both achieved their place in the record books.

The construction of the first 'City' had been preceded by the fitting of a larger Standard No 4 boiler to one of the 'Atbaras', built in 1901, and in 1907–8 a further nine of that class were similarly modified to become 'Cities'. In addition, 17 of the 'Badmintons' were given the same type of boiler in 1905–10, but these were later replaced with smaller ones, showing how complex were the various contemporary considerations going on at Swindon.

The 'Cities' had a relatively short life in the top link, being successively displaced from various routes by their outside-cylinder successors, the 'Counties' (qv), although the rough-riding of the latter prevented them from ever approaching the record speeds achieved by the last of Swindon's double-framed express-passenger locomotives.

(*See also Locomotives*)

PWBS

CITY OF BATH

In 1903, the Prince and Princess of Wales (later King George V and Queen Mary) were travelling to Cornwall, and word was sent to the GWR that Their Royal Highnesses would like 'a good run'. As a result, 'City' Class (qv) 4-4-0 *City of Bath* (No 3433) worked the royal saloons, plus two ordinary coaches forming the advance portion of the 'Cornishman', non-stop from Paddington to Plymouth in just over 233½ minutes. The route in those days was via Bristol, so the average worked out at 63 mph, and the train arrived no less than 37 minutes early. The maximum speed was 88 descending Dauntsey Bank.

PWBS

CITY OF TRURO

On 9 May 1904, the 'City' Class (qv) 4-4-0 No 3440 *City of Truro* achieved an extremely high speed descending Wellington Bank with an Ocean Mail special, at a time when the GWR and the London & South Western Railway were competing for transatlantic ocean liner traffic (qv) between Plymouth and London. On this occasion, Charles Rous-Marten, who had started the series 'Locomotive Practice & Performance' in *The Railway Magazine,* recorded a speed of 102.3 mph, the details of which were hushed up by the GWR until 1922. Although doubts were subsequently cast on the exact speed attained, analyses have since indicated that *City of Truro* was almost certainly the first steam locomotive to attain 100 mph. It was preserved in 1931, and has twice since been restored for steaming, the last occasion being for the 'GWR 150' celebrations in 1985.

PWBS

City of Bath *No 3433 gave its Royal passengers 'a good run' in 1903, reaching 88 mph on Dauntsey Bank.* (GWR Museum, Swindon)

CLEE HILL BRANCH

The Ludlow & Clee Hill Railway Act of 22 July 1861 authorized this mineral line east from the Shrewsbury & Hereford line at Clee Hill Junction on the north side of Ludlow. It was opened on 24 August 1864 with the GWR and LNWR companies taking over the working from 1 January 1877 and acquiring the line from 1 January 1893.

The 6-mile route was single from Clee Hill Junction through Middleton to the loop at Bitterley. There, the 1 in 20 approach gradient was followed by a 1 in 12 rope-worked incline up to the Clee Hill Granite Co's sidings. Special instructions governed the working of the incline where the maximum descending load was 85 tons including a dummy truck.

GB

CLEVEDON BRANCH

As construction work proceeded on the completion of the Bristol & Exeter Railway's (qv) main line to Exeter, the company obtained an Act on 31 July 1845 for branches to Yeovil, Tiverton (both qv) and Clevedon. The latter was the first to open, on 28 July 1847.

In its best years, the 3½-mile single line from Yatton had a service of up to 30 trains each way on weekdays. They used one long platform at Clevedon station which stood near the town, beside the River Yeo and adjacent to the Weston, Clevedon & Portishead Light Railway with which there was a connection.

The branch was worked by train staff and one engine in steam, with a fixed Distant at Clevedon and the signal box there unlocked by the train staff key. Latterly, passenger trains had no guard.

GB

CLYNDERWEN–LETTERSTON JUNCTION LINE

Stations: Clynderwen, Llanycefn ($3\frac{3}{4}$ m), Maenclochog ($6\frac{3}{4}$ m), Rosebush ($8\frac{1}{4}$ m), Puncheston ($12\frac{1}{2}$ m), Letterston ($17\frac{1}{2}$ m)

This route originated as an $8\frac{1}{2}$-mile branch to serve a slate quarry near Rosebush. It opened in 1876, carrying passengers from 19 September, but closed again at the end of 1882. Then came revival as the North Pembrokeshire & Fishguard Railway which reconditioned the original line and extended it 9 miles to Letterston with opening on 14 March 1895 for goods and 11 April for passengers.

After figuring in the revived plans for a port at Fishguard (qv), the line became a secondary route after the 1906 opening of the direct access to the port. It lost its passenger service from 25 October 1937 and closed completely from 16 May 1949, apart from a section from Letterston Junction to the MoD depot at Trecwn.

GB

COAL TRAFFIC

Coal was very quickly established as a basis of the GWR freight operation. First loads reached Bull's Bridge (Hayes) from South Wales in 1854, there being transferred into barges for the passage to the Thames docks. On 14 November 1854 the Frome/Radstock branch opened for coal, and in 1856 a deal was struck with the Ruabon Coal Co, which turned out to be highly profitable for both parties. A considerable traffic between South Wales and Birkenhead grew up from 1856—coal to Bute docks, red ore on the return working.

At its zenith, the volume of coal shipped from Newport (Gwent) was 6m tons per annum, but this figure pales into insignificance when compared with the Cardiff (and Penarth) figure of 15m tons of Taff Vale and Rhymney coal, and Barry's 11m. Inland coal travelled via the marshalling yard at Pontypool Road, and thence either through the Severn Tunnel or north by way of Abergavenny. More coal trains than expresses ran through the tunnel, and earned more money too.

The 'Jellicoe Specials', trainloads of South Wales coal which ran to Grangemouth to fuel the Navy at Scapa Flow during the Great War, were also made up at Pontypool Road. They went via Hereford, Shrewsbury, Chester, Warrington and Carlisle, the GWR working them as far as Warrington. Later the Brecon & Merthyr and Mid-Wales lines were also used, to reach Shrewsbury via Moat Lane and Newtown.

Until Felix Pole (qv) became General Manager, coal was habitually carried in wooden-bodied wagons having a 10 to 12 tons capacity, many of which were owned by the collieries. Pole introduced a 20-ton steel four-wheeler which, he argued, would carry almost twice as much, and create a 35% saving in siding space. He was thus able to offer a 5% reduction in charges, but since few collieries could actually accommodate the new wagons the response was at first lukewarm. The first 20-ton wagon was tipped at Port Talbot in August 1924, but the strike of

Coal traffic *A sea of private owner coal wagons in Cadoxton Yard, Barry, Barry Railway. Eleven million tons per annum were moved by the Barry Railway at its zenith.* (GW Society)

1926 upset things, bringing many South Wales pits to the verge of bankruptcy.

(See also Container traffic, Rolling-stock, goods, and entries for individual places and lines)

CA

COAT OF ARMS

From the beginning, the GWR adopted the combined arms and crests of the cities of London and Bristol as its own coat of arms. Over the years this varied in detail and several versions were used. The London motto, which appears beneath the shield bearing the red cross of St George with the sword of St Paul in the upper left-hand quarter, means 'O Lord direct us'. The Bristol motto, under the shield bearing a representation of a castle and a ship, translates as 'By virtue and industry'.

See also Locomotive liveries

MCHB

COLEFORD BRANCH

Stations: Monmouth Troy (22 miles from Severn Tunnel Junction), Newland (25½ m), Coleford (28 m)

A tramroad linked Monmouth (qv) and Coleford as early as 1817, but it was 1 September 1883 before the GWR's conventional line was opened over a similar course. This extended the 1861 branch of the Coleford, Monmouth, Usk & Pontypool Railway on from the wharf at Wyesham Junction through two tunnels at Redbrook and the converted tramway tunnel at Newland to a modest station on the south side of Coleford. Intended originally to convey Forest of Dean coal to South Wales, the line had to rely on its limited passenger and general goods traffic but failed to survive the economy measures of the First World War when it was closed on 1 January 1917, except for a short section from Coleford to Whitecliff Quarry.

GB

COLLETT, CHARLES BENJAMIN

Chief Mechanical Engineer, 1922–41. Churchward's successor, Charles Benjamin Collett was not everyone's choice for the appointment, even though he was Churchward's deputy and had been with the GWR for 29 years, and over the years many have written with less than wholehearted enthusiasm for his personality and achievements. Of the former it can be said that he possessed determination and was usually able to persuade the Board to take his point of view. He took much less interest in the affairs of his men and that of the town than any of his predecessors, leaving such considerations to various able assistants, notably W. A. Stanier.

Few Chief Mechanical Engineers, particularly in the 20th century, concerned themselves with detailed aspects of locomotive design, and Collett left his staff to do much of the design work during his 19-year reign at Swindon. In that period the principles laid down by Churchward (qv) were faithfully adhered to. However, they were not slavishly followed, and Collett should be given credit for achieving what few CMEs ever managed—overseeing the introduction of a variety of designs all of which were successful and which in many instances were improvements on the work of one who was recognized as a great innovator. William Stanier, who had been with the GWR since 1892 and who many thought should have succeeded Churchward, stayed at Swindon until 1931, when he moved to Crewe to take charge of locomotive and carriage affairs on the LMS.

Charles Benjamin Collett
(GWR Museum, Swindon)

The 'Kings' (qv), the finest 4-6-0s ever to run in the British Isles (although the three 'Queens' of the Great Southern Railway of Ireland probably ran them close) were perhaps Collett's finest achievement, although the mixed traffic 'Halls' (qv) proved invaluable to the company. In this respect Collett has never been given sufficient credit, for had the 'Halls' not existed, Stanier's very similar Class '5MT' 4-6-0 for the LMS, upon which such praised has been heaped, would surely never have seen the light of day.

Like Dean, Collett probably stayed in his post too long. Innovations on the LMS and the LNER, and later on the Southern too, saw the GWR pushed back into last place in design matters. Eventually Collett retired at the age of 70 in July 1941.

(See also Locomotives)

MCHB

COLWALL

After climbing for 7½ miles, the last 2½ at 1 in 80, the Worcester–Hereford line (qv) came to its summit at Colwall, the station following the 1,589 yd Colwall Tunnel which took the route through the Malvern Hills. The rock at the eastern end of the original tunnel had defeated two contractors before the line was finally opened on 13 September 1861, and the tunnel's limitations were later to lead the GWR to provide a new bore operational from 2 August 1926. A form of tokenless 'lock and block' signalling was used on the single line section through the new tunnel which was 22 yards longer and on a slightly easier gradient than its predecessor.

GB

CONTAINER TRAFFIC

Container traffic is not quite the modern concept that many believe it to be. Indeed, one of Brunel's ideas to overcome the break of gauge problem (qv, Broad Gauge) was a system of moveable wagon-bodies which could be carried on either a broad or narrow gauge frame. This came to nothing, but there was an early method of coal-carrying on the Taff Vale Railway (qv), which involved coal-boxes, four of which were carried at a time on special platform wagons. This was superseded by more traditional wagons, but container traffic expanded

ROAD-RAIL CONTAINER SERVICE

offers a door-to-door service, without handling *en route,* thus eliminating the risk of damage.

Packing can be reduced to a minimum, which economy is further reflected in reduced carriage charges.

Different types of containers, suitable for all descriptions of merchandise, are operated, including Insulated and Ventilated Stock for perishable traffic, and specially fitted stock for the conveyance of Bicycles.

An illustrated brochure is obtainable on application to The Chief Goods Manager, Great Western Railway, Paddington Station, London, W.2.

Container traffic *A container mounted on a lorry is loaded from the factory in this 1937 advertisement.*

throughout the 1930s and by 1938 the GWR had built up a fleet of open container wagons. These had been intended originally for carrying cast-iron baths, but during the war it was found that their usage could cover a much wider field than that. A demountable road/rail tank suitable for various liquids was also developed. As Nationalization became inevitable, considerable expansion in this type of traffic was visualized, and the GWR was busy building numbers of all types of wagons, together with the marshalling yards that it foresaw as being necessary for the traffic.

(See also Rolling-stock, goods)

CA

'CORNISHMAN'

In 1890, although the abolition of the Broad Gauge was only two years off, the GWR introduced a new train between Paddington and Penzance, which was shortly afterwards given the name 'Cornishman'. Faster than the 'Flying Dutchman' (qv), it nevertheless had accommodation for 3rd class passengers, and was booked to leave Paddington at 10.15 am, ahead of the 'Dutchman'. On 20 May 1892 it became the last Broad Gauge (qv) train to leave London for Penzance behind the locomotive *Great Western*. On that occasion it made many extra stops, while the 'Dutchman' ran no further than Plymouth. After the gauge conversion (qv) was complete, the first up narrow gauge 'Cornishman' reached Plymouth before time, and rolled into Paddington 4 minutes early.

After the abolition of the compulsory halt for refreshments at Swindon in 1895, the 'Cornishman' was scheduled to reach Bristol in $2\frac{1}{4}$ hours, to set a new record of $118\frac{1}{2}$ miles for a non-stop run on the GWR. After the introduction of the 'Cornish Riviera' (qv) as the company's principal West of England train in 1904, the name 'Cornishman' lapsed for just over 30 years, until it was resurrected in 1935 as part of the new summer schedules, introduced that year to mark the company's Centenary (qv). With the 'Riviera' running nominally non-stop to Truro, a second section was provided for the stations no longer served by stops or slip coaches (qv), and was given the name 'Cornishman'. This departed from Paddington at 10.35, and had the same 4-hour non-stop booking to Plymouth of the 'Riviera', before that train started running through to Devonport for its locomotive change. With four stops in Cornwall to serve the principal branch lines, the 'Cornishman' reached Penzance in $6\frac{1}{2}$ hours from Paddington.

PWBS

'CORNISH RIVIERA EXPRESS'

In 1904 the GWR accelerated its main Paddington–Penzance service to reach Penzance in 7 hours, and the new service markedly boosted traffic. The first leg of the journey was the world record non-stop run to Plymouth, the 245.6 miles via Bristol being completed at an average of over 55 mph. Capitalizing on the interest raised by this remarkable new schedule, *The Railway Magazine* organized a competition in July 1904 to find a name for it. Over 1,200 entries were received, while a further 700

THREE GUINEAS FOR A NAME FOR A TRAIN!

An Interesting and Easy Competition.

EVERY READER HAS AN EQUAL OPPORTUNITY OF OBTAINING THE THREE GUINEAS.

The most important railway event of the present season is the daily running by the Great Western Railway of a train between Paddington and Plymouth, and *vice versa*, without an intermediate stop. This is the longest non-stop run yet performed in regular service. The best trains on our railways are known by popular names, such as the "Flying Dutchman," the "Wild Irishman," the "Flying Scotchman," etc. In the number and appositeness of these popular titles for express trains, the Great Western Railway has been particularly favoured.

Such world famous trains as those performing the non-stop run between London and Plymouth are justly entitled to a distinctive appellation; and for the purpose of obtaining a suitable cognomen for these expresses, we offer a

PRIZE OF THREE GUINEAS

for the most suitable name for the non-stop train leaving Paddington for Plymouth at 10.10 a.m. and the return train due in London at 5 p.m. Provisionally, we have christened the trains the "3 T.F.," that is, the "3 Towns Flyer," (Plymouth, Stonehouse, and Devonport being known as the "3 Towns"). This title is, therefore, inadmissible in the Competition.

All that a Competitor has to do is to think of a word which is, or words which are, in the Competitor's opinion, most suitable for a popular name for the new train. Then write the title so chosen on Coupon to be found on advertisement page xvi. of this issue state briefly on the Coupon the reason for choosing the title, add name and address, enclose the Coupon in an envelope addressed "Great Western," RAILWAY MAGAZINE, 30, Fetter Lane, Fleet Street, E.C., and post the letter so that it reaches the Editor not later than the first post on Monday morning, August 8th.

Mr. J. C. Inglis, the General Manager of the Great Western Railway, has kindly consented to consider the various titles suggested and the reasons adduced for the choice of such titles, and will award the prize to the person who, in his opinion, has chosen the most suitable title for the new express.

The decision of Mr. Inglis will be final, and neither he nor the Editor will enter into any correspondence regarding the Competition or the award.

If two or more Competitors have suggested the title which Mr. Inglis considers the most apposite, the Three Guineas will be equally divided between them.

The Competition offers to readers of the RAILWAY MAGAZINE an intellectual, but at the same time a perfectly simple, manner of earning Three Guineas; so easy, indeed, that every reader can compete with an equal opportunity of being successful.

Nor is the prize of Three Guineas the only advantage the successful Competitor will obtain. His name will become known (and will be handed down to future generations of railway officers and *railwayacs*) as the originator of the title of "   " for the 10.10 a.m. ex Paddington. The name and address of the successful Competitor, together with the title chosen for the train, will be published in the RAILWAY MAGAZINE for September. Competitors can send in as many different titles as they like, but a separate Coupon must be used for each name suggested for the train.

'Cornish Riviera Express' *Happily, with the help of* Railway Magazine *readers the GWR eventually came up with a more romantic title than '3 Towns Flyer'!* (GWR Museum, Swindon)

were sent to the railway, and were therefore ineligible. Eight of the valid ones included 'Riviera' in the suggested title, including two which actually chose 'Cornish Riviera Limited'. The General Manager of the GWR finally selected 'The Riviera Express', but by the time the name was adopted officially, it had become the 'Cornish Riviera'.

At different times in its life, 'Express' and 'Limited' have both been used as a suffix, but the train was always known to the staff just as 'The Limited'. For the summer of 1906, when the new route via Westbury was opened, the train ceased to be a seasonal working, and adopted its time-honoured departure time of 10.30 am. By now it was only taking 4 hours 10 minutes to Plymouth, but coaches were slipped *en route* for Westbury and Exeter. Later the train was to be unique in taking no fewer than three slip portions (qv) out of Paddington, the additional one being dropped at Taunton, from where it worked forward to North Devon. By the time the First World War caused the schedules to be eased, the train was getting to Penzance in 6½ hours.

When the 'Kings' took the train over from the 'Castles', the run to Plymouth was cut to the round 4 hours, and Penzance was reached in 6 hours 20 minutes. For the company's Centenary (qv) in 1935, some extremely fine new stock was introduced, and the summer timetable showed the down train on ordinary weekdays running non-stop to Truro. However, as the 'Kings' were barred from crossing Saltash Bridge (qv), a service stop to change locomotives actually took place at Devonport. On Saturdays, when the holiday hordes descended on the West of England main line, the train was nominally non-stop to St Erth, where the stock reversed for St Ives. Three other Saturday trains in those timetables carried the name 'Cornish Riviera', but at peak times there would often be further relief workings.

PWBS

CORNWALL MINERALS RAILWAY

The Cornwall Minerals Railway was incorporated by an Act of 21 July 1873 which authorized lines from Newquay and Treamble to Fowey (qv) plus branches to Melangoose Mill and Carbis. The moving spirit behind the scheme was entrepreneur W. R. Roebuck and his plans were based on the earlier enterprises of a local industrialist, J. T. Treffry, who had built a canal from Ponts Mill to Par as early as 1842. Treffry went on to complete horse-worked lines from Par Harbour to Bugle Inn (1847) via a 1 in 10 incline at Carmears and a 10-arch viaduct south of Luxulyan, and from Newquay Harbour to East Wheal Rose and St Dennis (1849).

Anticipating a minerals boom period, Roebuck's CMR acquired the Treffry routes and reconstructed them for a hurried opening on 1 June 1874. The new main line from Fowey to Newquay avoided the earlier incline and viaduct, and also Toldish Tunnel near Indian Queens, and rebuilt the Trenance Viaduct at the Newquay end. There were also lines from Tolcarne Junction, Newquay, to East Wheal Rose (extended to Treamble and Gravel Hill) and to Carbis (and Carbean 1893).

The CMR network was expanded by the absorption of the Newquay & Cornwall Junction Railway's 1874 line from Burngullow (qv) to St Dennis Junction and then of the Lostwithiel & Fowey company's 1869 line, the latter having been a competitor for the shipment business through Fowey. But Roebuck's timing was wrong and the CMR experienced a period when traditional mining was diminishing and china clay (qv) growing only slowly. A Fowey–Newquay passenger service was introduced on 20 June 1876 as a way of seeking financial compensation.

The GWR began to work the CMR system from 1 October 1877 and took it over from 1 July 1896.

GB

CORNWALL RAILWAY

Backed by the GWR, the Cornwall Railway obtained its Act for a line from Plymouth to Falmouth on 3 August 1846, having triumphed over the rival Cornwall & Devon Central scheme for a link to the LSWR system. The poor financial climate halted construction work for several years, the company's shares became unsaleable, and only underwriting by the 'Associated Companies' (qv) enabled completion of the Royal Albert Bridge (qv) and a single line on to Truro. This was brought into use on 4 May 1859 and the Falmouth branch (qv) added on 24 August 1863. A 'Joint Committee' of its own, GWR, Bristol & Exeter and South Devon Directors managed the railway, which was amalgamated with the GWR by an Act of 24 June 1889.

GB

CORSHAM

Corsham was one of the original stations on the GWR main line and was opened with completion of the final section on 30 June 1841. It was served by Swindon/Chippenham–Bristol passenger trains but was more important for its stone traffic forwardings.

The excavation of Box Tunnel (qv) had revealed vast stone beds under Box Hill. Exploitation followed quickly, with a mineral railway linking the galleries and emerging as a siding beside the main line at the east end of the tunnel. By 1864 stone forwardings invoiced by Corsham had reached an annual figure of 100,000 tons, and by 1890 this had been increased by a network of quarry railways which led to Corsham goods yard. At the stone wharf there, the huge blocks of stone were received from the feeder lines and horse-drawn drays for loading to open wagons and subsequent forwarding.

GB

CORWEN

Corwen was the principal intermediate station on the GWR's Ruabon–Barmouth line (qv). It was also a junction with the LNWR/LMS line from Denbigh which the GWR had once tried to lease as a means of access to the North Wales coast. As it was, the Denbigh line arrived in October 1864, and the GWR-backed Llangollen & Corwen Railway on 8 May 1865; the two used a new permanent station from 1 September 1865, the route continuing west from there (as the Corwen & Bala) on 16 July 1866.

The two single-line routes from the east approached Corwen's two-platform joint station via a scissors crossover, with the route west singling again beyond the substantial goods depot and the engine shed, 45 ft turntable and water crane area opposite.

GB

CORYTON BRANCH

Stations: Cardiff Queen Street, Whitchurch (5½ m), Coryton Halt (5¾ m)

The line from Heath Junction to Treforest was opened by the Cardiff Railway (qv) on 15 May 1909. Denied the use of the junction at the latter point for coal by the Taff Vale Railway (qv), it introduced a railmotor (qv) to Rhydyfelin via Whitchurch, Tongwynlais and Upper Boat on 1 March 1911, and made little or no use of the end portion over the Taff Viaduct to Treforest.

Under GWR control the route was singled beyond Coryton (1928) and the passenger service cut back to that point from 20 July 1931. This consisted of some 50 trains on weekdays over the double-line section to Whitchurch via halts at Heath Low Level, Birchgrove and Rhiwbina, and then on to Coryton Halt where a run-round loop was provided.

GB

'COUNTY' CLASS

There were two different 'County' Classes on the GWR, dating from 1904 and 1945. The former were 4-4-0s in the new Churchward (qv) style, which were intended for the lighter express passenger workings, particularly over routes that had weight restrictions. As trains became longer, and more 4-6-0s appeared, they tended to get moved on to less demanding duties, but, until 1927, they were the largest class permitted over the Stonehouse viaduct, and so monopolized the Bristol–Wolverhampton services. With large outside cylinders and a short wheel-base, they had a tendency to roll badly, and crews were known to use pungent language about their riding. The last of the 40 in the class was withdrawn in 1933.

After the Second World War, Hawksworth (qv) wanted to obtain the power of a 'Castle' (qv) using two cylinders only, and produced the first of his 'Counties' soon after the end of hostilities. In several respects they resembled his 'Modified Halls' (qv, 'Hall' Class), but had continuous splashers and a new design of flush-sided tender, which subsequently became the standard 4,000-gallon type. The appearance of the new locomotives also marked the return of lining-out after the years of wartime austerity. Less obvious was the use of a boiler pressed to 280 psi to achieve the required tractive effort, although in the mid-1950s this was reduced to 250 psi. The first of the class was built with an attractive double chimney, but, in the late 1950s, all the class were fitted with a shorter version, which, although still with a traditional copper cap, did not look as well as the single ones or that originally fitted to No 1000. The last of the 30 members of this class were withdrawn in 1964.

(*Illustrations overleaf. See also Locomotives*)

PWBS

COWBRIDGE

Cowbridge station was a terminus from 18 September 1865 when the Cowbridge Railway opened its 5 m 49 ch line from Llantrisant (qv) until 1 October 1892, when the 6 m 29 ch of the Cowbridge & Aberthaw Railway was opened. The small Vale of Glamorgan town then got a new through station with the original one becoming the goods depot, but the position changed again when the GWR ended passenger services south of Cowbridge on 5 May 1930.

The Taff Vale Railway (qv) worked the local Cowbridge lines from opening, leasing them subsequently and then taking over completely. In the GWR era, the surviving Cowbridge–Llantrisant service was improved to ten trains each way on weekdays,

'County' Class *4-4-0 No 3826* County of Flint *of the 1904 batch of 'Counties', and Hawksworth's 4-6-0 No 1000* County of Middlesex *of 1945.* (Both GWR Museum, Swindon)

with a pick-up goods to serve Cowbridge goods yard and the limestone quarry.

GB

CREWE BRANCH

Stations: Wellington, Crudgington ($4\frac{3}{4}$ m), Peplow ($8\frac{3}{4}$ m), Hodnet (11 m), Tern Hill ($13\frac{3}{4}$ m), Market Drayton ($16\frac{3}{4}$ m), Adderley ($20\frac{1}{4}$ m), Audlem (22 m), Nantwich ($27\frac{1}{2}$ m), Crewe (32 m)

This was quite an important GWR branch and was used for the through carriages of the 'Bournemouth and Portsmouth to Manchester Express' and of a long-standing Worcester–Crewe service, as well as by ten domestic weekday trains which served the 14 intermediate stations and halts. There were also additional trains over the Wellington–Market Drayton section, the latter point being the junction with the North Staffordshire line from Stoke-on-Trent.

The northern end of the line originated with the Nantwich & Market Drayton Railway which was incorporated on 7 June 1861 and opened the 10 m 65 ch to Nantwich Junction on 20 October 1863. Incorporated two months later, the Wellington & Drayton Railway's 16 m 12 ch was not ready until 16 October 1867. By then the W&D had been absorbed by the GWR which was also working the N&MD, with amalgamation following on 1 July 1897.

The double-track route is reputed to have been the last to have time interval working replaced by absolute block signalling.

GB

CROSS HANDS BRANCHES

The GWR had two branches to Cross Hands, one west from Tirydail and the other north from Llanelly (qv). The shorter Tirydail line was the senior, its 4 miles having been opened on 6 May 1841 as the Great Mountain branch of the Llanelly Railway. The route included a $\frac{1}{2}$-mile, cable-worked incline of 1 in 12 and it served two collieries, a limestone siding and Penygroes Goods.

The other line to Cross Hands originated with the Llanelly & Mynydd Mawr Railway which acquired the 1806 Carmarthenshire Railway as the basis for its own 13-mile route of sharp curves and severe gradients opened on 1 January 1853. Coal was conveyed to the docks at Llanelly, with unofficial trips for colliers' work and holiday purposes. The L&MM line passed to the GWR at the Grouping and continued its work, serving four collieries and four goods depots.

GB

CRUMLIN VIADUCT

After successful testing with a load of 380 tons on each span, the completion of the Taff Vale Extension Railway (qv) across Crumlin Viaduct was marked by a ceremony, witnessed by 20,000 people, on 1 June 1857. The 1,658 ft long structure, rising 208 ft above Ebbw Vale, was one of the great railway civil engineering works in South Wales until its demolition after the line closure in 1964. It had taken four years to build and cost £62,000, but within a few years there were rumours of weaknesses, disproved when seven locomotives and a heavy train were used for further tests.

The viaduct consisted of ten 150 ft spans raised on eight latticed ironwork piers, plus a masonry one on the intermediate ridge. From Crumlin Junction at the east end a $1\frac{1}{4}$-mile branch descended to Llanhilleth on the Western Valleys line.

GB

CUT-OFF AND AVOIDING LINES

A number of GWR main lines took some-

Crumlin Viaduct *Some of the ten spans of this remarkable lattice ironwork bridge.* (GWR Museum, Swindon)

what devious routes to reach their destinations, and over the years the company found itself at a disadvantage with its competitors. The principal examples were the West of England and the Birmingham lines.

Cwmmawr branch (GWR Magazine, 1922)

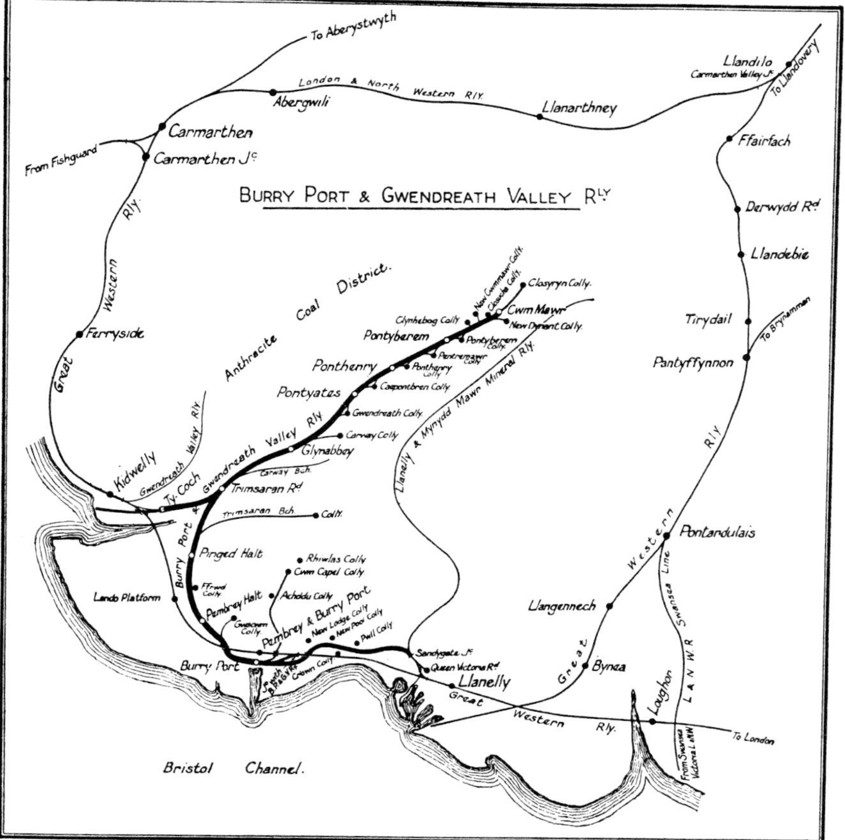

Until 1906 all expresses between Paddington, Exeter and beyond travelled via Bristol, and this meant that the rival LSWR route through Salisbury and Honiton was nearly 20 miles shorter. With the linking up of the 'Berks & Hants' (qv), the Weymouth and the Durston to Yeovil branches with 32 miles of new cut-off lines, the advantage passed to the GWR (qv Reading–Taunton line). In 1933 further improvements were made when by-pass lines were constructed around Westbury and Frome (both qv).

On the Birmingham route, the GWR, which worked all its trains via Oxford, was in fierce competition with the LNWR. The latter had a 16½-mile advantage, and in 1910 the GWR opened, jointly with the Great Central Railway, a new route which, branching off the old Bristol main line at Old Oak Common instead of Didcot, headed straight through the Chilterns by way of High Wycombe to Aynho Junction and Banbury (qv, Great Western & Great Central Joint Railway).

The most spectacular cut-off work carried out by the GWR was the building of the Severn Tunnel (qv). This opened in 1886, and when the South Wales & Bristol Direct Railway (qv) from Wootton Bassett, west of Swindon, to Patchway, north of Bristol, came into use in 1903, the distance from Swindon to Newport came down from 81¼ miles to 52.

Just before the First World War, the Swansea District Line (qv) from Neath to the Llandovery–Llanelly line was opened to avoid Swansea and enable the speeding up of the Irish and transatlantic boat trains to and from Fishguard (qv), but a projected extension westwards was never completed. There were other abortive cut-off plans, notably that of the Looe branch in the 1930s.

MCHB

CWMAMAN BRANCH

The GWR provided a 'Motor Car—One class only' shuttle service over this 2¾-mile branch from Black Lion Crossing Halt, Aberdare (qv), to Cwmaman Colliery Halt, calling at four other tiny platforms *en route*. This was originally a Vale of Neath (qv) coal branch which opened from Dare Junction in September 1858, passed to the GWR in 1865, and lost its passenger service on 22 September 1924.

GB

CWMMAWR BRANCH

Stations: Burry Port, Pembrey (1½ m), Trimsaran Road (5 m), Glyn Abbey (6 m), Pontyates (8 m), Ponthenry (9 m), Pontyberem (11 m), Cwmmawr (13 m)

One of the 'preliminary absorptions' under the Railway Act of 1921, the Burry Port & Gwendraeth Valley Railway passed to the GWR on 1 January 1922. Its 21 operational miles had earned £11,416 in 1920 and permitted a 10% dividend, no mean achievement for an enterprise that had twice been in the hands of the Receiver.

Originating as a canal and tramroad system, the BP&GVR was an 1866 amalgam of three enterprises, including the Burry Port Harbour Company. From there the 1869 'main line' crossed the South Wales main line (qv) on the level, and from Trimsaran climbed steeply to the coalfields and terminus at Cwmmawr, with branches to Trimsaran Colliery and Kidwelly Quay. The BP&GVR's eastern arm to Llanelly (qv) and its branch to Cwm Capel Colliery also crossed the GWR on the level. After some illicit passenger activities, increasing coal traffic revived the company, allowing the route to be modernized and realigned and passengers carried legally, to Pontyberem from 2 August 1909 and on to Cwmmawr from 29 January 1913.

Traffic between the BP&GV and GWR systems was exchanged via sidings east of the latter's Pembrey & Burry Port station. The service of four daily passenger trains to and from Cwmmawr operated from a separate, but adjacent, BP&GVR station.

GB

CYMMER

High up in the Afan Valley, Cymmer was served by three rail routes, the Rhondda & Swansea Bay line (qv) through Cymmer Afan station, the South Wales Mineral Railway's line through Cymmer Corrwg and on to Glyncorrwg and North Rhondda Colliery, and the GWR's branch to Abergwynfi (qv) which used Cymmer General. It also had three major collieries, a small goods depot, mileage sidings and a viaduct link between the GWR and SWMR lines. The latter's passenger service was withdrawn on 22 September 1930.

GB

DAWLISH

From Dawlish Warren, through Dawlish and its tunnels to Teignmouth, Brunel chose a route along the shore of Babbacombe Bay for the atmospheric propulsion (qv) to be used on the South Devon Railway (qv). It came to be the despair of permanent way men repairing the havoc caused by winter storms, but the delight of summer holidaymakers waving to passing trains or looking out through the Vita glass windows of the 'Cornish Riviera Express'.

Dawlish (Steamchest Collection)

A station, well placed for both town and sea, was brought into use at Dawlish on 30 May 1846. It lost its pumping station with the demise of the atmospheric system, was converted to standard gauge in 1892, got a second platform with the doubling of 1902–5 and a new signal box in 1920.

GB

DEAN, WILLIAM

Locomotive & Carriage Superintendent, 1877–1902. There were some who expected that Joseph Armstrong senior's (qv) brother, George, would succeed him, but William Dean had been assistant to Joseph and was the logical choice. Dean had been at Swindon since the age of 28 and was still a relatively young man of 37 when he became Locomotive & Carriage Superintendent. He held the post for 25 years, but even so outlasted George Armstrong by only five years, for the latter went on happily and more or less independently in charge in the northern reaches of the GWR's empire until he retired at the grand age of 75.

William Dean took as great an interest in the affairs of his work people as did his predecessor. However, the GWR came to be looked upon with more and more disfavour by its customers as the century drew to an end, and although Dean had little to do with this sad state of affairs, it is significant that he designed nothing up-to-date for the last years of the Broad Gauge. Indeed, he was not allowed to, for the finances of the GWR were far from healthy, and Gooch, the Chairman (qv), and Tyrrell, the Superintendent of the Line (qv), were old men, the latter in particular being a reactionary who saw no reason why anyone should want to travel in excess of 40 mph. Some replacements of the original Gooch 4-2-2s were necessary and 13 were turned out between 1878 and 1888 whilst Dean was in charge; although they had contemporary cabs, they were in all other respects true to Gooch's design of 1847, albeit most impressive-looking machines.

A design which many regard as the most elegant ever seen began as a Broad Gauge express engine. Dean built eight 'convertible' 2-2-2s, Nos 3021–8, at Swindon Works between April and August 1891, and as such they were nothing special to look at. A year later, after the last Broad Gauge train had run (qv), they were altered to standard gauge and worked alongside others of the class which had been built specifically for standard gauge. In 1893 No 3021 was derailed in Box Tunnel (qv Accidents) and Dean decided that the design was faulty with too much weight at the front end. He therefore lengthened the frames, fitted a bogie under the smokebox and so the classic '3031' 'Achilles' Class was created.

The Dean bogie singles had fairly short lives, for like all such locomotives they proved unable to handle the vastly

William Dean (GWR Museum, Swindon)

increased weight of the corridor expresses which became the norm in the first decade of the 20th century. On the other hand, Dean's standard goods engines seemed to go on for ever. There was nothing revolutionary about the 'Dean Goods'; they were developments of Armstrong's engines,but everything about them seemed right. They were strong, tough, economical, and possessed a fair turn of speed; 260 were built between 1883 and 1899. They served abroad in both World Wars and 54 passed into BR ownership. In trials against a new LMS-designed 2-6-0 in 1949, a 50-year-old 'Dean Goods' was the clear winner and it was only in 1957 that the class finally disappeared. Happily, one, No 2516, is preserved at the Great Western Museum at Swindon.

With the end of the Broad Gauge and the retirement of the reactionary Tyrrell, the GWR entered a golden era, one which recaptured the great pioneering spirit of Brunel and in which Dean played his part to the full. The Midland Railway had led the way in carriage design, but in 1891 Dean established the GWR's pre-eminence when he introduced the first complete corridor train in this country (qv Rolling-stock, passenger). Like the Midland, Dean made considerable use of the clerestory and his train consisted of four clerestory-roofed vehicles. They also had steam heating and lavatories, and on entering regular service in March 1892 proved instantly popular. The bogies and suspension were particularly advanced and soon trains of corridor carriages were running on all the GWR's principal long-distance services. No ordinary Dean corridor carriage survives but a number of special vehicles have been preserved, whilst a particular gem is No 1941, a non-corridor bogie third from 1901 which has been restored over 25 years at Didcot.

Dean's last years were full of sadness. After the death of his first wife he married again, but his second wife died in 1889. His two daughters were also dead by 1900, leaving him with one surviving son. Towards the end of the 1890s his memory and mental powers began to fade, and although he remained nominally in charge of GWR locomotive matters until his official retirement in June 1902, in reality Churchward (qv) was running things from around 1899. The company and those he worked with treated Dean decently, and a house was bought for him beside the sea at Folkestone, where he died on 24 September 1905 at the age of 65.

(See also Locomotives)

MCHB

DEVIL'S BRIDGE BRANCH

Stations: Aberystwyth, Llanbadarn (1 m), Capel Bangor (4½ m), Aberffrwd (7½ m), Devil's Bridge (11¾ m)

This 60cm-gauge scenic line, best known as the Vale of Rheidol Railway, survived years of varying fortunes to pass into BR hands and become its last surviving steam railway. The GWR had acquired it along with the Cambrian Railways (qv) who had bought the narrow-gauge enterprise in 1913 after 11 years of independent operation.

Schemes for a line up the Rheidol Valley dated back to 1861, but the first real development resulted from the Vale of Rheidol Light Railway Act of 6 August 1897 which produced a single line inland from Aberystwyth (qv) in August 1902 (passengers 22 December 1902). With two Davies & Metcalfe locomotives the VoR began carrying lead and timber down to a harbour branch at Aberystwyth, soon building up a business in tourists keen to savour the scenic upper reaches of the route and the famous Rheidol Falls.

Changes over the years included movement of the Aberystwyth terminus (1925), extra stopping places at Nantyronen, Rhiwfron, Glanrafon and Rheidol Falls, closure of the harbour branch (1924), summer-only passenger services (1931), and war-time closure (1939–45).

GB

DEVIZES

The single line which reached Devizes from Holt Junction on 1 July 1857 was to be linked with the Berks & Hants Extension line (qv) from Hungerford on 11 November 1862, to give the town some through Paddington–Bristol trains in later years. These were additional to the Newbury–Bristol, Trowbridge and Westbury services, plus locals to Patney & Chirton.

Devizes station, which originally had an overall roof, consisted of curved main and island platforms reached via the 190 yd Devizes Tunnel at the London end. There were down sorting sidings and a sizeable up goods yard.

Pan's Lane Halt lay on the Patney side of Devizes, and Bromham & Rowde Halt on the Holt Junction side.

GB

DIDCOT

Didcot got its first station when the Oxford Railway (qv) was opened on 12 June 1844 and lost it to a serious fire on 11 March

Didcot *Three railwaymen pose before the self-advertising nameboard at Didcot, 1913.* (GW Society)

1885. The complex of five narrow platforms under an overall roof was then replaced with a layout better able to cope with the increase in Didcot's own traffic and that arising from the opening of the Didcot, Newbury & Southampton Railway (qv) on 13 April 1882.

The west curve, operational from 15 February 1886, was a feature of the Didcot alterations and led to a layout that featured a triangular junction west of the station which itself was part of a larger triangle with the station platforms along its base line. Reaching its final form with alterations in 1932, the complex included a large locomotive depot which occupied the area now used by the Great Western Society.

Beyond the station lay the goods yard and the GWR's provender store. This tall 1884 brick building, with its hoists, water towers and adjacent sidings, supplied fodder for the many cartage and shunting horses at work throughout the system. Didcot also had three major private siding areas, including large ordnance and RAF depots, and handled a considerable amount of wartime freight traffic.

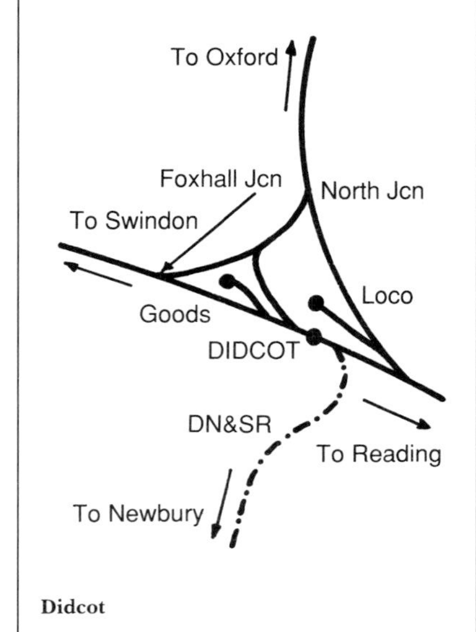

Didcot

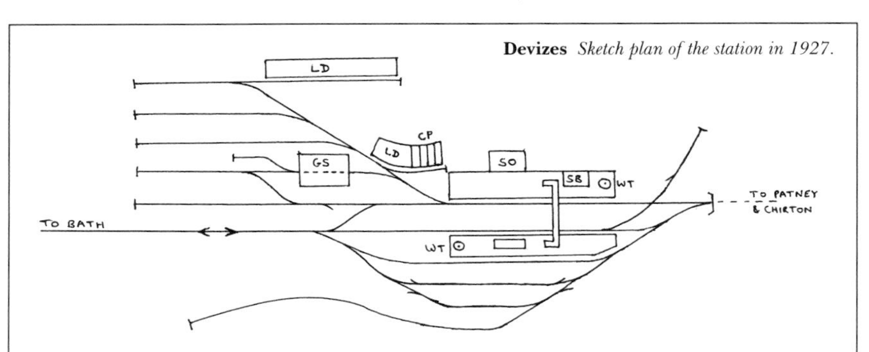

Devizes *Sketch plan of the station in 1927.*

Many long-distance trains called at Didcot and some London services terminated there. The (mainly local) DN&S trains used Platform 1 on the down side.

GB

DIDCOT–BANBURY LINE

Stations: Didcot ($53\frac{1}{4}$ miles from Paddington), Culham ($56\frac{1}{4}$ m), Radley ($58\frac{1}{2}$ m), Oxford ($63\frac{1}{2}$ m), Kidlington (69 m), Bletchington (71 m), Heyford ($75\frac{1}{4}$ m), Aynho ($80\frac{1}{4}$ m), Kings Sutton ($82\frac{3}{4}$ m), Banbury ($86\frac{1}{4}$ m)

The GWR's Oxford Railway (qv) linked the main line and the university town from 12 June 1844, its Oxford & Rugby Railway (qv) project carried the route forward to Banbury (qv) from 2 September 1850 and two years later the new link to Birmingham was brought into use (qv Banbury–Birmingham line).

The easily graded route made a number of waterway crossings, starting with the Thames between Appleford Halt and Culham. The Abingdon branch then joined at Radley and the Thame line at Kennington Junction on the approach to Oxford, with the Worcester line departing from Wolvercot Junction to the north. The latter was linked to the LNWR by the opening of the Yarnton loop on 1 April 1854. This carried a Worcester–Euston service for a while and later became an important freight exchange route.

On the Oxford–Banbury section, the Blenheim branch (qv) joined near Kidlington, which also had a bacon factory siding. There was a cement siding at Bletchington, the Princes Risborough (qv) line then joining at Aynho and the Cheltenham line (qv Banbury–Cheltenham line) at Kings Sutton, with water troughs between the latter points. They were used by the line's Paddington–Birmingham–North West services, local stations being served by various Paddington–Oxford and Reading–Banbury trains.

GB

DIDCOT, NEWBURY & SOUTHAMPTON RAILWAY

Stations: Didcot, Upton & Blewbury (3 m), Churn ($6\frac{3}{4}$ m), Compton ($8\frac{1}{2}$ m), Hampstead Norris ($10\frac{1}{2}$ m), Pinewood Halt ($12\frac{3}{4}$ m), Hermitage ($13\frac{1}{2}$ m), Newbury (18 m), Woodhay ($21\frac{1}{4}$ m), Highclere ($23\frac{1}{2}$ m), Burghclere ($25\frac{1}{2}$ m), Litchfield (28 m), Whitchurch ($31\frac{3}{4}$ m), Sutton Scotney ($37\frac{1}{2}$ m), Worthy Down Platform ($40\frac{1}{4}$ m), King's Worthy ($42\frac{1}{2}$ m), Winchester ($44\frac{1}{4}$ m)

Worked by the GWR from the outset, the DN&SR had ambitions to be a major north–south artery, a cut-off route for Welsh coal to Southampton and to serve neglected rural areas of Berkshire and Hampshire. However, despite having got its Act fairly easily on 5 August 1873, six years of inactivity followed and the company narrowly escaped abandonment. A new Board of Directors then revitalized the concern and got the $17\frac{1}{4}$ miles to Newbury East Junction opened on 13 April 1882. Conflict with the LSWR resulted in suspension of work on an independent access to Southampton in favour of completing a separate station at Winchester on 4 May 1885. An agreement in 1889 then changed the situation and led to the opening of a link to the LSWR main line on 1 October 1891.

Completed at last, the $44\frac{3}{4}$-mile route had cost £$1\frac{1}{4}$ million but its traffic levels only permitted dividends of around 3% on debenture stock. Something of an unavoidable nuisance to the GWR, the D&NS passed to that company at the Grouping.

The majority of D&NS trains called at all stations and took over 3 hours to cover the $56\frac{3}{4}$ miles to Southampton. Between Didcot and Newbury (qv) they crossed the Berkshire Downs with summits at Churn and Hermitage, two more summits then being needed between Enborne Junction and Whitchurch to surmount the northern Hampshire Downs, with a fifth just north of Worthy Down. A gradient of 1 in 106 applied over more than half the route and there were many cuttings, embankments and bridges, plus a tunnel before Winchester (Chesil) and a 2,014-ft viaduct beyond. Working was by electric token.

The D&NS made a vital contribution during the Second World War and was doubled between Didcot and Woodhay to this end, but it declined again when hostilities ceased.

GB

DIESEL RAILCARS

In 1934 the GWR put the first of its streamlined (qv) diesel railcars into service, the single-car unit being the first of 38 of this sort, of several differing designs. The experience gained was to influence the widespread introduction of diesel multiple-units on BR in the 1950s, the vast majority of which were fitted with four-speed epicyclic gearboxes as pioneered on the GWR cars. The prototype (No 1) was used on the Paddington–Slough services, possibly to keep it near the AEC works at Southall, which had provided the single 121-hp engine. Early experience showed it to be underpowered, and all subsequent cars had two such motors. The 44-seat cars Nos 2–4, complete with buffet, were designed for a supplementary

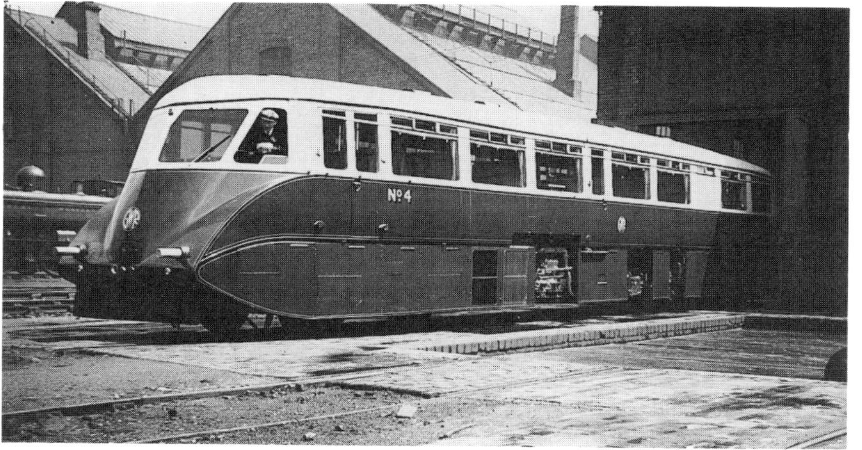

Diesel railcars *AEC railcar No 4, containing 44 seats and a buffet and designed for Birmingham–Cardiff expresses.* (Steamchest Collection)

Diesel railcars *Side view and plan of No 4.* (GWR Magazine, 1934)

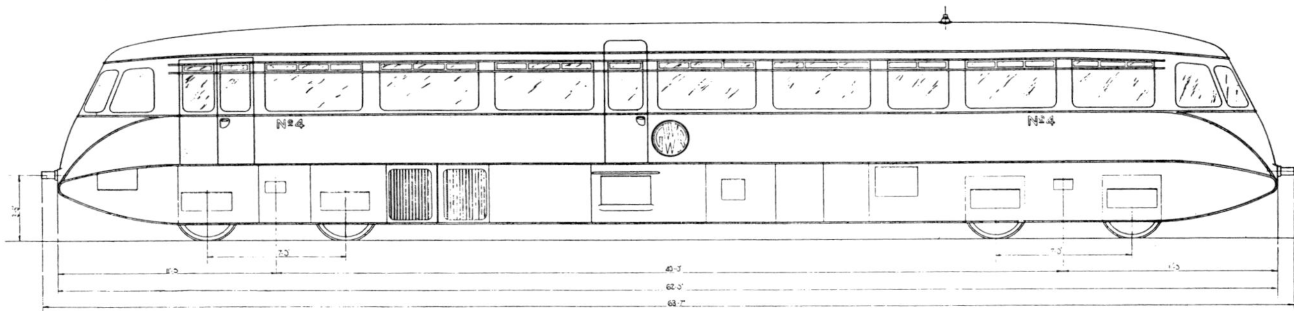

308

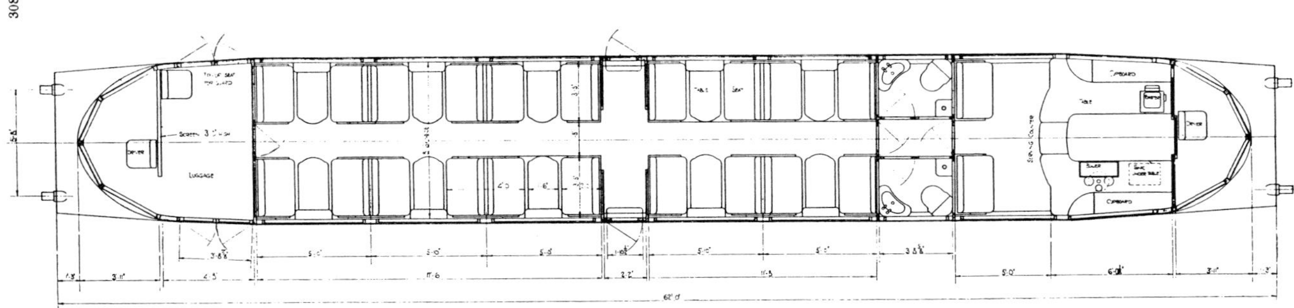

charge express service between Birmingham and Cardiff, where they reached speeds of up to 80 mph.

The two final cars of the pre-war batch differed considerably from the others. No 17 was designed for parcels traffic, and became associated with the delivery of Lyons' confectionery. The mechanical equipment on the final member of this batch was varied so that it could haul a trailing load, which set the pattern for the final 20 cars, authorized in 1938, but which were not delivered until 1940–42. These were all constructed to a common basic design, which owed more to railway than automotive practice, and the streamlining was simplified to avoid the use of panels curved in two dimensions. Some had a low gear ratio to enable them to operate with trailing loads on branch lines. The last four were true multiple-units, with a single cab each, which either operated back-to-back or with an ordinary coach marshalled between them.

(See also Rolling-stock, passenger)

PWBS

DINAS MAWDDWY BRANCH

Stations: Cemmes Road, Cemmaes ($1\frac{1}{2}$ m), Aberangell ($4\frac{1}{4}$ m), Mallwyd ($5\frac{3}{4}$ m), Dinas Mawddwy (7 m)

One Edmund Buckley promoted and financed the Mawddwy Railway as part of a dream of transforming the ancient Welsh market town of Dinas Mawddwy into a garden city. The 7 miles of railway along the Dovey Valley from Cemmes Road on the Cambrian's Welshpool–Machynlleth (both qv) line was authorized on 5 July 1865, opened in October 1867 and cost him £40,000. But Buckley's dreams ended in financial failure and this, with the decline of the local slate industry, ended passenger services on 17 April 1901 and freight on 8 April 1908.

The CamR rescued the Mawddwy branch and reopened it on 29 July 1911, but passenger traffic only warranted three trains each way and succumbed to omnibus competition on 1 January 1931.

GB

DIRECTORS

Thirty Directors were named in the original Act, but these were soon rationalized into two committees of 12 representing the two spheres of action of the railway, at London and Bristol:

London

Benjamin Shaw (Chairman) (qv)
Ralph Fenwick
George Henry Gibbs (qv)
Robert Frederick Gower
Riversdale William Grenfell
Robert Hopkins
Edward Wheler Mills (qv)
Henry Simonds
William Unwin Sims (qv)
William Tite (qv)
George Wildes
John Woolley

Bristol

Robert Bright (Deputy Chairman) (qv)
Henry Bush
Charles Bowles Fripp
Thomas Richard Guppy (qv)
William Singer Jacques
George Jones
Peter Maze
Thomas Pycroft
Nicholas Roch
Robert Scott
William Tothill
John Vining

The last survivors of this group were Mills and Simonds, both of whom stood down when the Board was reconstructed after the amalgamation of the South Wales and West Midland companies in 1863. The number of Directors was further reduced to 16 in

July 1867, when the list was:

Sir Daniel Gooch (Chairman) (qv)
Charles Alexander Wood
(Deputy-Chairman) (qv)
Richard Bassett
Francis L. Bodenham
Captain T. Bulkeley
Lewis L. Dillwyn MP
William C. King
Edward Leeming
Richard Michell
John W. Miles
Hon F. G. B. Ponsonby (qv)
C. R. M. Talbot MP (qv)
Rowland G. Venables
Edward Wanklyn
Sir W. Williams-Wynn, Bart MP (qv)
Edward Smith

The Board was increased in size to 18 in 1876 at the amalgamation with the Bristol & Exeter Railway (qv), and by one further member when the South Devon (qv) joined the fold in 1878. There were more additions from 1 July 1889, when Cornwall Railway representatives came in, following amalgamation, among them Col the Hon C. E. Edgcumbe (qv), and Robert Tweedy, who had been Chairman of the smaller company since 1864. He had also served on the Joint Committee (qv Associated Broad Gauge Companies) since its inception in 1859. In 1891 it was decide to elect two Deputy-Chairmen instead of one, and Viscount Emlyn and Hubbard (both qv) were appointed.

By the Grouping the total number of Directors had risen to 23:

Viscount Churchill (Chairman) (qv)
Sir Ernest Palmer
(Deputy-Chairman) (qv)
Lord Barrymore
Frank Bibby
T. Robbins Bolitho
Sir Aubrey Brocklebank
F. W. Grierson
Lord Inchcape
J. F. Mason
F. B. Mildmay MP
Charles Mortimer
Sir H. B. Robertson
G. A. Wills
J. W. Wilson
Sir W. Williams-Wynn (qv)
Lord Plymouth
(representing the Barry Railway)
Lt-Col Sir H. A. Yorke and J. Shaw
(both Alexandra Docks)
Lt-Col David Davies (Barry Rly)
Lord Glanely
(Cardiff, Rhymney Railways)
W. Heward Bell (Rhymney Rly)
G. Birkley Forrester (Taff Vale Railway)
Sir H. Mather Jackson, Bart
(Alexandra [Newport & S Wales]
Docks & Railway,
also the Rhymney Rly)

Two 20th-century Directors, Stanley Baldwin and Harold Macmillan (both qv), became Prime Minister.

CA

DITTON PRIORS BRANCH

Stations: Cleobury Mortimer, Cleobury Town Halt (2 m), Detton Ford Siding ($4\frac{1}{4}$ m), Prescott Siding ($5\frac{1}{4}$ m), Stottesdon Halt ($6\frac{3}{4}$ m), Aston Botterell Siding ($8\frac{1}{2}$ m), Burwarton Halt ($9\frac{1}{4}$ m), Cleobury North Crossing ($10\frac{1}{4}$ m), Ditton Priors Halt (12 m)

Despite modest traffic levels and a rural location, this light railway had a credit balance of £11,828 and paid a first dividend of $1\frac{1}{2}$% on its ordinary shares for 1918. Four years later it was absorbed into the GWR which maintained a passenger service until 26 September 1938 and a public goods service until 11 September 1939. After that the route was just used for the traffic of an Admiralty depot.

Local enterprise had led to the granting of the original Light Railway Order to the Cleobury Mortimer & Ditton Priors Light Railway on 23 March 1901, but opening was not until 1 July 1908 (passengers 19 November).

The CM&DP route was single with intermediate sidings and was worked by 'one engine in steam'. Mixed trains were used in the earlier years.

GB

DIVIDENDS

The GWR paid its first dividend, of $1\frac{1}{2}$%, in 1840, and for almost a decade they grew rapidly. However, money shortages in the 1850s (the lowest dividend ever paid was $1\frac{1}{4}$% in 1858) and the financial crisis of 1866 took their toll. A scheme for making dividends payable in shares rather than in cash was projected, but by then economies effected under the Chairmanship of Gooch (qv) were beginning to bite, and from 1868 resumption of payment in cash was made; the dividend rose from $1\frac{3}{8}$% that year to $2\frac{5}{8}$ in 1869, $3\frac{3}{8}$ in 1870, $4\frac{15}{16}$ in 1871, 6 in 1872 and $6\frac{1}{4}$ in 1873.

Trade depression and a coal strike in South Wales caused a recession in 1874 and 1875, to $4\frac{1}{2}$ and $4\frac{1}{4}$ respectively. It fell back further, to $3\frac{3}{4}$, in 1878, but by 1883 had recovered to $6\frac{3}{8}$, and did not fall below $5\frac{1}{4}$ for the next five years. Apart from one year at $3\frac{7}{8}$ (1898), the dividend subsequently did not fall below $4\frac{1}{4}$. In 1921 it was $7\frac{1}{4}$, its highest level since the halcyon days of 1844–7 when it had stood at $7\frac{1}{2}$ and 8.

After Grouping the GWR alone among the 'Big Four' retained its good dividend record, its shares standing well above the other three companies even during the Second World War. At the final Shareholders Meeting, it was the shareholders themselves who insisted that the Directors should receive compensation for their loss of office, which, however, they refused.

CA

DOCKS AND HARBOURS

After the Grouping the GWR became the largest dock-owning company in the world, having taken over that title from the North Eastern Railway as a result of absorbing the South Wales installations owned by the new constituent companies. In addition it took over the one at Swansea (qv) directly from its trustees. The full list is as follows:

Wholly owned		***Jointly owned***
Aberdovey	Llanelly	Chelsea
Barry	Newport	Fishguard
Brentford	Newquay	Lydney
Bridgwater	Penarth	Neyland
Briton Ferry	Plymouth	Rosslare
Burry Port	Port Talbot	
Cardiff	Saltney	
Fowey	Swansea	

These varied considerably in size, and, as will be seen, several were located on inland waterways, but all had their own particular uses. For example, from its position west of London, the GWR found it convenient to load cargos on barges at Brentford, which then carried them to the Port of London for transfer to ocean-going ships.

The biggest tonnages were handled at those ports dealing with minerals, which included the china-clay exports from Fowey, where the loading facilities were considerably extended during the Grouping era. However, it was the South Wales ports, spread along 50 miles of the northern shore of the Bristol Channel, which handled the lion's share of the company's dock business. In the days when many ships were coal-fired, the advantages of Welsh coal for bunkering purposes were fully exploited, and to attract vessels to GWR ports all the necessary ancilliary facilities were provided, in addition to enabling ships to off-load the cargos they had brought with them. The ports were well situated for quick onward deliveries by means of GWR train services to the West Midlands as well as the Home Counties. Considerable quantities of food, some of it still 'on the hoof', were regularly imported through the South Wales ports, and there were fish docks at Swansea and Cardiff, with their own trawler fleets. Vast areas of sidings were provided to assemble hundreds of wagons of coal from different collieries, ready to be loaded into ships whenever they appeared over the horizon.

The Bristol Channel has an extremely high tidal range, and this necessitated the ports being constructed with lock-gates, which complicated the working arrangements, and the muddy waters of the estuary caused silting problems. During the 1920s and 1930s, the newly formed Southern Railway invested considerably in its dock installations at Southampton, which benefitted from the well-known 'dwell' on the high tides, which obviated the necessity of lock-gates. As a result, the GWR lost considerable business to Southampton, and the Port of London. Coupled with the change to oil fuel for ships, the profitability of the GWR's South Wales ports declined in the early 1930s, and some of the docks ceased to be used during this period. In the Second World War, the installations became very important terminals for the arrival of food and munitions from North America, in spite of the extensive bombing raids made on them by the Luftwaffe. Hold-ups occurred with the arrival of 'Lease-Lend' materials from the USA, and the unprecedented step was taken of seconding C. M. Jenkin Jones from the LNER to sort the problem out.

Some of the GWR's harbours were extensively involved with passengers, Plymouth and Fishguard being used for transatlantic services. The liners did not enter the docks, but lay outside to enable the passengers and mail to be transferred to and from the land by tender. With eastbound services particularly, the 'Ocean Liner Specials' (qv) frequently achieved very fast times on their way to London, the most notable run being that of *City of Truro* (qv) and *Duke of Connaught* in 1904. The GWR operated its own ships between Weymouth and the Channel Islands, and on the Anglo-Irish services out of Fishguard, the latter being worked by a jointly owned subsidiary company, the Fishguard & Rosslare Railways & Harbours Co.

In view of the extensive use of Weymouth by the GWR, it may seem surprising that the harbour was not theirs, particularly since the pier was served by a branch line running through the streets of the town. The facilities were, however, owned by the town, although the railway actually drew up the plans for the major extensions in the 1930s, and guaranteed the loan for the works. Weymouth was only one of the 39 additional ports served by the GWR, but not all these were particularly prosperous during the inter-war years. Down in the West of England, for instance, the cable-worked incline serving Portreath Harbour was taken out of use in 1936, ten years after the similar installation at Newquay had been abandoned. On the other hand, in 1925 the GWR took over the operation of the ferries across the Dart between Kingswear and Dartmouth, the latter boasting the only GWR station that never had any railway tracks (qv Kingswear branch).

(*See also individual entries*)

PWBS

DOGS

Fifty or so years ago the GWR had 25 sheep-dogs on its roster, necessary to control the frequently straying sheep of South Wales. The company also found another use for dogs, for many spent their lives at stations on the GWR system as collectors for the GWR Widows & Orphans Fund. Met by most, perhaps, was 'Tim' at Paddington, who arrived as a sick stray from Exeter, recovered, and spent the rest of his life on duty between 9.30 am and 6.45 pm with a tin attached to his collar. He remained 'on duty' even after his death on 8 September 1902, mounted in a glass case on Platform 1, and earned over £1,000 for the Fund.

'Prince', presented to the staff at Reading in 1908 by the eminent KC Sir Rufus Isaacs, had, by the time of his death in 1912, collected £220 11s 2d (£220.56p). 'Jim' (Kingswear) liked to prowl about the boats in the harbour, but one day fell asleep on a collier. Though well cared for during his subsequent voyage to Newcastle, he was wary of this vessel afterwards. 'Jack' (Fishguard) used to assist in the loading of cattle as well as collecting, but 'Rover' (Kidderminster) forsook collecting duties for the company of a shooting party and never came back.

On a sadder note, 'Charley' (Windsor) died in 1898 after swallowing coins thrown for him, but the only idler seems to have been 'Twister' (Merthyr) who one year did not even earn enough to pay for his licence. Up to 1911, GWR dogs had collected almost £3,000 for their Fund.

CA

DOLGELLEY

Near Dolgelley the River Wnion is joined by the Mawddach just before the latter widens to estuary status. Following the former, the Bala & Dolgelley Railway had brought its trains to the small, pleasant township of Dolgelley on 4 August 1868, and on 21 June 1869 had been linked with a Cambrian Railways (qv) extension of the 1865 line to Penmaenpool to complete what became the GWR access route to Cardigan Bay.

Dolgelley had a conventional two-platform station between the river and the gently rising hillside and was well served by trains off the Ruabon line towards Pwllheli and by a local shuttle to and from Barmouth (all qv).

GB

DOVEY JUNCTION

Located at the head of the Dovey estuary, Dovey Junction was purely an interchange point between the Cambrian Railways (qv) lines on either side of the widening waterway, and had no road access. The senior of the two routes was the Aberystwyth & Welsh Coast Railway line south of the estuary which had been opened on 1 July 1863 and had initially had a branch to the Ynysglas–Aberdovey ferry. After the idea of crossing the mouth of the River Dovey had been abandoned, the 'Deviation Line' north of the estuary was opened from Dovey Junction to Aberdovey on 14 August 1867 to link up with the 1863 line north through Towyn. It involved extensive earthworks and tunnelling at Aberdovey where there was a double track branch plus wagon transporter on the pier.

Dolgelley *The station, looking west.* (Steamchest Collection)

Both routes crossed waterways on their approach to the curved, converging platforms at Dovey Junction, each of which had an adjacent loop. There was also a large refreshment room for the comfort of those forced to wait at this lonely location.

GB

DOWLAIS BRANCH

Stations: Nelson & Llancaiach, Trelewis Platform (1 m), Bedlinog ($3\frac{1}{2}$ m), Cwm Bargoed (7 m), Dowlais Cae Harris ($9\frac{1}{2}$ m)

The high plateau and great ironworks at Dowlais were served first by tramroads and later by conventional lines which climbed laboriously up the narrowing Bargoed valleys, approached at a higher level from Brynmawr (qv) and Pontsticill Junction or, like the Taff Vale, used a steep incline up from Merthyr (qv). The joint line of the GWR and Rhymney (qv) Railways used the Bargoed Taff for its 1 in 40 climb through increasingly bleak countryside to the station, loco shed and goods depot complex at Cae Harris, serving the ironworks and collieries there plus other collieries *en route*.

Authorized originally under a GWR 'Various Powers' Act of 15 July 1867, the line was opened for goods traffic on 20 December 1875 (passengers 1 February 1876). It carried a service from Ystrad Mynach/Nelson with as many as nine extra trains on Saturdays. In later years '56xx' 0-6-2Ts handled most of the workings.

GB

DROITWICH SPA

Important traffics at Droitwich included the products of the local salt industry, the visitors to the brine baths and the wagons exchanged between the GWR and MR/LMS systems. The latter's interest in the joint GWR/LMS station dated back to services on the line opened by the Oxford, Worcester & Wolverhampton Railway (qv) from Worcester and forward to rejoin the MR main line at Stoke Works on 18 February 1852, OW&W services then commencing on 1 May with the opening of the Stourbridge line.

Droitwich station, which was rebuilt in 1899 with special attention to the needs of invalid visitors, consisted of twin platforms, with the up side goods yard following and then the separation of the Stourbridge and Birmingham lines before they crossed the Droitwich Canal.

GB

EALING BROADWAY

This major inner suburban station first became a junction with the opening of the District Railway's line from Turnham Green on 1 July 1879. A Windsor–Mansion House service was operated via a connection with the relief lines from 1 March 1883 to 30 September 1885, after which the junction was later removed.

The GWR (New Railways) Act of 11 July 1905 then added the Ealing & Shepherds Bush Railway which ran from new platforms at Ealing via North Acton Junction and White City to Wood Lane. Opening for goods, including a branch to the West London line, was on 16 April 1917 and to passengers on 3 August 1920. The electric passenger train service was operated by the Central London Railway via an end-on junction at Wood Lane and under an agreement of 23 August 1911.

GB

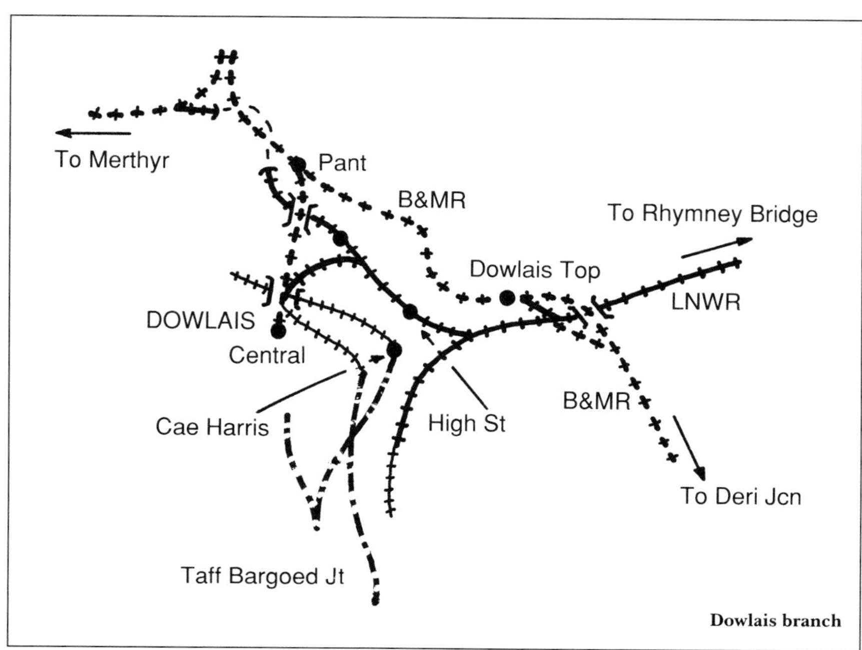

Dowlais branch

Ealing Broadway (GW Society)

EASTON BRANCH

Stations: Melcombe Regis (Weymouth), Westham Halt (¼ m), Rodwell (¾ m), Sandsfoot Castle Halt (1¼ m), Wyke Regis Halt (2¼ m), Portland (4¼ m), Easton (8 m)

The single line linking Weymouth with the Isle of Portland operated under joint GWR and LSWR/SR agreements which reflected the settlement of the original inter-company difficulties over access to Weymouth (qv). It carried a substantial passenger service, especially between Weymouth and Portland, and dealt with large quantities of coal and other traffic for the Admiralty plus stone from private sidings at Portland and Easton. A major physical feature was the viaduct over Radipole Lake where the original timber structure was replaced in 1908 by a combination of 700 ft and 250 ft embankments linked by five 108 ft steel girder spans carried on 8 ft cast iron cylinders.

The section to Portland was authorized to the Weymouth & Portland Railway on 30 June 1862 and opened on 16 October 1865. Its leasing and working arrangements by the GWR and LSWR were also applied to the Portland Breakwater Railway (known as the Admiralty Line) and to the Easton & Church Hope Railway. The latter had been incorporated on 25 July 1867 to build a line northwards from Easton, but had to be rescued by the two main-line companies. The result became an extension from Portland over 34 chains of the Admiralty line and then on to Easton—opened for goods on 1 October 1900 (passengers 1 September 1902).

From 30 May 1909 passenger services worked to and from a new station at Melcombe Regis instead of reversing at Weymouth Junction, and from 1931 the alternate-year working was abandoned in favour of working by the SR.

GB

EBBW VALE BRANCH

Stations: Aberbeeg, Cwm (2¾ m), Victoria (4¼ m), Ebbw Vale (6 m)

This busy, double-track GWR branch followed the course of the Ebbw River from Aberbeeg (qv) up to the great iron and steel works at Ebbw Vale. *En route* it served Marine and Graig Fawr collieries at Cwm, miners' trains operating between there and Beaufort which lay 52 chains beyond the Ebbw Vale Low Level station at which the ordinary branch passenger services terminated.

The complex of collieries and iron and steel plants between Victoria and Ebbw Vale involved 26 private sidings and nearly 60 miles of industrial railway, the latter giving access to a further eight collieries. At the north end lay the single-platform Ebbw Vale GWR station, about ¼ mile from the LNWR/LMS High Level and with its short, single-line extension to the coal and ballast sidings at Beaufort.

The line was also known as the Beaufort branch, the ironworks there being one of the reasons for the original 1798 tramroad opened by the Monmouthshire Railway & Canal Co (qv) and taken over by the GWR in converted, conventional form in 1880 (operationally 1875). At the other end of the timescale was Tyllwyn Halt, north of Victoria and dating from 29 November 1943.

GB

EDGCUMBE, COL THE HON CHARLES ERNEST

Director, 1889–1915. Born in October 1838, the second son of the Earl of Mount Edgcumbe, he was a JP for Cornwall and Devon and a director of the Princetown, the West London Extension and the Cornwall Railways. In his capacity with the latter he joined the GWR Board at amalgamation (1889) and served for 26 years until his sudden death in London on 14 September 1915. He is buried at Maker, near the family seat on the west bank of the Tamar estuary, and was succeeded on the GWR Board by Francis Bingham Mildmay MP.

CA

ELECTRIFICATION

The GWR was far and away the least electrification-minded of all the 'Big Four' main-line companies. There were tentative proposals in the 1930s to electrify all the lines west of Taunton, possibly to ease the problems of haulage up the steep banks in West Devon and the sharply curving Cornish main line, although it has also been suggested that they were merely a ruse to persuade the Welsh colliery owners to bring down the price of their coal. Despite the extensive electrification carried out by BR since 1948, very little of the former GWR network has been dealt with. The likeliest candidates would be the main line from Paddington to Bristol and the suburban lines to Reading and Oxford, but although there have been proposals and some estimates these have only been tentative.

Nevertheless, electric trains have run in and out of Paddington suburban station since 1906. The GWR was involved with the construction of the first underground railways in London, the Metropolitan and the Hammersmith & City (qv), opened in the 1860s. The GWR was joint owner of the latter, and when electrification came at the turn of the century it was the GWR which carried out the work, although the 20 six-car trains built in 1906 carried the names of both the Metropolitan and GWR. These were withdrawn by London Transport in the late 1930s, to be replaced by wholly owned LPTB stock, but the GWR remained part owner of the track and sub-stations until Nationalization. A fascinating survival of the GWR's venture into electrification is Brake 3rd No 3755, beautifully restored to its original crimson lake livery at Didcot Railway Centre. This was built in 1921, one of 36 non-corridor carriages designed to operate services between Maidenhead, Reading and various suburban destinations and Aldgate. Between Bishops Road, which became Platforms 13–16 of Paddington station (qv) in 1933, and the City, the trains were hauled on the underground section by Metropolitan Railway electric locomotives (one of these, *Sarah Siddons*, survives) but this service ended with the outbreak of the Second World War.

There were two other GWR London underground electric ventures. The first was the Ealing & Shepherds Bush Railway (qv Ealing Broadway) authorized in 1905 and owned jointly with the Central London Railway, which provided the trains, although steam-hauled GWR trains also used the metals. The other was the Central Line extension to West Ruislip, parallel to the GWR's Birmingham main line. This was built by the GWR, electric trains began to operate as far as Greenford in 1947 and right through to West Ruslip a year later.

Finally, mention should be made of the Mersey Railway, an independent concern but one which worked closely with the GWR; most GWR passengers bound for Liverpool transferred across the platform at Rock Ferry, the penultimate station before Birkenhead Woodside (qv), finding it more convenient to complete their journey in a Mersey Railway EMU.

MCHB

EMLYN, VISCOUNT FREDERICK ARCHIBALD VAUGHAN CAMPBELL

Chairman 1895–1905. Born at Windsor on 13 February 1847, the eldest son of the second Lord Cawdor, he was appointed a Director of the GWR in 1890, in succession to Talbot, and a year later joint Deputy-Chairman with Hubbard. At the end of June 1895 he succeeded F. G. Saunders (all qv) in the Chair, and thus became the youngest Chairman of a British railway.

Throughout his period of office he spent much time on company business. Under his Chairmanship the lease of the refreshment rooms at Swindon, for long a bone of contention between the Company and the lessees, was bought for £100,000, and at last passenger trains were not required to stop there. Carriages were improved, services speeded up, bus/rail services were integrated and several of the cut-offs (qv) put in hand.

In March 1905 he resigned from the Board when offered the post of First Lord of the Admiralty in Balfour's administration. He became Lord Cawdor on 29 March 1898, and died in a London nursing-home on 8 February 1911. He is buried at Cheriton, Co Pembroke.

CA

EVESHAM

Evesham lies at the centre of a vast fruit-growing area and in 1927 the GWR was obliged to provide a sizeable new goods yard to cope with the rising level of fruit and vegetable forwardings which could reach 200 wagons a day in busy periods. This yard, with its sidings, cart roads, weighbridge and warehouses, lay on the up side after the GWR's Oxford–Worcester line (qv) had crossed the River Avon. Opposite lay the exchange siding with the MR/LMS Ashchurch–Redditch line.

The GWR and LMS stations lay side by side east of the river, the former comprising down side buildings and a 500 ft platform plus an up side island with a long loading dock behind. It had been opened with the Oxford, Worcester & Wolverhampton Railway (qv) line from Norton Junction on 1 May 1852 and become a through station with the extension eastwards on 4 June 1853.

GB

EXETER

Exeter was a busy and important railway centre in the GWR era, handling a notable range of trains on the West of England main line plus others linking Devon and Cornwall with Birmingham and the North. The main GWR station, Exeter St Davids, also dealt with Waterloo trains which had divided at Exeter Central to go forward via Cowley Bridge Junction to Plymouth and North Devon. The short, steep link from Central via the 184 yd St Davids Tunnel was used by LSWR/SR local trains as well, and the GWR had its own local services to Taunton, Dulverton, Heathfield and Torbay. The latter called at Exeter St Thomas, 2 m 74 ch beyond St Davids.

The first Exeter station was one of

Evesham *The station, looking west.* (Lens of Sutton)

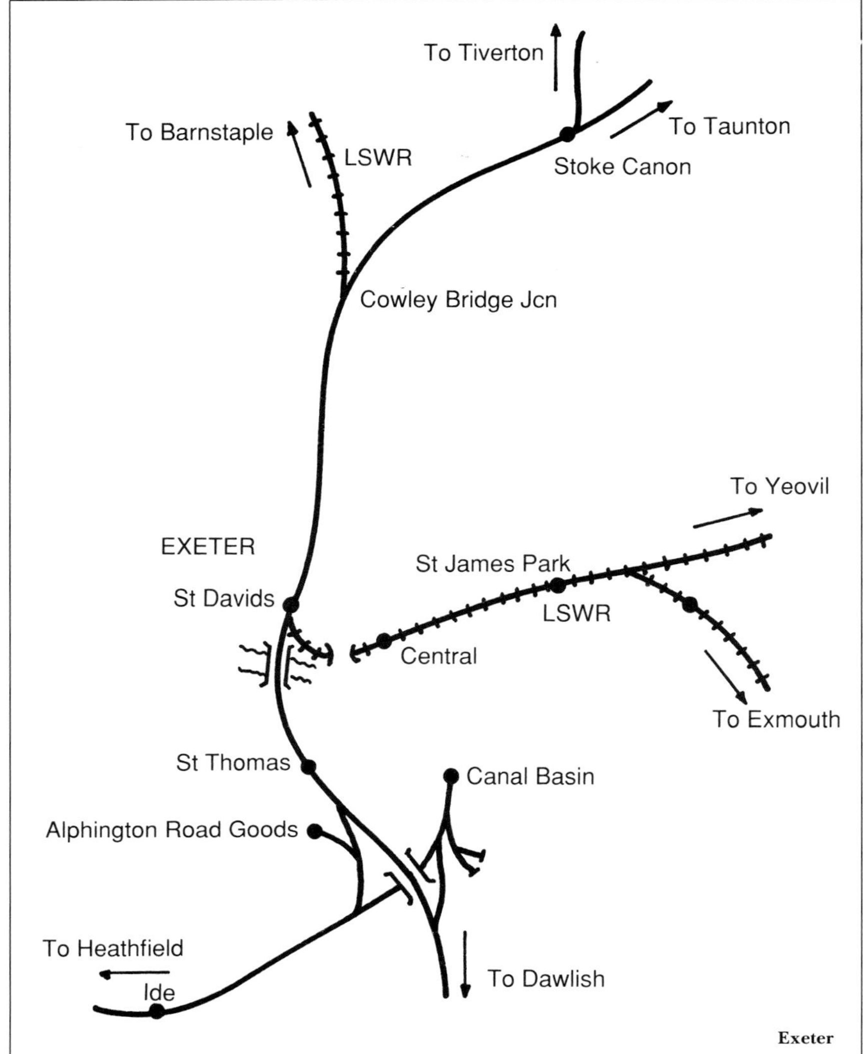

Exeter

Brunel's single-sided affairs. It opened with the arrival of the Bristol & Exeter's (qv) line from Beam Bridge on 1 May 1844 and was used by South Devon Railway trains (qv) westwards from 30 May 1846, an engine house being provided on the up side near the bridge over the River Exe. Other South Devon Railway (qv) trains worked to and from St Thomas station to avoid sharing traffic receipts with the B&E.

The B&E began operating trains on the Exeter & Crediton line from 12 May 1851, but the LSWR took these over from 1 February 1862 when the connecting line between the two systems was opened. The extra traffic prompted a new station at St Davids, opened two years later and then replaced by a 1911–14 rebuilding. The end product was a sizeable complex with long down side buildings and platform, a centre island for LSWR/SR trains and a GWR up island. There was a down side bay, near the Traffic Superintendent's office, and around the station were carriage sheds, up side loco and goods depots and the Red Cow level crossing. Various improvements were made in later years and a new marshalling yard, Exeter (Riverside), opened in 1943.

Exeter St Thomas lay on a raised section with buildings at street level and two platforms, once part-covered by an overall roof. Alphington Road goods depot then lay along the curving descent of the Heathfield line which also had a freight connection to City Basin on which trains had to be accompanied by a shunter and two 'Traffic Porters' to work the level crossings.

GB

EXETER–DULVERTON LINE

Stations: Stoke Canon ($3\frac{1}{2}$ miles from Exeter), Brampford Speke ($4\frac{1}{4}$ m), Thorverton ($6\frac{1}{4}$ m), Up Exe (7 m), Cadeleigh ($10\frac{1}{4}$ m), Tiverton ($14\frac{1}{4}$ m), Bampton ($21\frac{1}{4}$ m), Dulverton ($24\frac{3}{4}$ m)

This delightful GWR branch linked the main line at Stoke Canon with the Taunton–Barnstaple line (qv Barnstaple branch) at Morebath Junction. It followed the wooded valley of the River Exe for most of the journey, the Exeter–Tiverton trains crossing the river four times and those through to Dulverton only leaving it at Bampton. Single, and worked with five electric staff sections, the line had halts at Burn, West Exe, Bolham, Cove and Morebath Junction, and through journeys took 70 minutes.

The route was built in two parts, that from Morebath Junction to a point 2 m 17 ch north of Tiverton being authorized by the Tiverton & North Devon Railway Act of 19 July 1875, opened on 1 August 1884 and absorbed by the GWR from 1 July 1894. The GWR provided the link to the Tiverton Junction line (qv) and into Tiverton, which got a new station on 1 May 1885 when the line south to Stoke Canon was opened. The latter had been incorporated on 30 June 1874 as the Exe Valley Railway and had passed to the Bristol & Exeter (qv) on 19 July 1875.

GB

EXETER–PLYMOUTH LINE

Stations: Exeter St Davids ($173\frac{3}{4}$ miles from Paddington), Exeter St Thomas ($174\frac{1}{2}$ m), Exminster ($178\frac{1}{2}$ m), Starcross ($182\frac{1}{4}$ m), Dawlish Warren ($184\frac{1}{4}$ m), Dawlish ($185\frac{3}{4}$ m), Teignmouth ($188\frac{3}{4}$ m), Newton Abbot ($193\frac{3}{4}$ m) Totnes ($202\frac{1}{2}$ m), Brent ($209\frac{1}{2}$ m), Wrangaton ($211\frac{1}{2}$ m), Bittaford Platform ($212\frac{3}{4}$ m), Ivybridge (215 m), Cornwood ($217\frac{1}{4}$ m), Plympton ($221\frac{3}{4}$ m), Plymouth Mutley ($225\frac{1}{4}$ m), Plymouth

Exeter *The west end of Exeter St Davids during the reconstruction of 1911-14, the former over-all roof being dismantled in the background.* (National Railway Museum, York)

North Road ($225\frac{3}{4}$ m), Plymouth Millbay ($226\frac{1}{2}$ m)

The line opened by the South Devon Railway (qv) from Exeter to Plymouth between 1846 and 1849 was one of the best-known and loved stretches of railway on the GWR. Its course down the Exe estuary, along the coast through Dawlish (qv), up the Teign to Newton Abbot (qv) and on through the green Dartmoor foothills was delightful, but the curves and climbs legacy of the 'atmospheric caper' (qv) have troubled later generations of railway footplate, permanent way and operating staff.

The section to Aller Junction, for the Torquay line, was level, with watertroughs at Exminster, small tunnels west of Dawlish and considerable vulnerability to winter storms. The route then rose at 1 in 36–84 to the 264 yd Dainton Tunnel, dropped equally steeply to Totnes and then had 9 uphill miles, through the 869 unnecessary yards of Marley Tunnel, to the summit at Wrangaton. Rattery Viaduct lay on this section and five more followed on the descent to Plymouth (Glaze, Bittaford, Ivybridge, Blatchford and Slade) which included the $1\frac{1}{2}$ miles of 1 in 42 down Hemerdon bank.

Heavy trains needed pilots or bankers on the South Devon line and the local Exeter–Plymouth workings had no easy task in restarting from some intermediate stations. Operation got easier after doubling began in 1862, but the route has always been beautiful but difficult.

GB

FAIRFORD BRANCH

Stations: Oxford, Yarnton ($3\frac{3}{4}$ m), Eynsham ($7\frac{1}{4}$ m), South Leigh ($9\frac{3}{4}$ m), Witney (12 m), Bampton ($15\frac{3}{4}$ m), Alvescot ($17\frac{3}{4}$ m), Kelmscott & Langford ($20\frac{1}{4}$ m), Lechlade ($22\frac{1}{4}$ m), Fairford ($25\frac{1}{2}$ m)

This long single-line branch west from the Oxford–Worcester line (qv) at Yarnton Junction was built to serve Witney's blanket-making industry and for many years inwards wool traffic and outward blanket

Fairford branch *Lechlade station.* (Lens of Sutton)

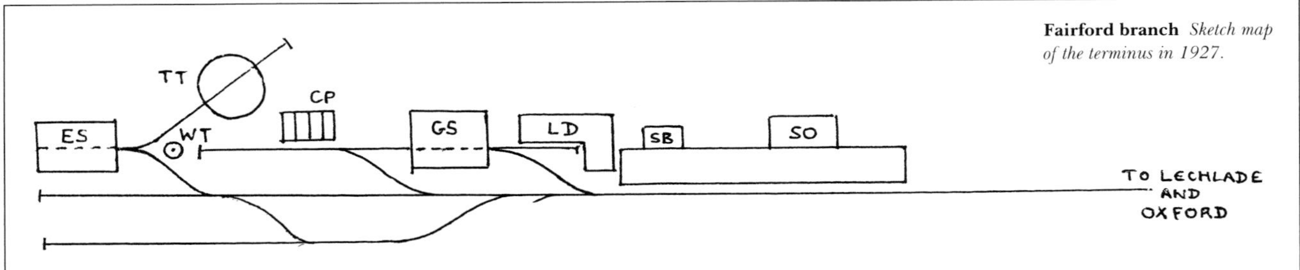

Fairford branch *Sketch map of the terminus in 1927.*

'specials' were a feature of its freight business. The Witney Railway was incorporated on 1 August 1859 with an authorized capital of £50,000 and powers to construct an 8 m 13 ch line which was duly opened on 14 November 1861. It was worked by the West Midland Railway on the 'one engine in steam' basis and in return for 50% of the gross receipts.

After several false starts and being caught between MR/GWR rivalries, the East Gloucestershire Railway's plans for a line from Cheltenham to Witney and Faringdon (qv) was cut back to a 14 m 10 ch extension of the Witney Railway to Fairford. This was opened, with the GWR working the traffic, on 15 January 1873 when the old Witney terminus was replaced by a new through station.

The GWR acquired the two local railways from 1 July 1890 and improved services, equipment and operating methods. By 1929 the line was carrying over 120,000 passengers annually and around 100,000 tons of freight, nearly half to and from Witney. A 50 mph speed restriction applied over the total length of 21 m 57 ch, the ruling gradient was 1 in 100 and working was by electric tablet to Bampton and electric train staff beyond.

In 1906 the branch was used for pioneer Automatic Train Control (qv) experiments.

GB

FALMOUTH BRANCH

Stations: Truro, Perranwell ($4\frac{1}{4}$ m), Penryn ($8\frac{1}{4}$ m), Penmere Platform ($10\frac{1}{4}$ m), Falmouth ($11\frac{3}{4}$ m)

The railway interests responded to Falmouth's need for a rail link with London to protect its position as a packet port, but although the Cornwall Railway (qv) secured an Act for a line to Plymouth on 3 August 1846 nothing seemed to go right for the enterprise. Falmouth lost tonnage to Southampton, fears that an influx of navvies would lead to food shortages induced rioting, contracting firms failed, and the Cornwall Railway ran out of money. Eventually the 'Associated Broad Gauge Companies' (qv) came to the rescue, opening between Plymouth and Truro, obtaining new powers and letting new contracts for the Falmouth section, and finally opening the 11 m 68 ch single line on 24 August 1863. A connection to the new docks followed in 1864.

Until 1893, when a new Penwithers Junction was provided, the branch had separate single-line access to Truro (qv) alongside the main line. As constructed it had two significant summits involving gradients of 1 in 60–66, two tunnels (Sparnick, 491 yds, and Perran, 374 yds) and eight timber viaducts. Between 1923 and 1934 four of the latter were rebuilt (Carnon, 252 yds; Perran, 113 yds; Ponsanooth, 215 yds; and College Wood, 318 yds) and the others converted to embankments, the works including some re-alignment and a completely new station at Penryn.

In addition to its 37 weekday passenger trains, the branch used to handle considerable amounts of freight, especially through Penryn and the docks. A train was bombed at Penmere in 1941.

GB

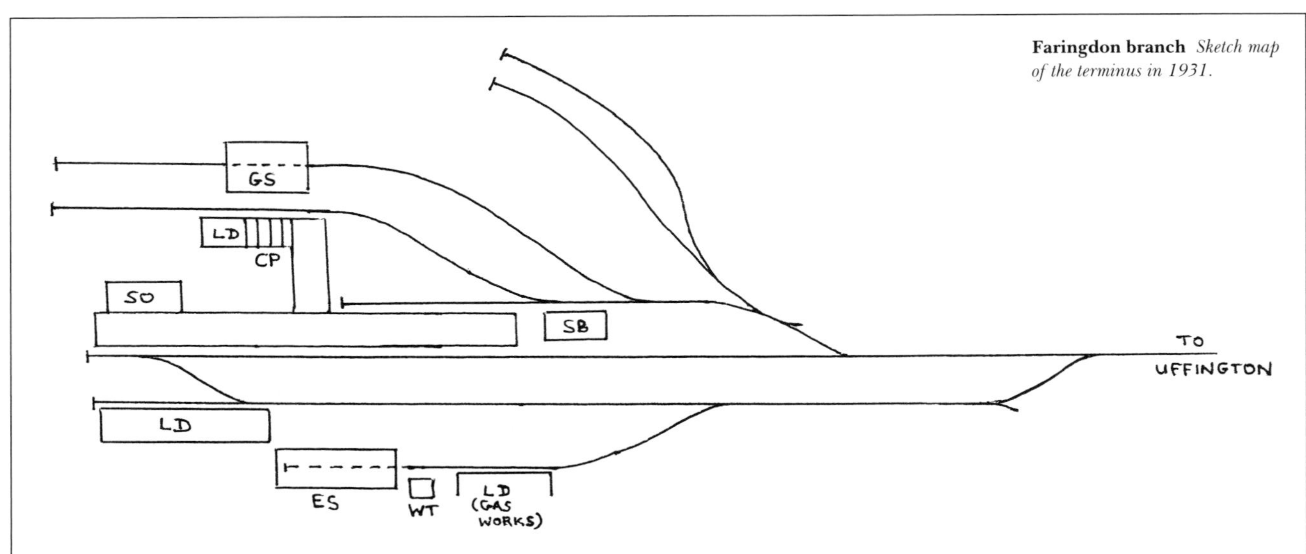

Faringdon branch *Sketch map of the terminus in 1931.*

FARINGDON BRANCH

The Faringdon Railway Act of 13 August 1860 authorized a 3 m 49 ch broad gauge branch from the GWR main line at Uffington north to the small town of Faringdon. Opened on 1 June 1864, the single line was worked by the GWR from the outset and became part of the GWR system from 1 July 1886.

Traffic on the branch was never very heavy, the weekday passenger service dropping to four each way by 1938 and then ending altogether on 31 December 1951. They had used the outer face of the up island at Uffington and set off past the triangular dock there for the combination of single platform plus run-round, engine and goods shed lines at the terminus. Control was by train staff and a ground frame at Faringdon.

GB

FIRE FLY

Following the opening of the GWR, when locomotives of various manufacturers' own designs were used, Gooch produced the first of his standard types, known as the 'Fire Fly' Class, after the initial one, built by Jones, Turner & Evans of Newton-le-Willows in 1840. They were 2-2-2s with outside sandwich frames, and bore the brunt of the traffic until the Swindon-built 4-2-2s appeared. Shortly after its delivery, *Fire Fly* worked a Directors' Special over the 36 miles from Paddington to Reading and back, taking only 45 minutes for the down journey, and reaching a maximum of 58 mph on the return. At the time of writing, a full-size working reproduction is under construction.

PWBS

FISHGUARD

The economic depression caused by the 1849 Great Famine in Ireland led the South Wales Railway (qv) to abandon its port plans for Fishguard in favour of Neyland (qv). Nothing of significance then happened until an 1876–82 local line from Clynderwen to Rosebush became part of the North Pembrokeshire & Fishguard Railway which reconditioned the original line and extended it to Letterston in 1895. The interests behind the NP&F obtained powers for an extension to Fishguard with port facilities there and at Rosslare. Threats to link the whole enterprise with the LNWR at Swansea brought GWR acquisition of the NP&F, its extension to Fishguard & Goodwick from 1 July 1899 and an agreement for the Fishguard & Rosslare Railways & Harbours Co (as a GWR and Great Southern & Western Railway of Ireland concern) to complete and work the connecting railways, the harbours and the steamer services.

Fishguard *'The Dawn of an Ocean Port. Shade of Brunel: "Fishguard as Ocean Port of Call, and opened by the biggest Liner in the world!"'* (GWR Magazine, 1909)

Fishguard *Panoramic view over Fishguard Harbour station on its blasted-out 'shelf', showing some of the 1,200-foot quay.* (National Railway Museum, York)

The circuitous, single-line course of the NP&F was not suitable for main-line running, so a new line was constructed over 10¾ miles north from a junction at Clarbeston Road, through the 243 yd Spittal Tunnel to Letterston Junction and then down at 1 in 50 to the harbour site. There, a shelf was blasted from the sheer cliff to provide for a 1,200 ft quay, a two-island platform station, sidings and cattle sheds. The new works, plus three steamers on the Rosslare service and two (ex-Neyland) on the Waterford route, came into operation on 30 August 1906.

In addition to the boat-connecting trains to and from Paddington, local services operated from Clarbeston Road to Fishguard, calling intermediately at Wolf's Castle Halt (6 m), Welsh Hook Halt (7¾ m), Mathry Road (9¾ m), Jordanston Halt (11¾ m), Fishguard & Goodwick (15 m), where the loco shed was situated, and then over the double line portion to Fishguard Harbour (15½ m).

The Rosebush line, which suffered closures in the 1917–21 period and then lost its passenger trains from 25 October 1937, had stations at Llanycefn (3¾ miles from Clynderwen), Maenclochog (6¾ m), Rosebush (8¼ m), Puncheston (12½ m) and Letterston (17¼ m).

(See also Dock and harbours, and Ships and shipping services) GB

FLOWER TRAFFIC

In the later GWR years the movement of cut flowers by passenger train reached significant proportions. The main growing areas were the Scilly Isles and the Channel Islands and the volume of business frequently rose to special train level, especially when prices in the market were good. Train-load quantities were only reached on the routes from Penzance and Weymouth to Paddington, with cartage on to Covent Garden, but vanloads were forwarded to many provincial destinations and smaller quantities of boxes were conveyed as normal parcels traffic.

(See also Freight services, Channel Islands traffic and Scilly Islands traffic) GB

'FLYING DUTCHMAN'

In December 1847 the GWR introduced a new express to Exeter, taking 4 hrs 25 mins over the roundabout route via Bristol, and stopping at Swindon for the compulsory 10-minute refreshment stop. It was booked to cover the 52 miles to Didcot in 55 minutes, and in the following year Gooch (qv) could boast that the train was achieving times of 48 to 59 minutes over this stretch, enabling him to claim later that he was the

'Flying Dutchman' (GWR Museum, Swindon)

'father of express trains'. In 1849 a famous horse called Flying Dutchman had won the Derby and the St Leger, having presumably been named after Wagner's opera, which had had its first performance at Dresden in 1843. The exploits of the racehorse prompted the GWR's staff to apply this nickname to their record-breaking train, which subsequently became widely used. In 1848, however, it had dropped back to a 4½-hour schedule to Exeter after the insertion of an extra stop at Chippenham, but was still booked over the initial stretch at an average of more than 57½ mph.

After the doldrums and financial stringency of the 1860s, the train made a comeback in the later days of the Broad Gauge, when it had become a London–Penzance express, leaving Paddington at 11.45 am. Running non-stop to Swindon, it was booked to average just over 53 mph on this stretch, although Ahrons found its timekeeping was not wonderful, particularly when it loaded to seven instead of the usual five eight-wheeled coaches (these were not bogie vehicles, as the inner axles were fixed, while the outer ones were pivoted like pony-trucks). It was hauled by one of the renewed broad gauge singles of the 'Rover' Class. PWBS

FOWEY BRANCHES

Stations: Par, St Blazey (½ m), Fowey (4½ m)
Lostwithiel, Golant (3¾ m), Fowey (5¼ m)

The first railway to Fowey was that of the Lostwithiel & Fowey Railway, authorized on 30 June 1862 and opened on 1 June 1869. The port then got a second route with the arrival on 1 June 1874 of the Cornwall Minerals Railway's (qv) line from St Blazey, the two competing so keenly for the available business that the L&F went under and was closed on 1 January 1880. It was revived by its rival from 16 September 1895, the two routes being joined at Fowey and passing to the GWR in the following year.

The CMR line from St Blazey, which involved a long tunnel through Great Pinnock Hill, carried passenger trains from 20 June 1876 to 8 July 1929 and for many years was the principal route. The 24 weekday passenger trains on the L&F route worked from the down side, country-end

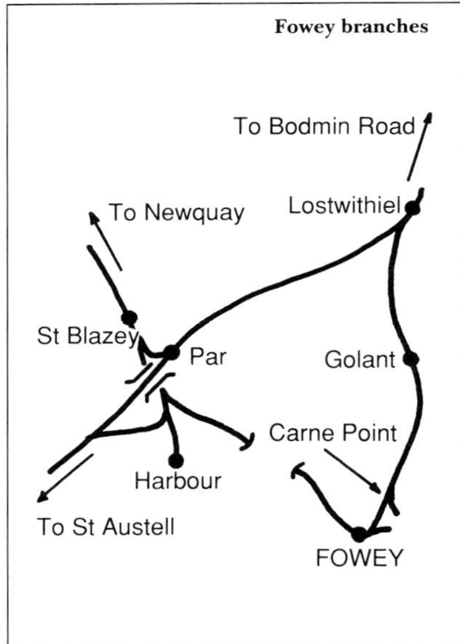

bay at Lostwithiel and then followed the west bank of the River Fowey. Along the Carne Point–Fowey section of the L&F line, the GWR provided eight jetties for unloading china clay to cargo vessels.

GB

FREIGHT SERVICES

Freight on the GWR began in a small way, in September 1839, largely through the agency of carriers, though it does not seem to have been much publicized. By 1850 the system was provoking adverse criticism from among the shareholders—receipts were roughly one-third of those generated by passengers (£99,850 as against £295,100 at 30 June 1850), or just over 25% of the total.

A goods service to Birmingham opened in February 1853, and the following year the original passenger station at Paddington (qv) became the goods depot when the new station was opened. Freight traffic doubled in five years, though even then its receipts were little more than half those from passengers. New efforts were made, and James Grierson (qv) was appointed Chief Goods Manager. Part of the problem was the 'break of gauge' (qv Broad Gauge), and receipts did not attain passable levels until the end of the 1860s, when noticeable increases in 'narrow' gauge mileage had been made.

Freight services *A typical goods station scene at Handsworth & Smethwick in 1933, showing the wide variety of goods moved in the days of the railway as 'common carrier'.* (GW Society)

As one of the foremost users of vacuum-fitted freight stock, the GWR ran overnight services to and from a wide variety of destinations. Many of these trains acquired nicknames—the Exeter goods, leaving Paddington at 10.45 pm, was the 'Flying Pig', and there was 'The Tip', both revivals of names from Broad Gauge days. The 9.45 pm Cardiff–Chester (Saltney) and the 8.20 pm Kidderminster–Paddington were the 'Spud' and the 'Carpet' respectively, and there was a 4.20 am departure from Westbury to Wolverhampton named the 'Moonraker' in allusion to its Wiltshire beginnings. Some of these trains were not light, the Paddington–Birkenhead grossing up to 800 tons, no easy matter for a '47xx' 2-8-0. These locomotives were also used on the long Newton Abbot and Plymouth runs.

In February 1930 no fewer than 75 of these services bore names, including the 'Tinman' (Margam–Bordesley), the 'Bacca' (Bristol–Paddington), the 'Sparagras' (Worcester–Crewe) and the 'Sauce' (Paddington–Worcester)—no prizes for guessing what each carried! Thanks to such marketing, receipts improved; in 1912 they had been only slightly higher than those for passengers, but by 1936, in spite of road competition, this figure had risen to 58% of the total.

A constant problem was to ensure that enough fitted wagons were sent to Cornwall for the highly-prized flower, fruit and broccoli traffic (all qv), which could be variable in timing and/or quantity according to the

Freight services *A 'league table' of Divisions' miles-per-hour averages was given every three months in the* GWR Magazine. *The figures 'speak well for the efforts and co-operation of the staff, and we are pleased to be able to record such creditable performances'.* (GWR Magazine, 1920)

GOODS TRAIN WORKING.

Miles per Hour of all Goods and Mineral Trains, for three months ended May 23rd, as compared with the average for the three months ended January 31st.

Position.	Division or Section.		
1	**Exeter**	**25·86%**	**Increase.**
2	**Worcester**	**19·4 %**	,,
3	**Bristol**	**13·09%**	,,
4	**London**	**11·4 %**	,,
5	**Swansea**	**4·87%**	,,
6	**Westbury**	**3·7 %**	,,
7	**Plymouth**	**3·19%**	,,
8	**Gloucester**	**2·67%**	,,
9	**Monmouthshire**	**1·1 %**	,,
10	**Llynvi & Ogmore**	**1 %**	,,
11	Cardiff	6 %	Decrease
12	Pontypool Road	6·25%	,,
13	Chester	9·87%	,,
14	Birmingham	10·38%	,,

whim of the weather. The broccoli specials (qv), often made up of cattle wagons (suitably cleaned, of course) were given priority treatment all along the line. Specials also ran from Penzance in connection with the flower traffic (qv Scilly Islands traffic).

Specials for potatoes, the early varieties packed in hampers and the later ones in sacks, ran from the West Country too, to the north via Didcot and to the west via Bristol. London traffic was worked forward from Didcot.

(*See also Rolling-stock, goods*)

CA

FROME

BR preserved the overall roof at Frome, a good example of a Brunel station complex, although the design was implemented by one of his assistants, J. R. Hannaford. On 7 October 1850, the ailing Wilts, Somerset & Weymouth Railway (qv) arrived as a single line from Westbury (qv). A line north from Frome to tap the North Somerset coalfield at Radstock was added on 14 November 1854, the WS&W route extended to Yeovil (qv) on 1 September 1856 and an avoiding line around the south of Frome (Clink Road Junction to Blatchbridge Junction) in 1933.

The triangular junction with the Radstock line preceded the wooden station and up side goods yard at Frome and had a set of sidings for branch traffic. A ground frame at Frome West controlled the connections to Frome Mineral Loop Lines.

GB

FRUIT TRAFFIC

In GWR terms this heading is a wide one, ranging over strawberries from France, the West Country and Worcestershire, bananas shipped by Elders Fyffes to Avonmouth, apples from Somerset and the Evesham area, with other soft fruit such as plums, also from Evesham. Large quantities of strawberries arrived at Plymouth from Brest (there was a particularly heavy crop in 1909, when the season lasted from 18 May to 25 June); red, white or blue strings denoted quality, and the GWR took them, and the home crop, by express van-trains to places as far away as Edinburgh, London and Dublin.

Bananas were carried in increasing quantities during the years on either side of 1900—from 10,000 bunches in the whole of 1884 to 200,000 during a single week in 1910. The fruit was stowed on beds of straw in specially ventilated, steam-heated vans, as many as 4–500 bunches for a single cargo, loaded in an operation lasting about eight hours.

(*See also Freight services*)

CA

GAUGE CONVERSION

By 1870 it had become obvious that mixed-gauge lines were much less economic to maintain than track laid solely to broad or

Gauge conversion *Poster advertising the arrangements for the conversion weekend of Friday 20 May-Sunday 22 May 1892.* (GWR Magazine)

GREAT WESTERN RAILWAY

ALTERATION OF GAUGE

OF THE MAIN LINE

BETWEEN

EXETER AND TRURO

AND OF THE FOLLOWING

BRANCH LINES-

Newton Abbot and	Moretonhampstead	Tavistock	and	Launceston
Newton Abbot	Kingswear	Truro	..	Falmouth
Churston	Brixham	St. Erth	..	St. Ives
Totnes	Ashburton			

NOTICE IS HEREBY GIVEN that the lines of the Company between the above-mentioned points will be altered from the broad to the narrow gauge commencing on the night of Friday. May 20th, 1892.

During the time the alteration is being made the Lines specified will be closed, and all traffic upon them entirely suspended until the work is completed, which is expected to be on the night of Sunday, May 22nd.

In connection with the alteration of the Gauge, the following special arrangements will be in operation:—

PASSENGER TRAFFIC.

FRIDAY, MAY 20th.

The 10.15 a.m. Train from Paddington will call at several additional Stations as far as Plymouth and at all Stations beyond Plymouth.

The 11.45 a.m. Train from Paddington will not run beyond Plymouth

The 5.0 p.m. Train from Plymouth to Penzance will not be run.

The running of some of the Branch Trains West of Plymouth will be altered.

SATURDAY, MAY 21st.

The ordinary Train Service between Penzance and Truro, and on the Helston Branch will be discontinued, and a special service of Passenger Trains will be in force.

SUNDAY, MAY 22nd.

No Trains will be run between Penzance and Truro, or between Plymouth and Tavistock

MAIL TRAIN ARRANGEMENTS.

The 9.0 p.m. Mail Train from Paddington on Friday, May 20th, Saturday, 21st, and Sunday, 22nd, and the 8.23 p.m. Up Mail Train from Plymouth on Saturday, May 21st, and Sunday, 22nd, will be run between Exeter and Plymouth (North Road) via the London and South Western Company's route, the Up Mail will be due to leave North Road for Paddington at 8.30 p.m.

On Monday, May 23rd, the Night Mail Train will be run from Plymouth (North Road) to Penzance, leaving North Road at 4.40 a.m., and calling at all Stations. This Train will be in continuation of the Mail Train leaving Paddington at 9.0 p.m., on Sunday, May 22nd.

A STEAMER will be run between Plymouth and Falmouth on Saturday, May 21st and Sunday, 22nd, in connection with the London Night Mail Trains, calling at Fowey. 1st and 2nd Class Passengers will be booked locally by this Steamer.

GOODS TRAFFIC.

Intending Senders of Coal, Mineral, General Goods and other traffic to and from Stations between Exeter and Penzance, including Branches, are requested to take notice that the Company will not be able to receive traffic for conveyance, to or from Stations on that section of the Railway, for a short period prior to Friday, May 20th, until after the conversion has taken place.

PLYMOUTH TRAFFIC. By arrangement with the London and South Western Company an uninterrupted communication for General Goods Traffic will be maintained between Plymouth and Stations East of Exeter (inclusive), during the alterations

For full particulars see Pamphlets, which can be obtained at the Stations.

Paddington, April, 1892

HY. LAMBERT, General Manager

JUDD & Co., Limited, Printers [illegible]

GREAT WESTERN RAILWAY.

CONVERSION OF GAUGE, 1892.

South Devon and Cornwall District.

Inspector __________

No. of Gang

Ganger's Name

Mileage on which he is to work

Nearest Station

Sleeping Berth

To leave __________ *Station at* ____ *hrs.* ____ *mins.*

on __________ *day,* *May,* 1892.

To return from __________ *Station at* ____ *hrs.* ____ *mins.*

on __________ *day,* *May,* 1892.

Gauge conversion *Ticket for recording the movement of gangers to their various stations ready for the conversion.* (GWR Magazine)

narrow gauge. In 1869 just over 130 miles had been converted to narrow (ie standard) gauge, and during the next ten years a further 648.5 miles were altered. By 1892 423 miles 32 chains, over half (252 m 26 ch) of it already mixed, remained to be changed, all of it on or branching from the Paddington–Penzance line, and it was decided to carry out the work over one weekend, 21–22 May.

Arrangements for housing and feeding the gangs, drawn from all over the system, had to be made—they were accommodated in goods sheds, station waiting rooms and, in some difficult cases, tents. During the evening of 20 May, stock was worked eastwards, broad gauge vehicles to Swindon, where special sidings had been laid, and narrow stock to Weston-super-Mare. As each section was cleared, Station Masters were required to confirm that nothing remained, and a certificate was then issued so that work could begin. Equipment had been prepared and laid ready—on baulk track (qv Permanent way), the transoms were shortened, and longitudinal timbers moved inward and refastened. On sleepered track, replacement chairs had already been set to the narrower gauge, and it was then just a question of laying rails in their new positions.

Gauge conversion *'This is to certify that the Line between Kingswear and Newton Abbot is ready to be re-opened to traffic. . .' A notice issued to the Torquay Station Master on Sunday 22 May 1892.* (GWR Magazine)

GREAT WESTERN RAILWAY.

"CONVERSION OF GAUGE."

This is to certify that the Line between Kingswear and Newton Abbot is ready to be re-opened for Traffic, and the ordinary working of Trains between those points can be resumed on Monday, the 23rd.

Traffic Inspector.

To the Station Master Torquay Station.

Meticulous attention to detail, even down to naming individuals in respect of a particular duty, ensured that the entire operation was completed ahead of time, in 31 hours instead of the 48 hours allowed, a remarkable achievement which drew from the Directors a congratulatory and well-merited telegram to all who had taken part. Main-line services had been maintained between Paddington and Exeter meanwhile, on the narrow gauge via Salisbury.

CA

GENERAL MANAGERS

For many years the General Manager's post on the GWR was not what it had come to be on other lines. In GWR reckoning it was a secretarial post; its holder's duties included dealing with public communications, leased and joint lines, compensations, claims, prosecutions, Government enquiries, Parliamentary and legal business in connection with new works (including the correspondence these caused), copying and distribution of correspondence, and responsibility for train working and its irregularities. He was also in charge of his own Department (which must have been a comfort to him), though he may have been surprised to find that this included the refreshment department.

The holders of the post were:

James Grierson	1863–87
Henry Lambert	1887–96
Sir Joseph Wilkinson	1896–1903
Sir James Inglis	1903–11
Frank Potter	1912–19
Charles Aldington	1919–21
Felix Pole	1921–29
Sir James Milne	1929–47

(*See also individual entries, and Administration and management*)

CA

GIBBS, GEORGE HENRY

Director, 1833–40. Born at Exeter on 24 August 1785, he spent much of his early life in Spain. He was a Director of the GWR from 1833 to 1840, when he retired through ill health, and died in Venice on 21 August 1842. He was a strong Anglican, and a bequest of £500 to the GWR formed the nucleus of the endowment which established the church of St Mark, New Swindon. He also left, through his diary and letters, an invaluable account of the early days of the company (see Bibliography).

CA

GLOUCESTER

Until the opening of the Severn Tunnel (qv), Gloucester was an important junction on the GWR's South Wales main line (qv). The Welsh expresses ran via Swindon and

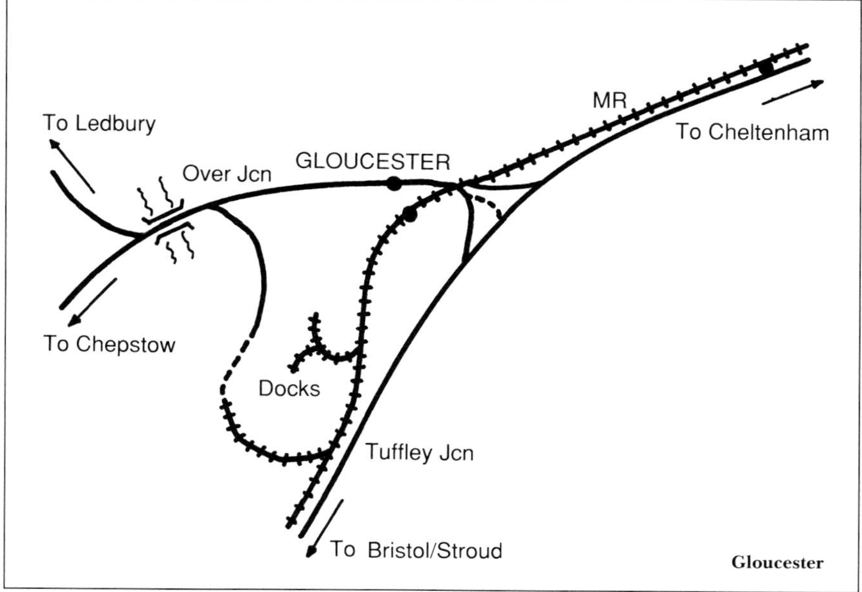

Gloucester

Stroud and round the east side of Gloucester to the city centre station. Their departure carried them over the River Severn, past Over Junction where the Ledbury line (qv) departed, and then down the west bank of the river to Chepstow (qv). Gloucester lost some status when the most important trains were diverted via the Severn Tunnel but regained it with the opening of the new Bristol–Birmingham route in 1908, handling also the Cheltenham/South Wales/Paddington services and a variety of local workings at its four-line, two-platform station.

The GWR's newly acquired Cheltenham & Great Western Union Railway (qv) had reached Gloucester on 12 May 1845, just after the Midland had snatched the Bristol & Gloucester line which, with the Birmingham & Gloucester, had given them the important Bristol–Birmingham route. The GWR could now get to Cheltenham over the C&GWU line of 8 July 1844 and the South Wales route was to follow in 1850–52, but this was only partial compensation.

Gloucester station lay at the western end of a triangle with the Avoiding Line on which there had also been a turntable-served station originally. Both the latter soon fell into disuse with the Avoiding Line then being revived from 25 November 1901 (passengers 1 July 1908). The GWR station was connected to its Midland/LMS neighbour by a long footbridge. Both companies had District Offices at Gloucester and both served the docks area and its private sidings, the GWR access being from Over Junction and through Llanthony Wharf Yard.

GB

GLOUCESTER–HEREFORD LINE

Stations: Gloucester, Oakle Street (5¼ m), Grange Court (7½ m), Longhope (11 m), Mitcheldean Road (14 m), Ross-on-Wye (18 m), Fawley (22 m), Ballingham (23 m), Holme Lacy (26 m), Hereford (30 m)

The line from Gloucester to Grange Court (qv) was opened by the Gloucester & Dean Forest Railway on 19 September 1851 as part of the GWR's route to South Wales. On 5 June 1851 the Hereford, Ross & Gloucester Railway was incorporated and had opened 5 miles of its route between Grange Court and Hopesbrook by 11 July 1853. But this followed a modest Severn tributary and was the easy bit. Ahead lay tunnels, including the 1,208 yd Ballingham Tunnel, and several viaducts over the River Wye, these delaying completion to Hereford until 1 June 1855. The HR&G was amalgamated with the GWR seven years later.

The route had a summer service of eight trains each way on weekdays and was used by through 'North and West' trains when the Severn Tunnel was closed. It had three intermediate halts.

GB

GLOUCESTER–SEVERN TUNNEL JUNCTION LINE

Stations: Gloucester (114 miles from Paddington), Oakle Street (119½ m), Grange Court (121½ m), Newnham (125 m), Awre (128¼ m), Lydney (133½ m), Woolaston (136 m), Chepstow (141½ m), Portskewett (146 m), Severn Tunnel Junction (148¾ m)

This line down the west bank of the Severn, following an easy course between the river and the higher ground of the Forest of Dean, was the GWR's principal route to South Wales prior to the opening of the Severn Tunnel (qv). Thereafter it still carried some trains from Paddington via Gloucester, plus services from Birmingham and locals from Cheltenham, but its status was never quite the same.

The original intention had been to cross the Severn from Standish, but when permission was refused the South Wales Railway (qv) was extended to Awre to meet a similar extension of the Gloucester & Dean Forest Railway from Grange Court (qv). Gloucester was linked with Chepstow (qv) from 19 September 1851 and the Wye crossing completed the route from London to Swansea from 19 July 1852.

After shedding the Ledbury line (qv) at Over Junction and that to Ross-on-Wye (qv) at Grange Court, the Chepstow line came nearer to the Severn at Newnham and passed through its 232 yd tunnel to Bullo Pill. There connection was made with the Forest of Dean Railway and its line to Bullo Pill dock, followed by the junction at Awre with the Forest of Dean Central. The Severn & Wye route (qv) over the Severn Bridge crossed the main line north of the junction between the two at Lydney. Then followed a long, straight stretch to Wye Valley Junction, Chepstow, Portskewett (which once had a short branch to Portskewett Pier to connect with the New Passage Ferry) and then over the west end of the Severn Tunnel to join the South Wales main line (qv) ahead of Severn Tunnel Junction station.

GB

GLYNCORRWG BRANCH

Known in GWR working instructions as the North Rhondda Branch, because it ran on beyond Glyncorrwg to North Rhondda Colliery, this line had originated with the South Wales Mineral Railway (qv) and had been inherited when the working of the Port Talbot Railway was taken over in 1908. After acquiring its Act on 10 August 1853 and being leased to the Glyncorrwg Coal Company two years later, the SWM route was opened progressively to 10 March 1863. It ran from Neath Harbour Junction via the 1½-mile Ynys-y-Maerdy incline to Tonmawr, where it had a junction with the PTR and colliery branches, and then through Gyfylchi Tunnel to the Afan Valley, Cymmer (qv) and on to the collieries beyond.

Essentially a coal railway, and difficult to work, the SWM did operate colliers' trains and services on holiday occasions. A more formal passenger service then ran between Cymmer and Glyncorrwg from 1918 to 1930, but after that only colliers' trains at the north end of the route. The GWR closed the incline section on 1 June 1910.

GB

GOBOWEN

The Shrewsbury & Chester Railway (qv) opened a station at Gobowen on 14 October 1848 and added the 2½-mile branch south-west to Oswestry (qv) on 23 December of that year. In its GWR years Gobowen comprised long up and down platforms with London-end bays plus a goods yard, cattle pens, engine shed and stabling sidings. It enjoyed good main-line and local services, the latter including

Oswestry–Ruabon workings among the 30 weekday trains each way over the branch.

GB

GOOCH, SIR DANIEL, BART

Locomotive Superintendent 1837–64, Chairman 1865–89. Born in Bedlington, Northumberland, in 1816, son of the manager of an iron foundry, as a youth Daniel Gooch knew George Stephenson, William Hedley and Timothy Hackworth. At 15 he took up employment at an ironworks in Tredegar, learning all he could. He had a varied early career, working under Robert Stephenson at the Vulcan Foundry, Warrington, with his brother Thomas on the London & Birmingham Railway, as a draughtsman under James Stirling at Dundee, and in October 1836 he became the partner of Sir Robert Hawks at a new works in Gateshead. This latter project failed, and, still not quite 21, whilst working with his brother Tom on the Manchester & Leeds Railway he applied to Brunel for the post of Manager of the GWR's 'Engine Manufactory'. The celebrated letter is kept at the GWR Museum at Swindon. Brunel (qv) appointed Gooch on 18 August 1837, and he was to serve the company for 52 years.

Sir Daniel Gooch (GWR Museum, Swindon)

No locomotives existed at the time of Gooch's appointment, and when the first Brunel-designed examples did arrive they were found to be unreliable and underpowered. Gooch persuaded Brunel to buy two locomotives he had designed for Robert Stephenson's company which were intended for export to America but were still in Newcastle. Altered to the 7-foot gauge, the first was named *North Star* and hauled the inaugural Directors' train on 31 May 1838. Gooch quickly became a close friend of Brunel, recommending to him that Swindon (qv) become the GWR's 'principal engine establishment'. He designed a series of engines for the GWR, built first of all by outside manufacturers, but from 1841 at Swindon. He married Margaret Tanner from Bishop Wearmouth in March 1838.

In 1864 Gooch left the GWR to lay the Atlantic cable with Brunel's SS *Great Eastern*, and the following year he entered parliament as MP for the Cricklade division of Wiltshire. However, throughout the country railways were in a state of financial depression and the GWR was on the edge of bankruptcy. The Company turned to Gooch, and in 1865 he was elected Chairman. He visited the Chancellor of the Exchequer in the hope of alleviating the situation but it took a long period of austerity, which Gooch resolutely saw through, before the GWR recovered. He was knighted in 1866.

At the age of 68 Gooch was the very first man to pass right through the Severn Tunnel (qv), crawling through where the headings of this, the greatest engineering feat of its time, had just met. Like Brunel, he was a great advocate of the Broad Gauge (qv) but in his old age he realized that it would have to go. He died, in office, greatly respected, at the age of 73 on 15 October 1889, and was buried at Clewer near Windsor.

(*See also Locomotives*)

MCHB

GOODENOUGH, H. T.

Telegraph Engineer, 1891–1902. He died 'in harness'.

AV

GRAND, KEITH WALTER CHAMBERLAIN

Born in 1900 and educated at Rugby, Grand joined the GWR in 1919 at Park Royal Goods station, from where he moved first to Ealing Broadway, then to the District Superintendent's Office at Paddington. After another move, this time to the General Manager's Office in 1922, he was appointed General Agent for the United States and Canada in 1926. He returned to England three years later, and from 1 January 1931 was Commercial Advertising Agent to the Superintendent of the Line. Exactly a year later he became Commercial Advertising and Publicity Agent. He was appointed Divisional Superintendent, Swansea, in 1936, but returned to Paddington as Assistant to the General Manager in 1937. Two years later he became Principal Assistant, and, in October 1941, Assistant General Manager. He succeeded Milne as General Manager from 1 January 1948, but with the title of Chief Regional Officer, Western Region. He died on 17 September 1983.

CA

'GRANGE' CLASS

Although a 4-6-0 with 5 ft 8 in driving wheels was outlined in Churchward's (qv) standardization plans as early as 1901, the type did not materialize until 1936, and then as 'renewals' of his 1911 'Moguls'. The 300-plus examples of the latter were used widely throughout the system, but were then getting old. Some trouble had also been experienced with the wear on the flanges of the leading coupled wheels in certain areas where the line was severely curved. A heavy casting had been mounted behind the front buffer-beam to reduce this by putting more weight on the pony-truck, but this reduced their route availability.

In the mid-1930s it was decided accordingly to renew the 2-6-0s as two different classes of 4-6-0, one with a smaller boiler to enable them to run over the 'Blue' routes, and the other with the Standard No 1 version. The resulting classes were named after 'Manors' (qv) and 'Granges', and all the latter reused the driving wheels and motion of withdrawn 'Moguls'. The 'Granges' were thus very similar to the 'Halls' (qv), but could readily be differentiated by the slightly raised running plate over the cylinders. Starting in 1936, 80 'Granges' were turned out from Swindon before the war put an end to the conversions. The first three locomotives were initially fitted with cast-iron chimneys, but a copper-capped version was later used, which had a distinctive outline, although routine boiler changes subsequently saw some of these appear on 'Halls'. The class was numbered in the 68xx series, and were all named after smaller country houses, neatly following on from the 'Castles' and 'Halls'. They were used for mixed-traffic duties on all the main lines, and were shedded as far apart as Paddington, Penzance, Fishguard and Birkenhead.

(See also Locomotives)

PWBS

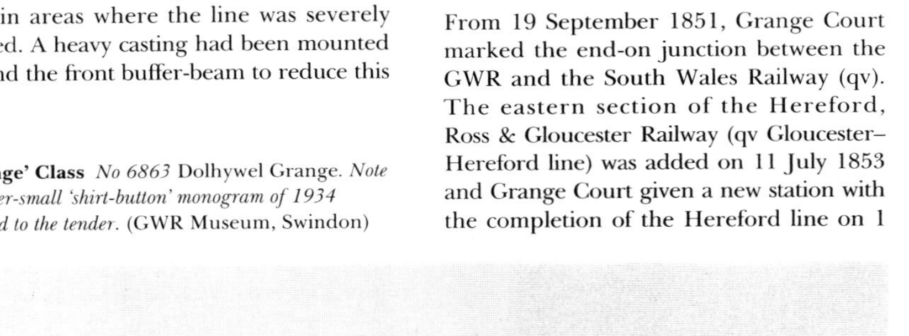

'Grange' Class *No 6863* Dolhywel Grange. *Note the over-small 'shirt-button' monogram of 1934 applied to the tender.* (GWR Museum, Swindon)

GRANGE COURT

From 19 September 1851, Grange Court marked the end-on junction between the GWR and the South Wales Railway (qv). The eastern section of the Hereford, Ross & Gloucester Railway (qv Gloucester–Hereford line) was added on 11 July 1853 and Grange Court given a new station with the completion of the Hereford line on 1 June 1855. As Grange Court Junction, GWR, it consisted of centre island and outer platforms, with the two routes converging at the south end and joining at the north.

GB

GREAT MALVERN

The Worcester & Hereford Railway (qv) opened from Malvern Link through Great Malvern to Malvern Wells on 25 May 1860, the through route being completed in 1861 and Great Malvern's impressive station in 1863. The latter had up side main buildings in the Gothic style, surmounted by an ornate clock tower and including a private waiting room for Lady Foley. There was also an up side loading dock, while the down side featured a large Station Master's house and a hotel fed with boiler coal via a siding, wagon turntable and tunnel. The hotel later became a girls' school with private subway access.

From 16 May 1864, trains on the Midland line to Ashchurch began to use Great Malvern, travelling over 44 chains of GWR metals between a down side bay and the junction. The main platforms were used by South Wales–Birmingham and Hereford–London trains, plus Hereford locals and those originating at Ledbury (qv) and Malvern Wells.

GB

GREAT WESTERN & GREAT CENTRAL JOINT LINE

Stations: South Ruislip (11¾ m from Paddington), Ruislip Gardens (12¼ m), Ruislip & Ickenham (13½ m), Denham (16¼ m), Denham Golf Club Platform (17¼ m), Gerrards Cross (19 m), Seer Green (21¾ m), Beaconsfield (23¼ m), High Wycombe (28 m), West Wycombe (30¼ m), Saunderton (33 m), Princes Risborough (36¼ m), Haddenham (41½ m)

Co-operation between the GWR and the expanding MS&LR (later Great Central) system had begun with the former advancing capital for a link from the latter's

Great Malvern *Note the Gothic-style main buildings and the diesel railcar at the down platform.* (Lens of Sutton)

London Extension to Banbury (qv). The GW&GC Railways Joint Committee then came into being on 1 August 1899 to improve the GWR's route to Birmingham and give the GCR an alternative to the London access over the heavily graded Metropolitan route. It was to improve the High Wycombe–Princes Risborough (both qv) line of the GWR, complete construction from the former to Old Oak Common (qv), and build a new line from the latter to the London Extension at Grendon. There was a GCR link from Northolt Junction to Marylebone, the 1863 Aylesbury branch (qv) from Princes Risborough was taken over in 1907, and a GWR extension linked Ashendon with Banbury via Bicester (qv) and Kings Sutton.

Goods traffic on the new line began on 20 November 1905, GCR passenger services on 2 April 1906 and GWR ones on 1 July 1910. The latter came to consist mainly of Paddington–Oxford, High Wycombe/Princes Risborough and Aylesbury services with a few longer-distance trains like the 'Birmingham & North Express' to Pwllheli.

The new line had flyover junctions at each end (Ashendon and Northolt Junction) and was double track throughout with separate platform lines.

GB

GREAT WESTERN RAILWAY MAGAZINE

For nearly 60 years, the *Great Western Railway Magazine* provided the company's employees with information on progress, new developments, welfare matters and staff changes. It sprang from the GWR Temperance Union and a desire to inform railwaymen dispersed throughout the system of what was going on. The first issue was published in November 1888, and the high standard and familiar format were retained right up to Nationalization.

GB

GREENFORD LOOP

Stations: West Ealing ($\frac{3}{4}$ m from Ealing Broadway), Drayton Green Halt ($1\frac{1}{4}$ m), Castle Bar Park Halt ($1\frac{3}{4}$ m), South Greenford Halt ($2\frac{1}{2}$ m), Greenford ($3\frac{1}{2}$ m)

The Greenford loop linked the main and GW&GCJR (qv) High Wycombe lines, running from one triangular junction between West Ealing and Hanwell over a succession of embankments to another just east of Greenford. It was authorized to the GWR by the Acton & Wycombe Railway Act of 6 August 1897 and then carried a 'circular' service for the Royal Show at Park Royal in 1903, a year in which additional spurs were authorized. A halt at Castle Bar Park, which served the GWR Athletic ground, was added when regular railcar (qv) services began on 1 May 1904. At first these took in Greenford (from 1 October), Southall, Willesden Junction and the West London line, but later auto-trains (qv) took over and the service was simplified into an Ealing Broadway (qv) /West Ealing–Greenford/Ruislip/Gerrards Cross pattern of some 110 workings between 5 am and midnight on weekdays.

GB

THE

Great Western Railway Magazine

FOR ALL INTERESTED IN RAILWAYS.

Published Monthly—

Ordinary Edition, 1*d*.	Annual Subscription,	3*s*.	(post free).
Art Edition - 2*d*.	,, ,,	4*s*.	,,
Insurance Edition, 2*d*.	,, ,,	4*s*.	,,

SPECIAL FEATURES:

Great Western Operations—Traffic Working Statistics —Technical Railway Articles—Locomotive Engineering, Signalling and General; New Great Western Engines, Stock and Structures; :: Current Events in the Railway World, etc. ::

The Magazine may be obtained at all Railway Bookstalls, and the various Stations and Offices of the G.W.R., or direct from the Editor, Paddington Station.

Great Western Railway Magazine *A 1937 advertisement.*

GRIERSON, JAMES

General Manager, 1863–87. Born on 10 October 1827, Grierson was appointed Secretary of the joint GWR/Shrewsbury & Chester Committee in 1851 and Traffic Manager of both lines three years later.

He became Chief Goods Manager at Paddington in 1857, and the company's first General Manager in 1863, just before his 36th birthday. He had control of only the Traffic and Goods Departments, but as a skilled negotiator had much to do with the West Midland Railway (qv) amalgamation. Also during his period of control both the Bristol & Exeter and South Devon Railways (both qv) were absorbed. His ability was not in doubt, and despite the fact that his power was restricted by the unenterprising attitude taken by some of his colleagues, in particular the drastic economy policy followed by Tyrrell (qv), the then Superintendent of the Line, he and Gooch (qv) were instrumental in improving the fortunes of the company. Able and popular, he served for 24 years before dying in office, on 7 October 1887, at his Marlow home. He is buried at Barnes Cemetery, W London.

CA

GROUPING

The railways' working deficit for 1919–20 was £41,349,530 (£200 billion at today's prices), and was estimated to become £54.5m the following year. It became clear that unless some sort of unification was to take place among the railways, they would probably grind to a swift and ignominious halt. Negotiations were lengthy, and when the railways were released from Government control following the First World War in August 1921, they were not permitted to return to their competitive ways. By the Railways Act of 1921 (11 & 12 Geo V c, 55), which was given the Royal Assent on 19 August—to take effect from 1 January 1923—four Groups were formed, having approximate geographical boundaries and consisting of the railway companies within those limits.

The GWR suffered less under these arrangements because it remained more or less the same entity, expanded by the absorption of several smaller companies. Its allotted territory included most of Wales and the Marches, Somerset, S Devon and most of Cornwall. Including leased and worked lines, this made it the third in size of the 'Big Four'; at 3,800 route miles, it was just under half the size of the largest, the LMS. No less than 3,565 of this mileage had been owned by the seven constituent companies, the six additional to the GWR itself being the Barry, Cambrian, Cardiff, Rhymney, Taff Vale, and the Alexandra (Newport & S Wales) Docks & Railways (all qv). These were absorbed from 1 January 1922.

Another 26 companies joined the GWR Group as subsidiary undertakings at various dates:

Grouping *'Hooray! Never even blew me cap off!' 'None of the companies which survive the amalgamation upheaval have come out of it with so much enhanced prestige as the Great Western' – South Wales News leading article, November 1922.* (GWR Magazine)

From 1 January 1922
Port Talbot Railway & Docks
Princetown
Rhondda & Swansea Bay
Ross & Monmouth
West Somerset
Cleobury Mortimer & Ditton Priors LR
Neath & Brecon
Brecon & Merthyr Tydfil Junction
Burry Port & Gwendreath (sic) Valley
Vale of Glamorgan
Wrexham & Ellesmere
Lampeter, Aberayron & New Quay

From 1 January 1923
Didcot, Newbury & Southampton
Gwendraeth Valleys
Llanelly & Mynydd Mawr
Penarth Extension
Penarth Harbour Dock & Railway
South Wales Mineral
Mawddwy
Van
Welshpool & Llanfair
Liskeard & Looe

From 1 July 1923
Midland & South Western Junction
Teign Valley

Neither the Exeter nor the Forest of Dean Central Railways had sorted out their affairs by this date, but were subsequently absorbed after an Amalgamation Tribunal.

(*See also individual company and line entries*)

CA

GREAT WESTERN RAILWAY.

PADDINGTON STATION,
LONDON, W. 2,
October, 1923.

DEAR SIR, OR MADAM,

I beg to inform you that the Directors are now prepared to issue Certificates of Stock of the Great Western Company in exchange for the Certificates of Stock of the Penarth Harbour Dock and Railway Company which has been amalgamated with this Company.

If you will be good enough to fill up the attached form and forward it to the Registrar of the Company at this Station accompanied by the Stock Certificates which you hold the Certificates for Great Western Stock will be forwarded to you with as little delay as possible.

The undermentioned Railway Companies have also been amalgamated with, or absorbed by, the Great Western Company :—

Alexandra (Newport & S. Wales) Docks & Railway Company
Barry Railway Company
Cambrian Railways Company
Cardiff Railway Company
Rhymney Railway Company
Brecon & Merthyr Tydfil Junction Railway Company
Burry Port & Gwendreath Valley Railway Company
Cleobury Mortimer & Ditton Priors Light Railway Company
Neath & Brecon Railway Company
Port Talbot Railway & Docks Company
Rhondda & Swansea Bay Railway Company
Ross & Monmouth Railway Company
Taff Vale Railway Company
Vale of Glamorgan Railway Company
West Somerset Railway Company
Wrexham & Ellesmere Railway Company

Certificates for Stocks, Shares, and Securities of any of these Companies may also be forwarded for exchange for Certificates of the Great Western Stock into which they have been converted.

I am,
Your obedient Servant,
A. E. BOLTER,
Secretary.

Grouping *Document advising shareholders of absorbed railways that the GWR was ready to exchange its own Certificates of Stock for those of the old companies, which were to be forwarded to Paddington with the attached form.* (W. Adams Collection)

GUPPY, THOMAS RICHARD

Born in 1797, he was one of the prime founders of the GWR. He became an original Bristol Director, and later, for a short time, a Director of the Bristol & Exeter Railway (qv) also. He achieved a certain notoriety at the opening of the railway when he walked from one end of the carriage roofs to the other while the train was at full speed! Despite this he survived to the ripe old age of 85. He was closely involved with Brunel (qv) in the construction of his steamships, the *Great Britain* and the *Great Western*. He became Manager of the Cwmavon Copper Works in 1844, and practised in Naples from 1849, as a mechanical engineer from 1854. He died in Portici, Naples, on 28 June 1882.

CA

HALESOWEN BRANCH

Stations: Old Hill, Coombes Holloway Halt (1 m), Halesowen (1½ m)

The short GWR branch from Old Hill to Halesowen continued south as a joint GWR/Midland line to join the latter's Bristol–Birmingham route at Northfield Junction, Longbridge. The 1 m 43 ch GWR portion had been authorized by a West Midland Railway (qv) Act of 17 July 1862, with opening on 1 March 1878, while the 5 m 70 ch joint line dated from the Halesowen & Bromsgrove Railway Act of 5 July 1865, with opening not taking place until 10 September 1883. Powers in the 1862 Act for a branch to Halesowen Basin were revived by the GWR in 1898 and this 54 ch line opened on 2 April 1902.

The GWR operated a local service between Old Hill and Halesowen until 5 December 1927, using push-pull or railmotor (qv) units to work up to 18 services each way on weekdays. By then the Kings Norton–Halesowen service had already ended, apart from trains carrying workmen to and from the Longbridge car works. The line to Halesowen continued to be important for goods, the Canal Basin having a 12-ton crane and four private sidings.

GB

'HALL' CLASS

In 1924 Collett (qv) fitted No 2925 *Saint Martin* with 6-foot diameter wheels and a side-window cab in response to a request from the Running Department for an improved version of the Churchward (qv) 'Moguls', and the result was to influence British mixed-traffic locomotive designs until the end of steam. *Saint Martin* proved satisfactory, and the initial production batch which started to appear in 1928 numbered no fewer than 80. Over the next 10 years the class increased to a total of 186, with additional locomotives being added to stock every year except 1932 and 1934. Named after Halls, most of which were situated in GWR territory, they differed in minor details only from the prototype, and were versatile and popular. Construction continued during the Second World War, but from 1944 a number of modifications to the design was made by Hawksworth (qv), who had succeeded Collett as CME in 1941.

The main differences with these 'Modified Hall' Class locomotives, numbered from 6959 upwards, were the use of three-row superheaters and full-length plate frames, the latter necessitating a new design of cylinder casting. By the time the

'Hall' Class *4-6-0 No 4947* Nanhoran Hall. (GWR Museum, Swindon)

last of them was built in 1950, the class totalled 330, of which 70 were of the 'Modified' variety. From the middle of 1941, wartime shortages prevented name-plates being fitted, and the words 'Hall Class' were painted on the centre splasher. All the locomotives concerned were named in the usual way after the war. The idea of a two-cylinder 4-6-0 with 6-foot wheels was taken from Swindon to Crewe by Stanier, and resulted in his Class '5MTs' and the BR standard version which followed, while Thompson, on the LNER, used the same basic layout for his equally successful 'B1s'.

(*See also Locomotives*)

PWBS

HALTS AND PLATFORMS

When competition with road transport became a problem, the GWR more than any other line instituted a policy of opening small wayside stations called 'haltes' to counter it. They were the brainchild of T. I. Allen (qv), and were intended as unmanned stopping-places for the steam railmotors (qv) which he introduced in 1903. The more English spelling of 'halt' was adopted by 1905, and up until 1947 the GWR opened almost twice as many as any other company. By the outbreak of the Great War, 145 were in use, and though some closed as a wartime economy, 169 were opened between 1927 and 1935. Appleford Halt, between Didcot and Oxford, was curious in that tickets could only be obtained from the Post Office, a 100 yds or so from the platform. When the Post Office was closed, passengers had to travel ticketless and pay at their destination.

The 'platform', a term borrowed from Scotland, was usually longer and was manned by a senior-grade porter. The first opened was at Rodmarton (Tetbury branch, qv) on 1 September 1904—the last to lose its title was Wootton Wawen, between Bearley and Henley-in-Arden, on 6 May 1974. In all, about 420 halts and platforms were opened by the GWR between 1903 and 1947, and a further 36 were taken over with the Cambrian Railways (qv) at the Grouping.

CA

HAMBRO, SIR CHARLES JOCELYN

Chairman, 1940–5. The eldest son of Sir

Halts and platforms *Rudimentary sleeper-built Whitehall Halt on the Hemyock branch, and more substantial Wootton Wawen Platform, on the Bearley to Henley-in-Arden line, the last to lose its title in 1974.* (Lens of Sutton/Steamchest Collection)

Eric Hambro, he was born in London on 3 October 1897 and as joint Managing Director of the well-known banking house, he joined the GWR Board in September 1930. He became Deputy-Chairman in 1934 and six years later was elected to succeed Lord Horne (qv). On his own resignation in 1945, his place as Chairman was taken by Lord Portal (qv), though he continued to serve on the Board. He died on 28 August 1963.

CA

HAMMERSMITH & CITY RAILWAY

The GWR subscribed £185,000 to the world's first underground railway, the Metropolitan line from Bishop's Road to the City of London, and was the Metropolitan's partner in the Hammersmith & City Railway. The association allowed the GWR to operate through City services from its suburban stations and branches as well as sharing those on the Hammersmith line and via that point to Richmond.

GWR broad gauge trains began operating between Bishop's Road and Farringdon Street on 10 January 1863 and, despite a subsequent round of disputes and changes, GWR steam locomotives continued to work through to the City until 1 January 1907 when Metropolitan electric locomotives took over the Paddington–Aldgate portion. The through services themselves then lasted until 16 September 1939.

The GWR-Metropolitan partnership in the 1861 Hammersmith & City Railway was confirmed by a joint agreement of 1 July 1867 which made the companies equal partners in the 2 m 38 ch mixed gauge line opened from the site of Westbourne Park to Hammersmith on 13 June 1864 and the link to the West London line (qv) which followed on 1 July. All services were 'narrow' gauge from 1 June 1869, including those via the 1870 link to the LSWR at Hammersmith, and used the new flyunder west of Royal Oak from 1878.

(*See also Electrification*)

GB

Hammersmith & City Railway *The GWR & Metropolitan station at Hammersmith, just behind the bustle of the Broadway.* (Lens of Sutton)

HART, WILLIAM ALBERT

Born at Bradpole, Dorset, in 1846, Hart entered railway service in 1866, in the Passenger Department at Swansea. He was transferred to Portskewett Junction in the same year, and moved in 1867 to the Divisional Superintendent's Office in Newport. After a further move to Cardiff, he went as Station Master to Slough and Bristol, before becoming Station Master at Paddington in 1879. He became Superintendent of the London Division in 1893, in which post he was responsible for the comfort of royal travellers journeying between London and Windsor. In 1897 Queen Victoria presented him with a silver tea and coffee service as a token of gratitude, and King Edward later gave him a pin of diamonds and rubies. He died on 2 April 1910 and is buried at Bradpole.

CA

HATTON JUNCTION

The original station, just plain 'Hatton', was opened by the GWR on 1 October 1852 as part of the Birmingham & Oxford Junction Railway (qv) line from Fenny Compton to Snow Hill. It became a junction from 10 October 1860 when the Stratford-on-Avon Railway was opened, and eventually handled services to Stratford, Honeybourne and Cheltenham as well as Leamington Spa/ Warwick– Birmingham locals.

Hatton Junction station was sited near the Warwick & Birmingham Canal and consisted of a main up platform plus down island and coal yard beyond. The Stratford (qv) and Birmingham lines parted beyond the country end overbridge with the 1897 avoiding line then following.

GB

HAWKSWORTH, FREDERICK WILLIAM

Chief Mechanical Engineer, 1941–47. Hawksworth was the GWR's last CME. True to tradition, he was a long-time servant of the company—indeed, his apprenticeship was longer than any of his predecessors, for it had lasted 43 years. He had designed the frame of the company's only 'Pacific', *The Great Bear* (qv), back in 1907, but there was no opportunity for him to repeat such a spectacular coup during his short period in charge.

Despite what Bulleid was up to on the Southern Railway, the GWR, taking on much war work, could only find the opportunity to build a limited number of tender and tank 0-6-0s, some more 'Halls' (qv), the latter incorporating modifications to the frame and cylinders, and some Stanier-design LMS 2-8-0s. Hawksworth would have liked to have introduced a 'Pacific' but had to be content with the high-pressure, double-chimney, two-cylinder 'County' Class (qv) 4-6-0s. Neither a failure nor an outstanding success, the 30 engines of this interesting class were a footnote rather than a key element in the long story of GWR locomotive design. 'Castle', 'Hall' and 'Manor' 4-6-0s, but no 'Counties', continued to be built in the early days of British Railways. Hawksworth stayed on after Nationalization as CME of the Western Region. He retired on the last day of 1949, and with his going his post disappeared too.

(*See also Locomotives*)

MCHB

Frederick William Hawksworth
(GWR Museum, Swindon)

HAY BRANCH

Stations: Pontrilas, Abbeydore ($2\frac{1}{4}$ m), Bacton ($3\frac{1}{2}$ m), Vowchurch ($6\frac{1}{4}$ m), Peterchurch ($7\frac{3}{4}$ m), Dorstone ($10\frac{1}{2}$ m), Westbrook ($13\frac{1}{4}$ m), Greens Siding ($14\frac{1}{4}$ m), Clifford ($16\frac{1}{2}$ m), Hay ($18\frac{3}{4}$ m)

Like many small railway enterprises, the Golden Valley Railway saw itself becoming part of a major rail route, in this case from the Severn to the Mersey. Needless to say, its hopes were not realized. Having obtained its enabling Act on 13 July 1876, the company managed to open the section between Pontrilas and Dorstone on 1 September 1881, but then took until 27 May 1889 to reach the Welsh border at Hay. Operating losses forced the closure of this section after only eight years, with closure of the remainder following on 20 April 1898.

The GWR purchased the remains of the Golden Valley enterprise from the liquidator on 1 July 1899 and reopened it as a conventional single-line branch from 1 May 1901. The passenger service, which lasted until 15 December 1941, varied from four to six trains on weekdays. Trains used a down side bay at Pontrilas and took 73–77 minutes to call at the intermediate stations, each with timber buildings, a single operational platform and a goods line. 'One engine in steam' working applied, the train staff unlocking ground frames for goods shunting.

GB

HAYLE

Cornwall's pioneer Hayle Railway was authorized by an Act of 27 June 1834 to link the Cornish tin and copper industry with the busy port of Hayle. Opened in stages from 1837, the railway had a 12-mile main line from Hayle to Tresavean with rope-worked inclines at Angarrack and Penponds and 5 miles of branches to Portreath harbour, to the Crofty and Roskear mines, and into Redruth. It carried

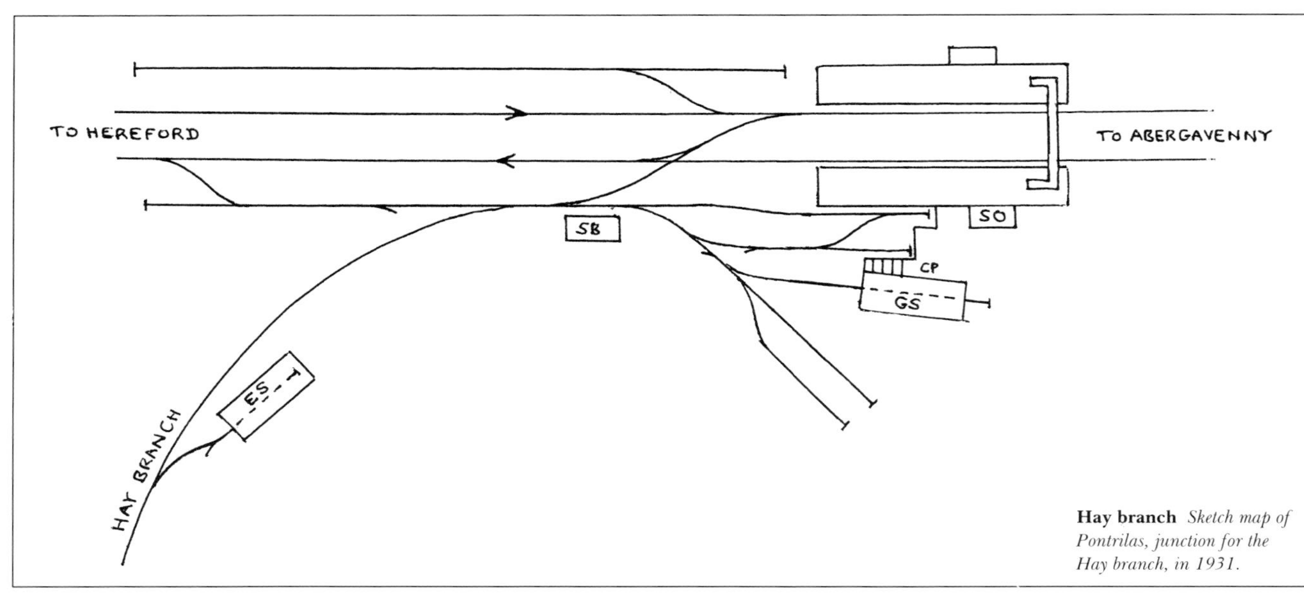

Hay branch *Sketch map of Pontrilas, junction for the Hay branch, in 1931.*

Hay branch *Pontrilas, looking north, with the Hay branch swinging away to the left. A mixed branch train stands at the bay platform.* (Steamchest Collection)

a passenger service from 22 May 1843, but was absorbed into the West Cornwall Railway (qv) by that company's Act of 3 August 1846.

The original Hayle Railway terminus in Foundry Square closed on 16 February 1852 and was replaced by the WCR station on 11 March. A connection down to the wharves was retained as the Hayle Wharves Branch and this continued in use, with a horse providing the motive power, until 1967.

The WCR route crossed the Hayle River by a high viaduct with the station and Hayle Wharves connection at its London end, a loop from the latter passing outside the up platform. An old engine house stood in the angle between the two lines with a small goods depot opposite.

GB

HELSBY BRANCH

Stations: Hooton, Little Sutton (1¾ m), Ellesmere Port (3¾ m), Ince & Elton (7 m), Helsby (9 m)

The long, straight double track east from Hooton (qv) to the Chester–Warrington line (qv) at Helsby was authorized to the Birkenhead Railway on 1 August 1859 and opened under GWR and LNWR ownership on 1 July 1863. It was later linked to the Cheshire Lines Committee via Helsby and carried through Birkenhead (qv) services in addition to the branch trains. Some of the latter terminated at Ellesmere Port which had grown steadily first with the opening of the Manchester Ship Canal (1894) and then with the development of the docks and the Stanlow refinery complex (1922). The branch had 13 private sidings at Ellesmere Port, with another 17 served via the MSC lines.

GB

HELSTON BRANCH

Stations: Gwinear Road, Praze (3 m), Nancegollan (5¼ m), Truthall Platform (7 m), Helston (9 m)

The remote and modest West Cornwall Railway (qv) station at Gwinear Road became a junction when the 8 m 67 ch Helston branch was opened on 9 May 1887. Its nameboard later read 'Gwinear Road. For Helston, The Lizard, Mullion and Portleven', the latter points being reached by bus services from the Helston terminus, and a reminder that the GWR's first use of 'motor cars' was from Helston to The Lizard on 17 August 1903 (qv Omnibus and chara-banc services).

A single line with a passing loop at Nancegollan and worked in its later years by electric train staff, the branch had been authorized by the Helston Railway Act of 9 July 1880 and was worked by the GWR until full absorption from 1 July 1898. From the south side of the down island platform at Gwinear Road the route headed past that station's main sidings before beginning the 25-minute journey to Helston's complex of single platform and goods, carriage, engine and road motor sheds. It carried significant quantities of flowers, vegetables, livestock and parcels in addition to the 8–10 weekday passenger trains each way.

GB

HEMYOCK BRANCH

Stations: Tiverton Junction, Coldharbour Halt (2¼ m), Uffculme (2¾ m), Culmstock (5 m), Whitehall Halt (6¼ m), Hemyock (7¼ m)

Authorized under the original 'light railway' legislation of 1868, the Culm Valley Light Railway was incorporated on 15 May 1873, opened on 29 May 1876 and sold to the GWR for £33,000 four years later.

Hemyock branch *Uffculme station.* (Lens of Sutton)

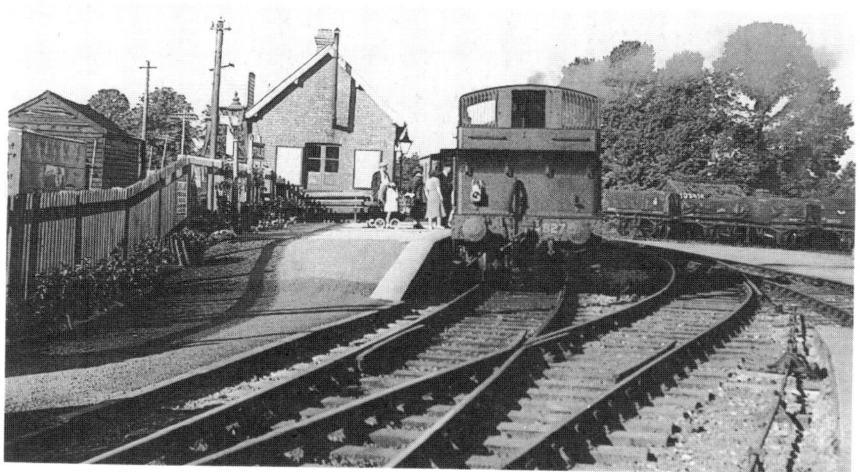

The line curvature restricted trains to 15 mph, with GWR 0-4-2T engines hauling special coaches, and all vehicles limited to 13 tons 18 cwts per axle (except for grain vans). Working was by 'one engine in steam' with a train staff and special provision for propelling empty stock from Uffculme to Tiverton Junction. Hemyock's single-platform terminus lay beside the River Culm and included engine, carriage and goods sheds and a siding for milk tanks to and from the dairy.

GB

HENLEY-ON-THAMES BRANCH

Stations: Twyford, Wargrave (1¾ m), Shiplake (2¾ m), Henley-on-Thames (4½ m)

From a country-end, up side bay at Twyford, this 4 m 49 ch branch ran north to the Thames at Henley, crossing the river by means of Shiplake Viaduct on the way. The GWR originally sought authority for it in 1846, received it on 22 July 1847, revived it in 1853 and finally opened the route on 1 June 1857. The gauge was converted at record speed between 9.30 pm on 24 March 1876 and 9.30 am the following day, and the route was doubled just before the station at Wargrave was added in 1900. Between 1905 and 1908 the line was used for Automatic Train Control (qv) experiments.

Henley-on-Thames branch *A notice convening a meeting to support the railway to the town, October 1852.* (GWR Magazine)

HENLEY RAILWAY.

PUBLIC MEETING

Having received a requisition numerously signed to convene a Meeting of the Inhabitants of this Town and Neighbourhood, for the purpose of considering the best means to be adopted for introducing a Railway into the Town.

I hereby *convene* a Meeting of the Inhabitants of this Town and Neighbourhood for the above purpose, to be held in the TOWN HALL, on THURSDAY, the 28th of OCTOBER instant, at Three o'Clock in the Afternoon.

EDWARD YOUNG,
Mayor.

Henley, 16th October, 1852.

C. KINCH, PRINTER, HENLEY.

The branch enjoyed a good service, including morning through trains to Paddington and evening returns, including one slip coach (qv) service. Traffic rose to a peak in Regatta Week when all three platforms at the Henley terminus would be busy and every siding needed for stabling.

GB

HEREFORD

Hereford's status as an important junction on the 'North & West' main line gave it some excellent long-distance services on that route (eg Birkenhead and Manchester to Cardiff and the South West) and on the route to Paddington via Oxford. The Birmingham–Cardiff expresses called and the city enjoyed local services on its five radiating lines, including trains to Wolverhampton via Shrewsbury, and Gloucester via Ross-on-Wye.

The Shrewsbury & Hereford Railway was the first to serve the cathedral city, its trains operating from Barr's Court station from 6 December 1853. Those of the Newport, Abergavenny & Hereford Railway (qv) began serving Barton on 2 January 1854, that company completing a link to the S&H at Barr's Court Junction soon after. This was, in fact, done on behalf of the Worcester & Hereford Railway (qv) whose route east from Shelwick Junction was completed by the West Midland Railway (qv) on 15 September 1861. In 1862 the LNWR and GWR companies leased the S&H, in 1874 the Midland's station at Moorfields was closed and its trains transferred to Barr's Court, and in 1893 the Barton passenger services followed suit. This later allowed abandonment of the former NA&H line north of Redhill Junction in favour of a

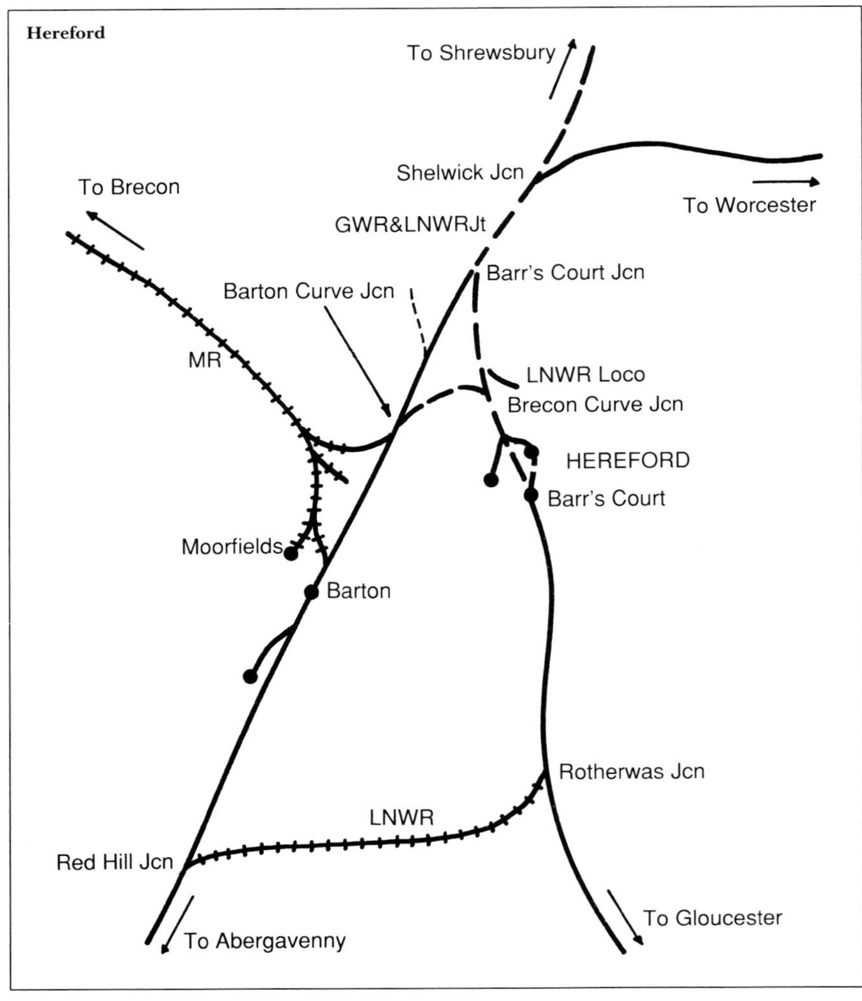

link to Rotherwas junction on the line opened by the Hereford, Ross & Gloucester Railway on 1 June 1855.

Barr's Court station consisted of a long narrow Gothic building with strong gables on the down platform, an up island and up and down side goods depots at the north end. Barton remained open for goods, including control of Bulmer's siding, and the area had several engine sheds, permanent way depots and a breakdown van.

GB

HIGHBRIDGE

Highbridge was an exchange point between the GWR and Somerset & Dorset systems, the latter's Glastonbury–Burnham-on-Sea line crossing the GWR on the level at the London end of Highbridge station. The GWR platforms straddled the River Brue and were linked to those of the S&D, both companies having goods lines and special instructions for the transfer of freight traffic. GWR exchange wagons were worked via the Permissive down goods loop or the up connection to Highbridge Wharf.

GB

HIGHWORTH BRANCH

Stations: Swindon, Stratton (2¼ m), Stanton (4¼ m), Hannington (5¼ m), Highworth (6½ m)

The Highworth branch was a very unpretentious single-line railway which ran northwards from a junction on the London side of Swindon (qv) to the small town of Highworth. The route was tortuous, the service sparse and the stations just a combination of platform, goods loop and small shelter or timber building.

Incorporated as the Swindon & Highworth Railway on 29 July 1875, the local venture could not raise the funds to complete construction and was taken over by the GWR on 1 July 1882. Opening followed on 9 May 1883.

The GWR provided a service of 4–5 trains each way on weekdays, catering primarily for people working in Swindon. Operation was by train staff and 'one engine in steam' until 1941 when electric token working was introduced.

GB

HIGH WYCOMBE BRANCH

Stations: Maidenhead, Cookham (3 m), Bourne End (4½ m), Wooburn Green (5¾ m), Loudwater (7¼ m), High Wycombe (9¾ m)

This line started life as part of the Wycombe Railway, authorized by an Act of 27 July 1846, leased to the GWR and opened as far as High Wycombe on 1 August 1854. Carrying through services from Paddington as well as local trains, it ran due north from Maidenhead (qv) to cross the Thames just before the Bourne End junction for the Marlow branch (qv). The single line then looped through Wooburn Green and followed the River Wye into High Wycombe which was rebuilt for the opening of the GW&GCJR (qv) Acton line with through lines, staggered platforms and a bay for branch trains. Bourne End consisted of a branch platform plus passing loop platforms which could also be used by branch trains.

GB

HOLIDAY AND EXCURSION TRAFFIC

When the GWR was born in 1835, very few people in Britain could afford a holiday. The railways, more than any other factor, made holidays for all, or almost all, possible, and the GWR probably played a greater part in this, in relation to its size, than any other line.

The years immediately after 1900 saw the GWR publicity (qv) machine move into top gear. 'Why go abroad, when there is a perfectly good Riviera at home?' was the slogan—and not just in summer, for the Devon and Cornish seaside towns were advertised as all-the-year-round resorts. Nevertheless it was the summer months which saw vast numbers heading westwards.

On Summer Saturdays the 'Cornish Riviera' (qv) and other West of England expresses would run in several parts and all manner of coaches would be provided. Although large numbers of fine corridor carriages were built from the 1890s onwards, it was still common in the 1930s for excursion trains to be made up of long rakes of non-corridor vehicles usually employed on suburban services in the London and Birmingham areas. A rake of three non-corridor sets would provide seats for over 850 passengers, nearly double that of a similar-sized corridor train with a restaurant car, but with no lavatories the long journey must have been agony for some.

Heavy seaside traffic continued after the Second World War (16,433 passengers arrived at Torquay on an August Saturday in 1957), Weston-super-Mare could expect in excess of 30,000 on a Bank Holiday, Porthcawl ('The Brighton of Cardiff') might expect 10,000, while 5,000 came on each summer Saturday to Newquay's thrice extended platforms and Butlin's holiday camp at Minehead stretched the single-track branch to the limits of its capacity.

There was also other regular excursion traffic, for hop-pickers to Hereford and Worcestershire, railway enthusiasts to Swindon, Swindon employees and their families on the annual 'Trip' works outings (qv Swindon Works), and in the 1930s rakes of saloon carriages, several of which have been preserved, were specially built to challenge the growing popularity of the road motor coach. The days when hundreds of carriages were kept specially for a few summer outings are long gone, but holiday traffic on BR's Western Region to Devon and Cornwall is still so heavy that no one is allowed on a holiday train on summer Friday nights and Saturdays without a reservation.

MCHB

HONEYBOURNE

The original Honeybourne station was provided by the Oxford, Worcester & Wolverhampton Railway (qv) on 4 June 1853, the route being doubled two years later and a 9½-mile branch to Stratford-on-Avon (qv) added on 12 July 1859. The latter was to become part of the GWR's new route from Bristol to Birmingham following the opening of a new line to Cheltenham on 1 August 1906 (qv Cheltenham–Birmingham line).

The new route passed beneath the Oxford line east of Honeybourne but had spurs to link it with the new four-platform station provided there. The latter enjoyed a service to Cheltenham and calls by Leamington/Stratford–Worcester trains in addition to those on its original route.

GB

CROSS COUNTRY SERVICES to and from the SOUTH COAST RESORTS The whole journey without change!

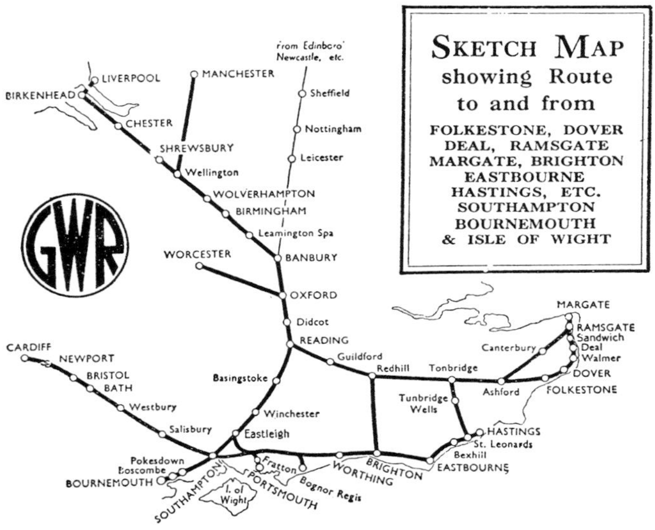

Through Express Services are run by the G.W.R. between the following centres and South Coast Resorts, with connections to and from intermediate stations.

BIRKENHEAD, CHESTER SHREWSBURY, WOLVERHAMPTON BIRMINGHAM, LEAMINGTON SPA BANBURY, OXFORD and BRIGHTON, HASTINGS, RAMSGATE MARGATE, FOLKESTONE, DOVER & DEAL		BIRKENHEAD, CHESTER MANCHESTER, SHREWSBURY WOLVERHAMPTON BIRMINGHAM, LEAMINGTON SPA, BANBURY, OXFORD and SOUTHAMPTON, PORTSMOUTH & BOURNEMOUTH

CARDIFF, NEWPORT, BRISTOL (Stapleton Road), BATH and WORTHING, HOVE & BRIGHTON

RESTAURANT CAR TRAINS

For full particulars see the Company's Official Time Tables and Notices.

Holiday and excursion traffic *Reading and Banbury, and their Southern and LNER (GCR) connections, form the hub of this 1937 advertisement from* Holiday Haunts *for through holiday services from Merseyside and the Midlands to the South Coast.*

Honeybourne

HOOTON

This multi-platform station on the Birkenhead Joint Lines of the GWR and LNWR had branches east to Helsby (qv) and west to West Kirby (qv). In addition to the branch services the station handled a large number of local trains from Birkenhead (qv) and Rock Ferry plus Birkenhead–Chester semi-fasts and longer-distance trains. It had a small goods depot, an exchange siding and private sidings serving brick and water-works companies.

The main line was opened by the Chester & Birkenhead Railway on 23 September 1840, the Helsby branch added on 1 July 1863, and that to Parkgate on 1 October 1866, with extension to West Kirby on 19 April 1886.

GB

HORNE, VISCOUNT SIR ROBERT STEVENSON

Chairman, 1934–40. Born on 28 February 1871, he entered politics as Unionist MP for Glasgow Hillhead in 1918, and was at once appointed Minister of Labour. He became President of the Board of Trade from 1920–21, then Chancellor of the Exchequer until 1922. After leaving Parliament he took a number of Directorships, among them the GWR, of which he became Chairman, succeeding Viscount Churchill (qv) in 1934. One of his first tasks was to see the GWR through its Centenary celebrations (qv), which he did most ably. He died suddenly on 3 September 1940, at Farnham, his place as Chairman being taken by Sir Charles Hambro (qv).

CA

HORSES

Until the 1930s, horses reigned supreme on the GWR, as on other lines, in teams of one, two, three or four hauling the delivery vans which plied between station and customer.

Hooton *'Junction for Neston, Parkgate, Heswall, West Kirby, Ellesmere Port and Helsby' proclaims the nameboard as a '43xx' 2-6-0 passes through with a freight.* (Steamchest Collection)

Even after road motor vehicles (qv) superseded them in these duties, many were retained, and, for their care, a team of vets was also on the payroll. Apart from their health, GWR working horses were the responsibility of the Chief Goods Manager—when T. H. Rendell (qv) took over this office in 1904, there were 2,700 horse on the company's books. They were used also for goods yard work, and most stations had at least one shunting horse, Birmingham Snow Hill no less than the humblest wayside station. And it was in Birmingham on 4 May 1914 that a parade of GWR horses took place, prompting the *Great Western Railway Magazine* to hope that it might become a regular event, as indeed it did. At Nationalisation, BR owned more than 8,000 horses, the last, Charlie, of Newmarket, not retiring until 21 February 1967.

CA

Horses *A finely turned out pair of dray horses pose outside the Royal Waiting Room at Windsor & Eton station.* (National Railway Museum, York)

HOTELS

The GWR's involvement with hotels was a complex one, dating back to the mid-1800s. These activities were closely associated with the operation of station refreshment rooms and, later, their restaurant cars. The running of such establishments has always been particularly subject to current management fashions and the prevailing wisdom on whether to concentrate on the company's core business, or go in for vertical integration. As a result, the number of hotels owned or operated by the GWR during its existence changed frequently. For instance, although several hotels were taken over in 1875 when the GWR amalgamated with the Bristol & Exeter Railway (qv), they were all let to other organizations to operate. Even their showpiece, the Great Western Royal Hotel at Paddington, was initially leased to a number of the Directors and shareholders. At the end of 1923, the GWR annual report showed that it owned the following hotels:

Albion, Plymouth
Fishguard Bay, Fishguard
George & Railway, Bristol
Great Western, Taunton
Great Western Royal, Paddington
Marine, Penarth Dock
Portishead, Portishead
Tregenna Castle, St Ives

Hotels *An advertisement for the Tregenna Castle Hotel, St Ives, from the 1937 edition of* Holiday Haunts.

When the railway was nationalized at the beginning of 1948, only six were handed over to the British Transport Commission, in spite of the company having bought and enlarged a new one during the intervening period. Of these six, only half were owned and worked by the GWR, two others being worked by other companies, while the last was not owned by the railway, but worked by them. It is thus impossible to provide here a detailed account of the whole of the GWR's hotel business, and we can only deal with some of the highlights of its better-known establishments.

Pride of place must inevitably be given to the Great Western Royal Hotel at Paddington (qv), which formed the front of the London terminus, and had its own entrance direct from the 'Lawn'. Two weeks after the present station came into operation in 1854, it was visited by Prince Albert and the Prince of Wales, and the 'royal' connection was established. The lease referred to above expired in 1896, and the hotel was thereafter operated directly by the GWR, and the management of all its hotel and catering activities was subsequently based there. It was enlarged on a number of occasions, and by 1907 lifts and electric lights had been installed, while, in the days before the telephone, guests could send messages by pneumatic tube from their rooms to the kitchen and telegraph office. The Chief Engineer's plans to replace Brunel's train shed in the late 1920s with concrete ones would also have affected the hotel, but these excesses were fortunately avoided. Although comfortable and well-appointed, the hotel never had illusions of grandeur, unlike the Midland's at St Pancras, and, as a result, it has remained in use as a very popular hotel through to the present day, although it was sold off by British Rail, like all their other hotels.

Down in west Cornwall, the GWR leased Tregenna Castle at St Ives (qv), with its extensive grounds, in 1878, and it was converted into a hotel. It was supervised by the small group of Directors who were currently looking after the one at Neyland which the GWR had acquired when they had taken over the South Wales Railway (qv). The property was purchased outright in 1895. During the period between the two World Wars, it was repeatedly extended, and a golf course was laid out for the convenience of guests. The Home Farm in its grounds, which provided dairy produce for the hotel, was also noted for the prizes won by its cattle at agricultural shows in the area.

Another GWR hotel in the West Country which was always busy at holiday times was the Manor House Hotel at Moretonhampstead (qv), which was purchased and converted by the company in 1929, only to require a further extension in 1935. It could boast a full 24-hole golf course, which put it 'one-up' on the Tregenna Castle. On the other hand, over in West Wales, the Fishguard Bay Hotel had eight miles of its own fishing waters, which were restocked with trout in 1925.

Between Liskeard and the popular resort of Looe (qv), the branch passenger service was complicated to operate, with trains having to reverse at Coombe Junction. Using some of the low-interest money available from the government in the 1930s, the GWR proposed to build a line direct to Looe from St Germans (qv), with a hotel being constructed alongside the new terminus. A fast shuttle service to and from Plymouth was to have been operated by streamlined diesel railcars (qv). Although preliminary work on the line started before the war, the scheme was never revived, although reference was made to the hotel in C. Barman's book *Next Station* (GWR, 1947). The 1930s plans for a new hotel at Snow Hill, Birmingham, were also abandoned. During the Second World War, the Manor House Hotel was requisitioned from 1940 until 1946, and part of the Fishguard Bay Hotel was used by the armed forces.

As part of the GWR's post-Second World War refurbishment plans, some additional hotels were to have been provided. Two of them, each with some 200 rooms, would have been in South Wales, and the one at Swansea was to have had a sun-terrace where guests could gaze out across the sea towards Mumbles. Neither was built, and the same happened to a smaller one being planned for Swindon at the same time.

(*See also Refreshment rooms*)

PWBS

HOWBEACH COLLIERY BRANCH

Successor to an 1830 scheme to provide a tramroad for the undeveloped central area of the Forest of Dean, this line was eventually authorized to the Forest of Dean Central Railway by an Act of 11 July 1856, with support from the Commissioners of Woods and despite opposition from the Severn & Wye Railway (qv). Twelve years of financial, legal and constructional difficulties followed before completion by the GWR and opening on 25 May 1868. Even with the GWR working the line for half of the gross earnings, the traffic warranted only 'one engine a day, every other day', and the interest and land rental charges pushed the owning company deeper and deeper into debt. No shareholders could be located when the enterprise passed to the GWR at Grouping!

The single line west from Awre Junction steadily steepened to 1 in 58 over its 4½-mile length. Worked by 'one engine in steam' and limited to 10 mph, it had an intermediate goods station at Blakeney which had a curved trackside loading dock and a 3-ton crane and was fairly busy during the Second World War. Working beyond Blakeney ceased in the 1920s and the rest of the line closed on 2 August 1949.

GB

HUBBARD, ALEXANDER

Director, 1878–1908. Hubbard was born in Rochester, but rose in public life in the West Country, becoming a JP, Mayor of Plymouth and Chairman of Plymouth Great Western Docks Company. He was also a director of both the Cornwall and South Devon Railways (qv), becoming Chairman of the latter in 1874. He was appointed to the GWR Board on the absorption of the SDR (1878). He was elected joint Deputy-Chairman with Viscount Emlyn (qv) in 1890, and though he stood down from this office in 1906 he remained a member of the Board until 1908.

CA

INGLIS, SIR JAMES CHARLES

General Manager, 1903–11. Born in 1851 in Aberdeen, as a Civil Engineer most of his work was done south of the Border, and he was concerned in the building of the Alexandra Docks, Newport (qv), the harbour at Newlyn and the Batter Breakwater at Plymouth. He was appointed Assistant Chief Engineer in 1892, succeeding to the post of (Civil) Engineer the same year. On the death of Sir Joseph Wilkinson (qv) in 1903 he was made General Manager, but became increasingly frustrated at the lack of financial control held by his new Department, in particular the high costs incurred by the Locomotive & Carriage Superintendent's Department. Knighted in January 1911, he formulated a plan to make the General Manager a 'Commander in Chief', as elsewhere, but died at Rottingdean on 19 December, before orders for his accepted plan were issued. He was buried at Kensington Cemetery.

CA

INSELL, ROBERT J.

Signal & Telegraph Engineer, 1923–28. Insell joined the GWR in 1881, becoming Chief Draughtsman at Reading Signal Works in 1893. He became Assistant to A. T. Blackall (qv) in 1900, and Chief Assistant in 1903. He was appointed Signal & Telegraph Engineer on 14 June 1923. He was a progressive engineer, and enthusiastic about the possibilities of power-operated signalling. He and C. M. Jacobs (qv) were the driving force behind the invention of the Audible Signal and Automatic Train Control (qv) and the installation of electric and electro-pneumatic signalling at several locations between 1905 and 1928 (qv Signalling). He suffered a painful accident in January 1925 from the effects of which he died on 25 March 1928.

AV

IRON DUKE

The first of the Gooch's (qv) famous '8-foot singles' was *Iron Duke*, built at Swindon in 1847, which gave its name to the class of 4-2-2s which typified his broad gauge express locomotives. It remained at work until 1871, when, like others of the class, it was 'renewed', the second locomotive of the same name appearing two years later. In Gooch's words, the original locomotives were responsible in 1848 for the working of . . . the express [from Paddington, which] was in the constant practice of running the 53 miles to Didcot, without stopping, in 48 to 59 minutes . . .' *Iron Duke* itself was one of those which reached 78 mph down Dauntsey Incline. A working reproduction was built for the National Railway Museum at York in 1985.

PWBS

JACOBS, CHARLES M.

Signal & Telegraph Engineer, 1928–36. Joining the GWR's Telegraph Department in 1882, he became Technical Assistant to the Telegraph Superintendent in August 1896, Electrical Assistant to the Signal Engineer in 1903, Assistant Signal Engineer in 1923, and Signal & Telegraph Engineer after the death of Insell (qv) in 1928. He retired in February 1936.

AV

JIGSAW PUZZLES

The famous series of GWR jigsaw puzzles began with No 1, 'Caerphilly Castle', sold at the British Empire Exhibition at Wembley in May 1924. The puzzles were sold beside the actual locomotive on display (qv), but at 5s each there was not a lot of interest. The

Jigsaw puzzles *'King Arthur on Dartmoor' of 1931.* (W. Adams Collection)

GWR therefore dropped the price to the cost price of 2s 6d, and subsequently sold 78,000. From then on the puzzles were considered as entirely promotional, and were all sold at cost.

GWR publicity (qv) was very imaginative and effective during this period, but the originator of this excellent idea has not been identified. During the next 15 years, over a million puzzles were produced by Chad Valley at Birmingham for the GWR, with three main subjects: railway, scenic views and historical scenes. The complete list of all known puzzles that went into general production and were publicly available is as follows:

'Caerphilly Castle' 150 pieces. Issued 1924, withdrawn 1927/28.

'The Cathedral'. This is a rarity being the only one which is double-sided, showing Exeter Cathedral on one side and a railway map of England and Wales on the other. 150 pieces. Issued 1926, withdrawn 1935.

'The Railway Station'. From Frith's famous painting. Despite the single title this came in a box with a twin puzzle showing Paddington Station. Both 150 pieces. Issued 1926, withdrawn 1929.

'Windsor Castle' 150 pieces. Issued 1926, withdrawn 1929/30.

'The *St Julien*' (a railway steamer) 150 pieces. Issued 1926, withdrawn 1928.

'*St Julien*' A three-quarter view of the same ship. 150 pieces. Issued 1927, withdrawn 1931.

'*King George V*' 150 pieces. One of a class which was the most powerful in Britain. Issued 1927, withdrawn 1936.

'Cornish Riviera Express' 150 pieces. Issued 1927, withdrawn 1936.

'The Freight Train' 150 pieces. Issued 1927/28, withdrawn 1930.

'Speed' 150 pieces. Issued 1928, withdrawn 1930.

'Britain's Mightiest' Another view of *King George V*. 150 pieces. Issued 1927/28, withdrawn 1930.

'Oxford' View up the High Street. 150 pieces. Issued 1927/28, withdrawn 1930.

'Swansea Docks' 150 pieces. Issued 1928, withdrawn 1932.

'Ann Hathaway's Cottage' 150 pieces. Issued 1930, withdrawn 1933.

'A Cornish Fishing Village' 150 pieces. Issued 1930, withdrawn 1933.

'Glorious Devon' 150 pieces. Issued 1930, withdrawn 1933.

'Springtime in Devon' Fingle Bridge 150 pieces. Issued 1930, withdrawn 1933.

'The Vikings Landing at St. Ives' Originally 375 pieces, increased to 400. Issued 1930, withdrawn 1936.

'St David's Cathedral' 150 pieces. Issued 1930, withdrawn 1934.

'Warwick Castle' 150 pieces. Issued 1930, withdrawn 1933.

'The Torbay Express' 375 pieces. Issued 1930, withdrawn 1934.

'Mountains of Killarney' 150 pieces. Issued 1931, withdrawn 1935.

'Windsor Castle' 150 pieces. Issued 1931, withdrawn 1933.

'King Arthur on Dartmoor' 375 pieces, then increased to 400. Issued 1931, withdrawn 1936.

'Bath' or 'Beau Nash's Bath' Street scene in Bath. 150/200 pieces. Issued 1932, withdrawn 1936.

'Stratford on Avon' View of Harvard House. 375 pieces, increased to 400. Issued 1933, withdrawn 1938.

'The Cheltenham Flyer' 150 pieces, increased to 200. Issued 1933, withdrawn 1936.

'Henley Bridge' 200 pieces. Issued 1933, withdrawn 1935.

'Historic Totnes' 200 pieces, decreased to 150. Issued 1933, withdrawn 1939.

'Piccadilly Circus' 200 pieces. Issued 1933, withdrawn 1937.

'The Romans at Caerleon' 200 pieces, then 150. Issued 1933, withdrawn 1939.

'The Royal Route to the West' Another view of *King George V* in the foothills of Dartmoor. 200 pieces, later 150. Issued 1933, withdrawn 1939.

'Brazenose College, Oxford' 400 pieces. Issued 1933, withdrawn 1939.

'Locomotives Old and New' Shows *Lord of the Isles* being overtaken by *King George V*. 200 pieces, later 150. Issued 1934, withdrawn 1939.

'Drake Comes West' 400 pieces. Issued 1934, withdrawn 1939.

'The Night Mail' 200 pieces. Issued 1934, withdrawn 1936.

'The Model Railway' 200 pieces, later 150. Issued 1935, withdrawn 1939.

'London Highways' 200 pieces. Issued 1935, withdrawn 1936.

'The Fishguard Army 1797' 200 pieces, later 150. Issued 1935, withdrawn 1939.

'The Streamline (D) Way' Shows a diesel railcar with a 'ghost' picture of *King George V* behind. 200 pieces, later 150. Issued 1935, withdrawn 1938.

'Windsor Castle from the Air' 200 pieces, later 150. Issued 1937, withdrawn 1939.

'GWR Locomotives in the Making' 200 pieces, later 150. Issued 1937, withdrawn 1939.

'Cornwall—Preparing for a Catch' 200 pieces, later 150. Issued 1937, withdrawn 1939.

This information was supplied by Rev Tom Tyler and Felicity Whiteley. Full details and illustrations of the GWR puzzles and others produced by Chad Valley can be found in their book Chad Valley Promotional Jig-saw Puzzles *(Magic Fairy Publishing, 1990) available from the publisher, Tel 0730 63459.*

JOINT LINES

The GWR became involved with numerous joint lines, the first of which was the Birmingham, Bristol & Thames Junction Railway (later to become the West London Railway, qv). This was of mixed gauge south of its crossing with the GWR, though no physical connection existed other than a wagon turntable. In 1846 the line became jointly owned with the London & Birmingham Railway, and broad gauge trains then ran to Victoria, part of which was leased to the GWR until 1933, although no GWR trains used it after 1915. In the south, lines around Weymouth (qv) were jointly owned with the LSWR, while the Halesowen branch, the Severn & Wye and the Avonmouth railways (all qv) were held with the Midland Railway. A line from Northolt Junction to Ashenden Junction was owned with the GCR (qv GW & GCJR), together with the Aylesbury branch (qv) from Princes Risborough.

By far the GWR's most frequent partner was the LNWR, with which it ran lines in the Wirral (Helsby/Hooton, Hooton/W Kirby, Chester/Birkenhead, all qv), and, in the Welsh Marches, Shrewsbury/ Buttington (including the Minsterley branch), Shrewsbury/Wellington, and Shrewsbury/Hereford (all qv). There were also two in the Ludlow area, the Clee Hill mineral line (qv Stone traffic) and the short branch from Woofferton (qv) to Tenbury Wells. Three GWR/LNWR lines lay in South Wales—Llandovery/Llandilo, Rhymney/Nantybwch, and the Brynmawr & Western Valleys branch—while the Brecon & Merthyr line (qv) from Pant to Merthyr became GWR/LMS Joint after the GWR absorbed the Brecon company in 1922. The approaches to Aberystwyth (qv) from both Shrewsbury and Carmarthen were jointly owned with the Cambrian Railways (qv), there was a short section joint with the Taff Vale Railway (qv) near Merthyr Tydfil, and the Taff Bargoed and the Merthyr/Quakers Yard lines were held with the Rhymney (qv). After the Grouping (qv), the GWR took over these routes completely.

CA

KEMBLE

In addition to its status as a stopping point for the main-line services from Paddington to Cheltenham and to Cardiff via Gloucester, Kemble was the junction for single line branches to Cirencester and Tetbury (both qv). The former ran from an adjoining platform on the up side, while the latter veered off west immediately beyond the end of the down bay. The station buildings stood in the angle between the up main and Cirencester platforms, with the 415 yd, single-track Kemble Tunnel at the London end of the station complex.

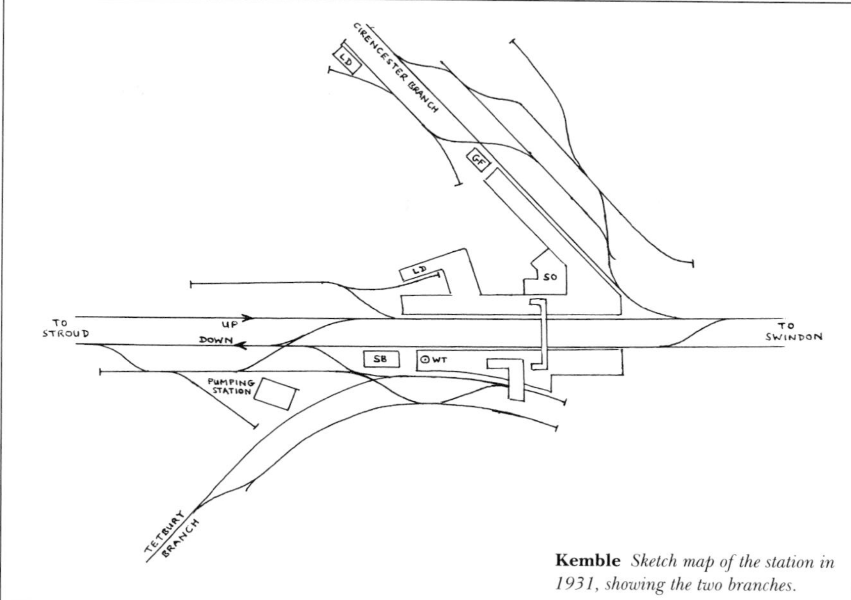

Kemble *Sketch map of the station in 1931, showing the two branches.*

The tunnel had been a condition of the landowner's consent for the original line, opened from Swindon to Kemble and Cirencester on 31 May 1841 and extended from the former to Standish on 12 May 1845. Squire Gordon had also refused to have a station on his land, and the original stopping point had been at Tetbury Road (later Coates) with just passenger exchange facilities at the actual junction. Kemble station proper came into use on 30 April 1872.

GB

KERRY BRANCH

This 3$\frac{3}{4}$-mile Cambrian Railways branch ran south from the main line at Abermule (qv Whitchurch–Aberystwyth line) to a generous one-platform station near the village of Kerry. Its single-line course curved at 1 in 43 up the wooded valley of the River Mule and served intermediate goods sidings at Fronfraith and Goitre, where the GWR opened halts after grouping. The passenger service, which began with the opening of the line on 2 March 1863 and ended on 9 February 1931, varied between one and seven trains each way on weekdays.

Timber traffic from the 60cm-gauge Kerry Tramway was exchanged at the goods depot at Kerry.

GB

KEYNSHAM

Keynsham was the only intermediate station opened with the Bristol-Bath section of the GWR on 31 August 1840. It subsequently acquired neighbours at Oldfield Park (1929), Twerton (1840), Saltford (1840) and St Anne's Park (1898), but lost one of the four tunnels on the section when the approaches to Bristol were widened. Served by Swindon/Chippenham/Bath–Bristol local trains plus those on the Avon Valley line, Keynsham was also notable for its paper mill and chocolate factory sidings.

GB

KIDDERMINSTER

Kidderminster had one of the most ornate station buildings on the GWR system. The two-storey frontage was in a very elaborate half-timbered style with dormers, awnings

Keynsham *Note the splendid 1880s-pattern covered latticework footbridge.* (Steamchest Collection)

and bargeboards adding to its dramatic overall appearance. It has been suggested that the 1863 structure had been destined for Stratford-on-Avon but was diverted in sectional form when the first Kidderminster station burned down.

Behind this grand frontage Kidderminster dealt with services on the old Oxford, Worcester & Wolverhampton (qv) route, to Tenbury Wells and Woofferton (qv), along the Severn Valley line (qv Worcester–Shrewsbury line) and the local workings to Bewdley. In the sugar beet season it was busy with wagons to and from the BSC factory, with all the shunting that entailed.

GB

KIDWELLY

Originally opened by the South Wales Railway (qv) on 11 October 1852, Kidwelly was a conventional two-platform station served mainly by local stopping services. East of the station the up side goods yard was followed by a connection to the Gwendraeth Valleys Railway and thence to the Burry Port & Gwendraeth Valley concern's branch to Kidwelly Quay. The GVR, which passed to the GWR under the 1923 Grouping, was a 3-mile, freight-only line to Mynydd-y-Garreg which had been authorized in 1866, opened five years later and then carried building materials, lime traffic and tinplate.

GB

'KING' CLASS

During the 1920s, trains, especially during the summer holiday season, were becoming heavier, and still more powerful locomotives than the 'Castles' (qv) were required. Collett (qv) therefore set about scaling up the 'Stars' (qv) as far as the loading gauge would permit. At the same time it was discovered that the Civil Engineer had largely completed a bridge-strengthening programme which would permit an axle-load of 22 tons for the new locomotives.

The GWR was pushing Nominal Tractive Effort as the measure of a locomotive's power, and the 'Castles' had been ousted from their pre-eminent position by the Southern's 'Lord Nelsons'. Collett was instructed to get the tractive effort of the new design over the 'magic' 40,000 lbs.f, which necessitated an interesting innovation with the design of the bogie. To accommodate the larger cylinders, the frame of the bogie was cranked, with the bearings inside on the trailing axle and outside on the leading one. Following introduction in 1927, the design was not without its initial troubles, but the main problem was cured by the provision of secondary coil springs on the leading axle, which added another unique feature to the locomotives' impressive appearance. To achieve the high nominal tractive effort, the diameter of the cylinders was fixed at $16\frac{1}{4}$ inches, but it has been suggested that only on the first of class were they initially bored out to this dimension.

The original intention had been to name the locomotives after cathedrals, but, as 'The Royal Road', the GWR was able to secure permission to use the names of Kings of England, working backwards from the reigning monarch, *King George V*. After his death in 1936, the last of the class, No 6029, had its name changed from *King Stephen* to *King Edward VIII*, and a similar process saw No 6028 become *King George VI* the following year. Because of their high axle-loads, the 'Kings' were initially only permitted to operate to the West Midlands via the Bicester line, going as far north as Wolverhampton, and to Plymouth on the West of England lines, via Westbury as well as Bristol. They were barred from the Severn Tunnel, although in their later years their route availability was widened to enable them to work over the West-to-North route. New boilers were provided for the class in the early 1950s, with much larger superheaters, and their steaming capacity was increased still further by the fitting of double chimneys.

(*See also Locomotives*)

PS

KING GEORGE V

After it was built at Swindon in 1927, *King George V* (No 6000) became the GWR's 'flagship' locomotive, and had a higher tractive effort than any other express locomotive in the country. That same year it

King George V *No 6000 stands at Ranelagh Bridge, Paddington, prior to the 1927 American trip; note the Westinghouse brake fitted beside the smokebox.* (GWR Museum, Swindon)

was sent to the Baltimore & Ohio Railroad's centenary celebrations in the USA, where it was presented with a brass bell, which is still carried on its buffer-beam. Withdrawn in 1962, it was put on the BR preserved list, and subsequently lent to Swindon Corporation. Four years later it moved to Hereford, where W. H. Bulmer had it on exhibition and used it to spearhead the 'Return to Steam' on British Railways. It moved back to Swindon and in 1990 was on show in the exhibition area of the Works along with other locomotives from the National Collection.

(See also 'King' Class)

PWBS

KINGHAM

Two years after the completion of the main line of the Oxford, Worcester & Wolverhampton Railway (qv), that company sponsored the opening of a 4½-mile branch to Chipping Norton on 10 August 1855, creating Chipping Norton Junction in the process. A second branch, to Bourton-on-the-Water, was opened on 1 March 1862 and the two extended to Cheltenham (1881) and Kings Sutton (1887) to create a through Cheltenham–Banbury route. A direct link between the two was provided on 7 January 1906 and was used by South Wales–Newcastle and Penzance–Aberdeen services.

Kingham, as Chipping Norton Junction was called from 1909, was a substantial and busy station with four platforms and a country-end dock. A footbridge led to the 1870 Langston Arms Hotel, and an engine shed was sited between the station and the direct line overbridge, which spanned the main and three loop lines.

GB

KINGSBRIDGE BRANCH

Stations: Brent, Avonwick (2½ m), Gara Bridge (5½ m), Loddiswell (9 m), Kingsbridge (12½ m)

From the south side of the down island platform at Brent, this scenic single line needed a deep cutting, a tunnel and 13 contacts with the River Avon to reach Kingsbridge, from whence an omnibus (qv) link operated to Salcombe. The stations had passing loops, with an intermediate signal box at Gara Bridge, and the service ranged from 5–8 trains each way on weekdays.

Kingham *A post-Nationalization view looking north: the bridge carrying the Cheltenham-Banbury line can be seen in the distance.* (Lens of Sutton)

An 1860 scheme raised £18,000 and laid 4 miles of track before collapsing. The Kingsbridge & Salcombe Railway was then incorporated on 24 July 1882 and passed to the GWR by an Act of 13 August 1888, with the line being opened on 19 December 1893.

GB

KINGSWEAR BRANCH

Stations: Newton Abbot, Kingskerswell (2 m), Torre (5 m), Torquay (5¾ m), Paignton (8 m), Goodrington Sands (8¾ m), Churston (11 m), Kingswear (14¾ m)

The South Devon Railway (qv) opened on 18 December 1848 from Newton Abbot to Torre, calling the latter Torquay until the extension to Kingswear was opened by the Dartmouth & Torbay Railway. That company's 9 m 53 ch route through quite difficult terrain had been authorized on 27 July 1857 with opening from Torquay to Paignton on 2 August 1859, to Churston on 15 March 1861 and, at last, to Kingswear on 16 August 1864. The South Devon worked the Kingswear line from the outset and leased it from 1 January 1866.

The northern section of the line has always been heavily used, but although the long-distance summer holiday trains terminated at Paignton the single line on to Kingswear still carried over 50 services each weekday. They climbed at 1 in 71/60 to the loop at Churston, where passengers changed for Brixham (qv), then dropped sharply down through the 495 yd Greenway Tunnel to the east bank of the River Dart. At one stage it had been planned to cross here to get to Dartmouth, but the east bank route was chosen instead, with a steamer ferry across the river from Kingswear.

At Kingswear the double-sided platform led directly to the GWR's pontoon and its three small steamers. There was also a riverside quay with travelling cranes, and an engine shed, turntable and goods facilities alongside the Churston road. Today the line from Paignton to Kingswear is operated as the Torbay & Dartmouth Railway.

GB

1949
Great Western Railway.
FERRY TICKET
DARTMOUTH TO
KINGSWEAR
TOLL 6d Z
1949

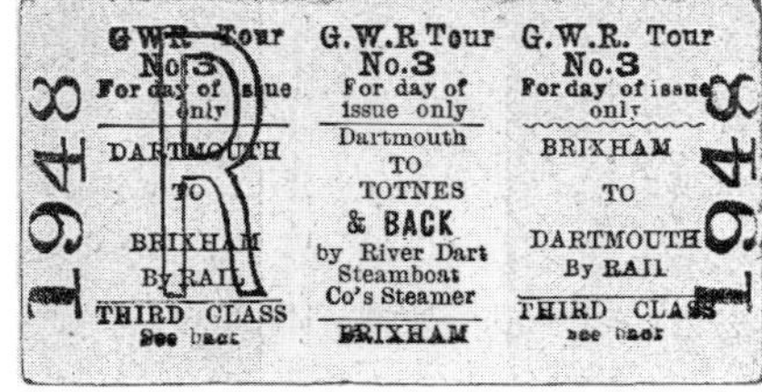
1948
G.W.R. Tour No.3 For day of issue only
DARTMOUTH TO BRIXHAM By RAIL
THIRD CLASS See back

G.W.R. Tour No.3 For day of issue only
Dartmouth TO TOTNES & BACK by River Dart Steamboat Co's Steamer
BRIXHAM

G.W.R. Tour No.3 For day of issue only
BRIXHAM TO DARTMOUTH By RAIL
THIRD CLASS see back
1948

Kingswear branch *GWR tickets for the ferry service across to Dartmouth, and a three-part Tour ticket, from Dartmouth to Brixham by rail, to Totnes and back by steamer, then back to Dartmouth.* (W. Adams Collection)

KINGSWINFORD BRANCH

In 1905 the GWR was authorized to extend a modest branch north from Kingswinford Junction, near Stourbridge (qv), to Oxley on the Wolverhampton– Shrewsbury line in order to create a route which would take freight traffic around Wolverhampton (qv). The original branch had been opened by the Oxford, Worcester & Wolverhampton Railway (qv) on 14 November 1858 and was subsequently extended to Baggeridge Junction, primarily to serve the Pensnett Railway, a development of the 1829 Shut End Railway.

The 12 miles from Kingswinford Junction to a triangular junction at Oxley became a through route on 11 January 1925 after years of desultory construction work. It carried a passenger service calling at nine intermediate halts from 11 May 1925 to 31 October 1932.

GB

LAMBERT, HENRY

General Manager, 1887–96. Lambert was born in 1833 in the east end of London. He began working for Pickfords (a constituent of the GWR) at the age of 14, and then the LNWR. He joined the GWR as Goods Superintendent at Paddington in 1865, then was appointed District Goods Manager (Swansea) in 1872. He returned to London four years later, becoming Chief Goods Manager in 1879. He succeeded Grierson (qv) as General Manager in 1887, but resigned in 1896 after a long illness. His place was taken by J. L. Wilkinson (qv).

CA

LAMBOURN BRANCH

Stations: Newbury, Speen (1¾ m), Stockcross & Bagnor Hall (2¾ m), Boxford (4¾ m), Welford Park (6¾ m), Great Shefford (8¼ m), East Garston (10 m), Eastbury Halt (11 m), Lambourn (12½ m)

Lambourn branch *The branch terminus. In the foreground are gas tanks probably used to replenish auto-train gas-lamps.* (Lens of Sutton)

The Lambourn Valley is racehorse-training country and many a well-fancied horse began its journey to a race meeting at Lambourn loading dock in a horse-box boarded with the name of the trainer to whom it was allocated. Other lines at the Lambourn terminus served the platform and run-round loop and the goods and engine sheds, although the latter was little used after railcars (qv) took over the branch service in 1936–37, starting each weekday with the 7.40 am to Newbury (qv) and ending it with the 8 pm arrival at Lambourn.

Although the Lambourn Valley Railway Act had been passed on 2 August 1883, work did not start for five years and later stopped for another seven (1890–97). Eventually the single line from Lambourn Junction, Newbury, and along the narrowing course of the River Lambourn was opened on 4 April 1898, but it was less than viable and sold out to the GWR from 1 July 1905. The latter provided a round of improvements including electric token signalling, a passing loop at Welford Park and a new station at Lambourn.

GB

LANE, MICHAEL

Principal Engineer of the GWR, 1860–68. Lane was associated with Brunel for much of his early career. As young men in their 20s they both worked on the Thames Tunnel (1825–27), Lane as foreman of bricklayers. Lane also worked under Brunel in Bristol Docks and Sunderland Docks. Except for a few months work on the construction of the Bath viaducts in 1838–9, and as Way and Works Engineer, and assistant to the resident engineer on the Western Division of the GWR (1841–2), Lane's career on the GWR only began in 1845, after being resident engineer of Hull Docks for 2½ years, when he moved back to Bath, and became Superintendent of the Permanent Way of a division of the GWR. He moved to Reading, and became 'Principal Engineer' of the GWR in 1860, after Bertram's retirement.

Lane was responsible for the introduction of the new narrow gauge line between Reading and Paddington in 1862, and rode on the footplate of the first train. He introduced built-up steel crossings to replace ones cast in blocks; the planting of railway banks to prevent slips; the establishment of the signalling works at Reading (qv) that commenced work in 1855 as a Civil Engineering Department factory, undertaking the repair and manufacture of mechanical signals from 1859; and the experimental use of steel rails, which he introduced into Paddington Yard in August 1867.

He also designed a mechanical interlocking apparatus for signal and point levers (qv Signalling), which had limited success, only about 10 installations being made. He saw to the introduction of interlocking throughout the GWR in 1865–6. He died at his home in Southall in 1868.

From information supplied by Vincent Tickner

LAUNCESTON BRANCH

Stations: Plymouth Millbay, Marsh Mills (4 m), Plym Bridge Platform (5 m), Bickleigh (7¾ m), Shaugh Bridge Platform (8¾ m), Clearbrook Halt (10 m), Yelverton (11 m), Horrabridge (12½ m), Whitchurch Down Platform (15½ m), Tavistock (16½ m), Marytavy & Blackdown (20 m), Lydford (23¼ m), Coryton (27½ m), Lifton (30¾ m), Launceston (35½ m)

The construction of this line had its roots in the 30-year-old rivalry between the broad and narrow gauge interests, the South Devon Railway (qv) supporting the two concerns which built it as much to keep the LSWR at bay as to meet the travel needs of the locality. From 1876 until 1890 an extra rail south of Lydford allowed the LSWR controlled access to Plymouth, but when its trains had gone the route settled down to a placid, rural existence with a good service as far as Tavistock and some five weekday trains each way extended to Launceston.

The South Devon & Tavistock Railway obtained its Act on 24 July 1854 and took five years to build a scenic 13-mile line through Bickleigh Vale, along the River Meavy to Yelverton and then north east to Tavistock. The line, which involved three tunnels and six viaducts, was opened on 22 June 1859. Three more rivers were used by the Launceston & South Devon Railway to open the 19-mile extension on 1 July 1865, the day the SDR took over the SD&T.

At Yelverton the junction station lay south of the tunnel and consisted of a passing loop with a V-shaped up platform for the Princetown branch (qv) trains. The 1859 Tavistock station, beside the River Tavy, was gutted by fire in 1887 and replaced by a standard GWR affair with an overall roof covering the platform lines and middle siding. Beyond Tavistock the GWR route crossed to the west of the LSWR and used adjoining platforms at Lydford before passing beneath its rival on the approach to Launceston. The branch was worked by electric train staff.

GB

LEAMINGTON SPA

Major works between 1936 and 1939 provided Leamington Spa with a new GWR station consisting of a three-storey down side building with a canopied frontage in the style of the period, a 670 ft down platform behind, then an up island beyond the through and platform lines. This complex and its bays dealt with the main-line service to Wolverhampton and beyond, stopping trains to Snow Hill and the service to Stratford-on-Avon. It replaced a piecemeal development of the original station which had been opened with the Birmingham & Oxford Junction Railway (qv) on 1 October 1852.

As originally planned the B&OJ line would have bypassed Leamington, but this was revised in 1848 when the GWR took over and an abortive approach was made to the LNWR to share a station. Instead the GWR finished up with separate broad and narrow gauge platforms. The LNWR station (Avenue Road) lay alongside the consolidated GWR one (Warwick Old Road/ General) with an exchange siding between the two. The main freight exchange sidings lay between the Warwick and Kenilworth lines at the west end, with the goods yard on the west side there and the engine shed at the east end beyond the divergence of the LNWR Rugby and GWR Banbury routes.

GB

LEDBURY

Ledbury was opened by the West Midland Railway (qv) on 13 September 1861 and became a junction when the Ledbury–Gloucester line (qv) was added from 27 July 1885. The latter acquired a halt at Ledbury Town in 1928 but the original station remained the most important and was well served by trains from Hereford to Worcester and beyond.

The junction between the two routes lay at the country end of the two-platform Ledbury station. At the other end was the 1,323-yd, narrow-bore, single-line Ledbury Tunnel which was fitted with treadles, clappers and an emergency tell-tale wire. The location had turntable, coaling, water and ash disposal facilities for the banking

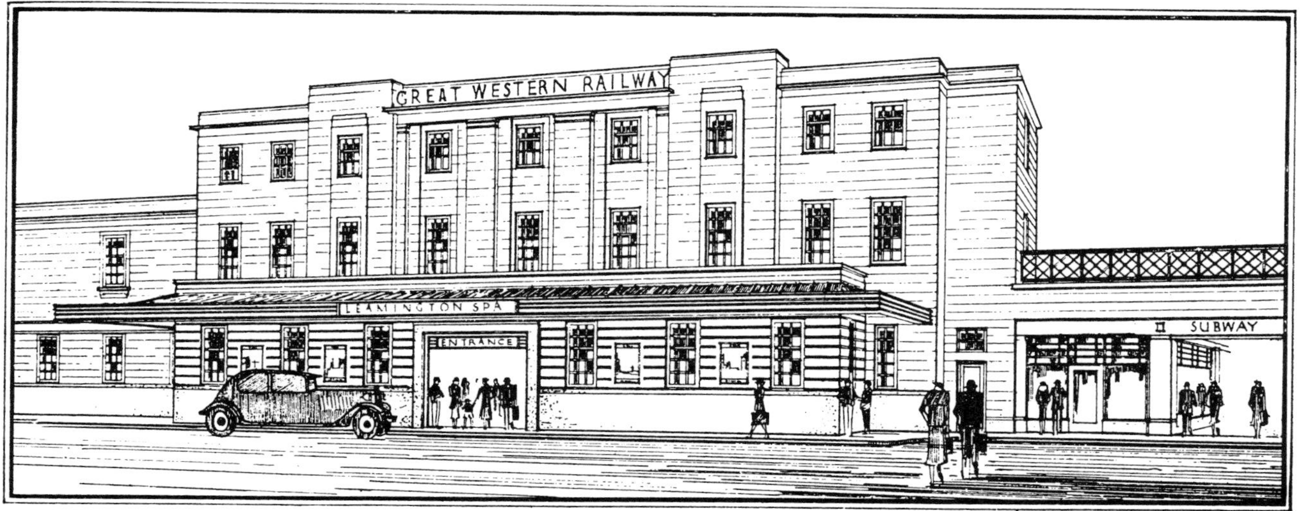

Leamington Spa *The new frontage proposed for the 1936-9 rebuilding of the station.* (GWR Magazine, 1937)

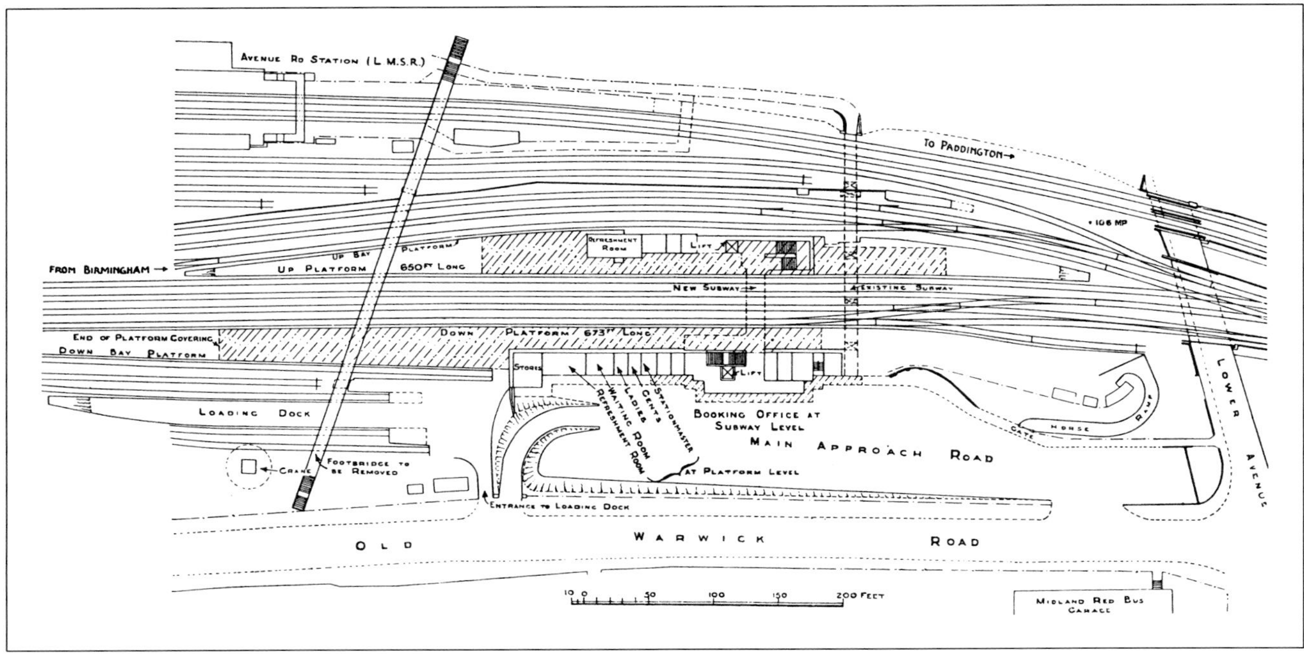

Leamington Spa *The new layout for the station.* (GWR Magazine, 1937)

engines used on the 1 in 70/80 gradient eastbound.

GB

LEDBURY–GLOUCESTER LINE

Stations: Ledbury, Dymock (5¼ m), Newent (9 m), Barber's Bridge (13½ m), Gloucester (19 m)

This route originated with Acts of 1873 authorizing the Ross & Ledbury Railway (28 July) and then the Newent Railway (5 August). The former only managed a 4 m 59 ch double-track line from Ledbury to Newent, opening this on 27 July 1885, the same day as the Newent Railway's 12 m 58 ch on to Over Junction. Both concerns were amalgamated with the GWR from 1 July 1892.

The general north-west course of the line from Gloucester followed the River Leadon most of the way, except for changing allegiance to tributaries on the Newent section. Traffic did not justify the double track at the northern end and this was removed in 1917 to create a three-section single line, with passing loops at Newent and Dymock and electric train staff working. A halt was opened at Ledbury Town in 1928 and three more in 1937–38, but traffic warranted only 4–5 trains each way taking about 50 minutes for the through journey.

GB

Ledbury *Looking west, towards the junction with the Newent and Gloucester line.* (Lens of Sutton)

LEOMINSTER

Through passenger services began on the Shrewsbury & Hereford Railway on 6 December 1853 and Leominster became a junction when the Leominster & Kington company completed its line from a point ½ mile north of the station on 2 August 1857. A second branch, this time from 1¾ miles south of the station, was opened by the Leominster & Bromyard Railway on 1 March 1884 and completed by the GWR 13 years later.

In addition to its substantial main-line platforms, Leominster had a separate, parallel island for its branch services plus a country-end engine shed and a substantial London-end goods yard complete with goods shed and travelling crane. An unusual signal box, raised high on brackets and with girder outriders to the branch plat-

Leominster *A post-Nationalization scene at Leominster, showing the elevated signal box and the branch island, in course of being lifted.* (Lens of Sutton)

form, presided over the main-line services and the branch trains to New Radnor (qv) via Kington and Worcester via Bromyard.

GB

LISKEARD

The original station was opened when the broad gauge Cornwall Railway (qv) began its service between Plymouth and Truro on 4 May 1859. A separate platform, at right-angles to the end of the up main line platform, was then added to provide a link with the Looe branch (qv) at Coombe Junction from 25 February 1901 (passengers 15 May). This 2 m 9 ch single line headed north from the branch platform and its run-round loop, turned south in a descending curve beneath the 150 ft high Liskeard Viaduct and completed a circle to arrive at Coombe Junction pointing north again. From there Looe trains reversed direction, freight workings to Moorswater and the ECLP siding continuing on beneath Moorswater Viaduct.

GB

LIVESTOCK TRAFFIC

The GWR was always happy to oblige in the matter of transporting livestock, its aim being to serve the countryside through which it ran. In early days livestock was carried in 'tilt' wagons, but in 1853, after Brunel insisted, custom-built cattle-wagons were introduced. Later, strict rules came into force in regard to the acceptance of livestock for transit, and each beast had to be examined for ' . . . injury, wounds or other defect' prior to loading, and if anything untoward was detected the ' . . . owner, consignor, owner's agent or representative' had to be informed and the fact noted on the waybill.

There were strict rules, too, governing the quantity of stock to be loaded in any one vehicle, and the speed at which it could be moved. It could be a complicated business, for each stock-fair or market must have an adequate provision of vans, not to mention an ample supply of horse-boxes to and from the various racecourses on the system before and after meetings. On the subject of livestock, it should not perhaps be forgotten that the GWR owned a herd of pedigree cattle. Kept at St Ives, Cornwall, for the supply of dairy products to the company's Tregenna Castle Hotel (qv Hotels), it also won a number of prizes at stock shows.

(See also Rolling-stock, goods)

CA

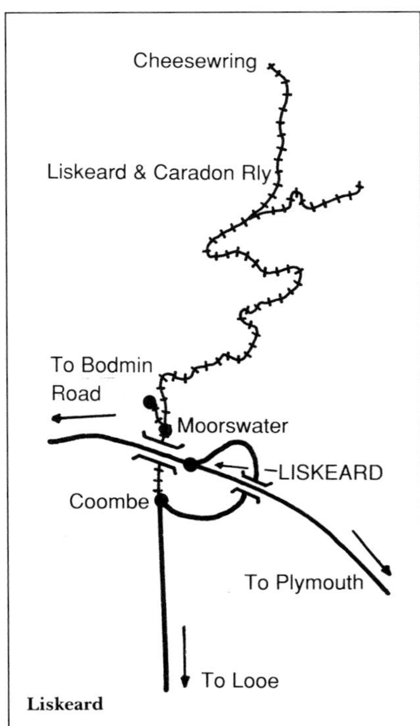

Liskeard

LLANELLY

By the time the South Wales Railway (qv) opened between Landore and Carmarthen on 11 October 1852, Llanelly had been a centre for metal and chemical manufacturing for over half a century. Docks and tramroads had been functioning for some time, including the 1833 Dafen branch and the 1839 Pontardulais line of the Llanelly Railway & Dock Co which had been incorporated by an Act of 19 June 1828. The SWR had to cross these and several industrial lines, and the local rail layout was not rationalized until the absorption of the Llanelly Railway as from 1 July 1889.

Under Grouping the GWR took over the Llanelly & Mynydd Mawr Railway and the Llanelly complex then consisted of the docks network south of the main line, the L&MM Cross Hands branch and two short colliery lines to the north, and to the east Llandilo Junction where the main docks route joined and the Pontardulais and Swansea lines separated. The single, conventional station was well served by main and Llandovery line trains, its GWR/LMS goods depot had a full range of facilities and the many local yards and sidings included those of the Llanelly Steel Co and several tinplate works.

GB

LLANELLY-LLANDOVERY LINE

Stations: Llanelly, Bynea ($2\frac{3}{4}$ m), Llangennech ($4\frac{3}{4}$ m), Pontardulais (7 m), Pantyffynnon ($11\frac{1}{2}$ m),

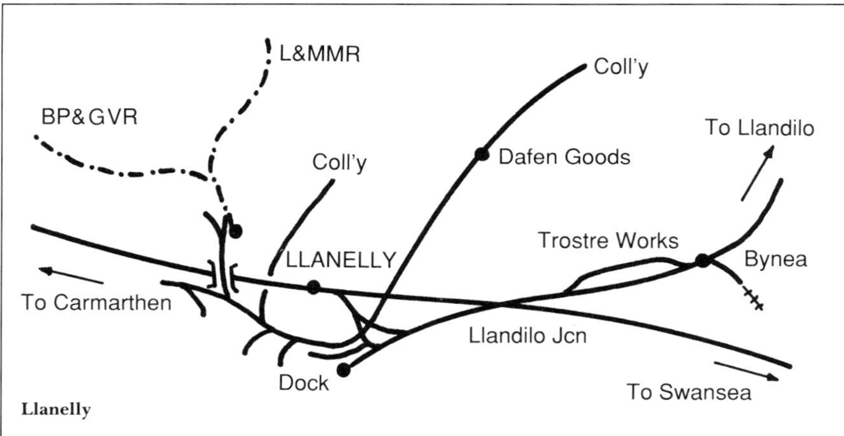

Llanelly

Tirydail ($12\frac{3}{4}$ m), Llandebie ($14\frac{3}{4}$ m), Derwydd Road ($16\frac{1}{4}$ m), Ffairfach ($18\frac{3}{4}$ m), Llandilo ($19\frac{3}{4}$ m), Talley Road ($21\frac{3}{4}$ m), Llangadock ($25\frac{1}{4}$ m), Llanwrda (27 m), Llandovery (31 m)

The Llanelly Railway & Dock Co was one of the Welsh railway pioneers, obtaining its enabling Act on 19 June 1828 and opening the horse-worked Dafen branch five years later. By 1 June 1839 the LR&D had opened a line between Llanelly and Pontardulais which was extended on to Llandilo by 24 January 1857, with a lease of the Vale of Towy Railway giving access to Llandovery from 1 April 1858. A partnership with the LNWR went sour and eventually lost the Llanelly company its 1865 Carmarthen (qv) branch from Llandilo Junction and the 1867 line from Pontardulais to Swansea, the GWR taking over what was left, including the share in the Vale of Towy, from 1 July 1889.

The train service on the Llanelly–Llandovery line reflected its origins. GWR 'all-stations' trains covered the whole route, LNWR/LMS local trains ran Llandilo–Carmarthen and Pontardulais–Swansea, with Swansea–Shrewsbury/Liverpool/Manchester/York and Euston trains using the Pontardulais–Llandovery portion. The route was a scenic one, following the valleys of the Loughor, Cennen and Towy rivers and crossing them or their tributaries five times. It made connection with the Swansea District Line (qv) at Morlais Junction and had coal routes east from Pantyffynnon and west from Tirydail.

GB

Llanfair Caereinion branch *Beyer Peacock 0-6-0T No 822 (GWR number)* The Earl *at an open level crossing.* (H. C. Casserley)

LLANFAIR CAEREINION BRANCH

Stations: Welshpool, Welshpool Seven Stars ($\frac{1}{2}$ m), Raven Square (1 m), Golfa ($2\frac{3}{4}$ m), Castle Caereinion ($4\frac{3}{4}$ m), Cyfronydd ($6\frac{3}{4}$ m), Heniarth ($7\frac{3}{4}$ m), Llanfair Caereinion (9 m)

Funded partly by a local authority loan and authorized by a Light Railway Order of 8 September 1899, the 2 ft 3 in-gauge Welshpool & Llanfair Light Railway was built at a cost of £56,900 between 30 May 1901 and opening on 9 March 1903 (passengers 4 April). It was worked by the Cambrian Railways (qv) under a 99-year agreement which gave them 60% of the gross receipts.

The W&L's four daily passenger trains in each direction ran from a small station adjacent to the Cambrian Railways' goods yard and followed a restrictive course through Welshpool (qv) before starting a 1 in 30 climb to Golfa. A summit 600 ft above sea level then preceded the descent at 1 in 45/50 to Cyfronydd and a section beside the River Banwy, after the six-arch Brynelin Viaduct, and on to the terminus at Llanfair Caereinion.

The GWR inherited the light railway at the Grouping but ended the passenger service on 7 February 1931. The line then continued with its stone, timber and agricultural traffic until 31 October 1956, and has subsequently been revived between Raven Square and the terminus.

GB

LLANFYLLIN BRANCH

Stations: Llanymynech, Llansantffraid ($3\frac{1}{4}$ m), Llanfechain (5 m), Bryngwyn ($6\frac{3}{4}$ m), Llanfyllin ($8\frac{1}{2}$ m)

Authorized to the Oswestry & Newtown Railway and opened on 10 April 1863, this $8\frac{1}{2}$-mile single line followed the River Cain for most of its journey from a bay platform at Llanymynech to the modest terminus in the foothills of the Berwyn Mountains. The passenger service consisted of five trains each way on weekdays, with additional services on Wednesdays and Saturdays, and there were public goods facilities at all the stations except Bryngwyn.

GB

LLANGOLLEN

Opposed by the LNWR but backed by the GWR, the Vale of Llangollen Railway obtained its Act on 1 August 1859 and had its 5¼-mile single line ready for opening on 1 December 1861 (passengers 2 June 1862). The Llangollen & Corwen Railway's extension westwards was completed on 8 May 1865, the route being worked by the GWR who absorbed the two lines in 1896 and doubled the section from Llangollen Line Junction (Ruabon, qv) to Llangollen Goods Junction two years later.

Llangollen station and its two curving platforms lay on a long narrow site so close to the River Dee that one platform was virtually on the river bank. There was an extensive goods yard with a canal wharf adjoining, and long stabling sidings for the holiday specials that brought hundreds of tourists to enjoy the local beauty spots.

GB

LLANGYNOG BRANCH

Stations: Oswestry, Porthywaen (4½ m), Blodwell Junction (6 m), Llanyblodwell (6¾ m), Glanyrafon (7¾ m), Llansilin Road (9¼ m), Llangedwyn (10¾ m), Pentrefelin (12¾ m), Llanrhaiadr Mochnant (14 m), Pedair Ffordd (15¼ m), Penybontfawr (16¾ m), Llangynog (19½ m)

Exploitation of the limestone, lead and slate resources of the Tanat Valley produced a number of local tramways, and schemes for even more. However, access from the Cambrian (qv) main line was eventually provided by the Tanat Valley Light Railway whose Light Railway Order was confirmed on 4 January 1899. Constructed and worked by the Cambrian, the TV line was formally opened on 5 January 1904 and carried public traffic from 6 January 1905, although every train in later timetables was qualified by a note to define its day or days of operation.

At the main-line end, the TV connected at Blodwell South Junction with the Nantmawr branch from Llanymynech. This had originally been opened on 13 August 1866 by the multi-titled Shropshire Railways, but closed on 22 June 1880 to be reopened by the Cambrian on 1 January 1886 after a period of lying derelict. From Blodwell North Junction another 1¼ miles of the TV led to the Cambrian's Porthywaen branch and its junction with the main line north of Llynclys.

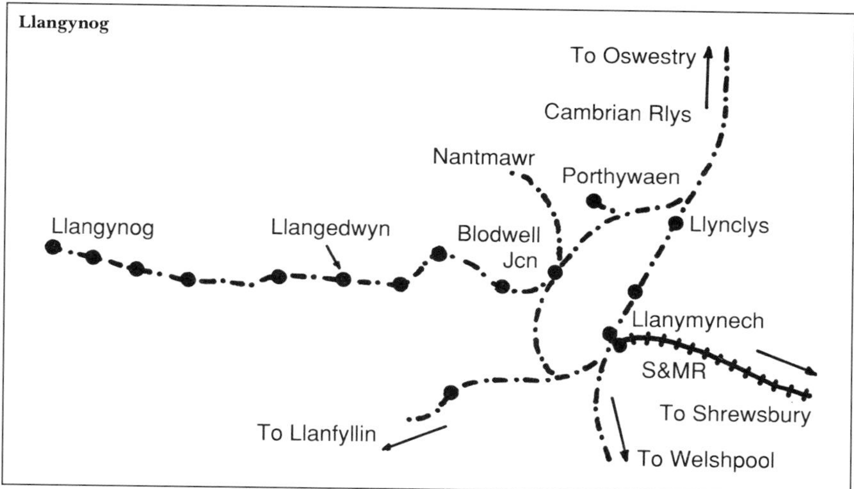

The single line of the TVLR climbed steadily throughout its course. Passing loops were provided at Llangedwyn and Llanrhaiadr, and several other points had goods loops and sidings. Facilities at Llangynog itself included a run-round line, an engine shed and a slate wharf which received traffic from the Craig Rhiwarth inclines.

GB

LLANTRISANT

This important junction on the GWR's South Wales main line (qv) lay halfway up the bank to Llanharan summit. It handled coal trains off the Ely Valley lines and branch passenger services to Penygraig (qv) and on the Pontypridd–Cowbridge/ Aberthaw route.

The line from Pontypridd (qv) arrived via Maesaraul and Mwyndy Junctions and its trains used either the country-end up side bay or the down island at Llantrisant, those for Cowbridge reversing direction there. The goods yard and running shed were also on the west side of the station.

GB

LOCOMOTIVES

Because of the GWR's uninterrupted existence for 113 years, the history of its locomotives forms a far more coherent story than that of any other British railway company. Over this span, only eight men had ultimate responsibility for its rolling-stock, and these included several of the most outstanding Chief Mechanical Engineers (qv, and individual entries) this country has produced. The other feature of the GWR which gave it an outstanding individuality was the adoption of the Broad Gauge (qv) on Brunel's advice. Although this initially set it head-and-shoulders above most of the other early railways, as the 19th century progressed it was to become somewhat of a burden on the fortunes of the company, until the last operational traces were swept away by the gauge conversion (qv) over the weekend of 20–23 May 1892, when all remaining broad gauge lines were converted to 'narrow' gauge (today's standard gauge of 4 ft 8½ in).

As well as spanning considerably more than a century, the history of the GWR's motive power has to encompass several thousand separate locomotives. Although the maximum number of broad gauge locomotives on the GWR's books at any one time was exactly 400, by 1 January 1948 their assets handed over to the British Transport Commission included a total of

3,857 steam locomotives. In spite of having been one of the earliest railways to adopt a standardization policy, a vast number of different designs were involved. In addition to those it had built or ordered itself, there were all the locomotives it took over when other companies were absorbed. As early as 1854 the first 'narrow' gauge locomotives had been added to its stock. These came from the Shrewsbury & Chester (qv) and the Shrewsbury & Birmingham Railways when they were absorbed, and throughout the GWR's existence many further railways were similarly taken over.

The biggest influx took place as a result of the Grouping (qv) following the Railways Act of 1921; this set up the 'Big Four' companies, which were to exist for the next quarter-century, and brought no fewer than 861 additional locomotives into GWR ownership. Our story must therefore be a highly selective one; in the main, the locomotives absorbed from other companies will have to be excluded, and space does not even permit reference to all those of purely GWR origin. For those wanting more information on this subject there is the 13-volume series *The Locomotives of the Great Western Railway*, produced by the Railway Correspondence & Travel Society, details of which are given in the Bibliography.

Historical background

Before considering any specific classes, a brief sketch of the company's operations from 1837 onwards will enable readers to set the details given later in context.

In the midst of building his superbly engineered line from Paddington to Bristol, Brunel (qv) issued a fairly broad specification for the first locomotives he ordered from a number of different manufacturers. In E. L. Ahrons's words, '. . . there never has existed such an extraordinary collection of freak locomotives as these which were built for the Great Western Railway, and delivered during the period of about eighteen months from November 1837'.

Fortunately their arrival took place just after the appointment of Daniel Gooch (qv), still only 20 years old, as the company's Locomotive Superintendent, and over the next decade his efforts and designs were to put the GWR's locomotive practice and performance ahead of any other railway in the world. From the initial classes he quickly selected one which would serve as the prototype for further construction, and ordered a further batch of broadly similar machines. Next he moved on to produce his own designs, but, as the GWR did not yet have its own construction facilities, a number of classes were obtained from different manufacturers. In 1846, however, Swindon Works (qv) turned out its first locomotive, appropriately named *Great Western*. It was a considerable success, and after the addition of an extra leading axle it formed the prototype for the famous broad gauge 'singles'. From then on, the GWR was to design and build virtually all its locomotives.

However, against the background of the 'Battle of the Gauges' and events described in the 'Broad Gauge' entry (qv), it is not surprising that the GWR's early lead with the development of steam locomotives should falter and be eclipsed, as the company's resources had to be expended in other directions. Gooch retired from the office of Locomotive Superintendent in 1864, to return as Chairman in 1865. The following year saw a major crisis in the country's railway industry, after the failure of a bank produced a 'domino effect', forcing other such institutions, and many contractors, into bankruptcy. This affected the GWR too, and drastic steps had to be taken in 1867 to restore the position. The economies ranged right across the company, with the number of Directors (qv) being reduced, and the crack 'Flying Dutchman' express (qv) even being taken off. Broad gauge carriages were not repaired, but replaced by narrow gauge ones, and in 1870 39 broad gauge locomotives were scrapped, none of them having run since at least 1865. Resources were thus already being diverted away from those services.

In 1864 Joseph Armstrong (qv) moved from Wolverhampton to Swindon to take over from Gooch, his appointment being significant because of his previous responsibilities for the company's narrow gauge locomotives. Following this and the financial crisis, construction of new broad gauge locomotives was halted in the autumn of the following year, after only 46 locomotives of Armstrong's design had been produced, and six of these were classed as 'Renewals'. It was not until 1871 that construction of broad gauge locomotives recommenced at Swindon, with the appearance of the first three of the 'Rover' Class 4-2-2s, and these too were officially considered to be rebuilds

Locomotives Great Western, *Swindon's first locomotive, built in 1846.* (GWR Magazine, 1895)

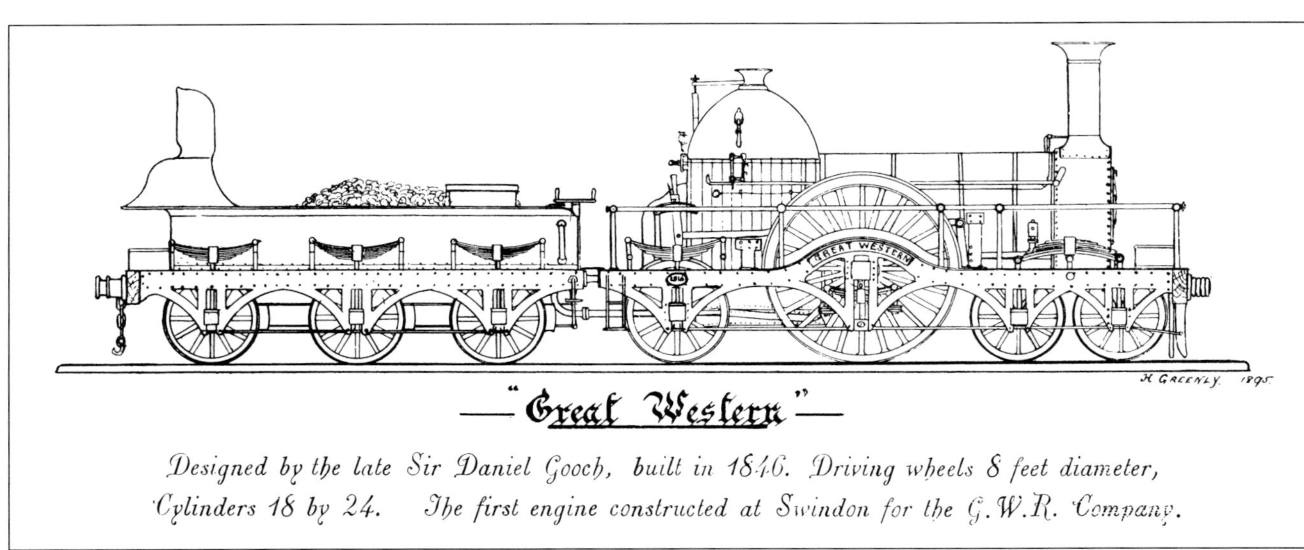

or renewals of the 'Iron Duke' Class. In the same period, more than 130 of Armstrong's 'Standard Goods' 0-6-0s were to be constructed, but these were accompanied by only 30 passenger 2-2-2s (the 'Sir Daniel' Class), which was a clear indication of the company's current priorities.

Joseph Armstrong died in 1877, and William Dean (qv) took over for the rest of the 19th century. He completed the renewal of 24 of the 'Iron Dukes', which saw the Broad Gauge era out, and for that reason were probably the most famous of all those which ran on Brunel's 7-foot tracks. Only nine had been renewed by 1877, and construction of the remainder lasted until 1888. Four years later the Broad Gauge had disappeared, but by the turn of the century Dean had developed a very characteristic style for what we must now refer to as his standard gauge locomotives. They had double frames, which proved somewhat prone to cracking, and relatively small parallel boilers, with, until the final years of the century, round-topped fireboxes. Tall chimneys and massive domes were provided, many of the latter on the passenger locomotives being provided with a brass cover. This would be polished at the start of the day's operations, and on occasions would be covered with a sack to protect it from soot and smuts until the locomotive had been attached to its train at the terminus. Trains were now heavier, and were increasingly likely to include corridor coaches, which had been introduced in 1892 (qv Rolling-stock, passenger). There was a strong family resemblance between many of Dean's locomotive classes, but although their size was increasing quite markedly, they still had a very traditional appearance.

Churchward (qv) followed Dean just after the turn of the century, when the *Belle Époque* was ushering in the Edwardian age, which saw our railways at their most influential. Business was expanding rapidly as the country became the powerhouse of the world, producing a maximum of 263 million tons of coal in a single year for the railways to move, while passengers travelled in new standards of luxury over many miles of newly constructed trunk routes, which finally removed the stigma of the 'Great Way Round' from the GWR. Before deciding on his new 'standards' , Churchward looked long and carefully at the world scene, as the documents that came to the National Railway Museum from the Swindon Drawing Office show, even buying a trio of French compound 4-4-2s which were used extensively on main-line expresses.

Many new ideas were tried out on a small scale before being adopted as standard, some changes being progressive over the years. Amongst these was the decision to use tapered boilers and Belpaire fireboxes, with the dome disappearing in favour of a brass bonnet surrounding the safely-valves, the fitting being combined with the top-feed arrangements. Drum-head smokeboxes replaced the Dean design, and hidden in their smoky depths were draughting arrangements that drew on the latest American university research. A few years later came the first trials of superheating, with Swindon ultimately developing its own particular version. New designs of valve gear were produced, the size of the rods being almost robust enough to move the locomotive itself rather than piston-valves just 8 or 10 inches in diameter. Again unseen by the casual observer were two new features that had an important bearing on the locomotives' performance: the gear was of the long-lap, long-travel variety, and a very efficient design of valve was adopted which combined steam-tightness with low rates of wear. On no other British locomotives did the exhaust steam come out in the same 'square-cut' puffs.

The first of Churchward's definitive locomotives was the 4-6-0 *William Dean* (qv) which appeared in the year he took over, so there was no doubt that he had started to develop his ideas during Dean's time as Locomotive & Carriage Superintendent. Locomotives to existing Dean designs continued to be built for a number of years, although they all tended to benefit from the fitting of tapered boilers. Plans were laid down for a range of designs, which included numerous standard features, ranging from boilers to blastpipes. There was no move to scrap any existing design until either it was worn out, or an economic case could be made from the use of less fuel and reduced maintenance costs. One class of the locomotives Churchward sketched out—the '16xx' pannier tanks—did not actually get built until after the GWR had been nationalized, a quarter of a century after he had retired. Although a few of the Swindon visual features were carried through, Churchward's designs set themselves apart in so many ways, but his standardization policy meant that all subsequent GWR locomotives clearly came from the same family.

After the First World War, the country's railways only just escaped nationalization, but instead it was decided that they should be merged into four large private companies, each of which, by and large, served a separate geographical area (qv Grouping). Alone among all the companies, the GWR was virtually unaffected, keeping its name but absorbing many small railways, of which only the six Welsh ones were important enough to be constituent, rather than subsidiary, companies. In the process the GWR acquired over 860 additional locomotives of non-standard designs, which had to be assimilated, the task falling to Collett (qv), who took over from Churchward on the eve of the Grouping.

Collett however, still had work to do on the GWR proper, and designed the company's two finest express locomotive classes in his first five years as CME. In the years that followed before the Second World War, as steam on the railways of Britain reached its zenith, the 'Castles' and 'Kings' (both qv) were to set many new standards for speed, haulage capacity and efficiency, and many other standard designs were produced to meet specific requirements or replace outdated locomotive types. Collett also produced the classic mixed-traffic 4-6-0, when one of the 'Saints' (qv) was given 6-foot diameter wheels, and, as well as leading to the construction of a large number for the GWR, the idea was subsequently copied extensively by the LMS, LNER and BR.

Collett also presided over the 'Swindonization' of the locomotives taken over by the GWR at the Grouping. They were a mixed bag, and many were scrapped unchanged. When the Swindon boiler inspector visited the Barry Railway (qv) sheds in 1922, no less than a third of their locomotives were 'stopped' because their boilers were unsafe, which indicates that their owner had maintained high dividends at the expense of the maintenance of assets. There were many GWR locomotives of considerable antiquity too, and Collett realized that, in spite of the economic difficulties caused by the Great Depression, savings could be obtained by replacing many of them with modern designs. Starting in 1929, for example, his design of large pannier tanks started to appear, the class finally reaching a total of no less than 853. Locomotives were not just renewed on principle, and as late as 1936 the 'Earls' were constructed by combining the boilers from one of Dean's 4-4-0 classes with the frames of another. When the noble gentlemen after whom they were named objected to the puny size of the locomotives concerned, the names were transferred to some of the 'Castles', and the 4-4-0s were thereafter unofficially referred to as the 'Dukedogs'. In 1934 Collett introduced the first diesel railcar (qv) for the GWR, setting

Locomotives *A later generation of* Great Western, *'Castle' Class 4-6-0 No 7007 of 1923, photographed still at work at Challow in 1960.* (Adrian Vaughan)

a trend which was to develop nationally in the early years of the BR era.

In 1941 Collett retired, having reached the age of 70, and the office of Chief Mechanical Engineer was taken over by F. W. Hawksworth (qv). The stresses and aftermath of the Second World War were to overshadow his period in charge of the railway's rolling-stock, but he nevertheless made a number of important changes before Nationalization (qv) changed the whole scene in 1948. Back in the 1900s, Churchward had adopted a relatively low degree of superheating for the main-line locomotives. With the passage of time and changing conditions, this was holding back some of the potential of the Swindon designs, and in 1944 Hawksworth started fitting larger superheaters to the 'Hall' (qv) locomotives currently being built. In post-war years this practice was to be extended to other passenger classes, starting with the construction of the first post-war 'Castles' in 1946, and the process continued after Nationalization right up to the final days of steam.

Another important change took place with the Hawksworth 'Halls', with the main frames being continued right through to the front buffer-beam, which removed a basic weakness in the Churchward two-cylinder design. The same design was to feature in his own 'County' Class 4-6-0s, which were to appear in 1945, being intended as a two-cylinder equivalent of the 'Castles'. They also featured the fashionable high boiler pressure of 280 psi, but, as with the Bulleid 'Pacifics', this was in due course to be reduced to the more normal 250 psi. Another Hawksworth change took place with the pannier tanks, with the completion of the first '94xx' design in 1947, by combining the two classic GWR features of a tapered boiler with pannier tanks. The result was a very attractive-looking locomotive, and a total of 210 were ultimately to be built, although, after the first ten, non-superheated boilers became standard.

Two more GWR classes of pannier tank were to appear in the first year after Nationalization. The first was a lightweight class for branch-line use, and some were sent all the way to northern Scotland to work the Dornoch branch. They were of classic GWR appearance, but the same could not be said about the final ten of the '15xx' Class. Although clearly of GWR lineage, they had outside cylinders and Walschearts valve gear, and were devoid of running-plates. Their very short wheelbase enabled them to traverse sharp curves, which resulted in several finishing their days working at collieries for the National Coal Board. Another of Hawksworth's post-war developments was the ordering of two gas-turbine-powered locomotives, but they, too, were not to appear until after Nationalization.

The locomotives

Broad Gauge

After that overview, we will now look at some of the GWR locomotive classes in more detail, starting with the broad gauge ones. Those built for the GWR, as distinct from the Associated Broad Gauge Companies (qv) such as the Bristol & Exeter and South Devon (qv) are listed in Table 1. The original 'oddities' are, in the main, excluded, but in Brunel's defence we should briefly discuss the reasons behind their peculiar designs. One of the objects of the 7-foot gauge was to enable fast trains to be operated, and in the 1830s engineers were very concerned about the lubrication of the locomotive's cylinders, the problem being worsened by high piston speeds. Accordingly the specification called for this not to exceed a maximum of 280 feet per minute at 30 mph. At the same time, he wanted locomotives that would not exert excessive forces on the track, so stipulated a maximum weight of $10\frac{1}{2}$ tons for the six-wheeled designs. Although the results were virtually unworkable, one can, nevertheless, see the logic of the specification, and one must remember that the rails laid on the initial stretch proved to be too light.

The contractors who responded to Brunel's original requirements used considerable ingenuity to meet the specification. In addition to the obvious course of providing small boilers and very large driving wheels, the most unusual locomotives were the two produced by R. & W. Hawthorn & Co. Using T. E. Harrison's patent, their engines and boilers were on separate frames, *Thunderer's* four driving wheels being driven through step-up gears. This increased their effective diameter from 6 to 16.2 feet. The second, *Hurricane*, had a more conventional engine portion, the absence of a boiler on it enabling the single driving axle to have wheels 10 feet in diameter, but adhesion weight would have been lacking.

It was fortunate that, in addition to the locomotives ordered to Brunel's specification, the GWR had purchased a couple of 'export rejects' from Robert Stephenson & Co. These were both 2-2-2s, intended for the 5 ft 6 in New Orleans Railway in the USA, which had cancelled the order. It was possible to modify them for Brunel's 7-foot gauge, and they were the only really reliable locomotives on the railway when it commenced commercial operations between London and Maidenhead in 1838. They were named *North Star* (qv) and *Morning Star*, and the former hauled the

Table 1: GWR broad gauge locomotive classes

Class	Wheel arrangement	Year introduced	Number in Class
'Star'	2-2-2	1837	12
'Fire Fly'	2-2-2	1840	62
'Sun'	2-2-2	1840	21
'Leo'	2-4-0	1841	18
'Hercules'	0-6-0	1842	4
Great Western	2-2-2	1846	1
'Prince'	2-2-2	1846	6
'Premier'	0-6-0	1846	12
'Banking'	0-6-0T	1846	5
'Pyracmon'	0-6-0	1847	6
'Iron Duke'	4-2-2	1847	29
'Corsair'	4-4-0T	1849	2
'Caesar'	0-6-0	1851	8
'Ariadne'	0-6-0	1853	102
'Sappho'	4-4-0T	1854	13
'Waverley'	4-4-0	1855	10
'Victoria'	2-4-0	1856	18
'Metropolitan'	2-4-0T	1862	22
'Hawthorn'	2-4-0	1865	26
'Sir Watkin'	0-6-0T	1865	6
'Swindon'	0-6-0	1865	14
'Iron Duke' renewals	4-2-2	1871	24

inaugural train.

At this point another peculiarity of all the GWR broad gauge locomotives must be mentioned. None of them was ever given a number, and they were solely referred to by name. This did not apply to the broad gauge locomotives operated by the Associated Companies, which became part of the GWR in 1876, nor those built as 'convertibles'. In view of the success of the first two 'Stars', a further batch, generally similar in design, was ordered, although domed fireboxes replaced the round-top type on the original pair. The class finally numbered 12. All of them had the word 'Star' in their names, setting a pattern which was to be followed far more extensively in the 20th century. Delivered in 1839–41, the last remained at work as late as 1871.

The general layout of the Stephenson 'Stars', with their slotted outside sandwich frames, was to influence many of Swindon's broad gauge passenger locomotives. The first to be designed by Gooch were the 'Fire Fly' (qv) Class, which numbered no fewer than 62, and were built by seven different makers. In appearance they were initially generally similar to the 'Stars', as was the next type to be built, the 'Sun' Class. The latter, however, had 6-foot driving wheels instead of the 7-foot ones of the 'Stars' and 'Fire Flies', to enable them to cope better with the steeper gradients west of Swindon. Eighteen locomotives were delivered in 1841–42, from three different manufacturers. Like all the early classes, there were appreciable differences between individual locomotives, even when new, let alone after some had been extensively modified, but space does not permit us to deal with such details.

Continuing to follow the mainstream of GWR top-link passenger designs, we come to the first complete locomotive built at Swindon. Appearing in 1846, it was appropriately named *Great Western*, and had the usual 2-2-2 wheel arrangement. Experience showed that there was too much weight on the leading axle, which broke out on the road, so it was converted to a 4-2-2. Pending the outcome of the trials with this large locomotive, Gooch had produced the six 'Prince' Class 2-2-2s in 1846–47. They were somewhat smaller, with *inside* sandwich frames, and were moved from the Exeter to the Birmingham route after the arrival of his '8-foot singles'. The latter formed the 'Iron Duke' (qv) Class, developed from *Great Western*, and 29 of them, in four 'Lots', were produced between 1847 and 1855.

The last batch of seven, named after battles in the Crimea War, were not built at Swindon, but by Rothwell. They continued many of the features that had characterized the earlier classes, but by this time domeless

Broad gauge *Gooch 4-2-2 single* Amazon, *as rebuilt.* (GWR Museum, Swindon)

boilers were being fitted, with raised, round-top fireboxes surmounted by a brass safety-valve bonnet. These locomotives were extremely fast, and frequently averaged over 60 mph between Paddington and Didcot in the late 1840s, putting the GWR in the forefront of world locomotive performance at that time. Although '8-foot singles' were to see out the broad gauge, the locomotives at work in 1892 were not those which Gooch had built, 24 of his 29 having been 'renewed' between 1871 and 1888, with a slight variation in names. On the first three, weatherboards were provided for the crew, but cabs then became standard, which, together with a different design of copper-capped chimney, changed their appearance appreciably. *Tornado* was the final one to be renewed, and the last broad gauge locomotive to be built. The renewals were officially known as the 'Rover' Class, after the first to appear.

Space only permits us to look in detail at the other extreme of the broad gauge stock, the 0-6-0 goods designs. The first locomotives on the GWR with this most common British wheel arrangement were the four 'Hercules' Class, designed by Gooch and built by Nasmyth, Gaskell & Co in 1842. They were the only broad gauge 0-6-0s to have *inside* sandwich frames, and were followed by the first of those built at Swindon. These were the 12 'Premier' Class locomotives, built in 1846–47. They were, however, not named after Prime Ministers, the other members of the class carrying plates as diverse as *Argo*, *Bellerophon*, *Bergion*, and *Jason*. They were known as '1st Lot Goods', and *Premier* was undoubtedly so named because it was the first engine to be built at Swindon, although its boiler came from outside. Their wheels were 5 feet in diameter.

The next six 0-6-0s formed the somewhat larger 'Pyracmon' Class, and were followed by the eight 'Caesars' in 1851–52. Again the title of the class is misleading, and the Roman scholar would find the names *Dido* and *Florence* somewhat of a surprise. After this Gooch started to construct his 'Standard Goods' locomotives, 102 of the 'Ariadne' or 'Caliph' Class being turned out between 1853 and 1863, in six different lots. The third of the class, *Europa*, was the only one to be rebuilt, and lasted to the end of the Broad Gauge era.

In the 1860s the problem of nomenclature of the different broad gauge classes cropped up, and some rationalization took place. The 'Caesars' and the 'Standard Goods' then all became known by the former name, while the two earlier types were referred to as the 'Fury' Class. In the space available there is no way in which we can follow every change of this sort; in the main, therefore, the information supplied throughout only applies to a locomotive as first constructed. The final broad gauge 0-6-0s were the 14 'Swindon' Class, built in 1865–66 by Armstrong. They were all sold to the Bristol & Exeter Railway in 1872–74, where they suffered the ignominy of being numbered. When they reverted to the GWR, after it had taken over the Associated Companies in 1876, they were renumbered.

Standard gauge 'Singles'

Having reached the narrow, or standard, gauge era, we will continue our examination of the GWR's main-line passenger locomotives, taking each wheel arrangement in turn, starting with the narrow gauge 'Singles', and concluding with the 4-6-0s. The details of the former are summarized in Table 2, and this, like all the subsequent Tables, is subject to the general note contained in the box on this page. The GWR had acquired its first narrow gauge locomotives in 1854, when they took over the Shrewsbury railways, and the following year Gooch ordered four new locomotives from Beyer, Peacock & Co, with a further four less then 12 months later. They were known as the '69' Class, and were smaller versions of his contemporary broad gauge 2-2-2s. More similar locomotives were required when the standard gauge services were extended to Paddington after the laying of mixed-gauge track, and in 1862 the ten 'Sharp's' were delivered from Sharp, Stewart & Co, which were very similar to the '69s'.

After Joseph Armstrong had become Locomotive Superintendent, Swindon produced its first standard gauge 2-2-2s, the first of which was named *Sir Daniel*, as a tribute to his predecessor. All told there were 30 of this class, which differed quite considerably from those previously obtained from outside sources. They had solid outside frames, with outside bearings for all axles, and the boiler was provided with a dome. They were a long-lasting class, but by the turn of the century had become too small for passenger work, and most were converted to 0-6-0s, and in this form one lasted until 1912. In 1873, Swindon turned out *Queen*, which gave its name to the class of 21 similar locomotives. *Queen* herself was particularly ornate, and, as the name implied, was intended for working the Royal Train (qv). She had a large brass dome, but the subsequent members of the class, built in 1875, were domeless. The situation was to change considerably over the years as rebuilding took place, and the boilers carried later were anything but standard in design. After 1899 they had Belpaire fireboxes.

Following Armstrong's death, Dean produced the 'Cobhams', which were replacements for the 'Sharp's', and reverted to outside sandwich frames, with elegant slots in them, looking especially handsome with their original domeless boilers and open splashers. Dean liked domes, however, and many boilers used subsequently had one mounted well forward, which did nothing for the locomotives' appearance. In 1891 Dean produced another locomotive design, which was, in time, to turn into a class which epitomized the elegance of Victorian locomotives. These were the '3001' 2-2-2s,

Note on the tables

By the middle of the 19th century the greater degree of similarity between locomotives of the same class makes it worth listing a number of important statistics about them. Unless otherwise indicated, in all subsequent Tables the dimensions, etc, refer to the first definitive member of the class, as it was built. Space does not, in the main, permit us to follow renumberings or rebuildings. The numbers of individual locomotives are given without quotation marks, but classes identified by a particularly numbered member are so distinguished. The GWR used to refer to classes in the form '57xx', that example being used to identify all 853 of the Collett heavy shunting pannier tanks. Under this system the second digit, in most cases, was maintained throughout the class, although there were too many locomotives in this particular class for this to be possible. Some classes intended for similar duties shared the same second digit, an example of this being the four-cylinder express passenger designs (and the 'Counties'), all of which had a zero as second digit.

Two particular statistics in the Tables may differ slightly from those which have normally been quoted in the past. These are the grate area and nominal tractive effort, both of which have traditionally been presented with spuriously greater accuracy than can actually be measured. I have accordingly only quoted grate areas to the nearest tenth of a square foot, and tractive efforts to the nearest 50 pounds force.

Table 2: GWR standard gauge 'single-wheelers'

Class	Year introduced	Number in Class	Cylinders: (No) Diameter x stroke (in)	Driving wheel diameter (ft in)	Grate area (sq ft)	Boiler pressure (psi)	Nominal tractive effort (lb.f)	Weight of loco (tons cwt)
'69'	1855	8	(2) 15½ x 22	6 6	13·6	—	—	30 6
'Sharp's'	1862	10	(2) 16 x 24	7 0	14·6	130	8,100	29 8
'Sir Daniel'	1866	30	(2) 17 x 24	7 0	16·6	140	9,600	29 13
'Queen'	1873	21	(2) 18 x 24	7 0	18·6	140	11,000	33 10
'Cobhams'	1878	10	(2) 18 x 24	7 0	19·3	140	11,000	34 14
'3001'	1891	80	(2) 20 x 24	7 7¼	20·8	160	14,100	44 4

eight of which had been built as convertibles, to keep the broad gauge adequately supplied with motive power during its last two years. As had been the case with the original *Great Western*, there was too much weight at the front for the single carrying axle, and after No 3021 became derailed (qv Accidents, 16 September 1893) they were all converted to 4-2-2s in 1894. A further 50 were built, and became extremely well known, monopolizing the express services between London and Newton Abbot.

Their most famous exploit was the run of No 3065 *Duke of Connaught* from Bristol to London on 9 May 1904. Taking over the 'Ocean Mail' special from *City of Truro*, (qv), the single-wheeler ran the 118.4 miles to Paddington in 99 minutes 46 seconds, at an average of 71.2 mph, reaching a maximum speed of 87. By the turn of the century, however, the day of the single-wheeler was over, and although some of the '3001' Class were fitted with larger Belpaire boilers, they were no longer able to cope with heavy main-line trains. The last were withdrawn during the First World War.

Standard gauge 'Singles' *Dean '3001' No 3019* Rover *after rebuilding to the 4-2-2 form.* (GWR Museum, Swindon)

Standard gauge 4-4-0s

In Table 3 (overleaf) are listed the GWR's standard gauge 4-4-0 locomotive classes. They can be divided into express passenger and mixed-traffic designs, as shown, and it is convenient to consider them in this order.

The first large-wheeled class comprised the four 'Armstrongs', which were nominally rebuilds of earlier locomotives, and were, in effect, larger versions of Dean's 'Singles'. With their greater adhesion they were able to cope better with 20th-century loads, and the last of them was not withdrawn until 1930. Next came the 'Badmintons', the first class to be built with Belpaire boilers. They had a typical Dean appearance, with outside cranks and coupling rods, the top of the frames being swept up in an elegant curve over each driving wheel. With business booming, this was a time for experiment, and, quite early on, two of the class were to differ appreciably from the rest. *Waterford* was built with the second prototype Standard No 2 domeless parallel boiler, and *Earl Cawdor* was given a side-window cab and a massive round-top boiler for a period of three years. From 1905 most of them received Standard No 4 boilers, to all intents and purposes turning them into 'Cities', although they lacked the latter's straight tops to the frames.

Next to appear were the 40 'Atbaras', which started the use of straight frames for express locomotives, and had Standard No 2 boilers. As was customary in the 1900s, boilers of many different designs were used on them after routine overhauls, and it is sometimes possible to date a photograph of a GWR 4-4-0 to within 18 months by identifying the type of boiler fitted. Many of these locomotives were named after battles and personalities connected with the Boer War, while others used placenames from elsewhere in the British Empire. In 1908 a further 20 similar locomotives were built, named after flowers, and fitted with boilers like those currently being carried by the 'Atbaras'. Even the first design of straight-top frames had shown weaknesses, and the 'Flowers' had deeper ones, but these still had to be strengthened in places after being in service.

The best known of the GWR's 4-4-0 express locomotives were the 'Cities' (qv), ten of which were built in 1901. Although the exploits of *City of Bath* and *City of Truro* (both qv) were the most spectacular, the recorded performance of other members of the class was also outstanding.

As already mentioned, the 'Cities' proper were subsequently joined by ten 'Atbaras' and 17 'Badmintons', which, from the traffic point of view, had the same capabilities. All these outside-framed express 4-4-0s were withdrawn in the late 1920s/early 1930s as part of Collett's replacement programme. The same applied to the Churchward 'Counties', which had outside cylinders and all the other features of his standard two-cylinder designs. They were

Table 3: GWR standard gauge 4-4-0s

Class	Year introduced	Number in Class	Cylinders: (No) diameter x stroke (in)	Driving wheel diameter (ft in)	Grate area (sq ft)	Boiler pressure (psi)	Nominal tractive effort (lb.f)	Weight of loco (tons cwt)
Express passenger								
'Armstrong'	1894	4	(2) 20 x 26	7 1	20·8	160	16,650	50 16
'Badminton'	1897	20	(2) 18 x 26	6 8	18·3	180	16,000	52 3
'Atbara'	1900	40	(2) 18 x 26	6 8½	21·3	180	16,000	51 12
'City'	1903	10	(2) 18 x 26	6 8½	20·6	200	17,800	55 6
'County'	1904	40	(2) 18 x 30	6 8½	20·6	200	20,550	55 6
'Flower'	1908	20	(2) 18 x 26	6 8½	20·4	195	17,350	53 6
Mixed-traffic								
'Duke'	1895	60	(2) 18 x 26	5 7½	19·0	160	16,850	46 0
'Bulldog'	1899	165	(2) 18 x 26	5 8	21·4	180	18,950	49 16
'Dukedogs'	1936	29	(2) 18 x 26	5 8	17·0	180	18,950	49 16

less successful than the outside-framed classes, however, being nicknamed 'Churchward's Rough Riders'. Their rigid wheelbase was only 8½ feet long, which was not much to oppose the lateral thrusts from the pistons in the 18 x 30 in cylinders. (Even at present-day preserved railway speeds, Stirling's No 1 can 'nose' quite markedly in response to the piston thrusts, and its cylinders are not only smaller, but it works at a lower boiler pressure.)

No more large-wheeled GWR 4-4-0 locomotives were built after 1912, which was in marked contrast with other companies of the later post-Grouping era. The LMS multiplied the Midland 'Compounds', while Gresley and Maunsell were still building their 'Hunts' and 'Schools' respectively after the GWR had scrapped the last of its similar express locomotives. These other classes were, however, all three-cylinder designs, which would have given them better riding characteristics.

We must now look at the smaller-wheeled Swindon 4-4-0s, of which there were only really two classes, the third being a latter-day combination of parts from the other two. Dean's 'Dukes' dated from 1895, and were designed to handle trains over the West of England banks which were being worked further east by his 'Singles'. Initially they were known as the 'Pendennis Castle' Class, after the name applied to the second member, but were later, more logically, referred to as 'Dukes', as the first locomotive was named *Duke of Cornwall*. At one time, however, they were also referred to as the 'Devon' Class, this being the part of the country where they were designed to work. Although obviously from the same stable as the 4-2-2s, they were nothing like as handsome, but were able to cope for much longer. Although they were replaced in the West of England fairly early on, their low weight enabled them to work certain lightly built lines, such as those of the former Cambrian Railways (qv), which had acquired no fewer than 20 by 1924. They were also used on the Midland & South Western Junction line (qv), which the GWR had also taken over at the Grouping. As will be mentioned later, certain of them were converted to 'Dukedogs' in the 1930s, and some of these hybrids lasted until 1960. The 'Dukes' had the curved-top frames that typified Dean's designs but, as with the larger-wheel versions, these were to prove lacking in strength, particularly after the provision of larger boilers.

Standard gauge 4-4-0s *Experimental 'Badminton' 4-4-0 No 3297* Earl Cawdor *with non-standard side-window cab and round-top boiler.* (GWR Museum, Swindon)

In 1898 one of the 'Dukes' was built with a larger domed boiler, the prototype for the later Standard No 2. The locomotive was No 3312 *Bulldog*, which was to become the prototype of a new class, although it visually still resembled the rest of the 'Dukes'. In 1906, however, it received a tapered boiler, but by this time a large number of proper 'Bulldogs' had already appeared, and looked very different. The first 40 had curved frames like the 'Dukes', and the next 100 had the straight type, with the final 15, built in 1909–10, being provided with a deeper version. Most of the class were named, many after places and geographical features in the West of England, although some of these were subsequently removed to avoid passengers confusing the name with the destination of their train. The final batch had bird names, most of them lasting into BR days, and some of them piloting 'Kings' over the South Devon banks in their final years. In the mid-1930s more locomotives capable of working certain lightly built branch lines were needed, and Swindon put a 'Duke' boiler on a 'Bulldog' frame. By the time the 29 conversions had been completed, more than half the class were shedded on the Cambrian lines. The story of their naming after Earls has already been described.

Standard gauge 4-6-0s *No 36, the GWR's first 4-6-0.* (GWR Museum, Swindon)

Standard gauge 4-6-0s

We now move on to the 4-6-0 wheel arrangement, the various classes being listed in Table 4. All the main ones have their own entries elsewhere, but a few comments are appropriate about the first two locomotives listed.

No 36 was the first 4-6-0 on the GWR, and one of the earliest with that wheel arrangement in the country. In appearance it was a classic Dean design, but, being intended for goods traffic, its small driving wheels did not necessitate any curves on the top of the outside frames, although small splashers were provided. It had a parallel boiler, with the usual large dome, and looked very handsome.

The same could not be said about the 'Krugers'. Only the first of these ten locomotives (No 2601) was turned out as a 4-6-0, the remainder being 'Moguls'. Their large boilers, with massive Belpaire fireboxes extending into a combustion chamber, may have appeared impressive to some, but the overall effect was ungainly. The first two were further disfigured with sandboxes saddling the boiler just behind the smokebox. No 2601 was also fitted with coil and volute springs which sprouted from the straight top of the running-plate. They were not a success, the 4-6-0 only lasting five years. Also in Table 4 are details of the GWR's only 'Pacific', *The Great Bear*, which has its own entry elsewhere.

Standard gauge 0-6-0 and 2-6-0 goods locomotives

When discussing the broad gauge locomotives earlier, reference was made to the numerous 'Ariadne' Class of 0-6-0s built in 1852–63. These were required to handle the increasing goods traffic, and clearly the railway would also need some corresponding narrow gauge locomotives. As shown in Table 5, there were less of these built in the same period, but their big expansion started in 1866, when construction of the 'Standard Goods' began. By the end of 1876 no fewer than 310 had been built, and the last was not withdrawn until the 1930s. Various details changed over such a long period, but they started life in a cabless form, subsequently acquiring weatherboards, and then short cabs, of what was to become the typical GWR shape. They had

Table 4: GWR standard gauge 4-6-0 and 4-6-2 classes

Class	Year introduced	Number in Class	Cylinders: (No) diameter x stroke (in)	Driving wheel diameter (ft in)	Grate area (sq ft)	Boiler pressure (psi)	Nominal tractive effort (lb.f)	Weight of loco (tons cwt)
4-6-0s								
No 36	1896	1	(2) 20 x 24	4 6	30·5	165	24,950	59 10
'Kruger'	1899	1	(2) 19 x 28	4 7½	32·2	180	27,850	60 8
No 100	1902	1	(2) 18 x 30	6 8½	27·6	200	20,550	67 16
'Saint'	1903	91	(2) 18 x 30	6 8½	27·1	225	23,100	70 4
'Star'	1907	73	(4) 14¼ x 26	6 8½	27·1	225	25,100	74 10
'Castle'	1923	171	(4) 16 x 26	6 8½	30·3	225	31,600	79 17
'King'	1927	30	(4) 16¼ x 28	6 6	34·3	250	40,300	89 0
'Hall'	1924	259	(2) 18½ x 30	6 0	27·1	225	27,300	75 0
'Grange'	1936	80	(2) 18½ x 30	5 8	27·1	225	28,900	74 0
'Manor'	1938	30	(2) 18 x 30	5 8	22·1	225	27,350	68 18
Mod 'Hall'	1944	71	(2) 18½ x 30	6 0	27·1	225	27,300	75 16
'County'	1945	30	(2) 18½ x 30	6 3	28·8	280	32,600	76 17
4-6-2								
The Great Bear	1908	1	(4) 15 x 26	6 8½	41·8	225	27,800	97 0

plain outside frames, and many variants of boilers were carried, with the Belpaire variety starting to appear in the 1900s. The 20 'Coal' locomotives were a small-wheeled version of the 'Standard Goods', being designed for the haulage of coal trains between Pontypool Road and Birkenhead.

They were followed by the 'Dean Goods', another long-lived class, which had inside frames. Some of the Armstrong standard locomotives had been 'called up' for service in the First World War (qv World Wars), and a few of them returned from as far away as Serbia, although others, which had gone to Salonika, saw their days out on the Ottoman Railway. The Dean 0-6-0s, on the other hand, were on army service in both World Wars, this requirement saving some of them from being scrapped: nine of the class which had already been withdrawn in 1939 were reinstated after hostilities had broken out. Some of those sent to the continent were destroyed at the time of the Dunkirk evacuation, but others were captured and used by the German and French railways, while, after the war, an appreciable number were sent to China under UNRRA auspices. Several of the class remaining at work in this country were not withdrawn until the 1950s.

Unlike the other Grouping companies, the GWR only built a comparatively small number of 0-6-0s during the 20th century, Churchward having produced none with that wheel arrangement. The 120 examples of the '2251' Class were designed by Collett to replace a number of older classes which had been taken over at the Grouping, although they appeared all over the system. Their tapered Standard No 10 boilers had been designed earlier to fit some of the locomotives taken over from the Taff Vale.

Standard gauge 0-6-0s and 2-6-0s *The long-lived 'Dean Goods', which eventually numbered over 200 examples. No 2426 is seen at Bristol in 1948.* (H. C. Casserley)

Instead of 0-6-0s, Churchward had continued building Dean's 'Aberdare' 2-6-0s, dating from 1900. Very different from the 'Krugers' which preceded them, they were effectively the freight equivalent of the 'Bulldogs'. The design was a neat one, with straight outside frames, their boilers varying during their early life like other contemporary GWR locomotives. Then, in 1911, construction was switched to the inside-framed, outside-cylinder Churchward equivalent, and nearly 350 of these '43xx' Class 'Moguls' were to be built. The last were constructed as late as 1932, and were provided with side-window cabs. They were an extremely versatile class, and appeared all over the system. In the late 1930s some of them were 'renewed' as 'Granges' and 'Manors' (both qv).

Standard gauge 2-8-0 goods locomotives

For their heaviest freight workings, the GWR used the 2-8-0 wheel arrangement,

Table 5: GWR standard gauge 0-6-0 and 2-6-0 goods and mixed traffic classes

Class	Year introduced	Number in Class	Cylinders: (No) diameter x stroke (in)	Driving wheel diameter (ft in)	Grate area (sq ft)	Boiler pressure (psi)	Nominal tractive effort (lb.f)	Weight of loco (tons cwt)
0-6-0s								
'57'	1855	11	(2) 15½ x 22	5 0	12·9	120	9,000	31 0
'79'	1857	24	(2) 16 x 24	4 6	12·9	120	11,600	29 16
'77'	1857	6	(2) 16 x 24	5 0	14·4	140	11,800	27 8
'131'	1862	28	(2) 16 x 24	5 0	12·9	—	—	30 0
'360'	1864	30	(2) 17 x 24	5 0	15·8	140	13,300	31 16
'Beyer'	1866	12	(2) 17 x 24	5 0	16·2	140	13,300	—
'Standard Goods'	1866	310	(2) 17 x 24	5 0	16·6	140	13,300	29 18
'Coal'	1874	20	(2) 17 x 24	4 6	16·9	140	14,900	30 0
'Dean Goods'	1883	210	(2) 17 x 24	5 0	16·4	140	13,300	33 0
'2251'	1930	120	(2) 17½ x 24	5 2	17·4	200	20,150	43 8
2-6-0s								
'Aberdare'	1900	81	(2) 18 x 26	4 7½	21·4	180	23,200	53 8
'43xx'	1911	342	(2) 18½ x 30	5 8	20·6	200	25,650	62 0

Standard gauge 0-6-0s and 2-6-0s *'Aberdare' 2-6-0 No 2632.* (National Railway Museum, York)

Standard gauge 0-6-0s and 2-6-0s *Churchward's inside-framed, outside-cylinder equivalent of the 'Aberdare', the versatile '43xx' 2-6-0 of 1911.* (GWR Museum, Swindon)

as shown in Table 6 (overleaf). After the prototype in 1903, 166 were constructed from 1905 onwards. In the First World War, Robinson's design of 2-8-0 for the Great Central was chosen for use by the Railway Operating Division (ROD), and after the end of hostilities large numbers of them were offered for sale at bargain prices by the Government. The GWR hired some and purchased a total of 100, 80 of them at £1,500 each. Their very different outlines were thereafter to be seen all over the GWR's main lines, although a number of Swindon features were to be incorporated during the course of the years. The class was known as the 'RODs', but the condition of some of them was not good. These were withdrawn fairly quickly, and their tenders used for the '2251' 0-6-0s being built at that time.

Construction of the Swindon '28xx' design recommenced in 1938, and these locomotives, numbered 2884–99 and 3800–66, had side-window cabs and other 'modern' features, like outside steam-pipes to the cylinders. Stanier's Class '8F' 2-8-0s were chosen as the national standard in the early part of the Second World War, and some were built at Swindon. In 1919 Churchward constructed a much larger 2-8-0, No 2700, with 5 ft 8 in driving wheels, for use on fast freight trains. To begin with, the Civil Engineer would not permit it to be fitted with a boiler any larger than the Standard No 1. In 1921 it was agreed that the much bigger Standard No 7 could be used, which increased the weight by $4\frac{1}{4}$ tons. Another eight similar locomotives were constructed, and they played an important role on the overnight fast freights over the main routes. With comparatively large driving wheels they came into the mixed-traffic category, and were also used for passenger trains on peak Summer Saturdays.

Standard gauge tank locomotives

Finally we will turn to the various designs of standard tank locomotives which were built in the 20th century. Details of these are given in Tables 7 and 8 (overleaf), the latter covering that GWR speciality, the pannier tanks. The story is a fairly complex one, and can only be summarized here.

Standard gauge 2-8-0s *Robinson GCR 2-8-0 in ROD service in France during the First World War. After the war, the GWR purchased 100 of these locomotives.* (GWR Museum, Swindon)

Table 6: GWR 2-8-0 goods classes

Class	Year introduced	Number in Class	Cylinders: (No) diameter x stroke (in)	Driving wheel diameter (ft in)	Grate area (sq ft)	Boiler pressure (psi)	Nominal tractive effort (lb.f)	Weight of loco (tons cwt)
No 2800	1903	1	(2) 18 x 30	4 7½	27·2	200	29,800	68 6
'28xx'	1905	166	(2) 18 x 30	4 7½	27·2	225	34,500	68 6
No 4700	1919	1	(2) 19 x 30	5 8	27·1	225	30,450	77 14
'47xx'	1922	8	(2) 19 x 30	5 8	30·3	225	30,450	82 0
'ROD'	Purchased 1919	100	(2) 21 x 26	4 8	26·2	185	32,300	74 7

Standard gauge 2-8-0s *'28xx' 2-6-0 No 2814* (Real Photographs)

Standard gauge tank locomotives *Churchward's pioneering 2-6-2T No 99.* (GWR Museum, Swindon)

For passenger work there were two main varieties of side tanks, both of which had the 2-6-2 wheel arrangement. The larger-wheeled '31xx' Class were used for the suburban services, and there were a number of variants over the years. The 'County Tank' 4-4-2Ts were also used on suburban trains in the London area, but were replaced in the 1930s with the '61xx' batch of 'Prairies'. For use on branch lines there were the '44xx' and '45xx' Classes, the latter having larger tanks. The other tanks primarily intended for passenger workings were the '48xx' 0-4-2Ts, designed by Collett for push-pull trains on the less-busy branch lines, to replace the assortment of earlier locomotives being used. Again a very neat design was produced, and the last 20, numbered in the '58xx' series, were not fitted for auto-train working. The '48xx' locomotives were renumbered in the 14xx series in 1946 when their original numbers were required for those 2-8-0s converted to oil-firing.

On the freight side, at the Grouping the GWR acquired a large number of inside-cylinder 0-6-2Ts from the Welsh constituent companies. These would blast their way, chimney first, up the valleys to the collieries with trains of empty wagons. On the return journey to the ports, with the aid of gravity, speeds were higher, and the pony-truck under the bunker provided useful guidance round the curves. As well as 'Swindonizing' many of the absorbed locomotives, the GWR produced 200 of its own design, numbered in the 56xx and 66xx series. The final 50 were constructed by Armstrong Whitworth. While not conforming to the Churchward layout, they nevertheless incorporated many standard parts, including the boiler.

Another non-standard design was the '1361' Class of five saddle tanks, built for dock work in 1910. Their short wheelbase enabled them to negotiate sharp curves, and one was employed in the wagon works at Swindon. As we will see later, a further six locomotives were produced in 1934 for similar purposes, but these were provided with pannier tanks rather than the saddle variety.

This leaves us with the two types of eight-coupled tanks, the history of which is intertwined. After a prototype in 1910, the class started to be built in appreciable numbers

Table 7: GWR side and saddle tank classes built after 1901

Class	Wheel arrangement	Year introduced	Number in Class	Cylinders: (No) diameter x stroke (in)	Driving wheel diameter (ft in)	Grate area (sq ft)	Boiler pressure (psi)	Nominal tractive effort (lb.f)	Weight of loco (tons cwt)
'31xx'	2-6-2T	1903	315	(2) 18 x 30	5 8	20·4	195	23,700	73 3
'44xx'	2-6-2T	1904	11	(2) 16½ x 24	4 1½	16·8	165	18,500	55 15
'County Tanks'	4-4-2T	1905	30	(2) 18 x 30	6 8½	20·4	195	20,000	75 0
'45xx'	2-6-2T	1906	175	(2) 17 x 24	4 7½	16·8	180	19,100	57 0
'1361'	0-6-0ST	1910	5	(2) 16 x 20	3 6	10·7	150	14,850	35 4
'42xx'	2-8-0T	1910	205	(2) 18½ x 30	4 7½	20·6	200	31,450	81 12
'56xx'	0-6-2T	1924	200	(2) 18 x 26	3 8	20·4	200	25,800	68 12
'48xx'	0-4-2T	1932	95	(2) 16 x 24	3 8	12·8	165	13,900	41 6
'72xx'	2-8-2T	1934	54	(2) 19 x 30	4 7½	20·6	200	33,150	92 12

Table 8: GWR 0-6-0 pannier tank classes built after Grouping

Class	Year introduced	Number in Class	Cylinders: (No) diameter x stroke (in)	Driving wheel diameter (ft in)	Grate area (sq ft)	Boiler pressure (psi)	Nominal tractive effort (lb.f)	Weight of loco (tons cwt)
'57xx'	1929	853	(2) 17½ x 24	4 7½	15·3	200	22,500	47 10
'54xx'	1931	25	(2) 16½ x 24	5 2	16·8	165	14,800	46 12
'64xx'	1932	90	(2) 16½ x 24	4 7½	16·8	165	16,500	45 12
'1361'	1934	6	(2) 16 x 20	3 8	10·7	165	16,300	35 15
'94xx'	1947	210	(2) 17½ x 24	4 7½	17·4	200	22,500	55 7
'16xx'	1949	70	(2) 16½ x 24	4 7½	14·9	165	18,500	41 12
'15xx'	1949	10	(2) 17½ x 24	4 7½	17·4	200	22,500	58 4

from 1912 onwards for short-distance mineral workings. The slump in the early 1930s resulted in little work for some of the locomotives, and it was decided to rebuild a number of them as 2-8-2Ts, the extra coal and water capacities enabling them to be used for longer-distance journeys. Ninety were scheduled for conversion, but only 54 had been dealt with when the Second World War started, and the remainder of the programme was cancelled. By then the position had swung back the other way, and ten more 2-8-0Ts were constructed in 1940. So, although the Table shows a total of 205 of the '42xx' Class, not all of these existed at the same time.

We will conclude our history with the 0-6-0 pannier tanks listed in Table 8. This very characteristic and almost unique arrangement was a feature of the GWR in the 20th century, and small boys were known to ask why some of the GWR's locomotives had square boilers! The almost flat sides and tops of the Belpaire fireboxes were, in fact, one of the main reasons for the change-over to pannier tanks, as it was very difficult to shape a saddle tank to fit over such a firebox, and shortening it to cover just the boiler barrel reduced the water capacity considerably. The other reason was the instability caused by water sloshing about in a saddle tank, this being considered partly to blame for the derailment at Loughor in 1904. The pannier type also gave better access to the inside cylinders and motion. The type was first

Standard gauge tank locomotives *'42xx' Class 2-8-0T No 4202.* (GWR Museum, Swindon)

Standard gauge tank locomotives *The ubiquitous '57xx' pannier tank, numerically the GWR's largest class. Here is No 8723 at Swindon.* (GWR Museum, Swindon)

Standard gauge tank locomotives *Post-Second World War 0-6-0 pannier tank No 9400, to Hawksworth's design.* (GWR Museum, Swindon)

used by the GWR in 1898, being fitted to a 4-4-0, but in 1903 it started to be fitted to the 0-6-0 tanks. Thereafter its use increased steadily, the feature being standardized for new construction from about 1910.

Space does not permit descriptions of the earlier GWR 0-6-0 tanks of either variety, and Table 8 concentrates on those built after the Grouping, when Collett set about the wholesale renewal of the older locomotives. The process started with the large locomotives used for heavy shunting and short trip-workings. These were the '57xx' Class, which, within 20 years, had expanded to a total of no less than 853 locomotives. This made then numerically the largest class on the GWR. Construction started in 1929, and 300 of them were at work within three years, all but 50 of these having been built by outside manufacturers. Eleven of the class were fitted with condensing equipment and feed-water pumps for use on the Metropolitan lines between Paddington and the sidings for Smithfield market. Between 1956 and 1963, with the need for them declining on BR, 14 of the non-condensing type were acquired by London Transport for use on their engineering trains.

The second type of Collett pannier tanks were those intended for working light passenger trains. They came with two different sizes of wheels, and most were equipped to work auto-trains, a total of 115 being constructed. The 1930s also saw the construction of the six Class '1361' dock tanks, which have already been mentioned in conjunction with the earlier '1361' Class.

It was not until after the Second World War that the final three types of pannier tanks appeared, the most numerous of them being the '94xx' Class, which combined the two very distinctive GWR features of pannier tanks and tapered boilers. Reference has already been made to these locomotives, as well as to the '16xx' and '15xx' Classes which were not built until after Nationalization.

Of necessity this account has had to skate over the finer details of the GWR's locomotive history, and those wanting to delve more deeply into this fascinating story are recommended to consult the references in the Bibliography.

PWBS

LOCOMOTIVE EXCHANGES

The first officially recorded exchange was in 1910 when, in response to criticism from the Board of the cost of his four-cylinder 'Star' Class (qv) express engines, Churchward (qv) arranged trials with the LNWR. No 4005 *Polar Star* won hands down and its success had much to do with the introduction soon afterwards of the four-cylinder 'Claughtons' on the LNWR.

In 1925, following the British Empire Exhibition at Wembley when the GWR displayed *Caerphilly Castle* (qv) alongside a Gresley 'Pacific' of the LNER and boldly proclaimed that its seemingly much smaller 4-6-0 was the more powerful, trials were arranged between King's Cross and Leeds and over the West of England main line. Once again Swindon triumphed (qv *Pendennis Castle*), and later Doncaster 'Pacifics' incorporated the lessons learned, notably higher boiler pressures and improved valve gear.

Third time was not so lucky for the GWR. Soon after Nationalization, a series of trials was organized between the locomotives of the former 'Big Four'. 'Kings' (qv) took part in the express locomotive category, 'Modified Halls' (qv Hall Class) in the mixed-traffic, and '28xxs' in the heavy goods. The 'King', both on its home territory and between King's Cross and Leeds, came out

Locomotive exchanges *'King' Class No 6018* King Henry VI *on the East Coast Main Line at Harringay in 1948.* (Steamchest Collection)

alongside the Bulleid 'Merchant Navy' as the heaviest consumer of coal. In the mixed-traffic category, the GWR locomotive was again shown to be heavy on coal, although not as bad as the Bulleid 'West Country' 'Pacific'. The 2-8-0 performed well—which was interesting, for as long ago as 1921 another engine of the class had run trials in Scotland and far outperformed a North British 0-6-0.

Swindon protested that its engines had had to use Yorkshire coal, whereas they had been designed for Welsh fuel which had a higher calorific value. Subsequent tests with Welsh coal showed the 'Hall' and the 2-8-0 in a more favourable light. The 'King' did less well, and within a few months experiments were being carried out with four-row high-degree superheaters. Eventually the entire class was modified with double chimneys and, like the similarly fitted Gresley 'A3' and 'A4' 'Pacifics', enjoyed an Indian summer.

MCHB

LOCOMOTIVE LIVERIES

The well-known livery applied to the GWR's latter-day steam locomotives can, like their mechanical ancestry, be followed a long way back through the company's history. While colour photographs were only available for comparatively little of the steam era, the GWR's well-developed publicity activities, plus the strong sense of its own importance, have ensured that much information is still available about earlier liveries.

Based on the evidence of a contemporary model, the Gooch Broad Gauge 'singles' had their outside frames painted dark brown, lined out with yellow. The wheels were a dark holly green, with yellow striping. On the boiler, the wooden lagging strips resembled varnished mahogany. There was much brightwork, with brass bands also encircling the lagging, and, even at this early stage, the need for a visual warning of the train's approach was met by painting the buffer-beams bright red. The NRM's reproduction of *Iron Duke* amply conveys the splendid overall effect. As far as is known, this livery continued until sheets of metal began to be applied to the outside of the boiler cladding, and these were then painted the same shade of green used on the wheels.

By Armstrong's time there was officially recorded information about the liveries, and the bands round the boiler were then being painted black, with white lining, which probably indicates that the use of brass had been abandoned in favour of iron. Flat areas, like cab side-sheets and tenders, were lined out in panels.

In 1881 Dean introduced a number of changes, the most striking being the use of Indian red for the outside frames and splashers, while the shade of green used was altered. He also started applying a chrome-orange stripe to the centre of the boiler bands, and the use of these with black lining was to continue until the end of the GWR, although the detail changed quite considerably. To begin with the wheels were green, but five years later they too became Indian red. In 1894 the green was again altered, this time to the middle-chrome or Brunswick shade which we know so well. The new livery was first applied to one of the Dean 'singles', *Achilles*, and perhaps more than any other class their splendid lines were enhanced by this striking paint scheme.

The 1900s were to see two further major changes, however, the first being the use of green for the splashers from 1903 onwards, and then, in 1906, black was used for the frames and wheels, which toned down the whole effect very considerably. Apart from the wartime years and various detailed changes that took place, especially with application of the company's name or initials, this livery was to last for the remainder of the company's existence, and was also adopted by British Railways for all its express passenger locomotives.

Maybe the GWR enthusiast is biased, but the absence of copper and brass brightwork on other companies' designs rendered the overall effect much less striking. There was, incidentally, one significant change in the way the BR version of this livery was applied to former GWR locomotives: the lining-out on the cab side was confined to a rectangular panel below the windows, whereas the GWR continued it up to cantrail level.

While on the subject of variations, it should be pointed out that Swindon and Wolverhampton liveries differed somewhat during the latter part of the 19th century. Harking back to the Oxford, Worcester & Wolverhampton Railway's (qv) traditions, the northern works compromised between them and what Swindon was using. A blue-green shade was applied to the boiler, cab and tender sides, while the clothing bands were lined out in black and white. Overall, variations in liveries were even more complex than the mechanical changes that took place during a locomotive's life, and one further point is worth making for the benefit of readers studying old illustrations of GWR (and some other companies') locomotives. In the early days of photography, the colour sensitivity of films was extremely uneven, and to overcome these limitations it was customary to paint the first of a new class in 'Works Grey' before taking its official portrait. Full lining out was applied, and this registered excellently on the large glass-plate negatives, but the relative shades on the resulting prints bore no relation to those observed by eye when one looked at a normally painted locomotive.

As well as the title 'GREAT WESTERN' in full, various different monograms were used from time to time on the tenders and

Locomotive liveries *Variations in tender liveries seen in preservation: pre-1904 florid monogram on* City of Truro; *'GREAT coat-of-arms WESTERN' on No 5029* Nunney Castle; *and the Second World War 'G W' flanking the arms on No 6998* Burton Agnes Hall. (All W. Adams)

side-tanks. Before the early 1900s a somewhat flamboyant version was used, with the three letters intertwined, then in late 1904 the coat of arms surrounded by a 'garter' and set between the words GREAT WESTERN became standard until about 1926. Least felicitous was the 'shirt-button' version adopted in 1934, which was far too emaciated and puny when applied to something as massive as a locomotive. There was considerable relief when the company reverted to the use of its coat of arms (qv) flanked by the block letters 'G W' during the Second World War for its principal passenger classes, a style which lasted until Nationalization. Other locomotives just used the three initials 'GWR'.

The coat of arms contained within the 'garter' was a design feature used also by other railways, although none of them could claim any actual connection with chivalry and the Order of the Garter. Their use of coats of arms was entirely unauthorized, except in a very few cases, and the GWR's was made up by putting those of London and Bristol side by side, without asking anyone's permission.

The classic curved GWR nameplate, with its individual brass letters bolted to the painted backplate inside a brass beading, dates from about 1905. Prior to that many different designs were used, some of the broad gauge locomotives just having the letters fixed to the frames. At the turn of the century a combined name and numberplate was used for several of the 'Bulldogs', some of them also containing a casting of the company's coat of arms. More details of the different variants, together with changes in livery, are given in the RCTS locomotive books, details of which can be found in the Bibiography.

PWBS

LOCOMOTIVE SHEDS

Originally all sheds, or depots, were under the control of Swindon. Around 1855 the Northern Division, the 'narrow gauge' territory north of Birmingham but also extending to include sheds west of a line from Leamington to Worcester and Aberdare, was set up. The Southern Division began to be sub-divided in the 1880s, and by the turn of the century there were the Paddington, Swindon, Bristol and Newton Abbot Districts. In 1918 a further re-organization saw GWR sheds divided into seven Divisions and the familiar codes appeared, stencilled on to locomotives. At the Grouping, the seven Divisions were Paddington (PDN) with six sheds, Bristol (BL) with seven, Newton Abbot (NA) with seven, Wolverhampton (WPN) with 11, Worcester (WOS) with six, Newport (NPT) with eight, and Neath (NEA) with ten. In addition there were a number of small subsheds. Two more Divisions were added after the Grouping, Cardiff Valleys and Central Wales.

Two basic designs were used for GWR

sheds, the straight through and the roundhouse; Old Oak Common (qv), the largest of its type in Great Britain, was the best-known example of the latter, with Didcot (qv) a perfectly preserved example of the former. Some of the older sheds were built of wood, but latterly most were of brick, although in some areas stone was used. Steel framing was a feature of latter-day sheds, such as at Southall (qv).

A great many people worked at a locomotive depot. Apart from drivers and firemen there were cleaners, shunters, storesmen, clerks, coalmen, fire-droppers, toolmen, tube-cleaners and steam-raisers, all of whom kept the engines running on a day-to-day basis, whilst the fitters, turners, coppersmiths, white-metallers, artisans and others carried out repair work. Running repairs were carried out at all main depots.

In 1947 Old Oak Common had the largest allocation of locomotives, 232, followed by Ebbw Junction, Newport, with 143, St Philips Marsh, Bristol, with 142, Cardiff Canton with 122, Tyseley with 116 and Swindon with 104. Part of Tyseley shed still exists as the Birmingham Railway Museum.

The accompanying list of GWR sheds is reproduced from *The British Locomotive Shed Directory* published by R. S. Grimsley in December 1947.

MCHB

London Division

Didcot	DID
Lambourn	
Newbury	
Winchester	
Old Oak Common	PDN
Aylesbury*	
Oxford	OXF
Abingdon	
Fairford	
Reading	RDG
Basingstoke	
Henley-on-Thames	
Marlow	
Wallingford	
Slough	SLO
Watlington	
Southall	SHL
Staines	

Bristol Division

Bristol Bath Road	BRD
St Philips Marsh	SPM
Bath	
Wells	
Weston-super-Mare	
Yatton	
Swindon	SDN
Andover Junction	
Chippenham	
Cirencester	
Faringdon	
Malmesbury	
Tetbury	
Westbury	WES
Frome	
Salisbury	
Trowbridge	
Weymouth	WEY
Bridport	
Yeovil	YEO

Newton Abbot Division

Exeter	EXE
Tiverton Junction	
Newton Abbot	NA
Ashburton	
Moretonhampstead	
Kingsbridge	
Penzance	PZ
Helston	
St Ives	
Laira (Plymouth)	LA
Plymouth Docks	
Princetown	
Launceston	
Moorswater	
St Blazey	SBZ
Bodmin	
Looe	
Taunton	TN
Barnstaple	
Bridgwater	
Minehead	
Truro	TR

Wolverhampton Division

Banbury	BAN
Birkenhead	BHD
Chester	CHR
Croes Newydd	CNYD
Bala	
Trawsfynydd	
Penmaenpool	
Leamington Spa	LMTN
Alcester	
Shrewsbury (Salop)	SLP
Ludlow	
Stourbridge	STB
Tyseley	TYS
Stratford-on-Avon	
Wellington	WLN
Crewe†	CRW
Wolverhampton (Stafford Road)	SRD
Wolverhampton (Oxley)	OXY

Worcester Division

Gloucester	GLO
Brimscombe	
Chalford	
Cheltenham	CHEL
Lydney	LYD
Hereford	HFD
Ross	
Kidderminster	KDR
Cleobury Mortimer	
Worcester	WOS
Evesham	
Honeybourne	
Kington‡	
Leominster‡	

Newport Division

Aberdare	ABDR
Aberbeeg	ABG
Cardiff	CDF
Llantrisant	LTS
Newport Ebbw Junction	NPT
Newport Pill	PILL
Pontypool Road	PPRD
Branches Fork	
Pontrilas	
Severn Tunnel Junction	STJ
Tondu	TDU
Bridgend	

Neath Division

Burry Port	BP
Carmarthen	CAR
Newcastle Emlyn	
Danygraig	DG
Port Talbot (Duffryn yard)	PT
Fishguard	FGD
Landore	LDR
Llanelly	LLY
Neath	NEA
Neath Bridge Street	
(N&B shed)	
Glyn Neath	
Neyland	NEY
Milford Haven	
Pantyffynnon	PFN
Swansea East Dock	SED
Whitland	WTD
Cardigan	
Pembroke Dock	

Cardiff Valleys Division

Abercynon	AYN
Barry	BRY
Cardiff East Dock	CED
Cathays	CHYS
Radyr	RYR
Ferndale	FDL
Merthyr	MTHR
Caeharris (Dowlais)	CH
Rhymney	RHY
Dowlais Central	
Treherbert	THT
Pwllyrhebog	

Central Wales Division

Aberystwyth	ABH
Aberystwyth (narrow gauge)	
Aberayron	
Brecon	BCN
Builth Wells	
Machynlleth	MCH
Corris (narrow gauge)	
Portmadoc	
Pwllheli	
Oswestry	OSW
Kerry	
Llanfyllin	
Llanidloes	
Moat Lane	
Welshpool (narrow gauge)	
Whitchurch LMS	

*Aylesbury was supplied with locomotives by Old Oak Common, Slough and Banbury.

†Crewe had a permanent allocation of two locomotives, but was also supplied by Wellington and Oxley.

‡Kington and Leominster were supplied with locomotives from both Worcester and Hereford

LODE STAR

In 1906 Churchward (qv) commenced building his 'Star' (qv) 4-6-0s, which were to become the basis of all GWR express passenger locomotives. The third to be built was No 4003 *Lode Star*. Most of them carried names that had previously been used for the broad gauge 'Stars' of the 1830s/1840s, but, in that earlier incarnation, the name had been spelt *Load Star*. No 4003 was one of the last of the class to remain in service, and was preserved after withdrawal in 1951. It was on display in the Great Western Railway Museum at Swindon when that opened in 1962, but is now at the NRM.

PWBS

LOOE BRANCH

Stations: Liskeard, Coombe Junction (2 m), St Keyne (3¾ m), Causeland (5 m), Looe (8¾ m)

From a separate platform at Liskeard (qv) this line circled down beneath the main line to reverse at Coombe Junction and then follow the East Looe River to a single platform station near the quay at Looe. Operation was by electric train token, with speed restrictions of 15 mph to Coombe Junction and 25 mph on to Looe.

The Liskeard & Looe Union Canal had been authorized in 1825 and opened in 1828, but increasing traffic from the Liskeard & Caradon Railway to the north led the canal company to obtain an Act of 11 May 1858 for a substitute railway which it opened on 27 December 1860 (passengers 11 September 1879). As the Liskeard & Looe Railway it obtained approval for a link from Coombe Junction to Liskeard in 1895 and opened it six years later.

The GWR took over the working of the L&LR and L&CR from 1 January 1909, but the latter's copper and granite traffic was already light and its lines were closed from 1 January 1917. As horse-worked routes they had been authorized in 1843 and opened from Moorswater to South Caradon in 1844 with a branch to Cheesewring in 1846. Extensions built included a deviation round Caradon Hill to avoid the Gonamena incline; those not built included a route on to Trewint and Launceston.

In later GWR years, ECLP had a siding at Moorswater for china clay loadings.

GB

LYDBROOK JUNCTION

After the Ross (qv) & Monmouth's line had opened on 3 August 1873, with public services beginning on the next day, Lydbrook achieved its junction status on 26th August 1874 when the Severn & Wye (qv) began freight services from Serridge Junction to provide another outlet for Forest of Dean coal. The latter route, which carried passenger services from 23 September 1875 to 8 July 1929, was successor to an early horse tramway.

GB

LYDNEY

The GWR station at Lydney lay on the road between the town and Lydney Harbour, which was on the west bank of the Severn 2 miles to the east. It had opened with the South Wales Railway's Grange Court–Chepstow East section (all qv) on 19 September 1851, and continued as an important calling point for both local and longer-distance services.

The Severn & Wye Railway's (qv) Lydney

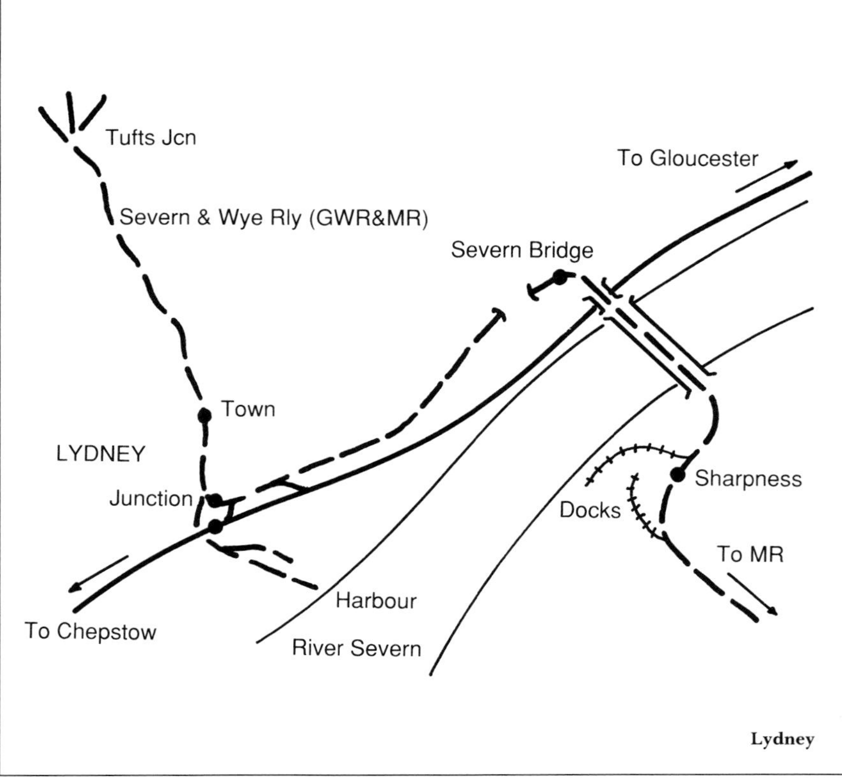

Lydney

Town station stood near the main road through Lydney, that company's docks branch of 9 December 1875 crossing the GWR line on the level and then dividing into the Upper Dock branch on the north side of the canal and the Lower Dock branch on the south. An S&W station near the GWR one was closed when the Severn Bridge Railway was added to the network on 17 October 1879, with new platforms opened on the west-north connecting curve which were to be linked by footbridge to the main-line pair. The two routes were physically connected at Lydney Junction before the later line climbed to cross the river by the 21-span Severn Bridge.

GB

LYTTELTON, LORD CHARLES GEORGE

Director, 1878–91. Born on 27 October 1842, he succeeded as the 5th Baron Lyttelton in 1876. Conservative MP for East Worcestershire in 1868 (Hagley Hall, Stourbridge, is the family seat), he represented the Constituency until 1874. He was appointed a GWR Director in 1878 in place of Wood (qv), became Chairman of the GWR Temperance Union, which launched the *Great Western Railway Magazine* (qv) in November 1888, and succeeded as the 8th Viscount Cobham on 19 April 1889. Elected Deputy-Chairman of the GWR in May 1890, he had to resign a year later when appointed a Railway Commissioner. He died on 9 June 1922.

CA

MACHYNLLETH

Machynlleth lies in the Dovey Valley on the former Cambrian Railways (qv) route from Whitchurch to Cardigan Bay. Its first station was opened with the Newtown & Machynlleth Railway's line on 3 January 1863 and handled through traffic from 1 July 1863 when the Aberystwyth & Welsh Coast Railway opened as far as Borth. Extension to Aberystwyth (qv) and absorption into the Cambrian Railways came in the following year.

Machynlleth was a passing point with staggered platforms and gabled stone buildings. In addition to the passenger trains north and south of the Dovey estuary it had a sizeable engine shed and a significant goods activity, including sidings for exchanging traffic with the adjoining Corris Railway (qv Aberllefenni branch).

GB

MACMILLAN, MAURICE HAROLD

Director, 1930–40. Born in London on 10 February 1894, from 1919–21 he was ADC to the Governor-General of Canada. In 1924 he was elected Unionist MP for Stockton-on-Tees, a Constituency he represented until 1929. He became a GWR Director in January 1930, and remained in office until 1940, when he was appointed a Government Minister. He was Prime Minister from 1957, following Sir Anthony Eden's resignation, until ill-health forced his own on 10 October 1963. On his 90th birthday he was created Earl of Stockton, and died on 29 December 1986 at his home, Birch Grove, Sussex.

CA

MAERDY BRANCH

Stations: Porth, Ynyshir (1 m),
Tylerstown (2½ m),
Ferndale (4¾ m),
Maerdy (6½ m)

The hard climb up the Rhondda Fach—1 in 60 steepening to 1 in 41—demanded a 24-minute allowance for the 20 weekday auto-trains (qv) or branch sets from Porth to Maerdy. On the way back they needed only 19 minutes to descend from the highest point on the Taff Vale system to the scissors junction beside the loco shed at Porth. The branch loco shed was sited at Ferndale.

The single-line Maerdy branch had been opened by the Taff Vale Railway (qv) in progressive stages (1849, 1856 and 1886), the Ferndale–Maerdy section involving the purchase of an earlier line. It was a coal line at first, with passenger services added in 1876 and extended to a single-platform station preceding the sidings of Maerdy Colliery in 1889.

GB

MAIDENHEAD

Although the Corporation of Maidenhead had opposed the first GWR Bill for fear of losing tolls on its bridge across the Thames, it no doubt celebrated the arrival of the special train at 12.19 pm on 31 May 1838 with which the GWR marked the opening of its first section of line. Public services then began on 4 June when 1,479 people were carried and paid £226 in fares. They had to use a wooden station east of the river, but got a nearer one on the High Wycombe branch (qv) when that opened in 1854 and a new main-line one west of the Thames in 1871.

The extension of the main line across the Thames came into service on 1 July 1839 using a remarkable Brunel brick bridge which had a rise of only 24¼ ft in the two main 128 ft spans. His critics made the most of some cracks which appeared in the eastern arch but were later confounded when it became clear that these were caused by easing the supports before the cement had set. After repairs, the centring was left in position to be on the safe side but then blew down in a gale without any repercussions for the daringly flat arch profiles.

Maidenhead enjoyed a good main-line and branch service, with some trains dividing there. It was one of several points which dealt with river excursions involving Salter's steamers, and there was a goods depot and private sidings.

GB

MAIL SERVICES

Only the GWR and LMS ran a Travelling Post Office train exclusively for mail. The GWR had in fact pioneered it, having run its inaugural train, between Paddington and Bristol, on 1 February 1855. The GWR called its train the 'Ocean Mails' because of the American traffic, this service being later extended to Plymouth: it left Paddington at 8.46 pm, reached Bristol at 12.30, Exeter at 3.20, and Plymouth at 5.45 am. At Plymouth, mail was transferred to and from the liners by tender, and, whisked swiftly to London by rail, would get there well before the ship had docked at Southampton. The up train ran to a similar schedule, leaving Plymouth at 7.10 pm and reaching Paddington at 4.19 am. At first only mail placed on the train at stations was sorted *en route*, but in 1866 pick-up apparatus was installed at Slough (qv).

This was by no means the first mail service, however—a 'Night Mail', also carrying passengers, first ran between Paddington and Twyford on 4 February

1840, and was extended with the line. Four sorting carriages were ordered in 1841. A regular service between Truro and Penzance (West Cornwall Railway, qv) began in 1864. The 'Cornwall TPO' later travelled between Falmouth and Penzance and was distinguished by the Duke of Cornwall's feathers and motto—'Ich Dien'—on the van sides: it was known to many as the 'Itch Dying' van.

The first train to traverse the newly narrowed gauge (qv Gauge conversion) in 1892 was the down 'Gloucester Mail', and after a gap of about 30 years, special mail trains returned in 1902, running between Paddington and Penzance. It was soon after this, but working an 'Ocean Mail' train down Wellington Bank in 1904, that 4-4-0 *City of Truro* (qv) attained immortality.

See also Ocean liner traffic

CA

MALMESBURY BRANCH

The Malmesbury Railway was incorporated on 25 July 1872, with the GWR providing much of the capital and completing the 6½-mile branch from Dauntsey in time for opening on 17 December 1877. From 17 July 1933 the branch was reduced to 3¾ miles by being linked to the South Wales main line at Little Somerford, its trains using the latter's up platform loop.

Malmesbury passengers were catered for by a weekday service of nine trains each way. Train staff working applied and the passenger trains operated without a guard.

GB

'MANOR' CLASS

To provide a 4-6-0 capable of operating over many of the company's secondary routes, Collett (qv) started in 1938 to 'renew' a number of the Churchward (qv) 'Moguls', giving them this wheel arrangement and a new Standard No 14 boiler. The result was the 'Manors', numbered in the 78xx series, and the 20 which were built before the Second World War all utilized the driving wheels and motion of withdrawn 2-6-0s. In 1950 there was a need for additional similar locomotives, and a further 10 were constructed from scratch. Like the 'Granges' (qv), the running-plate was raised over the cylinders, but the boilers of the 'Manors' were noticeably smaller. In the

'Manor' Class *No 7800* Torquay Manor. (GWR Museum, Swindon)

early 1950s, the work carried out by the testing department at Swindon indicated that their steaming capacity could be considerably improved by alterations to the smokebox arrangements, and a redesigned chimney was fitted which could be recognized by the absence of a deflector.

The class was capable of operating over the Cambrian Railways' routes west of Shrewsbury, and replaced the outside-framed 'Dukedog' 4-4-0s on these duties. In the declining years of steam, the chocolate and cream coaches of the 'Cambrian Coast Express' were regularly worked by one of them, fully-lined out in Brunswick green, and the up train would be double-headed by a pair of the class to deal with the gradients of Talerddig Bank. They also took over many of the piloting duties for the heavier trains over the South Devon banks, this time replacing the 'Bulldogs'.

(See also Locomotives)

PWBS

MARKET DRAYTON

Market Drayton was the point at which trains on the GWR's Crewe branch (qv) made connection with those on the former North Staffordshire Railway line to Stoke-on-Trent. The station consisted of a main up-side platform and a down island, with a sizeable goods depot behind the former. The junction between the two routes lay just to the north.

The section north of Market Drayton was opened by the Nantwich & Market Drayton Railway on 20 October 1863 and that to the south by the Wellington & Drayton Railway on 16 October 1867, the NSR line following three years later.

GB

MARKHAM COLLIERY BRANCH

This branch did carry a short-lived passenger service but its main function was that of a freight route serving several collieries, quarries and public goods depots. It started life as Hall's Tramroad, a horse-worked line which the GWR leased from the Countess of Llanover as a reaction to the LNWR's acquisition of the Sirhowy Tramroad. In GWR hands the section from Penar Junction up the Sirhowy Valley to Manmoel was converted to a conventional line from 18 March 1886, and that south to Hall's Road Junction, Risca, in September 1912. By that time the main route had been extended to Markham (16 July 1905) and a Cwmcarn branch added (April 1911).

The auto-trains (qv) introduced in 1927 between Crumlin/Pontypool Road and Penmaen and Oakdale Halts lasted only five years, although a Fridays-only service to the former continued until the war.

GB

MARLBOROUGH BRANCH

The GWR had agreed to work the Marlborough Railway before its incorporation on 22 July 1861 and eventually

Marlborough branch *The run-round loop and engine shed of Marlborough High Level, and below in the background the M&SWJR Low Level station.* (Lens of Sutton)

acquired it, by an offer of £120 of GWR stock for each £100 of the local company's ordinary stock, from 1 July 1896. The 5 m 49 ch broad gauge single line, with no intermediate stations, had been opened from the Berks & Hants Extension line at Savernake (both qv) to a station on the south side of Marlborough on 14 April 1864.

When the trains of the Swindon, Marlborough & Andover Railway (qv Midland & SW Junction Railway) started running throughout on 5 February 1883 they used the GWR's Marlborough branch from a point just south of the latter's High Level station through to Savernake. But the GWR charges, operation and general attitude proved unacceptable and the smaller railway opened a separate line from 26 June 1898. The situation changed again after Grouping when the northern section of the 1864 line was abandoned in favour of a new connection and use of the Low Level station at Marlborough.

GB

MARLOW BRANCH

Until 28 June 1873, Marlow folk had to make their rail journeys to and from Marlow Road on the 1854 Wycombe Railway line (qv High Wycombe line) from Maidenhead. They then got their own single-line branch running 2 m 60 ch from a junction at Marlow Road (Bourne End from 1874), along the north bank of the Thames and into a single-platform terminus, with run-round loop, loco and goods sheds and timber yard, at Marlow proper. The GWR had subscribed to the Great Marlow Railway, which was incorporated on 13 July 1868, and worked it from opening, with full amalgamation from 1 July 1897.

Electric token working was pioneered on the Marlow branch which enjoyed a good shuttle service plus some through Paddington and High Wycombe trains. The shuttle combination of 0-4-2T and trailer was known locally as the 'Marlow Donkey'.

GB

MARSHALLING YARDS

It has been estimated that every 100 miles travelled by a freight train involved 75 miles of shunting. As the volume of goods traffic grew, the GWR decided that Bristol would be conveniently sited as a marshalling centre, and yards were established at Bristol East, Bristol West and Stoke Gifford. Bristol East was converted to hump working in 1923, and this resulted in considerable savings in engine hours. The new layout's 14 sidings connected to the hump had a holding capacity of 468 wagons. The fact that there were also three yards in South Wales, not far from Bristol, at Severn Tunnel Junction (qv) Pontypool Road (qv and Coal traffic) and at Rogerstone, near Newport, another hump yard, reflects the amount of goods traffic emanating from that area and the importance the GWR attached to it.

There was also a large yard at Llandilo Junction, east of Llanelly, mainly for steel traffic. Smaller yards at Radyr (north of Cardiff) and Alexandra Dock (Newport) dealt mainly with coal. The yard at Severn Tunnel Junction, a modest arrangement of sorting sidings in 1920, grew to a full-scale yard in 1931, but closed in 1987. Banbury hump yard was also opened in 1931.

(*See also Freight services*)

CA

MATTHEWS, GILBERT

Superintendent of the Line, 1941–47. Matthews entered GWR service in 1908. He gained experience in station working in the London Division, and then went to the USA to study traffic operation on the Pennsylvania and New York Central railroads. On his return to the UK he was attached to the passenger train running department of the Superintendent of the Line's office, was appointed Chief Clerk to the Divisional Superintendent, Plymouth, in 1925, and seven years later appointed Assistant to the Superintendent of the Line, dealing mainly with staff matters. He became Operating Assistant in July 1934 and was appointed Divisional Superintendent, Swansea, in October 1937, but returned to Paddington as Principal Assistant to the Superintendent of the Line in January 1939. He succeeded F. R. Potter (qv) from 1 January 1941, and retired at Nationalization.

CA

MERTHYR TYDFIL

The first conventional railway to serve the growing coal and iron activity at Merthyr Tydfil was the Taff Vale (qv) which arrived at a Plymouth Street station on 12 April 1841. Ten years later it was connected to the great Dowlais ironworks by a steep $1\frac{3}{4}$-mile tramway which also carried passengers in its first three years of existence.

In 1853 the Vale of Neath Railway (qv) reached Merthyr from the west, descending at 1 in 80/50 via the 2,497 yd Merthyr Tunnel to a High Street station opened on 2 November. Next came the troubled but ambitious Brecon & Merthyr (qv), arriving from the north by a route of great viaducts and steep gradients on 1 August 1868. It used the by now GWR High Street station, with the Taff Vale transferring there in 1878 (leaving Plymouth Street as a goods depot) and the LNWR joining in 1879. From 1 April 1886 High Street also welcomed the Quaker's Yard & Merthyr Joint Railway (GWR and Rhymney) which arrived via the west bank of the Taff.

Merthyr's four radiating routes gave it two passenger services to Cardiff (via Pontypridd or Nelson) down the valley, those north to Pontsticill Junction (qv) and the Brecon–Newport line, others east via the LNWR to Abergavenny, and the local workings west via Abernant (3¾ m) and Llwydcoed (5½ m) to Hirwaun (7½ m).

After modification in 1867, the station had four main platforms under a glazed wooden overall roof, plus an up-side bay. A substantial goods depot lay beyond and a 7-line loco shed to the south. Although the ironworks traffic declined before the turn of the century, the GWR continued to carry vast quantities of coal, especially from the sidings along the ex-B&M and TVR routes.

GB

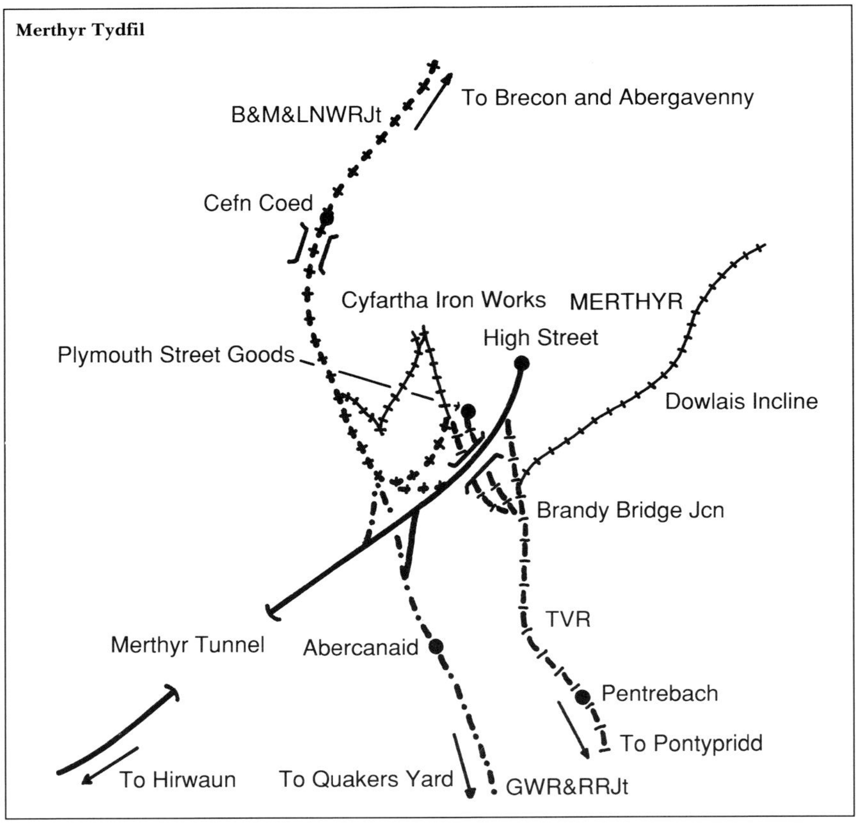

Merthyr Tydfil

MIDLAND & SOUTH WESTERN JUNCTION RAILWAY

The main line of the Midland & South Western Junction Railway ran from Andoversford Junction on the GWR's Cheltenham–Banbury line to Red Post Junction on the LSWR's Waterloo–Exeter main line, running powers into Cheltenham allowing the railway to fulfil its title. It derived originally from the Swindon, Marlborough & Andover Railway (qv Marlborough branch) whose Bill received the Royal Assent on 21 July 1873. Construction was delayed by financial constraints but the line eventually opened between Swindon and the GWR's Marlborough branch on 27 July 1881 and on from Savernake to Andover on 5 February 1883.

North of Swindon, the Swindon & Cheltenham Extension Railway had been incorporated on 18 July 1881 and was opened to Cirencester on 18 December 1883. Amalgamation into the M&SWJ followed in 1884 and then, after more financial problems, came opening through to Andoversford (and thus Cheltenham) on 1 August 1891. The GWR had been obstructive throughout the emergence of the new line, and one of Sam Fay's first tasks as its General Manager was to avoid dependence on that company's Marlborough branch by securing an Act for the Marlborough & Grafton Railway on 7 August 1896 and having it open from 26 June 1898.

Before the M&SWJ passed to the GWR under the 1923 Grouping it had opened a branch to Tidworth Camp in 1902 (goods 1 July, passengers 1 October) and doubled 28¾ of its 60¾ route miles using a loan from the Midland Railway. But it was hardly a prosperous line, paying 3% on its debenture stock and needing the rest of its earnings to pay off the loan.

(*See also Cheltenham–Andover line*)

GB

MILFORD HAVEN BRANCH

The Milford Haven Railway was incorporated by an Act of 5 June 1856 to build a broad gauge link to the South Wales Railway's (qv) Neyland line. The resultant 4-mile, 1 in 60 single-line branch was duly opened on 7 September 1863 and was worked by the GWR into which it was absorbed in 1896. Two industrial systems were connected to the GWR line at Milford, that of the docks undertaking and an industrial estate line running to an iron pier at Newton Noyes.

The small engine shed at Milford Haven provided pannier tanks for the local service via Milford Haven Branch Junction and on to Johnston, and also to marshal the fish-vans and other traffic handed over by the docks shunters. The branch was worked by electric token issued by the signal box at the end of the single, curving platform.

GB

MILK TRAFFIC

The existence of a railway network and an awakening demand for milk in Britain's growing towns and cities stimulated dairy farming at the end of the last century, and by 1900 milk traffic on the GWR had reached 2½ million gallons a year. The early rail movements were in tall 17-gallon churns carried in the guard's van of passenger services, but later the stubby and more

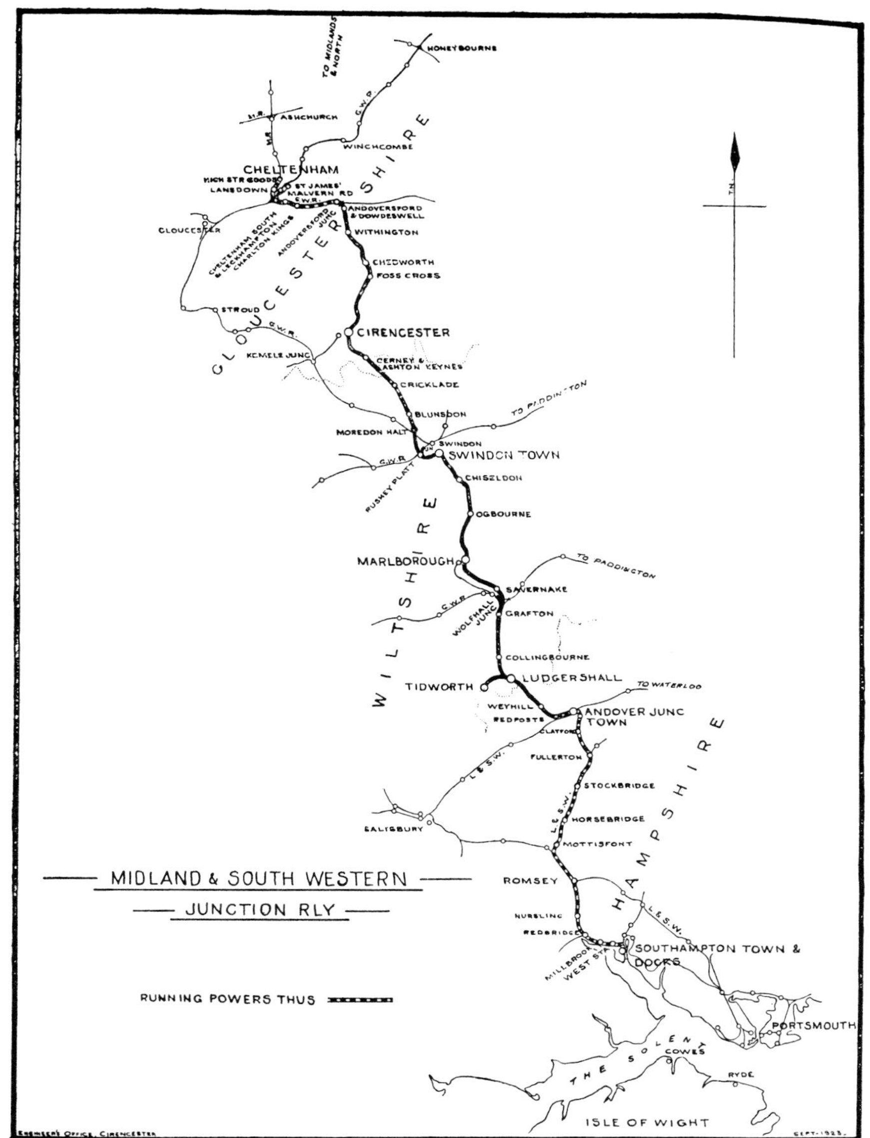

Midland & South Western Junction Railway
(GWR Magazine, 1923)

hygienic 10-gallon churns began to take over and the larger flows to pass in van loads.

By 1922 the GWR's milk carryings had risen to 75 million gallons, requiring 60 special trains daily and a fleet of 1,000 louvre-sided vans. Fixed and demountable rail tanks began to appear in the 1930s, working from creameries in the South West to distribution depots such as those of the London Co-operative Society at West Ealing, and United Dairies at Wood Lane.

(See also Rolling-stock, goods)

GB

MILLS, EDWARD WHELER

Director, 1835–63. An original member of the London Committee, he was a first Director of the GWR. As a partner in Glyn, Mills & Co from 1835–64, he was able to play a useful role as a link between the company and its bankers. He resigned in 1863.

CA

MILNE, SIR JAMES

General Manager, 1929–47. Following Pole (qv) was a difficult task, particularly during the '30s slump. Milne, however, not only succeeded brilliantly, but showed inspiring qualities during the war years.

He was born in Ireland, in 1883, and joined the GWR as a pupil in the Swindon Locomotive Department in 1904. He progressed via several posts in the offices of the General Manager and Superintendent of the Line, and in January 1916 became Assistant Divisional Superintendent, Plymouth. A transfer to the Ministry of Transport in 1919 was followed by a return to the GWR from 1 January 1922, as Assistant to the General Manager; he was made Principal Assistant later in the year. He became Assistant General Manager in 1924, and succeeded Pole in 1929. He retired from railway service at Nationalization, and died on 1 April 1958 at Woldingham, Surrey.

CA

MINEHEAD BRANCH

Stations: Norton Fitzwarren (2 miles from Taunton), Bishop's Lydeard (5 m), Crowcombe (9 m), Stogumber (11¾ m), Williton (15 m), Watchet (16¾ m), Washford (19 m), Blue Anchor (21¼ m), Dunster (23 m), Minehead (24¾ m)

The railway to Minehead was promoted by local people and survives today as the preserved West Somerset Railway. The holidaymakers it carries are a reminder of hectic summer Saturdays in the GWR era when the line handled 15 trains each way, compared with four in the opening years. In 1938, for example, the 9.35 am from Paddington got its passengers to Minehead non-stop by 12.55 pm, with a coach link on to Lynton and a cliff railway descent thence to Lynmouth.

Two local schemes brought the Minehead line into existence. The first was the West Somerset Railway, incorporated on 17 August 1857 and opening a 14 m 22 ch line to Watchet on 31 March 1862. Then came the Minehead Railway with a (second) Act authorizing the 8 m 10 ch extension on

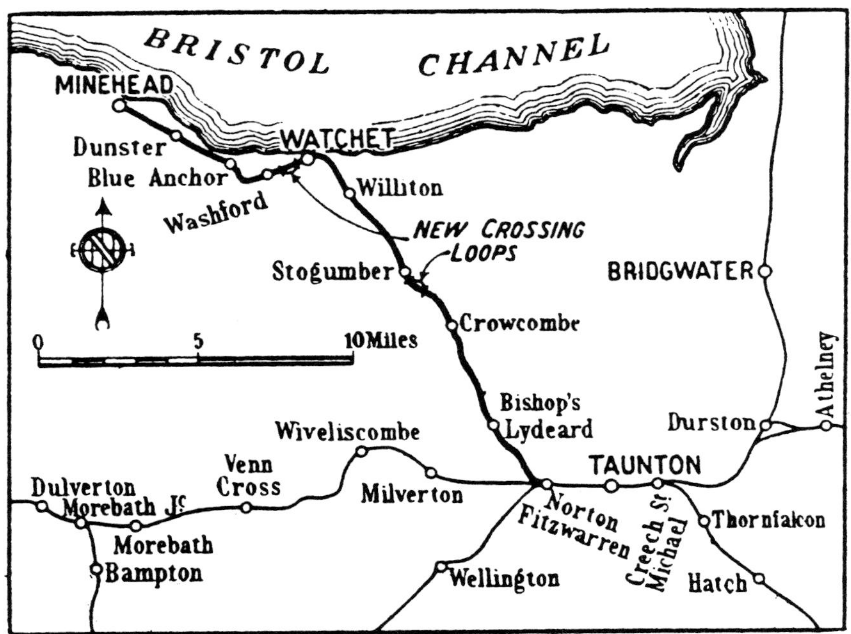

Minehead branch *Map of the branch showing the provision of new 750 ft passing loops, to be laid out for 40 mph running and with automatic tablet exchanging apparatus ready for the summer service of 1934.* (GWR Magazine, 1933)

29 June 1871 and opening it on 16 July 1874. The Bristol & Exeter Railway (qv) worked both lines.

As far as Dunster the line was single with passing loops, and its course below the Quantock Hills necessitated quite steep gradients to reach the summits at Crowcombe and Washford. Freight traffic arose mainly at Watchet and from its harbour branch, with passenger revenue highest at Minehead, which received a new station in 1905.

GB

MOAT LANE JUNCTION–BRECON LINE

Stations: Moat Lane Junction, Llandinam (2 m), Dolwen ($4\frac{3}{4}$ m), Llanidloes ($7\frac{1}{2}$ m), Tylwch ($10\frac{3}{4}$ m), Pantydwr ($14\frac{3}{4}$ m), St Harmons (16 m), Rhayader ($21\frac{1}{2}$ m), Doldowlod ($24\frac{3}{4}$ m), Newbridge-on-Wye ($28\frac{3}{4}$ m), Builth Road ($32\frac{3}{4}$ m), Builth Wells ($34\frac{1}{4}$ m), Aberedw ($38\frac{1}{4}$ m), Erwood (41 m), Boughrood & Llyswen ($45\frac{1}{4}$ m), Three Cocks Junction (48 m), Talgarth ($50\frac{1}{4}$ m), Trefeinon ($52\frac{3}{4}$ m), Talyllyn Junction ($55\frac{3}{4}$ m), Brecon ($59\frac{3}{4}$ m)

Passengers from the Welshpool line joined the Mid-Wales line at Moat Lane Junction and set off for Llanidloes over the course of the Llanidloes & Newtown Railway opened on 9 October 1859. There the River Severn was abandoned as a companion in favour of the River Dulas which was followed to a summit at Pantydwr, 947 ft above sea level and the highest point on the Cambrian Railways (qv) system. Next came a difficult section through Marteg Tunnel, taking the line on to join the River Wye on its descent from the Cambrian Mountains. This was followed all the way from Rhayader, beneath the Central Wales line at Builth Road and on to join the Hereford–Brecon line at Three Cocks Junction. This southern section of the through line had been authorized by Mid-Wales Railway Acts of 1 August 1859 and 3 July 1860 and was opened in 1864 (goods 1 September, passengers 21 September).

Many of the trains on the Mid-Wales route were worked by Cambrian 0-6-0 locomotives because of restrictive axle loadings on the southern section. By the time they had called at 17 stations and five halts, their passengers had spent two hours in getting to Talyllyn Junction, which would double if they went on to Cardiff or Newport. Freight varied from special jobs like the materials for the Elan Valley dams to livestock during the autumn cattle sales and milk from the Builth Wells creamery.

Worked by the Cambrian Railways from 2 April 1888 and amalgamated with that company from 1 July 1904, the Mid-Wales line passed to the GWR at Grouping.

GB

MONMOUTH

Monmouth's main station was Troy, situated to the south of the town with a substantial goods depot alongside. Its twin platforms were preceded by a 148-yard tunnel at the Usk end and followed by the separation of the Chepstow and Ross-on-Wye (both qv) routes, which became single as they diverged to cross the River Wye by viaducts of very different design. An old tunnel beneath the station approach commemorated an abortive 1865 scheme for a line to Pontrilas.

The Coleford, Monmouth, Usk & Pontypool Railway had reached Troy on 12 October 1857, and the Ross & Monmouth Railway began public services to May Hill, Monmouth's other station, on 4 August 1873. The GWR linked the two from the following 1 May after which May Hill remained just an ordinary affair of a single wooden platform and simple wooden buildings.

GB

MONMOUTHSHIRE RAILWAY & CANAL CO

Amalgamated with the GWR from 1 August 1880, this company had been incorporated by an Act of 1792 under which it built two canals to bring industrial products to the estuary at Newport. The western canal arm ran to Crumlin (qv) and the eastern one to Pontnewynydd. Both used tramroads as feeders, the Blaenavon one dating back to 1795 and the Aberbeeg and Ebbw Vale lines to 1798 (all qv).

After changing gauge from 3 ft 4 ins to 4 ft 2 ins, the MR&C eventually obtained an Act of 31 July 1845 which authorized a standard gauge line from Newport Docks to Trevethin Junction, Pontypool, and the adaptation of its existing lines for standard gauge use. Six Acts (1848, 1852, 1853,

Monmouth *Troy station looking north, the Ross-on-Wye line continuing downhill to the left and the Chepstow line swinging eastwards over the Wye viaduct; an auto-train approaches from the latter route, while another appears to be stabled at the end of the yard on the left.* (Steamchest Collection)

1865, 1874 and 1876) and ten lines (Newport–Pontypool 1853, Pontypool–Blaenavon 1854, Newport Old Dock Branch 1854, Third Line Junction–Trosnant Junction 1857, Abertillery–Cwmtillery 1858, Nantyglo Gate–Nantyglo 1858, Cwmffwdoer/ Cwmnantddu branches 1871, Talywain branch 1873, Newport Gaer branch 1879, and Talywain Branch Extension 1879) later, the MR&C became part of the GWR which had worked it from 1 August 1875.

GB

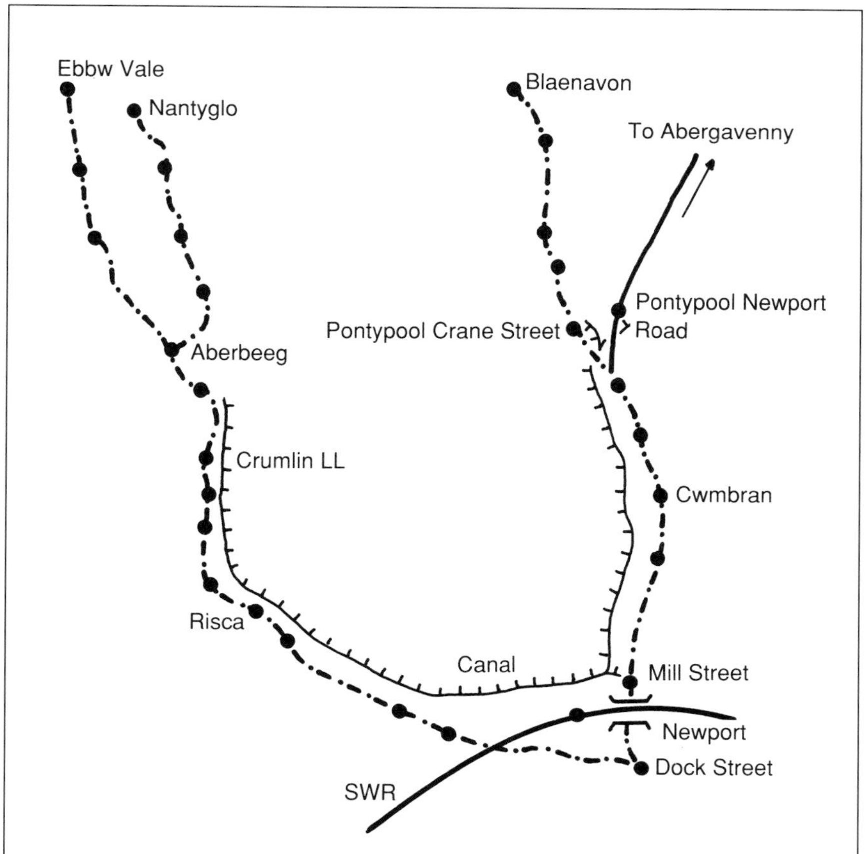

Ebbw Vale
Nantyglo
Blaenavon
To Abergavenny
Pontypool Newport Road
Pontypool Crane Street
Aberbeeg
Crumlin LL
Cwmbran
Risca
Canal
Mill Street
Newport
Dock Street
SWR

Monmouthshire Railway & Canal Co

MORETONHAMPSTEAD BRANCH

Stations: Newton Abbot, Teigngrace ($2\frac{1}{4}$ m), Heathfield ($3\frac{3}{4}$ m), Brimley Halt ($5\frac{1}{2}$ m), Bovey (6 m), Hawkmoor Halt ($7\frac{3}{4}$ m), Lustleigh ($8\frac{3}{4}$ m), Moretonhampstead ($12\frac{1}{2}$ m)

With a ruling gradient of 1 in 49, the 12 m 28 ch Moretonhampstead branch ran north from the main line at Newton Abbot and along the course of the River Bovey to a twin-track, single-platform covered station on the edge of Dartmoor. Operation was by electric train staff with crossing points at Heathfield and Bovey, the former being the junction for the Teign Valley route to Exeter.

The original broad gauge line had been authorized to the Moretonhampstead & South Devon Railway by an Act of 7 July 1862, with opening from 4 July 1866 and working by the South Devon Railway (qv) with which the smaller concern was amalgamated from 1 July 1872. The GWR introduced a bus service to Chagford in 1906, another to Princetown in 1909 and later established a hotel (qv Hotels) for the increasing tourist business.

Part of the southern portion of the branch utilized the route of the 1820 Haytor Tramway.

GB

MORETON-IN-MARSH

This Cotswold town was the first to join the railway age, having been the headquarters of the 1826 Stratford & Moreton Railway, a 17-mile tramway that was to become the GWR's Shipston-on-Stour branch (qv) from 1 July 1889. The station opened by the Oxford, Worcester & Wolverhampton Railway (qv) on 4 June 1853 thus became a junction in 1889 with an up-side platform for the morning and evening branch trains which lasted only until 8 July 1929.

GB

Moreton-in-Marsh *The station, looking north.* (Steamchest Collection)

MORRIS, JOSEPH

Superintendent of the Line, 1904–10. Born at Whittington, Shropshire, in 1845, he entered GWR service as a Clerk at Oswestry in 1861. He moved to the Superintendent's office in Chester in 1864, was appointed Chief Clerk in 1870, Assistant Clerk in 1879, and became Superintendent of the Northern Division in 1886. In 1891 he moved to Paddington as Assistant to Burlinson (qv), and was appointed to succeed Allen (qv) as Superintendent of the Line from 1 January 1904. He retired at the end of 1910, and was awarded the insignia of the RVO 5th Class.

CA

MOTOR VEHICLE TRAINS

Like the other Grouping companies, in the 1920s the GWR encouraged motorists to take their cars by train, the arrangements virtually being a continuation of the earlier practices for the transport of the landed gentry's carriages by rail. However, long before Eurotunnel started to consider transporting cars under the sea, the GWR provided such a service beneath the Severn (qv Severn Tunnel). This saved the considerable detour via Gloucester, and operated between Severn Tunnel Junction (qv), on the Welsh side of the Bristol Channel, and Patchway and Pilning on the other. Normally vehicles were carried at Owner's Risk on open wagons, although tarpaulins could be hired to protect them from sparks and sooty water. Given sufficient notice, a

Motor vehicle trains *'. . .avoid tedious Motoring over congested and uninteresting roads' advises this 1937 advertisement.*

FACILITIES FOR MOTORISTS.

Private Motor Cars are conveyed for rail journeys in Great Britain by Passenger Train or other Similar Service at Owner's Risk at reduced rates of:—

3d. per mile for single journey.

4½d. per mile for return journey.

(i.e., 3d. per mile outward journey, 1½d. per mile homeward journey.)
Minimum distance 50 miles single journey.

Provided not less than one First-class or two Third-class adult Passengers travel between the same points and by the same route. These facilities do not apply to cars accompanying passengers to and from shows or Exhibitions.

TRAVEL BY RAIL DIRECT TO THE DELIGHTFUL G.W.R. HOLIDAY LANDS and avoid tedious Motoring over congested and uninteresting roads. Full particulars from G.W.R. Stations and Offices.

covered carriage truck could be provided, and the higher Company's Risk rates were then charged.

PWBS

MOTT, CHARLES GREY

Director, 1868–1905. Born in 1833, he was appointed a Director of the GWR in 1868, and was very much concerned with the company's welfare in the Merseyside area. For 37 years he was a member of the joint LNWR/GWR Committee, as well as being involved with other railways both in Britain and abroad, and active in the problem of traffic questions in and around London. On his instigation, electricity was installed by the City & South London Railway (the southern section of the present-day Northern Line), and, partly as a result of this, he was unofficially designated the 'Father of the Tubes'. At the time of his death, on 7 November 1905, he was, at 72, the longest-serving member of the GWR Board. He is buried at Harrow Weald.

CA

NATIONALIZATION

Whilst all the 'Big Four' main-line railways opposed Nationalization, the GWR was most vehement and Sir James Milne (qv), the company's last General Manager, refused the post of the first Chairman of the Railway Executive. For a decade and more, the Western Region of British Railways, as the GWR became, carried on almost as though nothing had changed, except for the colour of its coaches, and even many of these went back to chocolate and cream in the late 1950s. But the Region was running into severe financial trouble, and at the beginning of the 1960s a management re-organization coincided with dieselization, and the old Great Western died quickly.

The GWR's territory had been reasonably self-contained, but in the areas where it was in competition with other companies, the Western Region absorbed former Southern Railway lines west of Exeter, LMS ones south-west of Birmingham and in Central and South Wales. However, the

Nationalization *No clue to the thoughts of the railwayman surveying the new BR emblem in this official Great Western photograph!* (GWR Museum, Swindon)

general public was hardly aware of this, for the Southern and London Midland Regions continued to operate the lines and provide the carriages and motive power.

In the early 1950s the Western was the largest Region of British Railways, with 4,350 route miles, but later revisions and closures considerably reduced this. Notable losses in the 1960s and '70s were the Bristol–Stratford-on-Avon–Birmingham main line with the transfer of through trains to the former LMS route, the down-grading of the company's other west-to-north main line via the Severn Tunnel and Shrewsbury, the transfer of almost all the through Paddington to Birmingham trains to the Euston route after electrification, and the singling of the Castle Cary to Weymouth line with the Channel Island boat trains transferring to the rival Bournemouth and Waterloo route.

The GWR had led the way with the introduction of diesel railcars (qv) in the 1930s and had a gas turbine locomotive on order from Switzerland, which was delivered in 1950. This latter proved a failure, and although the pioneer Advanced Passenger Train was also gas turbine-powered, this particular avenue proved a dead-end. Likewise, Nationalized Swindon went its own way with diesel-hydraulic transmissions; the 2,700hp 'Westerns' were the most handsome of all the big main-line diesels and were held in great affection by enthusiasts, but along with the less powerful 'Warships' and 'Hymeks' they succumbed to the more conventional diesel-electric. The original Mk II carriage was designed and built at Swindon, though subsequent production took place at other BR works. The mistake made by the GWR in its later years, and the Western Region in its early ones, was surely not to have gone electric.

MCHB

NEATH

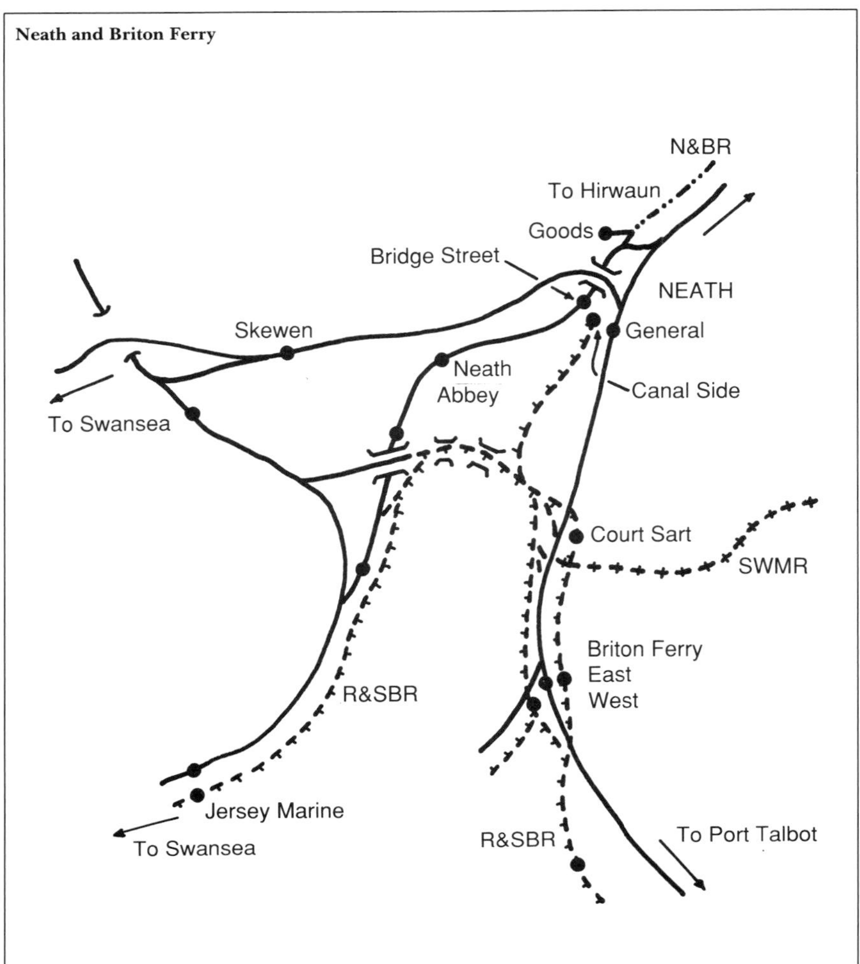

Home of the Abbey Ironworks, Neath was reached by the South Wales Railway (qv) on 18 June 1850, with four other railways following—the Vale of Neath (qv) (1 September 1851), the Swansea & Neath (15 July 1863), the Neath & Brecon (qv) (2 October 1864) and the Rhondda & Swansea Bay (qv) (14 December 1894). The SWR and R&SB routes approached along the east side of the Neath River which the latter crossed to continue its journey to Swansea via Jersey Marine and the sandy coastal dunes. The inland (VoN and N&B) routes were linked to the S&N's parallel course to Swansea leaving the main line to loop inland via Skewen. There and at Jersey Marine the Swansea District line (qv) was linked to the SWR and R&SB crossings of the river.

Served additionally by the GWR-acquired docks at Briton Ferry (qv), Neath was a busy traffic location for the GWR when all the independent companies had passed to it by the Grouping. In addition to Neath General station on the main line, the ex-R&SB Canal Side terminus adjacent continued in use until 1935, and there were west bank route stations at Bridge Street and Neath Abbey. Neath General was the main goods depot for public traffic, but there were four smaller depots and 17 private sidings, mostly for tinplate traffic but including the Vale of Neath brewery and the connection to the Neath Abbey Estate Railway.

GB

NEATH & BRECON RAILWAY

Stations: Neath Riverside, Cilfrew (2 m), Crynant (5¼ m), Seven Sisters (8½ m), Onllwyn (10 m), Colbren Junction (10¾ m), Craigynos (14 m), Cray (20½ m), Devynock & Senny Bridge (24 m), Aberbran (28 m), Cradoc (30 m), Brecon (32½ m)

This enterprise started life with an Act accorded to the Dulais Valley Railway on 29 July 1862 and authorizing a line from Drim Colliery, Onllwyn, to a junction with the Vale of Neath (qv) at Cadoxton. Before opening on 2 October 1864 a further Act had authorized the climb on to Devynock and through the Vale of Usk to Brecon (qv), this being brought into use on 3 June 1867.

After absorbing the Swansea Vale & Neath & Brecon Junction Railway and opening its line from Colbren Junction to the Swansea Vale Railway at Ynysygeinon on 10 November 1873, the N&B found itself hosting MR Swansea–Brecon services. Seeking a better deal for these resulted in a brief flirtation with the Manchester, Sheffield & Lincolnshire Railway in 1889! Other unconventional features of the N&B were its Fairlie locomotives, a saloon for the use of singer Adelina Patti, and the goats provided as a milk supply for the lonely Bwlch crossing loop.

The N&B and its 40-mile system passed into the GWR Group on 1 January 1922. After the LMS Swansea services ceased at the end of 1930, the GWR provided three Neath-Brecon trains each way on weekdays to supplement those to Colbren and Craigynos.

GB

NELSON BRANCHES

Stations: Pontypridd, Cilfynydd (1¼ m), Travellers Rest (2¾ m), Nelson (5 m)

The Taff Vale Railway (qv) built two connections between its main line north of Pontypridd (qv) and the GWR at Llancaiach. The first derived from the company's 1836 Act of incorporation and was opened for 3 m 29 ch from Stormstown Junction and up the Nant Cae-dudwg on 25 November 1841. It originally involved a 1 in 11 incline but was later re-aligned to avoid this.

The second route began with an 1887 mineral branch from Pont Shon Norton Junction to Albion Colliery which was extended to Ynysydwr Junction on the original route in 1900. A passenger service began on 1 June of that year and was continued by the GWR until 12 September 1932. The seven trains each way on weekdays called at the two intermediate stations plus halts at Berw Road and Llanfabon Road.

Single with a crossing loop at Cilfynydd, the 1887–1900 route was 5 m 36 ch long, had a ruling gradient of 1 in 40 and three electric train staff sections.

GB

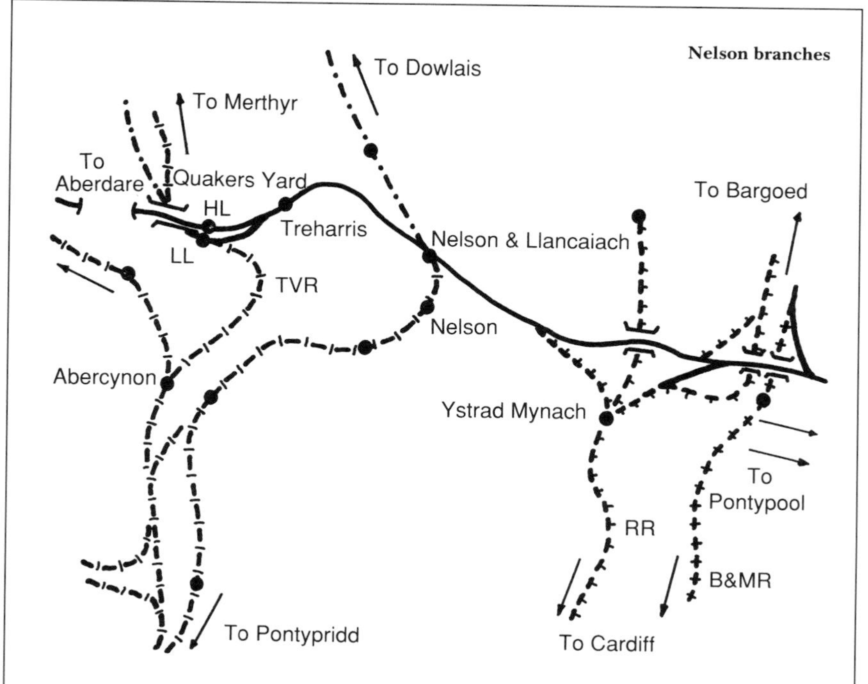

NEWBURY

The first station at Newbury was opened when GWR trains started running between Reading and Hungerford (qv Reading–Taunton line) on 21 December 1847. Activity increased as the town grew bigger and the railway was extended to Devizes in 1862, and again in the 1880s when the Didcot, Newbury & Southampton Railway (qv) trains arrived from Didcot on 13 April 1882 and extended on to Winchester on 4 May 1885. Lambourn branch (qv) trains were added from 4 April 1898 so that by the time the new West of England through route came into being in 1906 Newbury was badly in need of improved facilities.

Work started on a new station for Newbury in May 1908 and it was brought into use on 29 May 1910. Platform loops served the 1,065 ft up platform and the 950 ft one on the down side, the former having bays for the Lambourn and Didcot services and the latter a country-end bay for Winchester trains. The 206 ft up side main buildings, in red brick with Bath stone dressings, included booking, parcels, cloakroom, waiting and telegraph facilities plus refreshment and tea rooms panelled in fumed oak. (See layout plan overleaf)

A large goods depot stood at the London end of the Newbury complex and beyond that Newbury Racecourse station, which was first used for the meetings on 26–27 September 1905. On race days a service of 'sixty-minute specials' ran to and from Paddington, excursions operated from provincial centres and cheap tickets were available from local stations.

GB

NEWCASTLE EMLYN BRANCH

Stations: Pencader, Llandyssul (3½ m), Pentrecourt Platform (5¼ m), Henllan (7½ m), Newcastle Emlyn (10½ m)

Although the branch enjoyed a service of seven trains each way on weekdays, including one school train, traffic could normally be handled by an 0-4-2T locomotive and a single coach. This took 28–30 minutes for the 10½-mile journey via passing loops at Llandyssul and Henllan and along the course of the River Teifi to a terminus east of the small town of Newcastle Emlyn. The single-platform station there included a run-round loop, engine shed and turntable, and a goods shed and dock.

The line originated with the 1854 Carmarthen & Cardigan Railway which managed to get to Llandyssul by 1864 but then fell upon troubled times which only ended with acquisition by the GWR from 1 July 1881. By this time the Whitland &

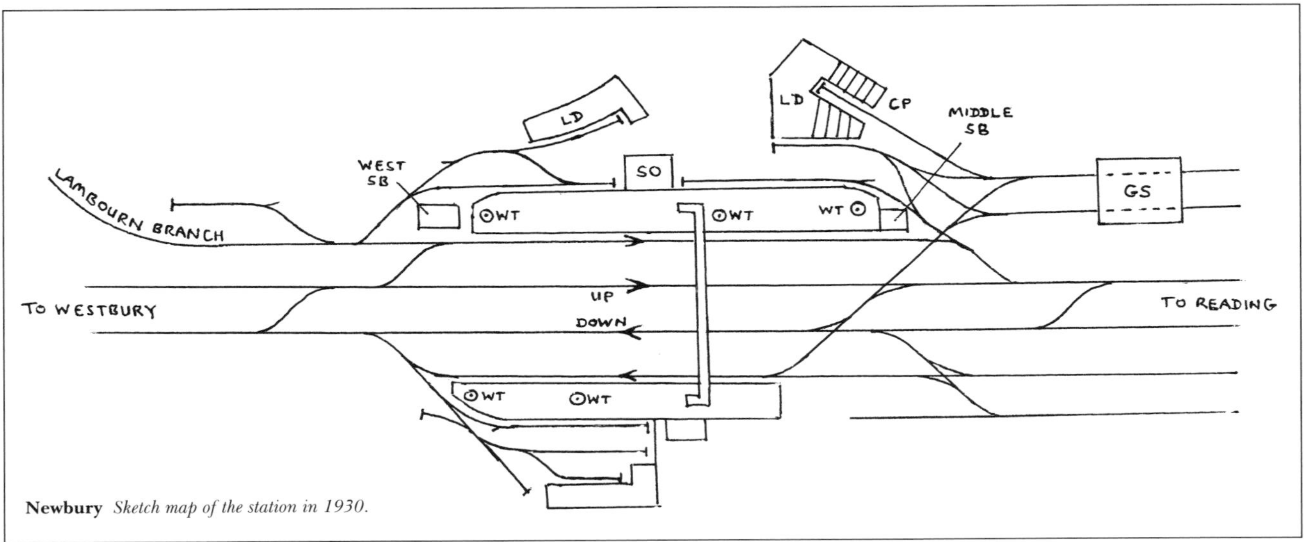

Newbury *Sketch map of the station in 1930.*

Cardigan Railway was in part operation and another route to Cardigan was not needed. Instead, the GWR opened to Newcastle Emlyn on 1 July 1895, extending the up platform and loop at Pencader at the same time.

GB

NEWPORT

As its High Street suffix affirmed, the GWR station at Newport was near the centre of the town. The frontage (1923–30) consisted of a sizeable administrative block leading to the main down platform and the up island beyond, a bridge over the River Usk standing at the London end and the twin tunnels beneath Stow Hill to the west. The two long platforms handled services on the main and Hereford lines (qv Newport, Abergavenny & Hereford Railway), out towards Pontypool (qv) via Maindee Junction and on the Western Valleys lines via Bassaleg (qv Newport–Brecon line). The latter included trains on the old Brecon & Merthyr route (qv) and LNWR services to and from Nantybwch.

Newport's railways fell into four groups, shaped by geographical factors and prompted by its development as a coal port. In addition to the east-west main line, two groups of lines arrived from the north, the Eastern Valleys lines via the course of the Usk and the Western Valleys lines via the Ebbw. Most led to the docks access lines which lay south of the main line and formed the fourth group.

The senior rail route was that of the main line, opened by the South Wales Railway (qv) on 18 June 1850 and reaching High Street station via the junction for the East Usk branch and the triangular Maindee Junctions with the Hereford route. West of the station, Gaer, Ebbw and Park junctions formed a triangle between the Cardiff and Western Valleys lines, with routes from Park Junction passing over the main line to the Alexandra Docks, to Old Dock and to the Eastern Valleys line.

The lines inland from Newport developed from the canals and tramroads of the Monmouthshire Railway & Canal Co (qv) which opened a conventional line to Pontypool on 1 July 1852 and used a station at Mill Street, Newport, from 9 March 1853. From 4 August 1852, passenger trains on the converted Western Valleys line had been running to Dock Street station, the GWR transferring both lots of services to High Street on 11 March 1880, by which time trains from Pontypool were using the 1874 Pontypool, Caerleon & Newport line via Llantarnam and Maindee Junction, and a new link from Park to Gaer Junction had been opened (1 May 1879).

The Alexandra Docks & Railway (qv) added the North Dock lines to the Newport rail system from April 1875 and was then involved in the Pontypridd, Caerphilly & Newport Railway scheme to divert Glamorgan valleys coal from its traditional Cardiff routes. The South Dock followed on 6 June 1893 and the East Usk Railway (Act of 6 August 1885 and vested in the GWR by

Newcastle Emlyn branch *The terminus station.* (Steamchest Collection)

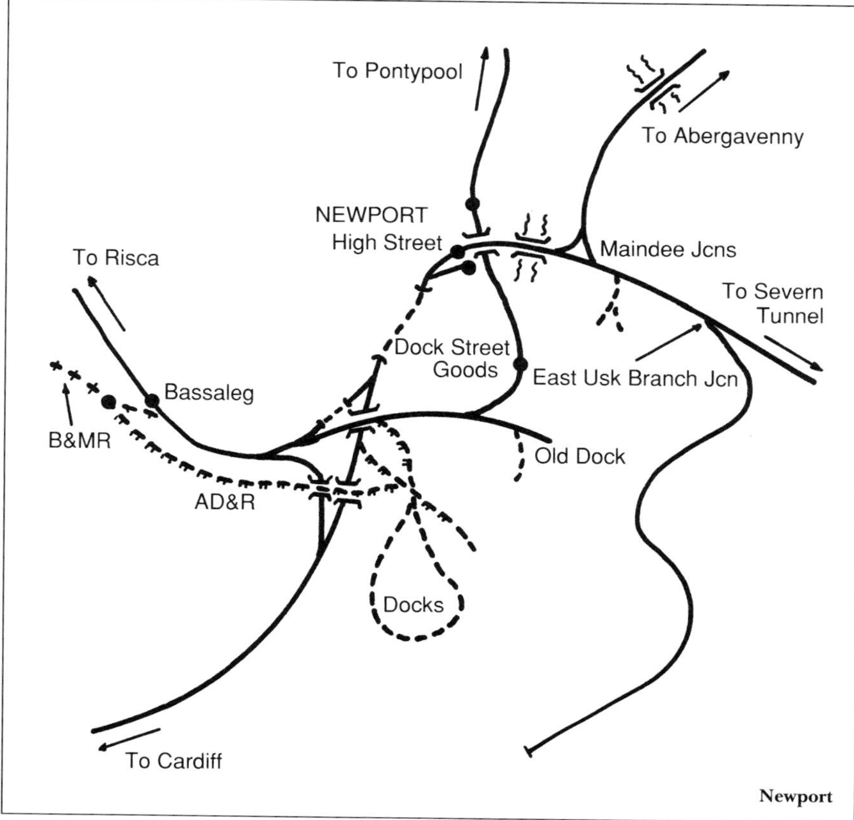

Newport

Act of 28 June 1892) in April 1898 to complete the main elements of the Newport network.

The docks at Newport had a water area of 135 acres and supporting their activity were 57 coal hoists, 13 transit sheds and 100 miles of sidings. The GWR had goods depots at High Street, Mill Street and Dock Street (for carted, coal and station-to-station traffic respectively), a large loco depot at Ebbw Junction (successor to Bolt Street, Dock Street and Pill) and a host of sidings serving works, warehouses and its own traffic and engineering functions.

GB

NEWPORT, ABERGAVENNY & HEREFORD RAILWAY

Incorporated by an Act of 3 August 1846, the NA&H opened between Hereford (Barton) and Pontypool (Coed-y-gric) (both qv) on 2 January 1854, having acquired three early tramroads in the process. Initially traffic was worked by the LNWR and the journey to Newport was completed over the Monmouthshire Railway & Canal Company's (qv) route.

A second Act, of 9 July 1847 but amended 4 August 1853, authorized the Taff Vale Extension Railway from Pontypool to Middle Duffryn, and this was opened in stages between 20 August 1855 and 5 October 1864. Other NA&H lines included the Llanhilleth branch down from Crumlin Viaduct (qv) (5 September 1855), the Maesycwmmer Loop (28 December 1863), the Hengoed Loop and the Bird-in-Hand branch, Pontllanfraith (both 30 November 1893).

A Barlow-rail line, the NA&H became part of the West Midland Railway (qv) on 1 July 1860.

GB

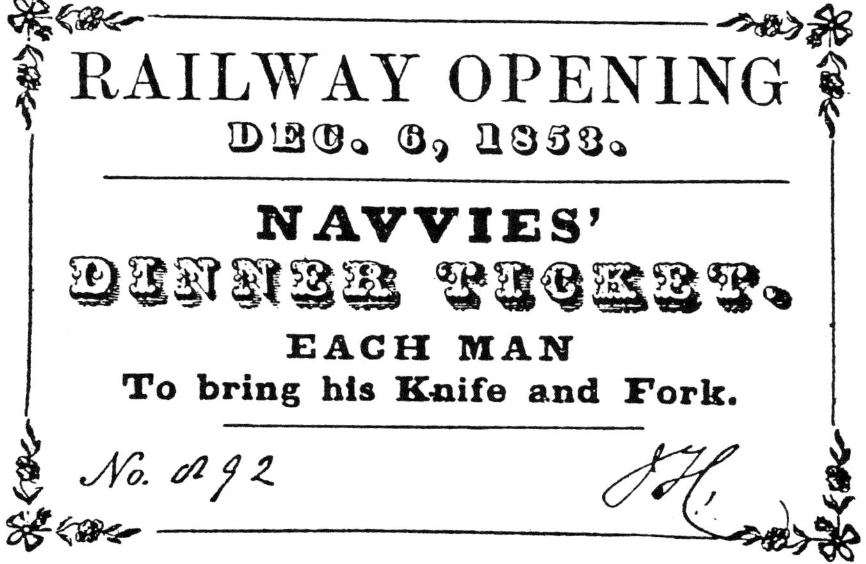

Newport, Abergavenny & Hereford Railway
Junketing for the labourers! (GWR Magazine)

NEWPORT–BRECON LINE

Stations: Newport High Street, Bassaleg (3 m), Rhiwderin ($4\frac{1}{4}$ m), Church Road ($6\frac{1}{4}$ m), Machen ($7\frac{3}{4}$ m), Trethomas ($9\frac{1}{2}$ m), Bedwas ($10\frac{3}{4}$ m), Maesycwmmer ($15\frac{1}{4}$ m), Fleur-de-Lis Platform ($16\frac{1}{2}$ m), Pengam ($17\frac{1}{4}$ m), Bargoed ($18\frac{3}{4}$ m), Darran & Deri (21 m), Fochriw ($23\frac{3}{4}$ m), Dowlais Top ($26\frac{1}{2}$ m), Pant ($28\frac{1}{4}$ m), Pontsticill Junction ($20\frac{3}{4}$ m), Dolygaer ($31\frac{1}{2}$ m), Torpantau (33 m), Pentir Rhiw (37 m), Talybont-on-Usk ($40\frac{1}{4}$ m), Talyllyn Junction ($43\frac{1}{4}$ m), Brecon (47 m).

This was a route of contrasts, wild and beautiful scenery on the northern section and busy industrial activity down through the Rhymney Valley to Newport. With its 22 stations and two halts the journey took about 150 minutes for the four weekday services which completed the through journey in each direction. These connected at Pant with the 5-minute shuttle to Dowlais Central via Pantyscallog and at Ponsticill Junction (qv) with the Merthyr line. Other trains ran to the New Tredegar branch (qv) from or via Pengam and on the Pengam–Ponsticill section.

The first through passenger services began on 1 September 1868 when the Brecon & Merthyr Railway (qv) completed the obligations which allowed it to use the Rhymney Railway (qv) between Deri and Bargoed which linked its northern and southern portions, the latter deriving from the acquisition and upgrading of the 1836 Rumney tramroad. The 1 m 22 ch, 1 in 40 branch to Dowlais was added on 23 June 1869 and trains used High Street, Newport, instead of Dock Street from 11 March 1880.

After parting company with the Western Valleys line, the northbound ex-B&M route headed for Machen where the repair shops were located until 1927 and where the 1865 ex-Rumney branch took a separate up and down course towards Caerphilly (qv). There was a connection with the Pontypool Road–Neath line (qv) beyond Maesycwmmer and the junction with the New Tredegar branch north of Pengam. The Dowlais–Pant complex then preceded Ponsticill Junction and the union with the Merthyr branch.

On the northern section, now used in part by the Brecon Mountain Railway, the colliery connections and 1 in 82–99 gradients gave way to an empty landscape and a 1 in 40 rise to a 1,314 ft summit near Pantywaen Junction, followed by another climb at 1 in 47/55 to a 1,313 ft summit at the end of the 667 yd Beacon Tunnel. Then came the descent of Seven Mile Bank to Talyllyn Junction and, finally, Brecon (qv).

GB

NEWPORT–SHREWSBURY LINE

Stations: Newport High Street, Caerleon (2¾ m), Ponthir (4¼ m), Llantarnam (5¾ m), Lower Pontnewydd (7¼ m), Pontypool Road (10 m), Nantyderry (14¼ m), Penpergwm (17 m), Abergavenny (19½ m), Abergavenny Junction (20½ m), Llanvihangel (23½ m), Pandy (26 m), Pontrilas (31 m), St Devereux (34½ m), Tram Inn (36¾ m), Hereford (43½ m), Moreton-on-Lugg (47¾ m), Dinmore (50½ m), Ford Bridge (53½ m), Leominster (56 m), Berrington & Eye (59¼ m), Woofferton (62¼ m), Ludlow (67 m), Bromfield (69¼ m), Onibury (71½ m), Craven Arms & Stokesay (74½ m), Marsh Brook (79 m), Church Stretton (81½ m), Leebotwood (85 m), Dorrington (88 m), Condover (90 m), Shrewsbury (94¼ m)

The line from Newport northwards, GWR as far as Hereford (qv) and then joint with the LNWR, carried through services from South Wales/South West to Birkenhead/Liverpool/Manchester, plus Cardiff–Birmingham services via Worcester, freight over the same routes and such local trains as could be fitted into the paths remaining. North of Abergavenny Junction (qv) the line was used by LNWR/ LMS services to and from Merthyr (qv).

The route was a scenic one, passing through a hilly green landscape filled with woods and watercourses. It involved summits at Pontypool Road, Llanvihangel and Church Stretton and the separate tunnels at Dinmore where geological reservations limited the original line to a single bore for the first 40 years. Northbound freight trains had banking assistance on the 1 in 82/95 climb to Llanvihangel, but the banking engines were not normally coupled up.

This line was born on 3 August 1846, the date of the Act incorporating the Shrewsbury & Hereford and Newport, Abergavenny & Hereford (qv) companies, the latter a successor to earlier tramroads and the former being leased to the GWR, LNWR and West Midland (qv) companies after the usual conflict between rival interests. Opening between Shrewsbury (qv) and Ludlow took place on 21 April 1852, on to Hereford on 6 December 1853 and south to Coed-y-gric (Pontypool, qv) on 2 January 1854. From there to Newport trains used the Monmouthshire Railway & Canal Co's (qv) line until that of the Pontypool, Caerleon & Newport via Maindee Junction was available in 1874.

GB

NEWQUAY BRANCH

Stations: Par, Luxulyan (4¼ m), Bugle (6¼ m), Roche (8¾ m), St Columb Road (14¼ m), Quintrell Downs Platform (18¼ m), Newquay (20¾ m)

This mainly single-line branch developed out of early tramways conveying mine and quarry output to the sea at Par and Newquay (qv Cornwall Minerals Railway). It became a through route from Newquay to Fowey (qv) from 1 June 1874 with a passenger service from 20 July 1876 and a connection from St Blazey to Par from 1 January 1870. Through running from the main line became possible after the gauge conversion (qv) of 1892 and Saturday services to and from Paddington later became a feature of the summer branch timetable.

From Par the route turned north through the St Blazey depot area and climbed through North Hill Wood to the beginnings of the central Cornish plateau at Luxulyan. This section had three viaducts, a 50 yd tunnel and views of the original tramway viaduct. Bugle was the junction for the first of the china clay connections, with a second group at St Dennis Junction just before an 1874 deviation to avoid Toldish Tunnel. The route then headed west to reach Newquay via Tolcarne Junction with the Perranporth (and Treamble) line (qv) and Trenance Viaduct. Accommodation at Newquay consisted of three platform faces, carriage sidings, a goods depot and an engine shed, plus, until 1926, a freight incline to the harbour.

GB

NEW RADNOR BRANCH

Stations: Leominster, Kingsland (4¼ m), Pembridge (8 m), Titley (12 m), Kington (13¾ m), Stanner (16¾ m), Dolyhir (17¾ m), New Radnor (20¼ m)

This modest single line west from Leominster (qv) to the edge of the Radnor Forest originated with an Act of 10 July 1854 which authorized the Leominster & Kington Railway. It ran for 13¼ miles from a junction north of Leominster and was opened on 2 August 1857, subsequently passing from the contractors to the GWR via the West Midland Railway (qv). Three

Newquay branch *Newquay station.* (Lens of Sutton)

extensions were made to the original line, an L&K branch to Presteign authorized in 1871 and opened on 10 September 1875, a line from Titley to Eardisley authorized to the Kington & Eardisley Railway in 1862 and opened on 3 August 1874, and that company's line on from Kington to New Radnor, authorized in 1873 and opened on 25 September 1875.

New Radnor branch (GWR Magazine)

The two companies were worked by the GWR and taken over in 1897–8. Kington came to be the focal point of the system with six weekday trains from Leominster, of which three continued to New Radnor. From Kington the branch via Titley and then north to Presteign had another three trains each way, and that south to the Midland's line at Eardisley three more, both these lines operating between 9 am and 7 pm.

These rural routes with their simple stations and halts were very vulnerable to road competition. The Eardisley line was closed to passengers from 1 July 1940 and the others in the 1950s.

GB

NEWSPAPER TRAFFIC

It was claimed in 1911 that more newspapers were carried by the GWR than by any other railway. What sparked it off was the fact that the London newspaper proprietors realized early in the century that their sales in the provinces would be handicapped by the availability of local papers unless their own product could be available in centres such as Bristol, Plymouth, Exeter and so on. So a new train, leaving Paddington at 3.05 am, was established (later retimed to 2.30 am), calling at Swindon, Bristol, Taunton, Exeter and Plymouth. It connected at Swindon with a train to South Wales, and at Plymouth with a Penzance service.

In 1911 the GWR was able to assist the Press in another way, too, when on 13 July it ran specials to Paddington from Ruabon and Chester with pictures of the Prince of Wales' Investiture at Caernarvon; the photographs were driven to the railheads and developed during the rail journey. A similar operation on Coronation day that year enabled film of the procession to be shown at cinemas in Birmingham within three hours of the event.

CA

NEWTON ABBOT

For many years GWR expresses to the West carried both Plymouth and Torbay portions which were separated at Newton Abbot. From 1927 onwards the work was done at a new station constructed at a cost of £140,000 and consisting of two long islands plus a separate platform for trains on the Moretonhampstead branch (qv). Newton Abbot's goods depot was located along the latter which left the main line at the London end of the station area. The

Newton Abbot *The old station looking west during the rebuilding of 1927.* (Lens of Sutton)

Torquay/Kingswear branch (both qv) separated at Aller Junction to the west, while the locomotive maintenance depot lay to the south of the station.

The South Devon Railway (qv) had reached Newton Abbot from Teignmouth on 30 December 1846 and then opened to Totnes on 20 July 1847. The following years witnessed both the brief romance with atmospheric propulsion (qv) and the opening of the Torquay branch. For the latter a third train shed was added to the main-line pair, but the station facilities were all brought together in 1861 and the line from the east doubled four years later.

The SDR first hired its locomotives from the GWR and later made agreements with builders and contractors. A maintenance works was established and went on to perform this support activity for the Associated Companies' (qv) Cornwall and West Cornwall sections as well. Newton Abbot also undertook the marshalling of freight to and from its branches and gained a new yard for this purpose (Hackney) in 1911.

For many years the broad gauge locomotive *Tiny* was on display on Newton Abbot's up platform. Both it and the clocks presented by the townspeople in 1927 survived a bombing and machine-gun raid in 1940.

GB

NEW TREDEGAR BRANCH

Stations: Pengam (17¼ miles from Newport), Aberbargoed (19 m), Cwmsyfiog (20 m), New Tredegar (21¼ m)

In addition to its through Newport trains, the New Tredegar branch also carried workmen's trains to and from Pengam and Bedwas. From Aberbargoed Junction the single line followed the eastern side of the Rhymney Valley and originally continued beyond New Tredegar to Abertysswg, Rhymney (Lower) and on to the Rhymney Iron Co and Maerdy Pit. This latter section was closed from 14 April 1930 following a landslide.

The branch had originally been acquired by the Brecon & Merthyr Railway (qv) from

Neyland *Panoramic view of the station, yards and wharfs in 1926.* (GW Society)

the 1825 Rumney Railway, opening for standard gauge use taking place on 1 May 1866.

GB

NEYLAND

Having shelved its plans for a port at Fishguard in favour of Neyland, the South Wales Railway (qv) opened a single line from Haverfordwest on 15 April 1856 and organized an Irish packet service using the pontoons which had come from the bridging of the Tamar. Despite developments at Milford Haven, and later Fishguard (both qv), Neyland remained busy with its coal, livestock, fish and other freight traffics and with local and main-line passenger services, the latter using separate arrival and departure platforms at the rather functional station.

GB

NICHOLLS, RICHARD HOWELL

Superintendent of the Line, 1919–32. Born in 1868, Nicholls joined the GWR in 1884, and in 1890 applied successfully for a post in the Divisional Superintendent's Office at Paddington. He then undertook many jobs, including that of a lecturer at the Paddington School of Signalling, and was appointed Chief Clerk to the London Divisional Superintendent in 1904. When Aldington (qv) became Assistant General Manager in March 1919, Nicholls moved into his place as Superintendent and served in it until 31 December 1932, to be succeeded by H. L. Wilkinson (qv). He was awarded the OBE in 1920, and died at Cheltenham on 13 October 1946.

CA

NORTH STAR

All told there were four completely different GWR locomotives called *North Star*, but the first and the last were the most notable.

When the railway was being built, a 2-2-2 was purchased from R. Stephenson & Co, which had originally been ordered by the 5 ft 6 in gauge New Orleans Railway, who defaulted on the deal. It was delivered by barge to Maidenhead on 28 November 1837, becoming the first locomotive to run on Brunel's broad gauge (qv). It ceased work in 1871, and was put on one side in Swindon Works but scrapped in 1906. For the GWR's centenary (qv) celebrations in 1935, a non-working reproduction was built, which is now in the GWR Museum at Swindon.

North Star *Churchward's original 'Star', No 40 of 1906, as originally built as a 4-4-2.* (Real Photos)

In 1906, the first of Churchward's (qv) four-cylinder express locomotives was named *North Star* and, like its broad gauge ancestor, became the prototype of the 'Star' Class (qv). It was originally No 40, but in 1912 the number was changed to No 4000. It was built as a 4-4-2, to enable a more direct comparison to be made with the French-built de Glehn compounds, but was altered to the 4-6-0 wheel arrangement in 1909. Twenty years later it was rebuilt as a 'Castle' (qv), and was not scrapped until 1957.

(*See also Locomotives*)

PWBS

OCEAN LINER TRAFFIC

The GWR's attempt to attract ocean liner traffic, chiefly transatlantic, was largely concentrated on two ports, Fishguard and Plymouth (both qv); the latter proved the more successful. In the 19th century nearly all Atlantic voyages began and ended at Liverpool, and the GWR got a small share of this with its terminus at Birkenhead Woodside (qv), a short ferry-ride across the Mersey to the landing stage where the liners tied up; but it could not compete with the LNWR in speed between Liverpool and Birmingham and London, and had to settle for passengers heading for Wales and for some of the Midlands and West of England traffic.

At the beginning of the 20th century, Southampton began to attract transatlantic traffic away from Liverpool, partly because the ships could also call at Cherbourg, Le Havre or Hamburg. Rail travel is, of course, much faster than the swiftest ocean liner, and the GWR realized that if the liners could be persuaded to call at Plymouth, the overall time between New York and London could be reduced by several hours. German- and American-owned liners were the first to do so, followed by the French Line, establishing the port's best-known transatlantic link.

Plymouth Millbay docks had been owned by the GWR since 1878, but it was more convenient for liners to anchor in Plymouth Sound, so the GWR provided tenders which ferried passengers ashore. The GWR was in competition with the LSWR but this came to an end, tragically, in July 1906 when an LSWR express inexplicably crashed at high speed at Salisbury. Thereafter the GWR, which, with its new West of England cut-off (qv) route via Westbury, had the advantage in distance over the LSWR, had the ocean liner traffic to itself. Before this, in May 1904, some remarkably fast running had put the GWR into the record books culminating in the run of 9 May when an 'Ocean Mail' (qv) special completed the run from Millbay via Bristol to Paddington in 3 hours 46¾ minutes, 4-4-0 No 3440 *City of Truro* (qv, and Speed records) travelling down Wellington bank at a speed faster than man had ever gone before, allegedly 102.3 mph, although the precise figure has always been disputed.

Fishguard was opened at great expense as a port in August 1906, partly for the Irish Sea traffic to Rosslare and Waterford, but also to serve Liverpool-bound liners. The first to call was the Cunard 'Blue Riband' holder *Mauretania* on 30 August 1909. She anchored in Fishguard Bay at 1.12 pm, three tenders were waiting, and the first train was away by 2.11½ pm; by arriving at Paddington by 6.40 pm, it established a new record of 5 days, 3 hours, 32 minutes from New York to London. The GWR continued to run ocean liner specials to and from Fishguard until the outbreak of the First World War brought them to an end, never to resume—for Cunard transferred its New York services from Liverpool to Southampton in 1920.

Fishguard's loss was Plymouth's gain and the *Great Western Railway Magazine* for January 1935 recorded that on one day the previous July six ocean liners had called, 1,235 passengers had disembarked, and a special train had been provided for each ship. After using Pullman cars for a short period in 1929–30, in 1931–3 the GWR built what are universally regarded as its finest carriages, eight saloons for the Plymouth ocean liner traffic (qv Rolling-stock, passenger). Superbly appointed and of a most handsome appearance, patrons were charged 10s (50p) over and above the 1st class fare to travel in them. A typical formation was four or five Ocean, or Super, Saloons, as they were known, plus a kitchen car and vans, the motive power being a 'Castle' Class 4-6-0. The saloons were retained on these duties until the very end of liner traffic at Plymouth in 1962; named after members of the Royal Family, five have been preserved.

MCHB

OLDBURY BRANCH

Starting life as the Dudley & Oldbury Junction Railway by an Act of 21 July 1873, and later called the Oldbury Railway, this branch finally opened to goods traffic on 7 November 1884. It was worked by the GWR who acquired it from 1 July 1894 and ran a generous passenger service with steam railmotors (qv) until 3 March 1915. Goods traffic continued over the 1½-mile branch from the junction at Langley Green to Oldbury Goods, ¾-mile beyond the former passenger station and possessing a 30-ton crane. The line also served several private sidings.

GB

OLD HILL–DUDLEY LINE

Stations: Old Hill, Windmill End (1½ m), Blowers Green (3 m), Dudley (3¾ m)

This branch enjoyed a good auto-train (qv) service starting with the 6.3 am from Dudley and ending there at 11.19 pm. Between these times there had been 26 trains each way on weekdays, most calling at the smaller halts at Old Hill High Street, Darby End and Baptist End and one or two running through to Birmingham. At the Dudley end the branch proper began at Blowers Green Junction, south of Dudley Tunnel. A little further on lay Windmill End Junction where a 1 in 51 goods line dropped down for 57 chains to Withymoor Canal Basin (later Netherton Goods), a canal transhipment point with a small goods depot, a 12-ton crane and two private sidings.

The Netherton & Halesowen Railway was originally authorized by a West Midland Railway (qv) Act of 17 July 1862 and was opened on 1 March 1878. A GWR Act of 18 July 1872 covered the Withymoor branch which was brought into use on 10 May 1879.

GB

OLD OAK COMMON

At the turn of the century Old Oak Common was still a rural spot, but the Acton & Wycombe Railway, authorized by a GWR Act of 6 August 1897, would soon make it a junction, and the creation of the Great Western & Great Central Railways Joint Committee (qv) in 1899 held the promise of a place in the scheme for a new route to Birmingham. A special train conveyed the Prince of Wales via Old Oak Common to the Royal Showground at Park Royal on 25 May 1903, with public services following in June, full opening to Greenford (qv) in 1904, freight through to High Wycombe in 1905 and passenger services from 2 April 1906.

A second major event of 1906 was the completion of a new locomotive depot at Old Oak Common. It took over the work of Westbourne Park and grew into the largest shed on the GWR, and possibly in the world. Facilities included two 65 ft turntables, a repair shop with 12 52 ft pits, a 30-ton overhead crane, 80-ton traversing table, 290,000 gallon water tank and a large coaling stage. Old Oak Common had an allocation of some 200 locomotives of all types, with stabling for 112.

GB

OMNIBUS AND CHARABANC SERVICES

The GWR pioneered railway motorbus services in Great Britain and maintained a lead far ahead of all other companies until the late 1920s when legislation brought about the end of direct railway operation of bus services. The pioneer vehicles were two Milnes-Daimler 22-seaters bought second-hand at £850 each and put to work between Helston station (qv) and The Lizard on 17 August 1903. F.C.A. Coventry, a GWR employee since 1893, was in charge, and he remained head of road transport until his retirement in 1942. Further Milnes-Daimlers were bought and a Newlyn to Penzance service inaugurated. The first double-decker began work in Cornwall in March 1904. Next a Slough to Beaconsfield service was introduced. By the end of 1904, the GWR owned 36 buses, and they were running in north and east Cornwall, in Plymouth and Torbay, and in the Marlborough area. A number of these had been introduced instead of building light railways, and soon proved themselves economical and popular.

Sightseeing excursions operating in the summer months augmented the regular services, thus establishing the distinction between stage carriage work and touring. Chocolate and cream livery was applied to most vehicles. Luggage and all manner of goods, including livestock, were carried, whilst a leather uniform, necessary waterproof protection against the elements, was provided for drivers, who received between 21s and 29s a week.

Old Oak Common *A view across the carriage sidings in June 1939, looking towards Paddington. On the left is 'The Factory', and beyond it the smoke of Britain's largest steam shed can be seen. The enormous water-tower and coaling plant can just be seen beyond the end of the building.* (GW Society)

Services expanded through the Edwardian era all over GWR territory and a variety of vehicles was used, including some steamers. Tours ceased in August 1914, shortage of petrol reduced some bus services, women conductresses took over from absent men, and the works at Slough had to produce its own spares for the German-manufactured Milnes-Daimlers.

During the 1920s more comfortable vehicles, Maudslays, Guys, Thornycrofts, AECs, Burfords, Morrises, Chevrolets and Gilfords, appeared. Extensive long-distance coach services, tours ('Land Cruises') and regular bus services were all operated, and at the passing of the Railways' Road Power Bill in 1928 there were some 300 GWR passenger-carrying vehicles on the road.

After this date the GWR, along with the other railway companies, gradually gave up operating road passenger services in its own name, preferring to transfer its financial interest to existing bus companies, or to set up new ones. Staff either transferred to these companies or to the GWR's Road Motor Department (qv). The last GWR-operated bus service, a joint one with the Southern Railway in Weymouth using Maudslays, passed out of its hands to Southern National—which still works in that town—on 1 January 1934.

MCHB

Omnibus and charabanc services *A Thornycroft motor bus operating from Slough.* (GW Society)

LAND CRUISES
Season 1937

G.W.R. personally conducted "all expense" motor tours in England and Wales from May to September, affording maximum sightseeing without fatigue.

NORTH WALES

Land Cruise No. 1 (6 days). Mondays, May 17th to September 20th.—From LONDON (Paddington Station). By rail to Chester. By road to The Horseshoe Pass, Vale of Llangollen, Berwyn, Swallow Falls, Snowdon, Llanberis, Pass of Aberglaslyn, Criccieth, Harlech, Barmouth, Aberystwyth, Devil's Bridge and Shrewsbury. Return to LONDON by rail.

DEVON AND CORNWALL

Land Cruise No. 2 (6 days). Mondays, May 17th to September 20th.—From LONDON (Paddington Station). By rail to Torquay. By road to Buckfast Abbey, Dartmoor Forest, Tavistock, Launceston, Tintagel, Newquay, Perranporth, Penzance, Land's End, Lizard, St. Ives, Falmouth, Truro, Plymouth and Torquay. Return to LONDON by rail.

SOMERSET AND DEVON

Land Cruise No. 3 (6 days). Mondays, May 17th to September 20th.—From LONDON (Paddington Station). By rail to Bath. By road to Cheddar Gorge, Wells, Glastonbury, Weston-super-Mare, Exmoor, Lynton, Ilfracombe, Barnstaple, Clovelly, Exeter, Dawlish, Teignmouth, Newton Abbot and Torquay. Return to LONDON by rail.

Land Cruise No. 4 (13 days). Cruises No. 3 and No. 2 combined.

INCLUSIVE FARES FROM LONDON (Paddington Station)

Land Cruise No. 1 (6 days)	**£12**	**0**	**0**
Land Cruise No. 2 (6 days)	**£12**	**10**	**0**
Land Cruise No. 3 (6 days)	**£12**	**10**	**0**
Land Cruise No. 4 (13 days)	**£25**	**10**	**0**

Fares include first-class transportation and hotel accommodation, table d'hôte meals, gratuities at hotels and admission fees to places of interest visited.

Fares from provincial towns upon application.

Write for Illustrated "LAND CRUISES" Programme :—
Superintendent of the Line, G.W.R., Paddington Station, London, W.2.

Omnibus and charabanc services

OSWESTRY

Oswestry gained a unified station out of the 1923 Grouping. The terminus of the branch opened from Gobowen by the Shrewsbury & Chester Railway (qv) on 23 December 1848 was closed and its trains diverted to a new bay at the adjacent Cambrian Railways (qv) station from 7 July 1924. The GWR station, itself a replacement dating from 1866, became a goods depot and the ex-CR station gained extended platforms, a new signal box and track layout, and improvements to its loco depot. The changes equipped it to handle the branch service to Gobowen/Ruabon/Chester (all qv) plus the local and through trains from Whitchurch (qv) and west to the Cardigan Bay resorts. Oswestry also had a rather variable service to the Llangynog branch (qv) and connections to the LNWR via Shrewsbury and Wellington.

Following the GWR acquisition of the S&C company from 1 September 1854, the Oswestry & Newton Railway had opened between Oswestry and Pool Quay on 1 May 1860. Four years later the latter became part of the newly-formed Cambrian Railways along with the Oswestry, Ellesmere & Whitchurch Railway whose trains reached Oswestry on 27 July, two days after the amalgamation. Oswestry gained further stature with the opening of the Cambrian's headquarters offices, locomotive works and carriage and wagon works there.

GB

OXFORD

The shorter Great Western & Great Central Joint (qv) route to Birmingham did not seriously affect the status of the original GWR line through Oxford, and the university town enjoyed an enviable variety of train services. It had its originating and terminating Paddington trains, mostly via Didcot but some via Thame, other London trains heading for Birmingham, Wolverhampton and beyond, and yet others destined for the Worcester route westwards. The Oxford line was used for through north-south trains and their return workings from the South Coast to Manchester, Birkenhead, Bradford and Newcastle; a Weymouth–Birmingham service ran via Oxford and it also handled local Blenheim and Fairford branch (both qv) trains.

The Oxford educationalists had been as wary of railways as those of Eton (qv Slough) but the GWR-backed Oxford Railway (qv) obtained its Act for a line from Didcot on 11 April 1843 and had the 9 m 57 ch thereof ready for opening on 12 June 1844—despite the antics of one landowner in erecting a house of timber and brown paper in order to extort compensation from the railway. The wooden terminus at Oxford was subsequently replaced by a more central station from 1 October 1852 when the route to Birmingham via Fenny Compton was completed.

The Oxford, Worcester & Wolverhampton Railway's (qv) line from Evesham reached Wolvercot Junction, north of Oxford, on 4 June 1853, and the town was soon part of a gauge war in which the OW&W developed a link with the LNWR and threatened its own line to London. The

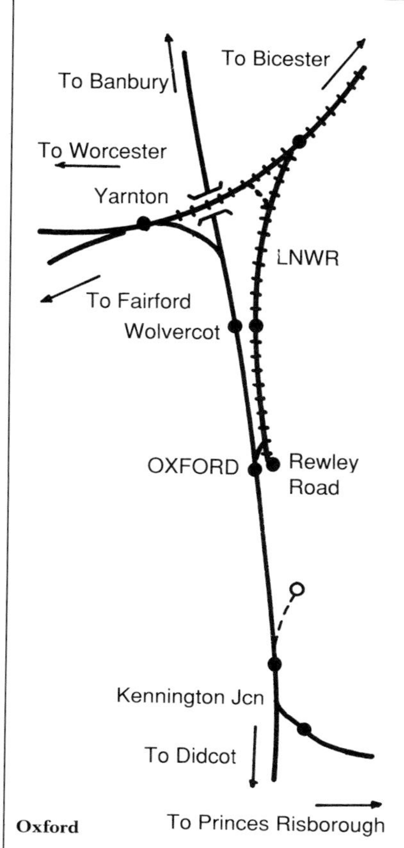

upshot was the acquisition of the OW&W line by the GWR in 1863—as a narrow gauge undertaking!

In its later form Oxford station consisted of up and down platforms with through lines, platform loops and north end bays. Wolverton and Oxford North junctions lay to the north, and to the south Becket Street Goods, Hinksey Yard and Kennington Junction. The LNWR station stood near the GWR one, while Oxford's engine shed lay on the opposite, down, side at the country end.

GB

OXFORD & RUGBY RAILWAY

This GWR-inspired project was authorized by an Act of 4 August 1845 and amalgamated with its parent in the following year. Construction was slow due to the financial difficulties of the period, and it was not until 2 September 1850 that a single broad gauge line was opened as far as Banbury (qv). New decisions then abandoned the works beyond Fenny Compton in favour of joining the Birmingham & Oxford Junction Railway (qv) there. This was achieved from 1 October 1852 and the route doubled and made mixed gauge.

GB

OXFORD RAILWAY

The Oxford Railway, which was incorporated on 11 April 1843, was a wholly GWR-funded project which was amalgamated with the parent company in 1844, a year in which the 9 m 57 ch line was opened from Didcot (qv) to a station on the south side of Oxford (qv) on 12 June. The objections from the university, which had turned the GWR's original branch proposals into a mere coach link from Steventon, had gradually moderated over the years.

GB

OXFORD, WORCESTER & WOLVERHAMPTON RAILWAY

Prompted by the traffic needs of West Midlands industry, this railway was authorized by an Act of Parliament of 4 August 1845 but then led such a chequered career that it acquired the nickname 'The Old Worse & Worse'. The project became involved in the gauge war (qv Broad gauge) and although supported initially by financial guarantees from the GWR, these were later to start an ongoing and acrimonious rift between the two concerns which was not resolved until the route became part of the GWR empire.

Despite considerable financial problems, the first section of the OW&W was opened between Abbots Wood Junction (MR) and Worcester (qv) on 5 October 1850. Dudley and Evesham (qv) were then reached in 1852, a year in which the OW&W sought to abandon its original broad gauge commitment and to promote its own extension towards London. The main line was completed through to Wolvercot Junction, Oxford, on 4 June 1853, but broad gauge rails had been laid on only part of it and by 1854 'narrow gauge' trains were running through to Euston via a junction with the LNWR at Yarnton. Wolverhampton (qv) was reached on 1 July of that year.

The OW&W opened various branches between 1854 and 1859, including lines to Chipping Norton and Stratford-on-Avon (qv). It became involved with the Newport, Abergavenny & Hereford Railway (qv) in rescuing the Worcester & Hereford (qv), and amalgamated with these to become the West Midland Railway (qv) by virtue of an Act of 14 June 1860. By the following year the pro-GWR faction on the OW&W board had prompted a working arrangement between the two companies and full amalgamation followed from 1 August 1863, adding 109 'narrow gauge' miles to the broad gauge empire.

GB

OXFORD–WORCESTER–WOLVERHAMPTON LINE

Stations: Oxford, Yarnton (4 m), Handborough ($7\frac{1}{4}$ m), Charlbury ($13\frac{1}{2}$ m),

Oxford-Worcester-Wolverhampton line
Charlbury station, looking towards Oxford. Note the Brunel 'chalet'-style building. (Steamchest Collection)

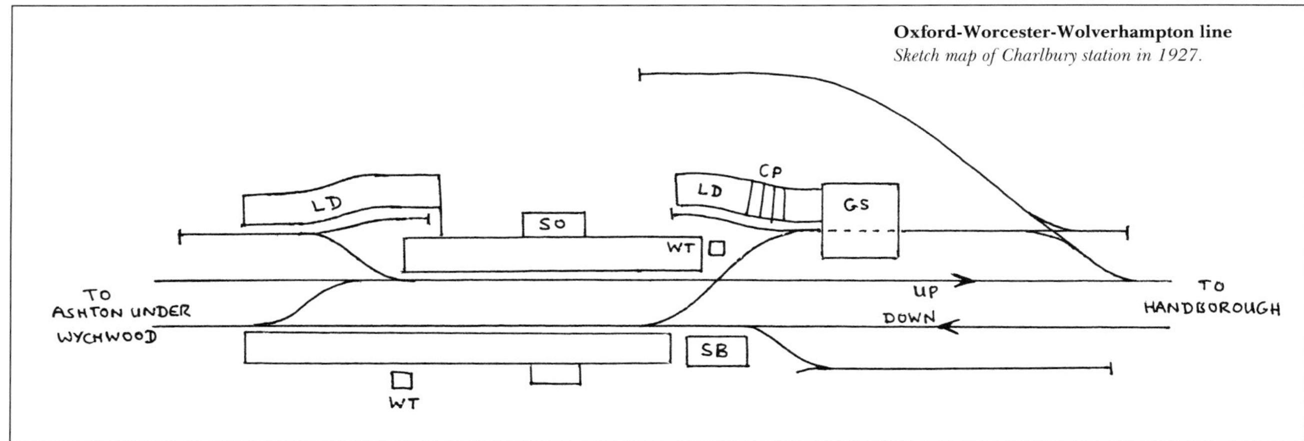

Oxford-Worcester-Wolverhampton line
Sketch map of Charlbury station in 1927.

Ascott-under-Wychwood ($17\frac{1}{2}$ m), Shipton ($18\frac{3}{4}$ m), Kingham ($21\frac{3}{4}$ m), Adlestrop ($24\frac{1}{2}$ m), Moreton-in-Marsh ($28\frac{3}{4}$ m), Blockley (32 m), Campden (35 m), Honeybourne ($38\frac{3}{4}$ m), Littleton & Badsey ($41\frac{1}{4}$ m), Evesham (44 m), Fladbury ($46\frac{3}{4}$ m), Pershore ($49\frac{1}{2}$ m), Stoulton ($53\frac{3}{4}$ m), Norton Junction ($54\frac{1}{4}$ m), Worcester Shrub Hill ($57\frac{1}{2}$ m), Fernhill Heath ($60\frac{1}{4}$ m), Droitwich ($63\frac{1}{4}$ m), Hartlebury (69 m), Kidderminster ($72\frac{1}{2}$ m), Churchill & Blakedown ($75\frac{3}{4}$ m), Hagley ($77\frac{1}{2}$ m), Stourbridge Junction ($79\frac{1}{4}$ m), Brettell Lane ($81\frac{1}{4}$ m), Brierley Hill (82 m), Round Oak ($82\frac{1}{2}$ m), Blowers Green ($84\frac{1}{2}$ m), Dudley ($85\frac{1}{4}$ m), Tipton ($86\frac{1}{4}$ m), Prince's End & Coseley ($87\frac{1}{4}$ m), Daisy Bank & Bradley (88 m), Bilston ($88\frac{3}{4}$ m), Priestfield ($89\frac{1}{2}$ m), Wolverhampton Low Level (91 m)

This was the route of the old Oxford, Worcester & Wolverhampton Railway (qv), carrying a good local service either side of Worcester (qv), through trains from Paddington, and others between Cardiff and Birmingham/ Wolverhampton. It had grown, slowly and painfully, from the Abbots Wood–Worcester section of 5 October 1850, opening in 1852 to Stoke Prior (18 February), Evesham (qv) (1 May), Stourbridge Junction (qv) (3 May) and then Dudley (20 December), in 1853 to Wolvercot Junction, Oxford (qv) (4 June) and to Tipton (1 December) and then on to Wolverhampton (qv) on 1 July 1854.

From Wolvercot Junction, north of Oxford, the line climbed gently to a summit beyond Moreton-in-Marsh (qv), following the River Evenlode from Handborough where Euston sections were once attached and detached, and on to junctions at Kingham (qv) and then Moreton. At the latter it prepared for the 1 in 100 drop of $4\frac{1}{2}$ miles through the 887 yd Campden Tunnel to the Vale of Evesham and junctions at Honeybourne (qv), Evesham and with the Midland Railway main line. More junctions followed the Worcester complex at Droitwich Spa (qv), Hartlebury and Kidderminster (qv), before the Birmingham and Wolverhampton lines divided at Stourbridge Junction and the latter ran via the steelworks connections at Round Oak and Dudley and more sidings at Tipton to meet the main line from Birmingham at Priestfield.

GB

PADDINGTON

Both Brentford (qv) and Vauxhall Bridge were among the contenders for the site of the GWR's London terminus, but the Act finally passed on 31 August 1835 provided for a junction with the London & Birmingham Railway and the use of its Euston station. That idea was later abandoned and a further Act of 3 July 1837 authorized a terminus in the Parish of Paddington. It was opened with the line to Maidenhead (qv) on 4 June 1838 and consisted of offices in the arches of Bishops Road Bridge, a wooden train shed with four platforms, a traverser to link the running lines, and an engine turntable and roundhouse.

Paddington's traffic grew rapidly from the 14 daily trains provided for the opening of the line to Bristol, and the GWR Directors were soon voting £50,000 for a new station on the present site. Work started in 1851 under Brunel's (qv) supervision and with the help of architect Digby Wyatt, the departure side being ready for use from 16 January 1854 and the arrival side from 29 May. Ten running lines were provided within the 700 ft long and 238 ft wide station interior, Nos 1,2,3, and 10 with platform access. Arched ribs of wrought iron supported the three roof spans (68 ft, 102 ft and 68 ft) whose design was clearly influenced by the Crystal Palace.

The Great Western Royal Hotel was built at the same time as the new station, opening in June 1854 and having cost some £60,000 (qv Hotels). It was part of Brunel's dream of a transport route from London to New York, and he was Chairman of the hotel company's board. The 112-bedroom edifice acted as the frontage for Paddington station and was designed in the style of Louis XIV by Philip Charles Hardwick, with sculpture by John Thomas. It was taken over by the GWR in 1896 and extensively modernized in the 1930s.

The station itself saw many alterations over the years. Bishops Road was added to handle the Farringdon service from 10 January 1863, and changes in 1878 and 1881–84 added platforms in place of carriage lines and removed the turntables from the concourse area known as 'The Lawn' (possibly derived from the original properties acquired for construction). More platform space was made available by the gauge conversion (qv) of 1892, and by 1911

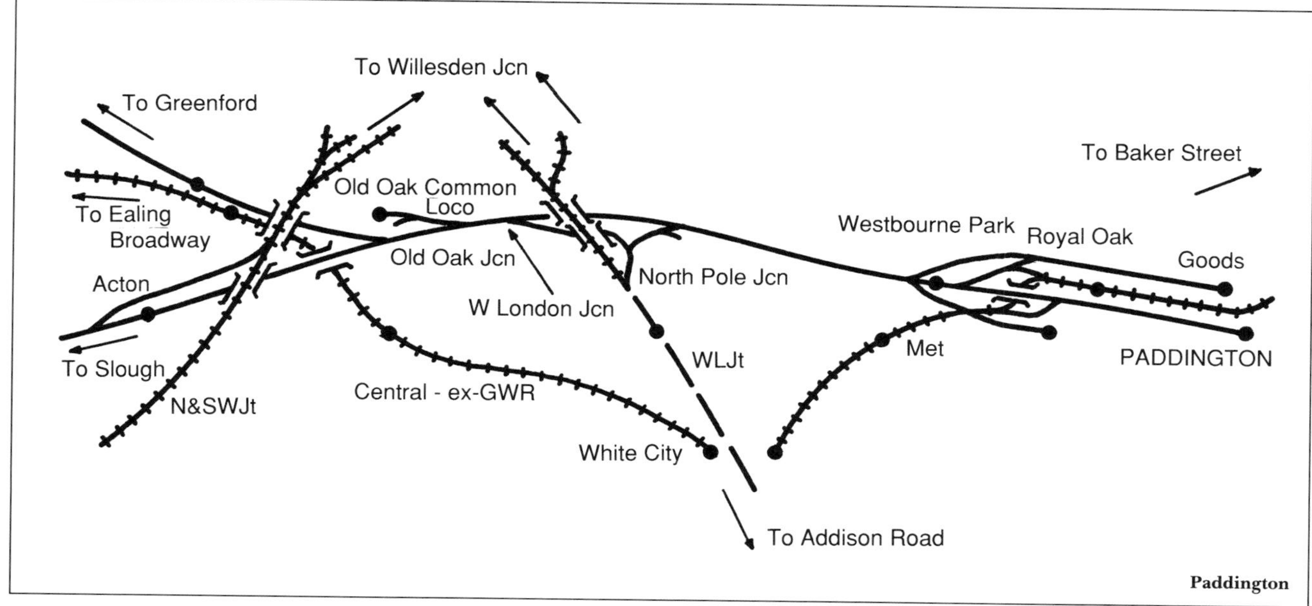

Paddington

the total face length had risen from the original 3,500 ft to 8,285 ft. Between 1913 and 1915 a fourth roof span was added, new arrival platforms 10–12 created and re-arrangement of the running lines out to Old Oak Common begun. The '20s saw the replacement of the cast iron roof columns by steel ones, the '30s brought clearance of The Lawn, a remodelling of Bishops Road and a new east side office block, and the 1940s some wartime bomb damage.

The train departures from Paddington rose steadily from 20 a day in 1855 to 154 in 1906 and 201 in 1931. The first all-mail train ran in 1855 (qv Mail services), the first through train to Penzance in 1867 and the 'Cornish Riviera' (qv) from 1 July 1904. Periods of major train service change attended the opening of the new West of England route in 1906 and the shorter route to Birmingham in 1910. Suburban services also expanded, in addition to the glamorous events like the introduction of Pullman cars (1929) and of named trains like the 'Bristolian' (qv) (1935). Paddington's signalling had to keep pace with the traffic expansion, signal boxes and semaphore signals appearing in the 1860s, colour light signals in 1922 and new electrically worked boxes in 1933.

Paddington also included a goods depot to the north of the approach lines, with sidings along the Grand Union Canal, and there was a turntable and engine sidings on the down side at Ranelagh Bridge. Beyond the Hammersmith & City line (qv) fly-under, the engine sheds at Westbourne Park had been closed in favour of Old Oak Common (qv) in 1906 and Paddington

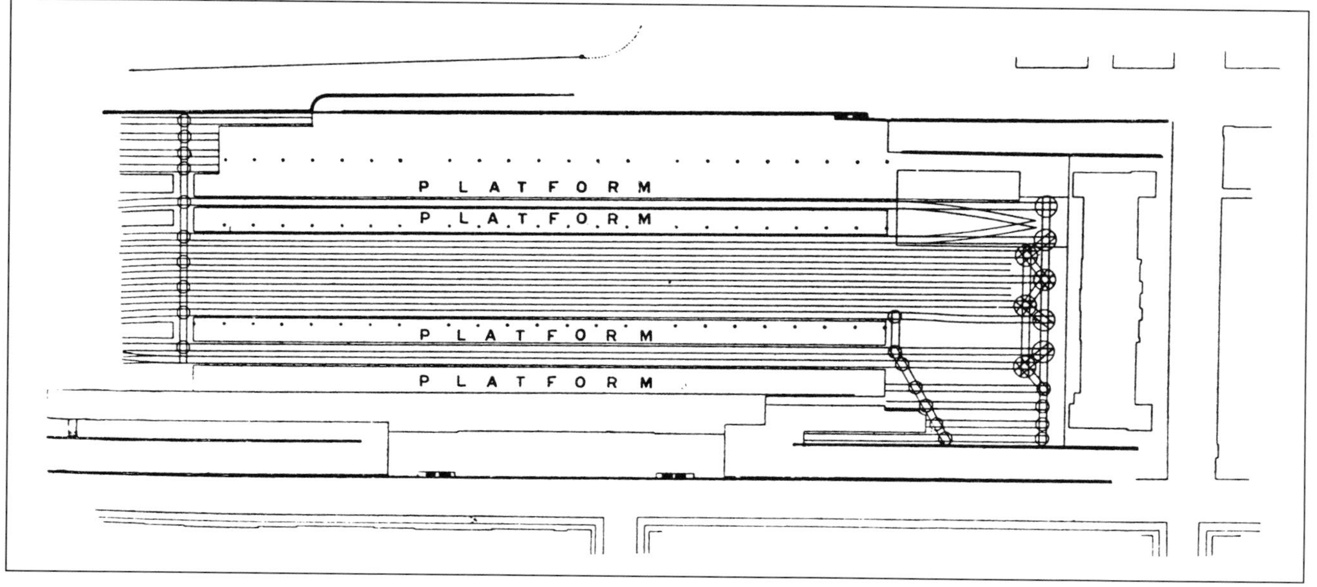

Paddington *Plan of the station as originally laid out.* (GWR Magazine)

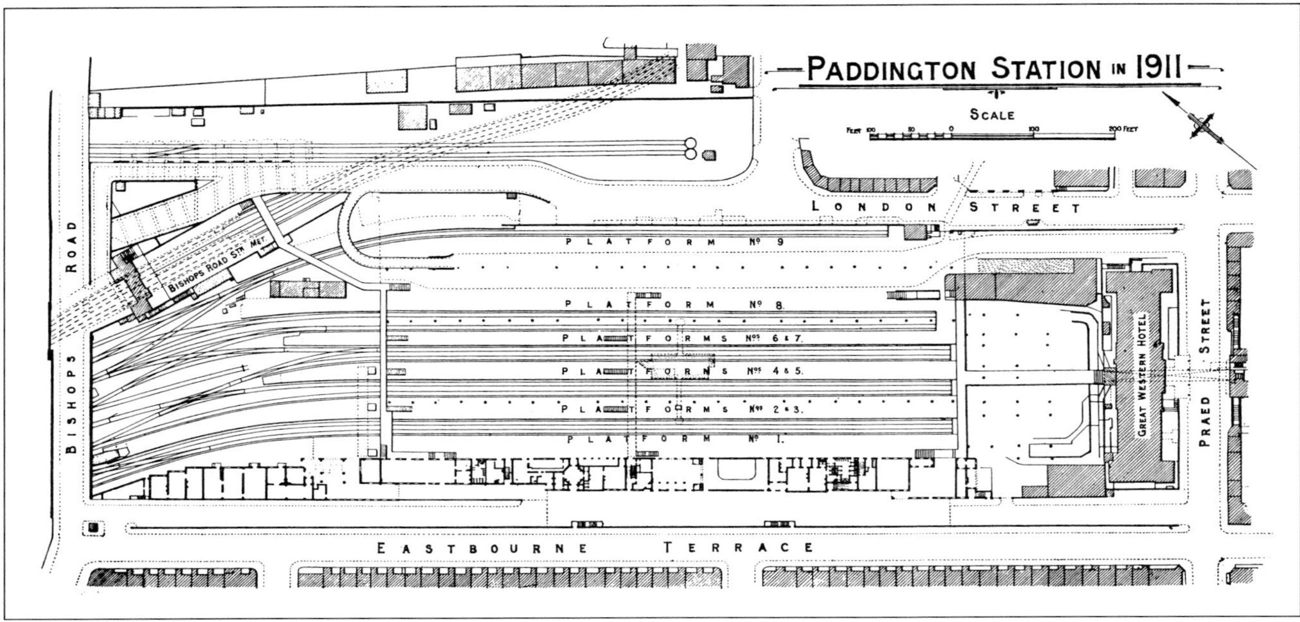

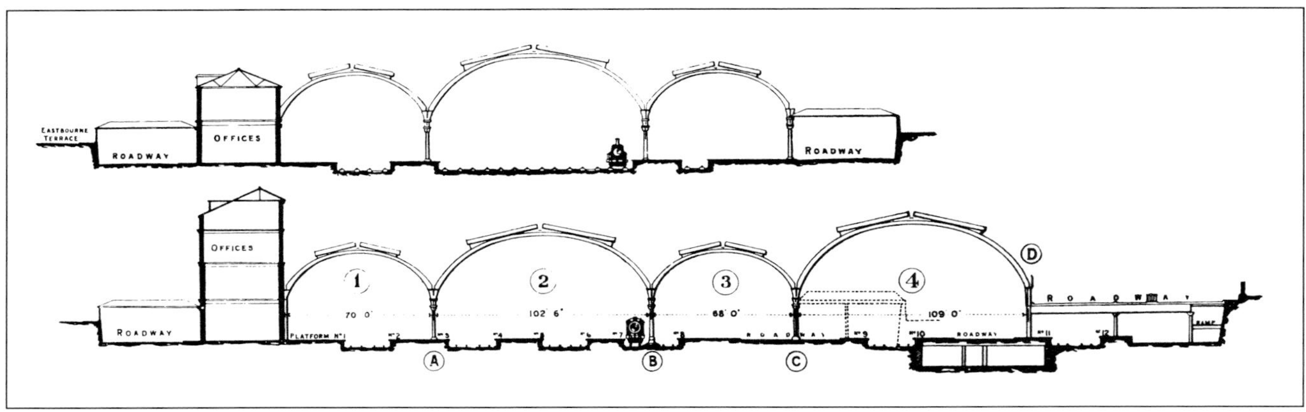

(Top) Paddington *The station in 1911.* (GWR Magazine)

(Above) Paddington *Comparison between the cross-sections of the station in 1854 and 1917, after the addition of the fourth roof span, looking westwards.* (GWR Magazine)

(Left) Paddington *The view from the end of Platform 1 in May 1922, showing the three original roof spans. The 'Cornish Riviera' prepares to depart.* (GW Society)

New Depot took their place. South of the main lines lay Westbourne Park station with its main, relief and H&C line platforms, and Crimea Yard. Further west lay Barlby Road Carriage Shed, Kensal Green Gas Works, the Engine and Carriage lines flyover, and West London Carriage Sidings.

GB

Paddington *Bustle on Platforms 4 and 5 some time during the 1920s.* (GWR Museum, Swindon)

PAGE, FREDERICK H. D.

Signal & Telegraph Engineer, 1936–47. Page moved from McKenzie & Holland, the signalling contractors, to the Taff Vale Railway in 1903. He became a draughtsman at Reading Signal Works in 1906, and an interlocking surveyor in 1912. After serving as Assistant to the Signal Engineer from 1923 to May 1925, he became Signal & Telegraph Engineer of the Cardiff District. He graduated to Assistant to the Chief Signal & Telegraph Engineer in 1928, succeeding to the post on 3 February 1936. He received the OBE in 1943, and retired on 15 April 1947.

AV

PAIGNTON

The Dartmouth & Torbay Railway (qv Kingswear branch) reached Paignton on 2 August 1859 and pushed on to Churston on 14 March 1861. Working was undertaken by the South Devon Railway (qv) whose modest early service was to grow considerably in the GWR years as the adjacent town and beach grew increasingly popular with holidaymakers. The long-distance services, arriving one after the other on summer Saturdays, terminated at Paignton's down platform with stabling in the sidings beyond in readiness for a return working from the up, all movements north of the station involving a level crossing over the busy main street.

Alterations in 1910 doubled the approach from Torquay (qv) and in 1925 Paignton gained extra down sidings in the area now used by trains of the preserved Torbay & Dartmouth Railway.

GB

PALMER, LORD ERNEST

Director, 1898–1943. Son of a founder of the famous Reading biscuit firm, he was an almost lifelong enthusiast of the GWR. Appointed a Director in August 1898, he quickly became Deputy-Chairman, in 1906. He was created a baronet in 1916 and a peer (for services to music) in 1933. He served as Deputy for four Chairmen, retiring from the Board in 1943.

CA

PAR

From 1 January 1870 a new link from St Blazey made Par the junction for the Fowey and Newquay branches (both qv). St. Blazey continued to be important for its ex-CR works, loco and clay traffic sidings.

GB

PARCELS TRAFFIC

This originated in postal traffic, which, of course, included parcels. Four- and six-wheeled vans were used at first for sorting and storage of mail, but by 1860 specific 'Travelling Post Offices' had taken over (qv Mail services). These were primarily concerned with letters, however, and regular parcels trains then began to run in order to supplement the letter service. They fell into two categories: the overflow of GPO parcels, and those parcels consigned directly via railway, from individuals, traders or through the company's agents.

Trains were mostly made up of corridor bogie stock, though consists were so varied that they defy generalization. Nor were the trains necessarily restricted to parcels, and a load might be supplemented by regular traffic in perishables—fish, milk, meat, flowers, fruit, and/or vegetables. Extra trains ran at Christmas, beginning about 15 December, when, during the latter days of the company, the parcels traffic was dealt with from the Alfred Road Depot at Paddington goods station, the main parcels line at Paddington itself being unable to cope. Connections along the route with scheduled passenger or special parcels trains ensured that the appropriate vans reached their destinations with minimum delay.

CA

PARSON, JOHN

Director, 1863–64 It has been alleged that much of the ill-feeling generated between the Oxford, Worcester & Wolverhampton Railway (qv) and the GWR was due to Parson's hostility to Gooch and Saunders (both qv). In due course, as a director of the West Midland Railway (qv) (which had absorbed the OW&WR in 1860), he obtained a seat on the GWR Board at the Amalgamation in 1863. He then became involved in a scandal over land which he bought, and then sold to the Hammersmith & City Railway (qv) (of which he was Chairman) at a large profit. He was removed from the Board in the following year, and Gooch, certainly, was relieved to see the back of him.

CA

PEMBROKE DOCK BRANCH

Stations: Whitland, Narberth (5¼ m), Templeton (8¼ m), Kilgetty (10¾ m), Saundersfoot (11½ m), Tenby (15¾ m), Penally (17 m), Manorbier (20¼ m), Lamphey (23¾ m), Pembroke (25¼ m), Pembroke Dock (27¼ m)

The Pembroke & Tenby Railway succeeded where the South Wales Railway (qv) had failed, obtaining Parliamentary blessing on 21 July 1859 for the route named in its title, opening it on 30 July 1863 and extending to Pembroke Dock on 8 August 1864. It then became even more of a thorn in the side of the GWR camp, extending to Whitland (qv) on 4 September 1866 and only foregoing its Carmarthen powers in return for the use of the SWR up line between Whitland and Carmarthen Junction.

Westwards, the route ran from Whitland to Narberth and then needed gradients of 1 in 47–52 to lift it over a high ridge to reach the coast at Saundersfoot and Tenby. The latter, which came to deal with substantial numbers of summer holidaymakers, was a passing loop with main down platform, up island and a goods yard which had once accommodated the original P&T terminus. Beyond Tenby the route continued west to a single platform at Pembroke and on to a two-platform station at Pembroke Dock. The latter had links into the dockyard and a ½-mile branch to Hobbs Point Pier.

GB

PENARTH LINE

Stations: Cardiff Queen Street, Cardiff General (1 m), Grangetown (2 m), Penarth Dock (3½ m), Penarth (4½ m), Lavernock (6½ m), Sully (8¼ m), Cadoxton (9¾ m)

Reflecting wider changes in South Wales generally, the Penarth line started life as a coal route to new docks at the mouth of the Ely River but became increasingly a line for Cardiff commuters and for visitors to the estuarial resort which grew up at Penarth itself. By 1938 the GWR had temporarily closed the docks, which had once reached an annual tonnage figure of 4.78m, but was running over 100 passenger trains a day over various sections of the route.

From Acts of 1856 and 1857 sprang authority for tidal wharves on the north side of the Ely River's entry to the Bristol Channel and for an enclosed dock opposite. The 6 m 2 ch access line from the supporting Taff Vale Railway (qv) at Radyr was opened to the tidal harbour in 1859, with the line from Grangetown Junction to the newly opened dock following in 1865. A subway linking the two was later available to foot passengers purchasing a penny railway ticket.

The Taff Vale took a 999-year lease of the Penarth Harbour Dock & Railway Co by an Act of 22 June 1863, extended one mile from Cogan Junction to Penarth Town on 20 February 1878 and on to the Barry Railway (qv) at Biglis (Cadoxton) on 1 December 1887. The PHD&R passed to the GWR on 1 January 1922 under the preliminary Grouping arrangements.

GB

PENDENNIS CASTLE

'Castle' Class (qv) No 4079 *Pendennis Castle* was involved in the famous locomotive exchange trials (qv) between the GWR and LNER in 1925. These took place after sister locomotive *Caerphilly Castle* (qv) had been on display alongside *Flying Scotsman* in the British Empire Exhibition at Wembley, where it was claimed to be Britain's most powerful express locomotive. Although much smaller than the Gresley 'A1', *Pendennis Castle* out-performed the 'Pacific' between King's Cross and Doncaster, giving faster times as well as using less coal. As a result, Gresley was later persuaded to copy the GWR's long-travel valves, which revolutionized the performance of his 'Pacifics'. After withdrawal in 1964, *Pendennis Castle* was preserved and is now in Australia.

Pendennis Castle *On display at the British Empire Exhibition, 1925.* (Steamchest Collection)

PWBS

PENYGRAIG BRANCH

Stations: Llantrisant, Coed Ely (4 m), Tonyrefail (5 m), Penygraig (7¼ m)

This line took its name from the Ely River whose course it followed north-west from the junction with the South Wales main line (qv) at Llantrisant. It was a steeply graded line, rising at 1 in 40 between Tonyrefail and Penygraig and steepening to 1 in 30 on the single-line, 'one engine in steam' extension to Clydach Vale. The principal traffic was coal but a workman's service on the extension developed into a useful

Llantrisant–Penygraig passenger service from 1 May 1901.

The Ely Valley lines originated with Acts of 1857 and 1858, the GWR working the services which began to Tonyrefail in August 1860 and through to Penygraig on 12 December 1862. A branch east from Mwyndy opened on 8 January 1862 followed in October 1865 by the Gellyrhaidd link with the Ely Valley Extension Railway and its line through Gilfach. The Penygraig–Clydach Vale section was authorized under the Ely & Clydach Valleys Railway Act of 5 August 1873 with opening on 10 August 1878.

GB

PENZANCE

Labelled in the timetables 'for St Just, Cape Cornwall, Land's End and Scilly Isles', Penzance was the GWR's far-west terminus, $305\frac{1}{4}$ miles from Paddington. Its first trains were provided on 11 March 1852 by the 'narrow gauge' West Cornwall Railway (qv) which had its headquarters at Penzance. Following leasing by the Associated Broad Gauge Companies (qv) in 1865, through passenger services to London were introduced from 1 March 1867 and eventually led to the 'Cornish Riviera' (qv) which began running on 1 July 1904, leaving Penzance at 10 am and due at Paddington at 5 pm.

Until 1921 the approach to Penzance was over a single-line, 51-span timber viaduct which necessitated trains being re-engined at Marazion. The viaduct was then rebuilt as a double-line causeway, and Penzance also got a new station in 1937. The complex included an engine shed at Long Rock, a goods shed (moved from Ponsandane to Penzance proper) and a line from the four-platform terminus to Albert Quay and the Scilly steamers. The location handled large quantities of fish from Newlyn, broccoli, and flowers from the Scilly Isles, with more broccoli being loaded at Marazion, station for St Michael's Mount.

GB

Penzance *The pre-1937 station.* (Steamchest Collection)

PERMANENT WAY

Brunel's 'baulk road' began everything. Bridge-rail, at 43 lb per yard, was spiked to baulks of pine, 30 ft long, 15 in wide and 7 in deep. To prevent the rails cutting into the baulks, a strip of hardwood, shaped to give an inward cant to the rails, was inserted beneath them. Baulks were laid lengthwise and attached to spacing timbers at 15 ft intervals. Each spacer, or transom, double at baulk joints, single at their centres, was bolted to a vertical pile of 10 in diameter, driven up to 18 ft into the track-bed. This was intended to give rigidity to the track, but so rigid was it that as the ballast settled the baulks flexed but the piles did not, giving a worrying up-and-down ride to the passengers. The piles were abolished, but the baulk road, now with the transoms fishtailed into the sides of the baulks and iron rods as additional spacers, continued to give a safe and comfortable journey for many years.

As mixed gauge became more common, transverse sleepers with cast-iron chairs superseded the baulks, and bullhead rail of 86 lb per yard the bridge-rail. This of course meant that fishplated railjoints and oak keys to secure the rails in the chairs became the rule. Eventually chairs/sleepers

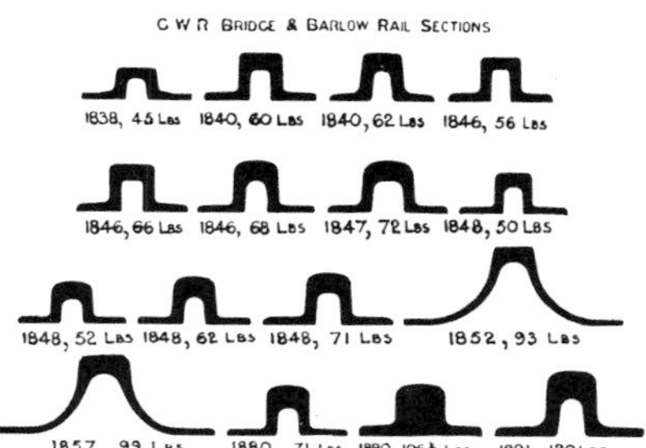

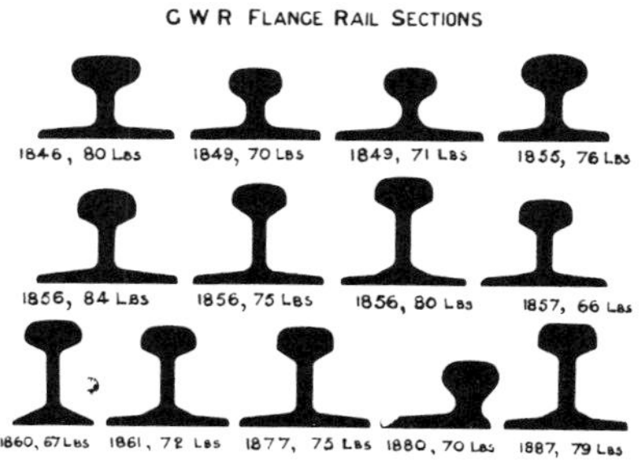

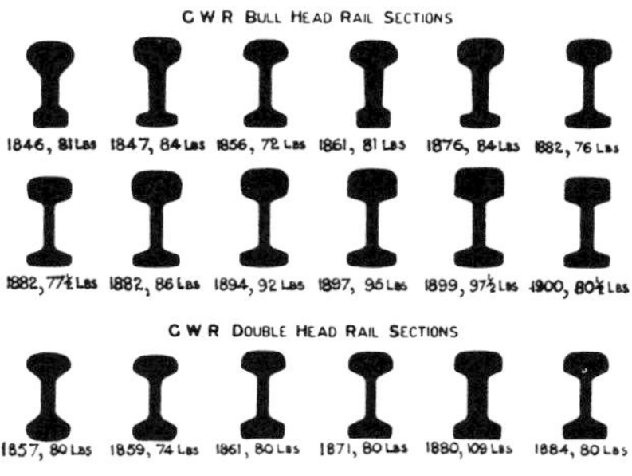

Permanent way *GWR rail sections, giving the year of introduction from the 1830s to the 1890s.* (GWR Magazine, 1913)

took over completely and in 1900 the GWR adopted the use of rails weighing $97\frac{1}{2}$ lb per yard. This was further amended in 1921, when the British Standard rail, at $94\frac{1}{2}$ lb per yard, was introduced. Steel keys began to take the place of the wooden ones—they curbed the tendency for rail-creep—and by 1947 flat-bottomed rail had been laid on 40 miles of main-line track. Some progress had been made with an early form of continuous welded rail, but since the butt-welding technique of the time could not be used on rails *in situ*, the longest practical length

Permanent way *Part of the broad gauge exhibit of the Great Western Society at Didcot, showing mixed gauge trackwork; note that the narrow gauge tracks change sides through the points. Note also the transoms dovetailed into the baulks and, on the right, the plate for the narrow gauge flange to run on while it is held in its correct course by the check rail opposite.* (Christopher Awdry)

became 300 ft, five 60 ft lengths. Prefabrication of track had also begun by this time, and it was then estimated that laying track in panels would save slightly less than a third of the man-hours required to lay traditional track.

To support the track and prevent it from moving, ballast was used from the start. Brunel used gravel at first, but early problems showed that what he was using was too small to be effective, and he quickly adopted larger sizes. But ballast is not used solely for rigidity—drainage is also important. Many early lines used ashes or earth, and while they were using unrottable stone sleeper-blocks this was fine. Brunel, however, was using timber supports for his rails, so that efficient drainage was vital. Sleepers also require rot-prevention treatment—Brunel used 'kyanisation', a long-drawn-out process which involved soaking the timbers in huge vats containing a solution of mercury bi-chloride. By 1840, however, creosote was becoming available, and treatment of timbers with this superseded the other, very messy, process. By the 1930s sleepers were being cut to size, and, as it were, force-fed with creosote—the average life of a creosoted sleeper is 20–25 years.

CA

PERRANPORTH BRANCH

Stations: Chacewater ($5\frac{1}{4}$ miles from Truro), St Agnes ($8\frac{1}{2}$ m), Perranporth ($13\frac{1}{4}$ m), Shepherds ($17\frac{3}{4}$ m), Newquay ($23\frac{3}{4}$ m)

The first section of this route dated back to 1849 when J. T. Treffry began the network of lines from Newquay Harbour that was to develop into the Cornwall Minerals Railway (qv). One of these served the East Wheal Rose mine at Newlyn and was later extended to Treamble and Gravel Hill, with the section from Shepherds to Tolgarn Junction, Newquay, becoming part of the GWR's new passenger branch when it opened throughout on 2 January 1905. The Chacewater–Perranporth portion had been operational from 6 July 1903.

The Perranporth branch started at a triangular junction with the main line west of Chacewater and took a winding course first north then east. Worked by electric train staff, the single line had passing loops at the main stations and involved quite severe gradients. Its Truro–Newquay services also called at seven halts *en route*.

The Treamble line continued in use for freight until 1917 and, again, as Clark's Siding, from 1926 to 1949.

GB

PLYMOUTH

Stations: Mutley ($225\frac{1}{4}$ miles from Paddington), North Road ($225\frac{3}{4}$ m), Devonport (227 m), Keyham ($227\frac{3}{4}$ m), St Budeaux Platform ($228\frac{3}{4}$ m); Millbay ($226\frac{1}{2}$ m)

One of Britain's notable early railway schemes was born at a meeting in Plymouth on 29 March 1819. This was the Plymouth & Dartmoor Railway (qv Princetown branch) which opened its 23 miles of 4 ft

Perranporth branch *Perranporth station.* (Steamchest Collection)

6 in gauge line on 26 September 1823 and began conveying Dartmoor granite down to the ships waiting at Sutton Pool. The South Devon Railway's (qv) new main line crossed the P&D route near the head of the Plym estuary when it opened a temporary station at Laira on 5 May 1848. It was completed through to a modest wooden station at Millbay on 2 April 1849 with the following three years then producing successively an extension into the new 13 acre GWR docks, an approach ticket platform and a Laira–Sutton Harbour branch along part of the old P&D route.

Millbay station was extended after absorbing the Truro and Tavistock services in 1859 and was rebuilt in 1900. It then consisted of a covered entrance area, a four-platform terminal, lines serving the fish dock and into the docks, and a long two-track goods shed. Between the site of the former ticket platform (closed 1896) and the separation of the routes east and west at Cornwall Junction lay a down-side carriage shed and an up-side loco depot. Traffic to and from the ocean liners passed via Millbay, the docks lines and the GWR's own steam tenders.

The Cornwall and South Devon lines were given a direct link from 17 May 1876, the year in which the LSWR gained access to Plymouth. The new station opened at North Road on 28 March of the following year and was a joint one although the GWR activity predominated, increasingly so as the LSWR went on to open Friary which handled the Turnchapel and Okehampton line services. Over the years the GWR emphasis moved from Millbay to the through platforms of North Road, where alterations were made in 1908 and 1938, and the locomotive activity from the Belmont area to the depot at Laira. These processes were finalized with the closure of the Millbay shed in 1931 and the station from 23 April 1941 after wartime bombing.

The GWR used Millbay as the originating point for its Yealmpton, Launceston and Princetown trains (all qv) and for the

Plymouth

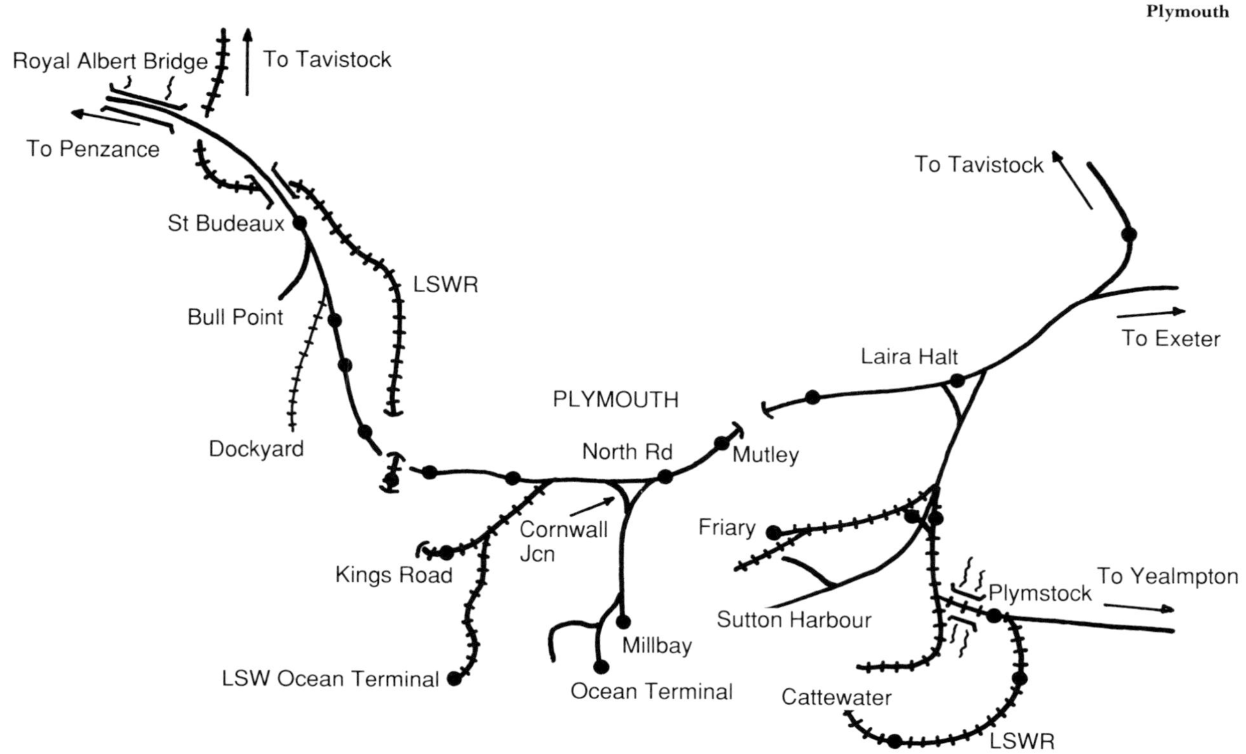

Royal Albert Bridge
To Tavistock
To Penzance
St Budeaux
LSWR
Bull Point
Dockyard
PLYMOUTH
North Rd
Mutley
Laira Halt
To Tavistock
To Exeter
Cornwall Jcn
Kings Road
Friary
Sutton Harbour
Plymstock
To Yealmpton
Millbay
Ocean Terminal
LSW Ocean Terminal
Cattewater
LSWR

prestige Plymouth–London service, but most of the through long-distance trains used the 1876 direct link with a connection provided to or from Millbay by trains of the extensive Plymouth suburban service. This operated between Plympton and Defiance Platform with some trains working to and from Millbay, some running in and out again, and others passing direct between North Road and Devonport. The rail-motors and later auto-trains (both qv) served halts at Laira, Lipson Vale, Wingfield Villas, Albert Road, Dockyard and Ford, and passed through the 183 yd Mutley and 125 yd Devonport tunnels.

In addition to the docks business, the GWR dealt with ordinary freight traffic at Millbay, North Quay Wharf and Sutton Harbour. There were several private sidings at Plymouth and the important link from Keyham into the dockyard system carried large quantities of materials, stores and special trains.

GB

POLE, SIR FELIX JOHN CLEWETT

General Manager, 1921–29. Born at Little Bedwyn, Wiltshire, on 1 February 1877, the second son of a schoolmaster, he entered GWR service in the Telegraph Department at Swindon on 12 October 1891, and became Telegraph Superintendent at Paddington two years later. He transferred to the Chief Engineer's Office in 1896 and to the General Manager's Office in 1904: he edited the *Great Western Railway Magazine* (qv) from 1903–19, was appointed Chief Clerk to the GM in 1913, Assistant to the GM in 1919 and Assistant General Manager on Aldington's (qv) promotion, later in the same year. He succeeded Aldington as General Manager in 1921, the youngest to hold the office since Grierson (qv). Knighted in 1924, he strongly opposed the strikers in 1926, and his astuteness ensured that several of their claims failed. He speeded up the services to Cheltenham (qv 'Cheltenham Flyer'), prompted the building of the 'Kings' (qv) and pulled off the visit to America of No 6000 *King George V* (qv). His final day of GWR service was 6 July 1929, after which he became Chairman of Associated Electrical Industries Ltd. His last years were clouded by blindness, but he mastered braille at the age of 70 and died at Reading on 15 January 1956.

CA

PONSONBY, HON FREDERICK GEORGE BRABAZON

Chairman, 1857–9. He was Chairman of Pilbrow's Atmospheric Railway and Canal Propulsion Company, an unsuccessful early atmospheric scheme, then was elected Chairman of the GWR in May 1857, succeeding Barrington (qv). During his short and successful period in office he secured, among other things, peace in the row with the Oxford, Worcester & Wolverhampton Railway (qv). He remained a GWR Director and died, unmarried, in London on 11 March 1895.

CA

PONTSTICILL JUNCTION–MERTHYR LINE

Stations: Pontsticill Junction, Pontsarn ($2\frac{1}{4}$ m), Cefn Coed (4 m), Merthyr ($6\frac{3}{4}$ m)

The 6 miles 20 chains from Pontsticill Junction on the Brecon–Newport line to Rhydycar Junction outside Merthyr (qv) formed a dramatic half circle, dropping at 1 in 50 to follow the loop of the Taff Fechan river and then joining the Vale of Neath line (qv) for the final access to High Street station. It had opened on 1 August 1868 in fulfilment of powers granted in the original Brecon & Merthyr Railway (qv) Act of 1 August 1859 and from 1 June 1879 had carried trains from the LNWR's Merthyr, Tredegar & Abergavenny line over the section from Morlais Junction. This portion between Morlais and Rhydycar junctions became joint property and passed to the GWR as such.

The B&M ran Brecon–Newport/Merthyr and Merthyr–Newport trains, the former dividing at Pontsticill Junction, but later services were mainly confined to the branch although a Llandrindod–Barry train did run this way. The route began at the island platform at Pontsticill and included the dramatic viaducts at Pontsarn and Cefn Coed on the section shared with the LNWR/LMS trains from Abergavenny.

GB

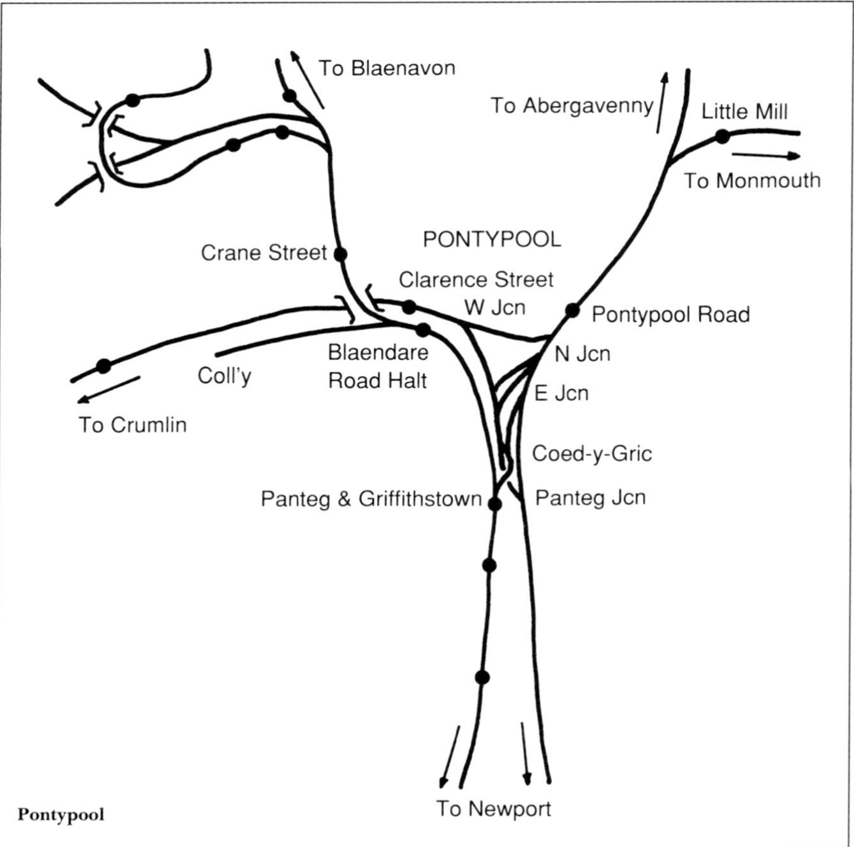

Pontypool

PONTYPOOL

By a series of complicated junctions, five GWR lines and seven routes were linked at Pontypool. It had four stations, a 90-engine loco shed, two major goods depots, five sizeable marshalling areas and over 20 private sidings, the latter involving dozens of local trip workings to position, clear and exchange the coal, brick and general goods traffic originating in or passing through the area.

The main development period had been the 1850s, with the Monmouthshire Railway & Canal Co's (qv) line from Newport opened on 1 July 1852 and extended to Blaenavon on 1 June 1854, the Newport, Abergavenny & Hereford's (qv) trains arriving in LNWR hands on 6 December 1853, the first section of the Pontypool–Neath (qv) line dating from 20 August 1855, and a link towards Monmouth (qv) established on 2 June 1856. The major subsequent additions to the network were the Pontypool, Caerleon & Newport line of 17 September 1874 and the Brynmawr route (qv), which carried a joint GWR/LNWR service, of 18 September 1879.

Trains on the Eastern Valleys route through Pontypool called at Blaendare Road Halt and Crane Street, other routes using Pontypool Road—and Clarence Street in the case of Neath trains. The GWR provided a new Pontypool Road station in 1909, located at the northern end of its four-platform predecessor and comprising a great 1,200 ft island, 52 ft 3 ins wide and with a bay for local traffic at each end. A separate administrative building housed the refreshment rooms and Divisional Superintendent's office.

GB

PONTYPOOL ROAD–NEATH LINE

Stations: Pontypool Road, Pontypool Clarence Street (1¼ m), Hafodyrynys Platform (5½ m), Crumlin High Level (6¼ m), Pentwynmawr Platform (7¾ m), Pontllanfraith (9 m), Hengoed High Level (11 m), Nelson & Llancaiach (14 m), Treharris (15¼ m), Quakers Yard High Level (16¼ m), Penrhywceiber High Level (17¾ m), Mountain Ash Cardiff Road (19 m), Cwmbach Halt (21¼ m), Aberdare High Level (22¾ m), Hirwaun (26¼ m), Glyn Neath (32¾ m), Resolven (35¾ m), Aberdylais (40 m), Neath General (41¾ m)

This was the GWR's dramatic inland route through South Wales, linking the North & West line with Swansea and carrying a significant through and local service as well as considerable quantities of coal and other industrial traffics. The first section, to Quakers Yard, involved the great Crumlin Viaduct (qv) and crossing eight 'valleys' lines. Then came a 6-mile stretch to Aberdare in company with the Taff Vale (qv), and finally a rise at 1 in 50 to Hirwaun and a 1 in 47/57 descent beyond.

The route originated with the Vale of Neath Railway (qv) (incorporated 3 August 1846), the Aberdare Valley Railway (2 July 1855) and the Taff Vale Extension line of the Newport, Abergavenny & Hereford Railway (qv), all in GWR hands by 1865. Aberdare to Neath was opened first, with the TVE reaching Middle Duffryn by four stages completed on 5 October 1864. By that time the AVR's section linking the two was open (1856), as was the VoN's branch to Merthyr (qv) (1853).

GB

PONTYPRIDD

Its location as the meeting point of the Taff and Rhondda predestined Pontypridd to become a major railway location. Its main station, rebuilt by the Taff Vale Railway (qv) in 1907, consisted of a great, curving island platform with five bays for the originating services which ran to Machen, Cardiff, Cowbridge and the Ynysybwl branch (all qv). Through trains ran from Newport and Cardiff to Merthyr and others to Treherbert and thus Swansea. Separate goods lines took freight trains round the up side, while valley to valley traffic, and reversing operations, went via the Rhondda Cutting triangle north of the station. Pontypridd had separate goods and locomotive depots.

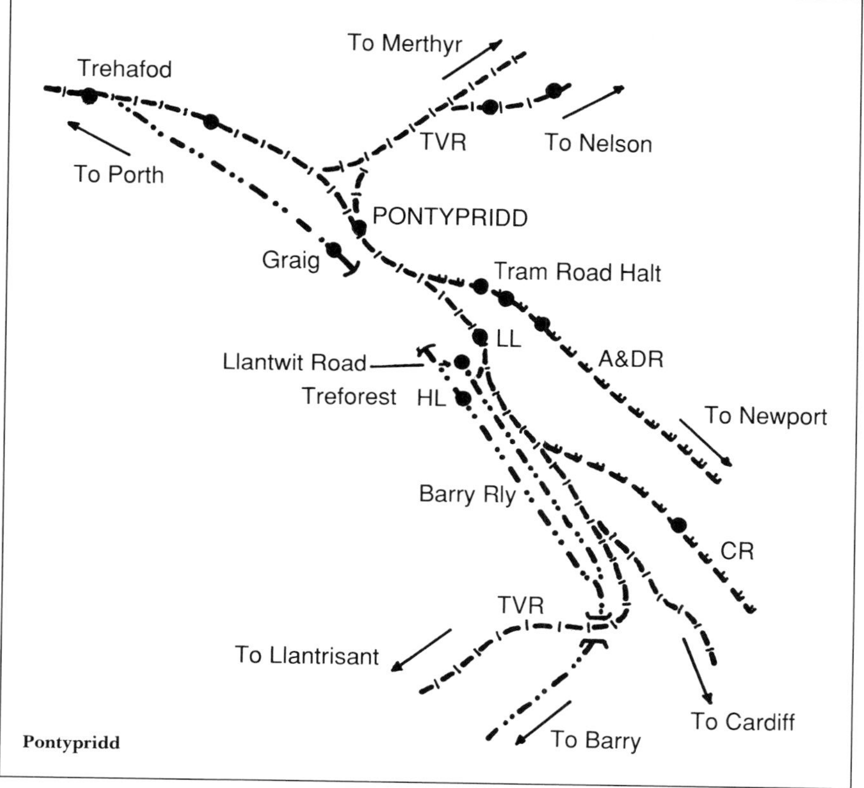

Pontypridd

The Taff Vale Railway had reached Pontypridd on 8 October 1840 using the floor of the valley and forcing the Barry Railway's (qv) later (13 May 1889) route to tunnel through from Treforest to Graig station and to the junction at Trehafod. In GWR years the Cardiff–Pontypridd and Barry–Porth services were routed to the ex-TVR station via Tonteg and Treforest Junctions from 10 July 1930. An earlier piece of rationalization had been the diversion of the PC&N/AD&R Newport trains from the Tram Road Motor Halt terminus into Pontypridd proper from 10 July 1922.

GB

PONTYPRIDD–ABERTHAW LINE

Stations: Pontypridd, Treforest (1 m), Church Village (5 m), Llantwit (5½ m), Cross Inn (7¾ m), Llantrisant (9¾ m), Llanharry (11 m), Ystradowen (13¼ m), Cowbridge (15½ m), St Mary Church Road (17¾ m), St Athan Road (20½ m), Aberthaw (21¼ m)

Although promoted by three nominally independent concerns, this line was a Taff Vale (qv) enterprise right from the start, the TVR absorbing the local companies in 1889/95 and then contributing the route to the GWR at the Grouping. Not that it amounted to much, for the whole exercise had been a territorial one and the traffic potential so modest that the Cowbridge–Aberthaw section lost its two weekday trains each way on 5 May 1930 and its freight facilities on 1 November 1932.

The first of the three constituents was the Llantrisant & Taff Vale Junction Railway, authorized on 7 June 1861 and linking Treforest and Maesaraul Junction on the Ely Valley Railway (5 m 20 ch) via the route of the Llantwit Vardre tramroad from December 1863 (passengers 21 January 1875). The Treferig Valley Railway added a 2 m 5 ch link to Treferig and Glyn collieries from April 1883 and the L&TVJ a 7 m 12 ch line to Waterhall Junction on the Radyr–Penarth line on 11 September 1886.

South of Llantrisant the Cowbridge Railway was incorporated on 29 July 1862 and opened over its 5 m 49 ch on 18 September 1865. The Cowbridge & Aberthaw Railway, authorized on 12 August 1889, then added another 6 m 29 ch from 1 October 1892. The latter followed the River Thaw to Aberthaw Low Level station and the lime and cement works there.

Despite the GWR's abandonment of the section below Cowbridge, the rest of the route enjoyed a much improved passenger service with 12 trains a day between Cowbridge and Llantrisant, 12 more on the Llantrisant–Pontypridd section and eight which ran through. The line had a limestone quarry south of Cowbridge and an iron ore mine at Llanharry.

GB

PONTYPRIDD–MACHEN LINE

Stations: Pontypridd, Caerphilly (7 m), Machen (10½ m)

The GWR passenger service on this line was made up of through Newport–Merthyr trains and various domestic combinations calling at six halts between Pontypridd and Caerphilly (qv) and three more on the Machen section. An 1887 service to Newport had been supplemented by railmotors (qv) from Pontypridd (Tram Road) in 1904, with auto-trains (qv) taking over subsequently, usually with an Abercynon 0-6-0PT.

The route had originated as the Newport-inspired Pontypridd, Caerphilly & Newport Railway incorporated on 8 August 1878 and intended to divert coal from Cardiff docks. Opening of the Pontypridd–Penrhos section took place on 7 July 1884, with running powers over the RR/B&M to Machen and Bassaleg then providing a connection with the Bassaleg–Alexandra Docks link which was authorized by an Act of 2 August 1883 and opened two years later. The PC&N became part of the Alexandra Docks & Railway (qv) from 31 December 1897.

On its first section the line climbed gently out of the Taff Valley to meet the Rhymney Railway (qv) at Penrhos Junction, the top of the latter's 1 in 47 'Big Bank' and meeting point with the Barry Railway (qv). Leaving the RR again at Caerphilly East Branch Junction for the B&M section, the descending lines separated before Machen, the down line dating from 1890 and following an easier course than the original 1 in 39 route which served Machen Forge, Pwlldu Colliery, Waterloo Halt and Waterloo Tin Plate Works.

GB

PORTAL, LORD WYNDHAM RAYMOND

Chairman, 1945–8. Born at Overton, Hampshire, on 9 April 1885, he won the DSO in 1918. His family had been connected with railway affairs for many years, and he was elected a GWR Director in 1927. He resigned when appointed an additional Parliamentary Secretary to the Minister of Supply, and became Minister of Works from 1942–44. He came back to the GWR on giving up that post, and in the next year was created a Viscount and succeeded Hambro (qv) as Chairman, the last to hold the position. When he took office, Nationalization was imminent, but he refused to let that colour his outlook. In 1947 a GWR-published document by Christian Barman called *Next Station: a Railway Plan for the Future* appeared, and contained the statement that '. . . the Great Western intends to maintain its position of leadership in the application of new forms of energy to railway traction'. And it did, though by then Lord Portal was no longer in charge. He presided at the last GWR General Meeting, on 14 March 1948, after which he resigned. He was made a GCMG in 1949, but died the same year at Laverstoke, Hants.

CA

PORTHCAWL BRANCH

Stations: Tondu, Kenfig Hill (3¾ m), Pyle (6 m), Porthcawl (9¾ m)

A 4 ft 7 ins gauge mineral tramway which linked Maesteg and Porthcawl harbour from 1829 was acquired by the Llynvi Valley Railway under an Act of 1847 and rebuilt as a broad gauge mineral line from 10 August 1861. Ogmore Valley Railway narrow gauge passenger services were added from 1 August 1865, the two railways combining as the Llynfi & Ogmore in 1866 and adding a dock at Porthcawl.

Pyle got a new station from 13 November 1876 with separate Porthcawl platforms, an underpass for Tondu–Porthcawl trains (worked by the GWR from 1873) and north/west plus east/south junction lines. Porthcawl then got its new station on 6 March 1916, a three-platform terminus on a redundant dock site, and the first 1½ miles of the branch south from Pyle was doubled in 1924 to cope with the growing day-tripper business.

Services on the Tondu–Porthcawl line consisted of some through trains, a few Newport/Cardiff–Porthcawl services and good, but separate, Pyle–Tondu and Pyle–Porthcawl workings.

GB

PORTISHEAD BRANCH

Stations: Bristol Temple Meads, Bedminster (1 m), Parson Street (1¾ m), Ashton Gate (3 m), Clifton Bridge (3½ m), Ham Green Halt (7 m), Pill (7¾ m), Portbury (9½ m), Portishead (11½ m)

After leaving the main line at a triangular junction south of Bristol, the Portishead branch headed north for the River Avon and used the beautiful Avon Gorge to breach the Gordano Hills before passing through Pill, traditional home of the river pilots, and then heading west to the pleasant estuary town of Portishead. Its generous service of trains, which catered for Bristol commuters and local Saturday trips to the estuary or Bristol City's football ground, included some through workings from Avonmouth (qv), Filton Junction and Stapleton Road. Freight traffic to and from the docks and sidings at Portishead included coal to the power station there.

The Portishead line was authorized to the Bristol & Portishead Pier Railway on 29 June 1863 and opened on 18 April 1867 with working by the B&E and eventual acquisition by the GWR from 1 July 1884. The original Portishead station consisted of a single platform on the line through to the pier with a second platform being added in 1930. From the coal yard a connection was made with the Weston, Clevedon & Portishead Railway, although in later years the GWR would not supply wagons to the impecunious WC&P without advance payment.

There were four tunnels on the Portishead line (of 59, 232, 88 and 665 yards), which was worked by electric train staff from Clifton Bridge and by token on the section to the Shipyard and Timber Jetty.

GB

'PORTS-TO-PORTS EXPRESS'

In GWR days, crews of ocean-going ships were usually paid off on arrival at a port, and a different one signed on when the vessel was ready to leave again. With turnrounds which were long by modern standards, it was sometimes necessary for sailors to travel to another port to get further work, and this was facilitated by this particular named train, which dated back to 1906. In the course of its journeys in each direction between Newcastle and Barry it used tracks owned by five different railways. It ran southwards from the busy shipping centre of the Tyne over the North Eastern main line, with a connection at Darlington from the ports on the Tees. From York it reached the Swinton & Knottingly Joint at Ferrybridge, one of whose owners was the Midland. At Sheffield Victoria the train reversed and, after the Grouping, attached a through coach from the ports of Hull and Goole. It continued over the Great Central to reach the GWR at Banbury, after which it crossed the Cotswolds to Cheltenham, using the third side of the triangle at Kingham (qv) to miss the station there. Another joint line with MR ownership took the train on to Gloucester, and then the GWR's original route to South Wales was followed as far as Cardiff. Here it switched to the Barry Railway for the short final leg. In 1922 the southbound journey was taking almost 10 hours, and the timings remained unchanged up to the beginning of the Second World War, although at the Welsh end it had, by then, been extended to Swansea. Six-coach sets, which included a restaurant car, were used for the main train, being made up from NER and GWR stock on alternate days.

PWBS

PORT TALBOT

The small dock opened at the mouth of the River Afan in 1835–37 and named after Emily Charlotte Talbot was destined to grow into a major port with a water area of

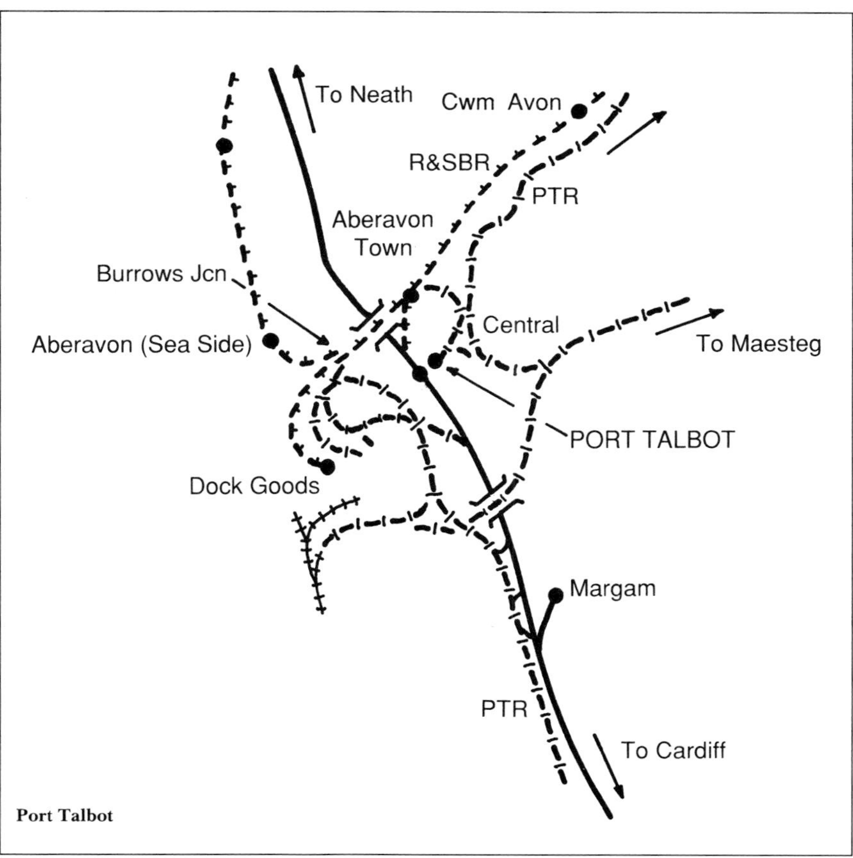

Port Talbot

123 acres. Its small, tramroad-served collieries, copper works and iron works begat much larger steel, tinplate and blackplate plant and the services of three railways, of which the 18 June 1850 line of the South Wales Railway (qv) was the first. The Rhondda & Swansea Bay Railway (qv) then reached the estuary in 1885 and nine years later the Port Talbot Railway & Docks (qv) enterprise was incorporated to build a new dock and three radiating coal lines. The PTR's passenger service to Blaengarw ended in the GWR era, but Port Talbot was well served on the main line and by trains on the ex-R&SB route from Swansea to Aberavon and on to Treherbert.

The east-west GWR main line ran from Margam goods and coal depot, through a conventional station near the docks access road, to a level crossing of the R&SB line. Three groups of works lay to seaward and their sidings were linked with the ex-PTR lines on either side of the main water area. The first R&SB station, Port Talbot Docks, closed on 14 March 1895 in favour of Aberavon Town and the ex-PTR Central terminus closed on 11 September 1933.

(See also Docks and harbours)

GB

PORT TALBOT RAILWAY & DOCKS

Stations: Port Talbot Central, Port Talbot Aberavon, Bryn (4 m), Maesteg (8½ m), Cwmdu (10 m), Lletty Brongu (12 m), Bettws (13½ m), Pontyrhyll (15 m), Pontycymmer (16½ m), Blaengarw (17½ m)

Essentially a dock-plus-coal railway, the Port Talbot Railway originated in much the same way as the Barry (qv) enterprise, and its promoters were also coal owners. They obtained their enabling Act on 31 July 1894 which authorized the acquisition of the harbour and dock built by the Talbot family in 1835–37 (qv Port Talbot) and the construction both of a new dock and of a line to Pontyrhyll on the GWR's Garw branch. Further 1896 Acts authorized the company's other two lines—east to Waterhall Junction (opened 19 December 1898) with access thence to Tondu over the Cefn & Pyle Railway, and north to the South Wales Mineral Railway at Tonmawr Junctions (opened 14 November 1898).

While the new dock at Port Talbot was being built, the PTR opened its main line up at 1 in 40 to Cwm Ceren tunnel, down to Maesteg and up again to Lletty Brongu on 31 August 1897, adding the further descent to Pontyrhyll Junction on 17 January 1898. A passenger service was operated from 14 February 1898.

At Port Talbot, where the PTR had its own Central station, the dock had proved costly to construct and slow to attract traffic, factors which influenced acceptance of a GWR offer to work the railway part of the undertaking from 1 January 1908. The whole enterprise then passed to the GWR at the Grouping with the passenger service one of the early casualties (beyond Maesteg 12 September 1932, completely 11 September 1933).

GB

POSTCARDS

More than 900 different official GWR picture postcards have been recorded (many more if print variations are counted). They were produced from around 1899 to 1942.

The first cards associated with the company were produced by the Picture Postcard Company for sale in slot machines on stations. They carry the company name and journey times for the scene depicted, but there is no evidence of company sponsor-

Postcards *A Series 1 card of the viaduct at Pontcysyllte, and a Series 2 example showing* Lord of the Isles, *both amongst the first issued by the GWR in 1904.* (John Alsop Collection)

ship. The first true officials appeared in March 1904 with a set of 25 for 1s (5p), or two a penny (one if stamped) from slot machines. The subjects included views, historical scenes and modern locomotives, and provided excellent low-cost publicity for the railway with the price covering production costs. Eight further sets were produced before the Great War, including a superb set of 12 posters, as well as a set of locomotives and a set to publicize the new Fishguard route to America.

A few more series came out in the 1920s, mostly Cathedrals, but there was an interesting set of aerial views of the docks. A final set of eight coloured views was issued in 1938 (most GWR cards were sepia).

The company also used postcards itself, to acknowledge enquiries for instance, and several series were printed starting in 1904 with an attractive set with the company crest by the picture. By 1912 the standard had dropped, the next five years seeing the use of more than 400 different commercial view cards overprinted by the GWR. These were generally used by goods depots.

Picture postcards were also available in restaurant cars, on board ship, and of course at the GWR hotels. These cards showed views, ships, and hotels respectively, the ships giving a good coverage of the 1927–39 period. Two curiosities were produced in 1927, double-size folding cards, one showing *King George V*, the other the 'Cornish Riviera Limited.'

1904 to 1912 were the peak years, with both numbers and quality dropping off thereafter. Second only to the LNWR in quantity, the general quality of the GWR cards was surprisingly no more than average. Nevertheless they provide today an interesting and comparatively inexpensive collecting theme.

Information supplied by John Alsop, whose book on railway postcards is listed in the Bibliography.

Great Western Railway,
General Manager's Office,
Paddington Station,
London, W.

G. W. R.
No. 5139
5 FEB. 1912
GENERAL MANAGER.

R S

11 o'clock

3rd.February 1912.

My dear Sir,

Railway Companies' (Accounts & Returns) Act 1911.

In reply to your letter of yesterday; as our dividend has not yet been declared and Mr.Whitelaw is very much engaged next week, it will be somewhat inconvenient for him to attend the meeting.

I think he could manage to be present however, provided a time is specified for dealing with this subject, and perhaps as Chairman you can arrange for this matter to be taken at 10-30, or at any other time which commends itself to you, so as to detain Mr.Whitelaw as little as possible.

Yours faithfully,

F Potter

Oliver Bury Esq.,
Kings Cross.

Frank Potter *A letter from the General Manager's Office signed by Potter and dated 3 February 1912, within a month of his having taken office.*
(W. Adams Collection)

POTTER, FRANK

General Manager, 1912–19. Born on 30 March 1856, he joined the GWR as a lad/clerk attached to the Goods Department at Paddington in 1869. After eight years he was promoted to the General Manager's Office, but in 1881 requested a transfer to Traffic and became Station Master at Shrivenham, Castle Hill (West Ealing), and West Drayton. He was made Chief Clerk in the office of the Superintendent of the London Division in 1888 and rejoined the General Manager's staff. He became Chief Assistant to Inglis (qv) (then GM) in 1904, succeeding him in January 1912. He became a member of the Railway Executive Committee in 1914, and was appointed Chairman of the General Managers' Conference of the Railway Clearing House. But the strain of the war years shortened his life; in March 1919, having declined a knighthood, he went to rest at St Ives, but died there on 23 July.

CA

POTTER, FRANK ROWE

Superintendent of the Line, 1936–40. The son of Frank Potter (qv above) he entered GWR service on 1 January 1895 as a booking clerk at West Drayton & Yiewsley. He was transferred to the London Divisional Superintendent's office in May 1897, and worked in the Train Department until 1900, when he moved to Slough as Goods Clerk. Returning to Paddington after a short time, he remained in the Superintendent's office until May 1907, when he was transferred to the staff of the Superintendent of the Line. He became Divisional Superintendent, Plymouth, in July 1911,

London in May 1913, and the first Superintendent of the Westbury Division in 1915. He was appointed Chairman of the Railway Clearing House Conference for 1916, and became Divisional Superintendent, Paddington, from 9 January 1922. Succeeding H. L. Wilkinson (qv) as Superintendent of the Line in 1936, he was himself followed by Matthews (qv) from 1 January 1941.

CA

POTTER, RICHARD

Chairman, 1863–5. Born in Manchester in 1817, he was elected to the GWR Board in 1849. A Gloucester timber merchant, his company made wooden huts for English and French troops in the Crimea—Brunel was also involved, designing a prefabricated hospital used at Renkioi. Potter resigned in 1856, but in 1860 became a Director of the West Midland Railway (qv). On that company's amalgamation with the GWR he came back to the GWR Board to be at once elected Chairman. He was an assiduous Chairman (he consolidated the GWR stocks and established a superannuation fund for the workpeople) but was not popular; he resigned in 1865 because the work was preventing attention to his private affairs. His successor was Gooch (qv), and he died at Box House, Minchinhampton, Glos, on 1 January 1892.

CA

PRINCES RISBOROUGH

The Wycombe Railway's line from High Wycombe (qv) to Princes Risborough was authorized by an Act of 17 August 1857 and extensions to Oxford (qv below) and Aylesbury by another of 28 June 1861. After opening as far as Thame on 1 August 1862, the Oxford line was completed two years later, by which time the Aylesbury branch (qv) had been operational since 1 October 1863.

Princes Risborough increased its railway status still further when the Watlington branch (qv) opened on 15 August 1872, the GWR station absorbing the work of the branch terminus in 1883–84 but then being rebuilt by the Great Western & Great Central Joint Committee, from 1 April 1906.

The new GW&GC line (qv), together with the 1910 Ashendon–Aynho completion, gave Princes Risborough a busy pattern of London–Oxford/Birmingham/Aylesbury services, plus its own originating trains. To cater for these the station had a generous layout of through lines, platform loops and country-end bays. The three separating routes had their junction at the north end, with the goods depot and private siding connections at the London end. Furniture was important among the freight forwardings.

GB

PRINCES RISBOROUGH–OXFORD LINE

Stations: Princes Risborough, Bledlow ($1\frac{1}{2}$ m), Thame ($5\frac{3}{4}$ m), Tiddington ($9\frac{3}{4}$ m), Wheatley ($13\frac{1}{4}$ m), Morris Cowley ($16\frac{1}{4}$ m), Littlemore ($17\frac{1}{2}$ m), Oxford (21 m)

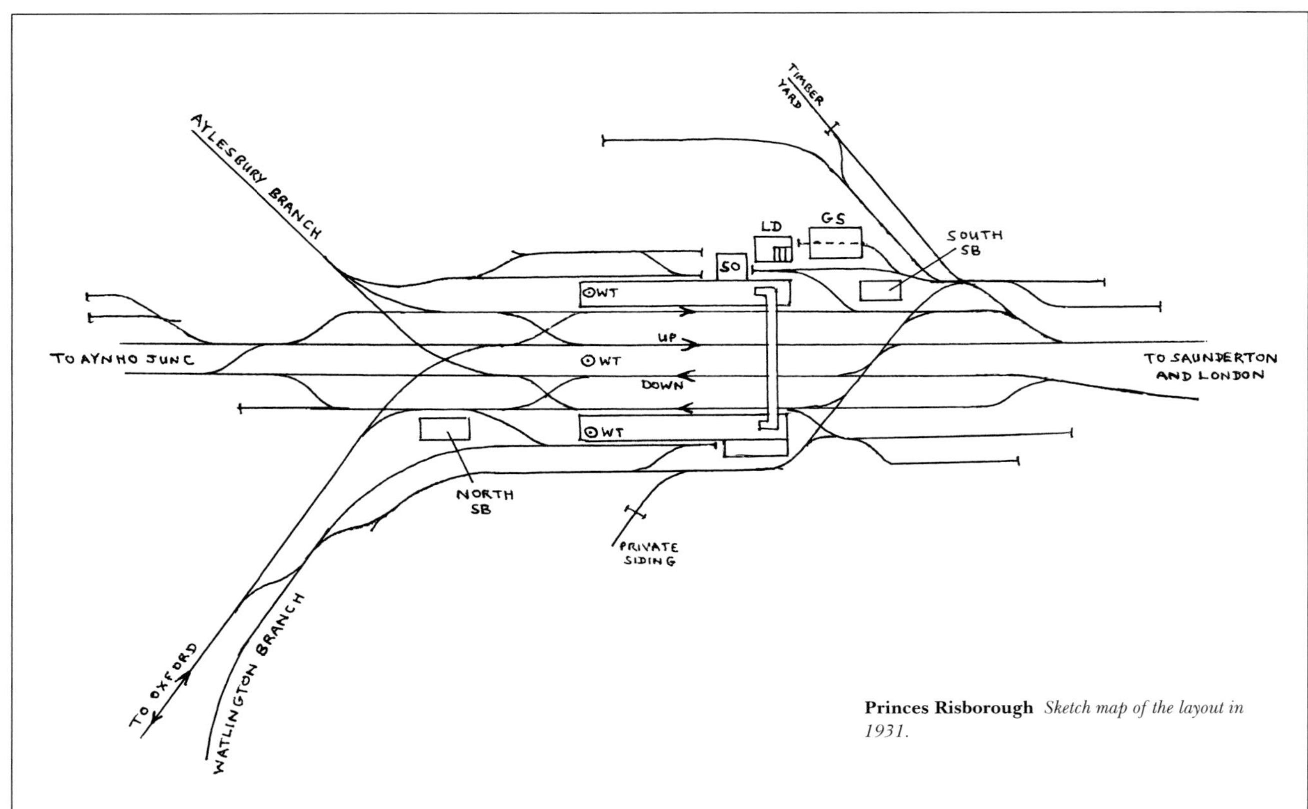

Princes Risborough *Sketch map of the layout in 1931.*

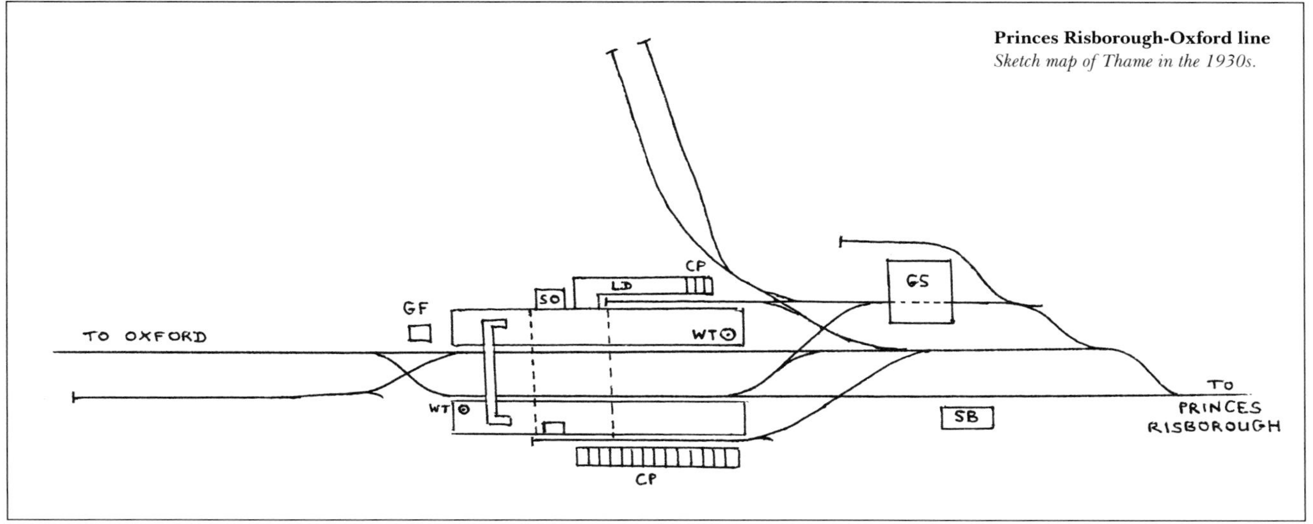

Princes Risborough-Oxford line *Sketch map of Thame in the 1930s.*

Princes Risborough-Oxford line *Thame station, with its overall roof, looking towards Oxford.* (Steamchest Collection)

Authorized to the Wycombe Railway by an Act of 28 June 1861, this line was opened as far as Thame on 1 August 1862 and completed to Kennington Junction, Oxford, on 24 October 1864. It became part of the GWR system from 1 February 1867 and increased its importance with the opening of the 'New Line' (qv GW&GC Joint line) via Northolt, which cut the Paddington–Oxford distance by 6¼ miles.

The line, which was single with passing loops and had halts at Towersey and Horspath, carried a mixture of through trains plus others to and from Thame and Morris Cowley. From Princes Risborough it headed straight for Thame, the principal intermediate station and notable for its 90 ft overall roof. Beyond Thame's passing loop the line followed the general course of the Thames, crossing it before Wheatley, approaching Horspath by tunnel and then sweeping round the south of Oxford via Morris Cowley and the car works sidings there.

GB

PRINCETOWN BRANCH

Stations: Yelverton, Dousland (1½ m), Burrator Halt (3 m), Ingra Tor Halt (6¼ m), King Tor Halt (9 m), Princetown (10½ m)

This bleak and lonely single-line branch was successor to the Plymouth & Dartmoor Railway, a 4 ft 6 in gauge line opened on 26 September 1823 to bring granite down from King's Tor to Sutton Pool. The section above Yelverton was then acquired for constructing the Princetown Railway which had been authorized by an Act of 13 August 1878. The new line opened on 11 August 1883 with trains worked by the GWR and running to and from Horrabridge until the junction station at Yelverton was brought into use from 1 May 1885.

After taking over the line on 1 January 1922, the GWR added three intermediate halts to the block post station at Dousland. Ten weekday trains used the V-shaped up platform at Yelverton and traversed the 10 m 39 ch, 1 in 40, winding, electric train staff route between there and the Princetown terminus, 1,373 ft above sea level. The branch handled traffic to and from Dartmoor Prison, some granite from King's Tor, and walkers to and from Ingra Tor, noted for its snake warning.

GB

PRIVATE SIDINGS

Though the GWR had access to many hundreds of private sidings during its history, it had control over none of them and owned none. A statutory right for a railway to connect with a private siding was generally made by a clause in the company's Act, individually until 1845, and by a 'blanket' clause under the Railway Clauses Consolidation Act, 1845, thereafter.

The right to connect was not restricted to the builders of the siding. Their successors could, if they wished, connect a hitherto unconnected siding, though the Board of Trade would wish to satisfy itself as to the practicability of working—the angle of the junction, for instance, or the gradient of the line. However, once a siding had been legally connected, the GWR (or any other railway company) had no right to discontinue or block the junction, and was liable to an exemplary fine if it did so. Indeed, the railway company rather than the trader was responsible for the maintenance of the junction, and any improvements had to be made by the railway company. Non-use was not grounds for closure—the trader retained the right to use his siding or not, as he wished.

Charges were made by the connecting company, but these could vary for individual traders only, for bulk traffic or in consideration of whether or not the railway company supplied trucks. Excess charges were recoverable at law. An extra charge could, however, be made by a company supplying and laying '. . . straw in trucks for preventing injury to traffic'. The connecting company was also responsible for insuring the goods it delivered, and in 1887 the GWR was successfully sued by a private owner in this regard.

Despite all this, the GWR clearly thought it worthwhile to maintain connections, particularly in South Wales, where even after Nationalization there were about 150 colliery and sidings where traffic was exchanged.

CA

PROJECTED LINES

Some of the ultimately abortive schemes proposed by the GWR were major enough, if carried through, to have affected profoundly the way the railway shaped. One of these, formed during the time when the GWR was contesting with the Chester & Holyhead Railway for the Irish mails, was a broad gauge line, only 3.5 miles longer than the Holyhead route eventually chosen, running from Didcot via Oxford, Evesham, Worcester, Ludlow and Newtown, tunnelling beyond Dinas Mawddwy to Dolgelley. It then headed for the sea, following much the same route as the present Cambrian Coast line, to reach Port Dinllaen, south of Caernarvon, whence ferries would have left for Ireland.

Another project, in 1846, aimed at the same destination from Worcester, but was withdrawn in view of the impending Gauge Commission (qv Broad Gauge). The Manchester & Southampton Railway was a proposal to link the north and south of England with a standard gauge line, avoiding a break of gauge. It was defunct by August 1848, and the Midland & South Western Junction Railway (qv) ultimately fulfilled at least part of its intentions. The East Gloucestershire Railway was promoted to link Witney with the M&SWJR at Andoversford, but got no further than Fairford (qv).

In the west, an alternative route to Looe, along the coast from St Germans (both qv), was proposed in the 1930s, and building began, but was abandoned before completion. At Helston (qv) it was found to be cheaper to run buses to the Lizard than to build a projected railway—this was the first railway bus service (qv) in the country. In 1905 the GWR sought powers for a link between its Bodmin branch and the Newquay line (both qv), avoiding the long detour through Par, and for a cut-off to avoid the South Devon banks. This would have left the present line just north of Aller Junction to follow a straighter route across Dainton. The line would then have swung inland to bypass Totnes, serving Dartington instead, and on a ruling gradient of 1 in 100 would have rejoined the South Devon Railway line just before Marley tunnel. It was never begun, and a Salcombe branch terminated 3 miles short of its objective, at Kingsbridge (qv). Just before the Second World War a scheme was projected for a deviation inland between Dawlish Warren and Bishopsteignton to avoid the weather-prone coastal section—the war put paid to that.

In Wales a proposed branch to New Quay from the Lampeter & Aberayron Light Railway came to nothing, as did also schemes for a branch to St Davids from Mathry Road, and an extension from New Radnor, via Rhayader and the Elan Valley, to Trawscoed on the Manchester & Milford line.

In England, a link was planned from the Severn Valley line between Bridgnorth and Eardington to the Shrewsbury/Birmingham line near Codsall, with a further branch southwards to Stourbridge. A Codsall/Stourbridge line *was* built after the Grouping, though not to the same route; the Severn Valley link never was. Oddest of all, perhaps, was the Mitcheldean Road & Forest of Dean Railway—built throughout, it was opened only as far as Drybrook Road. The section from there to Mitcheldean Road, though maintained, was never actually used!

CA

PUBLICITY

There was probably no railway more publicity conscious and adept at self-promotion than the GWR. Its most famous production was *Holiday Haunts* which ran, with interruptions during the war periods, from 1906 to the company's end. The statistics relating to it are staggering—200,000 copies were sold in each of the years 1928–31; its first edition ran to 334 pages, but by 1927 had reached 1,000; and during the peak years around 1930 2,400 miles of paper were used in its production. Its purchase price never exceeded 6d (2½p). GWR posters were not specially distinguished in their early days and the Advertising Department set up in 1886 achieved nothing memorable. However, the launch of the 'Cornish Riviera' express (qv) in 1904 was a masterstroke, particularly as it coincided with the opening of Churchward's reign and the company's pre-eminence in locomotive matters. The book *Cornish Riviera Express* sold ¼ million copies in its first edition.

The Publicity Department was given its first independent chief (William Henry Fraser) in 1924, and from then on it showed just what could be achieved by skilful public relations. Posters began to rival those of the LMS and the LNER, who employed some of the finest graphic artists then at work, and the one produced to commemorate the company's Centenary (qv) in 1935, featuring a 'King' and the 'Cornish Riviera' rake of Centenary stock carriages, has become a classic. Although by the mid-1930s the LNER and LMS streamliners were outpacing the GWR's crack 'Bristolian' and 'Cheltenham Spa Express' (both qv) (previously 'The Fastest Train in the World'), the Publicity Department had reached its zenith and to the general public the GWR was still the market leader.

Excellent relations were established with the national and local press and the publicity departments of not only the many seaside resorts the GWR served, but also inland ones such as the spa cities of Bath, Cheltenham and Leamington.

The dignified dark green livery of the locomotives with copper and brass accoutrements, and the chocolate and cream of the carriages, were a tremendous asset in establishing the company's unmistakeable image. Some 35,000 jigsaw (qv) puzzles of *King George V* and a similar number of the 'Cornish Riviera' were sold. Books (qv) produced by the company, bearing titles such

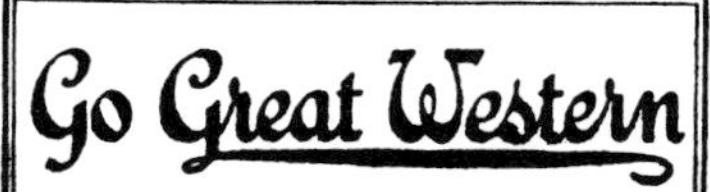

IT PAYS TO ADVERTISE IN

"*Holiday Haunts*"

THE G.W.R. OFFICIAL GUIDE
(Published Annually in March)

Full particulars of advertising rates will be supplied by the Superintendent of the Line, G.W.R. Publicity Department, Paddington Station, London, W.2.

WHEN WRITING TO ADVERTISERS PLEASE MENTION "HOLIDAY HAUNTS"

G.W.R. LANTERN LECTURES

The G.W.R. have interesting sets of lantern slides entitled

DEVON: THE SHIRE OF THE SEA KINGS. A Delightful journey through North and South Devon ... ... 75 slides

THE LORNA DOONE AND WESTWARD HO! COUNTRY. The beauty spots of Somerset and North Devon ... ... 74 slides

These and other sets of slides, accompanied by lecture notes, are lent for entertainments, scholastic purposes, bazaars, etc., free of charge, with the exception of any expense which may be incurred for carriage outside the Company's own delivery area. Application should be made to the Superintendent of the Line, G.W.R., Paddington Station, London, W.2.

Publicity *Three examples of GWR enterprise in the field of publicity: new mailing meters enabled the company to print its own frankings, as this example from 1926;* Holiday Haunts *provided a vast amount of advertising for the company and its customers for some 40 years; and Lantern Lectures were available for hire complete with lecture notes to drum up fresh holiday business.*

as *Cornish Riviera* (the place not the train this time), *Glorious Devon* and *Somerset* sold equally well.

The hard-working Press Department commissioned thousands of photographs of every aspect of the company's vast range of activities. Most of the negatives, often 12 x 10 in glass plates, have survived, one of the reasons why the GWR is the best documented of all the great railway companies. Stan Micklewright took many of these pictures from the late 1920s onwards; he retired to a village near Winchester and after his death a few years ago a thriving railway club was set up in his memory. Probably the greatest publicity coup achieved by the GWR was persuading the Prince of Wales, later King Edward VIII, to be its guest of honour at the Centenary Dinner at Bristol in 1935.

MCHB

PWLLHELI LINE

Stations: Barmouth ($25\frac{1}{2}$ m from Machynlleth), Dyffryn-on-Sea ($30\frac{1}{2}$ m), Pensarn ($33\frac{1}{2}$ m), Harlech (36 m), Talsarnau ($39\frac{1}{4}$ m), Penrhyndeudraeth ($41\frac{1}{2}$ m), Minffordd ($42\frac{1}{2}$ m), Portmadoc ($44\frac{3}{4}$ m), Criccieth ($49\frac{3}{4}$ m), Afon Wen (53 m), Abererch ($55\frac{3}{4}$ m), Pwllheli ($57\frac{3}{4}$ m)

On 22 July 1861 the Aberystwyth & Welsh Coast Railway obtained an Act authorizing the construction of a line along the Cardigan Bay coastline from Aberystwyth (qv) to Pwllheli. At the northern end the section between Afon Wen and Portmadoc was to be shared with the Carnarvonshire Railway, that company opening south to Afon Wen on 2 September 1867 and continuing to Penrhyndeudraeth until the A&WC line was completed on 10 October. By that time the A&WC had become part of the Cambrian Railways (qv).

The new line followed the coastal plain northwards to pass Harlech Castle and then make a great loop inland round the Traeth Bach estuary. Turning west via links with the Festiniog Railway at Minffordd, the Welsh Highland at Portmadoc and the Caernarvon line at Afon Wen, it came eventually to the terminus at Pwllheli. This was replaced from 19 July 1909 by a new five-line, two-platform station located $\frac{1}{2}$ mile beyond the 1867 location which was then occupied by the locomotive and goods functions.

On the approach to Portmadoc station and passing loop the A&WC crossed first the Gorseddau Tramway and then the Croesor Tramway, the latter becoming part of the Welsh Highland Railway's Snowdon mountain route from 1923 and having exchange sidings at Beddgelert Works. The line also had halts at Llanaber, Talybont, Talwin Bach, Llandanwg, Tygwyn, Llandecwyn, Black Rock and Penychain.

In later GWR days Pwllheli had a local service to and from Afon Wen, stopping trains to Barmouth and Machynlleth—the latter taking 3 hours for the $57\frac{1}{2}$ miles—and through coaches to Aberystwyth, Birkenhead, Birmingham and Paddington.

GB

RACE TRAFFIC

The GWR ran many race specials, and gave preferential treatment to all of them, but extra attention was always given to those trains (and passengers) travelling to Newbury or Cheltenham meetings. Newbury's dedicated Racecourse station (qv) was served by 60-minute trains from Paddington usually very well-patronized. The locomotive for the 'Members and First Class' train was especially selected, and a Running Inspector would travel on the footplate. Cheltenham was a 'top-link' turn, and the crew of the special often returned to London with the 'Cheltenham Flyer' (qv). In 1927 the GWR broke new ground by running specials to the Grand National at Aintree on 25 March. The first, leaving Paddington at 7.50 am, called at Ealing Broadway before running non-stop to Birkenhead; the second, a 1st class train, left London at 8.25 am, and ran non-stop throughout. In fact, the 'Non-stop' billing was nominal only—both trains halted at Shrewsbury to change engines. Onward travel from Birkenhead was arranged with Pickfords, a GWR subsidiary.

CA

Railmotors *No 2, one of the original railmotors of 1903.* (Lens of Sutton)

RAILMOTORS

In 1903 the GWR introduced the first of its steam railmotors, which consisted of a single saloon coach fitted with a boiler at one end, powering the small 0-4-0 engine on the bogie beneath it. Driving cabs were provided at both ends, so the unit could be operated easily in either direction without having to run the locomotive round as with a conventional train. By 1908 99 cars had been built, but there were 112 engine units, the surplus providing a pool for overhaul purposes. Unusually in GWR practice, the engines had outside Walschaerts valve gear. A number of auto-trailers were also built, but the railmotors often found it hard going hauling one of these as well. Most of the vehicles were fitted with retractable steps to enable passengers to be picked up and set down at various new halts (qv) which were built cheaply without raised platforms for the new services being worked by these units.

There were two main varieties of cars, for suburban and branch-line use, the latter being provided with a separate luggage compartment. All of them were fitted with gas lighting. The first of the GWR's auto-trains (qv) was introduced in 1905, using auto-trailers with a specially equipped tank locomotive, and, although railmotors continued to be constructed up to 1908, it became obvious that the auto-train concept was more versatile, and still gave similar economies of operation. The last of the railmotors was withdrawn in 1935, and most of

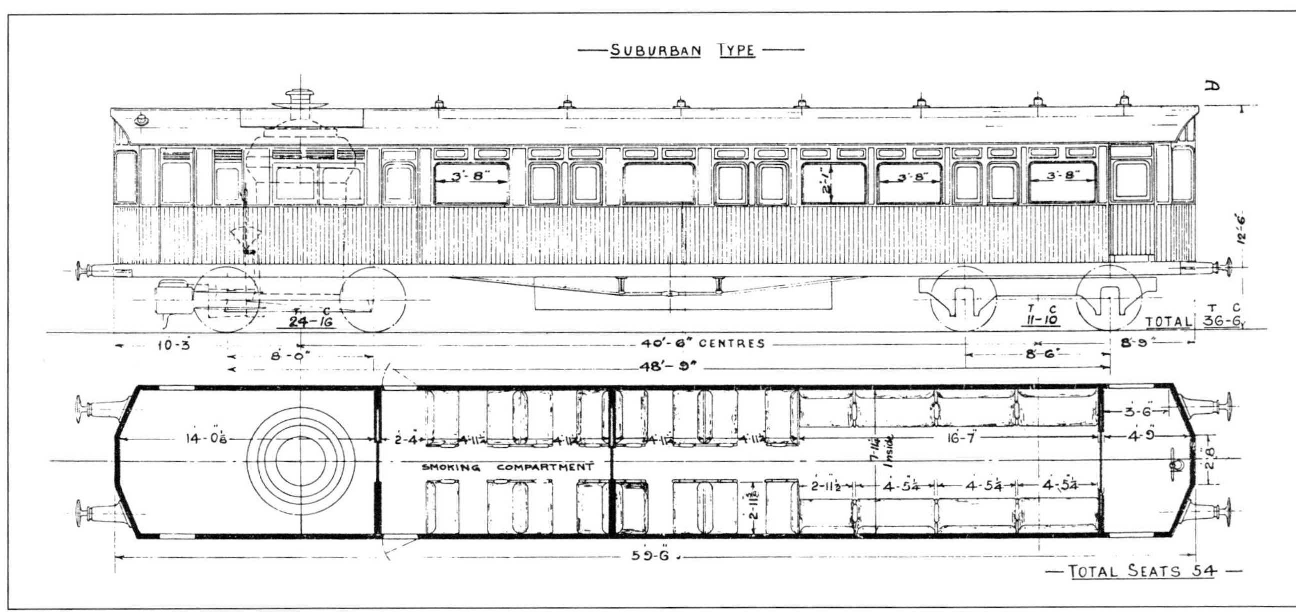

Railmotors *Side view and plan of one of the later 59 ft 6 in suburban examples.* (J. H. Russell Collection)

the cars were adapted for use as ordinary auto-trailers after being stripped of their power equipment.

PWBS

RAILWAY AIR SERVICES

The main-line railways obtained powers to operate air services in 1929 and the GWR followed this with a 1931 announcement of an experimental route linking South Wales and South Devon. Arrangements were

Railway Air Services *The extent of RAS services in 1936.* (GWR Magazine)

Railway Air Services *An air mail stamp granted by the Postmaster-General for mail by the new 1933 Birmingham-Cardiff-Devon service.* (GWR Magazine)

made with the infant Imperial Airways for the use of a six-seat, three-engined Westland Wessex, pilot and ground staff, and the service was ceremonially inaugurated on 11 April 1933. It linked Cardiff Airport with Haldon, near Teignmouth, and Roborough, near Plymouth, and had railway bus service connections to and from Cardiff General, Teignmouth, Torquay and Plymouth North Road stations. The flights left Cardiff at 9.15 am and 1.45 pm, took 1 hour 20 minutes on each leg and cost £6 for a return Cardiff–Plymouth journey. The service was subsequently converted to a single round trip from Castle Bromwich aerodrome to Cardiff, Haldon and Roborough, the first-named being linked with Snow Hill station; it ceased at the end of the summer.

By 1934 Railway Air Services had been formed by the 'Big Four' and Imperial Airways, and de Havilland Dragon Rapides were brought into use. The GWR extended its original route to Liverpool, then added a Birmingham–Bristol–Southampton–Isle of Wight service, but none of the operations was profitable. Further permutations and partners followed but the RAS operation eventually became mainly a ticket interchange facility.

GB

READING

Reading, a major GWR junction, had been reached by the original line from Twyford on 30 March 1840, the town being provided with the first example of Brunel's one-sided stations. The separate up and down platforms, served by tandem loops on the south side of the line, survived the addition of the Hungerford (21 December 1847) and Basingstoke (1 November 1848) extensions but were replaced in 1856 by a new layout of three through platforms and seven bays. A new SER station had then just been opened and a proper connection between the two systems was to follow.

Another round of changes took place at Reading at the turn of the century when the layout was remodelled to provide a main down platform, two islands and bays. The creation of the new route to the West of England in 1906 was followed by the addition of a goods branch to Reading Central (authorized 4 August 1905 as the Coley Branch Railway) two years later. The location also had an up side goods depot and several private sidings, including one for the considerable Huntley & Palmer biscuit traffic. Reading shed, with its allocation of around 100 locomotives, was sited in the triangle between the main and Berks & Hants (qv) lines, the GWR Signal Works (qv) and depot stood opposite, and a suburban station at Reading West lay along the B&H route.

Reading always enjoyed an exceptional passenger train service by virtue of its size and geographical location. In addition to local services and those to Bristol, South Wales and the South West, it handled Weymouth and Fishguard trains, those to Bristol via Devizes, to Oxford and the routes beyond, to Cardiff via Gloucester and from the SR via Birmingham to the North West.

GB

READING–TAUNTON LINE

Stations: Reading (36 miles from Paddington), Reading West (37 m), Theale ($41\frac{1}{4}$ m), Aldermaston ($44\frac{3}{4}$ m), Midgham ($46\frac{3}{4}$ m), Thatcham ($49\frac{1}{2}$ m), Newbury (53 m), Kintbury ($58\frac{1}{2}$ m), Hungerford ($61\frac{1}{2}$ m), Bedwyn ($66\frac{1}{2}$ m), Savernake (70 m), Pewsey ($75\frac{1}{4}$ m), Woodborough ($78\frac{3}{4}$ m), Patney & Chirton (81 m), Lavington (87 m), Edington & Bratton ($91\frac{1}{2}$ m), Westbury ($95\frac{1}{2}$ m), Frome ($101\frac{1}{4}$ m), Witham ($106\frac{1}{2}$ m), Bruton ($111\frac{3}{4}$ m), Castle Cary ($115\frac{1}{4}$ m), Keinton Mandeville ($120\frac{1}{4}$ m), Charlton Mackrell ($122\frac{1}{4}$ m), Somerton ($125\frac{3}{4}$ m), Long Sutton & Pitney (128 m), Langport East (130 m), Athelney (135 m), Durston (137 m), Taunton (143 m)

The need to relieve the pressure of increasing traffic on the GWR's Bristol main line was met first by quadrupling and then by the creation of new routes. The most significant of the latter was the establishment of the West of England main line by connecting three separate existing lines. These were the Reading–Devizes line which originated with the Berks & Hants

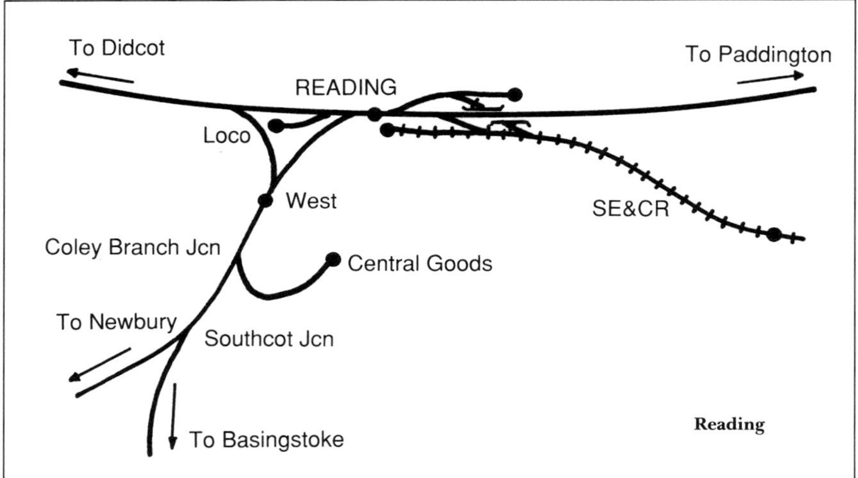

Reading

(Middle) Reading *The Southern (in the form of ex-LSWR Drummond 'L11' 4-4-0 No 156) and Great Western side by side at the country end of the station.* (Lens of Sutton)

BOURNEMOUTH
and the
SOUTH COAST

TRAVEL BY THE G.W.R.
Through Express Services and Restaurant Car Trains To and from the
NORTH AND MIDLANDS.

LIVERPOOL, BIRKENHEAD, MANCHESTER, WOLVERHAMPTON, LEAMINGTON SPA, OXFORD, with connections to and from many important centres.

For full particulars see G.W.R. Official Time Tables.

(Left) Reading *Reading West, on the Berks & Hants line, was the station used by through trains from the North and Midlands to the South Coast via Basingstoke – a 1937 advertisement.*

Railway (qv) (1847) and the Berks & Hants Extension Railway (1862), the section of the former Wilts, Somerset & Weymouth Railway (qv) between Westbury and Castle Cary (1856), and the Taunton–Yeovil branch (1853).

The first scheme to be completed was the Stert & Westbury Railway which was authorized to the GWR on 31 July 1894 and opened between Patney & Chirton and Westbury East Junction in 1900 (goods 29 July, passengers 1 October). Then came the Castle Cary & Langport Railway, authorized on 12 August 1898, opened to Charlton Mackrell in 1905 (1 July) and to Curry Rivell Junction in 1906 (goods 12 February, passengers 1 July). Finally the cut-off avoiding Durston was authorized as the Langport & Durston Railway on 15 August 1904 and opened in 1906 (goods 20 May, passengers 1 July). Through goods services over the new route began on 11 June 1906 and passenger trains from 2 July. The route achieved its final form when the Westbury and Frome avoiding lines were added in 1933 (qv Cut-off and avoiding lines).

Over the 1847/1862 lines to Patney the West Country expresses followed the course of the Kennet & Avon Canal, crossing over its Bruce Tunnel on the rise to Savernake (qv) and the traffic exchange wharf at Burbage. After the subsequent descent and passage over the new line to Westbury, the route rose again to a second summit at Brewham and descended to Castle Cary (qv). The second new section then followed an open course to the Somerset Levels, broken only by a 1,053 yd tunnel at Somerton. Finally came the union with the Bristol line at Cogload Junction, remodelled in the 1930–32 Taunton scheme to provide the down Bristol line with a flyover.

The new route achieved savings of 20¼ miles and 20-40 minutes.

GB

REDRUTH

The 4 ft gauge Redruth & Chasewater Railway had started carrying copper traffic to Point Quay in 1826 and was serving the Redruth mines by the following year. By 1838 they also had an outlet to the sea via the Hayle Railway which then contributed most of its route to the West Cornwall Railway (qv) which opened between Redruth and Penzance on 11 March 1852.

Redruth got a new station when the WCR line was extended to Truro, the old terminus and its 14-chain access becoming the West Yard goods and coal depot. A second goods depot, at Drump Lane, replaced the goods facilities at the second station from 17 June 1912.

GB

REFRESHMENT ROOMS

The first refreshment rooms were at Swindon, and were owned by Rigbys who built Swindon Works and many of the early stations. All trains stopped for 10 minutes and the GWR agreed there should be no other refreshment rooms between London and Bristol. Leased to Griffiths and then sold in 1848 to Phillips, the Swindon refreshment rooms were highly unsatisfactory, prices being high and quality poor. In a famous letter, Brunel wrote to Griffiths: 'I did not believe you had such a thing as coffee in the place; I am certain I never tasted any. I have long ceased to make complaints

Refreshment rooms *The infamous Refreshment Room at Swindon in 1852, and the same room (note the ceiling brackets) in more enlightened 1929.* (Both GWR Museum, Swindon)

TRAVELLERS___Save Time and Trouble

BEFORE STARTING YOUR JOURNEY

OBTAIN A SNACK BOX PRICE 1/-

These Snack Boxes contain a light meal and are obtainable at all G.W.R. Refreshment Rooms.

Refreshment rooms *Refreshments on the move (1937).*

at Swindon. I avoid eating anything there when I can help it.' (qv Swindon).

Later the hotel at Paddington (qv) offered refreshments and gradually other refreshment rooms were opened, but none was initially run by the GWR. The first was the South Wales Hotel at Neyland which was taken over with the South Wales Railway (qv) in 1863. However, all former Bristol & Exeter Railway hotels were let to contractors.

Then in 1890 the Directors changed their policy: a Catering Manager's office was opened at Plymouth and the running of refreshment rooms at stations in Devon and Cornwall was taken over by the GWR as the contractors' leases expired. By 1895 these numbered 11. In 1896 the GWR took over the Great Western Royal Hotel at Paddington and this became the headquarters of the Hotel and Refreshment Rooms Department. Elsewhere on the GWR, Browning and Wesley operated 23 refreshment rooms between Paddington and Birkenhead while various small contractors worked the others, but these were all gradually taken over so that by 1923 nearly all refreshment rooms on the GWR were operated by the company. When dining cars were introduced in 1896 they were staffed for two years by Brownings, but from 1898 the GWR operated these and all subsequent ones.

(*See also Hotels*)

MCHB

RENDELL, THOMAS HENRY

Rendell joined the GWR on 18 April 1870, working for seven years as a Senior Clerk in the Goods Department. From 1877 he was in the office of the Chief Goods Manager, moving to the General Manager's Office in 1891, where he became Chief Assistant to the General Manager in 1899. He was appointed Chief Goods Manager in succession to L. W. Maiden in 1904, but resigned in 1912 to become General Manager of the Barry Railway, from which post he retired in 1919.

CA

RHONDDA & SWANSEA BAY RAILWAY

Promoted by Swansea interests to better the GWR's performance in the carriage of Rhondda shipment coal, the Rhondda & Swansea Bay Railway had a long and complex gestation involving no fewer than eight Acts of Parliament between incorporation on 10 August 1882 and the agreement of 1 January 1906 under which the GWR began to work the system. The first R&SB line used the route of the Cwmafan Railway and the Afan River to reach Cymmer (qv) in 1885, and was completed through the 3,443 yd Rhondda Tunnel to the Taff Vale Railway (qv) at Treherbert on 2 July 1890 (passengers 14 March 1895). This was followed by extension to Briton Ferry (qv) on 30 December 1893 and to Swansea—via a swing-bridge over the Neath River—on 14 December 1894. Passenger services from Danygraig and a Court Sart–Neath branch date from 14 March 1895, with the former being extended to Swansea Riverside on 7 May and workshops being opened at Danygraig a year later.

Engined mainly with tank locomotives, the R&SB had 28 m 63 ch of railway operational by 1921. Its passenger trains, which included reciprocal through working to Cardiff over TVR metals, usually included a workmen's coach and it did a fair summer business in seaside excursions to Aberavon. The system passed to the GWR on 1 January 1922 under the Preliminary Absorption Scheme, the new owner's '45xx' 2-6-2Ts taking over many of the R&SB workings.

GB

RHOS BRANCH

Stations: Wrexham, Rhostyllen ($1\frac{3}{4}$ m), Legacy (3 m), Rhos ($4\frac{1}{4}$ m), Wynn Hall Halt ($5\frac{1}{2}$ m)

The Great Western Railway Act of 12 August 1889 gave retrospective blessing to the Ponkey Branch Railway which had opened from Ruabon (qv) to furnaces $1\frac{3}{4}$ miles to the north-west in 1861 and had been extended a further $1\frac{1}{4}$ miles to Legacy ten years later. A passenger service was carried for a time but the position changed in 1896 when the GWR created the Rhos branch by purchasing part of the old Pontcysyllte line, connecting it to the Ponkey branch at Legacy and adding $3\frac{1}{4}$ miles of new line through Rhos to join the main line south of Wrexham (qv).

After the new line opened on 1 October 1901 a railmotor (qv) service was instituted from 1 May 1905. This was cut back to Rhos from 22 March 1915 but then continued at an 18 trains a day level until 1 January 1931.

GB

RHYMNEY BRIDGE BRANCH

Stations: Cardiff Queen Street, Llanishen ($3\frac{1}{2}$ m), Caerphilly (7 m), Llanbradach ($9\frac{1}{2}$ m),

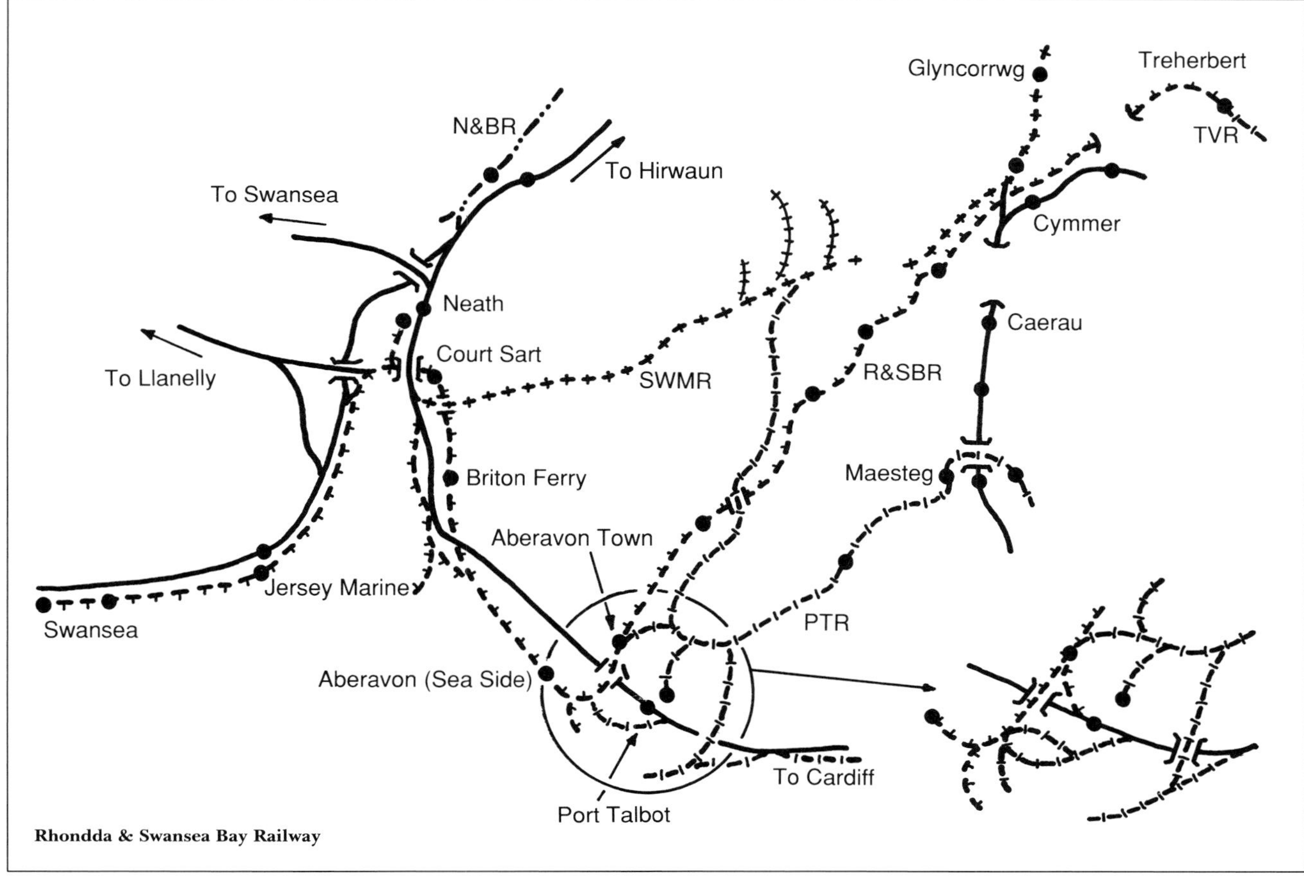

Rhondda & Swansea Bay Railway

Ystrad Mynach ($12\frac{1}{2}$ m), Hengoed ($13\frac{1}{4}$ m), Pengam (15 m), Bargoed (17 m), Brithdir (18 m), Tir Phil ($19\frac{1}{4}$ m), Pontlottyn ($21\frac{1}{2}$ m), Rhymney ($22\frac{1}{2}$ m), Rhymney Bridge (24 m)

This was the Rhymney Railway's (qv) main line, opened between Cardiff and Rhymney for passengers on 31 March 1858 after goods traffic had been carried in the previous two months. Initially RR trains used Taff Vale (qv) metals between Walnut Tree Junction and Crockherbtown Junction, Cardiff, but from 1 April 1871 the Rhymney had its own line from Adam Street Junction to Caerphilly (qv). Extension to Nantybwch by a joint line with the LNWR opened on 2 October of the same year.

In addition to its coal traffic, the line became an important through route for ordinary goods and for passenger services through to the LNWR/LMS system. Its domestic GWR passenger service was generous with some 70 trains a day on weekdays and 16 on Sundays, around 40% making the through journey. This included the 1,941 yard tunnel before Caerphilly, the opportunity for interchange there and at Hengoed, the link with the Newport–Brecon line (qv) at Bargoed and stops at the halts at Heath High Level, Cefn-On and Gilfach Fargoed.

At Ystrad Mynach the Penrhiwfelin goods branch and the Penallta Loop to the Pontypool Road–Neath line (qv) departed, the return connection being made just beyond Hengoed. Bargoed and New Tredegar collieries had their own subsequent connections with links at Rhymney to the Bute and Rhymney ironworks and to Dowlais.

GB

RHYMNEY RAILWAY

This was a successful South Wales railway concern, promoted by Cardiff dock and Rhymney coal interests and doing well enough to pay a 9% dividend before passing to the GWR at the Grouping. It differed from its neighbours in using the Westinghouse brake and preferring flat-bottomed rails but, like them, its mainstay was coal traffic.

The main Rhymney Railway Act received the Royal Assent on 2 July 1855 and authorized lines from Bute East Dock to Crockherbtown Junction and Walnut Tree Junction, Taffs Well, to Rhymney, with running powers over the Taff Vale Railway (qv) section between. Opening was progressive from September 1857, and passenger traffic began on 31 March 1858, the Rhymney company then adding the Bargoed–Deri portion of the Brecon–Newport line (qv) in 1864 and three important lines in 1871—its own Cardiff–Caerphilly line (1 April), the Penallta Loop (27 September) and the joint RR-LNWR line from Rhymney to Nantybwch (2 October). Later extensions included the Quakers Yard & Merthyr Joint line (1 April 1886) and the Senghenydd (qv) (1 February 1894) and Cylla (1 August 1906) branches.

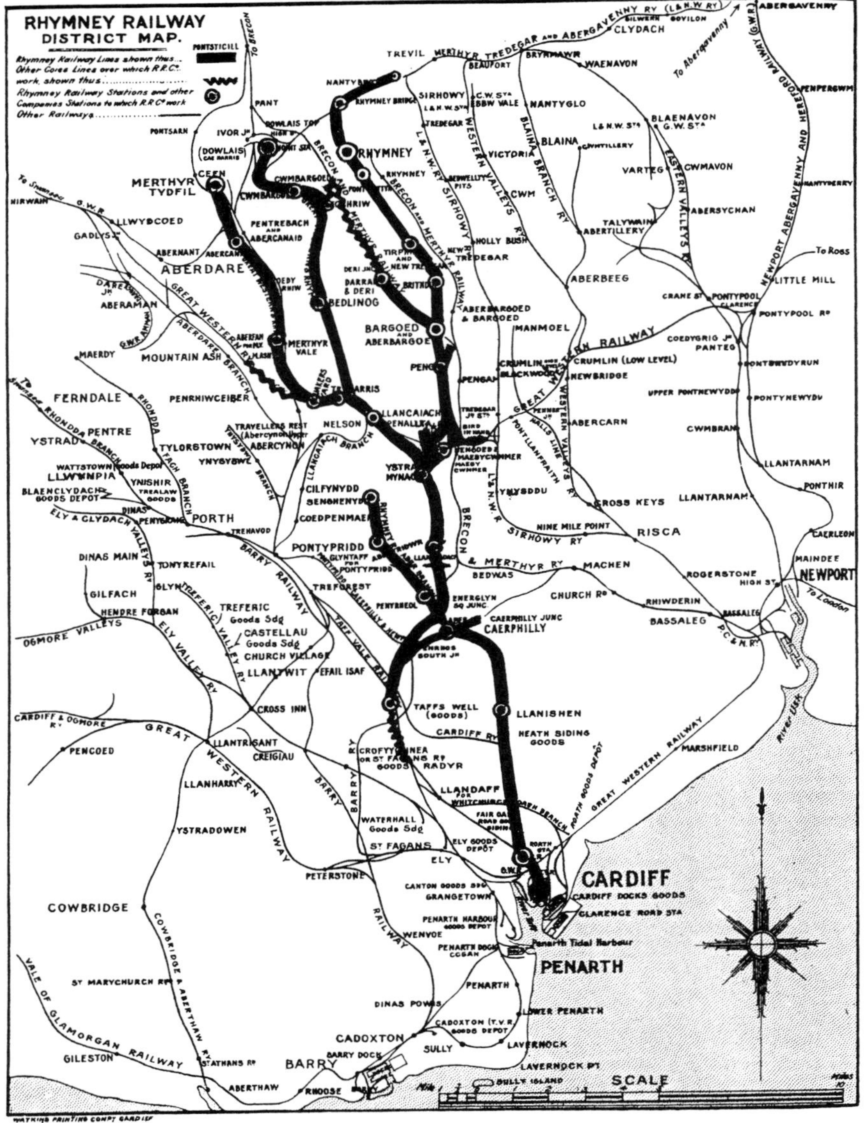

Rhymney Railway *Bargoed & Aberbargoed station looking north, junction for the Deri line (left) and that to Rhymney (right).* (Steamchest Collection)

Rhymney Railway (GWR Magazine, 1922)

Just prior to the Grouping the Rhymney system totalled 51 miles of which 38½ were owned. The company had 123 locomotives, 133 coaches and 1,041 wagons.

GB

ROAD MOTOR DEPARTMENT

The GWR put its first mechanical road vehicle, an experimental Thornycroft, to work in 1902 at Hockley, Birmingham. It was steam powered and although nearly all subsequent vehicles were petrol-engined, the Basingstoke firm of Thornycroft would be one of the company's chief suppliers. In 1900 there were some 3,600 horse-drawn vehicles in service with the GWR. They were phased out gradually, although there were still 1,700 horses (qv) on the GWR payroll in 1937, 500 of them in London, and they had not all disappeared by Nationalization.

The Motor-Car Department, as it was known, spread its empire as wide as, indeed wider than, the rail network extended, and it owned a huge variety of vehicles, ranging from motor tricycles, electric parcels vehicles and mechanical horses to cattle trucks and articulated lorries. Country lorry services began in 1908, the vehicles being based at stations where each day they would deliver to the surrounding district parcels and goods brought in by train. The motor took some while to displace the horse, but as the surface of rural roads improved during the 1920s so the service expanded until some 120 vehicles were in operation by 1930. Vehicles of around 4-ton capacity were chiefly employed.

The railhead service was a more specialized operation, where contracts were agreed with particular firms' carting agents to carry out collection and delivery on a regular basis. This would usually be based at a large station, rather than a branch-line one, and the vehicles would operate within a radius of 30 miles. The swiftest possible delivery times could be guaranteed and the vehicles would be painted in the customer's own livery if it wished, rather than the GWR's, the driver

Road Motor Department *A wide variety of GWR steam (Foden) and internal combustion (mostly Thornycroft) road motors at Theale station.* (National Railway Museum, York)

also wearing the customer's uniform. The chocolate firms of Cadburys and Rowntrees were two examples, the GWR operating a large number of 2-ton delivery vans in their respective liveries.

A business which expanded throughout the 1930s was container traffic (qv). The four main-line companies got together to promote this door-to-door service, advertising it as 'convenience without handling'. Although the containers were quite small and the cranes lightweight by present-day standards, this was the beginning of the now universal containerization system.

Right at the end of the GWR's existence, a major re-organization brought about the Zonal Goods system. Starting at the end of 1945 in Birmingham, by October 1947 there were 36 zones. The system was built around main railheads and sub-railheads, which, if it was more convenient, were linked by road rather than rail. There was a greater concentration on full rail wagon loads at the railhead; lorries to the sub-railhead ran non-stop, local deliveries then being carried out from the latter.

MCHB

ROATH BRANCH

As part of its escape from the crippling congestion at Bute Dock, Cardiff (qv), the Taff Vale Railway (qv) obtained powers for a line to the new Roath Dock on 6 August 1885 and opened this 5-mile route round Cardiff on 23 April 1888. It left the TVR main line at Roath Branch Junction east of Llandaff and ran via a connection to Newport Road Goods to reach the dock railway system at Roath Dock SE Junction.

GB

ROLLING-STOCK, GOODS

Although the GWR was founded in 1835, the first train to convey passengers did not run until 1838, and the actual conveyance of goods traffic did not begin until one year later, in September of 1839. At that early time, the vehicles, made by private contractors, were of two types only, ie open 'Box' wagons and 'Tilt' wagons. Made especially for the broad gauge, these early vehicles were originally painted light red with no markings whatsoever, as Brunel had declared that 'it was highly improbable that the Company's vehicles would ever leave the Great Western Railway's system, so there was little point in either branding or marking the waggons'.

The open 'Box' wagons were so called because the underframe had a flat top with side and end stanchions, between which 'boxes' could be fitted to carry the various types of merchandise, similar to the more modern container flats. The 'Tilt' wagons, later known as 'Bonnet-end trucks', had closed-in sides with semi-circular ends, with hoops joining each side, upon which tarpaulins could be spread and fastened, like the old covered wagons of the American pioneers in appearance.

The majority of these early broad gauge wagons ran on four wheels of 4 ft diameter, although there were several open 'Box' wagons which were fitted with six wheels, being the first such vehicles to run in the UK. At this time all wagons were built of

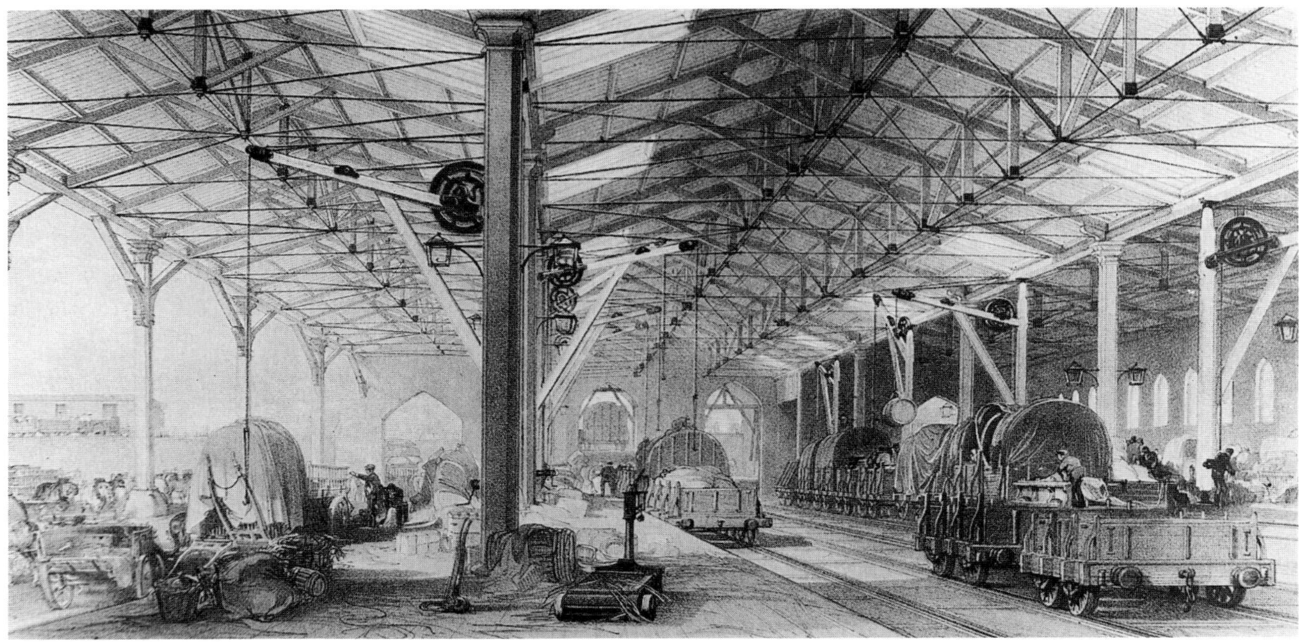

Broad gauge open 'Box' wagons designed to carry early containers, including some 'Bonnet-end trucks' with tarpaulins. (J. H. Russell Collection)

Type	Wheels	Length	Width (inside)	Tare	Capacity	Cost
'Tilt'	4	17'6"	8'9"	5t 2c	6t	£136
'Box'	6	20'0"	8'6"	5t 2c	9t	£179
'Box'	4	17'6"	8'6"	5t 0c	6t	£131

wood, with unsprung buffers known as 'dead-buffers', and drawbars fitted with coiled springs. All axle bearings were lubricated by grease, a mixture of animal fats, which melted as the bearings became warm whilst running. (Oil axleboxes did not appear until much later in 1897.)

Originally, the goods wagons were operated by local carriers acting as railway agents and using the vehicles to convey their various merchandise between Hayes and Maidenhead, and in 1840 one such enterprising agent, a Mr Dibben, was charging 'persons in the lower stations of life' 3s 6d each to travel with and in the goods wagons from Twyford, so instigating the beginning of 3rd class travel on the GWR.

It was soon found that wagons built entirely of wood had a very short life, so from 1841 iron was used for both frames and bodies. The 'dead-buffers' were replaced by a more flexible form, using large transverse springs at the centre of the underframe and connected to the drawbars.

The majority of these iron vehicles were constructed at the newly opened works at Swindon, and to quote from a table which Gooch presented to the Gauge Commissioners in 1845, the dimensions were as shown in the accompanying table. Goods trains on the GWR in 1845 were just a string of 'Tilt' and open 'Box' wagons coupled together by means of a five-link coupling, and smaller safety chains. It was from these first two styles of goods or freight wagons that all the subsequent hundreds of variations of vehicles designed and built by the company eventually evolved.

Brake vans did not exist, and guards travelled on any vehicle which happened to be equipped with some form of braking, usually one of the six-wheeled 'Box' wagons. No protection against inclement weather was provided, and it was not until 1852 that special vehicles for the use of the guard were built. These were known as 'Break Vans' (at this period, any retarding mechanism was still known as a 'break', the word 'brake' coming into use later). Although called vans, not all were closed in, but were constructed of iron and fitted with a hand-brake which could be applied from above the frames of the vehicle. Some 'Break Vans' were old passenger vehicles which had been condemned for the conveyance of travellers, gutted, and given an extra lease of life running at the rear of goods trains. All were painted grey at this time. The Rule Book of 1852 states: 'No Goods train may start without at least one efficient Break Van, which must be the last vehicle on the train. If there are two Break Vans, the second should be placed about the centre of the train, and a guard must ride in each.'

The development of the goods stock steadily increased; cattle wagons appeared in 1853, as the carriage of livestock in 'Bonnet-end' wagons was found to be detrimental to both animals and vehicles alike.

In 1854, the GWR took over the Shrewsbury & Chester (qv) and the Shrewsbury & Birmingham railways, so becoming the new owner of 2,600 standard gauge wagons of all types. At this date, the goods rolling-stock of the broad gauge numbered 3,200 assorted vehicles. In 1863, when the West Midland Railway (qv) was amalgamated into the GWR, the broad gauge goods stock totalled 5,689, consisting of 1,076 open goods wagons and cattle trucks, 2,023 covered goods wagons, 2,194 coal, coke, permanent way and departmental wagons, 284 timber trucks, 31 furniture vans, and 81 goods brake vans. The standard gauge stock totalled 8,284, which included 4,220 from the WMR and 148 from the Shrewsbury & Hereford Railway. By 1867, the totals stood at 11,526 standard gauge wagons and vans, and 6,588 broad gauge vehicles, to which was added in 1876 a further 2,175 from the Bristol & Exeter (qv), and 810 from the South Devon (qv) when these two railways were absorbed.

By this time the decision had been taken to abandon the broad gauge, and as the track mileage was gradually reduced, so was the stock of wagons and vans, a great number being broken up before and after the taking over of the B&ER and SDR. The only goods vehicles built for the broad gauge after 1876 were some four- and six-wheeled open fish wagons, designed for the fast fish traffic from the West Country. Finally in 1892 the end came, and apart from a few wagons broken up at Lostwithiel, Bridgwater and Newton Abbot, the whole of the broad gauge stock was gathered together on 15 miles of temporary track at Swindon for demolition. The accompanying photograph is of great interest in showing how the development of the goods stock had progressed from the open 'Box' and 'Tilt' wagons of 1839 to the many versatile designs of the 1890s.

Before leaving the broad gauge and its wagon stock, it may be of interest to record the unusual novelty of a mixed gauge goods service, which ran in 1871 between Truro and Penzance on mixed gauge track. Worked by a standard gauge locomotive, marshalled behind it were the standard gauge wagons, and sandwiched between these vehicles and the wider broad gauge trucks was fitted a special match-truck. These non-load-carriers were constructed with wide dumb buffers and sliding shackles to enable the vehicle to accept the draw and buffing gear of both the broad and standard gauge rolling-stock.

These mixed trains ran in West Cornwall right up to the abolition of the broad gauge in 1892 (a similar phenomenon with passenger trains was operated on the Windsor branch during the 1860s and '70s). It must have been interesting to observe these mixed trains at stations where points existed, to see the standard gauge wagons smartly side-stepping to either the left- or right-hand side of the track.

To return to the standard gauge goods stock, in the 1860s many of the examples which had been taken over from the various railway companies which had been absorbed into the GWR consisted of open 'Box' wagons, cattle trucks and 'Bonnet-end' wagons, all of the four-wheeled variety. They were from many sources, some purchased from private wagon builders and others built by the WMR. From 1867 the GWR itself began to construct large numbers of freight vehicles at its works in Saltney and Worcester, which practice continued right up to 1874. However, in 1871 the Swindon factory also started to build standard gauge freight stock, the first vehicles being four 20-ton six-wheeled flat goods wagons, which did not prove to be very useful, having a life of only approximately 40 years (later known as 'Beavers', they were numbered 13619–22).

This is perhaps a good place to record the system of identification used on the GWR to trace the many and various types of wagons built at this time. Initially, each batch of vehicles was given a Lot letter, which served to distinguish each order. For instance, Lot A of August 1867 was for the building of 50 two-plank wagons at Worcester. However, as it was apparent that the alphabet would be quickly used up, it was decided in 1869, when Swindon began construction of freight vehicles, to change the Lot letters to Lot numbers. Lot 1 dealt with at Swindon was for an order for 200 two-plank open wagons.

The year 1874 saw the final orders for wagon building at both Worcester and Saltney, Lot 118 being the last batch from the former, and Lot 130 ending construction at the latter.

Up to 1893, there was just one sequence of Lot numbers for both the carriage and wagon stock. After January of that year, all the Lot numbers from 683 onwards referred only to passenger and 'brown'

Broad gauge stock gathered at Swindon for breaking up. (J. H. Russell Collection)

vehicles, the goods stock being ordered on a new series. Carriage and wagon building from then on were always kept separate.

When it is realized that the huge increase in the conveyance of freight at the turn of the century meant that by 1902 the GWR owned a total of 59,036 goods and departmental wagons, it can be seen that some form of classification of the various types and uses of the vehicles had become necessary. Thus, in 1905 each group of vehicles was given a Diagram letter, followed by a number as variations of the particular group appeared. A simple example dealing with ballast wagons would be as shown in the accompanying table.

Diagram	Date built	Types	Weight	No built
P.1	1890–91	bogie ballast wagon	20T	30
P.2	1899	4-wheeled " "	14T	362
P.3	1896	" " "	10T	40
P.4	1896	" " "	8T	205

Also to assist in abbreviating the telegraphic code which was used for the transmission of messages via the Morse needle instruments, vehicles were identified by code names, eg instead of having to send 'Goods Brake Van', one code word, namely 'Toad', was used. A complete list of Diagrams and code names for goods stock is given in the adjacent table.

By the year 1908, the total number of wagons owned and maintained by the GWR had risen to 72,496, rising further to 83,480 in 1913, and 13 years later, the period spanning the First World War, the grand total was 88,580.

At the cessation of hostilities in 1919, the rather ancient one-, two-, and three-plank open wagons were scrapped, on average 1,500 per annum, their replacements being new opens and covered vans built at Swindon.

The Grouping meant that large numbers of goods vehicles were also absorbed from the Welsh railways, and although many were condemned out of hand, nevertheless by the year 1927 the sound vehicles and other new wagons built at the factory had raised the total to more than 98,000.

After the formation of the Railway Clearing House (RCH), the four main-line companies formed a 'common-user' pool of standard opens and covered vans which could move freely along the various companies' tracks without attracting demurrage fines. From 1922, out of a total of 481,000 wagons owned by the 'Big Four', the GWR contributed 65,000 common-user vehicles. All other goods rolling-stock, apart from these, were branded 'Return to GWR. Non Common-User' and had to be returned to the parent company within six days, otherwise penalty fines were raised against the company retaining the vehicles. Location checks of all wagons were carried out at major junctions by RCH 'Number-takers', who rendered their records daily to the RCH for the calculation of charges.

Between the wars, the freight trains of the GWR were classified into eight different grades of priority or importance as follows:

'C' headlights: Trains which were either of all 'fitted' (vacuum-braked) rolling-stock, all with oil axleboxes, capable of speeds of 40–50 mph, or 'partly fitted', with not less than one-third of the consist braked.

'D' headlights: Express freight, with a

Diagram	Variants	Type	Telegraphic code names
A	1–10	Girder wagons	Pollen A to F
B	1–10	Armour plate and roll wagons	Totem A, B; Serpent; Roll
C	1–29	Boiler trucks and trolleys	Crocodile A to M
D	1–2	Glass wagons	Coral A
E	1–4	Wheel and propeller wagons	Moral; Aero
F	1–4	Road-roller trucks	Loriot A
G	1–45	Flat and well trucks for road vehicles, covered motor car trucks, and covered trucks for motor car bodies	Loriot; Serpent Hydra; Mayfly Damo A, B; Asmo; Bocar; Mogo
H	1–10	Flat wagons	Beaver A, B and E; Gadfly; conflat
J	1–31	Rail and timber trucks	Beaver D, C; Gane; Macaw A to H.
K	1–4	Crane testing wagons	——
L	1–23	Match trucks	Match
M	1–5	Shunting trucks	——
N	1–34	Loco coal and mineral wagons	——
O	1–44	Open goods wagons	Tourn; Open A to C; Tube; Hyfit
P	1–23	Ballast wagons	——
Q	1	Provender wagons	——
R	1	Manure wagons	——
S	1–13	Fish wagons	Tadpole; Bloater; Insixfish
T	1–13	P way and sleeper wagons	——
U	1	Stone wagons	——
V	1–38	Covered goods and grain vans	Mink A to F; Grano; Tevan; Parto
W	1–14	Cattle wagons	Mex A, B; Bettle A, B and C
X	1–10	Meat vans	Mica A, B
Y	1–12	Fruit vans and Banana vans	Fruit A to D
Z	1–4	Gunpowder vans	Cone
AA	1–23	Goods brake vans	Toad A
BB	1	Stores vans	——
CC	1–8	Workshop and tool vans.	——
DD	1–6	Tank wagons	Cordon
EE	1–2	Flat wagons with demountable tanks	——
FF	1	Trestle plate wagons	——

A 'Crocodile F' loaded with a ship's propeller at Southall. (GW Society)

minimum of four braked vehicles, and not more than half the consist capable of 30 mph running.

'E' headlights: Express freight other than C and D, all wagons fitted with oil axleboxes, speed 25 mph.

'F' headlights: Through fast freight, not calling at intermediate stations.

'G' headlights: Locomotive and brake van only.

'H' headlights: Freight, coal, ballast, or empties trains, with through load to destination.

(Left and below) *Four-wheel wagon evolution: a pre-First World War wooden-bodied 10-tonner and the new 20-ton steel-bodied mineral wagon introduced by Felix Pole in 1924.* (J. H. Russell Collection/GWR Magazine)

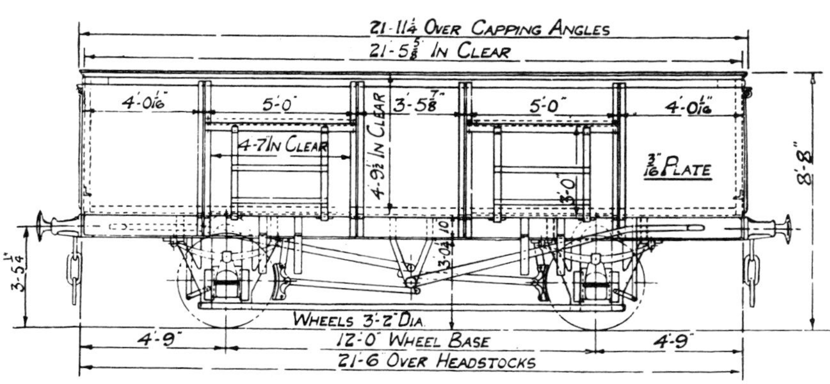

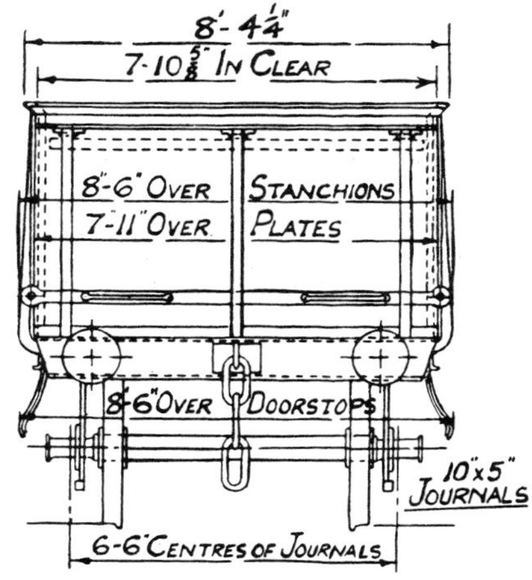

Classic GWR goods yard scene in the West Country in 1925. The sheeted wagon beside the crane is plated 'Return to GWR – Non Common User'.
(GW Society)

'J' headlights: As above, but calling at intermediate stations.

'K' headlights: Branch-line freight, ballast, or permanent-way train requiring to stop in section.

The last three categories were used for trains conveying coal, coke, etc, in private-owner wagons.

The express 'Vacuums', as they were called, were the premier freight trains of the GWR up to the outbreak of the Second World War, and ran mainly during the night and at high speeds for the period, thus ensuring the maxim of 'Next-day Delivery' claimed by all the principal Goods Depots throughout the system. The average loading of these fast trains was 50 vehicles, but this was dependent upon the route and gradients. At the other end of the scale, the coal and mineral trains ambling along at 20 mph under 'H' headlights, and routed along the Thames valley, had a maximum loading of 100 wagons. There were also many trains consisting purely of empties, being in the main private-owner wagons working back empty to collieries in Wales, the Midlands, and the North East, after delivery of their loads.

The GWR, like other railway companies, was known as a 'common carrier', which meant it was under legal obligation to convey any commodity that traders or merchants required it to so do. This meant that the variety of freight wagons available

(Below and above right) *Two patterns of GWR goods brake vans, a 16-ton four-wheeler and a 24-ton six-wheeler.*
(J. H. Russell Collection)

ranged in design from small four-wheeled timber trucks to the massive 120-ton Trolley with 24 wheels. There were wagons to carry cattle, grain, ballast, bananas, meat, fruit, oil, water, fish, motor cars, road-rollers, gunpowder and even manure—the list was impressive.

All freight trains on the GWR before 1948 were required to be made up with one of the very distinctive goods brake vans in the rear, and the accompanying photographs show two of these well-known vehicles. What perhaps is not so well known is the fact that the underframes of the goods brakes had hollow cavities which were packed solid with scrap iron. This was to raise the tare weight of the van to give the necessary heavy braking power.

JHR

ROLLING-STOCK, PASSENGER

The earliest passenger-carrying vehicles made for and used on the GWR were of the four-wheeled type, and were constructed specifically for the broad gauge. In design, these vehicles followed closely the pattern of the horse-drawn road stage-coach of the period, but of course were mounted on an iron underframe, within which ran two pairs of 4 ft diameter iron spoked wheels on long axles, mounted in small axleboxes lubricated with grease. These rather large wheels, so designed to reduce friction on the bearings, projected up above the solebars of the frame, and had to be either boxed in or, as seen in the accompanying illustration, given space between the insides of the solebars and the outsides of the carriage bodies.

The illustration below shows one of the earliest of the railway's attempts to accommodate the travelling gentry of the 1840s. Known as a 'Posting Carriage', this vehicle was designed as a saloon with a glazed door on each side. Bench seats with cushions ran all around the interior (with the exception of the doorways) and a central table was installed for the convenience of the travellers. (This pattern was followed for many years subsequently by the GWR, in their construction of 'Family Saloons'.) Another feature of this early design was the use of the 'clerestory', a raised central section of the roof which had small windows let into the sides to admit extra daylight to the interior. This 'clear-storey' has been used for centuries by masons in the high roofs of churches and cathedrals to achieve this effect. This particular feature is mentioned because the 'clerestory' roof style was adopted by the GWR for hundreds of main-line carriages right up to the turn of the century.

An illustration overleaf shows another early vehicle, which usually ran with the passenger-carrying stock. This was a 'Carriage Truck' and was used for the conveyance of the road carriages which well-to-do travellers used at each end of their rail journeys; they sometimes completed the journey inside their own private road coach mounted on the truck. Their horses were also catered for, being conveyed in strange little 'Horse Boxes', 9 ft 8 in long, 10 ft wide, and 7 ft 6 in high, running on four 3 ft diameter iron wheels .

From the foregoing it is possible to imagine a quaint little train in 1840 on the GWR made up of several of these various vehicles, and drawn by one of the 2-2-2 'Singles' of the 'North Star' Class (qv).

Other vehicles of this period for the conveyance of passengers consisted of very simple four-wheeled carriages, approx 18 ft long, with bodies set over the wheels. The 1st class travellers were seated in three separate compartments, each holding eight

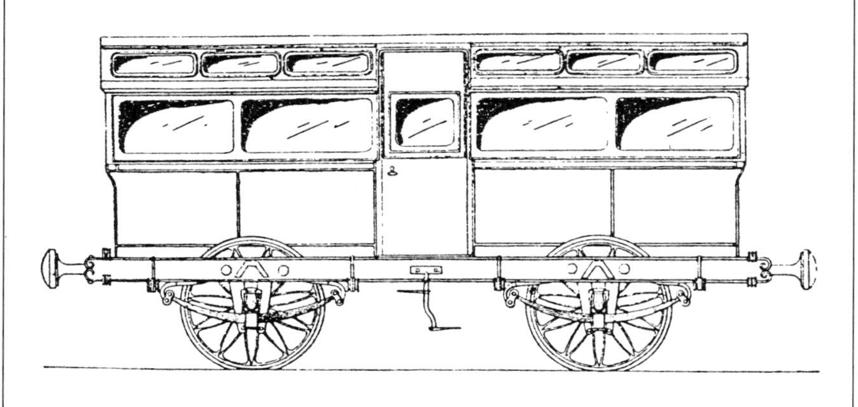

Broad gauge 'Posting Carriage'. (All drawings J. H. Russell Collection)

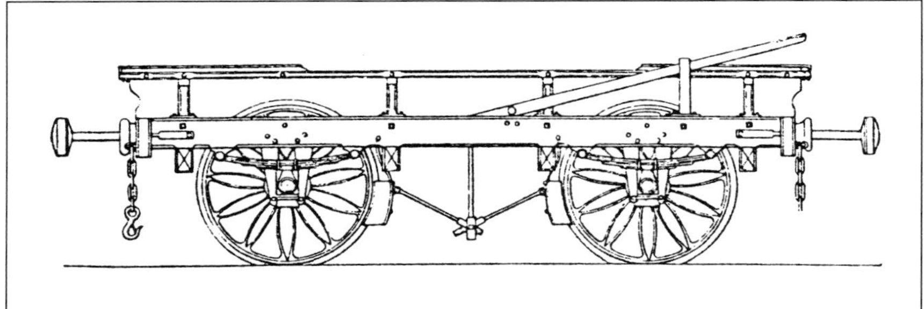

Broad gauge 'Carriage Truck'.

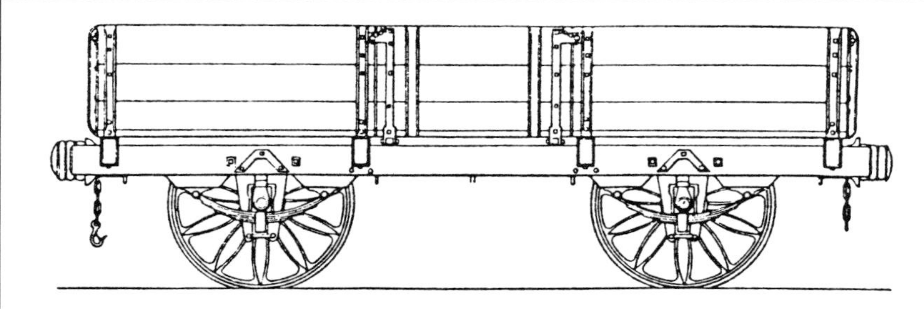

3rd class broad gauge open carriage.

Due to the Cheap Trains Act of 1844, the GWR was forced, much against its will, to provide carriages for the 'lower orders' which gave some protection from the elements. To replace the four-wheeled wagon type, a six-wheeled totally enclosed vehicle was therefore designed and built. Twenty feet in length, with only one door on each side, the interior was fitted with ten planks across the carriage, travellers having to jostle across each other to find seats. No windows were installed, but louvred shutters on each side, which could be closed completely in bad weather, supplied ventilation. Primitive clasp brakes were fitted which could be applied by the Guard, who travelled in amongst the 3rd class passengers.

In 1840 the GWR had constructed the first Royal Saloon (qv Royal Trains), originally on four wheels, but altered two years later to eight.

persons. The 2nd class were more confined, having four small compartments with open sides, each capable of squeezing in 12 people, while the 3rd class had to make do with a three-plank open wagon in which boards ran across the vehicle to act as seats.

This then was the beginning of passenger transport on the GWR, but in the mid 1840s it was found that the four-wheeled vehicles were unsatisfactory, tending to jump the track at speed. The problem was solved by Brunel, who decreed that from then on, all passenger carriages should be fitted with six wheels, old four-wheeled stock converted, and all new stock to be standardized with three axles instead of the former two. This meant longer bodies and heavier vehicles, but greater stability.

Again, three types were designed and constructed. The 1st class vehicle had four separate compartments, each holding eight persons. Seats were upholstered and trimmed with Moroccan leather, and each compartment had droplights in the doorways on each side, the design still being vaguely that of the 'post-chaise' road coaches. The 2nd class vehicles were longer than the 1st class equivalent, being 27 ft 2½ in against the 24 ft of the premier class. These vehicles were open at the sides and divided into six stalls, each of which could seat 12 passengers.

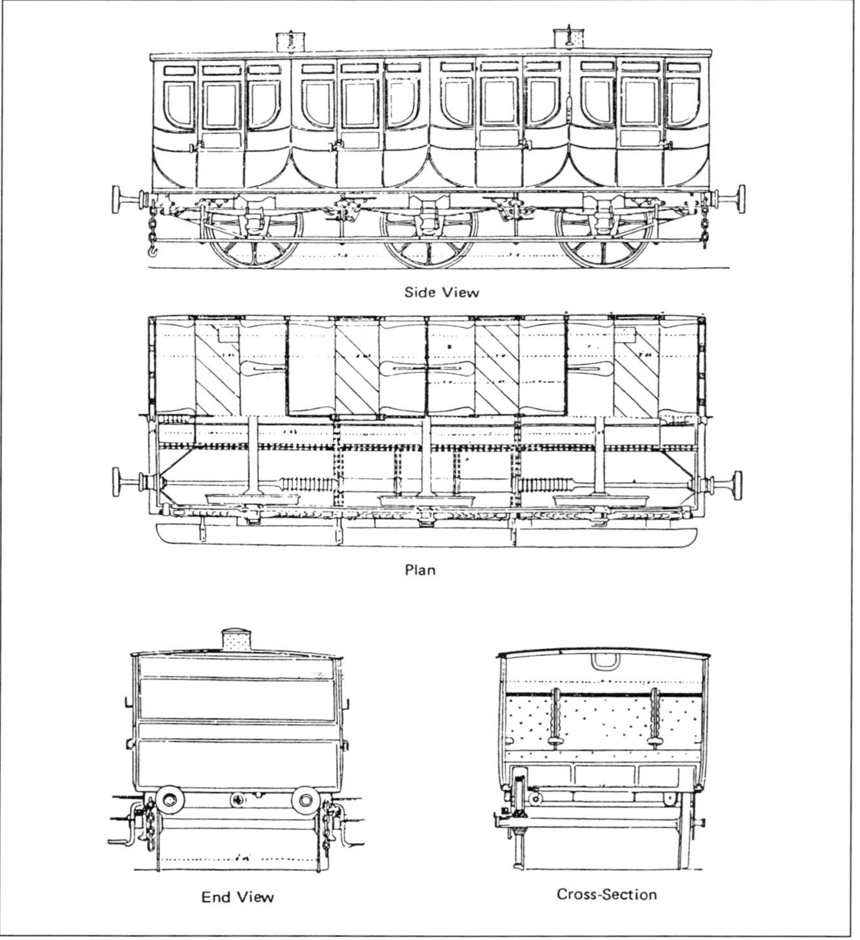

1st class broad gauge six-wheeled carriage, c 1851.

Later, in 1845, the company, building its own rolling-stock for the first time instead of using outside contractors, developed the six-wheeled 3rd class carriages by making the vehicles entirely of iron. Although looking more like a prison van than a passenger carriage, this design was an improvement on the 20 ft 9 in enclosed 3rds. For instance, there were now seven doors on each side, all fitted with a small window at the top. The vehicle was not divided into compartments, but the transverse seats had small 15 in high back rests. To convey passengers' luggage, a six-wheeled van was also designed similar, in essence, to the 3rd class vehicles, with iron sides, and having a compartment for a Guard.

It should be mentioned here that there were many other vehicles of all sorts running on the system, for use on local and branch lines, etc, but space precludes any details, so I can only generalize.

The year 1848 saw the building of the second Royal vehicle, the 'Queen's Carriage', which from the outset was fitted with eight wheels. Four years later, in 1852, eight-wheeled carriages were introduced on the GWR. Although 38 ft in length, these vehicles did not have a pivoting bogie as we know them, but a pair of four-wheeled trucks, one at each end. These were given slight sideways play to assist in the negotiating of curves. Known as 'Long Charlies', these coaches were Composites, having three 1st class compartments in the centre of the vehicle, and two rather cramped 2nd class compartments at each end, with what was presumably a closed-in luggage bay on the roof.

At about this time, the Directors decreed that all coaching stock, at that period wearing a livery of all-over dark brown, should now be painted in two colours, ie brown on the lower panels, and above the waist, white, which after many layers of varnish eventually became light cream. So started the well known 'chocolate and cream' livery of the GWR. However, it should always be remembered that from the 1930s onward, the colours would be more accurately described as milk chocolate and primrose yellow. (For a short period from 1922, all carriage stock passing through the Works was painted crimson-lake.) As other companies were taken into the GWR, so their inherited carriages swelled the numbers of broad gauge coaching stock. The Bristol & Exeter, for instance, handed over 263 carriages, and the South Devon a further 203 vehicles, all in 1876, plus the stock of the Cornwall Railway, worked by the GWR until 1889.

The new Swindon Works, which opened in 1869, spent the first seven years building standard gauge stock, then from 1876–88 produced a large batch of broad gauge six-wheeled carriages and a quantity of large roomy eight-wheeled coaches 46½ ft long, 10 ft wide and 8½ ft high. Two six-wheeled sleeping cars were built in 1877 and were the first such vehicles on the GWR, being 29 ft long and 10½ ft wide; they were superceded in 1881 by two eight-wheelers, 46½ ft by 9 ft. These were the first coaches to be constructed with standard gauge bodies running on broad gauge underframes, several more 8 ft by 8½ ft, as well as three eight-wheeled Post Office vans, following up to the year 1882. The idea was to facilitate the change-over from the broad gauge, which had already been decided upon and which actually took place in 1892 (qv Gauge conversion).

The year 1888 saw the introduction of independent pivoting bogies, and all carriage stock built after this date had standard gauge bodies, mounted on standard gauge frames, only the bogies being broad gauge. These carriages were known as 'Convertibles' and, together with other 10 ft wide carriages, had a central section running the length of the vehicle which could be removed when it was converted to standard gauge, bringing the width back to 8 ft. The last broad gauge vehicles built at Swindon were three Composites with narrow bodies on broad gauge frames, and 29 Brake 3rds constructed as convertibles in 1891. All saw many years' service on the standard gauge. Mention should also be made of the 'Fish' vehicles, which started off as broad gauge and were eventually converted to standard gauge; designed for the conveying of the fish traffic from the West Country, they were always on the carriage stock lists.

As the GWR ran two systems between 1860 and 1892, the broad gauge and the standard gauge to which the Northern Division was committed, it was the only railway company in the UK that had to build two separate types of rolling-stock. At first, the broad gauge stock was erected at Swindon and the standard gauge at Worcester and Saltney. Up to 1868, all the standard gauge carriages (except for four old Shrewsbury six-wheelers) were small four-wheeled non-corridor carriages, and during 1868–69 Worcester built 48 3rds, and Saltney 24 Composites, all of which were 21 ft in length. The first six-wheelers for the 'narrow' gauge were two 25 ft Composites, built at Swindon in 1870; 60 more followed within 12 months, half of which were stretched to 28 ft long. During subsequent years, large numbers of four- and six-wheeled vehicles of all kinds poured out of Swindon to replace the broad gauge stock on converted tracks. After 1874, all new carriage construction was concentrated at Swindon factory.

In 1874, a new Royal Saloon for Queen Victoria was made, the first narrow gauge vehicle to run on eight wheels, and was used mainly for trips between Windsor and Paddington. It was eventually reconstructed to form the Queen's Carriage in the new Royal Train of 1897.

During 1878, Swindon started producing bogie carriages for 2nd and 3rd class passengers in large numbers. At first these vehicles were 46½ ft long, but gradually the design was lengthened to 50 ft and more. At the same time, for local and branch-line services, hundreds of four-and six-wheeled coaches were made. In general, the main-line stock was built with the well-known clerestory roof, whilst the smaller carriages were turned out with either a single arc roof or, in many instances, a multi-arc roof. However, there were several examples of six-wheeled suburban stock which had the clerestory. The variety and variation of design was numerous in the extreme, and this might be a good place to explain the system used at Swindon Drawing Office to identify the many styles and types. Briefly, an order would be received for the construction of a batch of, say, 1st class eight-wheeled carriages. The order would be known as a Lot and given its consecutive number. After 1910, each type was alloted a initial Diagram letter, followed by a number for each specific change of style. So bogie stock was given A to Q and, ten years later, letters R to W were allocated to four- and six-wheeled vehicles. Therefore an example order might be 'A' for bogie 1st class, 1 if it was the initial diagram, and the Lot (or order) number was 551 of 1890, thus being known as A1 Lot 551 dated 1890.

William Dean (qv), who succeeded Joseph Armstrong at Swindon in 1877, was a carriage specialist. Originally Works Manager at Wolverhampton, his many designs of standard gauge coaching stock, plus his unique bogie and vacuum brake apparatus, carry his name to this day. In 1878, G. J. Churchward (qv) was detailed to help in the carriage side of the vacuum brake project, and so it was that these two famous engineers eventually became responsible for the quality and excellence of both locomotives and rolling-stock after it was decided to abandon the broad gauge in the 1890s.

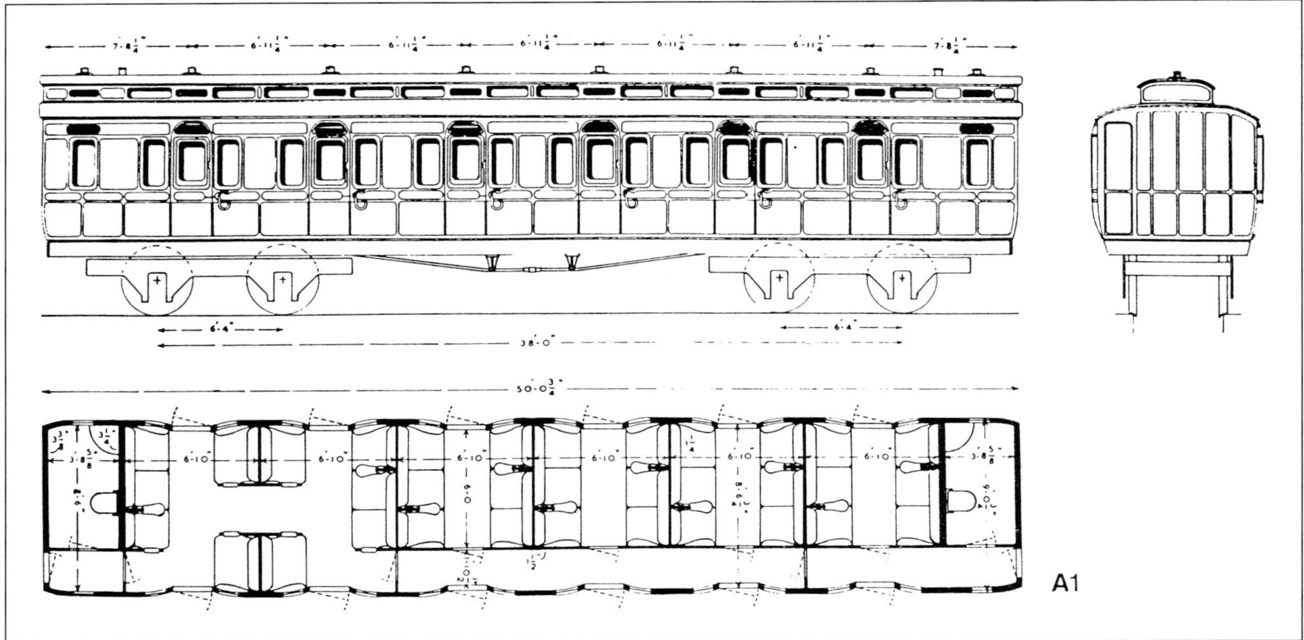

1st class 'bay-windowed' carriage from the GWR's first corridor train of 1891.

A notable example of the forward thinking of Dean and Churchward was the building in 1891 of the first corridor train on the GWR. Designed for the Paddington–Birkenhead service, the train consisted of four 'bay-windowed' clerestories, 50 ft in length, all fitted with *side* corridor bellows between each vehicle, plus a 40 ft non-corridor Brake Van of the normal low-roofed variety. The four passenger-carrying coaches consisted of a 1st class (our 'A1' example mentioned previously), a 2nd class, a 3rd class (C6 and C7), and a Brake 3rd (D5) at the rear. The 'bay-window' construction, which consisted of a series of bays between the compartment doors, did not last; the cost must have been prohibitive. This train did not enter regular service until 1892, but was such a success with the travelling public in the Northern Division that orders were placed at the factory for similar rakes of carriages to serve the West and South Wales. However, in these the 'bay-window' style was abandoned in favour of flat panelled sides with a 'tumble-home' at the bottom edges. The Brake 2nd, Brake 3rd and Composite were 56 ft long and ran on 8 ft 6 in wheelbase Dean bogies. This second series, known as the 'Cornishman', was completed in 1893 and still retained the side-corridor vestibules between vehicles. This feature was gradually moved to the central position as these early vehicles were superceded by more modern stock. Diagrams were A2, C8/9, D10/12 and E38/9.

The design of Dean era carriage stock remained standardized from 1893 until 1903, with a width of 8 ft 6 in and of clerestory construction for the many hundreds of vehicles built for main-line use; the only variety (which was infinite) was in the class, type and consequent length. Some shorter non-corridor clerestories were built for local and branch-line use, but these services were normally catered for with low-roofed stock of the four, six-and eight-wheeled patterns.

Typical Dean era clerestory carriage. (J. H. Russell Collection)

Sleeping cars were introduced from 1877 for use on the broad gauge, followed in 1881 by a design by Dean, which was to become the forerunner of modern Sleepers. This was a 'convertible' and saw long service on the standard gauge. In 1890 a 'bay-windowed' version, 50 ft in length, appeared, and between 1892 and 1897 four half Sleeper/half compartment Composites were built (Diagram J4), all of which were later converted to Corridor 3rds.

Dining cars (not used on the broad gauge) first appeared in 1896, again for 1st class passengers only. Three cars were built to Diagram H2, and were 56 ft long. A fourth was added in 1897, and a further two cars were put into service in 1900. In 1903, four more clerestory Dining cars were built, and for the first time catered for not only 1st class but also 2nd and 3rd classes in the same vehicle (Lots 1010–11, Diagram H7).

The year 1897 saw the construction at a cost of £40,000 of a special corridor train, suitable for the use of Queen Victoria on the occasion of her Diamond Jubilee. Originally the intention was for a complete new Royal Train, but Her Majesty insisted that the old Queen's Carriage be retained. Therefore this was rebuilt, and, together with five new cars, formed the complete train. The vehicles were made more or less to the standard construction, but were internally fitted out to suit royalty, and the clerestory roofs had domed ends, which distinguished the vehicles. The only other rolling-stock to be built with similar sloping ends were the Dynamometer Car of 1902, one Brake Composite to diagram E36 of 1892, a Saloon of 1894 to Diagram G3, and a Composite, Diagram E53, of 1897. The Royal Train vehicles were two brake vans to Diagram K12 Lot 838, one 1st (Diagram A5 Lot 839), and two 1st saloons (Diagram G4 Lot 840).

The years 1900–1 heralded the next step in carriage design on the GWR. This was the Milford Boat Train stock. Built to the clerestory pattern and with centre gangways on the open plan, these five-coach sets were designed for the Irish traffic from Milford Haven to Paddington, and were the first standard stock to be fitted with electric lighting. Apart from being open (ie there were no separate compartments), the other innovation was the fitting of large sliding doors to the luggage compartments of the Brake 3rds (Diagrams D32/36) and a tiny kitchen in the 2nd class coaches, whence buffet snacks could be dispensed (Diagram H5). These trains were built as Lots 935–938 of 1900, and Lots 964–967 of 1901, the vehicles being 1sts (Diagram A6), 3rds (C18), Brake 3rds (D32/36), and 2nds (H5–6).

Before moving on to more 'modern' stock, it is worth mentioning that between 1890 and 1903 Swindon Works built a total of 2,861 passenger carriages, not including 'brown' vehicles (ie non-passenger stock often running in passenger trains, such as parcels vans, 'Siphons', etc).

The Churchward era started on the GWR during 1903/4, the last clerestory carriage being completed late in 1904, just 12 months after the introduction of the steam railmotors (qv). These signalled the end of the Dean type of clerestory-roofed rolling-stock, as the new vehicles, which contained a four-wheeled steam locomotive at one end, were the first carriages to be erected with a high single-arc roof and vertical slab sides from solebar to cantrail, containing large windows with ventilators above. Given an independent series of diagrams, from A to R (which also applied to the accompanying trailer cars), 100 railmotors were built between 1903 and 1908. The first two were 57 ft long, followed by others at 59 ft 6 in, and a large number to the extreme length of 70 ft. Two other unusual steam cars were constructed for the GWR by Messrs Kerr Stuart in 1905. Of rather light design, these two were always very conspicuous in not being of Churchward outline.

The railmotors proved very popular, both on suburban services and branch lines all over the system and, to cope with the extra traffic generated, trailer cars were built, which were 3rd class only bogie vehicles, built to the same outline as the 'motors, and designed to run attached to the powered cars, acting as a set; they could be driven from either end, from a driver's compartment. In fact, the trailers outlived the 'motor by decades, being attached to small auto-locomotives as units (qv Auto-trains); many of the steam railmotors were converted into these trailer cars from 1915 until 1935, and so enjoyed a new lease of life.

The change from Victorian to Edwardian design on the GWR was startling. Moving from the rather cramped neatness of the 50 ft–56 ft clerestory coach to the massive opulence of the 70 ft long 'Dreadnought' stock of 1904–7 caused quite a stir amongst the travelling public. Adopting the name of the huge contemporary battleships of the period, these carriages were the largest passenger vehicles ever to run on the railways of Great Britain. Not only were they 70 ft long overall, but the width was 9 ft 6 in, which restricted their use to the main lines only. The first to appear were four Restaurant cars (H8) which catered for 1st, 2nd and 3rd class diners. Following on in 1905 were the Corridor 3rds (C23/24), Composites (E77), Brake 3rds (D42) and three 1st class Sleepers in 1907, the latter running on six-wheeled bogies (J6). Also in 1904/5 Swindon built 11 Travelling Post Office vehicles for the Ocean and Irish Mail services (qv), all to the 68 ft/70 ft configuration. One was provided with slip gear (qv), others had the pick-up/set-down mail gear, and a few of these big vans had longitudinal roof lights. ('Slip' carriages (qv) enabled the detachment of vehicles from a speeding express, and were operated by the Traffic Department from the early clerestory days until the last BR(WR) slip coach in 1960. Nearly all these carriages were Brake Composites (Diagram F) with internal corridors only, for obvious reasons.)

The next natural development from the 'Dreadnoughts' was the 'Concertina' type, again 70 ft long, but instead of the three doors on each side as with the earlier carriages, the new design had *inset* doors to each compartment, thus giving a concertina bellows effect.

The abolition of 2nd class accommodation took place in 1910, which explains why from 1910 no B Diagrams appear. The years from 1908 through the First World War to 1920 saw the advent of the 'Toplight' series of 57 ft coaching stock, taking their name from the additional small windows which were set above all the side windows except the doorways. This design feature started with the 'Dreadnoughts', and was used on main-line and suburban stock alike. During the war years 1914–19 the same configuration was used in the Ambulance Train vehicles which Swindon later converted back to main-line passenger use.

Churchward was succeeded by Collett (qv) in 1922, who continued to build carriages of a similar pattern as before, but instead of having coach-built sides, steel panels, almost flat, were now used, and the toplights were dispensed with. The carriage ends were formed into a convex curve, to enable shorter gangways to be fitted. A few were 70 ft long, but in the main, and from then on, 57 ft and 60 ft were the maximum lengths.

Following Gresley's example on the LNER, Collett experimented in 1925 with seven articulated trains. These eight-car sets consisted of a Brake 1st/1st twin (A16/17), a 1st class/Kitchen car/3rd class triplet (H30/31/32), and a 3rd/3rd/Brake 3rd triplet (C51/52). The main-line sets only

The case for the abolition of 2nd class accommodation. (GWR Magazine, 1909)

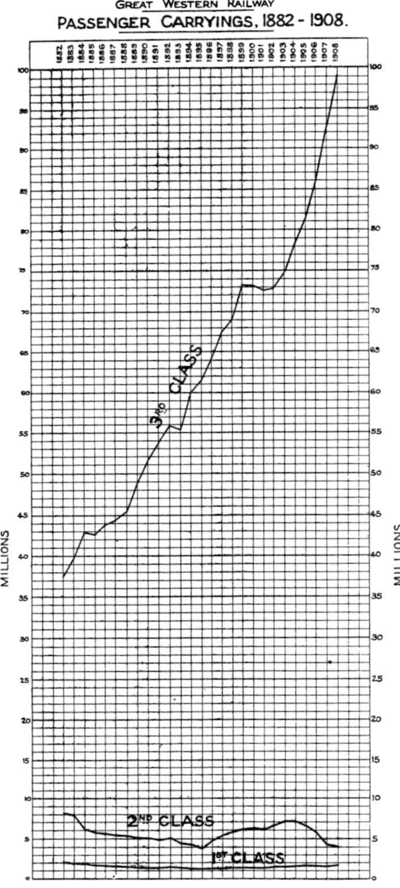

Diagram of Great Western train speeds.

Miles per Hour	1845 to 1847	1848 to 1850	1852 to 1860	1861 to 1864	1865 to 1866	1866 Winter	1867 to 1868	1869	1870	1871 to 1901	1902	1903 to 1906 Summer	1907 to 1912	1912 to 1913 Summer	Miles per Hour

Years. Miles per hour scale: 63, 62, 61, 60, 59, 58, 57, 56, 55, 54, 53, 52, 51, 50, 49, 48, 47, 46, 45. The Dotted Line shews speed from start to stop by Slip Coaches.

After the doldrums of the 1860s, average train speeds showed a marked improvement by the First World War. (GWR Magazine, 1913)

lasted 11 years, being broken up and rebuilt as individual coaches. The three suburban sets, however, consisting of six vehicles on seven bogies, made up of Brake 3rd/3rd/Composites, were not rebuilt and lasted until the 1960s. Made to Lots 1340–42, they were Diagrams C53, D93 and E126/133.

Between 1924 and 1933, Collett also designed and built a large number of two-coach permanently coupled non-corridor trains, known as 'B' sets. Used mainly in the Bristol Division, they also saw service on branch lines and local stopping trains. Each set was made up of two Brake Composites, with the Brake compartment at each end. Some sets had bow-ends, and others flat ends over the bogies. Diagrams were E116/129/135/140/145/147.

In this same period, the main-line corridor stock was known as the 'Cornish Riviera', being built specifically for this premier service. These vehicles were flush-sided, with smaller windows than usual, and measured 61 ft 4½ in long and 9 ft 5 in wide, which restricted their use drastically for many years. Diagrams were C59/60, D105/6, E137/8, and H35/6/7, plus three slips, F23.

The year 1934 saw the introduction of the 'Buffet' car on the GWR (H41), serving snack meals and drinks from a long counter which ran almost the length of the vehicle. Bar stools were provided, but no seats as such. In the same period, batches of 'Excursion' stock carriages were built. These coaches were open (no compartments) with a central gangway and seating on either side. Only two doors were fitted in each side, one at the end opposite the toilet and one half-way along the vehicle. This style was first introduced on the Milford Boat Trains of 1900/01 and still proved just as unpopular in 1934–8; in spite of passenger reaction, BR still continues the practice today.

The same year also heralded another experiment. An order had been placed with AEC of Slough for a lightweight diesel railcar (qv), and early in 1934 No 1 was added to the stock list. One of eventually 38 cars, No 1 was streamlined at both ends, and powered by a single six-cylinder diesel bus engine. Three more similar cars were built in 1934 (Nos 2–4) and were improved by fitting two engines, one on each side, plus a small buffet compartment. The next 14 cars were built by the Gloucester Carriage & Wagon Co, still using the AEC engines, between 1935 and 1937. The final batch of 20 were built by the GWR at Swindon Works during 1940–42, and although slightly streamlined were more angular and boxlike than previously. The last four cars, Nos 35–36 and 37–38, were built as twin sets, and were later strengthened by the addition of a Corridor 3rd sandwiched between the two units. Nos 17 and 34 were constructed specifically as Parcel Vans. Diagrams were U, V, W, X, Y, Z, and A1/A2/A3/A4.

The widest carriage stock ever built by the GWR was the series of 'Super Saloons' of 1931. These were the GWR's answer to the Pullman influence (only one train ran on the GWR with Pullman cars, the 'Torbay Pullman' (qv) of 1929) and were 9 ft 7 in wide. They were designed expressly for the Plymouth–Paddington boat trains and, being richly appointed, commanded a higher than 1st class fare. All eight were named after the Royal Family (Diagrams G60 and 61), and several are still in existence on preserved lines.

The 'Centenary' stock built 100 years after the birth of the GWR, was the successor to the earlier 'Cornish Riviera' stock. They were 60 ft long with large windows

RESTAURANT CARS ON PRINCIPAL G.W.R. TRAINS.

TARIFF.

BREAKFAST—Table d'Hôte - - - - - **3s. 6d.**
LUNCHEON—Table d'Hôte - **2s. 6d., and 3s.**
Ditto ditto (Cars on "Cornish Riviera Limited" and "Torbay Limited" Expresses and on Services operating between the G.W. and L.M.S., L.N.E., and Southern Lines) - - **3s. 6d.**
DINNER—Table d'Hôte - - - - - - **5s. 0d.**
Coffee - - - - - - - - **4d.** per cup.

TEAS.

Pot of Tea, with cut Bread and Butter - - - - **9d.**
Cake, Light Refreshments, etc., as Tariff exhibited in Cars.

The cuisine is directly controlled by the Great Western Railway Company

ENJOY MEALS EN ROUTE AT POPULAR PRICES

(Left and below left) *The interior of a GWR dining car of the 1920s, and a 1937 advertisement.* (GWR Museum, Swindon/Holiday Haunts)

Diagram	Type or Class
A	1st Class (8 wheels)
B	2nd Class up to 1905
C	3rd Class
D	Brake 3rds
E	Composites
F	Slip carriages
G	Saloons
H	Restaurant cars
I	—
J	Sleeping cars
K	Passenger Brake vans
L	Mail and Postal vans
M	Parcels and Sundry vans
N	Horse boxes
O	Milk vans and tanks
P	Carriage trucks
Q	Service vehicles
R	4- and 6-wheel 1st Class
S	4- and 6-wheel 2nd and 3rd Class
T	4- and 6-wheel Brake 3rds
U	4-wheel Composites
V	4- and 6- wheel Brake vans
W	4- and 6- wheel Parcel vans (later diesel railcars)
X	—
Y	Fruit vans (later Diesel Parcel van)
Z	Trailer cars

Note Steam railmotors used A to R diagrams, and other letters were used for trailer cars. Diesel railcars also used various, plus A and numerals.

and two recessed doors at each end. There were six types: 3rd (C69), Brake 3rd (D120), Composite (E149), Brake Composite (E150), Kitchen 1st (H43), and 3rd Diner (H44).

All corridor stock built between 1936 and the war years was standardized to a large degree, having doors only at each end, access to the compartments being via the corridor. Body widths were kept down to 9 ft to allow the vehicles to travel on other companies' networks, and the overall length varied from 57 ft 2 in to 60 ft 11 in, depending on the type.

Hawksworth-pattern carriage, the GWR's last design. (J. H. Russell Collection)

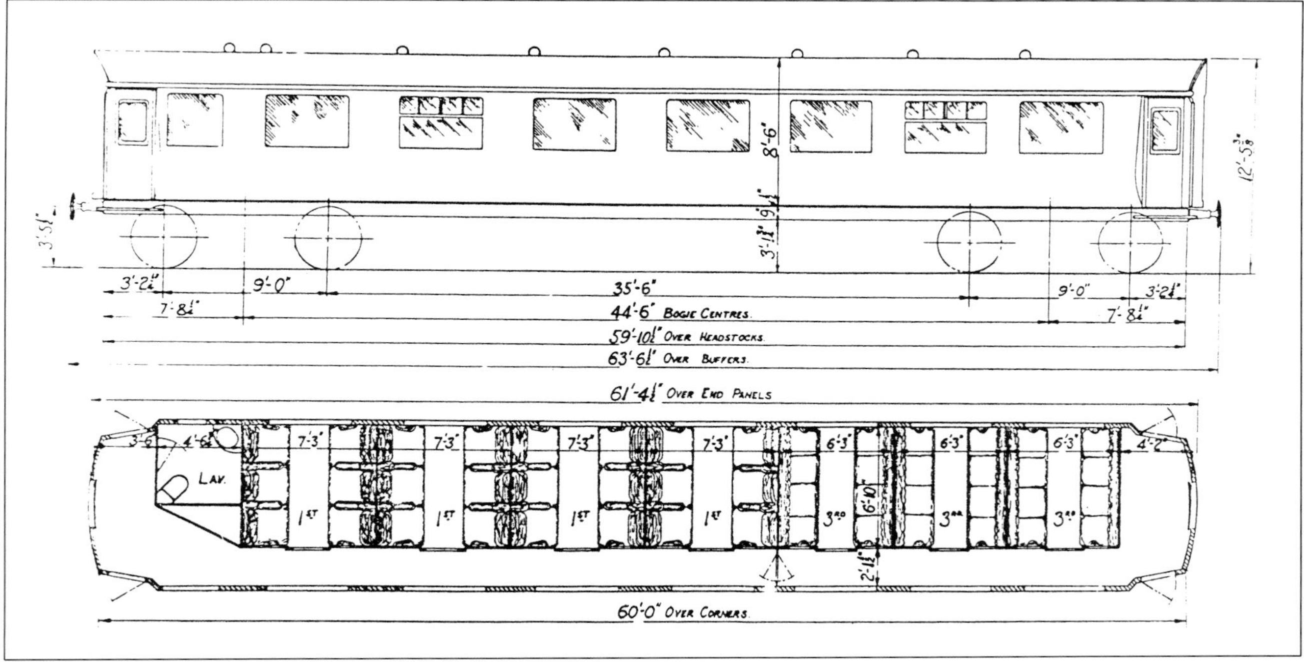

(Above) *1st/3rd composite 'Centenary' carriage.* (J. H. Russell Collection)

(Left) *A restaurant car of the 1930s.* (GWR Museum, Swindon)

The final design of passenger carriage built by the GWR was from drawings by Hawksworth (qv), the last CME. Basically the layout was very similar to the 1938 pattern, but with larger compartments and vestibules, which meant that the length had to go up to 64 ft. The main points of interest in the new vehicles were the use of fluorescent lighting, the large side windows, four doors on each side of the coaches, and the item which always distinguished them as 'Hawksworth' stock, the roofs, with Gresley-type domed ends. Diagrams were A23, C82–84, D131–33, and E164–5.

JHR

ROSS-ON-WYE

Ross-on-Wye was the meeting point of two modest GWR routes, that from Pontypool Road via Monmouth (qv below) and the one from Gloucester (qv Gloucester–Hereford line). Dating from 1 August 1873 and 27 July 1885 respectively,

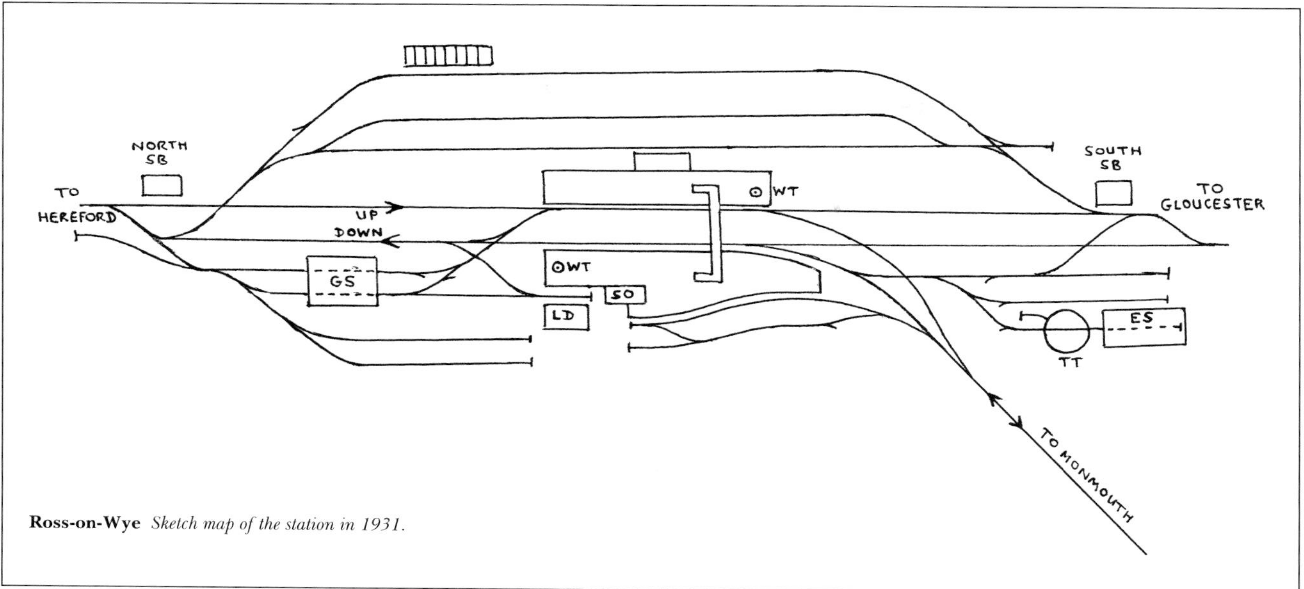

Ross-on-Wye *Sketch map of the station in 1931.*

the two lines joined at Ross Junction just east of the station and town. In addition to its passenger services, well patronized by tourists in the summer months, Ross had a sizeable goods depot with a 6½-ton crane.

GB

ROSS-ON-WYE–PONTYPOOL ROAD LINE

Stations: Ross-on-Wye, Kerne Bridge (4 m), Lydbrook Junction (5½ m), Symonds Yat (7½ m), Monmouth May Hill (12½ m), Monmouth Troy (13 m), Dingestow (16½ m), Raglan (19½ m), Llandenny (21¾ m), Usk (25 m), Glascoed Halt (27 m), Little Mill Junction (29 m), Pontypool Road (31 m)

From Ross to Monmouth this line followed the scenic course of the River Wye, connecting with the Severn & Wye system at Lydbrook Junction (qv), tunnelling to cross the necks of two loops, and reaching Monmouth Troy via the single platform at Monmouth May Hill and a viaduct over the river. Joined there by the Chepstow (qv) branch, it continued as a single line through more pastoral stations and halts to join the Newport, Abergavenny & Hereford line (qv) at Little Mill Junction. Usk, which had a 256 yd tunnel, was a passing point, and Little Mill had an additional station on the short branch to Glascoed ROF depot (opened 12 December 1938). Auto-trains (qv) provided most of the passenger services which took 1¾ hours for the through journey.

The Coleford, Monmouth, Usk & Pontypool Railway, worked by the NA&HR, had opened to Usk on 2 June 1856 and on to Troy on 12 October 1857. The GWR-worked Ross & Monmouth Railway had then reached May Hill on 3 August 1873 and been extended to Troy on 1 May 1874 to put a new through route under GWR control. The Ross & Monmouth company did, in fact, survive until grouping, paying 7s (35p) a share in its later years.

GB

ROYAL ALBERT BRIDGE

Linking Devon with Cornwall, the Royal Albert Bridge carried a single track 100 ft above the Tamar estuary by a combination of 17 curving approach spans and two magnificent main spans. The latter each

Royal Albert Bridge *Viewed from the Saltash side.* (Steamchest Collection)

accounted for 455 ft of the total length of 2,190 ft and relied on bowed tubular girders and suspension chains to support the rail deck. Although R. P. Brereton was in charge of the construction work, the bridge was designed by Brunel (qv) and carried his name in bold letters. On the opening day, 2 May 1859, the Prince Consort joined a Royal Train at 6 am from Windsor to arrive at Saltash at 12.15 pm and declare the bridge open. Public traffic began two days later. Terminally ill, Brunel was carried over the bridge a few days after it opened, lying on an open truck hauled by a Gooch locomotive.

Although the Cornwall Railway (qv) had a hard time raising money, the contractor, C. J. Mare, was eventually able to start work on the Tamar bridge early in 1853. It took two years to get the central pier lowered and settled and two more before the first span was floated into position on pontoons. These were subsequently removed and the spans raised by hydraulic pressure to allow the piers to be built up beneath them. On 11 April 1859 a train was run over the complete line from Plymouth to Truro, passing smoothly over the great bridge which had been conceived as a four-span structure with two tracks and costing £162,000, but had finished up with two spans, a single track and a cost of £225,000.

GB

ROYAL TRAINS

The GWR did not build a Royal Train as such, but the company did gain the distinction of constructing, in 1840, the first Royal Saloon, a four-wheeled broad gauge vehicle. This was modified to an eight-wheeler in 1842, and in it, on 13 June that year, Queen Victoria made the first railway journey undertaken by a reigning monarch. Another eight-wheeler was built between 1848–50, and featured bulged sides to give the Saloon more space. The Queen used this for all her GWR journeys until 1874. It was given bogies in 1877, converted to standard gauge two years later, and scrapped in 1903. A new Saloon was built in 1874, this time with a bulge in the roof as well as the sides: at first it ran on eight wheels, but soon acquired bogies. The Royal Train of this period comprised both the above Saloons, to which were added assorted six-wheelers, bogies and vans, lasting in this form until a new train was assembled in 1897 to mark the Queen's Diamond Jubilee.

Royal Trains *Kind Edward VII's funeral train passes through Ealing on Friday 20 May 1910 en route to Windsor behind No 4021* King Edward. (GWR Museum, Swindon)

This was made up of two Brake Vans, two 1st class attendants' and officers' Saloons, a Corridor 1st and the rebuilt 1874 Royal Saloon. The GWR had wanted to build a new train, but the Queen insisted that her customary saloon be left unchanged. With great ingenuity Dean (qv) managed to achieve this by building the Queen's private apartment, bulges and all, into a longer carriage.

No other royal vehicle was built by the GWR until 1940, when four special Saloons were made for use by VIPs and royalty on occasions when the ex-LNWR and LNER trains were not appropriate. Numbered 9001/2 and 9006/7, all are preserved, 9001 at the Birmingham Railway Museum, 9002 by the Great Western Society at Didcot, and the second pair by the NRM at York.

CA

RUABON

The advent of the railway helped Ruabon to exploit its edge-of-coalfield position and grow from a village to a substantial town serving a mixed pastoral and industrial community. The first trains arrived from Chester on 4 November 1846 with Ruabon becoming an interchange point when the Vale of Llangollen Railway opened from a junction ½ mile to the south on 1 December

Ruabon (Steamchest Collection)

1861 (passengers 2 June 1862). In that same year the GWR opened the first section of the line to Legacy in order to serve local ironworks. It subsequently extended this (1871) and acquired the Plas Madoc and Pontcysyllte branches (1896) to increase facilities for mineral traffic.

The express services to Chester and Birkenhead called at Ruabon, which was also the interchange, detaching and reversal point for those on the Barmouth line (qv below). Shrewsbury–Wrexham locals also called, plus those to Llangollen and Bala.

GB

RUABON–DOLGELLEY–BARMOUTH LINE

Stations: Ruabon, Acrefair (1½ m), Trevor (2½ m), Llangollen (6¼ m), Berwyn (7¾ m), Glyndyfrdwy (11½ m), Carrog (13½ m), Corwen (16¼ m), Cynwyd (18¼ m), Llandrillo (21 m), Llandderfel (23¾ m), Bala (28 m), Llanuwchllyn (32¼ m), Drws-y-Nant (38½ m), Bontnewydd (42 m), Dolgelley (45¼ m), Penmaenpool (47½ m), Arthog (52 m), Barmouth Junction (53 m), Barmouth (54½ m)

The lines of four GWR-backed railways eventually produced this difficult route of sharp curves and steep gradients from the Shrewsbury & Chester (qv), ¾-mile south of Ruabon, to meet the Aberystwyth & Welsh Coast/Cambrian line at Dolgelley (qv). The four railways were the Vale of Llangollen (opened to goods 1 December 1861, passengers 2 June 1862), the Llangollen & Corwen (8 May 1865), the Corwen & Bala (to Llandrillo 16 July 1866, Bala 1 April 1868) and the Bala & Dolgelley (4 August 1868). They were all worked, and subsequently absorbed, by the GWR.

The route carried local Ruabon–Bala/Barmouth trains serving some or all of the six intermediate halts, and through trains to Pwllheli. On their 118–150-minute journey the main intermediate traffic sources were Llangollen (qv), where the double-track station stood on a curve beside the River Dee, Corwen (qv) where the LNWR line from Denbigh joined, Bala Junction, where the branch to Bala and Blaenau Festiniog (both qv) departed, and Dolgelley (qv) where the Bala & Dolgelley/A&WC link had opened on 21 June 1869. On the single-line western section beside Bala Lake there was a private 'flag' station where a B&D/GWR Director had signals to halt trains and a flag to summon his steam launch across the lake. This section of the line has now reopened as part of the Bala Lake Railway.

GB

RUNNING POWERS

Running powers were an example, it is said, of co-operation between companies, though it could just as often work the other way. In return for a rental, arrived at by agreement, running powers could gain a company access to a station or across a stretch of line owned by another. A company was often reluctant to grant running powers unless it could perceive some advantage to itself, and conditions were often attached to the Agreement; on more than one occasion such an arrangement, far from being co-operative, led to friction. There was, for instance, a long-running battle between the GWR and the Midland Railway over access to Yate under an Agreement ratified in 1896, only settled in 1908 after Court Action.

The GWR sought and granted running powers to a lesser extent than any other company, its tacit policy being rather to absorb the smaller companies, thus rendering running powers unnecessary. There were, however, agreements with the Alexandra (Newport & South Wales) Dock (qv), Brecon & Merthyr (qv), GCR, LNWR, LSWR, Midland, Metropolitan, Rhymney (qv) and Taff Vale (qv) railways, the four Welsh companies being on the list because the GWR worked the local passenger service between Newport and Pontypridd. For a short section near Dolgelley, running powers were held across Cambrian metals, but in practice local engines took over GWR trains.

CA

RUSSELL, CHARLES

Chairman, 1839–55. Born in 1786, he served as Conservative MP for Reading from 1830–7 and 1841–7. While in Parliament he assisted the passage of the GWR Bill as Chairman of the Committee which examined it. He was elected Chairman of the GWR in 1839, and with Saunders and Brunel (both qv) became a champion of the broad gauge. He was a first Director of the Cornwall Railway (qv) when that company was incorporated (1846). Described by one writer as '. . . one of the greatest of early Victorian railway chairmen', Russell wished to resign from the office in 1853, but was persuaded to stay. Finally ill-health and age forced his departure on 2 August 1855. On 15 May the next year he committed suicide, his illness having affected his brain.

CA

ST AUSTELL

St Austell's first railway was a 2 ft 6 in gauge line opened in 1830 to convey clay to Pentewan Quay. The Cornwall Railway (qv) then arrived on 4 May 1859 with St Austell station assuming a conventional two-platform form in 1893 when the main line was doubled. The next development was in 1920 when the 1 m 33 ch Trenance Valley mineral line was opened north from a junction 28 chains beyond St Austell, with a passing point at Bojea and further sidings at Lower Ruddle and Baskell. In 1931 St Austell acquired a new up-side goods depot for its increasing china clay business.

St Austell was preceded by a 3½-mile climb from Par and followed by the St Austell and Gover Viaducts.

GB

ST FAGANS

St Fagans, on the South Wales main line (qv) west of Cardiff, was notable as the junction with the Barry Railway's (qv) coal route from Treforest and Porth to the docks. That company also tapped coal from the Ely Valley lines via a link from Peterston West Junction to Drope Junction and ran a Barry–St Fagans–Cardiff service via a second link to St Fagans East Junction.

GB

ST GERMANS

The 1859 route of the Cornwall Railway (qv) between Saltash and St Germans followed the Lynher River and required five timber viaducts to span its tributaries. Coinciding with the need to replace these with track doubling, the GWR undertook a route deviation, inland, on a better foundation and with easier curves and gradients. Opened in 1908 (goods 22 March, passengers 19 May), the new line had three masonry viaducts (Forder, Nottar, St Germans) and the 452 yd Wiveliscombe (Shillingham) Tunnel.

On the other side of St Germans a 1935 scheme had proposed a direct line to Looe. (qv Projected lines).

GB

ST IVES BRANCH

Stations: St Erth, Lelant (1 m), Carbis Bay (3 m), St Ives (4½ m)

St Erth, the main-line junction for the St Ives branch, used to be important for its forwardings of milk and broccoli traffic (both qv), as well as for the passengers changing for St Ives or travelling in the through carriages to and from the branch. The latter, authorized by an Act of 7 July 1873 and opened on 1 June 1877, was the last broad gauge line to be built. It was taken over by the GWR in 1878 and converted to standard gauge in 1892.

The single-line, 50 mph, electric train staff branch followed a steep coastal route along the western side of St Ives Bay with two intermediate stations and a one-time link to Lelant Quay. The GWR terminus at St Ives lay beyond Porthminster Viaduct and had a main platform, a short bay and a modest loco shed.

The GWR owned the Tregenna Castle Hotel at St Ives (qv Hotels).

GB

'Saint' Class *No 2981* Ivanhoe. (GWR Museum, Swindon)

'SAINT' CLASS

When Churchward (qv) started to revolutionize the whole basis of British steam locomotive design in the early 1900s, his first express passenger locomotives were the 'Saint' class 4-6-0s. The prototype was No 100 *William Dean* (qv), which appeared in 1902, and the following year saw the completion of No 98. This was designed in conjunction with his first 2-8-0, to become the first true example of his plans. Later that year series production of the new locomotives began, but several of the initial batch were turned out with the 'Atlantic' 4-4-2 wheel arrangement to facilitate comparison with the de Glehn compounds. The advantages of the extra adhesion provided by the third coupled axle were quickly apparent, and the 4-6-0 wheel arrangement became standard, with the earlier GWR 'Atlantics' being modified to conform. These first examples of the class were rather austere in appearance, with straight frames running through below the cabs, and a vertical break at the front end in front of the cylinders.

The initial batches were named after characters in Walter Scott novels, then 'Ladies', but, in 1907, on the series with 'Saint' names, the familiar curved framing appeared at both ends. It is for this reason that the whole class became known as the 'Saints'. A screw reverser also replaced the earlier use of massive hand-levers, which ordinary mortals could find difficult to move, particularly after the locomotive had been overhauled. The final members of the class to be built were the 'Courts', but the locomotives' numbers in the 29xx series were not in order of their building dates.

Over the years they were fitted with different types of standard boiler, and all had been superheated by 1912. Two members of the class were extensively modified. No 2925 *Saint Martin* was fitted with smaller wheels in 1924, to became the first 'Hall' (qv), and in 1931 No 2935 *Caynham Court* was fitted with rotary cam valve gear. In their early days the 'Saints' worked the main expresses, including the 'Cornish Riviera' (qv), but they were progressively displaced from these duties as the four-cylinder 'Stars' and 'Castles' (both qv) entered service.

(See also Locomotives)

PWBS

SALISBURY BRANCH

Stations: Westbury (16¾ miles from Bath), Warminster (21½ m), Heytesbury (25¼ m), Codford (27½ m), Wylye (31½ m), Wishford (36 m), Wilton (38¾ m), Salisbury (41¼ m)

Once the dust had settled on the early GWR versus LSWR rivalries, this line from Westbury (qv) to the LSWR/SR at Salisbury became part of an important through route carrying passengers to Bournemouth, Southampton, Portsmouth and Brighton, and Welsh coal for the bunkers of naval and commercial shipping. The use of Salisbury Plain by the Army for training purposes brought more traffic from 1895 onwards.

The climb at 1 in 70/76 from Westbury to Warminster was opened by the GWR on 9 September 1851 shortly after taking over the flagging Wilts, Somerset & Weymouth Railway (qv). But then local interests had to resort to law to compel completion of the stretch to Salisbury which eventually opened on 30 June 1856. The new line followed the course of the River Wylye to Wilton and then paralleled the LSWR/SR route to its own modest terminus adjoining that of its rival at Salisbury. From 12 September 1932 all passenger services were concentrated on the SR station at Salisbury, the GWR one remaining open for goods and coal.

GB

SALTASH

Saltash was the first GWR station in Cornwall, lying on a curve at the western end of the Royal Albert Bridge (qv). The original station opened by the Cornwall Railway (qv) on 4 May 1859 was rebuilt in 1880 and modified again when the route beyond the bridge was doubled. In GWR days there was a small goods yard on the up side at the country end and flower traffic (qv) was handled over the platforms in addition to the local passenger trains, some of which turned round there.

GB

SALTASH–PENZANCE LINE

Stations: Saltash (230 miles from Paddington), St Germans (235 m), Menheniot (240¼ m), Liskeard (243½ m), Doublebois (246¾ m), Bodmin Road (252½ m), Lostwithiel (256 m), Par (260¼ m), St Austell (265 m), Grampound Road (271¾ m), Probus & Ladock Platform (274¼ m), Truro (279¼ m), Chacewater (284½ m), Scorrier (286¼ m), Redruth (288½ m), Carn Brea (290½ m), Camborne (292 m), Gwinear Road (294½ m), Hayle (298 m), St Erth (299½ m), Marazion (303¼ m), Penzance (305¼ m)

The broad gauge Cornwall Railway (qv) reached Truro from Plymouth (both qv) on 4 May 1859 over a route involving five tunnels and 34 viaducts. From 11 May it was linked with the West Cornwall Railway's (qv) line on to Penzance (qv) but this was 'narrow' gauge and through running did not commence until its conversion in 1866 (goods 6 November, passengers 1 March 1867). The great gauge conversion (qv) back to standard gauge then took place over the weekend of 20–22 May 1892 and the main line was progressively doubled between 1893 and 1930.

The Cornish main line followed a tortuous course to minimize the effect of surmounting three summits (Doublebois, Burngullow and Redruth) and crossing inumerable waterways, and even the 'Cornish Riviera' express (qv) needed 2 hrs 18 min for the journey. Other long-distance trains, like the 'Owl' and the 'Waker' (as railwaymen knew them) took a little longer while locals, feeding the eight branch junctions, might need nearly 3½ hours to cover the 79½ miles west of Plymouth. The route was also busy with trainloads of broccoli, vegetables, fish, flowers, china clay and other goods.

GB

Saltash-Penzance line *Par station, looking southwest. Newquay trains used the outer island platform face (right).* (Steamchest Collection)

SAPPERTON TUNNELS

The Swindon–Gloucester line (qv) passed through the Cotswold ridge by means of two tunnels at Sapperton, the 352 yd Short Tunnel, which was on a rising gradient from Kemble (qv), and the 1,860 yd Long Tunnel, which had a 1 in 90 drop towards Stroud (qv). Brunel's original plan for the Cheltenham & Great Western Union Railway (qv) had envisaged a deep tunnel and fairly easy gradients, but when the GWR took over, pressures for economical completion led to a shallower and shorter tunnel section with steep gradients and sharp curves. Later up train enginemen were to curse the 1 in 60 rise up the valley of the Frome, with its reverse curves and the need to use a pilot or banker from Brimscombe. (See illustration overleaf).

GB

SAUNDERS, CHARLES ALEXANDER

The GWR's first Secretary, he was born in 1796 at Lewisham, but came of Scottish forebears. In 1833 he was appointed Secretary to the London Committee of the GWR. He became Secretary and General Superintendent in 1840, and was destined to play a vital part in the company's history. He was greatly responsible for raising capital in the West for the project, and became a close friend of Brunel. Later his persistance helped to bring about the Board of Trade's rethink in the matter of the Gauge Commissioners' report (qv Broad Gauge). With Russell, Gooch and Brunel (all qv) he more or less ran the GWR during its formative years, and when he retired in September 1863 his post was filled by three men—F. G. Saunders (his nephew) as Secretary, G. N. Tyrrell as Superintendent of the Line, and James Grierson as General Manager (all qv). The Board granted him a pension in recognition of his work—unprecedented at that time—and in November of that year he was presented with a silver centrepiece from Queen Victoria, in tribute for services to her during her railway journeys. He did not live long to enjoy either, dying in the following year, on 19 September.

CA

SAUNDERS, FREDERICK GEORGE

Chairman, 1889–95. Born on 24 December 1820, he was appointed Assistant Secretary to the South Wales Railway (qv) in 1844, becoming Secretary in Chief in December 1849. The Secretaryship of the GWR

Sapperton tunnels *Near the top of Sapperton bank, the western portal of Long Tunnel, little changed when this photograph was taken in July 1970.* (W. Adams)

became vacant on his uncle's retirement in 1863 (qv above), and nephew filled the uncle's place. On his resignation from this post in June 1886 he was made a Director and, in 1889, elected Chairman in succession to Gooch (qv). He retired at the end of June 1895, but remained a member of the Board until his death, at Caversham Grove, Reading, on 1 January 1901.

CA

SAVERNAKE

Savernake was the first summit along the West of England main line, its station the climax of a steepening climb from Newbury (qv) and prelude to an equally lengthy descent. The location, after opening on 11 November 1862 as part of the Berks & Hants Extension Railway (qv), became a junction for the Marlborough branch (qv) on 14 April 1864 and dealt with the latter's quota of Swindon, Marlborough & Andover Railway trains from 5 February 1883. These continued southwards via Wolfhall Junction until inter-railway problems prompted the SM&A's successor to build a new line from Marlborough, over the GWR line at Savernake and linked to it by down-side east and west spurs.

The GWR Savernake Low Level station was 250 yards from High Level. It consisted of up and down platforms, the former with the main buildings, and a country-end bay for Marlborough trains.

GB

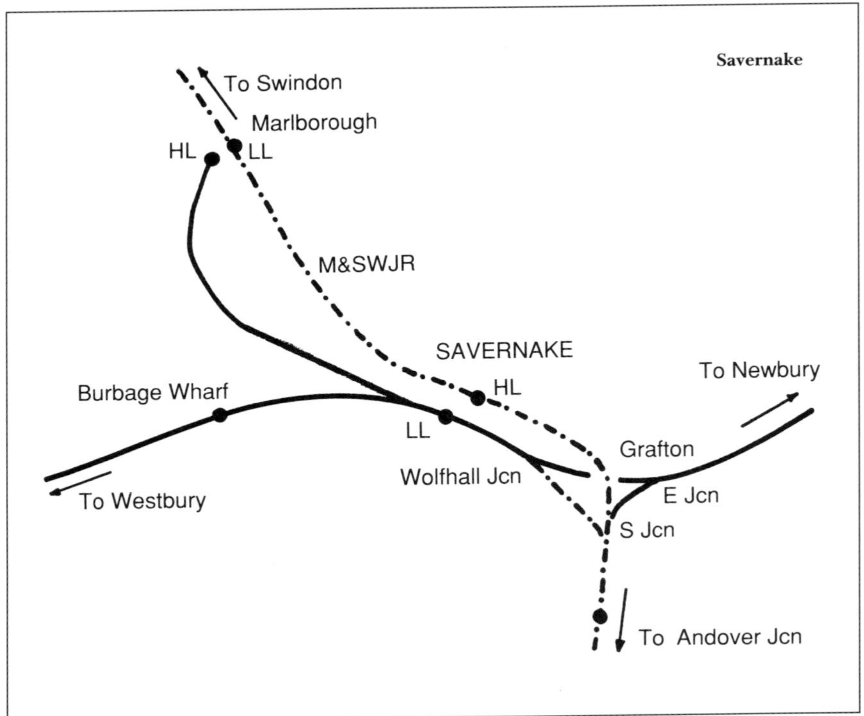

SCILLY ISLES TRAFFIC

One of the main industries of the Isles of Scilly has been flower growing, a traffic the GWR took pains to foster. By early this century steamers with up to 40 tons of flowers on board, packed in light wooden boxes, made up on the spot with timber sent down by goods train from Paddington, were leaving the Islands for the 3-hour journey to Penzance (qv). Two hours after arrival there, unloading and sorting done, both ordinary and special trains (given precedence, in some instances, even over passenger services) would depart, mostly for London, where they would arrive at about 3 or 4 am. Birmingham, Manchester, Aberdeen and N Ireland were likely to receive consignments also, and between January and May 1904 Penzance despatched almost 300 wagon-loads of flowers, about a third of which went by ordinary train. On 2 February 1926 a new steamer, *Scillonian*, made her maiden voyage. Built by a company in which the GWR had an interest, she cost £25,000 and was specifically designed to carry up to 50 tons of flower boxes.

CA

SENGHENYDD BRANCH

Stations: Cardiff Queen Street, Llanishen (3½ m), Caerphilly (7 m), Penyrheol (8½ m), Abertridwr (10 m), Senghenydd (11¼ m)

The Aber branch from Caerphilly (qv) was authorized to the Rhymney Railway (qv) by an Act of 25 July 1864 and its extension to Senghenydd by a subsequent statute of 25 July 1890. It was opened throughout on 1 February 1894 and duly passed to the GWR at the Grouping, that company providing some 20 weekday passenger trains and handling the output of the Windsor and Universal collieries.

West from Caerphilly the branch took the shorter of the Beddau loops to quit the RR main line at Aber Branch Junction and head at 1 in 49 up the valley of the Nant yr Aber. It was double track as far as Abertridwr and then single for the final stretch towards the heights of Mynydd Eglwysilan.

GB

SEVERN & WYE JOINT RAILWAY

The Severn & Wye Joint Railway was incorporated by a GW and Midland Railway Companies Act of 17 August 1894 which ratified the £477,300 purchase by the larger companies of the Severn & Wye & Severn Bridge Railway, itself incorporated on 21 July 1879 as the amalgamation of the Severn & Wye Railway & Canal and the Severn Bridge Railway.

The system had originated as a scheme for a canal and harbour at Lydney (qv) with connecting tramroads from the Forest of Dean, authorized by an Act of 1809 and opened over the next few years. As a conventional railway the main line from Lydney north to Lydbrook Junction (qv) was completed on 26 August 1874 and a passenger service began in the following year. The Severn Bridge Railway from Lydney to Sharpness was authorized by an Act of 18 July 1872 and opened on 17 October 1879.

The Midland Railway's Sharpness branch was included in the joint system which the main-line companies began to operate from 1 July 1894 by means of a management committee and stock and equipment contributions from both partners. The rest consisted of the main line through Lydney to Lydbrook Junction, the Coleford and Cinderford branches (both qv), the Mineral Loop and numerous colliery and other sidings. (See map overleaf)

GB

SEVERN TUNNEL

During the 1860s the GWR came under increasing pressure to improve the rail access to South Wales. From the beginning of 1864 the route via New Passage Ferry was available to passengers, but freight still had to travel via Gloucester, and commercial interests in the Principality began talking about the possibility of rival lines. Thus it was that the GWR board came to approve the proposals of Charles Richardson, the engineer of the Bristol & South Wales Union Railway (qv), for a tunnel under the Severn, obtaining Parliamentary approval for the decision on 27 June 1872 at a time when three rival schemes were in the offing.

Under Richardson's direction work on the Severn Tunnel began on 18 March 1873, but it was to be 5 September 1885 before Daniel Gooch (qv) was able to travel through by special train and 1 September 1886 before regular goods services commenced (passengers 1 December). By that time a workforce of up to 3,628 men had used 36,794 tons of cement and 76.4 million bricks in building the longest tunnel in the world. In the course of their endeavours the works had been flooded three times, twice by the Great Spring and once by an abnormal tidal wave, and great courage and resourcefulness had been demanded of everyone, from the new engineer Thomas Walker downwards.

Along its 4 m 628 yds the Severn Tunnel descended at 1 in 100 for 2 miles from the eastern portal to pass 44.7 ft below a deep channel known as The Shoots and then rose for a slightly longer distance at 1 in 90 to the Welsh portal. Water draining in from each end plus the culverted flow of the Great Spring combined to demand a pumping operation of 15–25 million gallons a day which, in turn, meant the constant operation of four Bull engines and ten 41–70 in beam engines with 20–37 in pumps and associated steam boilers. To keep the tunnel clear of fumes a 40 ft fan was needed. (See diagrams overleaf)

The new tunnel quickly proved its worth, with traffic levels rising and producing a level of congestion on the Bristol main line that led ultimately to the 1903 direct route from Patchway to Wootton Bassett (qv Cut-offs and avoiding lines). Doubling south of Filton, the loop from Dr Day's Bridge and increasing interchange at Stapleton Road were all part of the Bristol consequences. Indeed, by the 1920s local electrification, widening, a second tunnel or a bridge were all being considered as ways of increasing tunnel capacity, and a later option of a midway signal box was also examined.

GB

SEVERN TUNNEL JUNCTION

Located on the flat coastal plain on the Monmouthshire side of the Severn estuary, Severn Tunnel Junction was the site of a large marshalling yard and the point at which the old main line via Chepstow (qv) and its successor through the Severn Tunnel (qv above) joined. The station had a centre island and outer platforms to serve the double tracks of each route and for the

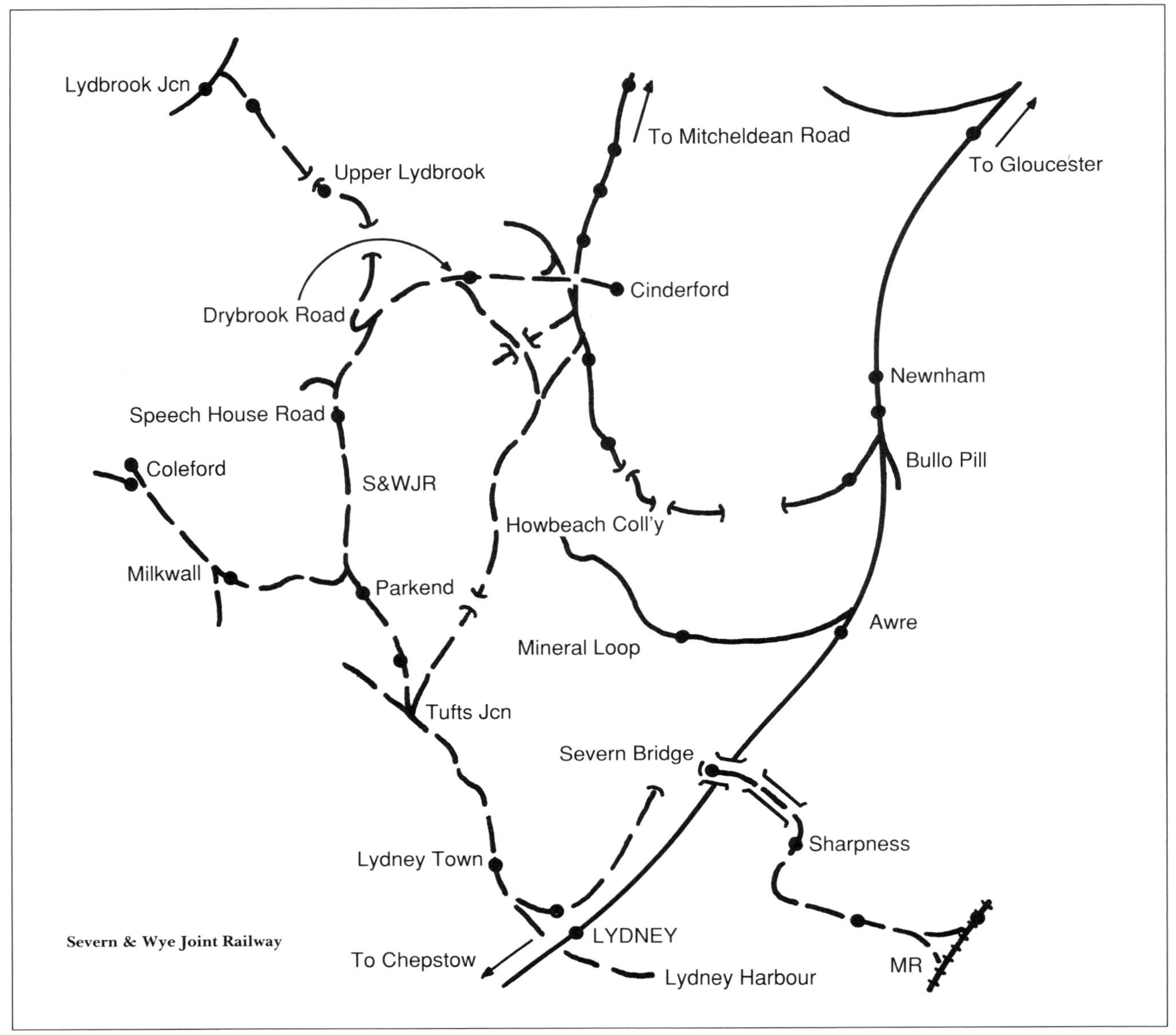

combination of 2-6-2T, carflat wagons and passenger coach that provided a motor vehicle train (qv) service under the Severn to Pilning. It was served by main-line, Bristol and Gloucester trains and initiated the auto-train (qv) services on the Wye Valley line to Monmouth (qv).

The marshalling areas grew, mainly through 1930s enlargement, into sizeable up and down hump yards which aggregated, separated and sorted freight wagons to and from South Wales. The up-side loco depot, opened in 1908, had an allocation of around 90 engines of which one-third were 2-6-2Ts whose duties included tunnel banking. These had their own up-side 'station' beside the brake kip, and the location was also a carriage and wagon examination point.

GB

SHAW, BENJAMIN

Chairman, 1835–7. An original member of the London Committee, Shaw was elected Chairman at the first General Meeting of the GWR on 29 October 1835. He does not appear to have made any great impression: he resigned from the Chairmanship on 9 October two years later, and came off the Board in about 1839.

CA

SHELBURNE, LORD HENRY PETTY-FITZMAURICE

Chairman, 1859–63. Born on 7 January 1816 in London, second son of the Marquis of Lansdowne, who sat in the House of Lords as Lord Wycombe, he succeeded as Lord Shelburne in August 1836. He was elected Liberal MP for Calne (Wilts) the fol-

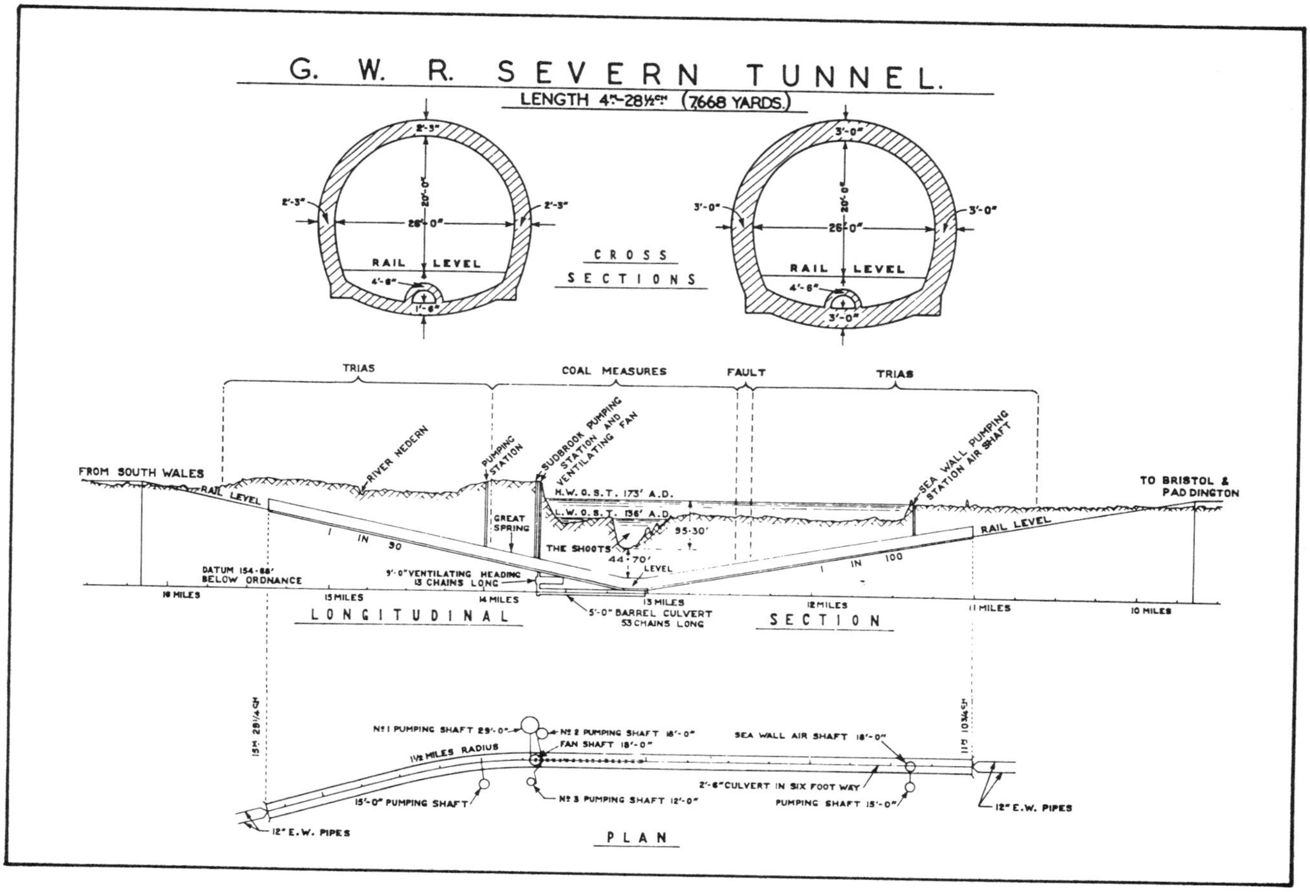

G. W. R. SEVERN TUNNEL.

LENGTH 4M-28½CH (7668 YARDS.)

CROSS SECTIONS

2'-3" 20'-0" 28'-0" RAIL LEVEL 4'-6" 1'-6"

3'-0" 20'-0" 26'-0" RAIL LEVEL 4'-6" 3'-0"

TRIAS | COAL MEASURES | FAULT | TRIAS

FROM SOUTH WALES | RIVER NEDERN | PUMPING STATION | SUDBROOK PUMPING STATION AND VENTILATING FAN | SEA WALL PUMPING STATION AIR SHAFT | TO BRISTOL & PADDINGTON

RAIL LEVEL | 1 IN 90 | GREAT SPRING | H.W.O.S.T. 173' A.D. | L.W.O.S.T. 136' A.D. | THE SHOOTS | 95·30' | 44·70' | LEVEL | 1 IN 100 | RAIL LEVEL

DATUM 154·68' BELOW ORDNANCE | 5'-0" VENTILATING HEADING 13 CHAINS LONG | 5'-0" BARREL CULVERT 53 CHAINS LONG

16 MILES | 15 MILES | 14 MILES | 13 MILES | 12 MILES | 11 MILES | 10 MILES

LONGITUDINAL SECTION

15M 29¼CH | 11M 10¾CH

Nº1 PUMPING SHAFT 29'-0" | Nº2 PUMPING SHAFT 18'-0" | FAN SHAFT 18'-0" | SEA WALL AIR SHAFT 18'-0" | 1½ MILES RADIUS | 15'-0" PUMPING SHAFT | Nº3 PUMPING SHAFT 12'-0" | 2'-6" CULVERT IN SIX FOOT WAY | PUMPING SHAFT 15'-0" | 12" E.W. PIPES | 12" E.W. PIPES

PLAN

Severn Tunnel *Plan, cross and longitudinal sections.* (BR)

Severn Tunnel Junction *'Castle' Class No 5046* Clifford Castle *passes through Severn Tunnel Junction with a heavy Paddington-South Wales train.* (G. H. Soole, G. Body Collection)

lowing year, and joined the GWR Board in 1858, possibly with a view to his taking over from Ponsonby (qv)—to whom he was related by marriage—in due course. He succeeded his father as 4th Marquis of Lansdowne in 1863, and Ponsonby sat in for him at the February meeting. Shelburne resigned shortly afterwards, his place being taken by Walpole (qv) as a stop-gap. He died of paralysis at Lansdowne House on 5 July 1866.

CA

SHIPS AND SHIPPING SERVICES

Like many of the other railways in this country which served ports, the GWR developed its own shipping services, the main ones being to the Channel Islands and Ireland. The former operated from Weymouth, while Fishguard was to replace New Milford as the port in West Wales used for the Irish routes. In addition there were a number of small tenders based at Plymouth, and at Fishguard for a short period, which were used to transfer passengers to and from transatlantic liners making calls at the ports. The smallest of the passenger-carrying ships were those which worked the ferry service between Kingswear and Dartmouth (qv Kingswear

Ships and shipping services *The first* St Andrew *of 1908, employed on the Fishguard-Rosslare service.* (GWR Museum, Swindon)

branch), the fourth of which was the *Mew*. Like several of the company's larger vessels, it was to have its moment of glory in the Second World War.

Shipping services from Weymouth (qv) dated back long before the railways, but the arrival of the GWR and LSWR at the port in 1857 started a rivalry between the two companies. Although the LSWR was already operating ships to the Channel Islands from Southampton, it decided to compete directly with the GWR's plans for services out of Weymouth. The latter, however, did not, at that time, have authority to operate shipping services, and so had to do it 'at arm's length' by means of a separate organization, the Weymouth & Channel Islands Steam Packet Company. It was specially set up for the purpose, and Brunel and Gooch were among the shareholders. These two rival services for Guernsey and Jersey from the same port provided far more capacity than was required, particularly as it was not even possible to travel to Weymouth by train from as close as Dorchester and catch that morning's departures. Although their existing service was not exactly prospering, a year later the Packet Company purchased a further ship for a service to Cherbourg, and some of the workings called at Alderney, but this route proved even less profitable. However, the LSWR's *Express* was wrecked in September 1859, and, after they had used a number of other ships intermittantly, they withdrew completely at the end of that year. The Packet Company, with guarantees from the GWR, soldiered on.

The situation was to change after 1871, when the GWR obtained its Steam Vessels Act, which gave it authority to operate ships from Weymouth and/or Portland to the Channel Islands, Cherbourg and St Malo, as well as from Milford Haven to Cork and Waterford. Although its direct operation of the Irish services was to start in 1872, it was not until 1889 that the GWR took over the Channel Islands services from Weymouth, which was part of the 'Great Awakening' that followed the appointment of Nathan Burlinson (qv) as Superintendent of the Line. The change coincided with the completion of improvements carried out in the port by Weymouth Corporation, which was to remain very closely connected with these services for the remainder of the GWR's existence.

Three new twin-screw steel ships were ordered, the *Lynx, Antelope* and *Gazelle*, but as these were not ready in time for the inauguration of the services, some iron-hulled paddle-steamers from Wales were used initially. When the new fast vessels did come into operation, there was a considerable speed-up in the service. In both directions the journey times to and from London came down to less than 12 hours, the biggest saving being from Jersey to Paddington, which had previously taken as long as 17 hours. For the remainder of the 19th century, the great rivalry between the two railways for the Channel Islands traffic continued, and on Good Friday 1897 the GWR's *Ibex* and the LSWR's *Frederica* were speeding to St Helier neck-and-neck when the former struck some rocks off Corbière. It had to put into Portelet Bay, and was subsequently beached for emergency repairs. Later that year the GWR took delivery of two new, and faster, ships, *Roebuck* and *Reindeer*, and the former made the crossing from Weymouth to Guernsey in only 3½ hours, while the daylight schedule from London to Jersey came down to just over 10 hours.

In 1899, the result of the headlong dashes across the Channel by the rival ships was to be far more serious, when the LSWR's *Stella* hit the Casquets in fog, and sunk with the loss of over 100 lives. Although all concerned hotly denied that there had ever been any racing, the all-out competition ceased, and agreement was reached to pool the receipts between the two companies, with tickets being valid by either route. During the summer each company would operate six times a week in both directions. From Southampton the LSWR would travel to the islands overnight, while the GWR sailed by day. In the winter months each railway would operate three southbound services a week, on alternate nights. The sailings to both mainland ports from the islands were by day throughout the year, but the frequency was less during the winter, with the routes alternating.

This established the general pattern for the two railways' subsequent operations to the Channel Islands, but the opening of the new line between Patney & Chirton and Westbury in 1900 (qv Cut-off and avoiding lines) did enable the GWR to cut its train times. The *Roebuck* and *Reindeer* had rendered the smaller vessels largely redundant, but other work for them was found at Plymouth, either as tenders to ferry passengers to and from the Atlantic liners, or on a new service to Nantes in France, which were authorized by a new Shipping Act of 1909. At the time of the Grouping, nothing much had changed with the Channel Island services since the turn of the century, but in 1925 the oil-fired turbine ships *St Julien* and *St Helier* came into service on the route from Weymouth, and were to see out the days of the GWR on this route. Two new cargo vessels, *Roebuck* (II) and *Sambur*, were introduced in the same year.

At the time of the GWR's 1871 Shipping Act, the Irish services from Wales were being worked by Ford & Jackson, who had an agreement with the GWR which was similar to the one at Weymouth. The railway company took over the operation and the ships in 1872, sailing from the port of Neyland (qv), although this was referred to as New Milford. The first of its own replacement vessels, *Limerick* (I) and *Milford*, arrived in 1873, but the former was wrecked and replaced the following year by another ship of the same name, which was also joined by *Waterford* (I). Two additional routes were tried during the remainder of the 19th century, but both were short-lived. The route to Cork only lasted for a year

Ships and shipping services *A 1937 advertisement for the company's shipping services to Ireland, the Isle of Man and Channel Islands.*

from 1875, before being passed over to another company, but in 1896 the *Voltaic* was obtained for the Wexford–Rosslare–Bristol route. In 1902 the GWR replaced two of the earlier steamers operating from New Milford by the twin-screw vessels *Great Western* (II) and *Great Southern*.

Plans for new railways in the south-western tip of Wales continued to be put forward well into the 20th century, and even at the time of the Grouping the GWR had unexercised parliamentary powers in that area. The year 1906, however, saw a major change in the shipping services across St George's Channel, with the opening of a stretch of railway serving their new port of Fishguard (qv), which had literally been blasted out of the cliffs. From it the GWR were able to operate the shortest of all the Anglo-Irish services, to Rosslare. The corporate structure was a complicated one, the operations being officially carried out by the Fishguard & Rosslare Railways & Harbour Company, although, from 1898, this had been jointly owned by the GWR and the Great Southern & Western Railway. The former undertook to work the port at Fishguard and the shipping services, for which they provided three new turbine steamers, *St George*, *St David* (I), and *St Patrick* (I), with *St Andrew* (I) joining them two years later. The services to Waterford and Cork were also moved to Fishguard, and the railway's direct interest in passenger sailings out of New Milford ceased. *St George* was sold to the Canadian Pacific Railway Company in 1912, but the other three vessels continued until they were replaced in the 1930s by larger ships with the same names, as was the *Great Western* (II). It was customary for certain ships from the Irish routes to move south into the Channel during the summer, as the Weymouth route had a much greater seasonality with passenger and freight loadings.

Mention has already been made of the calls by Atlantic liners at Plymouth (qv) and Fishguard. In addition to using some of the earlier cross-Channel vessels as tenders, a number of new ones were built. Until 1909 this traffic had only been handled at Plymouth, and the vessels reflected West Country seafaring history, carrying names such as *Sir Walter Raleigh*, *Sir Francis Drake* and *Sir Richard Grenville*, with *Sir John Hawkins* being added in 1929. The oldest of these tenders was the *Smeaton*, dating from 1883, but not all of them had a gross tonnage of more than 250 tons, so, like the tugs and other harbour vessels, do not appear in the accompanying table. After the completion of Fishguard, the Cunard Line started to make calls there with its Atlantic services, the first being by the *Mauretania* in August 1909. The railway company pulled out all the stops for the Blue Riband holder, and no fewer than three vessels clustered round the liner after it had anchored, including *Great Western* (II), which was normally used on the Irish services. In the First World War these calls stopped, and were never resumed, as Cunard subsequently switched its services from Liverpool to Southampton, leaving Plymouth to handle this type of business for all the shipping lines, British and foreign.

The GWR's ships became involved in the hostilities during both World Wars. In 1916 *Pembroke* was fired on by a U-boat, but *Ibex* was attacked three times, and struck back by sinking one of its assailants with gunfire.

Name	Built (purchased)
Malakof	1851 (1872)
Great Western (I)	1867 (1872)
South of Ireland	1867 (1872)
Vulture	1864 (1872)
Limerick (I)	1873
Milford	1873
Limerick (II)	1874
Waterford (I)	1874
*Pembroke**	1880
Smeaton	1883
Gael	1867 (1884)
Lynx	1889
Antelope	1889
Gazelle	1889
Cheshire	1889
Ibex	1891
Richard Grenville (I)	1891
Voltaic	1896
Roebuck (I)	1897
Reindeer	1897
Great Western (II)	1902
Great Southern	1902
Melmore	1892 (1905)
St George	1906
St David (I)	1906
St Patrick (I)	1906
St Andrew (I)	1908
Sir Francis Drake	1908
Atalanta	1907 (1910)
Bretonne	1893 (1910)
Waterford (I)	1912
Roebuck (I)	1925
Sambur	1925
St Julien	1925
St Helier	1925
Sir John Hawkins	1929
St Patrick (II)	1930
Sir Richard Grenville (II)	1931
St Andrew (II)	1932
St David (II)	1932
Great Western (III)	1934
St David (III)	1947
St Patrick (III)	1947

**Pembroke* was rebuilt from a paddle - steamer to a twin-screw vessel in 1896.

Its only ship to became a casualty got itself impaled on a warship in Scapa Flow after dragging its anchor. In the Second World War, however, the larger size of the railway's vessels resulted in most of them being requisitioned for war service, as troop carriers and ambulance ships. In 1944 *St David* (II) was bombed and sunk off the Anzio beachhead, and later the same year *St Andrew* (II) was badly damaged by a mine. *St Patrick* (II) had remained on the Anglo-Irish routes, but was bombed on three occasions, being finally sunk in 1941 with the loss of 30 lives. Six of the GWR's fleet had previously been involved in the evacuation from Dunkirk in 1940, *St Helier* making no fewer than seven round trips. A myriad of small ships was required to ferry soldiers out from the beaches, and the 32-year-old *Mew*, from Dartmouth, set off up the Channel at its full speed of 10 knots to assist. However, by the time it had reached Dover the evacuation was virtually over, and the authorities would not let it leave home waters.

With the war finished, the GWR reinstated its services to the newly liberated Channel Islands in 1945, initially only with the cargo steamers *Roebuck* (II) and *Sambur*. After being released from war service and overhauled, *St Helier* and *St Julien* returned to railway operations the following year. Replacements were ordered for *St David* and *St Patrick*, and these two very handsome vessels, using the same names, were completed with the shadow of Nationalization hanging over the GWR. They both had the company's coat of arms embossed on their bows, and, thanks to their official ownership by the Fishguard & Rosslare Railways & Harbours Company, they and their GWR livery were retained throughout their remaining days in BR service.

(*See also Channel Islands traffic*)

PWBS

SHIPSTON-ON-STOUR BRANCH

Stations: Moreton-in-Marsh, Stretton-on-Fosse (4¼ m), Longdon Road (6¾ m), Shipston-on-Stour (9 m)

The lower part of this branch dated back to 28 May 1821 when the 4 ft gauge Stratford & Moreton Railway was authorized as a horse tramway to distribute coal and goods from the Stratford Canal. The section from the canal to Moreton (qv) opened on 5 September 1826 with the short branch east to Shipston following ten years later, on 11 February 1836.

The Moreton sidings of the tramway bisected the route of the Oxford, Worcester & Wolverhampton Railway (qv) which acquired the smaller concern from 1 May 1847 and allowed private operators to run services on it from 1853 to 1859. The venerable old line then lay semi-derelict until the portion between Moreton and Shipston was resuscitated as a GWR branch from 1 July 1889.

Operated under the 'one engine in steam' regulations, the standard branch service consisted of four passenger workings and one out-and-home goods train. The former ceased on 8 July 1929.

GB

SHREWSBURY

Six rail routes met at Shrewsbury, three GW&LNW Joint lines—from Wellington, Hereford and Buttington—plus the GWR lines from Worcester and Chester and the LNWR Crewe line. Shrewsbury General station dealt with main-line services on the North & West route and from Paddington to Birkenhead and North Wales, plus a variety of local services and trains to mid-Wales via Welshpool.

The station itself was sited in a loop of the Severn, with the river passing beneath the platforms at the south end. It was a 'joint' location, consisting of main down-side buildings and platform and an up island, both with bays at the south end. The buildings, in mock Tudor style, were the work of T. K. Penson and Thomas Brassey, dating from 1849 but having been 'lifted' to accept an inserted ground floor level in 1903–04. To the south lay a triangular junction between the Hereford and Wolverhampton lines, the access to Shropshire Yard, Coleham Goods and the GWR and LNWR engine sheds. The purely GWR goods depot at Castle Foregate lay at the north end of the station, near Crewe Junction, and was followed by Coton marshalling yard.

Shrewsbury's first trains were those of the Shrewsbury & Chester Railway (qv below) which started using a temporary station there on 14 October 1848. They were joined at the new, permanent station on 1 June 1849 by those of the Shrewsbury & Birmingham, with the first Shrewsbury & Hereford workings commencing on 20 April 1852. The Crewe line was added in 1858 and the Welshpool and Severn Valley lines in 1862. The Shropshire & Montgomeryshire Light Railway of 1911 ran to a separate Abbey station not far from Abbey Foregate on the Wellington line.

There was always a great deal of activity at Shrewsbury and much shunting and transfer working between the various yards and sidings. Support facilities included an engine turntable at Severn Bridge Junction, yard and carriage sidings at Abbey

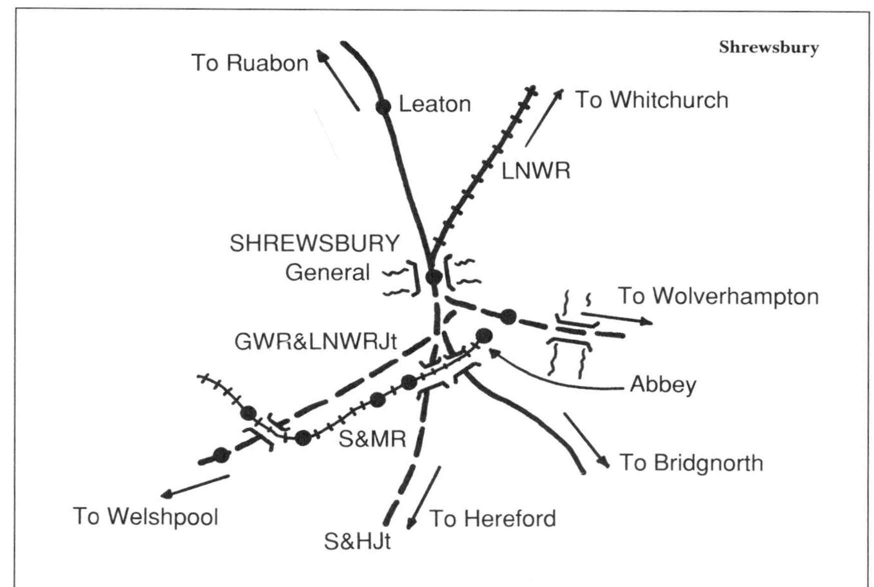

Foregate, a carriage shed at Coleham SVR and goods loops at Sutton Bridge Junction. Trains of goods wagons to and from the Wellington line stopped at Coleham for RCH number-taking.

GB

SHREWSBURY–BUTTINGTON LINE

Stations: Shrewsbury, Hanwood ($4\frac{3}{4}$ m), Yockleton ($7\frac{1}{2}$ m), Westbury (11 m), Breidden (14 m), Buttington (17 m)

In addition to its local passenger service, this was the through route for trains from London, Birmingham and Wolverhampton to the Welsh coast. It had been authorized on 29 July 1856 to the LNWR-backed Shrewsbury & Welshpool Railway, with opening on 27 January 1862 and purchase by the LNWR in 1864. A year later the local line was vested jointly in the GWR and LNWR, although the latter operated the services.

The S&W line involved a 12-mile climb to pass between the Long Mountain and Breidden Hill and on this section there were connections with the Shropshire & Mongomeryshire line at Meole Brace, with collieries at Cruckmeole Junction and a timber loading point at Yockleton. After the descent there was a brickyard siding at Buttington and the line had electric train staff exchange apparatus at Cruckmeole Junction, Westbury, Breidden and Buttington.

The S&W enabling Act also embraced a branch to Minsterley which was opened on 14 February 1861 and on which a joint passenger service called at Plealey Road (7 m from Shrewsbury), Pontesbury ($8\frac{1}{2}$ m) and Minsterley (10 m). From a connection just beyond Pontesbury came granite from the Snailbeach District Railways and barytes from Malehurst Siding, heavy trains being required to stop in advance of the descent through Plealey Road. There were also cattle forwardings from Minsterley and Pontesbury.

GB

Shrewsbury *The mock-Tudor buildings of Shrewsbury station, photographed in 1948.* (Real Photos)

Shrewsbury & Chester Railway *Cefn Viaduct.* (Steamchest Collection)

SHREWSBURY & CHESTER RAILWAY

The first constituent of the Shrewsbury & Chester Railway was the North Wales Mineral Railway which was incorporated on 6 August 1844 and opened its main line from Saltney Junction to Ruabon (qv) on 4 November 1846. The section from Wrexham (qv) to Ruabon and the 1847 branches to Saltney Goods, Minera and from Wheatsheaf Junction were authorized by subsequent Acts. The company also obtained an Act of 30 June 1845 for the Shrewsbury, Oswestry & Chester Junction Railway, designed to counter a threat from the London & Birmingham empire and authorizing an extension to Shrewsbury. This was opened on 16 October 1848 and the Oswestry (qv) branch added on 23 December of that year.

The NWM and SOC concerns were amalgamated as the Shrewsbury & Chester Railway by an Act of 27 June 1846 and, after a period of bitter conflict with the LNWR, joined the GWR from 1 September 1854.

GB

SIGNALLING

History of GWR signalling systems

Handsignals

From June 1838 until March 1840 handsignals were given by railway policemen at the lineside or at the entrance to stations. Both arms raised above the head meant 'Danger', one arm raised meant 'Caution', and one arm held horizontally across the track meant 'All Right'. From March 1840 a signal was erected on each side of all stations. This consisted of a post carrying a metal disc which was hoisted like a flag to the masthead to indicate 'All Clear', and was lowered to the ground to indicate 'Danger'.

'Capstans'

The first type of fixed signal on the GWR was situated at the rare facing points in running lines. This was the 'Capstan', a vertical, hollow, fluted, cast iron column about 4 ft tall, painted dark green, which stood close to the point blades. A connecting rod from the points was joined to a crank which was turned by a vertical rod rising through the centre of the capstan to a horizontal handle at the top. The handle moved through a quadrant frame and could be padlocked in the 'normal' or 'reverse' position. Above the handle was a disc; its face, a white disc with a red peripheral ring, was turned towards approaching trains when the facing points were set for the straight run, or was turned edge-on when they were set for the turnout.

'Disc & Crossbar' signals

From November 1840 Brunel's system of 'Disc & Crossbar' and 'Flag' signals were erected, and were brought into use from February 1841. This signal was operated by the policeman and consisted of a very tall wooden mast carrying the 'bar'—15 in deep by 8 ft long—below and at right-angles to a 4 ft diameter disc. Both bar and disc were perforated to reduce wind resistance and both were painted bright red for greatest visibility at long range. The bar indicated 'Danger—Stop', the Disc 'All Right'. In 1852 the bar of the 'Disc & Crossbar' signal relating to the down line was given downwards-pointing square lugs, and between 1852 and 1855 the bar of such a signal at a level crossing, which applied to both up and down lines, was given 'T' ends, ie both up and down projections. A 'Disc & Crossbar' signal on a branch line—approaching a trailing junction with a main line—consisted of two discs, one above the other, and two bars, also one above the other. Drivers approaching the facing points of a junction met an ordinary 'Disc & Crossbar' signal and the 'lie' of the points was indicated by the disc or apparent lack of a disc above the point capstan. The 'Disc & Crossbar' was the standard signal on the broad gauge GWR until 1865 when it began, slowly, to be replaced by semaphores; no new 'Disc & Crossbars' were built after 1869, but as late as 1881, second-hand lightweight 'Disc & Crossbar' signals, worked by lever from a signal box, were installed in new works (see 'Yeovil' in *Great Western Junction Stations* by Adrian Vaughan, Ian Allan, 1989).

Flag signals and Caution boards

Alongside the 'Disc & Crossbar' was the Caution flag signal consisting of an 'inverted triangle' frame on a mast. Hanging from the upper edge and gathered to a point at the base were two flags, or curtains, one red and the other green. These flag signals were, however, ill-considered; the wind tore them to shreds and they were soon replaced by a wooden 'Caution board'. One end of the board was pointed, the other end 'V'-shaped. When the pointed end was nearest the track the board showed a red 'Danger' face to approaching trains; when the 'V' end was nearest the track, a green 'Caution' face was shown. Night time signals were red for 'Danger', green for 'Caution', and white for 'All Right'.

Auxiliary signals

A distant sighting of the 'Disc & Crossbar' was essential as the trains had poor brakes and a good stopping distance was required. From 1852 an 'auxiliary' signal, either a 'Caution board' or a 'Disc & Crossbar', was placed 3–400 yards to the rear of the 'Home' 'Disc & Crossbar' at those locations where a distant view could not be obtained. The auxiliary signal was worked by hand or by a capstan and double wire, but later the signal was operated by a single wire and ground lever.

Time interval working

Only an interval of time could be maintained between trains in the absence of electrical communications. When shunting was blocking the line at a station, or for 3 minutes after a train had departed therefrom, the bar of the 'Disc & Crossbar' signal was turned 'on' to face oncoming traffic (the disc being edgeways-on was thus almost invisible to approaching trains). The red face of the Caution board was also turned to face the approaching train. After 3 minutes the bar was turned 'off' and the disc therefore turned 'on', and the Caution board was turned to show its green face to an approaching train. This indication was held for 7 minutes, after which the Caution board was turned edgeways-on to the trains.

In 1852 the time intervals were altered. After the passing of a passenger train the signals were held at 'Danger' for 5 minutes with a further 5 at 'Caution', after which the signals were set to 'All Right'. After a goods train the 'Danger' signal was 'on' for 8 minutes with a further 7 at 'Caution'. This thoughtful distinction between slow-moving goods trains and faster moving passenger trains was unique to the GWR. At the larger stations and all junctions and terminal stations the signals were always at 'Danger', and were 'taken off' only when a train required to enter and it was safe to do so.

Distance interval: signalling by electric telegraph, 1847–73
The electric telegraph was installed through Box Tunnel (qv) on 1 December 1847. The instruments had a 'clock face' dial, each number relating to a pre-arranged message. When an up train entered the tunnel, the Box Tunnel policeman caused the electrically driven pointer to indicate 12. The Corsham man, receiving this, understood 'Up train has entered tunnel'. The bar (and at night a red light) was put on at the Box end and no up train was permitted to enter the tunnel until the Corsham policeman transmitted 5—'Up Train is through tunnel'. The bar or red light at the Box end was then removed and the 'Caution' (proceed) aspect displayed for a certain length of time before the 'All Right' signal was put on.

A similar electric telegraph system was installed in 1852 on the steep inclines between Tetbury Road (near the present Kemble) through Sapperton tunnels (qv) and Brimscombe. The line from Birmingham Snow Hill to Hockley, opened on 14 November 1854, was signalled from the outset by electric telegraph, and shortly afterwards the system was applied to the section from Snow Hill station through the tunnel to Bordesley.

In 1855 a telegraph signalling system was installed from Gloucester to Over Junction, for Gloucester Docks.

Block working *Webb-Thompson Electric Train Staff instruments; the 'staffs' are stored in the base of the instrument before withdrawal. Llanybyther (Pencader-Aberystwyth), 1962.* (All photos in this section by Adrian Vaughan unless otherwise credited)

Block working *Tyers' No 7 electric tablet instrument (right), and (left) a GWR electric key token instrument showing the key tokens in the magazine. Yarnton Junction, 1955.*

Single line working

Electric telegraph and crossing order
Trains were advised forward to the opposite end of the section by single-needle telegraph, and the timetabled 'crossing places' were strictly adhered to unless very late running forced a telegraphic alteration. The first single tracks to be so controlled were Grange Court to Hereford (17½ miles) with a crossing loop at Ross (all qv), opened in two sections (July 1853 and June 1855), and the 60-mile Wilts, Somerset & Weymouth Railway (qv) with its 24¾-mile branch to Salisbury, opened in stages between 1851 and 1857, which was so signalled from 1856. Scores of miles of track were operated by telegraph alone without the security of a Train Staff (qv below); the WS&WR was not equipped with the train staff until 1877.

Train Staff & Ticket
This was introduced on the Princes Risborough–Oxford (Kennington Junction) line (qv) from November 1864. There was one wooden Train Staff and as many Tickets as required. If there was more than one train to go from 'A' to 'B', the first and subsequent trains carried a Ticket and the last one carried the Train Staff to 'B'. Once the Train Staff was at 'B', trains could only run from 'B' to 'A' until the staff returned to 'A'. The trains were not at first worked by the Absolute Block System (qv below) but went forward (provided they had the Staff or a Ticket) at their scheduled time, the subsequent 'follower(s)', if any, leaving according to time interval procedure (qv above). By 1870 the security of 'block' working by Spagnoletti instruments (qv below) had been added. In 1873, 494 miles of single track were signalled under Absolute Block regulations and 224 miles on time interval. In 1879 there were 626 miles under Absolute Block and 179 miles under time interval.

Absolute Block working
This was introduced with the Train Staff & Ticket on the single line between Bristol and New Passage in 1864, using Spagnoletti double line instruments (qv below) and bell. The Electric Train Staff was used from 1891 on the Dawlish seawall section. The Tyers No 7 Electric Train Tablet was used from 1909 on the Fairford branch (qv) between Yarnton Junction and Bampton, and the Electric Key Token from 1914 between Bourne End and Marlow (qv) (Figure 4).

The Tablet instrument had a complicated routine for removing or replacing a Tablet, but all three types of instrument had the same intention—to dispense only one Staff/Tablet/Token (S/T/T) at a time and not to dispense another until the first was replaced in the same instrument or the one at the other end of the section. The routine for removing or replacing the S/T/T was a co-operative one between the two signalmen concerned. The S/T/Ts were all keyed to fit only the instruments they belonged to.

Ganger's occupation key on single lines
This system was introduced from 1928. Before the permanent-way department obstructed a single line, the Ganger obtained a key from an instrument kept in a lineside hut. The key was released electrically by the co-operation of the signalmen at each end of the section using special instruments. The release of the key interrupted the electric circuits connecting the Train Staff instruments.

Spagnoletti's Disc Block Telegraph Instrument
C. E. Spagnoletti (qv) patented this device in 1863, and it became the standard GWR train signalling instrument. In 1880 there were 3,158 Spagnoletti, 322 Tyers, 20 Russell and 159 single-needle instruments in use for signalling trains.

There were separate 'keyed' and 'keyless' instruments in each signal box. The keyed instrument transmitted 'Line Clear' or 'Train on Line' to the box in rear and also displayed these messages. The white key was pegged down to bring the 'Line Clear' indication (or 'disc') into view, and the red key was pegged down, after the white key had been released, to display 'Train on Line'. These displays were repeated on the 'keyless' instrument at the box in rear. This system required four instruments on the 'block shelf'. The first 'keyed' and the 'keyless' instruments combined in one cabinet were probably introduced in 1905 when a more compact system was required above the miniature power frame at Didcot North Junction.

Block working *Spagnoletti 1863-type 'keyless' (left) and 'keyed' (right) block instruments and block bell (centre). Weston Rhyn, 1977.* (John Morris)

Absolute Block working on double lines

This system was developed from 1863, the object being to prevent more than one train occupying a block section between two signal boxes at the same time. Spagnoletti's instrument (qv above) was standard from the outset, but in the early period a Tyers instrument was used at some West Midlands and South Wales locations and on ex-Bristol & Exeter lines.

Between January and August 1863, the GWR was responsible for the operation of the double-track 'Underground' line of the Metropolitan Railway from Paddington (Bishops Road) to Farringdon with Spagnoletti instruments. They were also introduced from Paddington to West London Junction and from Ruabon to Cefn in 1863. In April 1865 the up line only, from Goring to Pangbourne, was made a 'block section', followed by Paddington to Ealing in 1867, to Slough in 1870, to Goring by December 1872, from Bristol to Thingley in 1872, and Thingley to Goring in December 1873. The Oxford branch was 'blocked' by 1874, Oxford to Leamington was complete by March 1880 and to Chester in 1883. The Bristol & Exeter Railway (qv) was already block signalled when it was absorbed into the GWR in 1876.

The 1863 block system assumed that the line was clear unless stated otherwise. The signals were normally in the 'All Right' position and the Spagnoletti instrument was pegged to 'Line Clear'. When a train passed Box 'A' the signalman there sent the 'Train on Line' code and the man receiving this unpegged his white and pegged down his red key. When that train passed within the protection of the Home signal at Box 'B', or in some cases when it had passed clear of 'B' station, the 'B' signalman placed his Home signal to 'Danger', sent 3 bell beats and pegged 'Line Clear' to 'A', whereupon 'A' lowered his signals once more for the section towards 'B'.

The bell codes in 1871 were:

	Beats
Passenger Train or Empty Engine on Line	1
Goods Train on Line	2
Line Clear	3
Branch Train (only on main line to junction)	4
Line Blocked	5
Stop Train Last Signalled	6
Testing	10

From November 1883 the 'open track' principle was abolished, the line was considered blocked until stated otherwise and the signals remained normally at 'Danger'. The Spagnoletti instrument had no means of showing 'Line Blocked', so this was indicated by the 'half and half' position, with both keys unpegged. The signalman at 'A' now had to ask 'Is Line Clear?' to 'B' before he could lower his signals. If the line at 'B' was clear to a specified 'clearing point' ahead of the Home signal, signalman 'B' repeated the bell code and pegged down his white key, whereupon 'A' lowered his signals. As late as 1886 the extent of the clearing point varied, from 457 yards at Abergavenny Junction to 18 yards ahead of the Home signal at Gloucester No 6 box. The standard clearing point ahead of the Home signal became 440 yards by 1904.

The 'Regulations for Train Signalling' stated: 'Unless special instructions are issued to the contrary, the line must not be considered clear, nor must a train be allowed to approach from the signal box in rear, until the preceeding train has passed at least ¼ mile beyond the home signal and all points within this distance have been placed in their proper position and the line is clear for at least ¼ mile ahead of the home signal.' (GWR Regulation 4, 1936)

GWR standard bell-codes

	Beats
Call Attention	1
(Emergency call attention A number of beats in rapid succession)	
'Is Line Clear?' for:	
Express passenger train, express diesel railcar, breakdown van train going to clear the line, 'light engine' going to assist disabled train, empty coaching stock timed at express speed? ('A' headlamps)	4
Ordinary passenger train, 'mixed' train, breakdown van train not going to clear the line? ('B' headlamps)	3–1
Branch passenger train (only on main line to junction)? ('B' headlamps)	1–3
Rail motor-car, auto-train or streamline railcar? ('B' headlamps)	3–1–3
Parcels, newspaper, fish, meat, fruit, milk, horse, cattle or perishable train composed entirely of vacuum-fitted stock with the vacuum pipe connected to the engine? ('D' headlamps)	5
Express freight, livestock, perishable or ballast train partly vacuum fitted with not more than one-third vacuum braked vehicles connected by vacuum pipe to the engine? ('D' headlamps)	4–4
Express freight, or ballast train conveying a stipulated number of vacuum-braked vehicles connected by vacuum pipe to the engine and authorised to run at a maximum speed of 35 mph?	2–2–3
Empty coach stock train not specially authorised to carry 'A' headlamps? ('D' headlamps)	2–2–1
Express freight, fish, meat, ftuit or cattle train, ballast train or breakdown van train not proceeding to an accident? ('E' headlamps)	3–2
Through fast freight train conveying through load? ('F' headlamps)	1–4
Light engine or light engines coupled together or engine and brake van? ('G' headlamps)	2–3
Freight, mineral or ballast train or train of empties carrying through load to destination? ('H' headlamps)	3–4–1
Freight, mineral or ballast train stopping at intermediate stations? ('J' headlamps)	3
Train conveying out of gauge or exceptional load? ('J' headlamps)	2–6–2
Branch freight train (only on main line to junction)? ('K' headlamps)	1–2
Ballast train, freight train or inspection train requiring to stop in section? ('K' headlamps)	1–2–2
Trolley requiring to go into or pass through tunnel	2–1–2
Train approaching	1–2–1
Train entering section	2
Section clear but station or junction blocked	3–5–5
Line clear to clearing point only	2–2–2
Engine assisting in rear of train	2–2
Train out of section, or obstruction removed	2–1
Engine arrived	2–1–3
Train drawn back clear of station	3–2–3
Blocking back inside home signal	2–4
Blocking back outside home signal	3–3
Blocking back outside home signal for train already in section	1–2–3
Shunt train for following train to pass	1–5–5
Opening signal box	5–5–5
Closing signal box	7–5–5
Testing bells	16
Time signal	8–5–5
Lampman or fogman required	9–5–5
Testing slotted signal	5–5–5–5
Take off slot train waiting	3–4
Cancel 'Is Line Clear?'	3–5
Emergency bell signals:	
Obstruction danger	6
Stop and examine train	7
Train passed without tail lamp	
To box in advance	9
To box in rear	4–5
Train divided	5–5
Train or vehicles running away on right line	4–5–5
Train or vehicles running away on wrong line	2–5–5

There were exemptions to this rule, for example under the 'Warning Arrangement' (Regulation 5). If, when the box in rear asked 'Is Line Clear?', the line was not clear in accordance with Regulation 4, some signal boxes were permitted to accept the train under the 'Warning Arrangement'. The signalman replied to the 'Is Line Clear?' with bell code 3-5-5, and the signalman receiving this gave warning to the driver that the section ahead was clear but that the clearing point at the signal box in advance was blocked.

Standard bell-codes

These codes were subject to revision over the years, but the list on the previous page is taken from 'GWR Regulations for Train Signalling on Double Lines', 1936.

Semaphore signals

Semaphore signal posts

First type: Wooden, parallel sides, square section with a pivot through the middle at the top of which the signal arm was attached. Very large 'ball and spike' finial.

Second type: Wooden, square section, tapered 1 in 50 to a cast-iron 'ball and spike' finial. The latter had at least 2 types of perforations in the ball, which was painted red on a stop signal and yellow on a Distant signal.

Lattice-work metal: Used at a few locations from the late 1890s. A large lattice-work gantry was erected over the up lines at Westbourne Park, Paddington, before 1902.

Concrete posts: First used about 1917.

Tubular steel posts: First used by contractors in the Basildon (Berks) intermediate block signals, 1907, and at Paddington with the American-style, three-position, upper-quadrant signal in 1914. The first GWR tubular steel posts appeared about 1925.

In 1929 the GWR stated that it had erected 170 wooden, 17 concrete and 9 tubular steel signal posts. By 1934 tubular steel posts had become the official replacement for wood.

Semaphore 'stop' signals

All running-line signal arms were painted red with a vertical white stripe and between 1865 and 1873 showed three positions: arm horizontal, 'Danger'; arm at 45° 'Caution'; arm within the post, 'All Right'. After 1 June 1873 the 'Caution' position was abolished and a handsignal substituted.

After the GNR Abbots Ripton crash of January 1876, the GWR commenced to mount a pivot casting on the outside of the post, and the 'All Right' was given when the arm was lowered to 60°.

Semaphore 'Distant' signals

These were placed a distance to the rear of the first stop signal, depending on the braking distance required, to give warning of the need to stop at that signal, or that the road was clear. The arms were red with a square end and a vertical white stripe, and showed a red light for 'Danger'. From 1876 they had a 'V'-notched end and a white chevron, but there was no differentiation between a Distant signal's red light and that on a 'Danger' signal. From 1925, starting in the Paddington–Southall area, Distant signals were given an amber light instead of red and a yellow arm with a black chevron. The change was completed throughout the railway in 1933.

Distant signals on single lines

All signal boxes on single lines once had working Distant signals, and directing Distant signals were, at some places, provided on the approach to low-speed divergences at crossing loops. From 1906, most Distant signals were 'fixed' by being bolted to the post. Where a box could be switched out and a 'straight run' through the station was possible, the lever operating the Distant signal was locked at 'Caution' until the box was switched out of circuit and the road set for the straight run. At level crossings, if there was no speed restriction over facing points, the Distant signals remained operative.

Distant signals approaching terminal stations

These were originally worked, but were fixed at 'Danger' from 1906 except in very special cases, eg Chelsea Basin.

Note that while Distant signal arms were red, they were, when horizontal, considered to be showing 'Danger'.

Slotted signals

When two signal boxes were so close together that the Starting signal of one acted as the Home signal for the other, that arm had to be controlled—'slotted'—by both signalmen. When the Distant signal for one box was placed below the Home or Starting signal of the box in rear, a slotting device prevented the Distant signal from being lowered until the stop signal had lowered.

The 'slotted' arm was lowered by the counterbalance weight on the left of the accompanying photograph. This weight was operated by gravity alone and was supported in the 'Danger' or 'Caution' position by both counter-balance weights on the right. The photograph shows one lever-operated counter-balance weight reversed, leaving the left-hand weight still supported by one weight. When both supports are removed, the slotted arm's weight drops to lower the signal.

Slotted signals *The arms counter-balanced on the right of the post are operated by two adjacent boxes, Hinksey North and Oxford Station South; only when both are pulled 'off' will the weight to the left fall and move the appropriate signal arm.*

Junction signalling

Semaphore signals indicating the route approaching a facing junction, were, at first, either two or more vertically arranged arms, the top arm applying to the straight run and the lower arm to the divergence, or on separate posts, the tallest referring to the main line at the junction, the shorter post applying to the divergence and placed to the left or right of the main post as appropriate. Sometimes the posts were separated by the entire width of the track bed, as at Kennington Junction (1874). The Distant signals applying to the junction signals were arranged in like manner. A working Distant signal was provided for all diverging routes at junctions irrespective of any speed restriction over the turn-out. Following the Aylesbury crash of 23 April 1904, directing Distant signals for diverging lines were removed unless a speed of 40 mph or more was permissible over the divergence. Additional stop signals to the rear of the junction signals were also arranged to show the direction set at the junction.

Bracket signals

These in use by 1880 and took the form of a timber main post located centrally under a timber crossbeam on which were mounted the short timber posts, or 'dolls', carrying the junction signals. The main mast and crossbeam were braced by cast-iron spandrels and later by 'X' bracing. The 'T'-shaped bracket for two-doll signals was finally superceded by the timber 'off-set' type of bracket signal which was in use by 1893. The older type continued in use for many years.

The soffit of the off-set bracket was a steel quadrant to accord with the curve of the roofs passing beneath, and was braced to the horizontal platform above by steel struts. Concrete main posts had a wooden 'doll' and a simple steel quadrant supporting the platform. Wooden main posts usually had wooden 'dolls', but in the Paddington 1928–33 colour-light signalling scheme, wooden main posts supported a platform 'T'-fashion which carried tubular steel 'dolls'. Tubular steel main posts supporting a traditionally curved bracket appeared in 1939/40. They invariably had tubular steel 'dolls'. In 1942 the curved soffit on these signals was replaced with a rectangular, 'N'-braced girder, and in 1944 solid steel plate replaced this type in rare instances. GWR tubular steel two-'doll' bracket signals had all the 'dolls' to the left or right of the main mast.

The arms on any bracket signal were arranged to indicate the layout of the junction ahead, with the highest arm applying to the fastest line—unless speed was equal over both divergences, when the arms were placed at the same height.

Bracket signals *A 1939-type tubular steel example, with a GWR 1942 tubular steel gantry in the background. BR(WR) arms on GWR spectacles. Hinksey North, 1970.*

Signal arms

Arms were originally wooden. The standard size for a main-line signal, since about 1887, was 4 ft by 1 ft, except when the arm was more than 26 ft above the rails, when the length was 5 ft. Posts more than 30 ft high were fitted with a mechanism to enable the lampman to raise and lower the signal lamp from ground level. All 'running' signal arms were red with a white stripe including, at first, Distant signals (qv above).

Until 1895 the 'spectacle' in front of the lamp was a single, circular frame (No 1, author's classification), holding a red glass. When the arm was lowered, the white light of the lamp was seen. In 1895 green became the colour for 'All Right', necessitating a two-glass spectacle (No 2), which was attached to each arm by a narrow casting. Installation of the 'No 2' spectacle took seven years, during which time some signals still showed a white light for 'All Right'. The No 2 spectacle was only used on arms fixed to timber posts.

Signal arms *1895-type spectacle with a BR(WR) arm. Newbury West, 1971.*

In the mid-1920s a vitreous enamelled steel arm with beaded edges and No 2 spectacle came into use.

3 ft, 4 ft and 5 ft arms for tubular steel posts were beaded-edged enamelled steel with a new spectacle (No 3), which was a solid casting as deep as the arm to which it was attached. The No 3 spectacle was used on steel and wooden posts. About 1946 an un-beaded arm with simple, right-angled stiffening was introduced.

Symmetrically balanced arms

These were designed for restricted clearances, and were wooden in 4 ft, 3 ft 9 in and 3 ft sizes, red with a vertical white stripe. They were pivoted at the centre of the arm, with a red light within the arm and a green light in the spectacle below. There were no steel arms in this form. Large diameter disc signals similar in appearance to ground disc signals (qv below) were used instead of symmetrically balanced arms at a few locations, notably Worcester and Gloucester.

Duplicate arm

This was fixed low so as to be seen below the arch of a bridge, and repeated the aspect of the top arm. Duplicate arms were 4 ft long, of the 'stop' or 'distant' types. The signal glass, red or amber, was within the arm, the green aspect in a spectacle above the arm.

Subsidiary signals (old style)

Shunt

Wooden, red, 3 ft long with a large white 'S'. The Shunt signal was placed below the lowest main arm and had a No 3-type spectacle. When lowered it permitted a driver to pass the section signal for the purpose of shunting, e.g. to draw the rear of his train clear of a set of points prior to reversing into a siding or across a crossover.

Calling-on

Wooden, red, 2 ft long with screwed-on small white letters 'CO'. The red light (where fitted) was within the arm, the green spectacle above the arm, both lights to the left of the post. When lowered, it permitted a driver to pass the main arm and proceed to the rear of a train ahead.

Warning

Wooden, red, 2 ft long with a screwed-on small white letter 'W'. Lights as Calling-on arm. It indicated to the driver that the section was clear but the station or junction ahead was blocked.

Signal arms *Backing signal with a beaded-edge steel arm and a three-stencil route indicator showing the opal glass background. Castle Cary, 1974.*

Backing

Wooden, red, 3 ft and 2 ft long, with two holes side by side. Route-indicating screw-on letters were applied when necessary.

Note: Shunt, Calling-on and Warning arms displayed red light 'Danger' and green 'Proceed'. Backing arms and signals within sidings displayed a white light at 'Danger', green 'Proceed'. Screw-on or painted letters were superceded by stencil Route Indicator (qv) displays.

Subsidiary signals (new style)

Steel-armed, vitreous enamel, beaded-edged subsidiary signals were in use from about 1930. The arms were 2 ft long, white, with a red horizontal stripe along each beaded edge. They were used in lieu of the old 'Shunt', 'Calling-on' and 'Warning' arms and showed a white light when at 'Danger', and a green 'Proceed' aspect. When lowered they exposed a letter 'W', 'S' or 'CO'. Illuminated at night, sometimes this was on a separate display.

Main line to goods loop/Goods loop to main

Red, 3 ft long, vertical white stripe and No 3-type spectacle. Red light at 'Danger'.

Signal arms *Old-pattern (left) and new pattern (right) subsidiary signals beneath a symmetrically balanced arm employed because of limited space or clearances. Exeter West, 1971.*

Siding to main line

Narrow, steel, red, 3 ft long with a white ring and elongated spectacle. Full depth arms had the No 3-type spectacle. White light at 'Danger'.

Goods loop to siding/Siding to siding

Steel arm, red, 2 ft by 9 in, white-ringed. Narrow, elongated spectacle. White light at 'Danger'.

Different length arms were used according to the status of the line, main running, loop or siding.

Ground disc signals

Originally the movement of the point blades operated a lamp case with a red or white and a green light/sector. Independent ground signals at points were cast-iron, miniature red semaphore arms, with cast apertures for lights introduced about 1895. From May 1915 a semi-circular white disc with a horizontal red stripe was bolted to existing ground signals. A new design introduced in 1915 was a tall, tapered casting, with a capped top and supporting a 16 in diameter white, beaded-edged steel disc with a horizontal red stripe and apertures for red/white and green lights. Up to three discs (reduced to 11 ¼ in diameter) were placed on these castings. In 1932 a short casting for up to three discs was introduced. Discs with a yellow stripe were used where it was permissible to pass the disc in the 'Danger' position.

Route Indicators

These were placed below or to one side of a signal, instead of using a bracket signal, and were used in goods lines/yards and at low-speed locations at stations. Cut-out metal letters were raised and displayed against an opal glass background, illuminated from behind at night. Indicators were introduced at Paddington in 1909, and saved the cost of large signals and several lamps, and reduced the number of signals in densely signalled areas.

Signal lights

From 1838 until 1895, the rule was that 'White is right and Red is Wrong, Green means gently go along'. The fitting of red/blue glasses on signals commenced in 1895 and was completed in 1902. The light was green when a yellow flame shone through a blue glass. Distant signal red lights were not generally differentiated from stop signal red lights until 1927, when an amber glass replaced the red and the arm was coloured yellow with a black chevron. This modification was not complete until 1933.

Power signalling

Opposite is a list of GWR power signalling installations.

Ground disc signals *Original miniature-semaphore-arm variety, with later disc attached. Witham, Somerset, 1974.*

Location	Brought into use	Taken out of use	Manufacturer/notes
Didcot North Junc	16.7.05	1927	Siemens point motors, signal fittings and relays.
Basildon (Berks) IBS	6.07	1965	Large number of Intermediate Block signals (including one in the Severn Tunnel, 11/1941-early 1944)
Wood Lane Junc	1908	19.6.38	Junction with the GWR's all-electric Ealing & Shepherds Bush Rly, now part of Central Line.
Yarnton Junction	31.6.09	30.7.29	McKenzie & Holland/Westinghouse (a)
Birmingham North	31.10.09	11.9.60	Siemens Bros (a)
Hockley South	21.7.12	1.12.68	Siemens Bros (a)
Birmingham South	1913	11.9.60	Siemens Bros (a)
Slough Bath Road	1913	8.4.31	McKenzie & Holland (b)
Paddington	11.1915	1927	Three-aspect, upper quadrant (c)
Wolverhampton South	7.1925		Three-aspect upper quadrant (d)
Winchester	3.22	6.33	Siemens Bros (e)
Newport East & West	29.5.27	9.12.62	Siemens Bros (e)
Rogerstone Hump	1.6.31	9.12.68	Descubes system (f)
Banbury Hump	7.31	15.8.71	Descubes system (f)
Westbourne Bridge	10.1.32	15.10.67	General Railway Signal Co (GRS) (g)
Cardiff East	28/5/33	27/3/66	Westinghouse (a)
Paddington Departure	2.7.33	15.10.67	GRS (g)
Paddington Arrival	13.8.33	19.11.67	GRS (g)
Cardiff West	7.1.34	27.3.66	Westinghouse (b)
Bristol Temple Meads Loco Yd	9.12.34	17.3.70	GRS (g)
Bristol Temple Meads West	26.5.35	12.4.70	GRS (g)
Reading Main Line East	16.3.41	4.1965	Siemens & General Electric Signalling Co (h)
Severn Tunnel down hump	1.10.39	12.82	S&GERS Co (f)
Severn Tunnel up hump	1941	24.4.65	S&GERS Co (f)

Notes on the table

(a) Miniature levers at 2½ in centres. Electric

(b) Electro-pneumatic.

(c) Three-position upper quadrant semaphores operated by track circuits. Raised vertically, 'All Right'; raised 45°, 'Warning'; horizontal, 'Danger'. Acted as section signal for Departure box on down main.

(d) Aspects as (c)

(e) Miniature levers at 2½ in centres. Electric. 'Route-setting', ie one lever set up an entire route and cleared signals.

(f) Push-button operation, electro pneumatic.

(g) Draw-slides. Electric.

(h) Miniature levers at 2½ in centres, 37-lever frame at London end of box to operate wartime 'New Junction' with SR Electric frame mechanically interlocked with 185-lever manual frame working main layout.

Interlocking systems

Mechanical interlocking of levers

The object of interlocking signal and point levers is to prevent the setting up of conflicting routes. The best interlocking machine was that using the principle of 'Initial and Final Motion' which should have three distinct phases: conflicting levers should be locked instantly a lever is moved; the mechanism should then remain at rest until the pulled lever is fully reversed; then the necessary levers should be unlocked. Most successful was the 'Tappet' system invented by James Deakin and patented by Stevens in 1870.

Lane's patent, 1865

The first interlocked lever frame built at Reading Signal Works (qv) was to Chief (Civil) Engineer Michael Lane's (qv) patent design of 1865 and was used at Didcot in that year. Lane's mechanism did not, however, adhere to the best locking principles. A rack was attached to each lever, and when the lever was reversed the rack drove a pinion which moved locking-bars horizontally to lock or release levers. This locking and releasing took place progressively over the stroke of the lever, and the mechanism soon became slack with wear.

Single Twist

Invented in the GWR Signal Works at Reading in 1870 and manufactured 1870–1890, this replaced the wear-prone rack by a 'twist bar', otherwise the locking action was identical to the Lane frame.

Each lever carried a pair of 2¾ in tall, vertical rollers just below floor level. Between these rollers passed a bar 2½ in deep, ¾ in thick and with a pronounced twist about its horizontal axis at the leading end. The lever's initial movement moved the rollers along the bar, the twist of which forced it to rotate. The movement thus derived drove a vertical connecting rod at the lower end of which was a toothed cog engaged in a short rack. The rack was forced sideways and moved the locking-bars. However, it locked and released in one movement which was unsatisfactory since a signal lever was released from its lock before the point lever to which it applied was fully reversed.

The levers were placed in a row parallel to the front wall of the box and were spaced at 5¼ in centres. When 'Normal' in the frame the levers were almost upright, leaning slightly towards the front wall; when reversed they were still fairly upright. Twist frames had, for the signalman to walk on, long, relatively flat cast-iron 'sweeps'. The sweeps lay between fixed 'quadrants' between the levers and clanked as one walked along them. The 'sweeps' were well

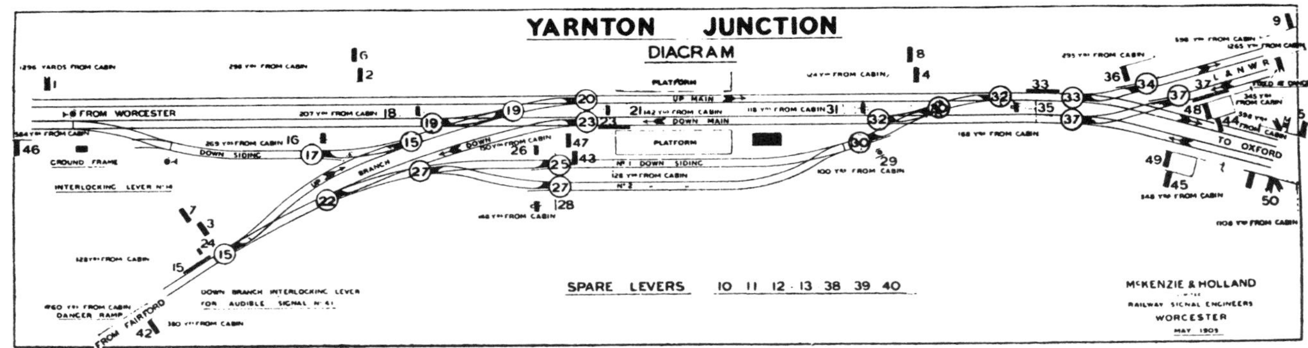

Power signalling *Diagram for the 1909 installation at Yarnton Junction.* (GWR Magazine)

made with 19 raised ribs to provide a foot-grip. Some 'sweeps' had a raised 'footrest' of doubtful value. A Twist frame was distinctive to the ear and eye. Below floor level the locking mechanism was cumbersome and required considerable height, requiring unnecessarily large signal boxes.

Double Twist
Manufactured 1890–1906, the twist bar was now given two rotational segments, one at the start of the lever's travel and one at the end so as to hold other levers locked until the releasing lever had been fully reversed. Otherwise the system was identical to the Single Twist and suffered from the same problem—wear in the many moving parts and complication of construction, alteration and maintenance. Some Double Twist frames lasted into the mid-1980s. The Radstock North frame is now at the Great Western Society site at Didcot, and Sarnau is at Scolton Manor, Haverfordwest.

Stud
Manufactured 1892–1908. The levers had $5\frac{1}{4}$ in and 4 in centres, and were identical to a Double Twist frame above floor level except where levers were at 4 in centres. Below the floor the locking was on the tappet principle. Each lever had a blade or blades attached horizontally and then curving downwards. These blades were edge-notched to accept locking studs. Some blades had a central slot and acted as a cam-plate to drive the locking studs sideways into or out of the notches. Studs were linked by bridle irons to carry the locking action along the length of the frame, but this system was not suitable for frames of more than 37 levers. Stud frames remained in use at various locations at least until 1970.

Horizontal Tappet
Manufactured 1904–1926. Between 1904 and 1908, the levers, at $5\frac{1}{4}$ in centres, looked like a Twist Frame from above. The first known example was installed at Cardiff West (75 levers) in December 1904. From 1908–1926, the levers were at 4 in centres, and the first known example was at Cleobury Mortimer (October 1908). The frame had a revised 'sweeps' design—a narrow casting lying loose between fixed quadrants between the levers. The levers travelled through an arc of 31.3° when reversed. Below the floor, Mk 1 and Mk 2 were very similar. Each lever had a horizontal, slotted cam-plate within which was a

Interlocking systems *'Double twist' frame. Note the wide 'sweeps' and rather upright levers. Uffington, 1962.*

Interlocking systems *The 'double twist' bars seen when the 'sweeps' are removed, the lever being 'normal' in the frame – note the twist at each end of the bar.*

Interlocking systems *'Stud' locking. Note the difference in 'sweep' design between the twist and stud frames. The locking blades are attached to the levers below the lever quadrants. Hamstead Crossing, 1964.*

roller attached to a connecting rod. When the lever was moved the connecting rod was driven vertically $1\frac{3}{4}$ in to a crank attached to horizontal tappet blades.

The tappet blades were edge-notched to take locking-nibs. Each row of locking-nibs across the frame was covered by three horizontal locking-bars which were or were not riveted to the various nibs according to requirements. The sideways movement imparted to one nib by its tappet blade was transmitted by the locking-bars to other nibs to lock/unlock other tappet blades and therefore the levers to which they were attached.

Interlocking systems *'Stud' locking. The locking blade of one lever can be seen projecting through the locking tray, the lever having been reversed.*

Vertical tappet

Manufactured 1909–1966. Between 1909 and 1923 the levers were at 4 in centres, with three-bar locking, and were identical above the floor to the later Horizontal Tappet frame. Below the floor the tappet mechanism was arranged vertically, the tappet blades being driven directly by the camplate and roller. In 1923 the 'three-bar' design was upgraded with two extra locking-bars across the rear face of each nib to achieve 'five-bar' locking and a greater number of locking permutations. Above the floor the appearance was unchanged.

In 1926 a new 'five-bar Vertical Tappet' frame was introduced. This was the final development of mechanical interlocking on the GWR. The Mk 3 Vertical Tappet had a revised design above the floor: the cast-iron 'sweeps' had a 'humped' appearance compared with all earlier frames; they occupied the full width between the levers and were bolted down, the reverse position notch being in the casting. There were four ribs between the reverse notch and the floor, and 11 ribs in the main part. Wooden blocks finished off the ends of the frame. The levers passed through a 40° arc; a signalman used to levers in a Double Twist frame found he was 'leaning over backwards' when pulling Vertical Tappet levers.

The largest five-bar frame installed was 206 levers at Newton Abbot East, but Reading Main Line West's 222-lever, three-bar frame was re-locked with a five-bar mechanism in 1943. The last large new frame to be built at Reading Works to this 1926 GWR standard pattern was 125 levers for Llandilo Junction in 1966.

Electric interlocking of block instruments and Distant signal

This was introduced in 1909. The block telegraph 'Line Clear' circuit to the box in rear was interrupted until the Distant signal arm was within 5° of horizontal and the lever was properly 'Normal' in the frame.

Electric interlocking of the section (stop) signal through the 'Line Clear' indication from the box in advance was in use from 1907 and was extended gradually over time, but many boxes never had this feature. The lever for the section signal was

Interlocking systems *The vertical tappet locking cam is fully extended, its lever having been reversed. The slot is shaped to drive a roller, seen in the bottom position of the recess, having moved the attached tappet blade downwards. Notched tappet blades and locks can be seen, together with the horizontal bars connecting various locks across the mechanism.*

Interlocking systems *Vertical tappet. Operating floor view, with 'leaning back' levers and 'humped' 'sweeps'. Hinksey North, 1970.*

Detonator placers *A two-lever frame to operate detonator placers on the up and down lines at Oxford Station South, 1970.*

electrically locked until 'Line Clear' was pegged by the signalman in advance, and the latter could not peg 'Line Clear' unless his Home and Distant signals were at 'Danger' and the levers were 'Normal' in the frame.

Other signalling equipment and devices

Block Switch
This was introduced generally from 1909 and over many years subsequently to permit signal boxes to be taken out of circuit at certain periods of the day or at weekends. By turning a switch in 'Box B', the block telegraph circuits into 'Box B' from 'A' and 'C' were connected directly between those two boxes.

Detection
Point blades and facing point bolts (qv below), when moved by the lever, moved detection slides, metal plates with rectangular ports cut into them. These detection slides lay at right-angles to the signal wires which also carried metal plates which had to pass through the notches when the signal wire was pulled. If the point blades or facing point bolt had not gone fully home, the detection slide ports would not be in line with the signal wire plates, which could not then pass; thus the signal could not be lowered.

To prove that a set of points had properly answered the lever, electric detection was introduced with the Didcot electric power signalling (qv above), but was not widely used until after 1923 and the development of the motor point (qv below).

Detonator placers
The signalman reversed a black-and-white-banded lever to place two detonators on the rail in an emergency and during fog or falling snow, when a train was approaching for which 'Line Clear' had not been obtained from the box in advance. Prior to 1915, 800 'placers' were in use; by 1919, 2,027 were in use. Most of these were separate two-lever frames for up and down line. In all new frames from 1919, full-size levers within the frame were provided for this function.

Facing point bolt
Driven by a lever in the signal box, this was a strong, steel bar which was a perfect fit in either of two ports cut in the stretcher-bar tying across the blades of a facing point. The distance between the ports was equal to the distance travelled by the blades from 'Normal' to 'reversed'. If the facing points did not move to within 1/32 in of the full distance, the bolt and its port were not in register and the bolt could not be inserted. The lever in the box could thus not complete its travel and the mechanical interlocking (qv above) locked the facing point lever and signal levers.

Fouling bar
This device prevented the facing point bolt (qv above) being withdrawn by the signalman when a train was close to the facing points. A steel bar 60 ft long lay inside and about 1 in below the crown of the rail, attached to the facing point bolt. When the bolt moved through its complete travel, the bar was raised and lowered. If a wheel flange was on the rail above, the bar touched it and was prevented from rising; hence the facing point bolt could not be moved. Track circuits (qv below) took over the function of the fouling bar but some bars survived into the 1970s.

Gates at level crossings
As a result of Acts of Parliament of 1839 and 1845, the railway had to be fenced off, entailing gates at road/rail level crossings. These were opened by hand by a signalman or mechanically from within the signal box by means of a wheel-driven pinion working in a long rack. Raising/ lowering the rack by turning the wheel drove rodding to swing the gates. This was a difficult job in a high wind especially where the gates were wide, such as at Silk Mill Crossing where they spanned four tracks. Wicket gates beside the main gates permitted pedestrians to cross the line when the main gates were closed across the road.

Fouling bar *An example in place against the right-hand rail in advance of a facing point; the rod-and-crank lifting mechanism can be seen. Kennington Junction.*

Motor points, battery operated

Points electrically operated by a 20-volt battery were introduced in October 1923 to abolish Beaconsfield West and Gerrard's Cross East, both controlling the remote end of the platform loops to/from the main line, thus permitting the operation of the points from the larger box at the station. Their operation was, however, unsatisfactory; it took 18 seconds to move the points.

Motor points, hand-generated current

This system was patented in 1923 by Nicholson & Roberts and marketed by Westinghouse. It allowed the abolition of the small signal boxes controlling Pencader Junction and Aberayron Junction in 1929, the junctions being worked from Pencader and Lampeter boxes respectively. It also permitted the enlargement of layouts with points remote from the operating signal box, which was particularly useful on the DN&S and M&SWJ sections during the wartime extension of the layouts.

Level crossings *Magnificent gates at Hamstead Crossing. Note also a good example of a Type 8 signal box (see Signal boxes entry). 1971.*

Train Describer

This was a clockwork-electric instrument to indicate the route required to be taken by an approaching train. The signalman rang the bell code for the train and pegged the destination on the lower, transmitting, face, to the box in advance. The upper face received descriptions from the box in rear. The receiving instrument's needle at the box in advance moved and indicated accordingly. It saved telephone calls and special bell codes. (See illustration overleaf).

Signal arm repeaters

Some signal lamp cases had a small lens at the rear facing the signal box through which the signal lamp shone and was seen by the signalman. When the arm was lowered a shutter obscured this light so the signalman knew that the arm had answered the lever. Some signal arms worked an electric switch so that an electric indicator in the signal box indicated the position of the arm.

Signal lamps were also linked to an electric circuit to prove that the flame was burning. When the lamp went out an alarm bell rang.

Track circuits

A small current was fed through the running

Signal arm repeaters *Tyers' distant signal arm repeater.*

Train describers *Tyers' train describer with (left) GWR 1946-pattern block instrument. Malago Vale, Bristol, 1973.* (John Morris)

rail, the other rail acting as the 'return wire', which maintained a relay operating certain locking circuits. When 'short-circuited' by a train's wheels the relay switched off those circuits, preventing the release of electric locks on signal and point levers, interrupting the block telegraph circuit so that 'Line Clear' could not be sent to the box in rear, and operating track circuit repeaters (qv below). The first known use was at the Basildon (Berks) signals in 1907 (qv above).

Track circuit repeater
This gave a visual indication of the presence of vehicles on the track. At first a free-standing instrument on the block shelf, later the indication was incorporated in the track diagram, first by a metal ball which lifted out of sight when that section was occupied, and later by a light which came on when the track was occupied.

AV

SIGNAL & TELEGRAPH ENGINEERS

The holders of this office on the GWR were:

Telegraph Engineer

C. E. Spagnoletti	May 1855–1891
H. T. Goodenough	1891–1902

Signal Engineer

Thomas Blackall	March 1885–June 1893
A. T. Blackall	June 1893–July 1903

Signal & Telegraph Engineer

A. T. Blackall	July 1903–July 1923
R. J. Insell	July 1923–March 1928
C. M. Jacobs	April 1928–Feb 1936
F. H. D. Page	Feb 1936–April 1947
A. W. Woodbridge	April 1947–(September 1959)

(See also individual entries)

AV

SIGNAL BOXES

The signal box was a brick or timber building housing the lever frame and block telegraph instruments (both qv signalling), so that the signalman could give or refuse permission for a train to approach. It was not to be confused with a 'ground frame box', some of which were larger than some signal boxes but whose function was concerned with shunting movements.

The first signal boxes were erected from 1863. As a general guide, the GWR employed Saxby & Farmer for signal boxes between Paddington–Slough and Oxford–Birmingham; McKenzie & Holland, Newport–Cardiff, West Midlands, Shrewsbury and Chester areas and supplied their own designs for the rest.

GWR-designed signal boxes

Almost all these early boxes were replaced by GWR standard buildings. No GWR-built signal boxes had decorated barge-boards at the gable ends or a walk-way around the windows.

The following descriptions of GWR-designed signal boxes is developed from the work done by Mr Reg Instone BA and Mr John Morris for the Signalling Record Society, and from *The Signal Box* by the Signalling Study Group. The 'Type' number is the Instone/Morris classification.

Note

GWS = *A Pictorial Record of Great Western Signalling* with plate number

GWA = *A Pictorial Record of Great Western Architecture* with plate number

Both books are by Adrian Vaughan and published by OPC (see Bibliography).

Type 1
The earliest known type, erected from 1873 or earlier. Rough brick construction, ordinary gable, low, pitched roof, eaves close to wall, tall chimney, small, house-type windows with small panes, outside steps to small landing at door. (GWA 540)

Type 2
From 1877. Hip gable roof resulting in short ridge due to short length of box. Tall, metal, circular, vent, rising to a point—'rocket' ventilator—on ridge. Some boxes so short that hipped roof rose to a point, sometimes surmounted by 'rocket' vent. Improved windows, larger area, with small, square panes. Brick base to floor level and brick rear wall extending around sides to windows. Vertical timber planking from floor to eaves, sometimes replaced by horizontal planks or even bricks. Outside steps. (GWS 88, example with new, horizontal planking)

Type 3
From 1879–80. Plain gables, brick rear wall, vertical planking floor to roof at front and sides. Large, multi-square-paned windows. Outside steps to landing running width of building. Some had porch added later. Generally located in GWR southern and western areas.

Type 3 *Sarnau, 1973.* (All photos in this section Adrian Vaughan)

Horizontal planking floor to windows and on porch. Multi-square-paned large windows.

Type 4
Used *circa* 1883 on Oxford–Worcester signalling, and Kidderminster–Rowley Regis, 1887–8. Brick base and rear wall, ordinary gables filled with horizontal planking. Steep pitched roof with large finials. Outside steps to door, sometimes covered by porch.

Type 5
From 1889. First GWR signal box to be built to standard sizes. All brick but plain gables filled with horizontal planking pierced by slatted ventilator. Finial at gable apex. 'Rocket' vent(s) on ridge tiles. Large, multi-square-paned windows. Outside steps to door. No external porch. Large and small boxes erected until 1901 in brick and in timber.

Type 5 *Witham, Somerset, 1973.*

Type 6
A narrower version of Type 5 in wood or brick for small stations, eg Conwil and Stow-on-the-Wold, often built on the platform.

Type 7
1896 with three modifications, 'b' to 'd', up to 1921. There was a timber equivalent for 7a/b/c classified Type 27a/b/c.

7a Original design. Smooth, bright red brick walls to hip gable roof, lead flashing covering junction of hip gables and roof proper, with tall, pottery finial at junction of hips and ridge. Ridge tiles with 'rocket' vents. Wide overhang eaves relative to earlier types, ornately shaped wooden brackets from wall to eaves. Chimney for semi-open fire/oven corbelled out from rear wall rising to ornate top. Staffordshire blue bricks, sharp-edged at quoins and around doors and locking room windows, which latter had iron frames and cast-iron sill projecting beyond wall. New pattern, upper floor window panes arranged '3 up, 2 down'. External stairs to door. No external porch. (GWA 512)

7b First modification, 1900. Lead flashing replaced by ridge tiles, removing need for finials. Curled 'hip hooks' at eaves to support hip gable ridge tiles. (See illustration overleaf).

7c Second modification, 1904. Expensive chimney abolished, free-standing stove installed with pipe through roof.

7d Third modification, 1906. Inside stairs to operating floor. Bull-nosed blue bricks at quoins. Locking room windows, wooden glazing bars, on bevelled blue brick sills, flush with wall. Extra window in end wall of locking room.

Type 8
Introduced 1922. Cheap Type 7, with Type 5 roof and Type 7 '3+2' pane layout and red/blue bricks. No external porch on brick-built examples. (GWS 102) There was an all-timber equivalent (Type 28), some having outside porch. (See illustration overleaf).

Type 9
1927–32. Steel-framed, concrete-block walls to hipped roof, with tiles hung from one corner in 'diamond' pattern. Internal stairs. Only 17 built, all in connection with track widening schemes. (GWA 518)

Type 10
1933. Steep-pitched, hipped roofs, narrower windows, concrete lintels over locking room windows. All built in connection with quadrupling, Olton–Lapworth; also at Long Rock, Penzance.

Type 7b *Kennington Junction, 1968. Note the electric key token set-down post and net.*

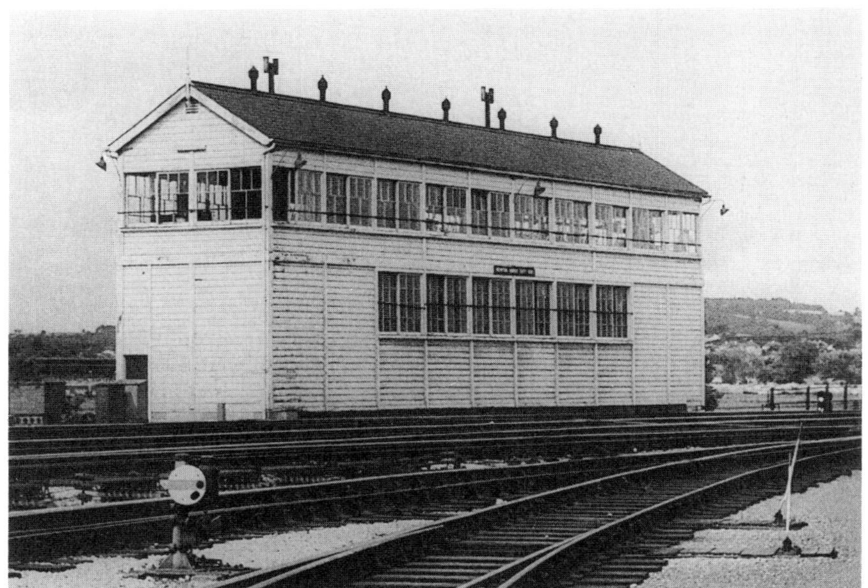

Type 28 *Newton Abbot East, 1971.*

Type 11
1932–9. All red brick or brick/wood, hip roof, tiles hung 'diamond' fashion, slates hung traditionally.

Type 12
1938–47. All brick, plain and hipped gables, roofs of slate asbestos sheeting. Larger, deeper windows nearly to floor, concrete lintels over locking room windows. Many detail variations due to wartime shortage of materials.

Type 13
1939–42. The 'ARP' (Air Raid Precautions) design. Solid brick walls and flat concrete roof. Large, deep windows. Haphazard choice of site for 'ARP' boxes; several new layouts built specifically to serve ammunition depots received non-'ARP' type boxes. (See illustration opposite).

Signal boxes housing power frames
Didcot North (Type 7b); Yarnton Junction (Type 27b on narrow brick pedestal); Slough Bath Road (Type 7d); Winchester (Chesil) (Type 8); Newport East (timber on pedestal); Newport West (Type 7); Birmingham North (second-hand Saxby & Farmer, raised on steel pillars, similar design to the Saxby & Farmer Paddington Arrival box of *circa* 1880—See GWA 511).

Bristol Temple Meads and Cardiff—brick, rectangular, flat roof and central bay projecting. Operating floor windows extended entire length of box, two shorter rows of windows below. Concrete strip carried immediately over each row of windows.

Paddington Arrival and Departure—similar to Type 13, ie all-brick, flat roofed.

'One-off' types
Reading Main Line East, Main Line West and Goods Lines East, 1896—red brick, yellow brick decoration, hip roofs, pottery finials and 'cockscomb' ridge tiles. Internal stairs. Main Line boxes had projecting bay window.

Bristol Temple Meads East—on platform, hipped roof and angled walls at east end, nicknamed 'The Coffin Box'. Up to floor level in stone with mullioned windows to match Elizabethan style of station.

Bath Nos 1 and 2 (East and West)—smooth Bath stone to match surroundings.

AV

SIGNAL WORKS, READING

Located against the north face of the station embankment on the east side of the Caversham Road, the Works commenced work in 1855 as a Civil Engineering department factory for the manufacture of points and crossings and the repair of permanent way wagons and tools. The repair and manufacture of mechanical signals began in 1859 and the construction of interlocked 'frames' of levers from 1865, the year in which the Chief Civil Engineer, Michael Lane (qv), patented his rack and pinion type of interlocking machine (qv Signalling).

Over many years the construction of signalling equipment and signal boxes increased in importance until the Works lost its wagon repair function and became

Type 13 *Hinksey North, 1968.*

wholly a 'Signal Works'. The Works burned down in 1874 and was rebuilt; an 1877 plan shows that it was still a 'Maintenance & Signal Works' concerned with the fabrication of wagons, points and crossings as well as signalling items. There was then a foundry, blacksmith's shop, sawmill, machine shop, carpenters', fitters', tinmens' and paint shops, clock and instrument repair shops and drawing offices. Between 1883 and 1890 the works became solely a Signal Works and the permanent way function was re-sited at Swindon. The Works were enlarged piecemeal over the years until the site was completely rebuilt during the period 1948–52. The site was razed in 1984 and the land sold for redevelopment.

AV

SIMS, WILLIAM UNWIN

Chairman, 1837–9. Like Shaw (qv), Sims was an original member of the London Committee, and on 26 October 1837 succeeded him as Chairman, G. H. Gibbs (qv) having been offered the post and declined. Sims supported Brunel in the broad gauge problems in 1838, but later came to feel that a change of Engineer might be necessary. Not a strong Chairman, he committed suicide while in office, on 17 November 1839; his sister had become insane, and the Inquest felt that this, combined with railway worries, had contributed to the tragedy. He was succeeded by Charles Russell (qv).

CA

SLIP COACHES

Detaching a coach or coaches at speed was a practice dating back to the earliest railways. The first GWR 'slip coach' was dropped from the 5.10 pm Paddington express at Slough for the Windsor branch on 4 November 1858. Stations large and small were served by slip coaches; in 1908 the GWR slipped at 79 locations every weekday. Up to three slip portions made up of one or more coaches could be conveyed at the rear of the main train. The 10.30 am Paddington–Penzance 'Cornish Riviera' (qv) between 1910 and September 1939 had slip portions for Weymouth dropped at Westbury, Minehead and Ilfracombe dropped at Taunton, and for Kingswear dropped at Exeter. However, this service of slips was seasonal; in the winter service of 1936, the train stopped at Exeter to detach an ordinary coach.

The slip guard uncoupled his coach from the main train by pulling a lever to withdraw a wedge from the pivoted drawhook, allowing the hook to drop and release the coupling. The same lever allowed the guard to apply the vacuum brake (qv) and bring the coach to a stand.

Slip coaches broke the fundamental safety rule that there must never be more than one train in a block section. Signalmen had to be acutely aware of slip coaches and special identification lamps were carried at the rear of the main train and slip portion(s).

Slip coach services were suspended in early 1917 and reinstated in May 1919. The services subsequently provided were:

1921	1928	1935	1952	1958
27	40	22	12	3

The last slip coach was dropped at Bicester off the 5.10 pm Paddington– Birmingham express on Friday 9 September 1960.

(*Refer to* A Pictorial Record of Great Western Signalling *pages 123 and 126—see Bibliography*)

AV

Slip coaches *A two-coach slip portion arrives at Banbury in 1939.* (Steamchest Collection)

SLOUGH

Although the GWR's first trains did call at Slough, the Directors kept their promise to Eton College not to build a station there! Failing in its attempts to get an injunction against this evasion, Eton eventually relented and Slough was provided with a two-section station on the down side of the line in June 1840. On 13 June 1842 Queen Victoria honoured it by making her first railway journey from there (qv Royal Trains).

Slough had other early distinctions. It was linked to Paddington by 'electro-magnetic telegraph' in 1843, the GWR set up the Reading Signal Works when it took over from the previous contractors at Slough in 1859, mail pick-up apparatus was introduced in 1866 (qv Mail services), and a sizeable engine shed was opened in 1868. In 1879–86 the station was rebuilt with ornate pavilions in the French Renaissance style.

In addition to the main-line passenger services, Slough handled the branch trains to Windsor (qv), some of these running to and from the main line via the triangular junction west of the station. A sizeable goods depot lay opposite and Slough had several private sidings, including one into the up-side trading estate.

Slough was the home of the GWR's Road Motor Department (qv) and also of 'Station Jim', a dog which helped to collect £40 for the GWR Widows & Orphans Fund before his death in 1896 (qv Dogs).

GB

SMITHFIELD GOODS

The 600-ft long, 250-ft wide GWR depot at Smithfield, opened on 3 May 1869, consisted of six sidings linked by turn-table and with hydraulic lift access to the meat market above. It was served via the Widened Lines with trains (maximum 28 wagons) reversing in at the Aldersgate end and departing from the Farringdon Street end.

GB

SODBURY TUNNEL

The 2 m 924 yd Sodbury Tunnel lay on the 1 in 300 descent of the South Wales main line (qv) from the summit at Badminton and on through Chipping Sodbury to the Severn estuary. Its construction was a major feature of the works for the GWR's South Wales & Bristol Direct Railway (qv) which came into through use for goods traffic from 1 May 1903 (passengers 1 July). Watertroughs (qv) were situated just west of the tunnel which itself discharged several million gallons of natural and drainage water daily. Some of the construction shafts were topped with ornamental towers, and were retained for ventilation.

GB

SONNING CUTTING

Brunel had originally intended the GWR main line to approach Reading through a tunnel beneath the Holme Park land of Robert Palmer MP, but subsequently decided upon a deviation to the south through a cutting 2 miles long and up to 60 ft deep. In the wet winter of 1838–9, with 1,220 men at work but 700,000 cubic yards still to excavate, he probably wished he hadn't!

Sonning Cutting was completed in time for opening to Reading on 30 March 1840 but it was the scene of the GWR's first bad accident on Christmas Eve 1841 when the engine *Hecla* and its mixed train ran into a landslip and eight people died (qv Accidents).

GB

SOUTHALL

Although the GWR main line was opened as far as Maidenhead on 4 June 1838, the station at Southall was not ready for use until 1 May 1839. It became a junction with the opening of the Brentford branch (qv) in 1859–60 and dealt with an increasing volume of suburban passenger business. There was a sizeable loco depot in the angle between the main and branch lines and the extensive goods business included private sidings for Daimler, Crown Cork, Quaker Oats and International Tea.

At one period there was a service from Southall to Clapham Junction.

GB

Southall *A pre-First World War view of the station, looking west.* (GWR Museum, Swindon)

SOUTH DEVON RAILWAY

Various proposals for an east-west line through Devon crystallized in the early 1840s into the South Devon Railway scheme which was incorporated by an Act of 4 July 1844. The GWR and Bristol & Exeter (qv) companies subscribed £350,000 to the project and Brunel was its engineer, recommending atmospheric propulsion (qv) which the Directors saw in action on the Dublin & Kingstown Railway.

The Exeter–Teignmouth section was opened on 30 May 1846 and on to Newton Abbot on 30 December, using locomotives hired from the GWR pending laying of the atmospheric pipes. These were brought into use on 16 August 1847, with passengers being carried from 13 September and the changeover completed by 23 February 1848. For a while all went well but failures and escalating costs brought a change back to locomotive haulage from 10 September 1848. Services had meantime been extended west to Totnes on 20 July 1847, to Laira on 5 May 1848 and into Millbay on 2 April 1849.

South Wales & Bristol Direct Railway *Chipping Sodbury station, typical of those on the new 1903 line.* (GWR Museum, Swindon)

Over the years the SDR extended its system to embrace branches to Kingswear, Tavistock, Launceston, Moretonhampstead and Ashburton (all qv). It was efficient and dedicated to improvement, and handed over 113 m 58 ch of excellent railway when amalgamated with the GWR from 1 August 1878 (qv, Associated Broad Gauge Companies).

GB

SOUTH WALES & BRISTOL DIRECT RAILWAY

Authorized to the GWR by an Act of 7 August 1896, this scheme provided for a new main line link from Wootton Bassett (qv) to Patchway, and for connections with the MR at Westerleigh, Berkeley and Standish. An estimate of £986,084 was accepted from S. Pearson & Son in 1897 and the 30-mile line was completed throughout for goods on 1 May 1903 (passengers 1 July).

GB

SOUTH WALES MAIN LINE

Stations: Wootton Bassett (83 miles from Paddington), Brinkworth (87 m), Little Somerford (89¾ m), Hullavington (94¼ m), Badminton (100 m), Chipping Sodbury (104½ m), Coalpit Heath (108½ m), Winterbourne (109¾ m), Patchway (113 m), Pilning High Level (116¾ m), Severn Tunnel Junction (123½ m), Magor (126 m), Llanwern (129¾ m), Newport (133½ m), Cardiff (145¼ m), Ely (147½ m), St Fagans (149¼ m), Peterston (152 m), Llantrisant (156¼ m), Llanharan (158¾ m), Pencoed (161½ m), Bridgend (165¼ m), Pyle (170¾ m), Port Talbot (177½ m), Briton Ferry (181¼ m), Neath (183 m), Skewen (185 m), Llansamlet (187½ m), Landore (189½ m), Swansea (191 m), Cockett (191¾ m), Gowerton (194¼ m), Loughor (196½ m), Llanelly (200 m), Pembrey & Burry Port (204 m), Kidwelly (209¼ m), Ferryside (213½ m), Carmarthen (220½ m), Sarnau (224½ m), St Clears (228 m), Whitland (233¾ m), Clynderwen (239 m), Clarbeston Road (245¾ m), Fishguard & Goodwick (260¾ m), Fishguard Harbour (261¼ m)

The original roundabout route via Gloucester and the South Wales Railway (qv) reached Carmarthen Junction on 11 October 1852, Haverfordwest on 2 January 1854 and Neyland (qv) on 15 April 1856. The port established there then dealt with the GWR's Irish traffic until the 1845 plans for Fishguard (qv) finally became a reality in 1906, by which time the Severn Tunnel (qv) had been open for 20 years and the direct route from Swindon for three.

The route of the 'South Wales & Bristol Direct Railway' (qv) dipped from Wootton Bassett Junction to a connection with the Malmesbury branch (qv), then rose at 1 in

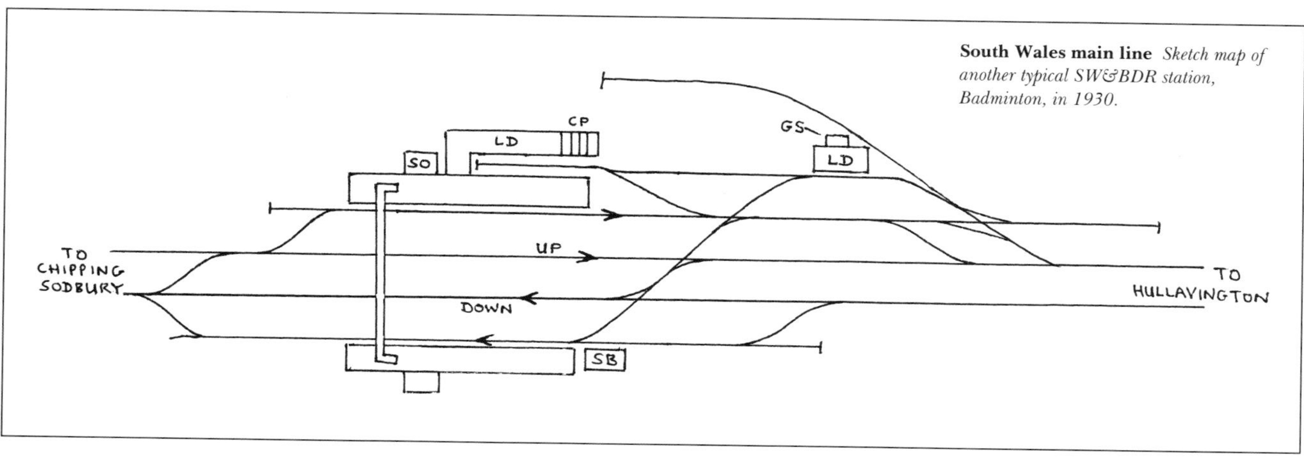

South Wales main line *Sketch map of another typical SW&BDR station, Badminton, in 1930.*

300 via the 506 yd Alderton Tunnel to top the Cotswold Ridge near Badminton station, where special privileges operated for the Duke of Beaufort and his visitors. The descent to the Severn then began with the 2 m 924 yds of Sodbury Tunnel (qv) and connected with the MR/LMS at Westerleigh Junction (qv) before shedding its Bristol link at Filton. The course of the Bristol & South Wales Union line (qv) was joined at Patchway as the separate high- and low-level tunnels testified.

Emerging from the 4 m 628 yds of the Severn Tunnel, the main line joined the Gloucester one and passed through Severn Tunnel Junction's freight yards to Newport (qv). There connection was made with the 'North & West' route to Shrewsbury as well as with the docks and valleys lines, including the Brecon & Merthyr route (qv). At Cardiff (qv) junction was made with seven routes north and two south, plus links to the extensive docks network.

Beyond Cardiff the main line turned inland and rose via the Ely Valley and connections with the Barry and Taff Vale systems (both qv) to a summit at Llanharan. More junctions followed at Bridgend (qv) and Pyle and with the steelworks and docks lines at Port Talbot (qv). From Port Talbot to Neath the route passed the Briton Ferry (qv) complex and had links with the former Port Talbot, Rhondda & Swansea Bay and Neath & Brecon systems.

Most main-line passenger services to West Wales ran into Swansea (qv) High Street station and out again, although direct running alternatives existed in the 1913 Swansea District Lines (qv), from the top of Skewen Bank, or the Landore Loop. There was a steep climb west to Cockett Tunnel and down again to cross the Loughor River and join the Central Wales line on the approach to Llanelly (qv), where junction was made with the docks line and that to Cross Hands (qv). Similar situations existed at Pembrey & Burry Port and at Kidwelly (qv) before the route turned north along the River Towy to Carmarthen Junction (qv).

The undulating West Wales end of the main line needed two short tunnels, one before shedding the Pembroke and Cardigan lines at Whitland (all qv) and the other after the departure of the Haverfordwest route at Clarbeston Junction. The main line then ran forward via three halts to a 1 in 50, single-line drop to Fishguard Harbour, after the Clynderwen–Letterston route (qv) had rejoined at the latter point.

GB

SOUTH WALES RAILWAY

A GWR-backed line, planned to cross the Severn from Standish and continue through South Wales to Fishguard (qv), the South Wales Railway was incorporated by an Act of 4 August 1845, with extension Acts following. The first section was opened between Chepstow and Swansea (both qv) on 18 June 1850 and a revised link with the GWR, via Gloucester and Grange Court Junction (qv), was completed by bridging the Wye at Chepstow from 19 July 1852.

Abandonment of the Fishguard works followed the Great Famine in Ireland, but extensions between 1852 and 1858 took the SWR to Neyland (qv) where facilities for a Waterford boat service were established. By an agreement of 1851 the GWR leased the South Wales concern, under a Joint Committee control arrangement, but problems over both working and financial matters led to full amalgamation from 1 August 1863.

GB

SPAGNOLETTI, CHARLES ERNEST

Spagnoletti was born on 12 July 1832, and at the age of 14 went to work in the Office of the National Debt, but soon left to work with Alexander Bain, a pioneer of the electric telegraph. Spagnoletti joined the newly formed Electric Telegraph Company in 1847 and invented the 'single needle' telegraph system. This was a matter of vital importance to electric communication as it was a simpler, cheaper system than those already in use. He was appointed Telegraph Superintendent of the GWR in May 1855 at £100 pa, the first such appointment on any British railway, but he was allowed to keep his connections with outside firms.

He developed ideas for civil as well as electrical engineering; his patent method of laying roads by interlocking concrete blocks sealed with bitumen was used throughout the London County Council area. He patented the 'Disc Block Telegraph Instrument', introduced on the Metropolitan Railway in January 1863, and did much to develop electricity generation and electric lighting; he was in charge of early installations on the GWR. He retired in 1891 and died in 1915.

AV

SPEED RECORDS

For long periods the GWR held British and world records for average and maximum speeds. In the early days of the Broad Gauge, *Iron Duke* (qv) and another of the class reached 78 mph down Dauntsey Incline, and these 4-2-2 locomotives were also involved in the fast running with service trains between Paddington and Didcot. As recounted by Gooch, they regularly covered the 53 miles in 48–59 minutes in 1848, a world record at that time. In 1904, *City of Truro* (qv) reached a speed of approximately 100 mph descending Wellington Bank with an Ocean Mail special, which was the fastest any steam locomotive had achieved anywhere in the world at that time. During the 1920s and 1930s, the 'Cheltenham Flyer' (qv) set up a number of British and world speed records in the course of its afternoon dash from Swindon to Paddington. Not only was its scheduled speed the fastest anywhere for many years, but *Tregenna Castle* (qv) set up another world record in June 1932, when it averaged 81.7 mph, start-to-stop, over the 77.3 miles. The first fully authenticated 100-mph speed on the GWR was achieved by *Builth Castle* (qv) in 1939.

PWBS

STAFF WELFARE AND HOUSING

Life expectancy in Swindon in 1849 was 25.7 years, and horrific as this was it had worsened since the arrival of the GWR works and the consequent overcrowding. The GWR set out to improve things by building cottages, the first being completed in 1841. The 'village' grew to eight streets, each cottage being built of stone with at least two bedrooms, a toilet and a small front garden. They were palatial for the time and still exist, modernized, except for one which is now a folk museum. A barracks was provided for single men, which later became a methodist chapel and is now the GWR Museum, Swindon.

Elsewhere, railway cottages or houses were built all over the system for employees to rent. Enginemen on 'lodging turns' either stayed in boarding or lodging houses, or, at busy centres such as Old Oak Common, Severn Tunnel Junction and Didcot, they spent the night in specially built accommodation blocks.

Staff welfare and housing *The GWR Park at Swindon.* (W. Adams Collection)

The GWR also built St Mark's C of E church, which still stands, a Mechanics Institute, a school and a library. A great annual Swindon event was the 'Trip' outing; the first was held in 1849, organized by the Mechanics Institute. A succession of trains would take the Swindon men and their families to the seaside; 26,000 employees and families travelled *circa* 1930. The GWR generally looked after its employees and their families and a position on the railway was much sought after, several generations often becoming GWR employees.

Around 1900, men worked eight, ten or 12-hour shifts, enginemen sometimes longer. The eight-hour day was introduced in 1919 but could not prevent a national strike later that year, largely the result of the cost of living rising by 110% since 1913. Station Masters and Inspectors as well as nearly all the Goods and Traffic Department and most footplatemen joined the strike, which resulted in the granting of a minimum wage of 52s (£2.60) a week. This was a significant weakening of the old, paternalistic attitude of the company to its employees, although a strong sense of loyalty prevailed amongst GWR men, and women, down to 1948 and beyond.

The total staff in 1918 was 80,000, and in 1935 100,000, the latter including 11,000 drivers and firemen. There were around 800 different kinds of employment on the GWR.

(*See also Swindon*)

MCHB

STAINES BRANCH

Stations: West Drayton, Colnbrook (3 m), Poyle ($3\frac{3}{4}$ m), Staines (6 m)

West Drayton & Yiewsley was one of the original GWR main-line stations and became busier with the addition of the Uxbridge (qv) and Staines branches in 1856 and 1884–5 respectively. Both departed on the up side by the station's West box and goods yard, the Staines branch then turning south and passing beneath the main line.

The Staines & West Drayton Railway was a local concern which was authorized by an Act of 7 July 1873 but needed revival by the

Staff welfare and housing *A Swindon 'Trip' outing in the 1930s, when as many as 26,000 GWR employees would travel to the coast in a fleet of trains.* (GWR Museum, Swindon)

GWR before the 2 m 60 ch to Colnbrook was opened on 9 August 1884, with a 3 m 20 ch extension to Staines on 2 November 1885. The line was single and worked by electric train staff, auto-trains (qv) and then diesel railcars (qv) providing the service of up to 17 trains each way daily. They ran to and from a single-platform station at Staines where the buildings were originally a private dwelling and where a wartime connection was installed to exchange traffic with the SR.

GB

STANIER, WILLIAM A.

Despite being chiefly celebrated as the architect of LMS locomotive development, William Arthur Stanier was thoroughly GWR in background. Born in Swindon in 1876 (his father was confidential clerk to Dean) he commenced his apprenticeship at the Works in 1892, subsequently moving to the Drawing Office in 1897, engaged on locomotive design work. He became Inspector of Materials in 1900 and Divisional Technical Inspector of Locomotives, Carriages and Wagons in 1902. He gained running shed experience during a temporary posting to Westbourne Park, and was made Assistant to the London Division's Locomotive Superintendent.

Stanier returned to Swindon in 1906 as Assistant to the Locomotive Works Manager, becoming Manager himself in 1920. He became Collett's Principal Assistant when the latter replaced Churchward in 1922, gaining from Collett's relative lack of interest in any duties beyond pure engineering.

Stanier had no desire to leave the GWR and very much wanted to be CME, but he was wooed away by the LMS in 1932, leaving with Viscount Churchill's blessing and the good wishes of the Swindon workforce who held him in high esteem.

With acknowledgements to Denis Griffiths, author of Locomotive Engineers of the LMS *(PSL, 1991).*

'STAR' CLASS

After settling the basic design features of his two-cylinder 4-6-0s in the early 1900s, Churchward (qv) moved on to a four-cylinder version for the GWR's principal express passenger duties. To provide a better comparison with the French compounds, the first of the new class was turned out as a 4-4-2 in 1906, and received the name *North Star* (qv), which had been carried by the first locomotive to run on the GWR, back in 1837. Although it had a number of different details compared with later locomotives, as well as the 'Atlantic' wheel arrangement provided initially, *North Star* was to set the pattern for all the remainder of the company's first-line express locomotives, right through to the 'Kings' (qv) of 1927.

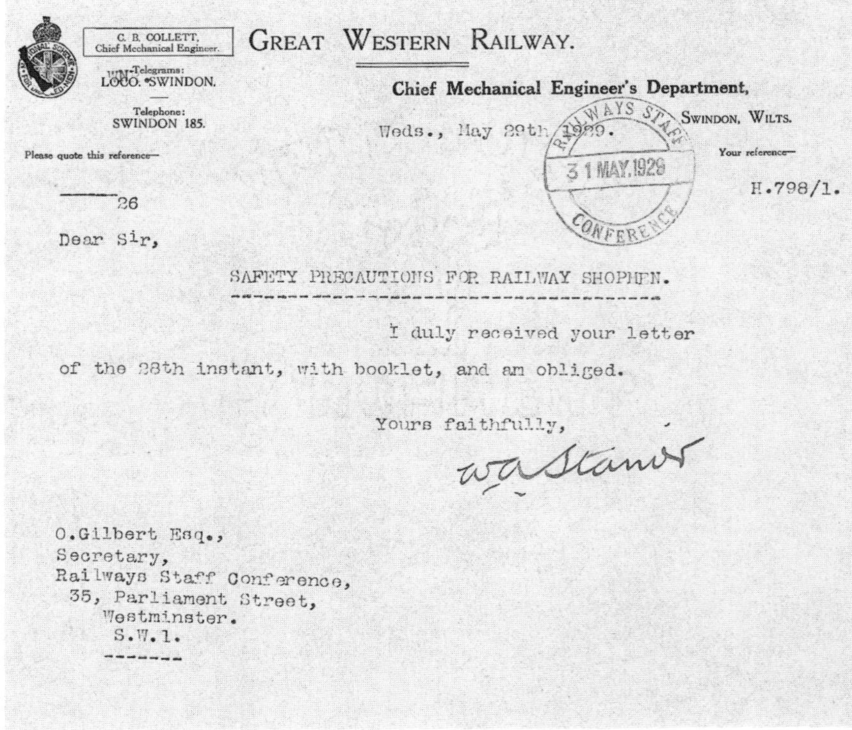

C. B. COLLETT,
Chief Mechanical Engineer.

GREAT WESTERN RAILWAY.

Telegrams:
LOCO. SWINDON.

Telephone:
SWINDON 185.

Chief Mechanical Engineer's Department,
SWINDON, WILTS.

Weds., May 29th 1929.

RAILWAYS STAFF CONFERENCE
31 MAY.1929

Please quote this reference—
——26

Your reference—
H.798/1.

Dear Sir,

SAFETY PRECAUTIONS FOR RAILWAY SHOPMEN.

I duly received your letter of the 28th instant, with booklet, and am obliged.

Yours faithfully,

W A Stanier

O.Gilbert Esq.,
Secretary,
Railways Staff Conference,
35, Parliament Street,
Westminster.
S.W.1.

William A. Stanier *A note signed by William Stanier in 1929 during his time as Principal Assistant to Collett.* (W. Adams Collection)

The first definitive batch appeared in 1907, and by the beginning of the First World War the class numbered 61, with a further 12 being added to stock in 1922–23. Walschaerts valve gear was used between the frames, with rocking levers to transmit the motion from the rear of the inside cylinders to the front of the outside ones, their detailed design compensating for the different angularity of the two sets of cranks. The first 10 locomotives were named after 'Stars', and these were followed by the 'Knights', 'Kings', 'Queens', 'Princes' and 'Princesses', with the post-war batch being named after abbeys. A number of renamings took place during the locomotives' lives: at the beginning of the First World War, the name *Knight of the Black Eagle* was replaced on No 4017 by *Knight of Liége* to mark the nation's sympathies with Belgium after the German invasion. A long and protracted argument then ensued over the correct accent for Liége, which was retained as an acute until the locomotive was withdrawn in 1949. Five of the class were rebuilt as 'Castles' (qv) during the 1920s.

(See also Locomotives)

PWBS

STARCROSS

Lying on the South Devon Railway (qv) route down the west bank of the widening Exe estuary, Starcross was preceded by Exminster watertroughs and linked to Exmouth by a ferry purchased by the GWR in 1898. The ferry pier stood at the end of the down platform opposite the tall sandstone building which housed the twin pumping engines for the SDR's ill-fated atmospheric (qv) system. Later on the building served as a chapel, then a museum.

The line was opened on 30 May 1846.

GB

STATION ARCHITECTURE

Though Brunel tends to monopolize discussion of GWR architecture, he was by no means on his own—Sir Matthew Digby Wyatt took a substantial hand at Paddington (qv), for instance—but perhaps the first major variant out of London is J. Danks' Slough (qv) station. The variety is great, from the small 'pagoda' stations of Brunel—Appleford is an example—through the larger 'verandah' type as at Charlbury and Mortimer, to those with overall roofs—Frome (built by one of Brunel's staff, J. R. Hannaford in 1850) is one of the few surviving examples. Cardiff Bute Road (1840), Chepstow and Bridgend (1850) (all qv) are all examples of Brunel's work.

Edward Wilson was possibly the designer of Worcester Shrub Hill (1865), R. E. Johnston of Hereford (1853) and A. W. Elmslie of Great Malvern (all qv), recently restored to his 1862 plan following a fire in April 1986. Francis Fox was responsible (1882) for Weston-super-Mare (qv), while Abergavenny (qv) (1854) was designed by Charles Liddell, who, with R. Gordon in 1857, was also involved with Hengoed Viaduct.

Larger stations on the original GWR main line were laid out with both platforms on one side of the track only—Slough, Reading, Taunton and Gloucester for example—but as traffic became heavier the impracticalities of this became apparent, and they were rebuilt. Many stations are constructed using local materials, perhaps one reason why GWR buildings usually blend so well with their surroundings. Some were built on very awkward sites—Bath (qv) for instance stands, in effect, on a viaduct, being built on arches between two crossings of the River Avon. Others, such as the South Devon Railway's Torre and Starcross (qv), were built for a specific purpose and bear traces of their 'atmospheric' origin.

CA

Station architecture *Brunel 'verandah'-type station buildings at Mortimer, between Reading and Basingstoke.* (Steamchest Collection)

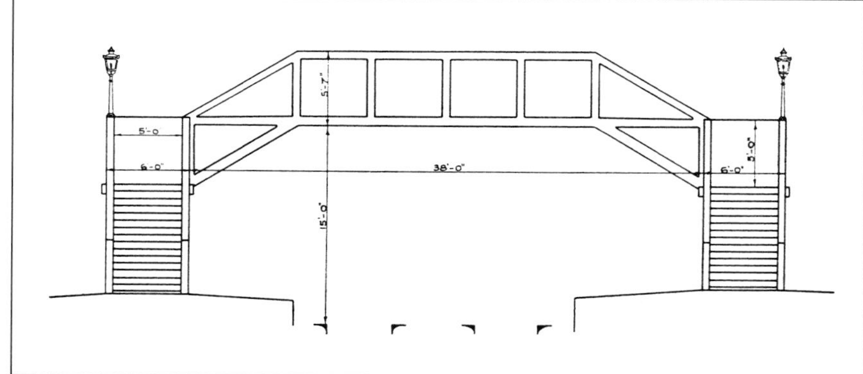

Station architecture *Standard GWR pre-cast concrete footbridge of the mid-1930s.* (GWR Magazine)

STOKE GIFFORD

Outside the double tracks of the South Wales main line (qv) at Stoke Gifford lay up and down loops and then ten freight sidings on each side. Beyond the northern group lay 'cripple' and brickworks sidings. The yard exchanged traffic between the main line, the Bristol–Birmingham route and the link to Avonmouth Docks (qv).

GB

STONE TRAFFIC

One source of GWR stone traffic, but by no means the only one, was Clee Hill (qv), to the east of Ludlow. It was served by the GWR and LNWR jointly through the Ludlow & Clee Hill Railway and the Cleobury Mortimer & Ditton Priors Light Railway, which the GWR absorbed from 1 January 1922. Railheads were at Bitterley and Ditton Priors respectively, and the stone quarried was from an outcrop of basalt, used in road-making from the 1860s, and later for railway ballast also. At the time of the Grouping more than three quarters of the total tonnage (300,000, Bitterley; 80,000 Ditton Priors) travelled via the Ludlow line.

The Foster Yeoman operation began from Dulcote Quarry, Wells, in 1930, when the newly formed company acquired a fleet of 130 private-owner wagons built by the Gloucester Carriage & Wagon Company.

CA

STOURBRIDGE

The Oxford, Worcester & Wolverhampton Railway (qv) opened a station east of the town of Stourbridge on 1 May 1852 and extended its line north to Dudley later that year (goods 16 November, passengers 20 December). The line towards Birmingham (qv Birmingham–Stourbridge line) dated from 1 April 1863 and the $\frac{3}{4}$-mile branch to Stourbridge Town from 1 October 1879. A new, substantial two-island platform station was provided at Stourbridge Junction in 1901, located 30 chains south of the original and with the branch to Town reversed to depart from the north end. A frequent shuttle service operated over the latter, while Stourbridge Junction dealt with trains from Paddington, the Hereford–Snow Hill and Worcester–Wolverhampton services, plus Cardiff–Birmingham railcars and an intensive local fast, semi-fast and slow service to Snow Hill.

The Town branch replaced an earlier incline to Stourbridge Canal but continued to serve the canal basin by an extension beyond the single-platform station and the large goods depot which followed. The route descended at 1 in 67 between the two Stourbridge stations and then at 1 in 27. It was worked as two separate freight and passenger lines from 1935 onwards.

GB

STRATFORD-ON-AVON LINE

Stations: Hatton, Claverdon ($1\frac{3}{4}$ m), Bearley (5 m), Wilmcote ($6\frac{1}{2}$ m), Stratford-on-Avon ($9\frac{1}{4}$ m), Milcote ($12\frac{1}{4}$ m), Long Marston ($14\frac{3}{4}$ m), Honeybourne ($18\frac{1}{4}$ m)

Although it started life as two separate branches, this line was to become part of the new Bristol–Birmingham route created by the GWR in 1908. To this end the Bearley–Honeybourne section was doubled and came to carry important through services from Birmingham and the North in addition to quite generous local services.

Stratford lost its first railway, the Stratford & Moreton tramway, on the day the Oxford, Worcester & Wolverhampton Railway (qv) opened its branch from Honeybourne, 12 July 1859. This used a terminus at Sanctuary Lane and the Stratford-on-Avon Railway (incorporated 10 August 1857) used another in Birmingham Road when it arrived from Hatton (qv) exactly ten months later. Both termini were closed on 1 January 1863 after the two lines had been linked, the new station later being used by Stratford-on-Avon & Midland Junction Railway trains until its own station was ready.

From the south Stratford was approached by a nine-arch brick viaduct and single-span steel bridge over the River Avon. The racecourse platform and the junction with the S&MJR then preceded the main station which was rebuilt in 1907 with the up platform converted to a 600-ft island and the down one lengthened to 550 ft. Visitors to the 'Shakespeare Country', encouraged by GWR publicity and the coach tours available, accounted for a significant part of Stratford's passenger business.

GB

STREAMLINING

In the mid-1930s 'streamlining' was an 'in' word, and was applied to many products in the same way as the word 'jet' was used in the 1960s. Streamlining was particularly associated with faster travel, and the railways naturally got in on the act, including the GWR. In late 1933 it introduced its first diesel railcar (qv), which was officially described as an 'Experimental Stream-lined Heavy Oil Rail Car'. Its appearance was certainly attractive, and generated a lot of interest and publicity, particularly when the next three cars started operating a fast business service between Birmingham and Cardiff.

Much less happy, however, was the GWR's other foray into streamlining, when two of its 4-6-0s, *King Henry VII* (No 6014) and *Manorbier Castle* (No 5005) appeared in the spring of 1935 with a number of surprising additions to their classic Swindon lines. Most prominent was the half-sphere fitted to the front of the smokebox door, which prompted the nickname 'Bullet Nose', but other fairings were also applied. The most obvious were those behind the chimney and safety-valve bonnet, while continuous splashers, with straight nameplates, merged into a wedge-shaped front for the cab. It is reputed that Collett (qv) had his arm twisted to streamline the company's locomotives, and got hold of a small model which he daubed with plasticine before giving it to the drawing office to translate into full-size modifications. Some of the new fittings were removed remarkably quickly, because they got in the way of servicing the locomotive, paralleling the similar disappearance of some of the panels on the railcars; by 1939 both locomotives were virtually back to their original condition.

PWBS

Streamlining *'Castle' Class No 6014* King Henry VII *in Swindon Works being prepared for the GWR's unhappy streamlining experiments.* (Steamchest Collection)

STROUD

From its Cotswold summit at Sapperton (qv) the Swindon–Gloucester line (qv) made a steep, curving descent along the route of the Thames & Severn Canal to the former woollen town of Stroud. This section was opened on 12 May 1845 and carried a good service of Paddington–Cheltenham/South Wales trains. The GWR's first steam railmotor (qv) service operated on the section between Chalford and Stonehouse from 12 October 1903.

In addition to its pleasant stone station buildings and goods shed, Stroud had a siding serving Stratford Mills and an adjoining MR/LMS station which lasted until 1947.

GB

Stroud *The goods shed sported this splendid piece of advertising until at least 1970, when this photograph was taken.* (W. Adams)

SUPERINTENDENT OF THE LINE

An office unique to the GWR, it was created in 1863 when Charles Saunders (qv) retired. His job was split into three, and the Superintendent of the Line became responsible for traffic. During the company's history there were nine holders of the office:

G. N. Tyrrell	1864–88
N. J. Burlinson	1888–94
T. I. Allen	1894–1903
J. Morris	1904–10
C. Aldington	1911–19
R. H. Nicholls	1919–32
H. L. Wilkinson	1933–36
F. R. Potter	1936–40
G. Matthews	1941–47

(*See also individual entries*)

CA

SWANSEA

Swansea was about to enter a period of major expansion as the South Wales Railway (qv) completed its line to a modest

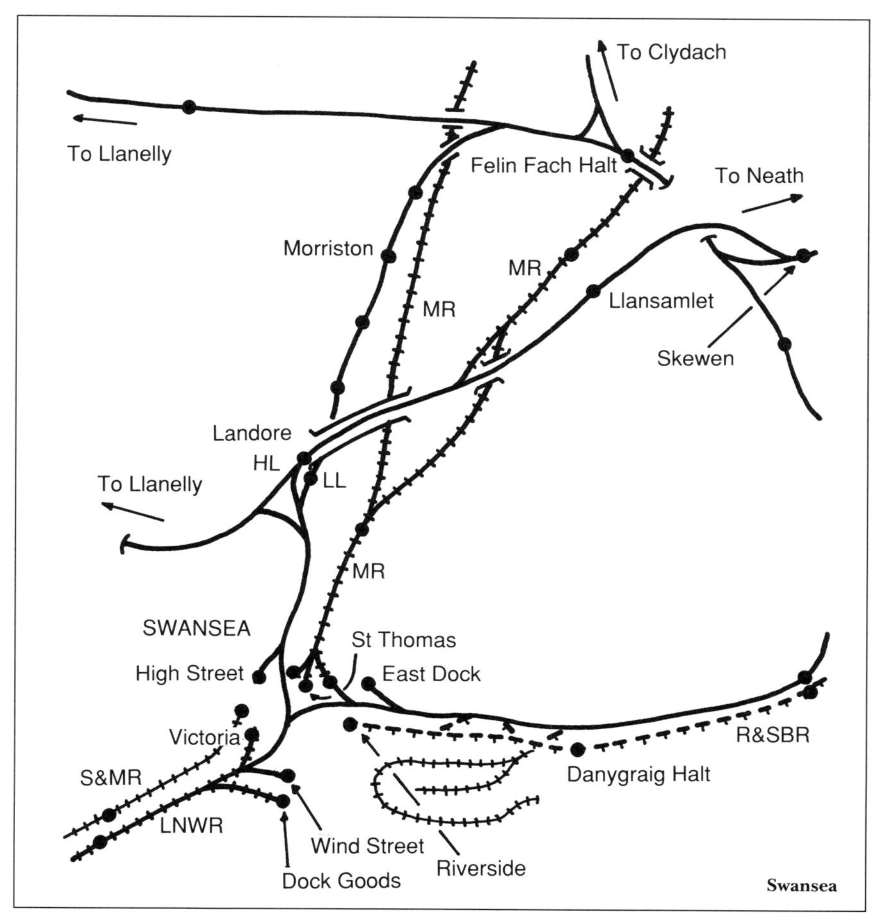

Swansea

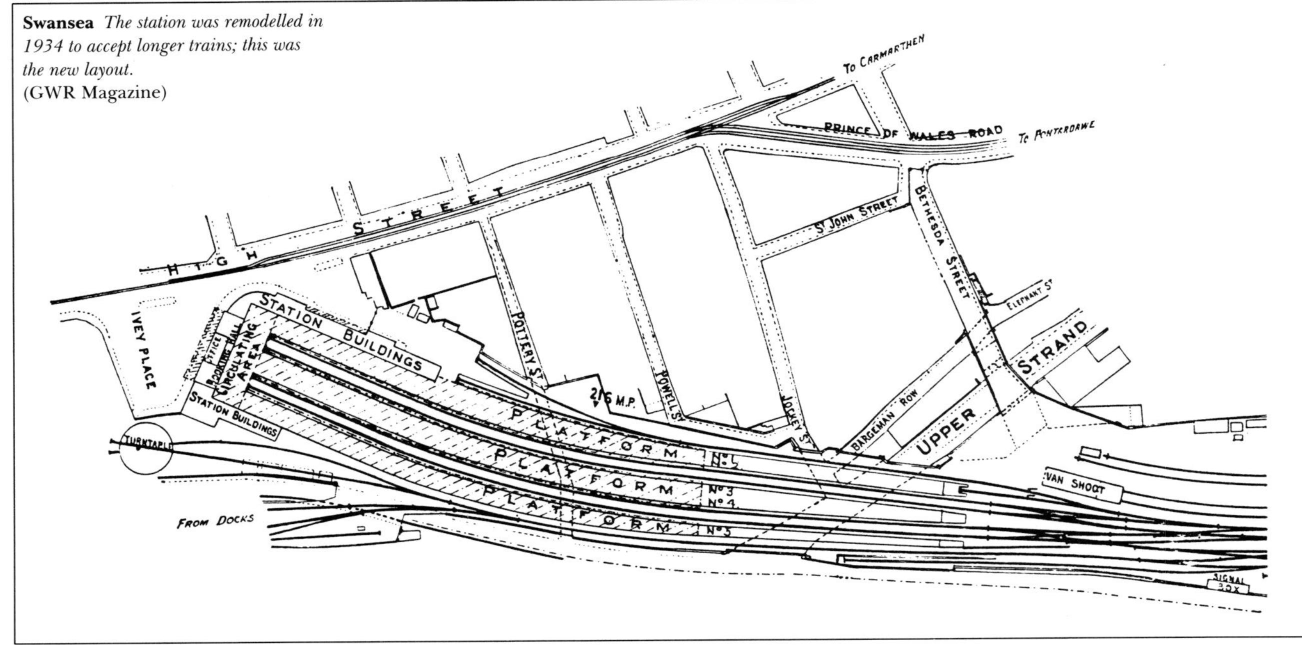

Swansea *The station was remodelled in 1934 to accept longer trains; this was the new layout.* (GWR Magazine)

wooden High Street station on 18 June 1850. The lower reaches of the Swansea Valley were to fill with metal and allied works which would later pass on 800 acres of industrial dereliction, and from the tiny North Dock of 1852 would grow a complex of five major docks within a port area of 226½ acres. The latter, and all the railways of the area, except the Midland's approach from Hereford via Pontardawe and the LNWR's from the Central Wales line via Gowerton, were destined to become part of the GWR.

The SWR access via Llansamlet involved a 400 yd viaduct to reach Landore whence the continuation to Carmarthen (qv) was operative from 11 October 1852. By that time the rail connection to the North Dock was already in use and was extended to service the South Dock when that was opened seven years later. This extension, authorized in 1857 as the Swansea Harbour Railway and also serving Wind Street Goods, was leased by the harbour trustees to the Vale of Neath Railway (qv) for 1,000 years from 1 July 1862, but the lines to the later docks east of the river (Prince of Wales 1882, Kings 1909 and Queens 1920) remained under the control of the 1854 Swansea Harbour Trust and passed to the GWR at the Grouping.

On 15 July 1863, the year the GWR took over the South Wales Railway, the Vale of Neath secured independent access to Swansea via the Swansea & Neath Railway which arrived via the coastal route from Neath and crossed the river to Wind Street Junction. Two years later, a year in which a coal train fell into the North Dock from an open S&N bridge, the GWR acquired the VoN and its subsidiary and transferred the passenger service from Wind Street to a new terminus called East Dock. In 1874 the Midland started using the Swansea Vale Railway's St Thomas station and in 1882 LNWR trains began running out from Victoria Road towards the Mumbles over a route which paralleled that of the 1804 Swansea & Mumbles Railway, the oldest public railway in the world.

Two more 'GWR sphere' lines opened before the turn of the century. The first was the company's own Morriston Railway, authorized on 25 July 1872 and opened from Hafod Junction through Landore Low Level to Felin Fran on 9 May 1881. Then came the Rhondda & Swansea Bay Railway (qv) which opened for freight on 14 December 1894 along a coastal route parallel to that of the Swansea & Neath. From 14 March 1895 it ran passenger services to a new Riverside terminus, initially using SHT lines beyond Danygraig where its workshops were located.

Swansea West Loop was opened to create the Landore triangle in 1906 and the Swansea District Lines (qv) route (Skewen–Llanelly) in 1913. Then came the Grouping which brought much-needed improvements at High Street but closed Riverside to passengers from 11 September 1933 and East Dock from 28 September 1936.

GWR activity in the Swansea area was considerable. The company had its main goods depot and warehouse at High Street, a 70-ton crane at Kings Dock, and nearly 100 sidings and depots for traffic and servicing activities. In addition to the long-distance and local passenger services, goods traffics included coal, oil, wood, metals, chemicals and food, and special flows such as the 10,000 loads of fish forwarded each year. Motive power was provided from Landore depot where extensive carriage sidings were also located.

GB

SWANSEA DISTRICT LINES

The 'Swansea District Railways' scheme was one of a group of improvements initiated by the GWR in the early years of this century. It had been authorized by the Great Western Railway Act of 15 August 1904 which provided for an avoiding line running north of Swansea and creating a direct route between the main line at Skewen and the Llandilo line just east of Llanelly. Intended to bypass the Swansea congestion and improve access to the anthracite coalfields, the line was opened between Skewen and a new marshalling yard at Felin Fran on 18 February 1912 and on to a triangular junction with the Llandilo line on 14 March 1913. An additional mini cut-off was formed by adding a link to Court Sart Junction on 9 May 1915, thus avoiding Neath.

To achieve an easier gradient the new line needed three tunnels, Lon Las (925 yds), Llangyfelach (1,953 yds) and Penllergaer (287 yds), the Tawe viaduct and a selection of cuttings and embankments. The Swansea–Morriston–Llandarcy Platform passenger trains used it for 2¼ miles, but the intermediate goods depots and private sidings were more important. Of extensions authorized west to Pembrey and north from Felin Fran to Gwaun-cae-Gurwen (GWR Act of 18 August 1911) only the two ends of the latter were built—as the Cwmgorse branch (11 December 1922) and the Pontardawe branch (3 August 1923).

GB

SWANSEA–TREHERBERT LINE

Stations: Swansea, Danygraig (1 m), Jersey Marine (3½ m), Court Sart (6½ m), Briton Ferry (7¼ m), Aberavon Seaside (10 m), Port Talbot Aberavon (11 m), Cwmavon (12¾ m), Pontrhydyfen (14½ m), Cymmer (18¾ m), Blaengwynfi (21 m), Blaen-Rhondda (24 m), Treherbert (24¾ m)

The Rhondda & Swansea Bay Railway (qv) ran half-a-dozen passenger trains each way daily on its main line, taking 81–85 minutes on the journey and connecting at Court Sart with the 1½-mile branch to Neath (qv) and at Cymmer (qv) with the 2¾-mile South Wales Mineral Railway branch to Glyncorrwg (qv). Although the GWR closed the Swansea section on 11 September 1933 and routed trains over its main line as far as Aberavon, it did increase their numbers and also ran a Treherbert–Aberystwyth service this way on specific dates.

The original R&SB line, opened progressively from 1885, ran east over the burrows from Swansea, looped north to cross the Neath estuary and then turned south to Aberavon. It then followed the Afan Valley inland, climbing to the 3,443 yards of Wales's longest tunnel at Rhondda to reach that place and a junction with the Taff Vale north of Treherbert (both qv).

GB

SWINDON

The 1840 decision to build a Locomotive Works where the GWR bypassed to the north of the old Swindon also made it essential to provide a station there. To conserve funds the GWR contracted with J. & C. Rigby, who had built other local stations, to provide one at Swindon in return for the refreshment room (qv) profits and an undertaking that all regular trains would make a refreshment stop. The GWR was to regret this arrangement, and it was 1895 before they were able to buy it out for £100,000.

Rigby's station was ready in 1842 and replaced the exchange platforms provided when the Cirencester line opened. It consisted of island platforms on either side of four through lines, with a footbridge linking their administrative, refreshment and hotel buildings. This remained the basic station layout except for access alterations on the down side and the addition of bays for the numerous originating and terminating services. The extensive goods activity included an Imperial Tobacco siding, and the loco shed along the Stroud route was expanded in 1871 and 1908.

Both Swindon and its railway activities grew steadily, a Carriage & Wagon Works being added to the Locomotive Works in 1869 and the latter expanding into the area originally acquired for the engines made redundant by gauge conversion. As part of its enlightened staff outlook the GWR backed the operational activity with company housing, gas, water and electricity, a school, church and park, a Mechanics Institute centre and a GWR Medical Fund Hospital (qv, Staff welfare and housing). By 1911 the town's population was 55,000, of which 12,000 were GWR employees.

GB

Swindon *An early postcard view of the London end of the station.* (Lens of Sutton)

SWINDON WORKS

Swindon was chosen as the site of the company's Works in 1840 by Gooch (qv) on the grounds that engines on the London to Bristol main line had to be changed there, it was the junction for the Cheltenham line, it was a convenient place to house the engines required to bank trains up the Wootton Bassett incline, and it was served by a canal which could bring in coal and coke.

In the spring of 1841 the Directors set aside £35,290 for the construction of the main part of the Works. Whilst not complete it was operational in time for the opening of the route between London and Bristol, and by 1843 423 men were employed there. At first locomotives were only repaired at Swindon, then, in early 1846, a goods engine *Premier* was built there with a boiler brought in from outside, and then, finally, the first completely original Swindon product, the celebrated *Great Western*, emerged in April 1846, a mere 13 weeks after being ordered. It proved remarkably speedy and powerful but rather heavy on the track, so an extra front axle was added and the classic 4-2-2 was created

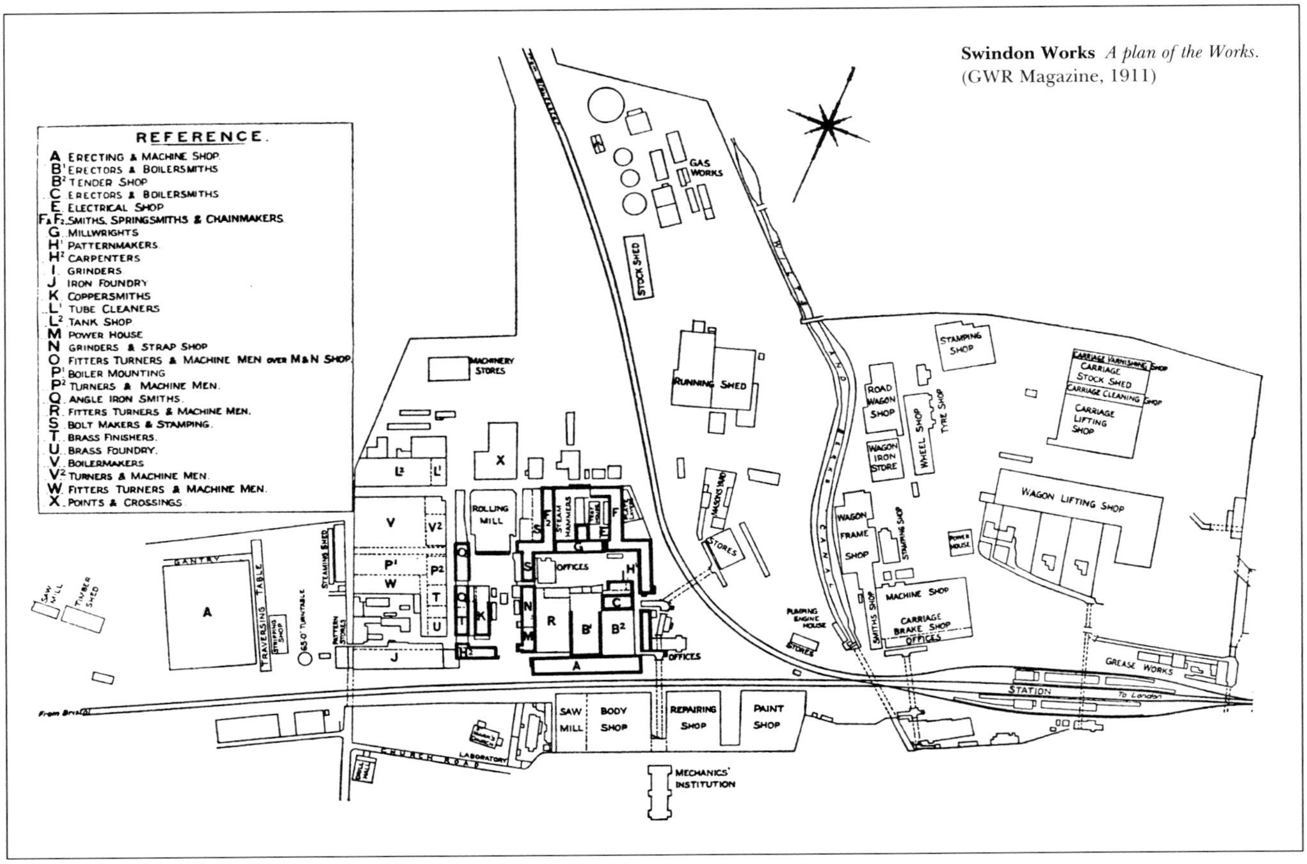
REFERENCE.
A ERECTING & MACHINE SHOP.
B¹ ERECTORS & BOILERSMITHS
B² TENDER SHOP
C ERECTORS & BOILERSMITHS
E ELECTRICAL SHOP
F₁ & F₂ SMITHS, SPRINGSMITHS & CHAINMAKERS
G MILLWRIGHTS
H¹ PATTERNMAKERS.
H² CARPENTERS
I GRINDERS
J IRON FOUNDRY
K COPPERSMITHS
L¹ TUBE CLEANERS
L² TANK SHOP
M POWER HOUSE
N GRINDERS & STRAP SHOP
O FITTERS TURNERS & MACHINE MEN over M & N SHOP
P¹ BOILER MOUNTING
P² TURNERS & MACHINE MEN.
Q ANGLE IRON SMITHS.
R FITTERS TURNERS & MACHINE MEN.
S BOLT MAKERS & STAMPING.
T BRASS FINISHERS.
U BRASS FOUNDRY.
V BOILERMAKERS
V² TURNERS & MACHINE MEN.
W FITTERS TURNERS & MACHINE MEN.
X POINTS & CROSSINGS
GAS WORKS
STOCK SHED
RUNNING SHED
MACHINERY STORES
ROLLING MILL
OFFICES
STORES
PUMPING ENGINE HOUSE
STAMPING SHOP
ROAD WAGON SHOP
WAGON IRON STORE
WHEEL SHOP
TYRE SHOP
WAGON FRAME SHOP
STAMPING SHOP
POWER HOUSE
SMITHS SHOP
MACHINE SHOP
CARRIAGE BRAKE SHOP
OFFICES
CARRIAGE VARNISHING SHOP
CARRIAGE STOCK SHED
CARRIAGE CLEANING SHOP
CARRIAGE LIFTING SHOP
WAGON LIFTING SHOP
GREASE WORKS
STATION
To London
From Bristol
SAW MILL
BODY SHOP
REPAIRING SHOP
PAINT SHOP
CHURCH ROAD
LABORATORY
MECHANICS' INSTITUTION
SAW MILL
TIMBER SHED
GANTRY
TRAVERSING TABLE
STAMPING SHED

Swindon Works *A plan of the Works.*
(GWR Magazine, 1911)

which served the GWR until the end of the Broad Gauge.

By 1847 1,800 men were working for the GWR at Swindon, many of them living with their families in company accommodation in what was called New Swindon, down the hill from the original town. The financial slump coinciding with the collapse of the Railway Mania hit the GWR hard and the workforce was so reduced that only 600 were left at Swindon by the end of 1847. Some 150 of these were drivers and firemen and the Works output was drastically reduced and there was much hardship. Things gradually returned to normal, and by the early 1850s the Works was once again expanding. With the absorption of the standard gauge railways north of Birmingham in 1854, Swindon began to build 4 ft 8½ in gauge locomotives.

The Works continued to grow throughout the 19th century, the mid-1870s being a period of great expansion which saw the Carriage Works reach its optimum extent. The gasworks was also built at this time, and a chemical laboratory was set up in the 1890s. When the Broad Gauge came to an end in 1892, 16 miles of sidings were laid out for condemned stock. The famous 'A' Shop, able to deal with the largest engines, was authorized in 1900 and by this time Swindon had become the largest Works in the world for the manufacture and repair of carriages and wagons.

In the early 1900s a trade recession, greater efficiency under Churchward (qv), and higher wages elsewhere led to a reduction in the workforce and increased union activity. Over 5,000 Swindon men served in

Leaving G.W.R. Works Swindon
479

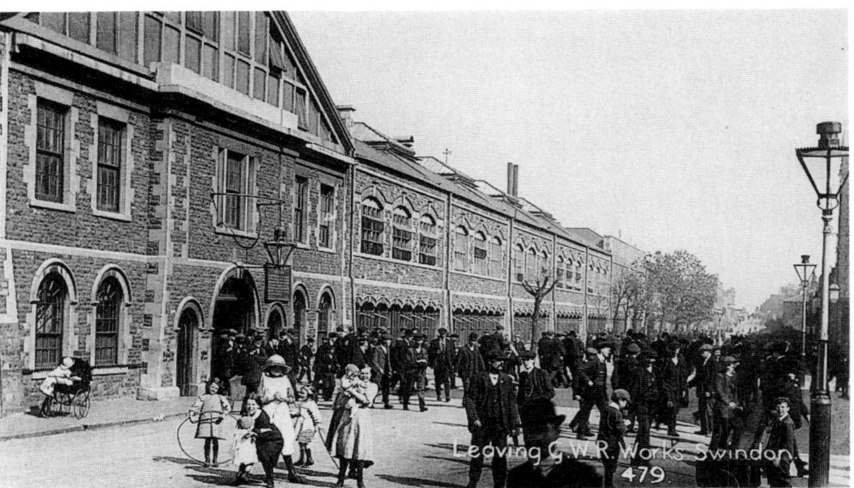

Swindon Works *The Tunnel Entrance of the Works in London Street.*
(GWR Museum, Swindon)

Swindon Works *A pre-First World War view of the Stamping Shop.* (GWR Museum, Swindon)

the forces in the First World War, the majority being GWR employees; some 1,000 were killed. Afterwards the unions gained better working conditions, notably a 47-hour week. At the Grouping some 14,000 men and women were employed by the GWR at Swindon. The last big alterations to the Works took place with the help of government money in 1930. The 'King' Class 4-6-0s (qv) of 1927–30 were the culmination of some 80 years of development, as were the contemporary Ocean Saloons and the 1935 Cornish Riviera 'Centenary' carriages (qv Rolling-stock, passenger).

During the Second World War, as in the First, Swindon was heavily engaged in military work. Diesel railcars (qv) had been built there since 1939 and after Nationalization this work increased. The last express locomotive of GWR design, 'Castle' (qv) No 7037, was completed in August 1950 and named *Swindon* by HRH Princess Elizabeth in November of that year at the Works. The last British Railways main-line steam locomotive, No 92220 *Evening Star*, was completed and named at Swindon on 18 March 1960 and five years later the Works's last British Railways diesel was built.

By 1967 the number of employees had fallen to around 6,000. Rumours of closure grew and although there was something of a revival in the late 1970s culminating in the building of 20 metre-gauge diesels for Kenya in 1979, the final closure announcement was made in the spring of 1985 in an extraordinarily tactless manner just as Swindon was preparing to celebrate the 150th anniversary of the GWR. There were then 1,500 employees. Closure was effected in 1986, but this was not quite the end for on 21 July 1989 Swindon Railway Workshops Ltd was officially inaugurated in No 20 Shop. Here former employees repaired and restored private and officially preserved locomotives, and some work was also carried out on contemporary rolling-stock for industry.

(*See also Armstrong, Joseph, Locomotives, and Rolling-stock, Passenger*)

MCHB

SWINDON–GLOUCESTER LINE

Stations: Swindon ($77\frac{1}{4}$ miles from Paddington), Purton ($81\frac{1}{2}$ m), Minety & Ashton Keynes ($85\frac{1}{2}$ m), Kemble (91 m), Chalford (98 m), Brimscombe ($99\frac{1}{4}$ m), Stroud ($102\frac{1}{4}$ m), Stonehouse (105 m), Gloucester (114 m)

Swindon Works *The Carriage Body Shop.* (GWR Museum, Swindon)

Swindon-Gloucester line *Chalford station, looking towards Swindon; steam railmotor No 2 in the platform.* (Steamchest Collection)

Sometimes known as the Golden Valley line, this 36¾-mile route was fairly level for the first 10 miles and then rose at 1 in 100/94 to the two Sapperton tunnels (qv) which carried it through the Cotswold ridge. Then came 7 miles of sharply curving descent at 1 in 60/90 to Brimscombe which once supplied the bankers for up freight trains and pilot engines for passenger workings. This section, which followed the course of the Thames & Severn Canal, was quite dramatic, while that gently onwards through Stroud reflected the pastoral face of the area's former woollen industry.

The route was authorized in 1836 to the Cheltenham & Great Western Union Railway (qv) which opened from Swindon to Kemble and Cirencester (all qv) on 31 May 1841 before running into financial difficulties and selling out to the GWR. The Kemble–Standish Junction section was then opened on 12 May 1845 to meet the line on to Cheltenham. The route was double track apart from the Kemble Tunnel section (doubled later), and came to carry trains like the 'Cheltenham Spa Express' ('Cheltenham Flyer', qv) plus London–Cardiff trains and a local railmotor (qv) service calling at seven additional halts between Chalford and Stonehouse.

GB

TAFF VALE RAILWAY

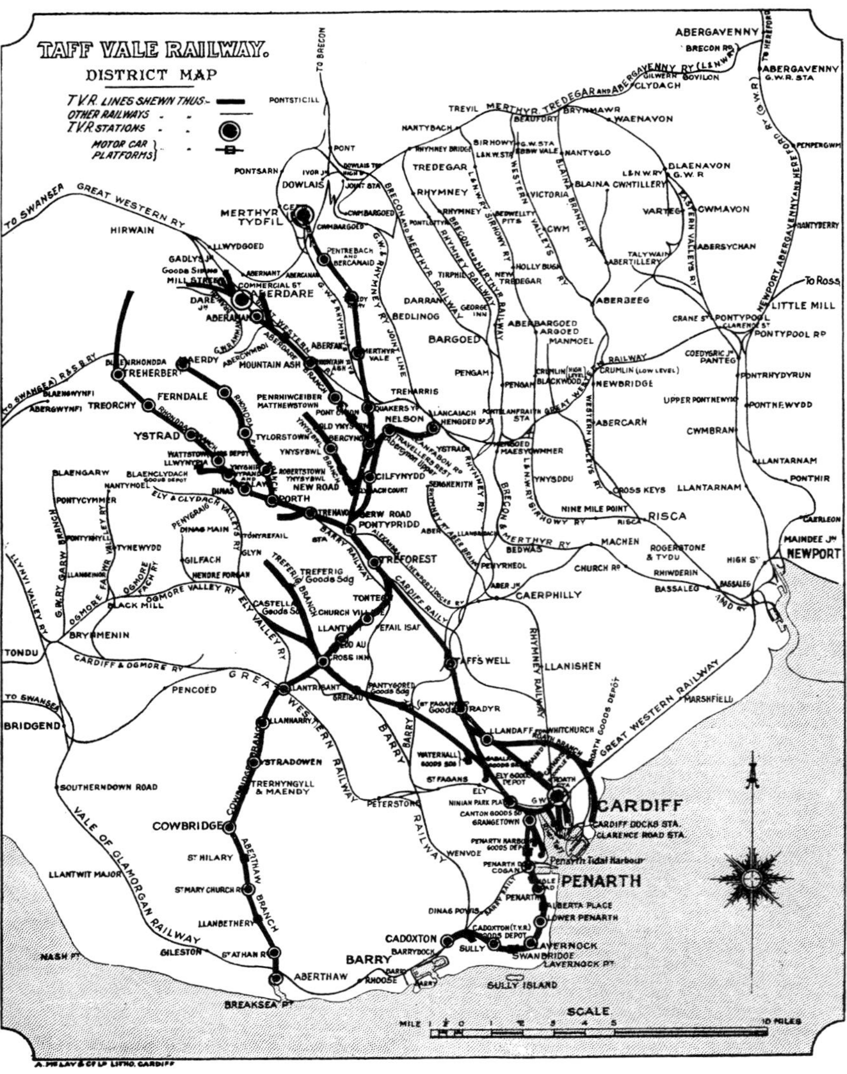

Taff Vale Railway (GWR Magazine, 1922)

The Taff Vale was the senior and largest of the independent South Wales railways, the company having obtained its original Act on 21 June 1836 and then grown to a route mileage of 124½ miles prior to its amalgamation with the GWR from 1 January 1922. The TVR main line had been opened from Cardiff to Abercynon on 9 October 1840 and extended to Merthyr on 12 April 1841, stationary winding engines being used on a double incline between Navigation House and Quakers' Yard until 1864.

From these beginnings the Taff Vale went on to lease and absorb eight smaller concerns—the Aberdare Railway in 1902; Cardiff, Penarth & Barry Junction, 1889; Cowbridge, 1889; Cowbridge & Aberthaw, 1895; Dare Valley, 1889; Llantrisant & Taff Vale Junction, 1889; Rhondda Valley & Hirwaun Junction, 1889; and Treferig Valley, 1889—also leasing the Penarth Harbour, Dock & Railway in 1863 and working the Penarth Extension Railway from 1878. It also opened a host of extensions and branches—to Llancaiach (1841); Rhondda (Dinas 1841, Treherbert 1856); East Branch/Bute West Dock (1848); Rhondda Fach (Ynyshir 1849, Ferndale 1856, Maerdy 1886); Eirw (1854); Pwllyrhebog (1863); Ynysybwl (1886); Cyfartha (1887); Pontshon-Norton (Albion Colliery 1887, Ynysydwr Junction 1900); Roath (1888); Clydach Vale (1889); Clydach Court (1900); and Llandaff Loop (1900).

After surmounting toll and congestion problems at Cardiff Docks by its Penarth developments and the new route round to Roath, the Taff Vale was badly affected by the advent of the Barry Railway and turned to passenger traffic to help recoup lost earnings. Improved services, auto-trains, railmotors (both qv) and the opening of new 'platforms' (qv Halts) all contributed to a recovery, although dividends rarely exceeded 4% in the later years.

The TVR headquarters was at Queen Street station, Cardiff, its Locomotive Works at Cardiff West Yard, and the Carriage & Wagon Works at Cathays, where the running shed also had nearly one-third of the company's 300, mostly tanks, engines.

(See also individual companies and locations)

GB

TALBOT, CHRISTOPHER RICE MANSEL

Born in 1802, Talbot, whose home was Margam Park, became Lord Lieutenant of Glamorgan, MP for Glamorganshire and a

Taff Vale Railway *Coal traffic at Taffs Well in the hands of 0-6-2 tanks in 1943. In the background is the Barry Railway's Walnut Tree Viaduct.* (GW Society)

friend of Gooch, though they had had early differences. As Chairman of the South Wales Railway (qv) he became a GWR Director on that company's amalgamation in 1863 and continued to serve for many years. When he died (at Margam Abbey on 17 January 1890), he was, though no longer active there, the oldest sitting member of the House of Lords.

CA

TALYLLYN JUNCTION

The Brecon & Merthyr Railway (qv) acquired that part of the 1812 Hay Tramroad between Talyllyn and Brecon and used it as part of the route opened from Pant on 1 May 1863. The tramroad's tunnel was widened into the 674 yd Talyllyn Tunnel which led directly to the twin platforms at Talyllyn Junction station and then the triangle connecting the Brecon, Newport and Mid-Wales routes. The station, which at one time had a staff of 80, dealt with a fair amount of interchange traffic and had the graves of a dog and a blackbird on the platform.

GB

TAUNTON

The original GWR/Bristol & Exeter main line via Bristol and the West of England main line created in 1906 met at Cogload Junction, 4¾ miles east of Taunton station. They brought considerable traffic for the town and its catchment area and for the branches to Minehead, Barnstaple and Chard (all qv). The demands for track and platform accommodation, especially at peak holiday periods, became so great that a major remodelling was undertaken between September 1930 and February 1932 involving rebuilding the station, qua-

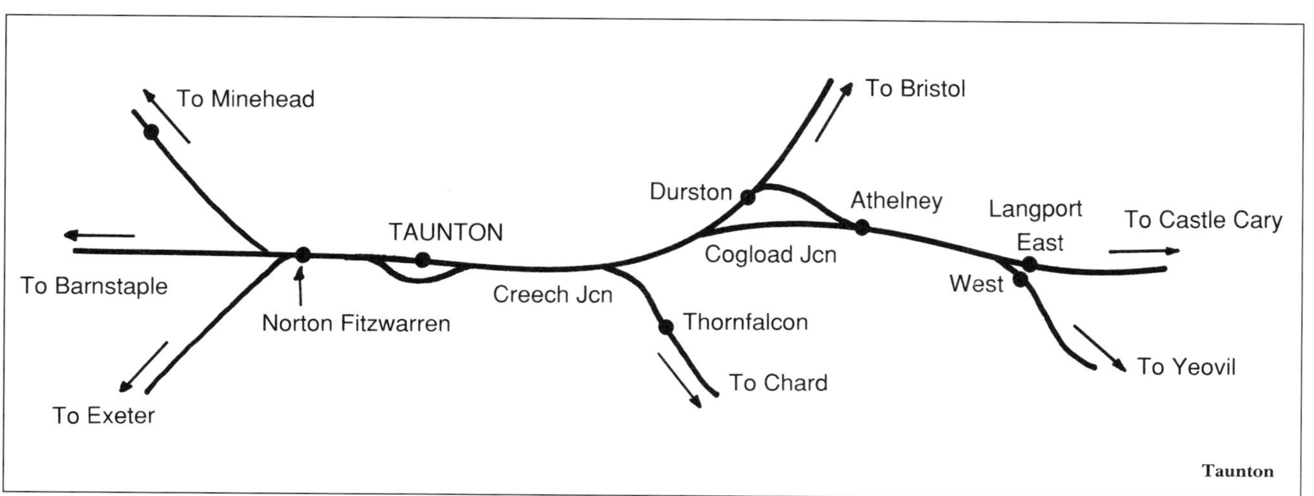

Taunton

drupling the track between Norton Fitzwarren and Cogload, and a flyover for down Bristol trains at the latter.

The Bristol & Exeter Railway (qv) had reached Taunton on 1 July 1842 and pushed on to Beam Bridge on 1 May 1843, giving the town a Brunel station with up and down sheds in tandem. This was replaced in 1868 and considerably altered in 1895, with an engine roundhouse and a goods avoiding line to the south being added in 1896.

The 1932 remodelling at Taunton produced a layout with two outer platforms served by the relief lines and a central island between the up and down main lines. Bays at the country end were used by Barnstaple and Minehead trains with more at the London end for the services to Chard, Yeovil and along the two main lines. Here, too, there was a sizeable goods yard with the engineer's concrete works opposite.

At Norton Fitzwarren, junction for the Minehead and Barnstaple branches, serious accidents in 1890 and 1940 killed 10 and 27 people respectively (qv Accidents). The station there had originated in 1873 and prior to remodelling had been used for ticket examination. To the east, the Chard line departed at Creech Junction near the main-line watertroughs.

GB

TEIGNMOUTH

Although its atmospheric (qv) system was not ready and steam locomotives had to be borrowed, the South Devon Railway (qv) opened the line from Exeter to Old Quay, Teignmouth, on Saturday 30 May 1846.

The Great Bear (GWR Museum, Swindon)

Seven trains each way were offered on weekdays and the 3rd class fare to London by ordinary train was 17/5d (87p). The cost doubled if the 'Express' was used from Exeter.

The two-platform station at Teignmouth, rebuilt in 1884, lay in a cutting on the coastal route running behind the town and harbour area. The latter had a siding for shipment clay traffic, and a goods depot was located behind the station's up platform.

GB

TETBURY BRANCH

Stations: Kemble, Rodmarton Platform (3 m), Culkerton (4½ m), Tetbury (7¼ m)

The 7 m 17 ch Tetbury branch was authorized to the GWR by an Act of 7 August 1884 and opened on 2 December 1889, but the Tetbury folk had wanted a railway for a much longer period. Indeed, the chairman of the opening ceremony, after mentioning earlier schemes, added that it had taken less time to build the Canadian Pacific Railway than to meet Tetbury's railway ambitions!

Once seen as part of a new route to South Wales, the branch soon settled down to a more humdrum existence. Over a single-line route which started off with a series of curves and then followed minor streams westwards, the branch set started work with the 7.50 am from Tetbury and finished back there at 7.52 pm having completed six round trips.

GB

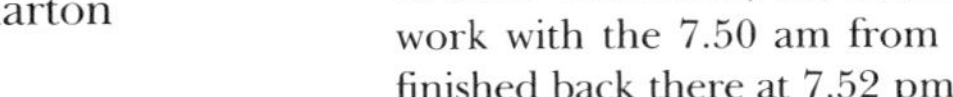

THE GREAT BEAR

This was the GWR's only 'Pacific', and, when built in 1908, was the first locomotive with that wheel arrangement in the country, which gained it considerable publicity for the railway. Mechanically it was a 'Star' (qv) with a larger boiler and a carrying axle under the firebox, whose inside bear-

Tetbury branch *The terminus, with the commodious goods shed in the left background and the single-loco engine shed with integral water tower glimpsed above the station awning.* (Steamchest Collection)

ings had a tendency to run hot. Its length and weight restricted it to the Paddington–Bristol main line, where it was quite often to be seen on nothing more exciting than a fast freight. It was dismantled at Swindon in 1924, and reappeared as a 'Castle' (qv) 4-6-0, still carrying the number 111, but now named *Viscount Churchill*, after the Chairman of the company (qv).

PWBS

THINGLEY JUNCTION–WESTBURY LINE

Stations: Melksham (6 miles from Chippenham), Holt (8¾ m), Trowbridge (11¾ m)

In addition to its local trains, which also served halts at Lacock, Beanacre, Broughton Gifford and Staverton, and those on the Devizes line, this section was part of an important GWR through route from Paddington and Wolverhampton to Westbury and Weymouth. It left the Bristol main line at Thingley Junction, was joined by the Devizes line at Holt Junction and then made a triangular junction, controlled by Bradford North, South and East signal boxes, with the Avon Valley line from Bathampton and on to Westbury. Melksham had a dairy products siding, there were Air Ministry sidings at Lacock, and a WD depot at Beanacre.

The route was the only section of the Wilts, Somerset & Weymouth Railway (qv) completed before a cash crisis brought acquisition by the GWR. That opening took place on 5 September 1848 and included a reversal junction at Thingley. Holt Junction dated from 1857 and the halts from 1905.

GB

TICKETS

The selection of GWR tickets illustrated on pages 236-8 (photographed by James N. Tory) are from the collection of Raymond V. J. Butt, who has also supplied the accompanying notes.

TIMETABLES

The GWR had no timetables at first. Saunders (qv), the Secretary of the GWR, wrote in April 1841; 'Our engines are so inefficient that time-table working was hopeless'. Up trains did not always run on the up line and vice versa, and 30 years later Gooch (qv) wrote: 'It was no uncommon thing to take an engine out on the line to look for a late train that we expected, and many times have I seen the train coming and reversed the engine and run back out of its way as quickly as I could'. However, such a situation could not last and once locomotives had become more reliable, proper working began.

In a nationwide survey the GWR, despite the advantage of the Broad Gauge, achieved nothing special. So, on 10 March 1845, a 5-hour schedule between Paddington and Exeter began. With stops the average speed was 43 mph, making it the fastest in the world. The Swindon stop was reduced to 1 minute, but the proprietor of the refreshment rooms (qv) objected, took the GWR to court and won, but despite having to put back the 10-minute stop the overall time was further reduced to 4½ hours. The 53 miles between Paddington and Didcot took 55 minutes, and a special in 1848 did it in 42½ minutes (qv Speed records). However, speeds barely increased from then until the end of the Broad Gauge.

In 1902, when West of England expresses still ran via Bristol, the 10 am out of Paddington reached Bristol in 2 h 5 min, Exeter in 5 hours, Plymouth in 6 h 34 min, and Penzance in 9½ hours. The 'Cornish Riviera' (qv) in July 1904 ran from Paddington to Plymouth non-stop in 4 h 25 min and Penzance in 7 h 10 min. The shorter Westbury route subsequently cut the schedule by 20 minutes (qv Cut-offs and avoiding lines).

The timetable was the responsibility of the Superintendent of the Line (qv). A meeting with all the Divisional Superintendents would be held at Paddington, and work on the summer timetable would begin in January. Minutes would be presented to the General Manager and he would consult with the traffic committee of the Board of Directors, which would take into account any extra mileage and judge whether the cost could be justified. Once the general outline had been agreed, the timetable clerks would have some six weeks to work out the details.

Public timetables were produced twice a year and in 1902 cost one penny; by 1939 the price had risen to 6d (2½p). Service timetables for the staff came out every three months. These ran to 1,500 pages and were printed by Wymans at the GWR printing works, Reading. Timetable clerks from all the divisions would get together and check the proofs, often working late into the night. The type used weighed 13 tons.

MCHB

TITE, SIR WILLIAM

Director, 1835–38. Born in London in February 1798, the man who later became architect of the Royal Exchange had a hand in many railway projects, making a large fortune as a land agent and architect during the age of railway expansion. Among his many designs were those for the London & Southampton Railway's terminus at Southampton, and stations at Gosport and Carlisle. He was appointed a Director of the GWR in 1835, and negotiated the purchase of the company's office in Princes Street, London. He resigned in 1838, J. Casson taking his place. He was knighted in 1869 and died on 20 April 1873.

CA

TIVERTON BRANCH

The small Devon town of Tiverton was linked with the GWR main line by a 4¾-mile branch east to Tiverton Junction. In later years the 13 services each way on weekdays were provided by an auto-train (qv), known affectionately as 'The Tivvy Bumper', which made its first journey from the bay at Tiverton at 7 am and finally ended its working day there just before midnight. The branch had an intermediate halt at Halberton and its trains used the curving outer face of the up island platform at Tiverton Junction.

The station at Tiverton was linked with Dulverton from 1 August 1884 but then became the goods yard when a new station was provided on 1 May 1885 to coincide with the opening of the line south to Stoke Canon Junction. After alterations in the 1930s, Tiverton consisted of a two-platform station plus up bay and dock, a down siding, and a goods yard for the oil, coal, livestock and agricultural traffic.

The Bristol & Exeter's (qv) Tiverton Road became Tiverton Junction with the opening of the Tiverton branch on 12 June 1848, a second branch to Hemyock (qv) then being added from 29 May 1876. A 1932 reconstruction gave it through main lines, platform loops and outer branch lines plus engine shed, goods sidings and butter platform.

GB

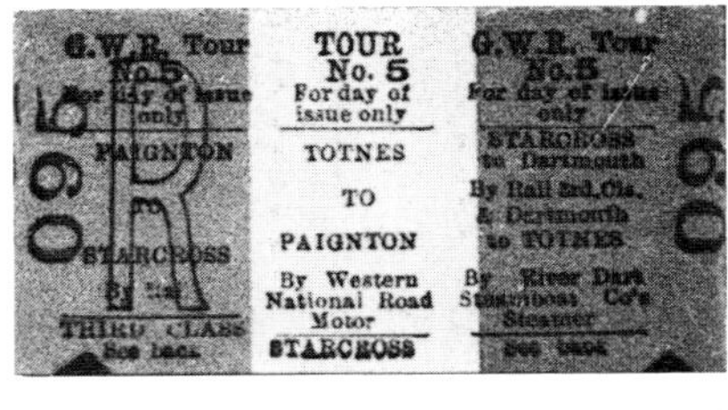

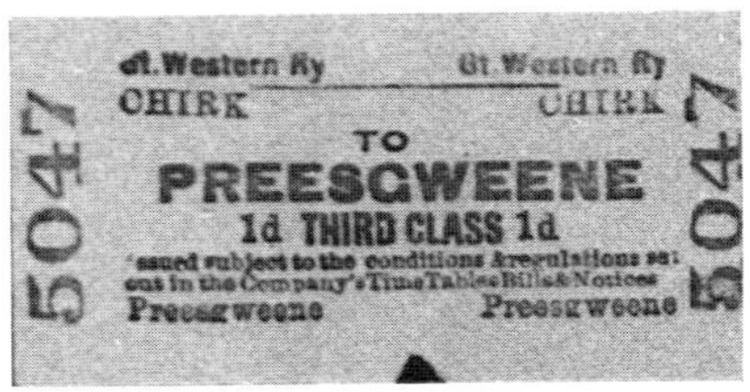

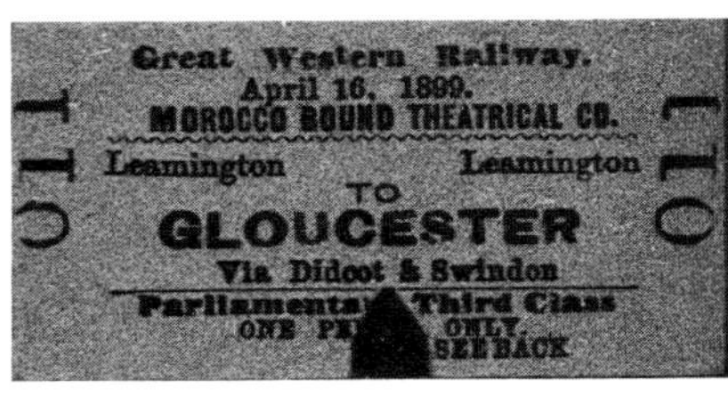

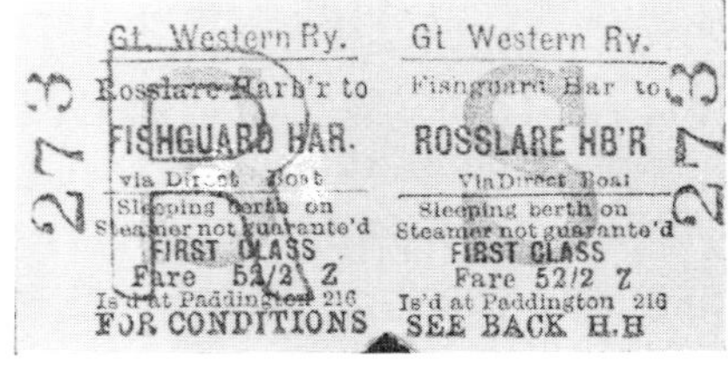

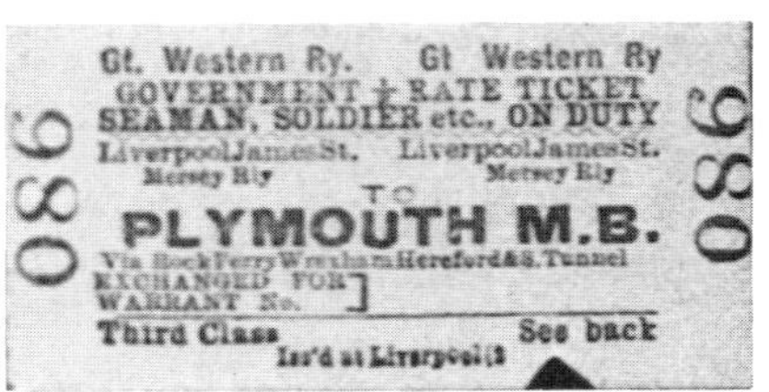

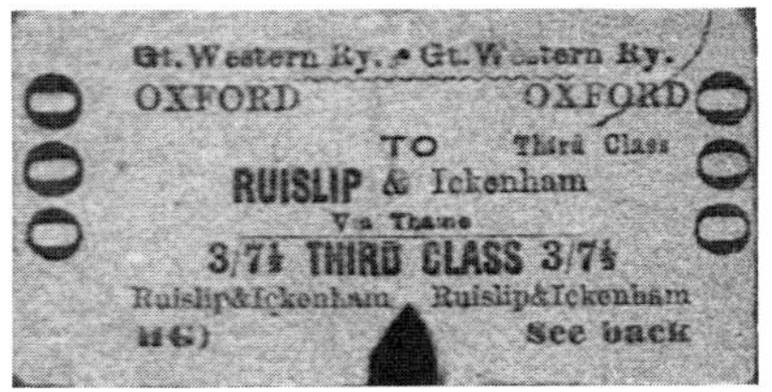

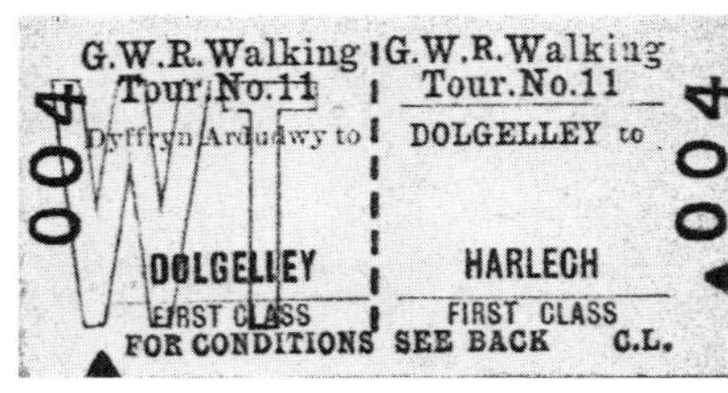

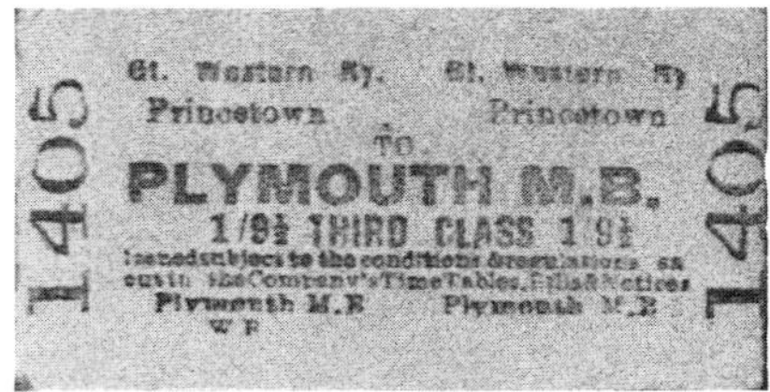

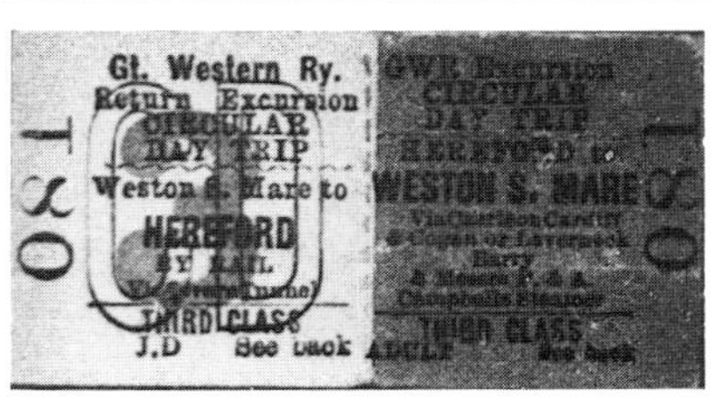

Great Western issues (above and above right)
243 *3rd single, Cheltenham South & Leckhampton-Cheltenham Spa St James, a short journey! A post-1925 print (when 'Spa' was added to the station name), it was not issued until 1960!*
5047 *3rd single, Chirk-Preesgweene, another short journey. A pre-1935 print (when Preesgweene was renamed Weston Rhyn).*

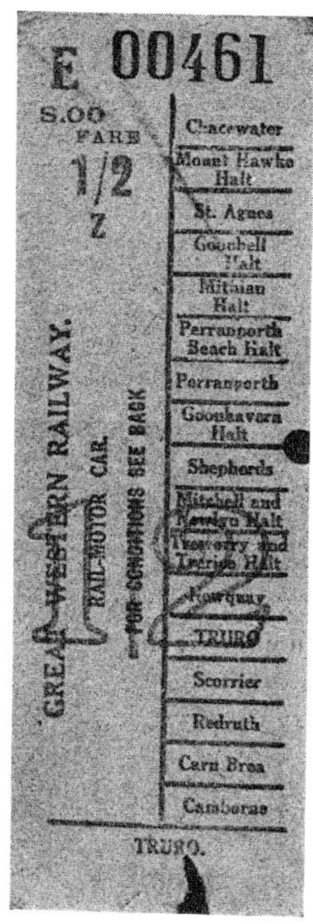

1504 *3rd Parliamentary single, Fowey-Liskeard.*
086 *3rd single, Liverpool James St (Mersey Railway)-Plymouth Millbay. An unusual GWR ticket, originating from a non-GWR station; at one time the well-known through train from Birkenhead to the South Eastern resorts started from James St, and although it was a short-lived event, the GWR continued to issue through tickets from the Mersey station.*
000 *3rd single, Oxford-Ruislip & Ickenham. Issued on 3 April 1906, the day after the Great Western & Great Central Joint line (qv) opened, making this journey possible.*
1405 *3rd single, Princetown-Plymouth Millbay. Issued in 1919 for a journey from the GWR's highest station over the tortuous branch down to Yelverton and thence to Plymouth.*
065 *2nd single, Slough-Acton. Issued in 1905 when 2nd class accommodation was still provided on London suburban services.*
1000 *3rd single, The Hawthorns-Birmingham Snow Hill. The Hawthorns was a GWR halt built in 1931 to serve West Bromwich Albion FC's ground. This ticket was issued just after the outbreak of war, on 21 October 1939.*
011 *3rd Parliamentary single, Leamington-Gloucester, for the Morocco Bound Theatrical Co, 16 April 1899. In the days when clubs, societies and other organisations invariably travelled by train, specially printed tickets were often provided.*
002 *3rd Parliamentary single, Swindon-Bristol. This ticket proves that seeing is not believing! It falls into the same category as the previous example, but because Liverpool Cricket Club's tour started on the LNWR, that company printed the tickets for all the stages of the tour; so, although headed Great Western Railway, it is in fact an LNWR print.*

2173 *3rd Parliamentary return, Torquay-Portsmouth Town – 'Soldier, Seaman, &c, on leave'. A relic of the Great War.*
004 *1st return, Dolgelley-Harlech, returning from Dyffryn Ardudwy. Walking Tours (note the 'WT' overprint on the return half) were a feature of the GWR, although one imagines that not many walkers would have availed themselves of 1st class accommodation!*
023 *3rd return, Blenheim & Woodstock-Oxford, plus cruise to Abingdon. The GWR made arrangements with a number of pleasure-boat operators for day tours, and some of the most popular were those with Salter Bros of Oxford, who maintained (and still do) a boat service along the whole of the Thames from Oxford to Kingston. Indeed, the only inland railway station to have a landing-stage was Tilehurst. Note the 'RR' (Rail and River) overprint on the return half.*
081 *3rd Circular return, Hereford-Weston-super-Mare. Another boat operation, this time in connection with P. & A. Campbell's of Barry. The outward journey was partly rail (to Barry) and then boat (to Weston), but the return was entirely by rail via the Severn Tunnel.*
095 *Starcross-Dartmouth, returning from Paignton. Another tour arrangement was with the River Dart Steamboat Co, but this ticket represents a rather more complicated tour involving not only the railway and the steamer company, but also the Western National Road Motor Co, hence the three-part ticket.*
273 *1st return, Fishguard Harbour-Rosslare Harbour. No railway travel at all was involved on this journey!*
824 *2nd single, Uxbridge Road-Gower Street. Although headed 'Gt Western Ry', this is technically a joint line issue, since Uxbridge Road was on the West London Railway, of which the GWR was joint owner with the LNWR. The large red 'O' overprint, also to be seen on the next ticket, indicated that from Bishops Road onwards, the journey was over the Outer (ie clockwise) rail of what is now the Circle Line.*
8284 *3rd Parliamentary single, Royal Oak-Edgware Road. Nowadays on the LRT Hammersmith & City Line, in 1898, when this ticket was issued, Royal Oak was on the joint Hammersmith & City Railway.*
053 *Dog single from Hammersmith, again on the joint Hammersmith & City Railway in what is now considered 'Underground' territory. Long after the line was formally transferred to LT, through tickets were issued from H&C stations to BR destinations, a relic of the former joint GWR and Metropolitan ownership (the same applied to ex-Met&GC stations).*
2333 *3rd single, Kensington Addison Road-Baker Street. Strictly speaking, this should be a West London Railway (GWR and LNWR joint) issue. At no point did this journey involve running over metals possessed solely by the GWR.*
E00461 *3rd single, railmotor issue. The range of destinations on this ticket comprises the Chacewater-Newquay branch and Truro to Camborne on the main line through Cornwall.*
307 *3rd Weekly Season, Buckfastleigh-Totnes. When one thinks of Season Tickets, one tends to think of commuters in and around the large conurbations. This example, for travel over what is now the preserved Dart Valley Railway, shows clearly the intricate 'safety' background devised by the GWR to deter counterfeiters.*

Joint line issues (below and overleaf)
827 *3rd Parliamentary single, Chester-Wallasey. Headed 'L&NW & GW Joint Rys', this journey commenced over the Birkenhead Joint Railway and ended up on the Wirral Railway. The ticket was printed by the LNWR.*
343 *3rd child single, Haddenham-High Wycombe. This is a GWR print for the GW&GC Joint line. After the Grouping, many of the tickets for this line were printed by the LNER as successors to the GCR.*
6594 *3rd single, Wood Lane Exhibition Station-Oxford Circus. This is a Hammersmith & City issue, printed by the GWR for a through journey on to the Baker Street & Waterloo Railway, hence the relatively rare 'BW' overprint.*
8363 (illustrated overleaf) *3rd single, Hammersmith-Latimer Road. Another Hammersmith & City issue, this time printed by the Metropolitan.*

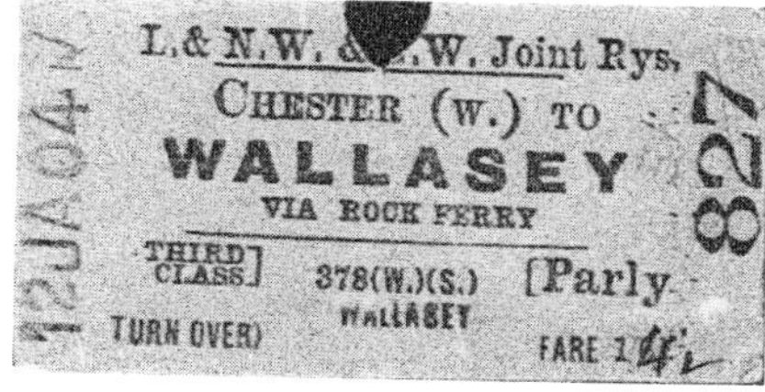

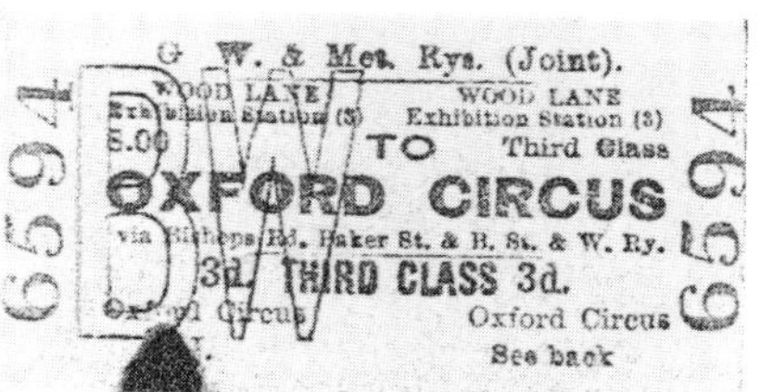

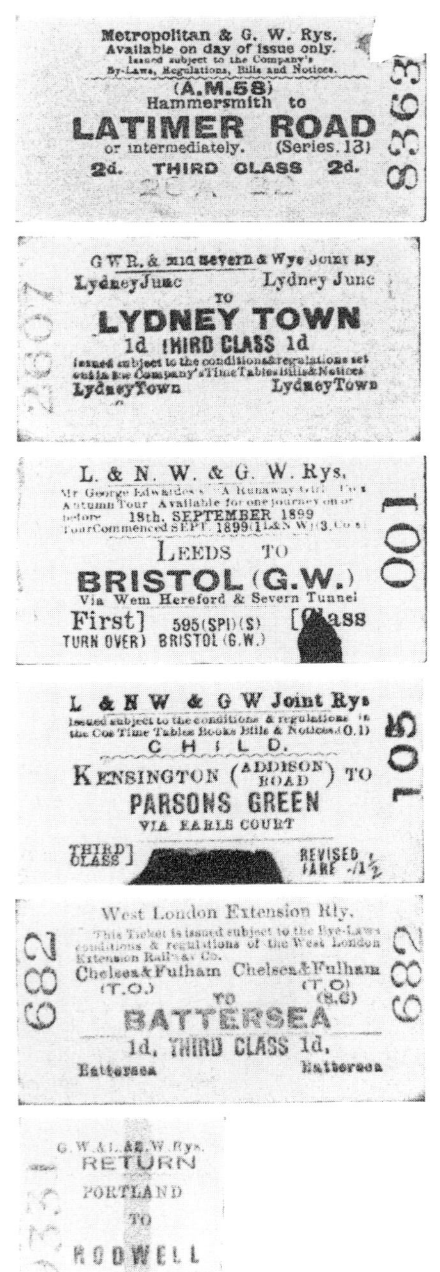

2607 *3rd single, Lydney Junction-Lydney Town. This was one of the few joint line issues involving the GWR's title with the name of the railway, in this case the Severn & Wye Joint Railway.*
001 *1st single, Leeds-Bristol. At the time that this ticket was printed, it was usual for parties undertaking a tour by rail to have sets of tickets specially produced for them, as here for 'Mr George Edwardes's "A Runaway Girl" Co's Autumn Tour' in September 1899. This LNWR print, headed 'L&NW & GW Rys', includes a journey over the Shrewsbury and Hereford joint line.*

105 *3rd child single, Kensington Addison Road-Earls Court. This journey commenced on WLR metals, joint GWR and LNWR, the ticket printed by the latter, and continued on the Metropolitan District Railway.*
682 *3rd single, Chelsea & Fulham-Battersea. One of the few joint line tickets printed by the GWR with the joint line company title printed at the head. The West London Extension Railway was, like the WLR to the north, jointly owned by the GWR and LNWR, who were also joined by the LSWR and LB&SCR. This ticket was issued in 1913.*
9331 *1st return, Rodwell-Portland (return half). A journey over the Weymouth & Portland Joint Railway, vested jointly in the GWR and LSWR.*

Constituent companies' issues (below and right)
Barry Railway 3121 *3rd Parliamentary single, Barry Island-Barry.*
Brecon & Merthyr Railway 948 *3rd Parliamentary return, Torpantau-Merthyr. This ticket was issued in 1953, 30 years after the B&M had ceased to exist.*
Cambrian Railways 580 *3rd Parliamentary child single, Builth Wells-Merthyr. This journey started on the Cambrian (formerly Mid-Wales Railway) and, after Talyllyn Junction, finished on the Brecon & Merthyr.*
Cardiff Railway 3066 *3rd return, Rhydyfelin-Cardiff. The Cardiff Railway was one of the smallest of the Welsh valley companies, and even this short journey finished up on the Rhymney Railway!*
Caradon Railway 1523 *Free Pass Return. The Looe & Caradon Railway was not authorized under the terms of its Act to carry passengers, but this legal delicacy was overcome by charging passengers for their belongings and issuing free passes for the passengers themselves!*
Manchester & Milford Railway 596 *3rd Parliamentary single, Aberystwyth-Treherbert. The M&M never went remotely near either Milford or Manchester, and this journey, by stopping trains, would probably have given the traveller a vision of purgatory. Starting on the M&M, he would have joined the GWR (former Carmarthen & Cardigan Railway) at Pencader Junction, then on to the former South Wales Railway at Carmarthen; a change to the Rhondda & Swansea Bay Railway at Briton Ferry would result in a final run on to the Taff Vale Railway to reach Treherbert.*
Midland & South Western Junction Railway 4344 *1st single Chiseldon-Swindon Town.*
Taff Vale Railway 58 *2nd single, Treforest-Porthcawl. The TVR was perhaps the most extensive of the Welsh valley lines, but most of this journey was on the GWR, to which company the traveller would change at Llantrissant (the spelling of which was altered to Llantrisant at the turn of the century).*

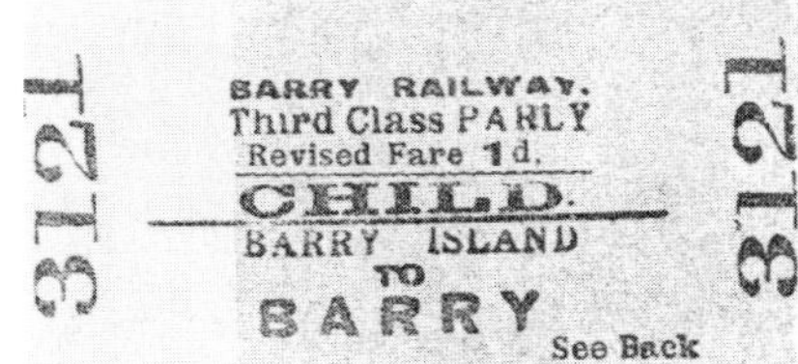

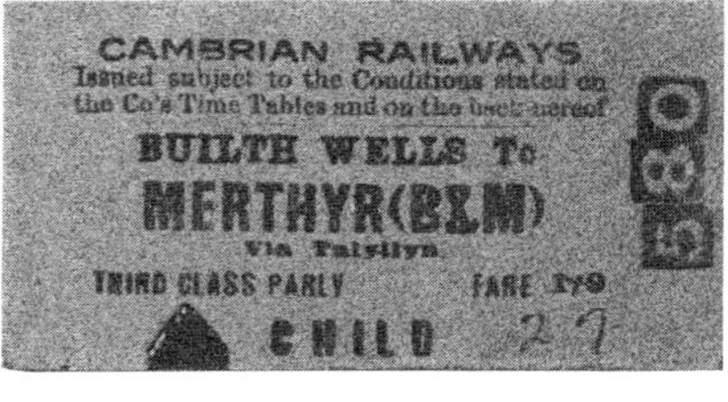

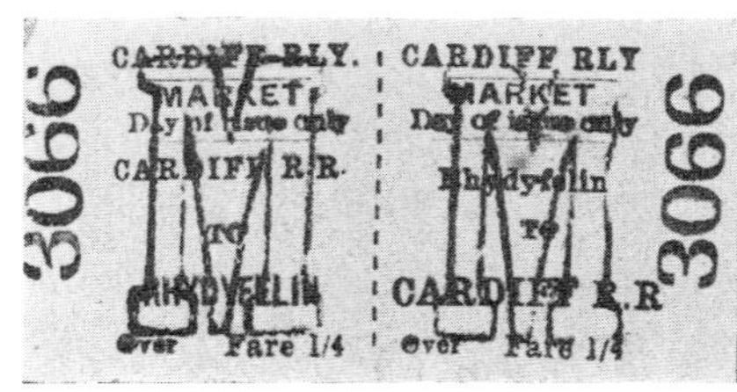

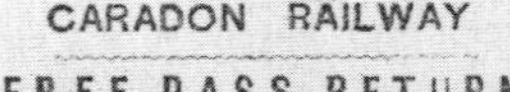

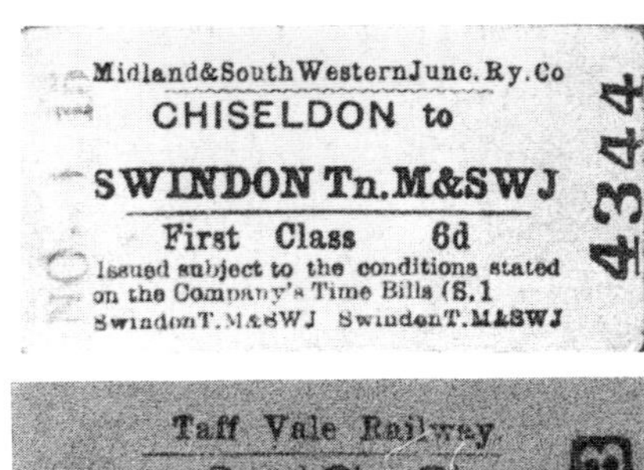

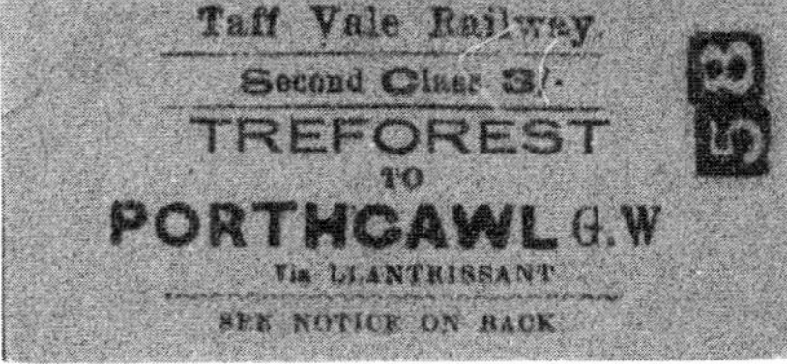

TONDU

Tondu was a major mid-Glamorgan railway centre with lines north up the Ogmore, Garw and Llynvi valleys, east to Llanharan, south to Bridgend and west to Pyle and Porthcawl. The GWR operated passenger services on all but the Llanharan route and carried countless wagons of coal and industrial products from the Llynvi Valley sidings to the docks at Barry, Penarth and Cardiff or the inland markets of England. Tondu station had separate platforms for the Bridgend and Porthcawl lines (qv), with the Abergwynfi (qv) and Nantymoel/Garw lines then separating at Middle box and a large loco depot and workshops was situated in the triangle formed by the direct link between the two.

The tramroad opened by the 1825 Duffryn Llynvi & Porthcawl Railway in 1829 had been taken over by the Llynvi Valley Railway in 1847 and later converted to a conventional railway, along with the 1834 Bridgend line which it acquired in 1854. In the same 1861–65 period the Ogmore Valley Railway opened the route to Nantymoel, the two companies then forming the Llynvi & Ogmore Railway from 1866 and being progressively absorbed into the GWR. Before the final amalgamation on 1 July 1883, four more lines had opened—Blackmill to the Ely Valley Extension Railway at Hendreforgan (1 September 1875); the Cardiff & Ogmore Valley Railway's line from Blackmill to Llanharan (2 October 1876); the line to Blaengarw (25 October 1876); and the line between Tondu and the C&O at Bryncethin Junction (1 May 1877). The Bryncethin Junction–C&O Junction Blackmill section and its seven-span viaduct closed in 1938.

GB

'TORBAY EXPRESS'

Torbay was always a popular 'watering place', regardless of the season, and had its own through services from London well before the First World War. Just before the war started, the departure time of the principal down service was changed to 12 noon, which became the traditional one for the 'Torbay Express' or 'Torbay Limited', as the train was known at different times. This was so strongly imprinted on its clientèle that the time remained unchanged when the GWR introduced 'clock-face' departures in 1924, although other West of England trains left at 30 minutes past the hour. Another unusual feature of the 'Torbay Express' was that, by the beginning of the Second World War, the up and down trains were both departing at the same time. By then the down service of this prestige GWR express was reaching Torquay (qv) in 3½ hours, with a 5-minute stop at Exeter, which kept it just out of the mile-a-minute bracket overall, although the working timetable showed it with an average of just over 60 mph to Exeter. The trains ran through to and from Kingswear (qv), calling at Paignton and Churston, the latter then the junction for the Brixham branch (qv), which resulted in the somewhat unusual sight of a 'King' on a single-track line.

PWBS

'Torbay Express' *The down train having just passed Dawlish.* (GWR Museum, Swindon)

'TORBAY PULLMAN LIMITED'

Between the two World Wars, the Pullman Car Company made agreements with several of our railway companies to use their 1st and 3rd class cars for various workings. Passengers paid the ordinary fare as far as the railway was concerned, but Pullman charged its own supplement and kept the profits from its catering activities. In the spring of 1929 Pullman agreed with the GWR to try its cars on the 'Ocean Liner Expresses' (qv Ocean liner traffic) between Paddington and Millbay Docks, and, at the start of the summer services that year, a new train, the 'Torbay Pullman Limited', was also introduced.

It ran in both directions on Mondays and Fridays only, down in the morning at 11 o'clock from Paddington, and back at 4.30 from Paignton. The London–Newton Abbot stretch was run non-stop in each direction, and a 'King' or a 'Castle' (both qv) was used on the six-car set, which included some of Pullman's new all-steel cars (the company was well in advance of the main-line railways in this respect). At the start of the 1929 winter timetable the train began running on Saturdays as well, but the service was not a success and was withdrawn the following year. Pullmans also disappeared from the 'Ocean Liner Expresses', although the GWR later introduced its own Super Saloons (qv Rolling-stock, passenger), which had many resemblances to the 1st class Pullmans. At this range it is difficult to determine why the 'Torbay Pullman Limited' failed to attract sufficient custom, but the earlier start of the down train may not have been popular with those used to the 'Torbay Express', while the supplementary fares were rather high.

PWBS

TORQUAY

Torquay's growth as a major holiday resort brought it an excellent service of long-distance and local trains, plus dozens of extras, like the 'Torbay Express' (qv), non-stop from Paddington on summer Saturdays.

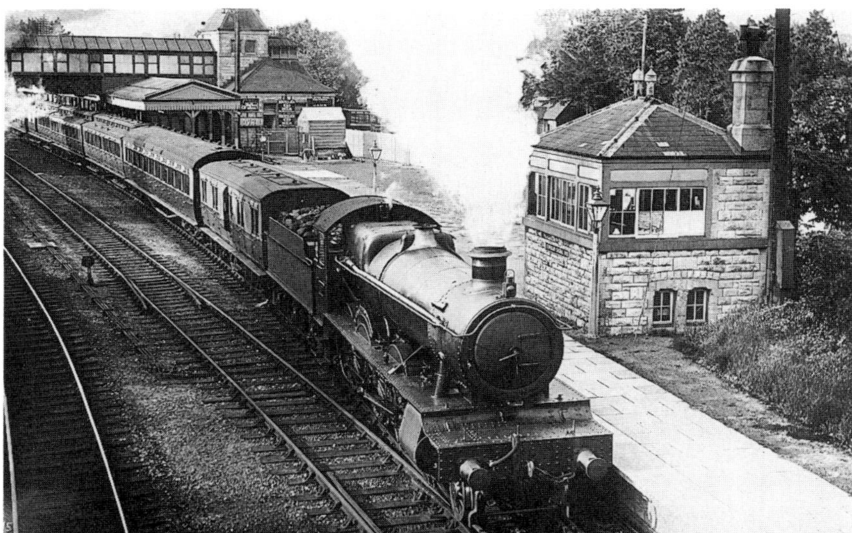

Torquay *A 'Hall' Class 4-6-0 gets a down train under way.* (Steamchest Collection)

The sight of palm trees in the station gardens meant that the holiday had really begun even if tickets, seat reservations and luggage-in-advance arrangements for the return still lay ahead.

The Dartmouth & Torbay Railway (qv Kingswear branch) station opened on 2 August 1859 was worked by the South Devon (qv) from opening. Its GWR form comprised up and down platforms with a trailing access siding between and with long single-storey buildings relieved by ornamental end towers.

GB

TOTNES

Devon's beautiful River Dart is navigable as far as Totnes and, until the Kingswear branch (qv) was opened, was used by Dartmouth travellers to reach the line opened by the South Devon Railway (qv) on 20 July 1847. It also provided the main ingredient of one of the GWR's most popular excursions, based on a train journey to Totnes and a river trip on *Kingswear Castle* or one of the other Dart steamers. The river also featured in the plans of the Buckfastleigh, Totnes & South Devon Railway which opened its 9¼-mile single-line Ashburton branch (qv) on 1 May 1872 and added a ¾-mile horse-worked connection from the main line to Totnes Quay on 10 November 1873.

After various modifications, especially in the 1930s, Totnes station came to comprise through lines plus platform loops, an up-side dock and scattered down-side goods facilities. The quay branch departed between the station and the river bridge and the Ashburton connection beyond the latter. A long signal box on the up platform was flanked by a creamery which incorporated a former SDR atmospheric system (qv) engine house. In addition to its passenger business Totnes handled milk, coal and timber traffic.

GB

Totnes *The station looking north as a down express passes through. Note the creamery on the left incorporating part of the former South Devon Railway atmospheric system engine house.* (Lens of Sutton)

TREGENNA CASTLE

Named after the GWR's own hotel (qv Hotels) at St Ives in Cornwall, 'Castle' (qv) No 5006 *Tregenna Castle* was noted for its record-breaking run with the 'Cheltenham Flyer' (qv) on 6 June 1932. It was in charge of the express when it cut over 10 minutes from what was already the fastest schedule in the world, running the 77.3 miles from Swindon to Paddington in 56 min 47 sec (qv speed records). This gave an average of 81.7 mph start-to-stop, which was also a world record. In the course of the journey the locomotive averaged 90 mph for 39 miles on end.

PWBS

TREHERBERT BRANCH

Stations: Cardiff Bute Road, Cardiff Queen Street (1 m), Llandaff (4¼ m), Radyr (5½ m), Taffs Well (7¼ m), Treforest (12 m), Pontypridd (13 m), Trehafod (14¾ m), Porth (16 m), Dinas Rhondda (17½ m), Tonypandy & Trealaw (18 m), Llwynypia (19 m), Ystrad Rhondda (21 m), Treorchy (22 m), Treherbert (23¾ m)

Having opened its line between Cardiff and Merthyr in 1840–41, the Taff Vale Railway (all qv) turned its attention to the Rhondda valleys, opening to a canal tramroad at Dinas in June 1841 but then waiting until the deep mines further up had proved their commercial potential. This done, the TVR opened to Treherbert for goods on 7 August 1856 (passengers 7 January 1863).

In the GWR era passenger activity warranted a service of some 60 trains on weekdays, most working through from one of the Cardiff stations to Treherbert. There a single island platform handled the Cardiff trains plus those on the Rhondda & Swansea Bay (qv) route to Swansea.

Along the Rhondda Fawr section from Pontypridd (qv), the ex-Barry route (with its Barry–Porth service) joined at Trehafod, the Maerdy branch (qv) departed at Porth, two colliery branches served Clydach Vale and Cwm-parc, and a third continued north from Treherbert to Mynydd Colliery. Other pits were served direct from the main line which also had four intermediate 'platforms'.

GB

TROWBRIDGE

Trowbridge, the country town of Wiltshire, got its first station on 5 September 1848 when the Wilts, Somerset & Weymouth Railway (qv) opened the Thingley Junction–Westbury line (qv). The Weymouth trains, those from South Wales/Bristol to Salisbury and beyond, and a variety of local railmotor (qv) permutations, gave Trowbridge passengers an excellent choice of services. There was an engine shed from 1875 to 1923 and the goods yard was usually busy with agricultural and allied traffics.

GB

TRURO

Truro figured in several early railway schemes, partly in its own right and partly because it lay on the route to the packet port of Falmouth. But nothing happened until the West Cornwall Railway (qv) reached a temporary station at Higher Town on 26 August 1852 and then replaced it by a terminus round by the river at Newham on 16 April 1855. Truro's main station came into use on 4 May 1859 when the Cornwall Railway (qv) arrived from the east, most of the West Cornwall trains using it from 11 May and Falmouth branch (qv) services from 24 August 1863.

Truro *The station looking north; a down train takes water. Behind the engine is the Falmouth bay.* (Steamchest Collection)

After expansion around the turn of the century, Truro consisted of a main down platform with a Falmouth bay, and an up island with sidings beyond. The 443-yd wooden viaduct on the down approaches was replaced by a masonry one in 1904 and the seven-road engine shed, which preceded the entrance to Higher Town Tunnel (70 yd), was closed in 1965.

GB

TUNNELS

The original route of the GWR had no tunnels between London and Swindon. Brunel knew, of course, that he would need to tunnel through the Cotswolds at Box (qv) on the descent to Bath, and great was the outcry when he began to do so. Twerton and three further tunnels (one now opened out) intervene in the Avon valley, between Bath and Bristol. The Cotswolds were pierced at Sapperton (qv) too, on the old Cheltenham & Great Western Union line (qv) from Swindon to Gloucester and Cheltenham, at Mickleton on the Oxford, Worcester & Wolverhampton line, at Harbury on the Birmingham route, and later at Chipping Sodbury.

The Bristol & Exeter had one tunnel, at Whiteball (qv), and the South Devon line had two, at Dainton and Marley, with several short ones along the coastal stretch between Dawlish and Teignmouth (qv Exeter–Plymouth line). There were several in Cornwall, the longest, at 1,173 yards, being Pinnock on the Fowey branch (qv) from St Blazey.

In Wales, however, it was a different story. Apart from anything else, three substantial tunnels were needed to get there, at Sodbury (qv), Patchway and Severn (qv). There were also tunnels on the Gloucester–Chepstow line, at Newham, and two near Newport. Rhondda (3,443 yds) and Merthyr (2,497 yds) (both qv) were each the means of linking one valley to another, as was also Cymmer (qv) (1,591 yds), north of Maesteg.

In West Wales, Maenclochog tunnel had the distinction of having been used for aerial target practice during the Second World War. That it re-opened afterwards is perhaps even more remarkable. The Cambrian section has several tunnels, none of any great length, while working inland towards Ruabon, the Berwyn tunnel, west of Llangollen and recently re-opened by the Llangollen Railway, runs to 682 yards. The other 'preserved' GWR tunnels are Foley Park (480 yards) between Bewdley and Kidderminster on the Severn Valley Railway, Greenway (495 yards) on the Torbay & Dartmouth Railway (qv Kingswear branch), and Greet, near Winchcombe (693 yards) on the Gloucestershire & Warwickshire Railway (qv Cheltenham–Birmingham line).

CA

TYRRELL, GEORGE NUGENT

Superintendent of the Line, 1864–88. He was born in London on 13 April 1816 and went to New South Wales for health reasons, but returned to England in 1842 and joined the GWR in that year, in the Traffic Department at Keynsham. After service at Exeter, Gloucester and Cirencester, and a period as Superintendent of the Northern Division, he succeeded Seymour Clarke as Superintendent at Paddington. He was appointed Superintendent of the Line from 1 February 1864, the first person to hold the title.

He was not, apparently, a progressive man, having a horror of high speeds, and GWR trains at this time earned an unenviable reputation for slowness; friendship with the contemporary Chairman, Gooch (qv), perhaps allowed Tyrrell undue freedom for such a policy. He was, however, responsible for establishing a good service through the Severn Tunnel (qv) on its opening in 1886. He retired at the end of June 1888, aged 72, and died at Slough on 12 July 1893.

CA

UNIFORMS

Coats and waistcoats were originally of a 'dark rifle green' corduroy edged with scarlet, with 'trowsers' in dark Oxford mixture. Gilt buttons were also specified. Scarlet edgings or stripes on the trousers indicated rank, and guards had a frock-coat and waistcoat. Porters had sleeved jackets, GWR painted on their glazed hats, and a badge with GWR and a number on one arm. After 1852, their green corduroy became brown for a while.

Everyone wore a top-hat: porters were the first to lose them, the guards following in 1852, when caps were substituted. The police did not lose their leather-crowned top-hats until 1859, when caps were substituted. Jackets were made more comfortable

Uniforms *Nineteenth-century uniforms from (top to bottom) 1863, 1876 and 1896, as illustrated in successive issues of the Rule Book.* (GWR Magazine)

Uniforms *GWR uniforms from the 1920s. Clockwise from above left: an Inspector's double-breasted overcoat; a Ticket Collector's serge jacket suit; a railmotor Conductor's cloth jacket suit; and a Carter or Motor Driver's cloth jacket and breeches suit.* (GWR Museum, Swindon)

at the same time. Engine crews, according to the Rule Book in force until after 1860, were required to '. . . appear in white fustian clothes', clean every Monday morning, or on Sunday if they were working that day.

Apart from the porters, the uniform of the general staff changed in 1863 from rifle green to dark blue—the porters continued to wear the green corduroy they had reassumed in 1859. In 1902 serge jackets supplanted the frock-coats of guards, signalmen and ticket collectors, while porters were given blue serge instead of green corduroy. Softer caps took the place of the straight, hard-sided variety that all grades below Station Master had worn since 1865. Station Masters (initially called Station Clerks) and Superintendents at first wore plain clothes, with a top-hat, naturally, but until 1865 no other badge of office.

CA

UXBRIDGE BRANCHES

Uxbridge was served by two GWR branches, one running 2 m 51 ch north from the main line at West Drayton to a terminus at Uxbridge Vine Street, and the other 1 m 77 ch south from Denham East Junction on the GW&GC Joint line (qv) to Uxbridge High Street.

The Great Western & Uxbridge Railway Act of 16 July 1846 was obtained by local interests which were unable to raise their share of the capital and sell out to the GWR as planned. However, the latter revived the powers in 1853 and opened the single-line branch from West Drayton on 8 September 1856. Converted to standard gauge in 1871 and doubled in 1880, the line had one intermediate station at Cowley and, before the Second World War, had a service of 46 trains each way on weekdays.

The GWR Act of 1 August 1899 authorized the Uxbridge & Denham Railway which opened on 1 May 1907 (goods 11 May 1914) and came to carry a modest morning and evening passenger service to and from Gerrards Cross. The latter service was withdrawn from 1 September 1939.

GB

VACUUM BRAKE

The GWR vacuum brake was developed from the Sanders-Bolitho automatic system, on trial from 1876–80. The advantage of this system over the 'simple' vacuum brake was that in the event of the continuous brake pipe parting, the brakes were automatically applied to the main train and the breakaway portion.

Vacuum brake *The final form of Armstrong's system on a 'four-cone' ejector engine. The air valve has a small handle above it which, when pulled forward, admits steam to one cone. The large handle to the right of the air valve is pulled forward to admit steam to the remaining three cones. Below this is the blower valve handle.* (Adrian Vaughan)

William Dean (qv) saw that the system could be refined and in 1880 gave the job to 24-year-old Joseph ('Young Jo') Armstrong, third son of Joseph Armstrong (qv). He was assisted by a talented draughtsman from the Carriage & Wagon Works, 24-year-old G. J. Churchward (qv).

A perfect vacuum, 0 lbs per sq in, will support a column of mercury 30 inches tall. The GWR vacuum was 25 inches, approximately 12.5 lbs per sq in *below* that of the atmosphere outside. All other vacuum brake systems worked on 21 inches, or approximately 10.5 lbs per sq in below atmosphere. These other systems maintained the vacuum by a constant steam jet, expensive in coal and prohibitively expensive if a greater vacuum than 21 inches was required. The GWR system maintained the higher vacuum economically by means of a crosshead-driven pump which drew air from the system, compressed it and forced it outside. It carried a valve which prevented a greater vacuum than 25 inches.

The original form of this brake consisted of a fixed piston in a sliding cylinder to which were attached the brake rods. The Slough crash (qv Accidents) demonstrated the slow-acting/slow-releasing nature of the brake and it was re-designed between 1903 and 1910. The sliding brake cylinder was replaced by a conventional design where the piston moved and the cylinder was fixed. The 'reservoir side' was now above the piston, the 'train pipe' side below, so that atmospheric pressure raised the piston to apply the brakes. A 'Direct Admission' valve was applied to each cylinder, and when the train pipe vacuum dropped to 15 inches of mercury, the 'DA' valve opened to admit atmospheric pressure direct to the underside of the piston.

When the brake piston rose it compressed the remaining air on the upper side and reduced the vacuum which, by reducing the difference between the pressures on each side of the piston, slightly weakened the brake. To this problem was added the fact that during prolonged braking, some air got past the IR band and reduced the reservoir vacuum still further. The other effect of lengthy periods of braking was the overheating of the crosshead pump as it compressed and ejected large volumes of air from the train pipe at times when air was required in the pipe. These problems were overcome by the invention at Swindon of the 'Vacuum Retaining Valve'.

This came into action as soon as the brake was applied and diverted the pump's action to the upper or reservoir side of the piston on the locomotive/tender only. By means of the 'pepper box valve', the pump was not allowed to create more than 23 inches of vacuum whilst it was cut off from the train pipe. Thus there was nothing to prevent the most rapid build-up of pressure below the piston while the greatest possible vacuum was maintained above the piston.

To increase the speed of release, a 'four-cone' ejector was introduced. There were two control handles: one admitted steam to three cones for rapid release of the brake when the train was stationary, while the other operated a single cone to maintain the vacuum during running if this could not be done entirely by the pump. Only the 'Star', 'Saint', 'Castle', 'King', 'Hall', 'Grange', 'County' ('10xx') and '47xx' Classes were fitted with this ejector.

AV

VALE OF NEATH RAILWAY

Incorporated on 3 August 1846 and funded partly by the South Wales Railway (qv), the Vale of Neath was amalgamated with the GWR on 1 February 1865. Its main line from Neath to Aberdare (both qv) had opened on 1 September 1851 and was linked with Pontypool Road (qv) as a through route from 5 October 1864. The company absorbed the Aberdare Valley Railway (Aberdare–Middle Duffryn, opened November 1856), the Swansea & Neath Railway (Swansea Wind Street Junction–Neath, 15 July 1863) and the Swansea Harbour Railway, and worked the Briton Ferry Dock & Railway (qv). It also opened lines to Merthyr (qv) (2 November 1853), Cwmaman (qv) (September 1858) and Bwllfa Dare (August 1861).

GB

VAN BRANCH

The 6¾-mile branch west from Caersws (qv Whitchurch–Aberystwyth line) was built to serve lead mines at Van but closed when they ceased production, only to reopen later to supply the Cambrian Railways' (qv) ballast requirements. It had been authorized by a Board of Trade Certificate dated 22 May 1873 issued under the 1864 Railway Construction Facilities Act, and had opened for freight on 14 August 1871. Passengers were carried on mixed trains from a separate platform at Caersws from 1 December 1873, but this activity only lasted six years.

After closing down in 1892, the Van line was reopened by the Cambrian on 1 August 1896, but was in Chancery immediately prior to vesting in the GWR at the Grouping. Finally closed from 4 November 1940, at various times it had halts or sidings at Trewythen, Red House, Trefeglwys, Cerist and Garth Road.

GB

WALLINGFORD BRANCH

Although its Act of 25 July 1864 authorized the Wallingford & Watlington Railway to cross the Thames to the latter point, this small local concern managed only a short single-line branch from the GWR main line to a single-platform station on the west side of the town of Wallingford. Opened on 2 July 1866, when Cholsey was opened as the junction station, the branch was worked by the GWR from the outset and absorbed in 1872.

The Wallingford branch had a good shuttle service of some 18 weekday trains each way, usually an 0-4-2T locomotive and auto-coach trailer. Goods traffic included milk tanks from the CWS creamery, road trailers despatched on 'Serpent C' wagons and the usual coal and general goods. The near level 2 m 52 ch line was controlled with a square train staff under 'one-engine-in-steam' regulations.

GB

Wallingford branch *The branch terminus.* (Steamchest Collection)

WALPOLE, RT HON SPENCER HORATIO

Chairman, 1855–56 and 1863. Born on 11 September 1806 at Stagbury, Surrey, Walpole, a lawyer politician, was Home Secretary in Lord Derby's 1852 Ministry, and again in 1858–9 and 1866–7, joining the GWR Board in 1853. He agreed temporarily to take over from Russell (qv) as Chairman during the 1855 Parliamentary recess, and began an enquiry into the company's financial affairs. In February 1856 the Chairmanship was taken by Lord Barrington (qv), Deputy Chairman since 1843. On the resignation of Lord Lansdowne (qv Shelburne), Walpole agreed to act again as stop-gap Chairman until the Amalgamation Act should be passed. He was succeeded by Richard Potter (qv), retired from the Board in 1866 and died at Ealing on 22 May 1898.

CA

WANTAGE ROAD

Paddington/Reading–Swindon trains served the five main-line stations between Didcot and Swindon—Steventon, Wantage Road, Challow, Uffington and Shrivenham (qv Bristol main line). (Until the Oxford branch opened, a road coach had been provided from Steventon and for a short period in 1842 the London and Bristol Committees of the GWR used a house there for meetings.)

Wantage Road station opened in 1846 and was rebuilt with platform loops in 1932. It served a large agricultural area and the goods yard was provided with a 12-ton crane and an exchange siding for the Wantage Tramway Co. The latter had opened a 2½-mile horse tramway to Wantage proper in 1875 (goods 1 October, passengers 10 October), converted it to steam in 1878 and by 1897 was reporting annual carryings of 37,846 passengers and 8,570 tons of freight. Ironically, a local GWR omnibus service undermined the tramway's passenger connections with main-line trains and they ended on 31 July 1925, although freight continued until 21 December 1945.

GB

WARWICK

Although the Leamington end of the Warwick conurbation was served by the LNWR/LMS loop from Rugby it was essentially a GWR town, its Coventry Road station placed within 2½ hours of Paddington and 25 minutes of Snow Hill by the line originally opened as part of the Birmingham & Oxford Junction Railway (qv) scheme on 1 October 1852. Goods traffic was catered for by the adjacent goods yard, with further full load and cranage facilities at Cape Yard.

GB

Watertroughs *An up Birmingham 2-hour express picks up water at Lapworth troughs between Rowington Junction and Hatton.* (Steamchest Collection)

WATERTROUGHS

Watertroughs on the GWR

Location (between)	**Length (yards)**
West of England Line	
Aldermaston and Midgham	560
Fairwood Junction and Clink Road Junction	553/495†
Cogload and Creech Junction*	560
Exminster and Starcross	560
Bristol and South Wales Routes	
Pangbourne and Goring & Streatley*	620
Keynsham and Fox's Wood	620
Badminton and Chipping Sodbury	524
Undy Crossing and Magor	560
Ferryside and Carmarthen Junction	620
Birmingham and Wolverhampton Line	
Denham and Ruislip & Ickenham	560
Aynho Junction and King's Sutton	560
Hatton and Rowington Junction	560
Oxford and Worcester Line	
Charlbury and Ascott-under-Wychwood	560
Shrewsbury and Hereford (Joint with LMS)	
Bromfield and Ludlow	613

* At these locations four sets of troughs were installed on the quadruple track.

† The longer troughs were on the down line. Elsewhere those on the up and down lines were the same length.

From the early 1900s, the GWR prided itself on its long-distance non-stop workings, its 245.6-mile world record with the 'Cornish Riviera' (qv) between Paddington and Plymouth via Bristol being established as early as 1904. Although the GWR's locomotives always had a low water consumption, especially after being superheated, workings such as this were only possible after watertroughs had been provided at suitable points. By the 1930s, troughs were installed between the points shown in the accompanying table.

Where necessary, the in-coming water was softened in a nearby lineside installation. The locomotive's scoop was hand-operated by a rotating handle on the front of the tender, and the part-spherical dome to deflect the water downwards was a prominent feature towards the rear of the tender top. In the early part of the century, some tank engines were fitted with scoops which could be used in either direction, the most notable being the 'County Tanks.'

These were built between 1905 and 1912, but the fitting was removed in the early 1920s, together with the prominent ducts on top of the side-tanks.

PWBS

WATLINGTON BRANCH

Stations: Princes Risborough, Chinnor (3¾ m), Aston Rowant (6¼ m), Watlington (9 m)

This pleasant rural branch line ran for 8 m 66 ch from a junction just north of Princes Risborough (qv), along the Oxford line and then south-west through the Chiltern foothills to a station about a mile from Watlington. Authorized to local interests on 26 July 1869 as the Watlington & Princes Risborough Railway, opened on 15 August 1872 but failing to cover its working costs, the line was eventually sold to the GWR for £23,000.

The branch passenger services averaged about five trains each way, starting at the Watlington end and finishing when the slip coach (qv) off the 7.10 pm from Paddington got back there. They called at the two intermediate stations and at four 'platform and shelter' halts (Bledlow Bridge, Wainhill, Kingston Crossing and Lewknor Bridge) of 1906–1925.

The auto-trains (qv) were controlled by train staff and 'one-engine-in-steam' regulations.

GB

WELLINGTON (SALOP)

In addition to calls made by the longer-distance main-line services, GWR stopping trains from Birmingham came out as far as Wellington, which was also the junction for GWR branch services to Crewe (qv) and Craven Arms (qv below), and for LNWR trains to Coalport and Stafford. The two-platform station with its central through lines and east-end bays was on the Shrewsbury & Wellington Joint section of the Shrewsbury–Birmingham line, although the GW&LNW owners had separate goods depots. Trains for Crewe departed westwards and left the Shrewsbury line at Market Drayton Junction, other branch services heading east to Stafford Junction where the joint line separated into its constituents. Motive power for the GWR branch services was provided from the three-road engine shed which had an allocation of about 20 locomotives, mostly 2-6-2Ts in the later years.

The line between Shrewsbury and Oakengates dated from 1 June 1849 and had been opened by the Shrewsbury & Birmingham Railway, with the LNWR deriving its share of the joint portion from the Shropshire Union Railways & Canal Co's Stafford branch of the same year. The Craven Arms line was then added in stages between 1857–67, and that to Nantwich completed on 16 October 1867.

GB

WELLINGTON–CRAVEN ARMS LINE

Stations: Wellington, Ketley (1½ m), Lawley Bank (3 m), Horsehay & Dawley (4 m), Lightmoor Platform (5½ m), Coalbrookdale (7 m), Buildwas (8¾ m), Much Wenlock (11½ m), Presthope (14¼ m), Longville (18 m), Rushbury (29¾ m), Harton Road (22¾ m), Craven Arms (28½ m)

This mainly single-track route grew up piecemeal and was operated in the same way, more passenger services running over parts of the route than throughout. Not that passengers were numerous, for the steam railmotor (qv) service introduced in 1905 was unsuccessful and the seven halts of the 1930s produced little extra business.

The Shrewsbury & Birmingham Railway had opened a branch from Madeley Junction to Lightmoor on 1 June 1854 but this was gradually supplanted by the Wellington & Severn Junction Railway's more direct route from Ketley Junction via Horsehay, authorized on 28 August 1853, opened on 1 May 1857 and given a passenger service when the GWR took over from the Coalbrookdale Iron Co on 1 July 1861. On the following 1 February the Much Wenlock & Severn Junction Railway (incorporated on 21 July 1859) produced another section of the eventual branch by opening the 3½ miles from Much Wenlock to the Severn Valley line at Buildwas.

The gaps in the through route were partly filled from 1 November 1864 when the GWR linked Lightmoor and Coalbrookdale, and the Wenlock Railway (Act of 22 July 1861) contributed the remaining section to Buildwas. The latter concern opened Much Wenlock–Presthope on 5 December 1864 and Presthope–Marsh Farm Junction on 16 December 1867 to complete the through route from Wellington. The independent companies were amalgamated with the GWR in the 1890s.

There were several sidings along the route, including that of the foundry at Ketley, the power station at Buildwas and a dairy siding at Much Wenlock. The Light-

Wellington-Craven Arms line *No 4046* Princess Mary *on a North to West express passes Craven Arms in 1933; it is being routed down the Hereford line.* (Michael Baker Collection)

moor–Buildwas section was double track, with the station at the latter point on two levels. Passenger services on the Madeley route ceased from 21 September 1925.

GB

WELLS

The first public train service to Wells began on 15 March 1859 and was worked by the Bristol & Exeter Railway (qv) over the Somerset Central Railway's 5½-mile line from Glastonbury to a station in Priory Road. East Somerset Railway trains from Witham (qv Witham–Wells line) began running on 1 March 1862 to a separate terminus in Priory Road, and Wells got a third station when the Cheddar Valley line opened through from Yatton (qv) on 5 April 1870. The link between the Yatton and Witham lines crossed the SCR/Somerset & Dorset goods yard lines on the level and was not passed for through running until 1 January 1878 when the ESR station was relegated to goods use and GWR traffic was concentrated on the 1870 Tucker Street. The latter's trains did not stop at Priory Road until 1934.

GB

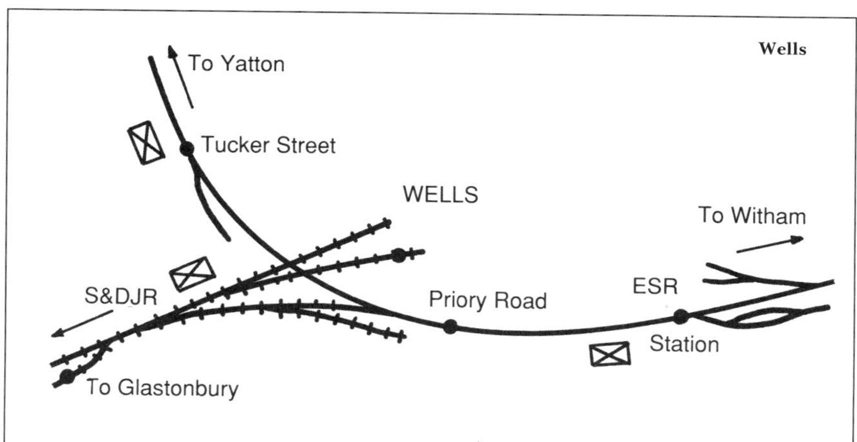

WELSHPOOL

The most remarkable feature of Welshpool was the dramatic station provided by the Oswestry & Newtown Railway for the opening of the line from Pool Quay on 14 August 1860. Its main feature was the up-side building in French Renaissance style and displaying gables, dormers and end towers to the front and a long awning on the platform side. The station also had a down island, with engine turntable and warehouses beyond, and an extensive up-side goods yard. The connection to the Welshpool & Llanfair line (qv, Llanfair Caereinion branch) and its station ran behind the cattle pens.

GB

Welshpool *A down train preparing to depart. Note the long awning and imposing buildings on the up side.* (Steamchest Collection)

WESTBURY

After the creation of the new main line to the West in 1906 (qv Reading–Taunton line), Westbury became an interchange point with the Weymouth and Salisbury lines (both qv) as well as handling local services like those to Devizes and the Trowbridge–Frome trains (all qv). It got a new station for this purpose with two 600-ft island platforms raised above road level, a goods depot at the country end and an engine shed and freight marshalling sidings beyond that. Up and down goods loops

Westbury *Looking towards the station from the south.* (Steamchest Collection)

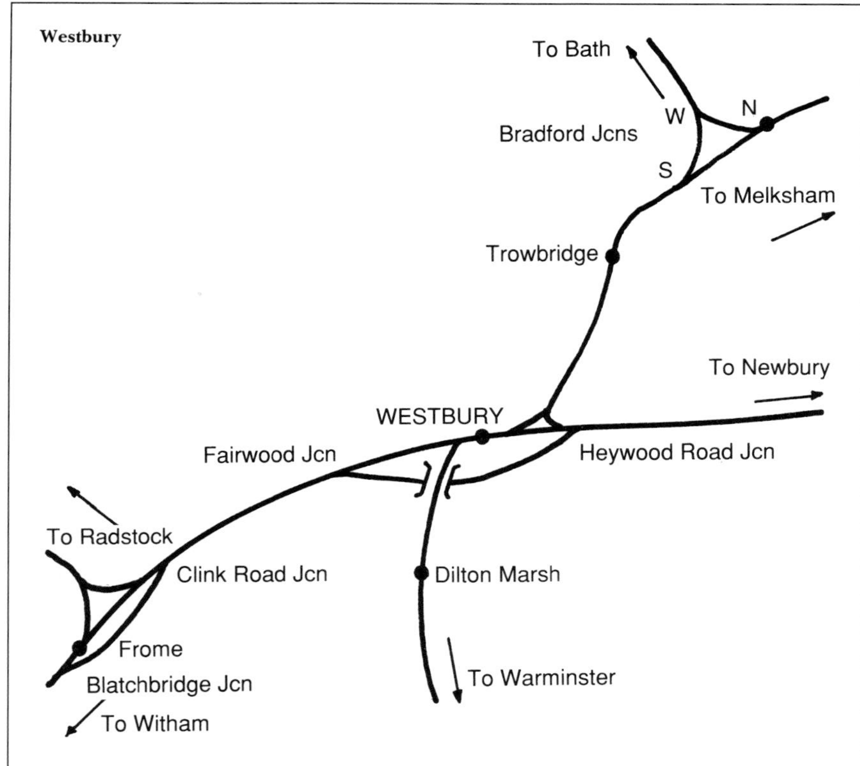

were built on either side of the station which also had a number of private sidings.

The first line to reach Westbury had been that of the Wilts, Somerset & Weymouth Railway (qv), opened from Thingley Junction (qv) on 5 September 1848 and extended to Weymouth over the period 7 October 1850 to 20 January 1857. By that time Westbury had been linked to Devizes, Bathampton and Salisbury and progressive doubling was to follow. In this century the new main line was opened between Patney & Chirton and Westbury on 29 July 1900 (passengers 1 October) and the 2¼-mile avoiding line between Heywood Road Junction and Fairwood Junction at the beginning of 1933. Westbury slip coaches (qv) were then detached at the former and brought in by the station pilot. A final addition, in 1942, was an east–north curve between the main and Avon Valley lines.

GB

WEST CORNWALL RAILWAY

The West Cornwall Railway's enabling Act of 3 August 1846 provided in Section 22 for the absorption of the Hayle Railway (qv). The latter had commenced operations eight years previously and comprised 12 miles of 'main line' from Tresavean to the port of Hayle plus branches to Redruth (qv), Portreath and the North Crofty and Roskear mines. By substituting viaducts for the HR's inclines at Angarrack and Penponds, the West Cornwall was able to use the earlier route between Hayle and Redruth and extend it to Penzance (11 March 1852), Penwithers Junction, Truro (25 August 1852), and Newham, Truro (16 April 1855).

Hard times for Cornwall's mining industry kept the West Cornwall Railway poor. Connection was made with the broad gauge Cornwall Railway at Truro (both qv) from 11 May 1859, but the WCR could not afford conversion from 'narrow' gauge to broad and this came about only after the Associated Broad Gauge Companies (qv) took over the working from 1 July 1865. An extra rail was laid and through broad gauge goods trains reached Penzance (qv) from 6 November 1866, passengers from 1 March 1867.

GB

WESTERLEIGH JUNCTIONS

The establishment of this link between the GWR's South Wales main line (qv) and the MR's Birmingham–Bristol line just north-east of the latter city revived some old rivalries between those two railways. The Bristol & Gloucester Railway, which grew out of two horse-worked lines to the River Avon, started life as a GWR-backed broad gauge project but was then snatched for the Midland in 1845 by the enterprise of that company's Deputy Chairman and an improvement on the GWR's niggardly take-over bid.

These early events deprived the GWR of a direct route from Bristol to Birmingham, but the emergence of the scheme for the South Wales & Bristol Direct Railway (qv) produced an opportunity to remedy this by providing a connection between the two routes at Westerleigh and running powers to get to the new GWR Cheltenham–Birmingham line (qv) via Honeybourne.

The two loops at Westerleigh were opened on 1 May 1903 but then closed again for five years while the two railways sorted out a new conflict. The Midland wanted the GWR to use its metals between Westerleigh and Bristol but, with a route of its own, this would have been unnecessarily costly for the latter. A court judgement and an appeal were necessary before the GWR got its way and began a passenger service over the Midland lines through Yate from 2 November 1908.

Westerleigh Junction consisted of a conventional triangle with East, West and North boxes and with the northbound line thence passing over the MR lines to reach the junction at Yate.

GB

WEST KIRBY BRANCH

Stations: Hooton, Hadlow Road (1½ m), Neston (3¾ m), Parkgate (4¾ m), Heswall (7 m), Thurstaston (9¼ m), Caldy (10¾m), Kirby Park (11¼ m), West Kirby (12 m)

This single GWR and LNWR Birkenhead Joint Lines (qv) branch originally ran from Hooton (qv) to a terminus at Parkgate. Opened on 1 October 1866, it had then been extended from a new Parkgate station and along the Dee estuary on 19 April 1886 to a fresh terminus alongside that of the Wirral Railway at West Kirby. A curve there linked the two systems, with a 'staff receiver and deliverer' for the use of through trains.

The Sectional Appendix stipulated: 'Trains on this line must be worked by tank engines'.

GB

WEST LONDON RAILWAY

Known in its early years as 'Mr Punch's Railway' for the unflattering comment it attracted from that journal, the West London grew from modest and erratic beginnings into a major cross-London route. The northern section, authorized as the Birmingham, Bristol & Thames Junction Railway on 12 June 1836, ran south from a junction with the London & Birmingham Railway to Kensington and crossed the GWR on the level in the process. A passenger service began on 27 May 1844, with both GWR and WLR trains calling at the exchange platforms where the two lines crossed from 3 June.

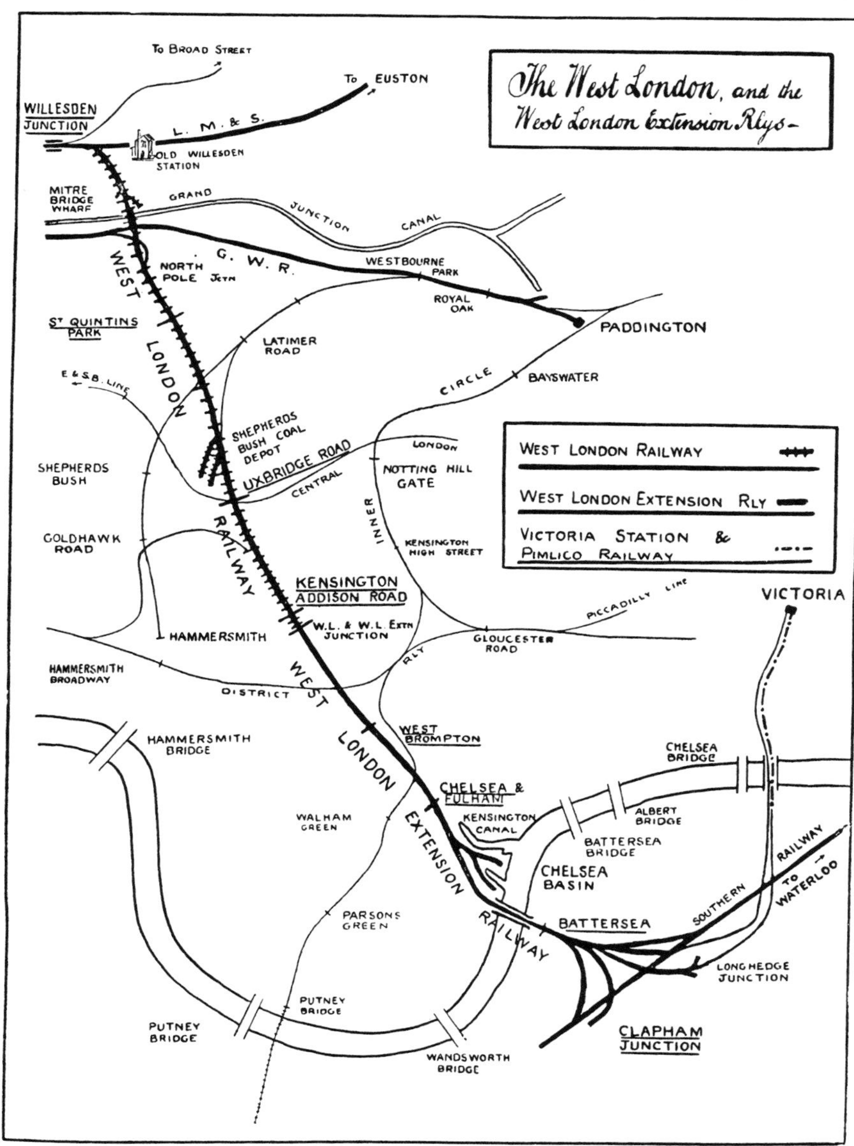

West London Railway (GWR Magazine, 1936)

For a while the West London fell upon hard times, and even though it was taken over by the GWR and LNWR companies by an Act of 31 July 1845 passenger services (from Harrow) were not restored until 2 June 1862. Three years before that the West London Extension Railway had been authorized to a GWR, LNWR, LSWR and LB&SCR partnership, with all four providing services over the route from 2 March 1863. Those of the GWR linked Southall and Victoria with calls at Hanwell, Ealing, Kensington, Chelsea and Battersea.

Linked to the GWR main line at Old Oak Common (qv) via North Pole Junction, the West London route had 11 assorted connections with seven different railways. GWR milk traffic (qv) used the route, as did that company's trains to the South Lambeth Goods Depot opened on 1 January 1911. Inter-company freight was exchanged at Lillie Bridge Sidings and parcels at the substantial Kensington Addison Road (later Olympia). Passenger services ranged from local ones, eg GWR trains to the City or the main line branches, to the 'Sunny South Special' from the North West to Brighton and Eastbourne.

GB

WEST MIDLAND RAILWAY

Deriving from an Act of 14 June 1860, the West Midland Railway was an amalgamation of the Oxford, Worcester & Wolverhampton, the Worcester & Hereford, and the Newport, Abergavenny & Hereford undertakings (all qv). One of the main objectives was the linking of the OW&W and NA&H systems by completion of the ailing Worcester & Hereford, this eventually being achieved on 15 September 1861.

When it passed to the GWR on 1 August 1863, the West Midland system contributed 190 miles of its own plus 77 miles leased or worked (Severn Valley Railway, Witney Railway and Coleford, Monmouth, Usk & Pontypool Railway) and was a major factor in its new owners eventually relinquishment of the broad gauge.

GB

WESTON-SUPER-MARE

The initial portion of the Bristol & Exeter Railway (qv), opened on 14 June 1841, included a 1½-mile branch to the growing

Weston-super-Mare
(Michael Baker Collection)

Bristol Channel resort at Weston-super-Mare. Until locomotives took over from 1 April 1851, passengers on this single, broad gauge line were conveyed in four-wheel carriages drawn by three horses in tandem. The branch was doubled and a new station provided on a site later to become the goods depot on 20 July 1866, when the ill-favoured Weston Junction was also replaced by Worle. From 1 March 1884 the branch was replaced by a loop rejoining the main line at Uphill Junction and provided with a new through station (Weston-super-Mare General) which was later given an up bay.

The destination of countless day-trippers and holidaymakers, Weston had a separate Locking Road excursion terminus which originated in 1866 and eventually achieved four-platform status. On the loop, Weston Milton Halt displaced Worle in 1922 to cater for the town's inland growth, and from 1897 to 1940 it enjoyed services on the Weston, Clevedon & Portishead Light Railway in addition to the many GWR local and long-distance services.

GB

WEYMOUTH

First as the Wilts & Somerset Railway and then as the Wilts, Somerset & Weymouth Railway (qv), the GWR route to Weymouth had emerged from the bitter rivalry with LSWR interests in the area. Its completion on 20 January 1857 marked a new era of co-operation, the line from Dorchester being laid mixed gauge and used by the trains of both railways. They also leased and worked the Weymouth & Portland Railway and the Weymouth Quay Tramway, both of which opened on 16 October 1865.

The original four-track covered station at Weymouth retained its period form throughout the whole GWR era although up-side LSWR and excursion platforms were added, plus a long double-sided down platform. The loco depot lay beside the down approaches and the goods shed between the station and the quay and

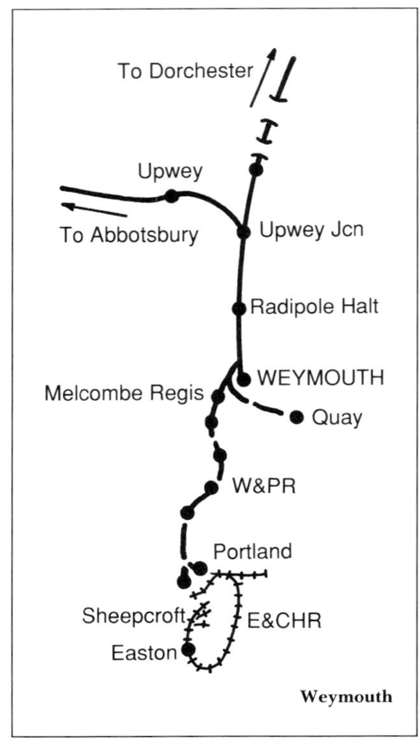

Weymouth

Weymouth *The steamer quay.* (Steamchest Collection)

Portland lines. The whole area was frequently very busy, with boat trains, Channel Islands traffic (qv) and incoming excursions adding to the workload.

On the 1-mile single line along the steamer quay, locomotives started to displace horses in 1880 and passenger trains used the route from 1 July 1889 when the GWR began operating the steamer service to the Channel Islands with three new twin-screw vessels from Lairds of Birkenhead (qv Ships and shipping services). Major improvements were made in 1925 when four new oil-fired steamers were introduced, from 13 July 1933 when accommodation at the quay and its station was considerably increased, and in 1938 when track curves were eased to allow the special long couplings previously necessary to be dispensed with.

The Portland branch trains originally had to reverse outside Weymouth station, but from 30 May 1909 they ran to and from the Melcombe Regis platform built just beyond the carriage sidings. They were worked by the SR in later years, with the GWR working the station and tramway.

GB

WHARNCLIFFE VIADUCT

In November 1835 the GWR let the first contract of its exciting new railway project. It went to Grissell & Peto and was for a viaduct over the Brent Valley, begun early in 1836 and completed in mid-1837. Of brick and masonry, the 860-ft structure rose 65 ft above the valley floor and had eight 70-ft arches. It was named after Lord Wharncliffe for his part in facilitating the GWR's Parliamentary proceedings, and bore his coat of arms. The viaduct was widened during the 1878–84 quadrupling.

GB

WHITCHURCH–ABERYSTWYTH LINE

Stations: Whitchurch, Fenn's Bank (3 m), Bettisfield ($6\frac{3}{4}$ m), Welshampton ($7\frac{3}{4}$ m), Ellesmere ($10\frac{3}{4}$ m), Frankton ($12\frac{3}{4}$ m), Whittington High Level ($16\frac{1}{4}$ m), Oswestry ($18\frac{1}{4}$ m), Llynclys (22 m), Pant ($23\frac{1}{4}$ m), Llanymynech ($24\frac{1}{4}$ m), Four Crosses ($25\frac{3}{4}$ m), Arddleen ($27\frac{1}{2}$ m), Pool Quay ($29\frac{1}{4}$ m), Buttington ($31\frac{1}{4}$), Welshpool ($33\frac{3}{4}$ m), Forden ($38\frac{1}{4}$ m), Montgomery (40 m), Abermule (44 m), Newtown ($47\frac{3}{4}$ m), Moat Lane Junction ($52\frac{1}{2}$ m), Caersws ($53\frac{1}{4}$ m), Pontdolgoch (55 m), Carno ($59\frac{1}{4}$ m), Talerddig ($61\frac{1}{4}$ m), Llanbrynmair ($64\frac{3}{4}$ m), Cemmes Road (70 m), Machynlleth (75 m), Dovey Junction (79 m), Glandyfi ($79\frac{3}{4}$ m), Ynyslas ($85\frac{1}{4}$ m), Borth ($87\frac{1}{4}$ m), Llandre ($89\frac{3}{4}$ m), Bow Street ($91\frac{1}{4}$ m), Aberystwyth ($85\frac{3}{4}$ m)

The Cambrian Railways' (qv) main line began at Cambrian Junction, just south of Whitchurch, quickly crossed into Wales and then headed across Fenn's Moss to meet the Wrexham branch (qv) at Ellesmere. Two minor summits followed, the second at Oswestry (qv) where the company had its headquarters and works. At Llynclys Junction, the Porthywaen and Tanat Valley lines departed westwards, followed by the Nantmawr and Llanfyllin lines at Llanymynech, a crossing of the River Severn near Pool Quay and then the junction with the GW&LNW Shrewsbury–Buttington line (qv).

Beyond Welshpool (qv), where traffic was transferred with the Welshpool & Llanfair Light Railway, the Cambrian trains followed an easy river and canal course to Newtown. The line varied between 200 and 300 ft above sea level and had only one branch, that from Abermule to Kerry (qv). Then came the lonely Moat Lane Junction (qv), where the Mid-Wales line departed, and Caersws, junction for the freight branch to Van (qv).

The route now involved a climb of 8 miles to reach the cutting and summit at Talerddig, 120 ft deep and 693 ft above sea level. Gold had supposedly been found here, but the CR trains which had been climbing at 1 in 100 and then 1 in 58 were glad to move on to the 14-mile descent to Machynlleth (qv), dropping at 1 in 56 initially but more gently after joining the Dinas Mawddwy branch (qv) and its companion River Dovey. At Dovey Junction, the Pwllheli and Aberystwyth (all qv) routes separated, the latter running south of the estuary and then via two secondary summits to the terminus.

Apart from the Buttington–Moat Lane Junction section, most of this route was single track signalled by Tyers electric tablet system in the Cambrian era. In the early years tank, 0-6-0 and 2-4-0 locomotives predominated, with 4-4-0s appearing soon after the turn of the century and the GWR just developing the established CR pattern. Serious accidents were rare, with the notable exception of the head-on collision near Abermule on 26 January 1921 when 17 people were killed.

In summer, about half the trains on this route were for holidaymakers from London and the North West. The local services included at least one 'all stations' train, the 10 am from Whitchurch perpetuating the 'Parliamentary' train tradition and taking 4 hr 12 min for the through journey. In the up direction the 2.50 pm from Aberystwyth took 5 hours to reach Whitchurch.

Principal opening dates are given in the Cambrian Railways entry.

GB

WHITEBALL

To reach Exeter the Bristol & Exeter Railway (qv) had to pass through White Ball Hill on the Somerset–Devon border. This involved a 1,092-yard tunnel cut to a depth of up to 200 ft with a curve at the London end and a rising gradient of 1 in 127 to the summit beyond the other portal. The bore had to have a 2 ft brick lining because of its mixed geology and for many years represented a test for engines and men, especially when restarting an up train on the 1 in 115 rising gradient through Burlescombe.

GB

WHITLAND

'Whitland. Junction for Pembroke and Tenby and Cardigan Branches' read the GWR nameboard at this West Wales station. Its first railway had been the South Wales main line (qv) opened on 2 January 1854, the Pembroke & Tenby line then following on 4 September 1866 and the Whitland & Cardigan Railway opening its first section, from a junction 2¼ miles west of Whitland, on 24 March 1873.

In GWR days Whitland consisted of an up platform with main buildings and country-end bay, a down island and then the goods depot and sidings beyond. There was an engine shed and turntable at one stage and a later milk depot siding.

GB

WILKINSON, H. L.

Superintendent of the Line, 1933–36. He entered GWR service in the District Goods Manager's office at Bristol in 1890, moved to the Divisional Superintendent's office there in 1892 and to the London Division in 1896. He was Assistant Station Master at Paddington for some years before appointment as Chief Clerk to the Superintendent, Cardiff Division, in 1910, returning to Paddington as Outdoor Assistant the next year. In September 1917 he became Divisional Superintendent, Paddington, and was appointed Assistant Superintendent of the Line from 9 January 1922. He took office as Superintendent on 1 January 1933, but retired through ill-health in August 1936, to be succeeded by F. R. Potter (qv).

CA

WILKINSON, SIR JOSEPH LOFTUS

General Manager, 1896–1903. He was born in Buckinghamshire in 1845, educated at Reading, and began with the GWR as a boy clerk in 1859. By 1876 he had risen to be Principal Assistant to the Goods Manager, and in 1885 he went to South America as General Manager of the Buenos Aires & Pacific Railway. When Lambert (qv) was appointed as General Manager of the GWR, Wilkinson was asked to return as Chief Goods Manager, which he did in May 1888, and during the six months of Lambert's subsequent illness he also acted as Assistant General Manager. He took over fully from Lambert in July 1896, and was instrumental in breathing new life into the company. He was knighted in 1902, but died on 16 June the following year after a short illness.

CA

WILLIAM DEAN

In 1902 Churchward (qv) built the prototype for all his standard classes, in the form of the 4-6-0 No 100, which was given the name *Dean*. Later this was changed to *William Dean*, to clarify the fact that it was named after his predecessor at Swindon. With outside cylinders, a high running-plate, and inside valve gear, the locomotive had the essential characteristics of all the successful classes that followed, and caused a considerable stir when it appeared. Initially it was fitted with a parallel boiler, rather than a tapered one, but this other hallmark of Churchward's designs was fitted a year later. The locomotive was later numbered 2900, to make it the first of the 'Saint' Class (qv), and was withdrawn in 1922.

PWBS

WILLIAMS, JOHN

Director, 1855–65. Williams came from Chester, and was appointed a GWR Director in 1855, but stood down ten years later so that Gooch (qv) could come on to the Board in his place. Gooch was elected on 2 November 1865, and William's resignation was ratified at the General Meeting on 2 March following.

CA

WILTS, SOMERSET & WEYMOUTH RAILWAY

A factor in the intense rivalry between the GWR and LSWR, the planned Corsham–Salisbury line of the Wilts & Somerset

William Dean *Originally numbered 100, this 4-6-0 was Churchward's prototype for all his subsequent standard classes.* (H. C. Casserley)

Railway was expanded into a GWR-backed Weymouth line scheme, incorporated by an Act of Parliament of 30 June 1845. The Wilts, Somerset & Weymouth Railway, authorized further variations in 1846 and 1847, opened the 13¾ miles from Thingley Junction to Westbury (both qv) on 5 September 1848, but then became a victim of the financial pressures of the period. The GWR took over from 14 March 1850, but managed only to extend to Frome (qv) by 7 October 1850 and to Warminster on 9 September 1851.

There matters rested with many of the forward works uncompleted until, spurred by a local pressure group and its writs of mandamus, the GWR resumed work, obtaining powers for the Devizes and Bathampton lines on 31 July 1854 and opening a Frome–Radstock branch on 14 November of that year. After linking Warminster with Salisbury (qv Salisbury branch) from 30 June 1856, 26 miles of single line was opened between Frome and Yeovil (qv) on 1 September and the difficult section on to Weymouth (qv) with its four tunnels (Holywill, 311 yards; Frampton, 660; Poundbury, 264; and Bincombe, 814) and nine viaducts, on 20 January 1857. On 2 February of that year the 9½-mile branch to Bathampton (qv) was opened — ten years after its construction — and the 8¼ miles to Devizes (qv) on 1 July.

After track doubling between 1875 and 1885 the route carried an increasing load of boat trains, Bristol, Birmingham and London services and local workings. It was not easy to work because of the steep gradients beyond Yeovil where down trains had a 5-mile climb steepening to 1 in 51 before Evershot summit.

GB

WINDSOR BRANCH

The Bills deposited by the infant GWR in 1833 included provision for a Windsor branch, but the Provost and Fellows of Eton College saw this as offering their boys easy access to the temptations of London, and the eventual 1835 Act precluded a station within 3 miles of the college. Attitudes had moderated by the time of the GWR (Slough & Windsor) Act of 14 August 1848, but the college still required access for recovering wayward pupils!

The 2 m 63 ch branch was opened on 8 October 1849, its single line from Slough (qv) following an embankmented route to the 203-ft wrought iron bowstring bridge over the Thames and on into a station opposite Windsor Castle. The route became mixed gauge in 1862 and standard in 1883. Modified then and in 1897, Windsor station grew into an impressive affair with three platforms and separate Royal waiting rooms provided to mark Queen Victoria's Diamond Jubilee. On the down side a line descended to a goods depot below the approach arches.

In later years weekday local services numbered nearly 80, plus inwards excursions. Earlier there had been through Paddington services including a slip coach (qv), and even one to Victoria via the West London (qv) route.

GB

WINDSOR CASTLE

In 1924, King George V and Queen Mary visited Swindon Works, and, at the end of their tour, His Majesty drove 'Castle' (qv) No 4082 *Windsor Castle* back to the station, with the Queen also on the footplate. This event was later recorded by brass plates fixed to the cab sides. When the King died in 1936, the locomotive was used to haul his funeral train from Paddington to Windsor. In 1952, after the death of his son, King George VI, the locomotive was not available, and for the funeral train on this occa-

WINDSOR CASTLE.

28th April,1924.

Dear Churchill,

The King and Queen wish me to thank you and your Staff for to-day's excellent arrangements at Swindon.

It was gratifying to Their Majesties to have this opportunity of becoming acquainted with this vast industrial centre and of seeing the various departments of the well-known Works of your Company.

The King and Queen have carried away the happiest recollections of their first visit to Swindon, and they much appreciated the loyal reception extended to them while proceeding on the engine "Windsor Castle" from Weighbridge to the Station, by the thousands of men and women upon whose skill and efficiency the prosperity and development of this important Railway Headquarters so largely depends.

Yours sincerely,

Clive Wigram

The Viscount Churchill,G.C.V.O.,

Windsor Castle *The letter of appreciation from the King and Queen.* (GWR Magazine) sion the name and number were exchanged with those of No 7013, formerly *Bristol Castle*. Both these renamed locomotives then retained their new identities until they were scrapped.

PWBS

WITHAM–WELLS LINE

Stations: Witham, Wanstrow (2½ m), Cranmore (5½ m), Shepton Mallet High Street (9 m), Wells Priory Road (13¾ m), Wells Tucker Street (14 m)

The Shepton Mallet promoters of the East Somerset Railway enjoyed GWR moral, if not financial, support. They obtained an Act on 5 June 1856, started work the following February, and opened the authorized 9 miles from Witham on 9 November 1858 to the delight of 'a prodigious multitude'. Financial backing from Wells (qv) brought another Act (on 14 June 1860) and extension to a terminus there on 1 March 1862. The GWR worked the local concern but its earnings were so modest that the prospect of gauge conversion in 1874 compelled the sale to the larger company.

From an up-side bay at Witham the undulating ESR route ran west through the Mendip foothills from which it derived limestone traffic via three goods sidings and the Waterlip Quarry line. The Witham–Wells/Yatton trains crossed over the Somerset & Dorset at Shepton Mallet and there was a connection to that company on the 1878 link which abandoned the ESR terminus at Wells for end-on connection with the GWR there.

Trains of the East Somerset Railway preservation scheme now operate west from Cranmore.

GB

WOLVERHAMPTON

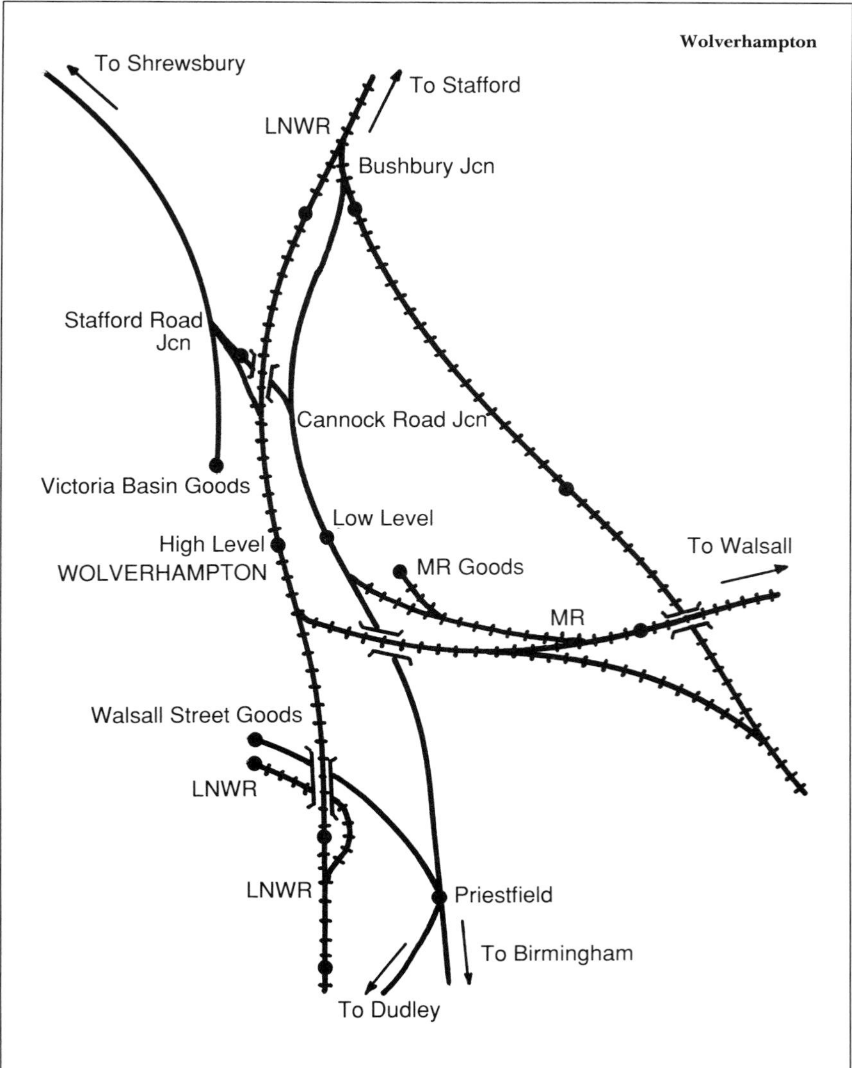

The GWR's Low Level station at Wolverhampton was a major calling point for its expresses from Paddington to Shrewsbury, Chester, Birkenhead and North Wales. It also initiated services to Weymouth and via Bristol and had a good pattern of more local trains on its three radiating lines and over the relatively short-lived Kingswinford branch (qv). The through trains on the main line were mostly re-engined at Low Level which consisted of a sizeable down-side building leading to the two long platforms with four lines between them and bays at three of the four ends. The location dated from 1854 with a major remodelling taking place in 1869.

Wolverhampton's first railway was the enterprising Shrewsbury & Birmingham which arrived at a temporary terminus on 12 November 1849 and then found itself obstructed in every way by the LNWR, only finally gaining access to Birmingham in 1854. The latter was a momentous year for Wolverhampton and the GWR, the Oxford, Worcester & Wolverhampton Railway (qv) opening to Low Level from 1 July of that year, the Birmingham, Wolverhampton & Dudley Railway opening on 14 November, and the S&B diverting its trains from Stafford Road. All had become, or were to become, GWR constituents.

The GWR's Wolverhampton goods depot was at Walsall Street, on a short 1855 branch from Priestfield. The area was also important for the Stafford Road Locomotive Works, established by the S&B in 1849 and extended in 1860 and 1881 (qv Armstrong). Locomotive building was transferred to Swindon (qv) in 1908, but Stafford Road remained busy with repair work and gained a new repair shop in 1932. Further along the ex-S&B route lay the important Oxley marshalling yards, preceded by Oxley viaduct and followed by the down-side loco shed. From Oxley Middle and North junctions, single-line connections were made to the Kingswinford branch.

GB

WOOD, SIR CHARLES ALEXANDER

Director, 1863–96. Born on 11 November 1810, he was appointed a Director of the GWR in 1863, in place of William Fenton, at the same time as Gooch (qv) was elected Chairman, and acted as Deputy-Chairman from 2 November 1865 until 1890. To judge from a reference to it as '. . . an encumbrance' during a meeting in 1866, he seems to have been a member of the anti-Broad Gauge lobby. He was knighted in 1874, and following his death in April 1896 was succeeded as Deputy-Chairman by Viscount Cobham (qv Lyttelton).

CA

WOODBRIDGE, ARTHUR

The GWR's last Signal & Telegraph Engineer, April 1947 to September 1959. He joined the GWR in 1926.

AV

WOOFFERTON BRANCH

Stations: Kidderminster, Bewdley (3½ m), Wyre Forest (8 m), Cleobury Mortimer (10 m), Neen Sollars (13½ m), Newnham Bridge (15¾ m), Tenbury Wells (19 m), Easton Court (21½ m), Woofferton (24¼ m)

This was a very rural piece of railway linking Kidderminster and the Hereford–Shrewsbury line via a pleasant course which crossed the Severn on Dowles viaduct and headed west through the Wyre Forest to pick up the course of the River Rea. Five trains each way made the through journey on weekdays with others running between Tenbury Wells and Woofferton. The former took 62–67 minutes in the down direction, including the call at Cleobury Mortimer which was the starting point for the Cleobury Mortimer & Ditton Priors Light Railway.

The western end of the branch was jointly owned by the GWR and LNWR/LMS, having been authorized to the Tenbury Railway by an Act of 21 July 1859, opened on 1 August 1861 and transferred to the main-line companies from 1 January 1869. The Tenbury & Bewdley Railway Act of 3 July 1869 produced the rest of the route, with opening on 13 August 1864, and vesting in the GWR in 1869.

GB

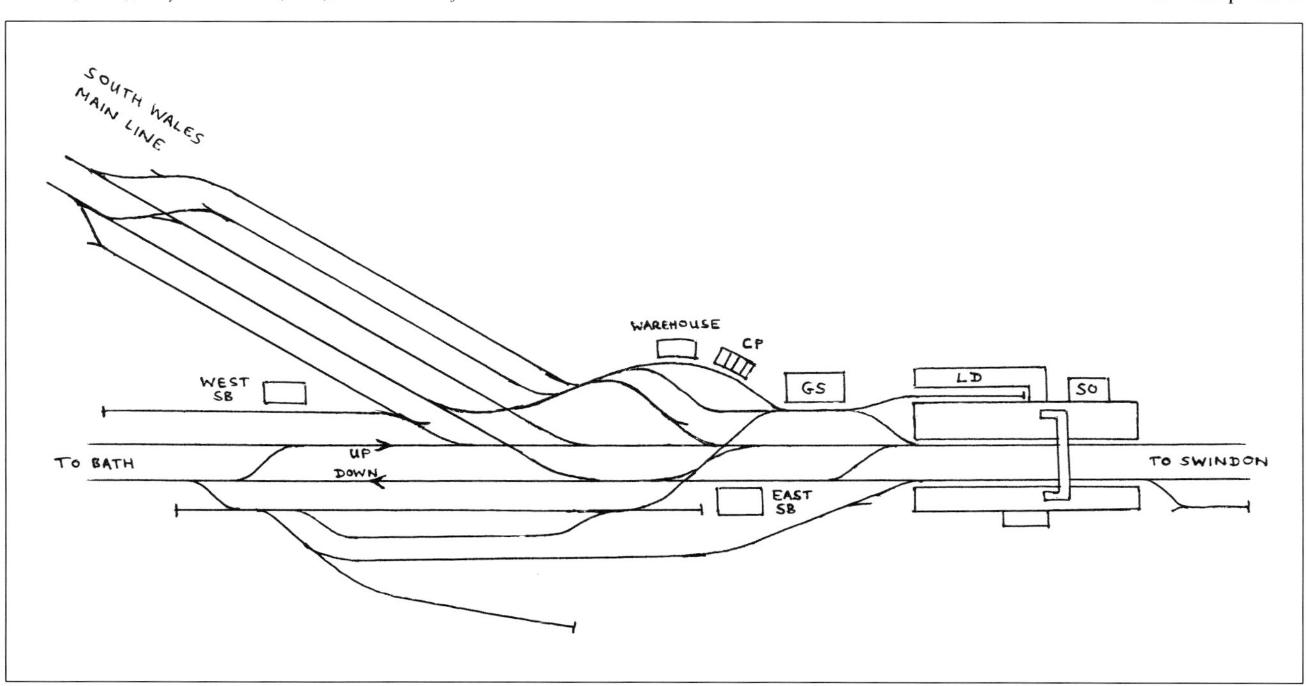

Wootton Bassett *Sketch map of the station and junction in 1929.*

WOOTTON BASSETT

The GWR main line reached Wootton Bassett Road, or Hay Lane, on 17 December 1840 and pushed on to Chippenham (qv) in the following year when Wootton Bassett got a new, Brunel-style station 2¾ miles west of the original on 30 July. This was then rebuilt for the 1903 opening of the South Wales & Bristol Direct Railway (qv) and enjoyed a good local service plus stops by some longer-distance trains on both routes. The junction lay west of Wootton Bassett's goods yard and had additional loops and sidings along both routes. From 1927 there was also a siding for United Dairies milk tanks.

GB

WORCESTER

The two stations at Worcester were situated on the main line from Oxford to Hereford, outside the base corners of a triangular link with the 212 yd Rainbow Hill Tunnel and the line to Droitwich (qv). The senior and largest was Shrub Hill, reached on 5 October 1850 by a branch from the Midland's Birmingham–Gloucester line and later becoming joint with the GWR as a result of the latter's eventual absorption of the Oxford, Worcester & Wolverhampton Railway (qv). West of the triangle lay the elevated and more central Foregate Street station, opened as part of the Worcester & Hereford Railway (qv) on 17 May 1860 and followed by an embankment leading to a viaduct over the River Severn.

The joint station at Shrub Hill was approached past the MR goods yard and shed and consisted of down-side main buildings and platform, four running lines and then the up island. It anticipated later practice in being signalled for each end to be used separately, and had the GWR goods yard and shed on its northern side. From the latter, lines crossed Tolladine Road to the coal yard and the sheet works, with goods lines separating these from the extensive Carriage & Wagon Works. A sizeable engine shed then lay within the triangle, with a line back over Tolladine Road to the Vinegar Works sidings. Another siding, the Butts Branch, started beyond the twin Foregate Street platforms and reached the riverside wharves by reversal.

Worcester was a busy and interesting location handling passenger services like the Cardiff–Birmingham express railcars (qv) and freight flows like tinplate to Metal Box. Among its unusual features were standard semaphore signals controlling road traffic across the Vinegar Works branch and a suspended cellar and water balance lift at Foregate Street.

GB

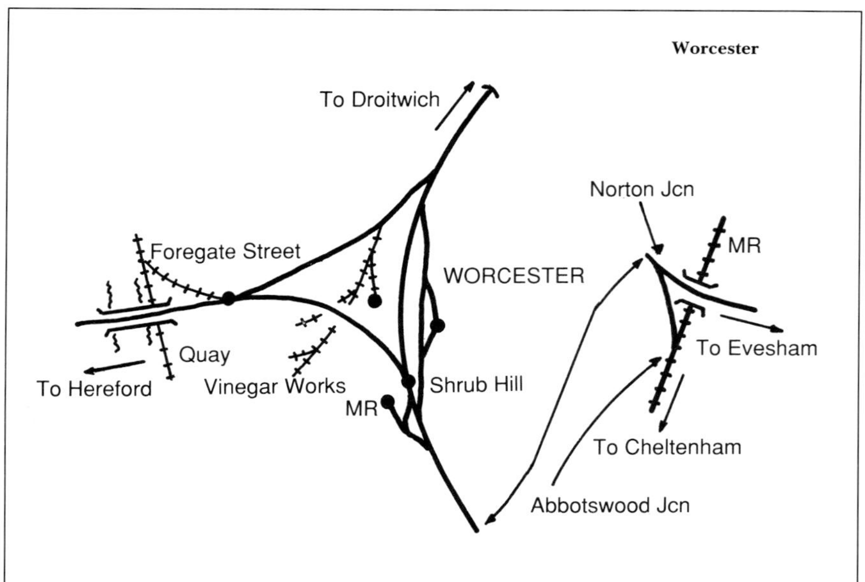

WORCESTER–HEREFORD LINE

Stations: Worcester Shrub Hill, Worcester Foregate Street ($\frac{3}{4}$ m), Henwick ($1\frac{1}{4}$ m), Bransford Road (4 m), Malvern Link (7 m), Great Malvern (8 m), Malvern Wells ($9\frac{1}{2}$ m), Colwall ($11\frac{1}{2}$ m), Ledbury ($15\frac{1}{2}$ m), Ashperton ($19\frac{1}{2}$ m), Stoke Edith ($21\frac{3}{4}$ m), Withington (25 m), Hereford ($29\frac{1}{4}$ m)

This line climbed moderately along the eastern slopes of the Malvern Hills with the gradient steepening to 1 in 80 as it passed through them via the 1,589-yd Colwall Tunnel and then descended through the 1,323-yd Ledbury Tunnel to the mellow countryside beyond. The original Colwall Tunnel was replaced in 1926 but the Ledbury one remained in its original, confined form which necessitated the use of corridor stock on all trains and had the GWR's footplate men coughing and spluttering in the smoke-filled atmosphere.

After years of in-fighting between rival railway interests the line authorized to the Worcester & Hereford Railway by an Act of 15 August 1853 was rescued by the Newport, Abergavenny & Hereford (qv), the Oxford, Worcester & Wolverhampton (qv) and Midland companies and opened from Henwick to Malvern Link on 25 July 1859, Worcester to Henwick on 17 May, Malvern Link to Malvern Wells on 25 May 1860 and on to Shelwick Junction (with the Shrewsbury & Hereford line) on 13 September 1861. It acquired branches to Ashchurch (1864), Bromyard (1874–77) and Gloucester (1885).

The route carried the GWR's South Wales–Birmingham service, Hereford–Oxford–London trains and various local workings including trains originating at Ledbury, Colwall and Malvern Wells (all qv). Its use was limited by the single-line tunnel sections and the need to bank heavy trains but it remained an important east-west artery for freight and passengers.

GB

WORCESTER–LEOMINSTER LINE

Stations: Worcester Shrub Hill, Worcester Foregate Street ($\frac{3}{4}$ m), Henwick ($1\frac{1}{4}$ m), Leigh Court ($5\frac{1}{2}$ m), Knightwick ($8\frac{1}{2}$ m), Suckley (10 m), Bromyard ($14\frac{1}{2}$ m), Rowden Mill ($17\frac{1}{4}$ m), Fencote ($19\frac{3}{4}$ m), Steens Bridge ($23\frac{1}{2}$ m), Leominster ($27\frac{1}{2}$ m)

From a junction at Bransford Road on the Worcester–Hereford line (qv above), this rural railway turned west along the River Teme to its principal intermediate station at Bromyard. It then continued through wooded countryside to a summit at Fencote before running parallel with the Hereford–Shrewsbury line into Leominster (qv). Single with passing loops and worked by electric train staff, it carried five through passenger trains each way on weekdays with one more over the Worcester–Bromyard portion.

The original plans of the Worcester, Bromyard & Leominster Railway, incorporated by Act of 11 August 1861, were to be truncated to the eastern portion of the route, with opening from Leominster Junction to Knightwick on 2 May 1874 and on to Bromyard on 22 October 1877. Worked and maintained by the GWR, the WB&L was taken over from 1 July 1888. From the same date the Leominster & Bromyard Railway was acquired, that company having been incorporated on 30 July 1874, opening from Leominster to Steens Bridge on 1 March 1884. The Steens Bridge–Bromyard section was then completed by the GWR on 1 September 1897.

GB

WORCESTER–SHREWSBURY LINE

Stations: Worcester Shrub Hill, Fernhill Heath (2½ m), Droitwich Spa (5½ m), Cutnall Green (9 m), Hartlebury (11¼ m), Stourport-on-Severn (14¼ m), Bewdley (16¾ m), Arley (20½ m), Highley (22¾ m), Hampton Loade (25 m), Eardington (27¼ m), Bridgnorth (29½ m), Linley (33¾ m), Coalport (36¼ m), Iron Bridge & Broseley (38¼ m), Buildwas (39¾ m), Cressage (43¾ m), Berrington (47¾ m), Shrewsbury (52 m)

Incorporated by the Severn Valley Railway Act of 20 August 1853, this line from Hartlebury to Shrewsbury followed the River Severn all the way from Stourport, along the edge of the Wyre Forest, through the gorge at Ironbridge and on, south of The Wrekin, to meet the Hereford line at Severn Valley Junction, Shrewsbury. Its course embraced sharp curves at Folly Point, summits near the colliery at Alveley and just south of Bridgnorth, Oldbury viaduct and Victoria Bridge, and the modest Knowlesands Tunnel. In the GWR era its all-stations trains took anything from 139 to 175 minutes to serve the five halts and 17 intermediate stations.

Leased by the West Midland Railway (qv) in 1860, the Severn Valley route was opened on 1 February 1862 and gained a loop from Bewdley to Kidderminster on 1 June 1878. This was mainly used by a connecting shuttle and trains on the Tenbury Wells branch, although some Kidderminster–Bridgnorth services operated. In addition to Bewdley the SVR had a second interchange point, with Wellington–Craven Arms (qv) trains, at Buildwas.

A portion of the route survives as part of the Severn Valley Railway preservation scheme.

GB

Worcester-Shrewsbury line *Arley station, now preserved on the Severn Valley Railway, looking north.* (Steamchest Collection)

WORLD WARS

The GWR felt the effects of the World Wars in many ways, both conflicts involving government control of the railways. Three of the company's vessels served as hospital ships in the first War, *Roebuck* being sunk at Scapa Flow in 1915. In the Second, another commandeered hospital ship, *St David*, was sunk at Anzio, whilst *St Patrick* was bombed and sunk approaching Fishguard on her regular run from Rosslare in 1941, 30 passengers and crew losing their lives (qv Ships and shipping services).

On the rails, 238 GWR carriages served as ambulance coaches between 1914 and 1918, and rather fewer between 1939 and 1945, some being converted, others being built as such. They became the property of

GREAT WESTERN RAILWAY.

(Circular No. 2386.)

General Manager's Office,
Paddington Station,
London, W.
5th August, 1914.

The Government have, for the time being, taken over the control of the Railway in connection with the Mobilization of the Troops and General Movements in relation to Naval and Military requirements.

The Management of the Railway and the existing conditions of employment of the Staff will remain unaltered, and all instructions will be issued through the same channels as heretofore.

FRANK POTTER,
General Manager.

World Wars *Circular from the General Manager advising staff of the Government control of the railways in 1914.* (GWR Magazine)

World Wars *One of the 238 GWR carriages serving in First World War ambulance trains.* (GWR Museum, Swindon)

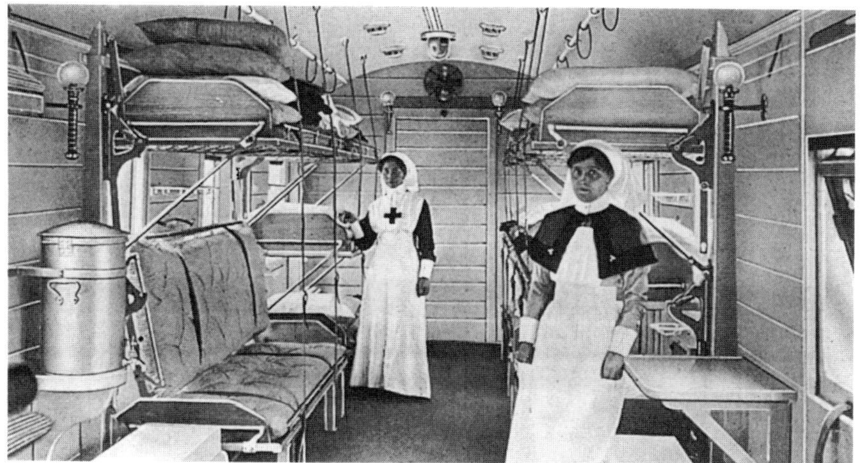

World Wars *Evacuees at Paddington in September 1939. (The carriage, No 5428, was later damaged in an air raid and subsequently rebuilt.) James Milne wrote to staff to express his 'appreciation of the magnificent services rendered by them in connection with the recent evacuation of London and other congested areas. I have every confidence that this is only typical of the efforts that will be made by all grades in the strenuous and difficult days that are ahead.'* (Michael Baker Collection)

the government and many were sent to Europe; afterwards most were bought back by the GWR and converted to normal use. At least one, Churchward 'Toplight' full brake No 1159, has been preserved at Didcot. A quite different use was found for two saloons completed in 1941 which were fitted with radio-receiving equipment and used by government officials and military leaders (qv Rolling-stock, passenger). Some 7,952 GWR employees volunteered in August 1914.

Engines were also taken over; many 'Dean Goods' 0-6-0s served abroad in both World Wars, while amongst a batch of brand new '43xx' 2-6-0s sent to France in 1917 was the now preserved No 5322. After

World Wars *A Second World War Air Raid Precautions exercise at Paddington.* (National Railway Museum, York)

World Wars *In August 1940 Newton Abbot station was damaged in an air raid. This is the up island; note the length of rail lodged in the roof!* (GW Society)

the First World War the GWR, like many companies, bought ROD 2-8-0s built for the Royal Engineers. They lasted much longer than those on other lines, the final one being withdrawn in 1958. During the Second War, American-built 2-8-0s worked briefly on the GWR, others being stored in South Wales, before all were sent abroad. British Riddles-designed (War Department) 2-8-0s had a much longer life over here, many surviving on the Western Region into the 1960s. Swindon built Stanier-designed '8F' 2-8-0s for service both at home and abroad, and one, No 8431, is preserved on the Keighley & Worth Valley Railway (qv Locomotives). In addition, munitions were produced in great quantities at Swindon and other GWR works.

During the Second World War a fixed annual payment of £6,670,603 was imposed on the GWR in 1941, but Nationalization arrived before promised payments for arrears of maintenance and the excessive wear and tear of wartime conditions could be made. The South Wales coal industry, in severe decline throughout the 1930s, lost its export market but home demand ensured its temporary revival. Passenger services were reduced, and crowds were sometimes so great at Paddington that Ministry of War Transport Regulations were ignored and extra carriages were provided on the extra carriages were provided on the authority of the Chairman. Restaurant cars disappeared, speed was reduced, blackout blinds were fitted to carriages, and journeys were slower, more uncomfortable and, occasionally, dangerous. GWR trains and stations were attacked by German aircraft on occasions, notably Newton Abbot and Plymouth and those in the Birmingham and London areas and the Home Counties. Snow Hill and Paddington were both damaged, but the GWR suffered less than the other members of the 'Big Four'. Much heroism was shown on occasions by GWR employees; 2,524 were killed in the First World War, 788 in the Second.

MCHB

World Wars *Successful completion of the GWR's 'Spitfire' Fund.* (GWR Magazine)

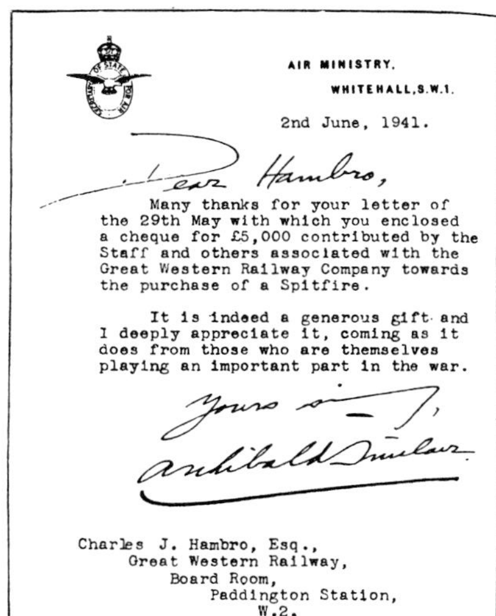

AIR MINISTRY.
WHITEHALL, S.W.1.

2nd June, 1941.

Dear Hambro,

Many thanks for your letter of the 29th May with which you enclosed a cheque for £5,000 contributed by the Staff and others associated with the Great Western Railway Company towards the purchase of a Spitfire.

It is indeed a generous gift and I deeply appreciate it, coming as it does from those who are themselves playing an important part in the war.

Archibald Sinclair

Charles J. Hambro, Esq.,
Great Western Railway,
Board Room,
Paddington Station,
W.2.

WREXHAM AND BRANCHES

Stations: Wrexham, Plas Power (2 m), Brymbo (3½ m), Coed Poeth (6¼ m), Berwig Halt (6¾ m)

The GWR main line through Wrexham originated with the North Wales Mineral Railway which was incorporated on 6 August 1844. The Act authorized the line

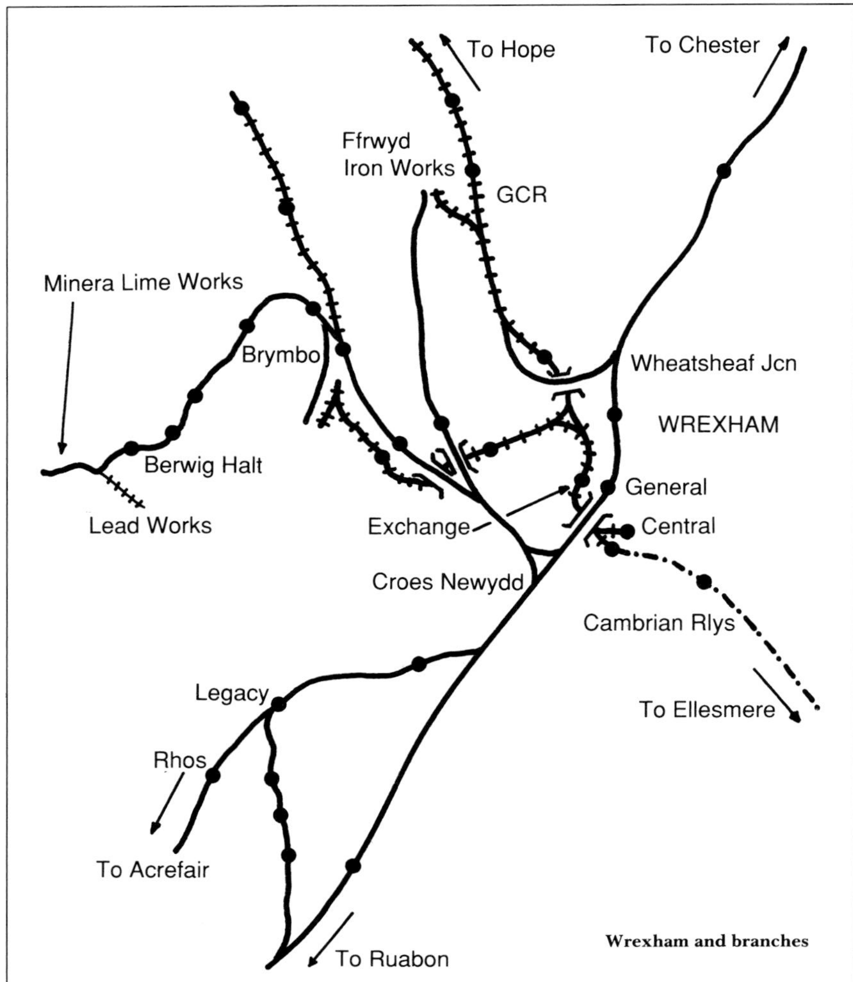

Wrexham and branches

from Saltney and this was opened to Wrexham and on to Ruabon (qv) on 4 November 1846, a few months after the North Wales Mineral and the Shrewsbury, Oswestry & Chester Junction Railway had combined as the Shrewsbury & Chester (qv). In pursuance of its mineral traffic interests, the NWM had also been authorized branches to Saltney Goods, Minera, Gwersyllt, Brynmally and Ffrwyd, all of which were opened in 1847.

Wrexham had three stations, the GWR General, the Great Central's adjoining Exchange, and Central, which was used by both GC and Cambrian-worked trains on the line to Ellesmere (qv below). General, which was rebuilt in 1910–12, was a substantial affair with main and Barmouth line platforms and an adjacent goods yard and interchange sidings. Locomotives for the extensive main-line, branch and freight workings were provided by Croes Newydd shed which had been opened in 1902 in the old roundhouse style.

Croes Newydd shed lay within the triangular junction with the 3¼-mile line to Brymbo which had been authorized by the Wrexham & Minera Railway Act of 17 May 1861, opened on 22 May 1862 and acquired by the GWR under an Act of 31 July 1871. This line was extended north to meet the LNWR at Llanfynydd by the Wrexham & Minera Extension Railway which was incorporated on 5 July 1865, opened on 27 January 1872 and had then become a GWR and LNWR joint line by an Act of 11 June 1866. A GWR railmotor (qv) service was operated as far as Berwig Halt on the Minera Lime Works line and a joint GWR and LNWR passenger service from Mold to Brymbo, the former ending on 1 January 1931 after 34 years of operation.

By the Moss Valley Railway (GWR) scheme authorized on 21 July 1873 the GWR opened a new route from Brymbo to the Ffrwyd Iron Works on 11 May 1882. With its Vron, Southsea, Brynmally and Caepenty colliery branches this completed the network serving the substantial coal and metal industries to the west of Wrexham proper.

GB

WREXHAM–ELLESMERE LINE

Stations: Wrexham Central, Marchwiel (2¼ m), Bangor-on-Dee (5¼ m), Overton-on-Dee (8½ m), Ellesmere (12¾ m)

This Flintshire branch, running east of the River Dee, linked the Cambrian system with a station at Wrexham Central and, beyond that, with the Great Central's Wrexham, Mold & Connah's Quay line which, in turn, was connected to the collieries and steelworks north-west of Wrexham. It had been authorized to the Wrexham & Ellesmere Railway on 31 July 1885 with MS&L and Cambrian backing and as part of a South Wales–Mersey route concept, but it was 2 November 1895 before the line was finally opened from the old WM&CQ terminus at Wrexham.

Although worked by Cambrian Railways (qv), the W&E remained independent until its absorption by the GWR on 1 January 1922, the company having paid 1920 dividends of 4% on its preference and 3½% on its ordinary stock. The GWR increased the number of halts to six and provided a service of eight trains each way on weekdays plus a few through workings, mainly freight. The route, which included a 190-ft bridge over the River Dee, was closed to passengers between 10 June 1940 and 6 May 1946, but remained busy with freight to and from the ordnance depot at Marchwiel.

GB

WYE VALLEY BRANCH

Stations: Severn Tunnel Junction, Portskewett (2¾ m), Chepstow (7¼ m), Tidenham (8¾ m), Tintern (12¾ m), St Briavels (16¼ m), Redbrook-on-Wye (19½ m), Monmouth Troy (21¾ m)

In 1938 this line carried five passenger trains each way daily, two of them railcars (qv) which cut the journey by 7–9 minutes despite the need to serve simple halts at Caldicot, Tutshill, Netherhope, Brockweir, Llandogo, Whitebrook, Penallt and Wyesham. They made an ideal vehicle for many excursion ticket holders visiting Tintern Abbey or travelling the whole of this attractive route which left the Gloucester line north of Chepstow (qv) and took a scenic wooded course along the River Wye.

A local enterprise seeking to revive former riverside industrial activity, the Wye Valley Railway obtained its Act on 10 August 1866 but did not get its line open until 1 November 1876. Construction costs had totalled £318,000, Tidenham Tunnel had to be lenghtened from the planned 715 yards to 1,188 yards, and revenue worked out at £5,200 a year against the £37,000 estimated! Little wonder that after 28 years of losing money, the line was sold to the GWR.

From 1928 Tintern was the only signalled location and also had a sawmill siding near the mouth of the 182-yd tunnel there.

GB

WYNN, SIR WATKIN WILLIAMS-

Born in London on 22 May 1820, he became the 6th Baronet of Wynnstay, Ruabon. He also became a GWR Director following the absorption (1854) of the North Wales Mineral Railway, the owners of which retained an hereditary right to appoint a Director. He appointed himself, and thus forged a family link with the GWR which lasted almost throughout the life of the company. He was MP for Denbighshire from 7 July 1871 until his death on 9 May 1885, when he was succeeded on the GWR Board by his nephew (qv below). The hereditary rights were abolished under the Railways Act of 1921, but by that time his nephew was established on the Board and thus able to continue the family connection.

CA

WYNN, SIR WATKIN WILLIAMS-

Born on 25 January 1861, he followed his uncle (qv above) as a hereditary Director of the GWR in 1885, serving the company for 58 years. He succeeded his father as 8th Baronet on 24 May 1944, and died on 9 May 1949. Three GWR locomotives were named for the family — *Sir Watkin*, a 2-2-2 built in 1866 (which became the 'name' engine for the Class), No 4119, a Dean 'Badminton' Class 4-4-0, called *Wynnstay* (after the family seat), and a 'Bulldog' 4-4-0, No 3375 *Sir Watkin Wynn*. This last was still running at Sir Watkin's retirement in 1943, and served the company for several more years.

CA

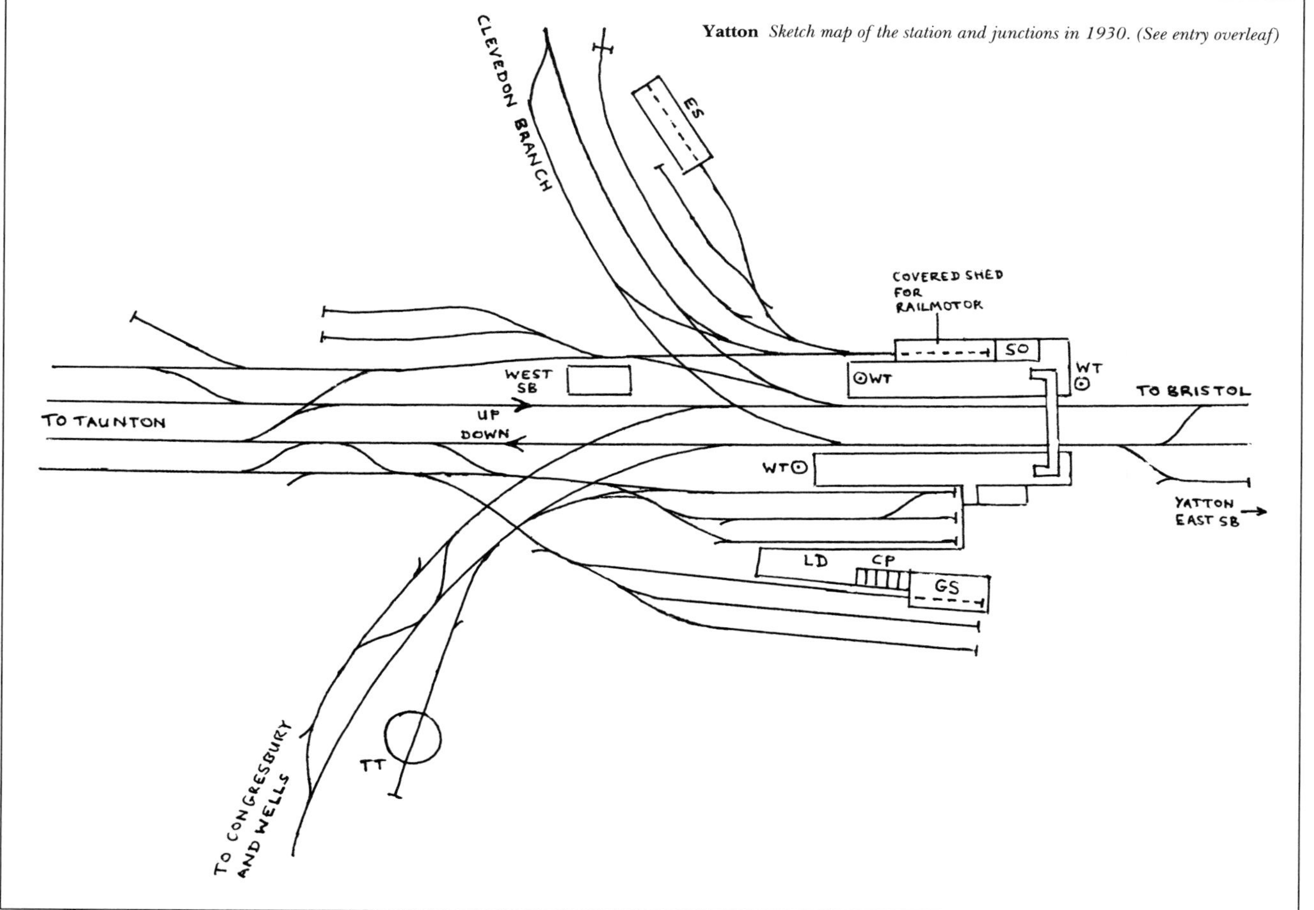

Yatton *Sketch map of the station and junctions in 1930. (See entry overleaf)*

YATTON

Yatton started life as Clevedon Road station on the Bristol & Exeter Railway's (qv) original line of 14 June 1841, and then became Yatton when the short branch to the coast at Clevedon (qv) was added on 28 July 1847. Before the GWR took over, the Cheddar Valley line had been opened as far as Cheddar itself on 3 August 1869 and extended to Wells (qv and below) on 5 April 1870. For 30 years the trains to Blagdon (qv) also operated from Yatton and along the Cheddar branch to their junction at Congresbury.

Added to the main-line services the three branch routes made Yatton a busy location with a substantial volume of exchange traffic between the two main-line platforms and their country-end bays, for Clevedon on the up side and the Congresbury line on the down. Extra running lines were provided north and south of the station, which had B&E-style buildings, and at one period coaches were slipped there. A small engine shed stood beside the Clevedon branch, with the station's goods depot and loading bank on the down side.

GB

YATTON–WELLS LINE

Stations: Yatton, Congresbury ($1\frac{1}{2}$ m), Sandford & Banwell ($4\frac{1}{2}$ m), Winscombe ($5\frac{1}{2}$ m), Axbridge (8 m), Cheddar ($9\frac{1}{2}$ m), Draycott ($11\frac{1}{2}$ m), Lodge Hill (14 m), Wookey ($16\frac{1}{2}$ m), Wells Tucker Street ($17\frac{1}{2}$ m)

The Cheddar Valley line headed south from its junction with the main line at Yatton (qv above) to Congresbury where it crossed the River Yeo and the Blagdon branch (qv) departed. After squeezing between Wavering Down and Shute Shelve Hill its course then followed the edge of the Mendip Hills to Wells (qv) where an end-on junction was made with the Witham–Wells (qv) line. The route was single with passing loops and worked by electric train staff with a key for the stone sidings at Sandford, Cheddar and Wookey, and for the paper mill at the latter point. The attractive stone-built stations included Cheddar which had an overall roof and invoiced much of the seasonal forwardings of strawberries.

The Cheddar Valley & Yatton Railway had been incorporated on 14 July 1864 as a Somerset & Dorset project. By agreement the Bristol & Exeter (qv) took it over in 1865, started work two years later, and opened to Cheddar on 3 August 1869 and on to Wells on 5 April 1870.

GB

YEALMPTON BRANCH

Stations: Plymouth Millbay, Plymouth North Road ($\frac{3}{4}$ m), Mutley ($1\frac{1}{4}$ m), Plymstock ($3\frac{3}{4}$ m), Billacombe ($4\frac{3}{4}$ m), Elburton Cross ($5\frac{3}{4}$ m), Brixton Road ($6\frac{1}{2}$ m), Steer Point (8 m), Yealmpton ($10\frac{1}{4}$ m)

Authorized by the Plymouth & Dartmoor Railway (South Hams Extension) Act of 28 June 1888, the GWR feared the LSWR might develop this scheme into a trunk route to Exeter. These fears were set at rest by an agreement dated 19 July 1894 which transferred the Plymstock Junction–Yealmpton section to the GWR with opening following on 17 January 1898. After the development years, the service settled down to seven railmotor (qv) services each weekday, but the route's vulnerability to early road competition led to its closure to passengers on 7 July 1930.

To get to the Yealmpton line GWR trains had to use the LSWR's Turnchapel branch to cross the Cattewater and reach the junction at Plymstock. At Elburton the route turned south for Steer Point and its steam ferry to Newton Ferrers before turning east again for the small passenger terminus and goods yard at Yealmpton. The route enjoyed a revival with the reinstatement of passenger trains from 3 November 1941 to 6 October 1947.

GB

YEOVIL

Yeovil's railways originated in an area and period of considerable inter-company rivalry. The result was a confusing and inconvenient pattern of lines which even two local shuttle services, a joint station and some imaginative train routing could not entirely overcome. The main-line stations at Pen Mill (GWR) and Yeovil Junction (LSWR/SR) lay on the town's eastern and southern outskirts and were linked by shuttle and other services with the better-placed Yeovil Town where the GWR had the main platform and the LSWR/SR the adjoining two. The location also had separate roofs and, at one time, separate Station Masters, but its goods yard was mainly devoted to LSWR traffic, the GWR using its depot at Hendford.

The Bristol & Exeter Railway branch from Durston (qv below) had opened to a station at Hendford on 1 October 1853 and was joined there by Salisbury & Yeovil trains on 1 June 1860. By then Pen Mill had been opened (1 September 1856) and linked with Hendford by a through line (2 February 1857) on which the B&E built the joint Town station to replace Hendford (1 June 1861). A GWR branch to Clifton Maybank, near Yeovil Junction, was in use for freight exchange from 1864 to 1937.

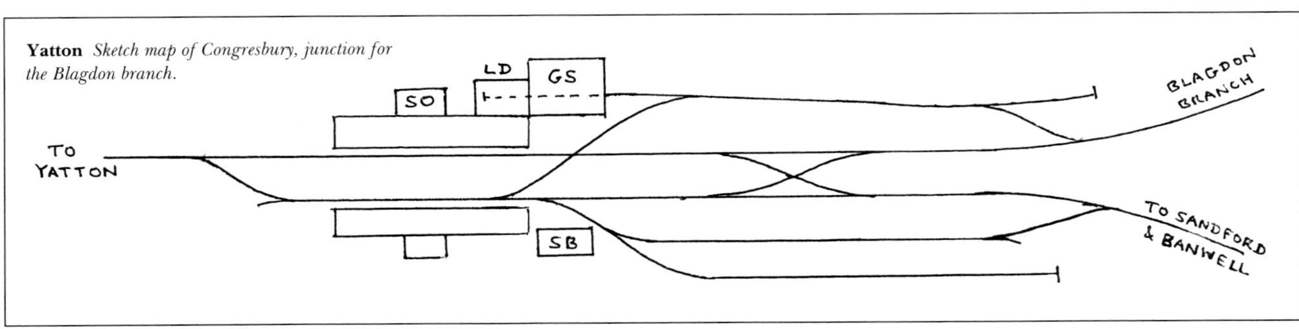

Yatton *Sketch map of Congresbury, junction for the Blagdon branch.*

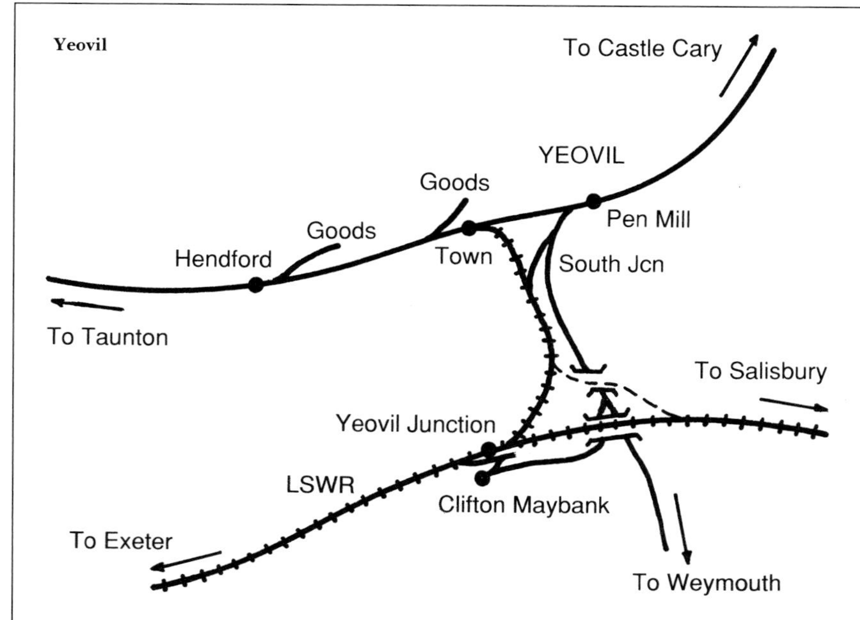

The GWR Weymouth (qv) line services used Pen Mill which consisted of up-side main buildings, the up line, a down island and some through sidings. The goods depot lay north of the station and the tiny loco depot in the angle between the Weymouth and Taunton lines. Noteworthy Pen Mill events included a nasty rear-end collision in 1913, station remodelling and resignalling in 1934–37 and a new GWR/SR connection at Yeovil South Junction in 1943.

GB

YEOVIL–LANGPORT LINE

Stations: Yeovil Pen Mill (127 miles from Paddington), Yeovil Town (127½ m), Montacute (132½), Martock (135¼ m), Langport West (140¼ m)

This single line, which carried a Yeovil–Taunton service, had started life as a Bristol & Exeter Railway (qv) branch from Durston on the Bristol–Taunton line. The section from Martock to Yeovil (Hendford) was ready by 1849 but the B&E's extra financial burdens when the GWR lease ended delayed completion of the remainder, with opening finally achieved on 1 October 1853 (goods 26 October).

Part of the original branch was embodied in the new West of England main line which opened in 1906 (qv Cut-off and avoiding lines) but the Yeovil trains continued to use the old route via Lyng Halt and Durston. The motor trolley system of maintenance was used on the branch which operated with electric train staff and token.

GB

YNYSYBWL BRANCH

Stations: Pontypridd, Ynysybwl New Road (3¾ m), Ynysybwl (4 m), Old Ynysybwl Halt (4½ m)

With intermediate halts at Clydach Court (2 m) and Robertstown (3½ m), this 4 m 69 ch single-line branch left the Merthyr line via a triangular junction beyond Pontypridd (qv) and headed up the Clydach Valley to the single-platform station at Ynysybwl. The Taff Vale Railway (qv) had extended the 1890 passenger service to Old Ynysybwl Halt on 17 October 1904, the branch then rising at 1 in 30 to Llanwonno Colliery, 2 miles further on.

Following a tortuous course along the north bank of the river, the Ynysybwl line had opened from the Abercynon direction in 1886 with the south curve at Clydach Court Junction being added in 1900 to allow the passenger service to run to and from Pontypridd. Closure of the upper portion of the route began in the 1930s.

GB

'ZULU'

Towards the end of the Broad Gauge days, several of the GWR's expresses acquired some rather unusual names, which were entirely unofficial although widely used. Amongst these was the 'Zulu', which in the down direction was the 3 pm from Paddington to Plymouth, introduced in June 1879. At that time the papers were full of news about the Zulu War, and the connection with the train was presumably the fact that the Zulu tribe was noted for its fleetness of foot. Like the 'Flying Dutch-

Yeovil *A 'County' Class 4-4-0 brings a train from Weymouth into Pen Mill station. Note the engine shed between the Weymouth and Taunton lines on the right.* (Steamchest Collection)

man' (qv), the 'Zulu' did not deign to convey 3rd class passengers, and was tightly timed over Brunel's 'billiard table' between Paddington and Swindon. Like the 'Dutchman', it averaged just over 53 mph to the Swindon stop, the fastest in Britain at the time. The stop at Swindon was a compulsory one (qv, and Refreshment rooms), then the train continued, averaging 47 to the Bath stop and 44 on to Bristol, but the next stretch to Taunton was again run at a high speed, this time just under 53 mph. An average of more than 47 mph was then required over the climb through Whiteball Tunnel and on to Exeter, but the single-line stretches further west brought averages down considerably.

In the up direction, the 'Zulu' was a train from Penzance, leaving there at 11.15 am and due into Paddington at 8.10 pm, after slipping a coach at Didcot for the north during its non-stop run from Swindon. In March 1891 the down 'Zulu' had the unusual distinction of being trapped in a snow-drift at Brent in South Devon for four days.

PWBS

A delightful GWR scene to end on: diesel railcar No 7 of 1935-7 runs into Great Malvern station. The platform-end notices, signal box and signals all establish a strong Great Western atmosphere. (GW Society)

APPENDIX A

Chronology of significant events, 1833–1948

1833	21 Jan	First Meeting of the Bristol committee that was to launch the Great Western Railway.
	7 Mar	Brunel appointed as Engineer.
	30 July	Bristol Committee's first public meeting.
	19 Aug	Great Western Railway title adopted at a meeting of the London and Bristol Committees.
1834	25 July	First GWR Bill rejected by House of Lords.
1835	31 Aug	Great Western Railway Act received the Royal Assent.
	29 Oct	Decision by GWR Board to adopt broad gauge.
1836	21 June	Taff Vale Railway obtained its Act.
1837	3 July	Act obtained for London terminus at Paddington.
	18 Aug	Gooch became Superintendent of Locomotive Engines.
1838	15 Jan	*North Star* steamed for the first time.
	4 June	GWR opened between Paddington and Maidenhead.
1839	9 Jan	Faith in Brunel and the broad gauge reaffirmed after difficulties and criticism.
		Electric telegraph in operation as far as Hanwell by April.
	1 July	Maidenhead–Twyford section opened.
1840	30 Mar	Twyford–Reading section opened.
	1 June	Reading–Steventon section opened.
	20 July	Steventon–Faringdon Road section opened.
	21 Aug	Trial trip between Bristol and Bath followed by opening on 31 August.
	25 Oct	GWR's first recorded accident, at Faringdon Road engine shed.
	17 Dec	Faringdon Road–Wootton Bassett section opened.
		The year was also notable for the opening of the first portion of the Taff Vale Railway, the building of the first royal carriage and the adoption of disc and crossbar signals. A decision taken on 6 October led to the establishment of Swindon Locomotive Works.
1841	31 May	Wootton Bassett–Chippenham section opened.
	14 June	Opening of Bristol & Exeter Railway between Bristol and Bridgwater.
	30 June	GWR line from London to Bristol completed with the opening of the Chippenham–Bath section, including Box Tunnel.
		In addition to the completion of the GWR main line, 1841 saw the opening of the Cheltenham & Great Western Union Railway from Swindon Junction to Cirencester on 31 May, with the GWR acquiring the enterprise on 1 July.
1842	13 June	The first railway journey by a reigning monarch. Queen Victoria travelled from Slough to Paddington.
	1 July	B&E line extended to Taunton.
	29 Sept	First excursion train from Bristol to London.
1843	2 Jan	Swindon Locomotive Works brought into regular use.
1844	1 May	1843 extension of B&E to Beam Bridge linked to Exeter.
	12 June	Branch opened from Didcot Junction to Oxford.
	8 July	B&G line opened from Bristol to Gloucester to link with 1840 Birmingham & Gloucester line.

1845	16 Jan	'Territorial' agreement between GWR and LSWR.
	12 May	Kemble–Standish section opened to give access to Gloucester via B&G.
	16 Dec	Commencement of broad versus narrow gauge locomotive trials.
1846	30 May	Exeter–Teignmouth line opened by South Devon Railway and extended to Newton Abbot on 30 December.
	18 Aug	Gauge Regulation Act passed.
		The year also saw the GWR purchase of the Birmingham & Oxford and Birmingham, Wolverhampton & Dudley concerns, the introduction of cloakrooms and the adoption of cardboard tickets. The GWR leased the South Wales Railway and the first Swindon locomotive appeared, *Premier* in February and *Great Western* in April.
1847	20 July	Newton Abbot–Totnes (SDR) opened; atmospheric traction then introduced progressively.
	23 Oct	GWR trains reached a new station at St James Square, Cheltenham.
	21 Dec	Reading–Hungerford branch opened.
1848	5 May	SDR reached Laira Green; extended to Plymouth (Millbay) on 2 April 1849.
	5 Sept	Thingley Junction–Westbury section opened by Wilts, Somerset & Weymouth Railway.
	1 Nov	Southcote Junction–Basingstoke opened.
	18 Dec	Newton Abbot–Torre opened.
		In 1848 the SDR abandoned its atmospheric system and the Shrewsbury & Chester line was completed.
1849		The Bristol & Exeter company took back the working of its line in May and the Windsor branch opened on 8 October.
1850	18 June	South Wales Railway opened from Chepstow to Swansea.
	2 Sept	Oxford (Millstream Junc)–Banbury opened.
	7 Oct	Westbury–Frome opened; GWR had acquired WS&W Railway on 14 Mar.
		Experimental introduction of the absolute block system through Box Tunnel. The GWR took over Oxford & Rugby Railway.
1851	1 July	GWR acquired the Kennet & Avon Canal.
	9 Sept	Westbury–Warminster line opened.
	19 Sept	Grange Court–Gloucester (G&DFR) opened and leased by the GWR. Link to east side of Chepstow Bridge also opened, a single line over the bridge itself following on 19 July 1852.
1852	11 Mar	West Cornwall Railway opened Redruth–Penzance, with Redruth–Truro Road section following on 25 August.
	21 Apr	Shrewsbury–Ludlow section of Shrewsbury & Hereford Railway opened (to Hereford for goods from 30 July).
	3 May	Oxford, Worcester & Wolverhampton Railway, which had opened its first section in 1850, was completed between Stourbridge and Evesham.
		During the year the Monmouth Company's Newport–Pontypool line opened, the mixed gauge route to Birmingham was completed and the electric telegraph linked London with Bristol. The South Wales Railway extended to Carmarthen on 11 October and the year also saw the first eight-wheel carriages employed on regular express services.
1853	4 June	Evesham–Wolvercot Junction (OW&W) opened.
		In this year, too, the B&E was opened to Yeovil from Durston, and the Ludlow–Hereford section started carrying passenger traffic.
1854	2 Jan	Carmarthen–Haverfordwest (SWR) opened and also Pontypool (Coedygric)–Hereford (NA&H).
	16 Jan	Departure side of new Paddington station brought into use; arrival side from 29 May.
	29 May	Gloucester–Standish line opened to allow Midland Railway access to Bristol.
	9 June	Great Western Royal Hotel, Paddington, opened.
	1 Sep	Amalgamation of the Shrewsbury & Bimingham and Shrewsbury & Chester concerns with the GWR.
1855	1 June	Grange Court–Hereford line opened, Charles Russell retired and C. E. Spagnoletti appointed Telegraph Superintendent.
1856	15 Apr	South Wales Railway reached New Milford and a service to S Ireland commenced using contractors' vessels.
	30 June	Warminster–Salisbury opened.
	1 Sept	Frome–Yeovil opened.
		The first GWR goods trains reached Birkenhead on 2 February to be followed by the first passenger trains on 1 May. The Didcot and Reading loops were opened with mixed gauge.

1857	20 Jan	Extension from Yeovil to Weymouth where a steamer service to the Channel Islands was introduced.
	24 Jan	Duffryn Junc–Llandilo opened by the Llanelly Railway which had started with horse operation in 1833 and linked Llanelly with Pontardulais and Garnant in 1839-40.
	2 Feb	Trowbridge–Bathampton opened.
	1 June	Henley-on-Thames branch opened.
		The year also brought the opening of the Bridport and Devizes lines and the Llandilo–Llandovery section of the VofT.
1858	4 Nov	First slip coach introduced (Slough).
1859	2 May	Formal opening of Royal Albert Bridge by the Prince Consort, allowing Cornwall Railway trains to run from Plymouth to Truro from 4 May.
	11 May	Cornwall and West Cornwall Railways linked at Truro.
	18 July	Brentford branch opened for goods.
	25 July	Henwick–Malvern Link opened (to Worcester 17 May 1860, to Malvern Wells 25 May 1860 and to Shelwick Junc 13 September 1861).
	2 Aug	Torre–Paignton opened (D&TR).
	15 Sept	Death of Brunel.
		Other events in 1859 were the establishment of the Reading Signal Works and the appointment of Lord Shelburne as Chairman.
1860		From 1 July the West Midland Railway emerged from the OWW, NA&H and Worcester & Hereford group, the Hatton–Stratford link opened on 10 October and the year also brought the installation of a McKenzie & Holland locking frame at Paddington and the first official use of the title of Station Master.
1861	1 July	GWR and West Midland Joint working began.
	14 Aug	The first narrow gauge train at Paddington.
1862	1 Jan	South Wales Railway amalgamated with the GWR.
		A number of branches were opened, including the Severn Valley, Devizes and Kington lines, and the 'Flying Dutchman' was reinstated.
1863	10 Jan	Metropolitan line opened and worked by GWR.
	30 July	Tenby-Pembroke opened; extended to Pembroke Dock on 8 August 1864.
	1 Aug	Great Western, West Midland and South Wales Railways amalgamated.
	24 Aug	Truro–Falmouth (CR) opened.
	8 Sept	Bristol–New Passage (for ferry) opened.
1864		Gooch resigned as Locomotive Superintendent but returned to become GWR Chairman on 2 November 1865. Joseph Armstrong took over the locomotive post.
1865	1 Feb	Vale of Neath (first portion opened to Aberdare in 1851) amalgamated with GWR.
	1 July	West Cornwall Railway acquired.
1866	4 Sept	Tenby–Whitland opened.
		In November broad gauge rails were added between Truro and Penzance and through broad gauge trains ran from Paddington to Penzance from 1 March 1867. GWR finances in a bad way as a result of loans falling due; wholesale economies.
1867		GWR began building more of its own rolling stock at Worcester, and the Hammersmith & City Railway was vested in the GWR and Metropolitan.
1868	1 June	Conversion era began with the conversion of one line between Whitland and Carmarthen Bridge for the P&T Railway.
1869		Grange Court–Hereford converted to narrow gauge, Oxford–Wolverhampton became entirely narrow gauge.
1871		A period of adding extra lines and station rebuilding.
1872	1 Feb	GWR took over steamer services from Milford Haven.
	11 May	The last broad gauge train in South Wales and, from 29 May, there was narrow gauge west of Swindon.
		The year also saw the Severn Tunnel Bill deposited (work starting at Sudbrook in the following March).

1874	1 June	Fowey–Newquay (CMR) opened.
	17 Sept	New Pontypool–Newport link.
		An eventful year with three bad accidents (West Drayton, Merthyr and Shipton), conversion to narrow gauge south of the Bristol main line and the start of quadrupling between Paddington and Taplow. The first bogie carriages.
1875		The Monmouthshire Railway was taken over and the vacuum brake first used for passenger rolling-stock.
1876	1 Jan	GWR absorbed Bristol & Exeter Railway.
	1 Feb	GWR absorbed South Devon, Cornwall and West Cornwall Railways.
	Mar-May	Narrow gauge line added as far as Plymouth.
1877	1 Jan	New sidings at Acton linked with Acton Wells Junction.
	1 June	The last broad gauge branch, to St Ives, was opened.
		The first sleeper saloon appeared in 1877, a six-wheel, four-berth vehicle, 29 feet long.
1878		The GWR acquired Millbay Docks and put in a connection from Plymouth North Road Junction.
1879		A year in which conversion in the West began with the Weston-super-Mare and Yeovil branches, the Severn Bridge was opened, iron wagons frames came into use and the 'Zulu' joined the 'Flying Dutchman' on the main line to the West. After three years of trials a form of automatic vacuum brake began to come into regular use. A setback occurred with the inundation of the Severn Tunnel workings by the Great Spring on 16 October.
1880		Electric lighting at Paddington.
1881	22 Aug	Carmarthen & Cardigan Railway amalgamated with GWR.
	26 Sept	Severn Tunnel headings joined.
1882		The first train lavatories were brought into service and gas began to replace oil lighting. 3rd class accommodation was made available on all but certain expresses (all trains from 1890).
1883		More Severn Tunnel problems with flooding in October first by the Great Spring and then by a tidal wave in the Severn.
1884	1 Mar	Weston-super-Mare loop opened.
1886	9 Jan	Experimental coal train ran through the Severn Tunnel, through Bristol–Cardiff passenger services commencing on 1 December.
	1 Sept	Whitland & Cardigan Railway taken over.
		Oil boxes began to replace grease boxes on carriages.
1887	6 Apr	GWR took over working of B&CDR's Kings Sutton–Chipping Norton line on opening to complete new route to Cheltenham begun in 1881.
	27 May	Bodmin branch opened.
1888		Appearance of the first *Great Western Railway Magazine.*
1889		The GWR took over the working of the Channel Islands steamers in August. Sir Daniel Gooch died on 15 October.
1890	June	New express, the 'Cornishman', began running between Paddington and Penzance.
	1 Sept	Bristol Port Railway & Pier acquired to complete the (1874-85) link to Avonmouth.
	11 Nov	Serious accident at Norton Fitzwarren. Work on quadrupling between Taplow and Didcot began; completed in 1896.
1891	9 Mar	A great blizzard seriously affected lines in the West of England.
		The year also saw the adoption of the Electric Train Staff system.
1892	7 Mar	First corridor train with full lavatory facilities began running Paddington to Birkenhead.
	20 May	The last broad gauge trains left Paddington and Penzance at 10.15 am, conversion of the remaining broad gauge in the West of England following on 21 and 22 May.
		The external version of the communication cord made its appearance (brought inside coaches from 1900).

1893		Steam heating was introduced in this year and doubling started on the Plymouth–Penwithers Junc section, except the Royal Albert Bridge (eventually completed in 1906).
1894	1 July	Sharpness branch opened by Midland Railway.
		The period of doubling on from Penwithers Junction to Penzance began in 1894 and was finally completed in 1930.
1895	1 Oct	The first trains not to make a refreshment stop at Swindon, more following in 1896 and using the newly installed watertroughs.
1896	May	First dining cars introduced, Paddington to Plymouth and Cardiff.
	1 July	Cornwall Minerals Railway taken over.
1897		A year which saw oil axle boxes used for freight rolling-stock, 20-ton wagons for locomotive coal, the virtual end of longitudinal track and the first of the Port Talbot Railway & Docks lines opened.
1898	12 Feb	Control acquired of the North Pembrokeshire & Fishguard Railway.
1899		Non-stop services from Paddington to Exeter and Birmingham introduced.
	16 June	Bad accident at Slough.
1900	1 Oct	Stert–Westbury opened (for goods in July) as part of the new line to the west of England.
1902		Six-coupled 4-6-0 locomotives introduced.
1903	3 June	Old Oak Common–Park Royal–Hanwell/West Ealing route opened.
	1 July	Wootton Bassett–Patchway opened for passengers.
	14 July	*City of Bath* with a 130-ton Royal Special ran Paddington to Plymouth via Bristol at an average of 63 mph. The first such non-stop run had taken place on 10 March.
	17 Aug	First GWR motor bus service, Helston to The Lizard.
	12 Oct	First railmotor service, Stonehouse–Chalford; a prelude to the introduction of numerous rural halts. In this eventful year dining facilities were made generally available to 3rd class passengers (first instance 1900) and the vacuum brake began to be used on goods wagons.
1904	9 May	Record 227-minute Plymouth–Paddington run by *City of Truro* and *Duke of Connaught*, former achieving 103.3 mph down Wellington Bank.
	1 July	The world's longest non-stop run, between Paddington and Plymouth, inaugurated as the 'Cornish Riviera Express', known as 'The Limited'.
	1 Aug	First section of Honeybourne–Cheltenham line opened; completed 1 August 1906.
		Steel was used experimentally for a coach roof in 1904 and the first ten 'County' Class locomotives were built. The year also saw Exminster watertroughs brought into use and an experimental fast freight service from Acton to Bristol.
1905	20 Nov	GW&GC Joint line opened throughout for goods. Didcot North signal box (38 levers) opened, with power operation, carriage lighting improved by the use of incandescent gas mantles, Dawlish tunnels widening completed (Teignmouth at end of 1884).
1906	1 Jan	First ATC installation, on the Henley branch.
	17 Mar	Old Oak Common locomotive depot opened.
	11 June	Curry Rivell–Cogload cut-off first used for goods (for passengers from 2 July).
	30 Aug	Opening of Fishguard Harbour and a new link to Ireland.
		Other events of 1906 included the appearance of the first six-coupled, four-cylinder locomotives, the Aldermaston–Midgham watertroughs brought into use, and the working of the Rhondda & Swansea Bay Railway taken over.
1907		In August the GWR introduced semi-automatic signals linked with track circuits, between Pangbourne and Goring, and the four-cylinder 'Stars' appeared.
1908	1 Jan	Port Talbot Railway lines taken over.
	1 July	New Wolverhampton–Bristol route/service via Honeybourne.
		The 142-ton *The Great Bear* 4-6-2 appeared in the year that locomotive construction was concentrated on Swindon; ATC was installed between Slough and Reading.

1909	1 Jan	The GWR took over the Liskeard & Caradon and Liskeard & Looe concerns.
1910	4 Apr	Ashendon Junc–Aynho Junc opened (1 July for passengers).
	9 May	Stoke Gifford–Avonmouth opened.
	1 Oct	2nd class abolished.
1913		The peak year for South Wales export coal—38 million tons—and the Safety First movement began. The Swansea District Lines opened in 1913-14, and Paddington station was extended in 1913-15.
1914	5 Aug	The Government took over the railways.
1917	1 Jan	Wartime service curtailments.
1919	1 Feb	Introduction of the eight-day week.
	26 Sept	Railway strike, until 5 October.
1920	3 Aug	Ealing & Shepherds Bush Railway opened (goods 1917) using three-position upper quadrant automatic signals.
1921	19 Aug	Railways Act passed. Most trains got back to their pre-war speeds and an Aberdeen–Penzance service was introduced.
1922	1 Jan	Grouping brought the Barry, Cambrian, Cardiff, Rhymney, Taff Vale and Alexandra Docks & Railway concerns into the GWR group. For specific dates of absorption, see 'Grouping' entry.
1923	1 Jan	At Beaconsfield West, points and signals were operated by electric motors. The first 'Castle', No 4073 *Caerphilly Castle,* made its appearance.
1924		King George V and Queen Mary visited Swindon in April, 20-ton mineral wagons for South Wales coal were introduced in August, and the year saw the start of car-carrying trains through the Severn Tunnel.
1925		Locomotive exchange trials with the LNER.
1926		Railways affected by the General Strike from midnight on 3 May until 14 May. *Launceston Castle* went to the LMS for trials.
1927	20 July	*King George V*'s maiden trip with the 'Cornish Riviera Express' before shipment to the USA for the Baltimore & Ohio centenary.
		Newton Abbot got a new station replacing the South Devon Railway two-shed type.
1928		The 'Hall' Class of workhorses appeared, and the Royal Assent was given for a GWR Bill which led to the company's involvement in the Western National and South Wales Motors omnibus concerns.
1929		Sir Felix Pole resigned as Chairman, Manor House Hotel at Moretonhampstead was opened and the Tregenna Castle at St Ives extended.
1930		Major extension of ATC authorized.
1931		Cogload flyover brought into use and main line between Cogload and Taunton quadrupled.
1932		The 1931 quadrupling was extended on from a new station at Taunton to Norton Fitzwarren. On 6 June a successful bid was made with the 'Cheltenham Flyer' to win the world start-to-stop speed record (No 5006 *Tregenna Castle*, 81.7 mph Swindon–Paddington).
1933		The year brought the opening of the Westbury and Frome avoiding lines (in March). In April GWR began an air service between Cardiff and Haldon (for Torbay) and Roborough (for Plymouth) using an Imperial Airways Westland Wessex.
1934		A sad start was the death on 3 January of Lord Churchill, but 1934 also saw the rebuilding of Cardiff station, the introduction of experimental AEC diesel railcar No 1 on Paddington–Didcot services, and an express diesel railcar service from Cardiff to Birmingham.

1935		Centenary year, with new stock for the 'Riviera Express', the rebuilding of Bristol and special centenary celebrations in Bristol (31 August) and London (30 October).
		'The Bristolian' began running from 9 September.
1937		GWR Staff Association formed from the Great Western Social and Educational Union.
1939		Report on Taunton–Penzance electrification. Outbreak of war, take-over of railways by the Government, and the evacuation of children began on 1 September.
1940		A year in which GWR ships were at Dunkirk and there was a bad crash at Norton Fitzwarren on 4 November, killing 27 and injuring 56.
1941		Severe bombing at Plymouth in April and May. C.B. Collett retired in July, to be replaced by F.W. Hawksworth.
1942		Gloucester–Cheltenham widened to four tracks.
1945		Lord Portal succeeded Sir Charles Hambro in a year in which the 4-6-0 'County' Class locomotives appeared.
1946		As part of the post-war recovery, new 64-foot Hawksworth coaches came into service, gas turbine experiments began and the first GWR oil-fired steam locomotive appeared.
1947		Special demonstration of the ATC system. 'Manor' 4-6-0s allocated to Newton Abbot and Laira.
1948	1 Jan	Vesting date under the Transport Act 1947—the effective Nationalization of Britain's railways.
	5 Mar	Final meeting of the Great Western Railway Co.

Details by courtesy of British Rail (Western)

A significant date in the history of the Newcastle Emlyn branch: the opening of Pentrecourt Platform, 1 February 1912.
(Steamchest Collection)

APPENDIX B

Gradient Profiles of the GWR, 1947

Reproduced from *Gradients of the British Main-Line Companies* (published in 1947 by The Railway Publishing Co Ltd for *The Railway Magazine*) by kind permission of Ian Allan Ltd.

JOINT LINES

LOCATION OF MILEPOSTS

Up side, from zero at Paddington. On the West of England main line the posts from Westbury to Castle Cary are calculated via Swindon and Trowbridge, and from Taunton onwards via Bristol (Temple Meads). On the North main line a separate series starts from zero at Northolt Junction, and a second separate series from zero at Ashendon Junction; from Aynho Junction (Banbury) onwards the posts are calculated via Oxford. On the South Wales main line the posts from Severn Tunnel Junction onwards are calculated via Gloucester.

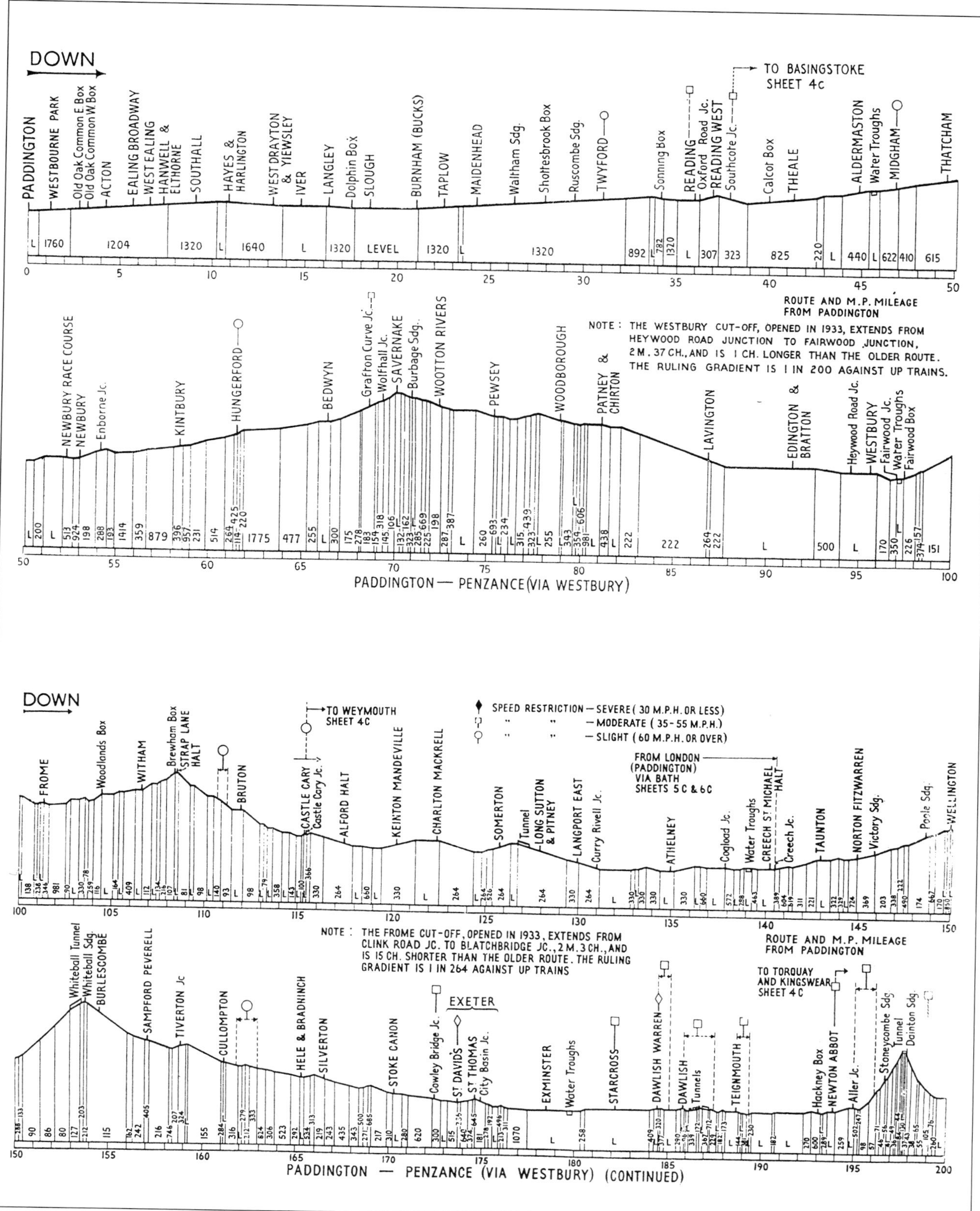

DOWN
PADDINGTON
WESTBOURNE PARK
Old Oak Common E. Box
Old Oak Common W. Box
ACTON
EALING BROADWAY
WEST EALING
HANWELL & ELTHORNE
SOUTHALL
HAYES & HARLINGTON
WEST DRAYTON & YIEWSLEY
IVER
LANGLEY
Dolphin Box
SLOUGH
BURNHAM (BUCKS)
TAPLOW
MAIDENHEAD
Waltham Sdg.
Shottesbrook Box
Ruscombe Sdg.
TWYFORD
Sonning Box
READING
Oxford Road Jc.
READING WEST
Southcote Jc.
TO BASINGSTOKE SHEET 4c
Calcot Box
THEALE
ALDERMASTON
Water Troughs
MIDGHAM
THATCHAM
ROUTE AND M.P. MILEAGE FROM PADDINGTON
NOTE: THE WESTBURY CUT-OFF, OPENED IN 1933, EXTENDS FROM HEYWOOD ROAD JUNCTION TO FAIRWOOD JUNCTION, 2 M. 37 CH., AND IS 1 CH. LONGER THAN THE OLDER ROUTE. THE RULING GRADIENT IS 1 IN 200 AGAINST UP TRAINS.
NEWBURY RACE COURSE
NEWBURY
Enborne Jc.
KINTBURY
HUNGERFORD
BEDWYN
Grafton Curve Jc.
Wolfhall Jc.
SAVERNAKE
Burbage Sdg.
WOOTTON RIVERS
PEWSEY
WOODBOROUGH
PATNEY & CHIRTON
LAVINGTON
EDINGTON & BRATTON
Heywood Road Jc.
WESTBURY
Fairwood Jc.
Water Troughs
Fairwood Box
PADDINGTON — PENZANCE (VIA WESTBURY)
DOWN
TO WEYMOUTH SHEET 4C
SPEED RESTRICTION — SEVERE (30 M.P.H. OR LESS)
— MODERATE (35-55 M.P.H.)
— SLIGHT (60 M.P.H. OR OVER)
FROME
Woodlands Box
WITHAM
Brewham Box
STRAP LANE HALT
BRUTON
CASTLE CARY
Castle Cary Jc.
ALFORD HALT
KEINTON MANDEVILLE
CHARLTON MACKRELL
SOMERTON
Tunnel
LONG SUTTON & PITNEY
LANGPORT EAST
Curry Rivell Jc.
FROM LONDON (PADDINGTON) VIA BATH SHEETS 5C & 6C
ATHELNEY
Cogload Jc.
Water Troughs
CREECH ST MICHAEL HALT
Creech Jc.
TAUNTON
NORTON FITZWARREN
Victory Sdg.
Poole Sdg.
WELLINGTON
NOTE: THE FROME CUT-OFF, OPENED IN 1933, EXTENDS FROM CLINK ROAD JC. TO BLATCHBRIDGE JC., 2 M. 3 CH., AND IS 15 CH. SHORTER THAN THE OLDER ROUTE. THE RULING GRADIENT IS 1 IN 264 AGAINST UP TRAINS
ROUTE AND M.P. MILEAGE FROM PADDINGTON
Whiteball Tunnel
Whiteball Sdg.
BURLESCOMBE
SAMPFORD PEVERELL
TIVERTON Jc
CULLOMPTON
HELE & BRADNINCH
SILVERTON
STOKE CANON
Cowley Bridge Jc.
EXETER
ST. DAVIDS
ST THOMAS
City Basin Jc.
EXMINSTER
Water Troughs
STARCROSS
DAWLISH WARREN
DAWLISH
Tunnels
TEIGNMOUTH
TO TORQUAY AND KINGSWEAR SHEET 4C
Hackney Box
NEWTON ABBOT
Aller Jc.
Stoneycombe Sdg.
Tunnel
Dainton Sdg.
PADDINGTON — PENZANCE (VIA WESTBURY) (CONTINUED)

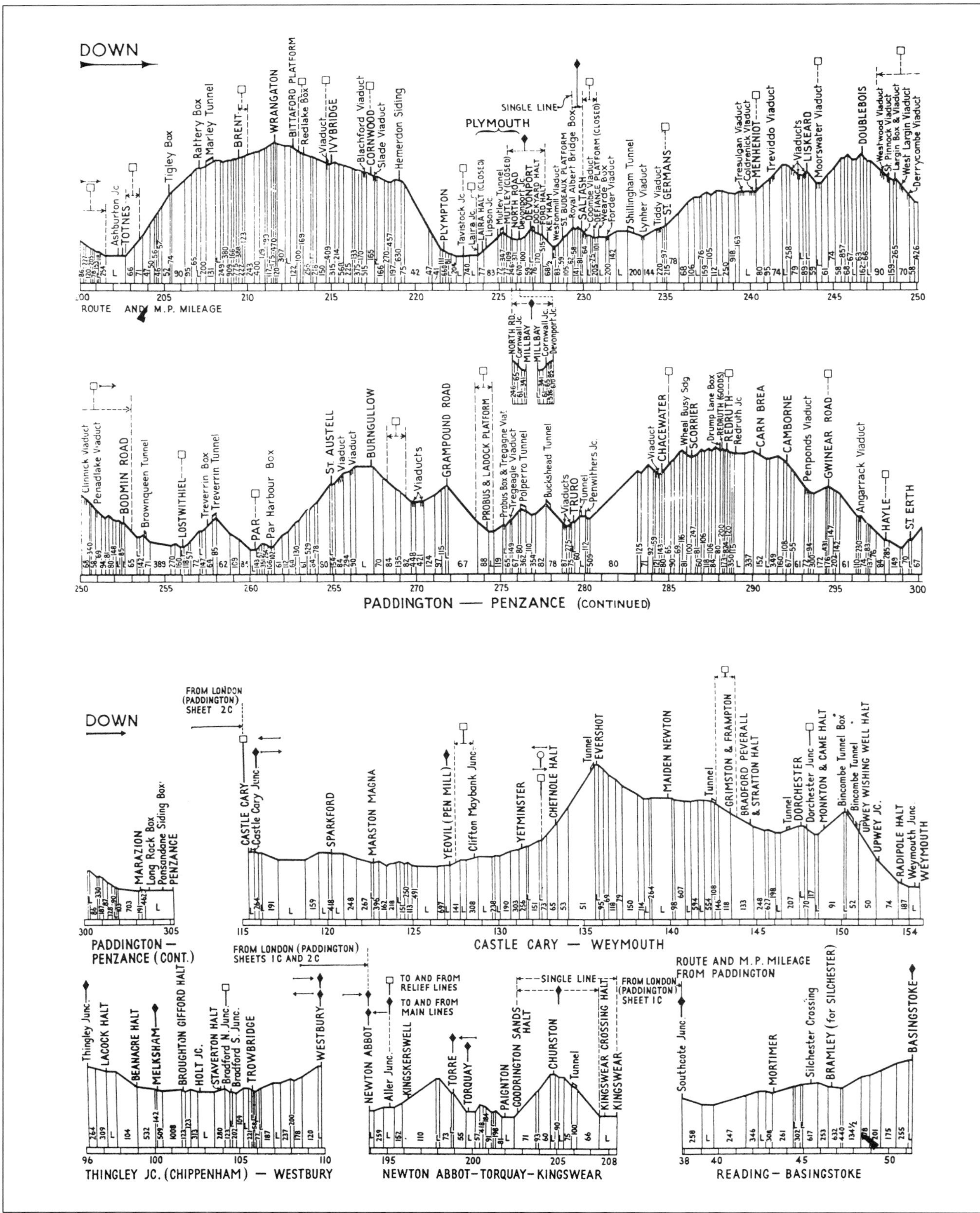
DOWN
ROUTE AND M.P. MILEAGE
PLYMOUTH
SINGLE LINE
PADDINGTON — PENZANCE (CONTINUED)
DOWN
FROM LONDON (PADDINGTON) SHEET 2C
PADDINGTON — PENZANCE (CONT.)
CASTLE CARY — WEYMOUTH
FROM LONDON (PADDINGTON) SHEETS 1C AND 2C
TO AND FROM RELIEF LINES
TO AND FROM MAIN LINES
SINGLE LINE
FROM LONDON (PADDINGTON) SHEET 1C
ROUTE AND M.P. MILEAGE FROM PADDINGTON
THINGLEY JC. (CHIPPENHAM) — WESTBURY
NEWTON ABBOT-TORQUAY-KINGSWEAR
READING — BASINGSTOKE

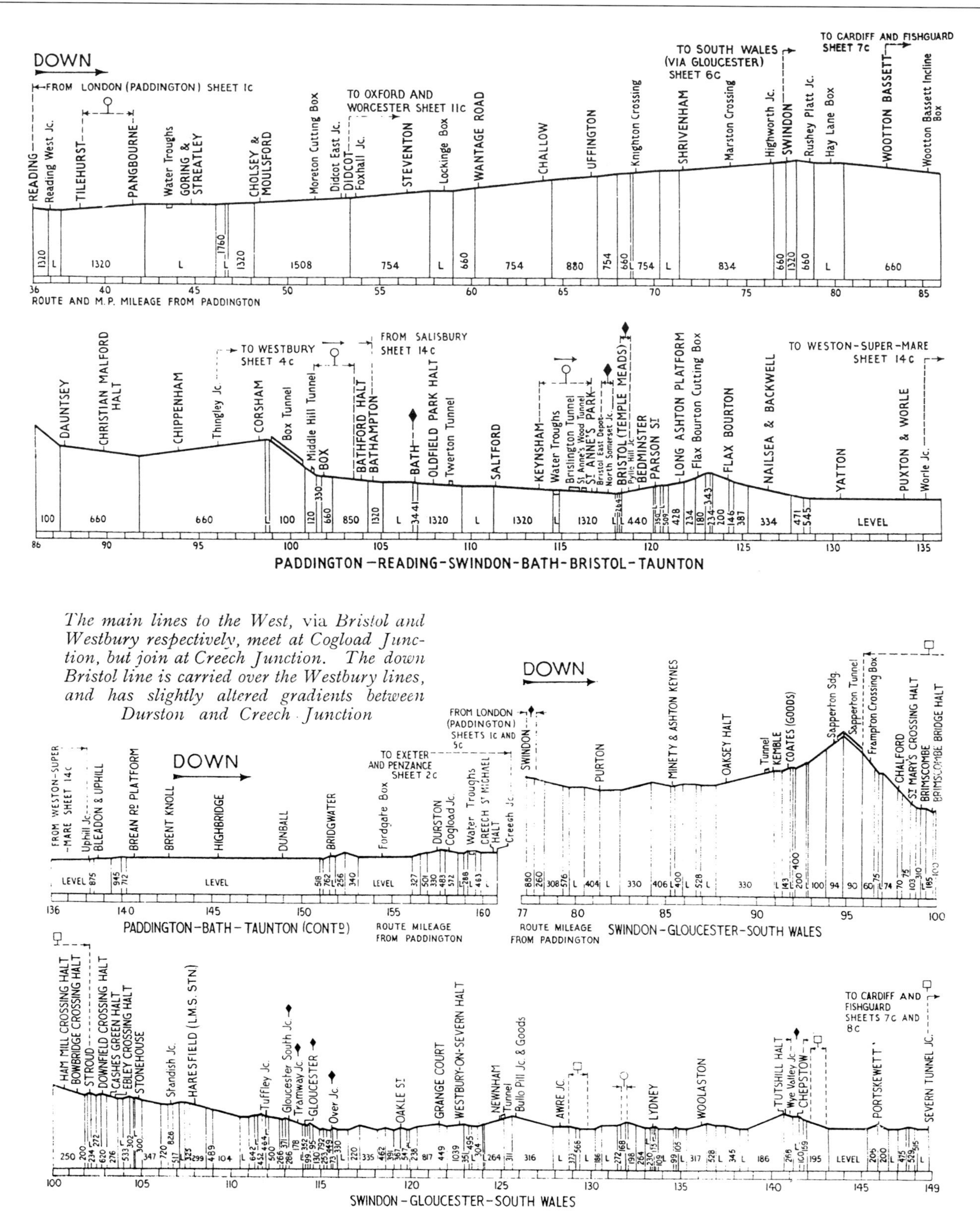

The main lines to the West, via Bristol and Westbury respectively, meet at Cogload Junction, but join at Creech Junction. The down Bristol line is carried over the Westbury lines, and has slightly altered gradients between Durston and Creech Junction

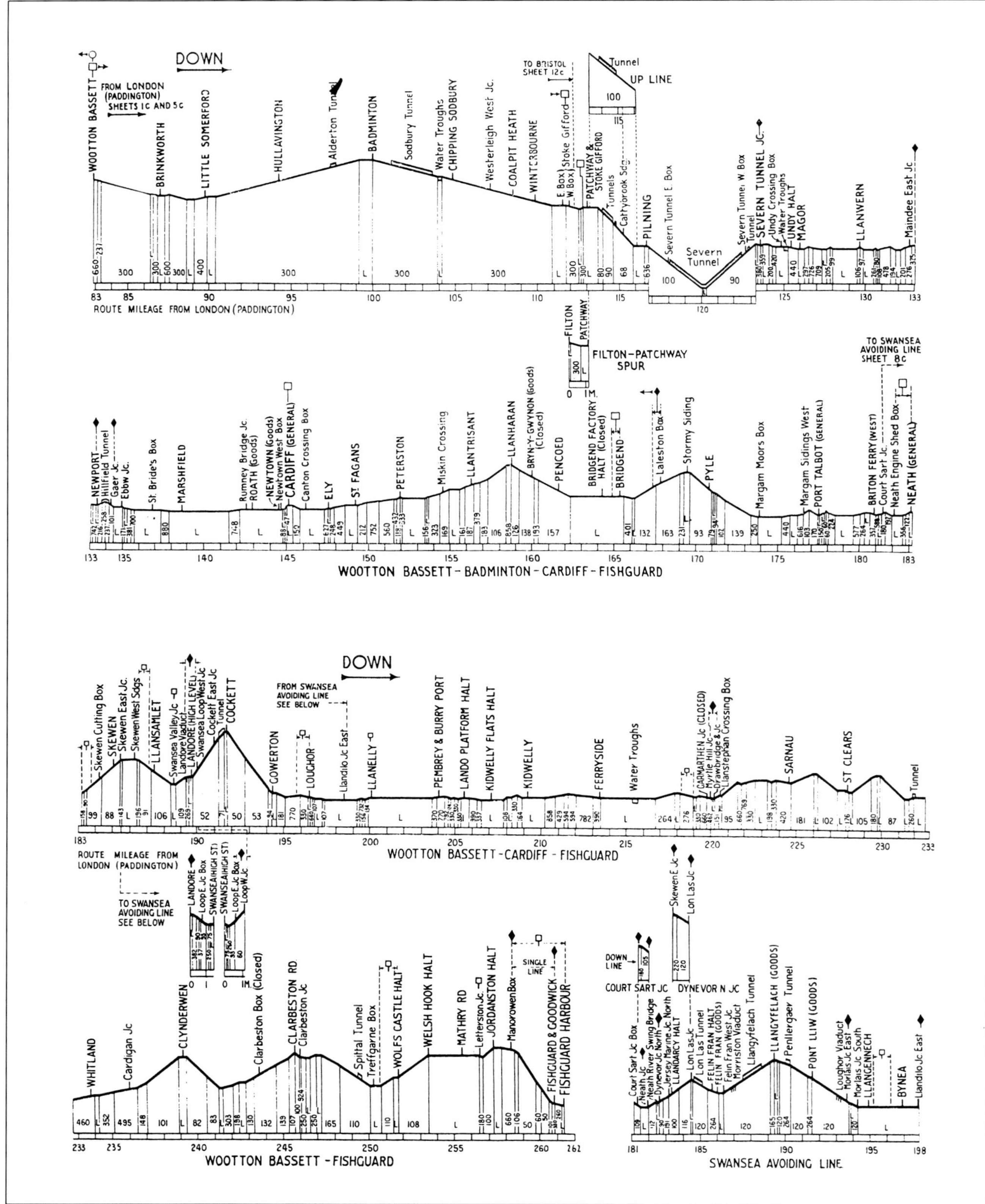
DOWN
FROM LONDON (PADDINGTON) SHEETS 1C AND 5C
WOOTTON BASSETT
BRINKWORTH
LITTLE SOMERFORD
HULLAVINGTON
Alderton Tunnel
BADMINTON
Sodbury Tunnel
Water Troughs
CHIPPING SODBURY
Westerleigh West Jc.
COALPIT HEATH
WINTERBOURNE
TO BRISTOL SHEET 12c
Stoke Gifford
PATCHWAY & STOKE GIFFORD
Tunnels
Cattybrook Sdg
Tunnel
UP LINE
PILNING
Severn Tunnel E. Box
Severn Tunnel
Severn Tunnel W Box
SEVERN TUNNEL JC.
Undy Crossing Box
Water Troughs
UNDY HALT
MAGOR
LLANWERN
Maindee East Jc
ROUTE MILEAGE FROM LONDON (PADDINGTON)
FILTON
PATCHWAY
FILTON-PATCHWAY SPUR
TO SWANSEA AVOIDING LINE SHEET 8C
NEWPORT
Hillfield Tunnel
Gaer Jc
Ebbw Jc.
St. Bride's Box
MARSHFIELD
Rumney Bridge Jc.
ROATH (Goods)
NEWTOWN (Goods)
Newtown West Box
CARDIFF (GENERAL)
Canton Crossing Box
ELY
ST FAGANS
PETERSTON
Miskin Crossing
LLANTRISANT
LLANHARAN
BRYN-Y-GWYNON (Goods) (Closed)
PENCOED
BRIDGEND FACTORY HALT (Closed)
BRIDGEND
Laleston Box
Stormy Siding
PYLE
Margam Moors Box
Margam Sidings West
PORT TALBOT (GENERAL)
BRITON FERRY (WEST)
Court Sart Jc.
Neath Engine Shed Box
NEATH (GENERAL)
WOOTTON BASSETT - BADMINTON - CARDIFF - FISHGUARD
Skewen Cutting Box
SKEWEN
Skewen East Jc.
Skewen West Sdgs
LLANSAMLET
Swansea Valley Jc
LANDORE (HIGH LEVEL)
Cockett East Jc
COCKETT
FROM SWANSEA AVOIDING LINE SEE BELOW
GOWERTON
LOUGHOR
Llandilo Jc East
LLANELLY
PEMBREY & BURRY PORT
LANDO PLATFORM HALT
KIDWELLY FLATS HALT
KIDWELLY
FERRYSIDE
Water Troughs
CARMARTHEN Jc (CLOSED)
Myrtle Hill Jc
Llanstephan Crossing Box
SARNAU
ST CLEARS
Tunnel
ROUTE MILEAGE FROM LONDON (PADDINGTON)
WOOTTON BASSETT - CARDIFF - FISHGUARD
TO SWANSEA AVOIDING LINE SEE BELOW
LANDORE
SWANSEA (HIGH ST)
WHITLAND
Cardigan Jc
CLYNDERWEN
Clarbeston Box (Closed)
CLARBESTON RD
Clarbeston Jc
Spittal Tunnel
Treffgarne Box
WOLFS CASTLE HALT
WELSH HOOK HALT
MATHRY RD
Letterston Jc
JORDANSTON HALT
Manorowen Box
SINGLE LINE
FISHGUARD & GOODWICK
FISHGUARD HARBOUR
WOOTTON BASSETT - FISHGUARD
DOWN LINE
COURT SART JC
DYNEVOR N JC
Skewen E Jc
Lon Las Jc
Court Sart Jc Box
LLANDARCY HALT
Lon Las Tunnel
FELIN FRAN HALT
FELIN FRAN (GOODS)
Morriston Viaduct
Llangyfelach Tunnel
LLANGYFELACH (GOODS)
Penllergaer Tunnel
PONT LLIW (GOODS)
Loughor Viaduct
LLANGENNECH
BYNEA
Llandilo Jc East
SWANSEA AVOIDING LINE

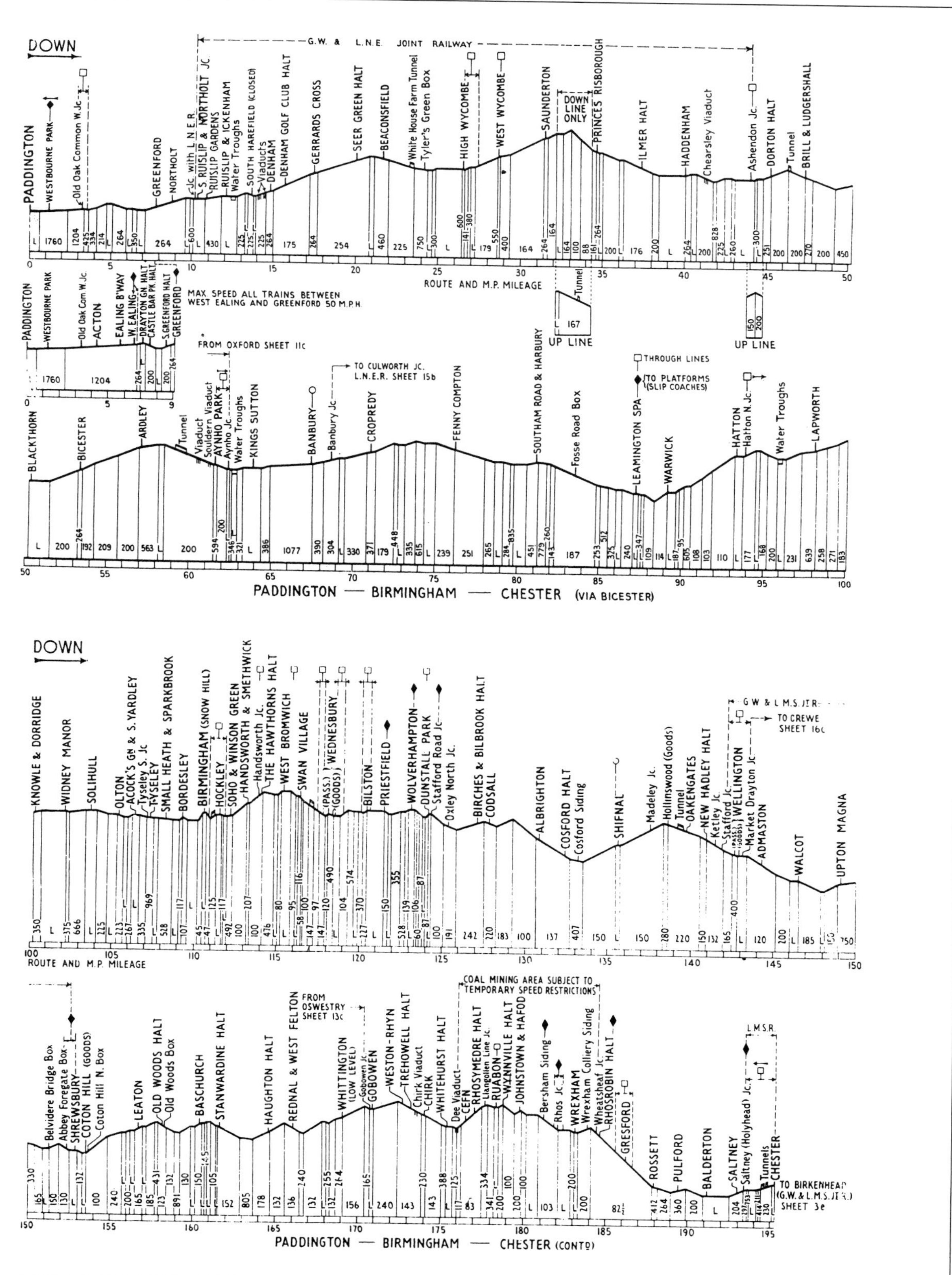
DOWN
G.W. & L.N.E. JOINT RAILWAY
PADDINGTON
WESTBOURNE PARK
Old Oak Common W. Jc.
GREENFORD
NORTHOLT
Jc. with L.N.E.R.
S. RUISLIP & NORTHOLT JC.
RUISLIP GARDENS
RUISLIP & ICKENHAM
Water Troughs
SOUTH HAREFIELD (CLOSED)
Viaducts
DENHAM
DENHAM GOLF CLUB HALT
GERRARDS CROSS
SEER GREEN HALT
BEACONSFIELD
White House Farm Tunnel
Tyler's Green Box
HIGH WYCOMBE
WEST WYCOMBE
SAUNDERTON
DOWN LINE ONLY
PRINCES RISBOROUGH
ILMER HALT
HADDENHAM
Chearsley Viaduct
Ashendon Jc.
DORTON HALT
Tunnel
BRILL & LUDGERSHALL
ROUTE AND M.P. MILEAGE
UP LINE
Tunnel
ACTON
EALING B'WAY
W. EALING
DRAYTON GN HALT
CASTLE BAR PK HALT
S. GREENFORD HALT
MAX SPEED ALL TRAINS BETWEEN WEST EALING AND GREENFORD 50 M.P.H.
FROM OXFORD SHEET 11c
TO CULWORTH JC. L.N.E.R. SHEET 15b
THROUGH LINES
TO PLATFORMS (SLIP COACHES)
BLACKTHORN
BICESTER
ARDLEY
Tunnel
Viaduct
Souldern Viaduct
AYNHO PARK
Aynho Jc.
Water Troughs
KINGS SUTTON
BANBURY
Banbury Jc.
CROPREDY
FENNY COMPTON
SOUTHAM ROAD & HARBURY
Fosse Road Box
LEAMINGTON SPA
WARWICK
HATTON
Hatton N. Jc.
Water Troughs
LAPWORTH
PADDINGTON — BIRMINGHAM — CHESTER (VIA BICESTER)
DOWN
KNOWLE & DORRIDGE
WIDNEY MANOR
SOLIHULL
OLTON
ACOCK'S GN & S. YARDLEY
Tyseley S. Jc.
TYSELEY
SMALL HEATH & SPARKBROOK
BORDESLEY
BIRMINGHAM (SNOW HILL)
HOCKLEY
SOHO & WINSON GREEN
HANDSWORTH & SMETHWICK
Handsworth Jc.
THE HAWTHORNS HALT
WEST BROMWICH
SWAN VILLAGE
(PASS.) WEDNESBURY (GOODS)
BILSTON
PRIESTFIELD
WOLVERHAMPTON
DUNSTALL PARK
Stafford Road Jc.
Oxley North Jc.
BIRCHES & BILBROOK HALT
CODSALL
ALBRIGHTON
COSFORD HALT
Cosford Siding
SHIFNAL
Madeley Jc.
Hollinswood (Goods)
Tunnel
OAKENGATES
NEW HADLEY HALT
Ketley Jc.
Stafford Jc.
(PASS.) (GOODS) WELLINGTON
Market Drayton Jc.
ADMASTON
WALCOT
UPTON MAGNA
G.W. & L.M.S. JT.R.
TO CREWE SHEET 16c
ROUTE AND M.P. MILEAGE
COAL MINING AREA SUBJECT TO TEMPORARY SPEED RESTRICTIONS
FROM OSWESTRY SHEET 13c
L.M.S.R.
Belvidere Bridge Box
Abbey Foregate Box
SHREWSBURY
COTON HILL (GOODS)
Coton Hill N. Box
LEATON
OLD WOODS HALT
Old Woods Box
BASCHURCH
STANWARDINE HALT
HAUGHTON HALT
REDNAL & WEST FELTON
WHITTINGTON (LOW LEVEL)
Gobowen Jc.
GOBOWEN
WESTON-RHYN
TREHOWELL HALT
Chirk Viaduct
CHIRK
WHITEHURST HALT
Dee Viaduct
CEFN
RHOSYMEDRE HALT
Llangollen Line Jc.
RUABON
WYNNVILLE HALT
JOHNSTOWN & HAFOD
Bersham Siding
Rhos Jc.
WREXHAM
Wrexham Colliery Siding
Wheatsheaf Jc.
RHOSROBIN HALT
GRESFORD
ROSSETT
PULFORD
BALDERTON
SALTNEY
Saltney (Holyhead) Jc.
Tunnels
CHESTER
TO BIRKENHEAD (G.W. & L.M.S. JT. R.) SHEET 3e
PADDINGTON — BIRMINGHAM — CHESTER (CONTD)

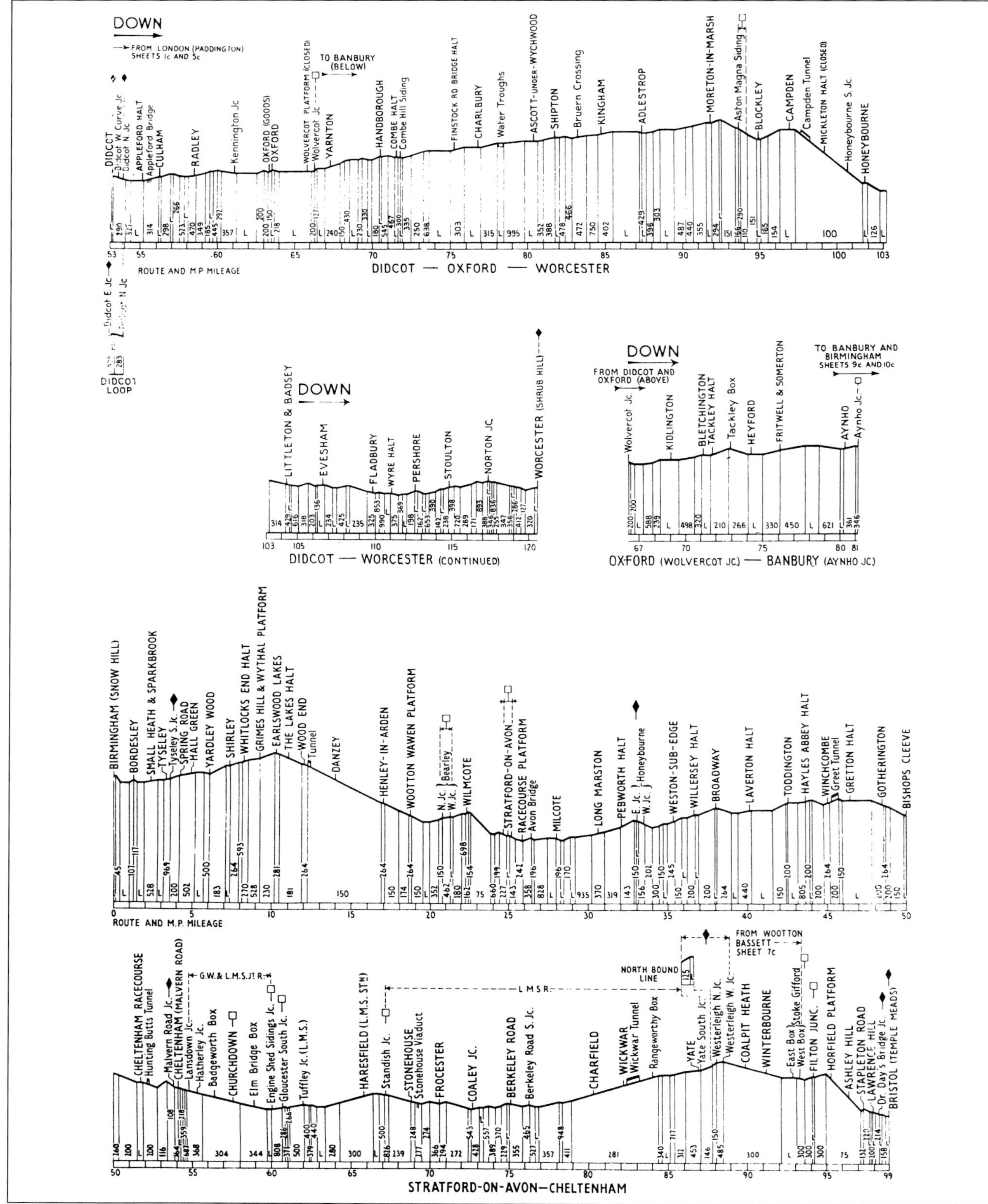
DOWN
FROM LONDON (PADDINGTON) SHEETS 1c AND 5c
TO BANBURY (BELOW)
DIDCOT — OXFORD — WORCESTER
ROUTE AND M.P. MILEAGE
DIDCOT LOOP
DIDCOT — WORCESTER (CONTINUED)
FROM DIDCOT AND OXFORD (ABOVE)
TO BANBURY AND BIRMINGHAM SHEETS 9c AND 10c
OXFORD (WOLVERCOT JC) — BANBURY (AYNHO JC)
STRATFORD-ON-AVON—CHELTENHAM
FROM WOOTTON BASSETT SHEET 7c
NORTH BOUND LINE
G.W. & L.M.S. JT. R.
L.M.S.R.

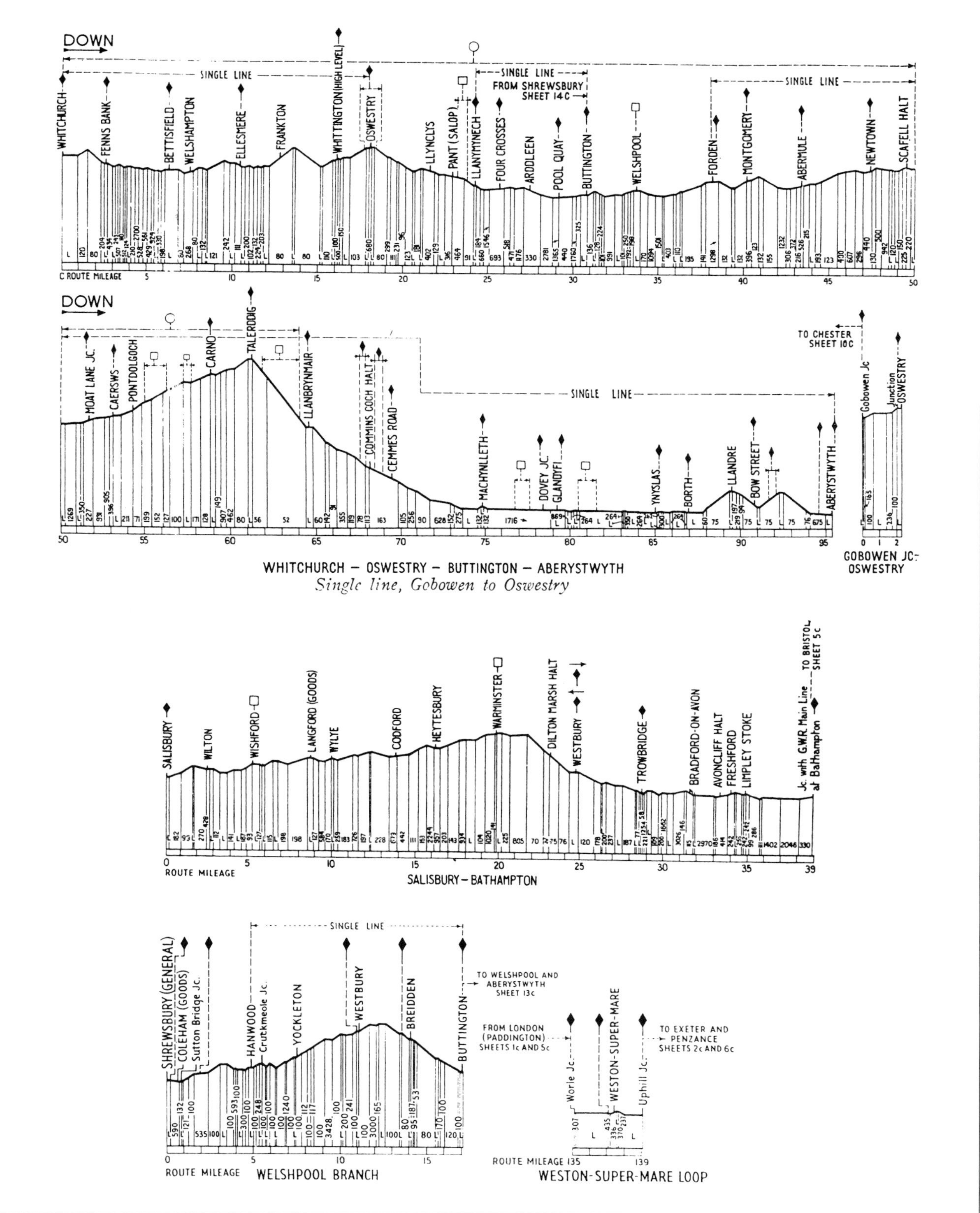

WHITCHURCH – OSWESTRY – BUTTINGTON – ABERYSTWYTH
Single line, Gobowen to Oswestry

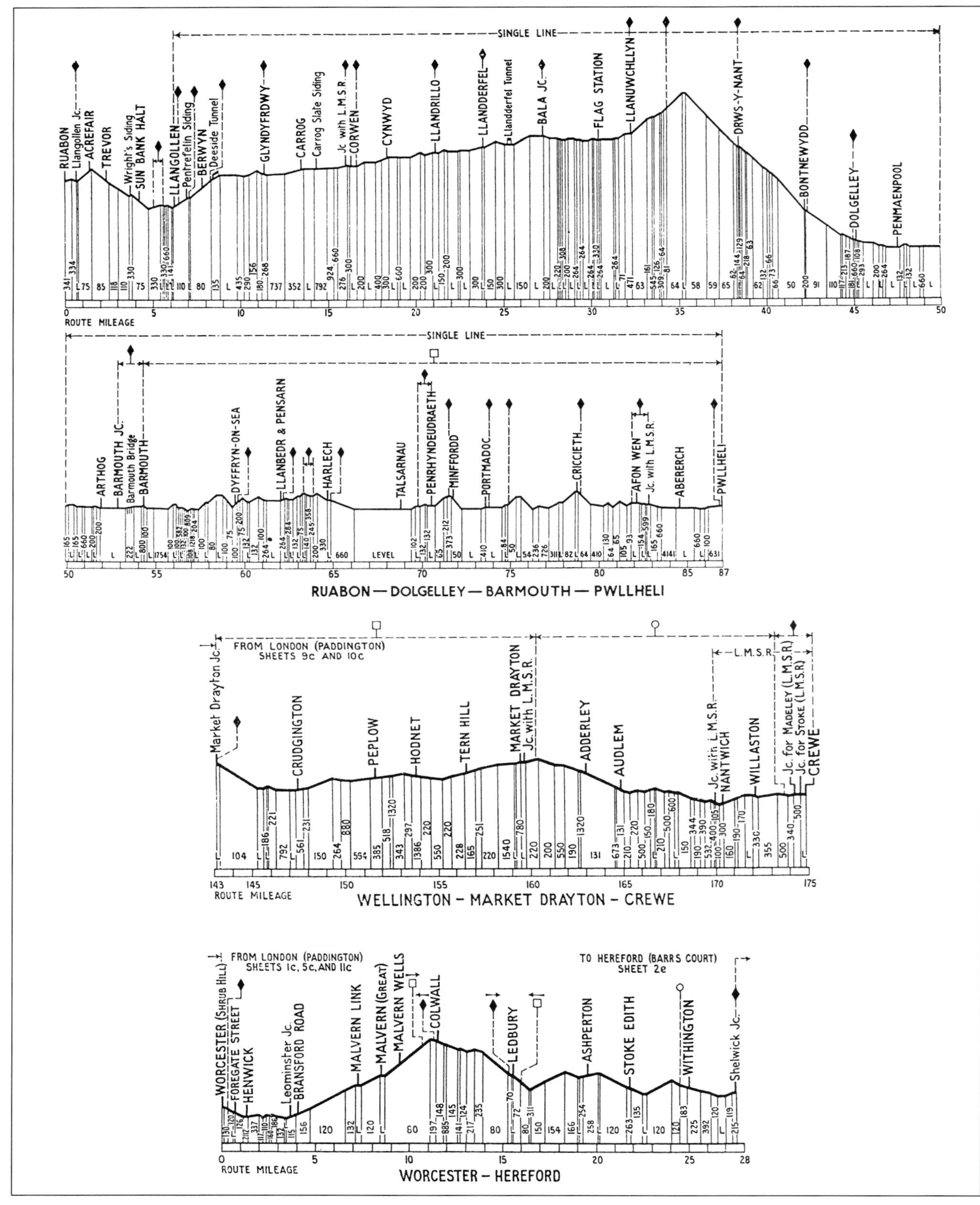
SINGLE LINE
RUABON
Llangollen Jc.
ACREFAIR
TREVOR
Wright's Siding
SUN BANK HALT
LLANGOLLEN
Pentrefelin Siding
BERWYN
Deeside Tunnel
GLYNDYFRDWY
CARROG
Carrog Slate Siding
Jc. with L.M.S.R.
CORWEN
CYNWYD
LLANDRILLO
LLANDDERFEL
Llandderfel Tunnel
BALA JC.
FLAG STATION
LLANUWCHLLYN
DRWS-Y-NANT
BONTNEWYDD
DOLGELLEY
PENMAENPOOL
ROUTE MILEAGE
ARTHOG
BARMOUTH JC.
Barmouth Bridge
BARMOUTH
DYFFRYN-ON-SEA
LLANBEDR & PENSARN
HARLECH
TALSARNAU
PENRHYNDEUDRAETH
MINFFORDD
PORTMADOC
CRICCIETH
AFON WEN
Jc. with L.M.S.R.
ABERERCH
PWLLHELI
LEVEL
RUABON — DOLGELLEY — BARMOUTH — PWLLHELI
FROM LONDON (PADDINGTON) SHEETS 9c AND 10c
Market Drayton Jc.
CRUDGINGTON
PEPLOW
HODNET
TERN HILL
MARKET DRAYTON
Jc. with L.M.S.R.
ADDERLEY
AUDLEM
Jc. with L.M.S.R.
NANTWICH
WILLASTON
L.M.S.R.
Jc. for MADELEY (L.M.S.R.)
Jc. for STOKE (L.M.S.R.)
CREWE
ROUTE MILEAGE
WELLINGTON - MARKET DRAYTON - CREWE
FROM LONDON (PADDINGTON) SHEETS 1c, 5c, AND 11c
WORCESTER (SHRUB HILL)
FOREGATE STREET
HENWICK
Leominster Jc.
BRANSFORD ROAD
MALVERN LINK
MALVERN (GREAT)
MALVERN WELLS
COLWALL
LEDBURY
ASHPERTON
STOKE EDITH
WITHINGTON
Shelwick Jc.
TO HEREFORD (BARRS COURT) SHEET 2e
ROUTE MILEAGE
WORCESTER — HEREFORD

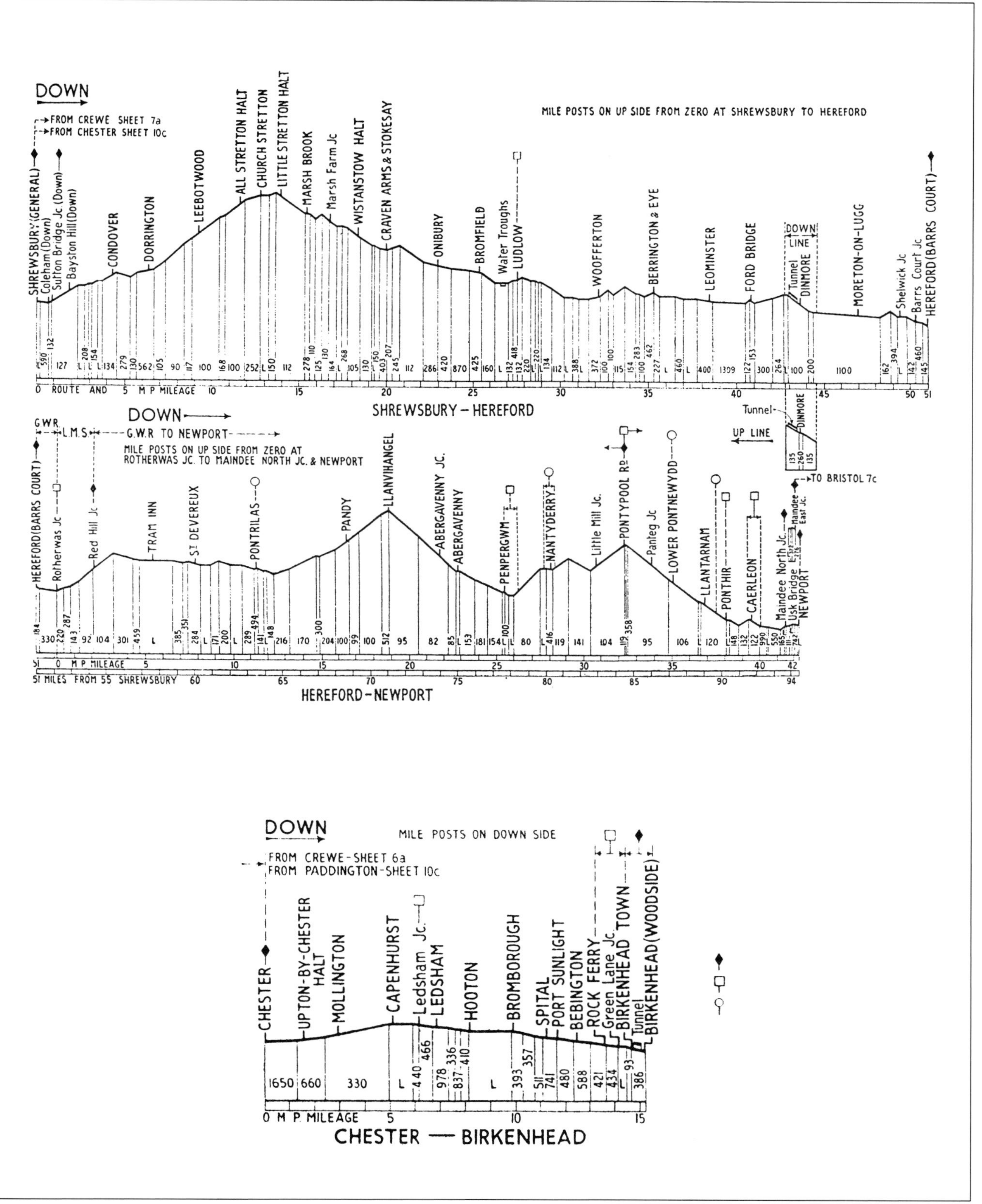
DOWN
FROM CREWE SHEET 7a
FROM CHESTER SHEET 10c
MILE POSTS ON UP SIDE FROM ZERO AT SHREWSBURY TO HEREFORD
SHREWSBURY - HEREFORD
DOWN
G.W.R TO NEWPORT
MILE POSTS ON UP SIDE FROM ZERO AT ROTHERWAS JC. TO MAINDEE NORTH JC. & NEWPORT
UP LINE
TO BRISTOL 7c
HEREFORD - NEWPORT
DOWN
MILE POSTS ON DOWN SIDE
FROM CREWE-SHEET 6a
FROM PADDINGTON-SHEET 10c
CHESTER — BIRKENHEAD

APPENDIX C

Complete list of named locomotives of the GWR and constituent companies

Compiled by Richard Semmens

This Appendix is based on information contained in the series of books *Locomotives of the Great Western Railway* published by the Railway Correspondence and Travel Society, whose cooperation is gratefully acknowledged.

Notes

Number

* An asterisk denotes that this is not the first name carried by this locomotive. For example, No 27* *Acton:* reference to the list by Class (in this case Absorbed railways—Birkenhead Railway) reveals that the locomotive was originally No 27 *Memnon*.

Name

Where a name was used successively on different locomotives in the *same* GWR class, or was used on more than one locomotive from the same absorbed railway, the locomotives are listed in numerical order.

Class

Class names are given in quotation marks (eg 'King'). Otherwise, the name of the absorbed railway from whom the locomotive was acquired is given (eg Brecon & Merthyr).

† Broad gauge locomotive

‡ Narrow gauge locomotive (less than 4ft 8 in)

Otherwise standard gauge

GWR named locomotives, alphabetically by name

No	Name	Class	Wheel arrangement
3704	*A. H. Mills*	'Bulldog'	4-4-0
4981	*Abberley Hall*	'Hall'	4-6-0
—	*Abbot*	'Waverley'†	4-4-0
4083	*Abbotsbury Castle*	'Castle'	4-6-0
—	*Abdul Medjid*	'Victoria'†	2-4-0
—	*Aberaman*	Taff Vale	0-6-0
17	*Aberaman*	Taff Vale	0-6-0
—	*Aberdare*	Taff Vale	0-4-2
7	*Aberdare*	Taff Vale	0-6-0
8	*Aberdare Valley*	Alexandra (Newport & South Wales) Docks and Railway	0-6-0ST
5013	*Abergavenny Castle*	'Castle'	4-6-0
—	*Abergwawr*	Taff Vale	0-6-0
6860	*Aberporth Grange*	'Grange'	4-6-0
4	*Aberystwyth*	Manchester & Milford	0-6-0
3712	*Aberystwyth*	'Bulldog'	4-4-0
4084	*Aberystwyth Castle*	'Castle'	4-6-0
6900	*Abney Hall*	'Hall'	4-6-0
—	*Acheron*	'Fire Fly'†	2-2-2
—	*Acheron*	'Hawthorn'†	2-4-0
—	*Achilles*	'Fire Fly'†	2-2-2
—	*Achilles*	South Devon/ South Wales Mineral	0-6-0ST
3031	*Achilles*	'Achilles'	4-2-2
—	*Actaeon*	'Fire Fly'†	2-2-2
—	*Active*	Alexandra (Newport & South Wales) Docks and Railway	0-4-0ST
27*	*Acton*	Birkenhead	0-4-0T
6991	*Acton Burnell Hall*	'Hall'	4-6-0
4982	*Acton Hall*	'Hall'	4-6-0
—	*Ada*	South Devon/Llynvi & Ogmore	0-6-0ST
4901	*Adderley Hall*	'Hall	4-6-0
3394	*Adelaide*	'Atbara'	4-4-0
3395	*Aden*	'Atbara'	4-4-0
11	*Aegeon*	Monmouthshire Railway and Canal Co	?
—	*Aelfred*	Lambourn Valley/Cambrian	0-6-0T
—	*Aeolus*	'Unclassified'†	2-2-2
3032	*Agememnon*	'Achilles'	4-2-2
—	*Ajax*	'Unclassified'†	2-2-2
—	*Ajax*	'Premier'†	0-6-0
—	*Ajax*	South Devon	0-6-0ST
—	*Ajax*	Severn & Wye and Severn Bridge	0-6-0
—	*Alan-a-dale*	Severn & Wye and Severn Bridge	0-6-0T
3456	*Albany*	'Bulldog'	4-4-0
3033	*Albatross*	'Achilles'	4-2-2
10	*Albert*	Birkenhead	2-2-2
—	*Albert*	Llanelly	0-6-0
—	*Albert*	Llanelly	0-4-2
3414	*Albert Brassey*	'Bulldog'	4-4-0
3062	*Albert Edward*	'Achilles'	4-2-2
—	*Albert Edward*	Swansea Harbour Trust	0-4-0ST
4983	*Albert Hall*	'Hall'	4-6-0
171	*Albion*	'Saint'	4-6-0
30	*Albion*	Cambrian	2-4-0
4984	*Albrighton Hall*	'Hall'	4-6-0
6931	*Aldborough Hall*	'Hall'	4-6-0
4902	*Aldenham Hall*	'Hall'	4-6-0
6930	*Aldersey Hall*	'Hall'	4-6-0
—	*Alexander*	'Victoria'†	2-4-0
3299*	*Alexander Hubbard*	'Badminton'	4-4-0
—	*Alexandra*	Llanelly	0-6-0
3061	*Alexandra*	'Achilles'	4-2-2
—	*Alexandra*	Alexandra (Newport & South Wales) Docks and Railway	0-4-0ST
32(?)	*Alexandra*	Cambrian/Brecon & Merthyr	0-6-0
4	*Alexandra*	Cambrian	0-6-0
11	*Alexandria*	Alexandra (Newport & South Wales) Docks and Railway	0-6-0ST
—*	*Alfred*	Llanelly	0-4-2
3415*	*Alfred Baldwin*	'Bulldog'	4-4-0
—*	*Alice*	Llanelly	0-4-2
4985	*Allersley Hall*	'Hall'	4-6-0
4985*	*Allesley Hall*	'Hall'	4-6-0
104	*Alliance*	'De Glehn Compound'	4-4-2
—	*Alligator*	'Pyracmon'†	0-6-0
7	*Allt*	Brecon & Merthyr/Neath & Brecon	0-6-0ST
—	*Alma*	'Iron Duke'†	4-2-2
—	*Alma*	'Rover'†	4-2-2
36	*Alma*	Taff Vale	0-6-0
—	*Alyn*	'Cambrian'	0-6-0ST
—	*Amazon*	'Iron Duke'†	4-2-2
—	*Amazon*	'Rover'†	4-2-2
3001	*Amazon*	'3001'/'Achilles'	2-2-2
—	*Amman*	Llanelly	2-4-0ST
—	*Amphion*	'Standard Goods'†	0-6-0
3272	*Amyas*	'Duke'†	4-4-0
4111	*Anemone*	'Flower'†	4-4-0
—	*Anglesea*	Neath & Brecon	0-6-0WT
—	*Annie*	Alexandra (Newport & South Wales) Docks and Railway	0-4-0ST(?)
—	*Antelope*	'Sun'†	2-2-2
—	*Antelope*	South Devon	4-4-0ST
27	*Antelope*	West Midland (Newport, Abergavenny & Hereford)	2-4-0
38	*Antelope*	Taff Vale	0-6-0
7	*Antelope*	Brecon & Merthyr	0-6-0
7801	*Anthony Manor*	'Manor'†	4-6-0
—	*Antiquary*	'Waverley'†	4-4-0
—	*Apollo*	'Unclassified'†	2-2-2
—	*Apollo*	West Cornwall	0-6-0
43	*Apollo*	Taff Vale	0-6-0
—	*Aquarius*	'Leo'†	2-4-0
—	*Arab*	'Fire Fly'†	2-2-2
6992	*Arborfield Hall*	'Hall'	4-6-0
5986	*Arbury Hall*	'Hall'	4-6-0
—	*Argo*	'Premier'†	0-6-0
—	*Argo*	'South Devon'	0-6-0
—	*Argus*	'Fire Fly'†	2-2-2
—	*Ariadne*	'Standard Goods'†	0-6-0
—	*Ariel*	'Unclassified'†	2-2-2
—	*Aries*	'Leo'†	2-4-0
6901	*Arley Hall*	'Hall'	4-6-0
2931	*Arlington Court*	'Saint'	4-6-0
6800	*Arlington Grange*	'Grange'	4-6-0
3273	*Armorel*	'Duke'/'Bulldog'	4-4-0
7	*Armstrong*	'Armstrong'	4-4-0
—	*Arrow*	'Fire Fly'†	2-2-2
6993	*Arthog Hall*	'Hall'	4-6-0
—	*Arthur*	'Llanelly'	0-6-0
1	*Ashburnham*	Burry Port & Gwendraeth Valley	0-6-0T
5966	*Ashford Hall*	'Hall'	4-6-0
6824	*Ashley Grange*	'Grange'	4-6-0
6	*Ashtead*	Weston, Clevedon & Portishead	0-6-0T
2932	*Ashton Court*	'Saint'	4-6-0
5976	*Ashwicke Hall*	'Hall'	4-6-0

No	Name	Class	Wheel arrangement
—	Assagais	'Sun'†	2-2-2
—*	Astley Green	Llanelly & Mynydd Mawr	0-4-0T(?)
4903	Astley Hall	'Hall'	4-6-0
4986	Aston Hall	'Hall'	4-6-0
3002	Atalanta	'3001'/'Achilles'	2-2-2
3373	Atbara	'Atbara'	4-4-0
6971	Athelhampton Hall	'Hall'	4-6-0
7009	Athelney Castle	'Castle'	4-6-0
—	Atlas	'Unclassified'†	2-2-2
—	Atlas	South Devon	0-6-0ST
28	Atlas	Taff Vale	0-6-0
18	Atlas	Brecon & Merthyr	0-6-0ST
3393	Auckland	'Atbara'	4-4-0
4101	Auricula	'Flower'	4-4-0
—	Aurora	'Sun'†	2-2-2
—	Aurora	South Devon	4-4-0ST
15	Aurora	Cambrian	4-4-0T
3455	Australia	'Bulldog'	4-4-0
—	Avalanche	'Avalanche'†	0-6-0(?)
3003	Avalanche	'3001'/'Achilles'	2-2-2
3332	Avalon	'Bulldog'	4-4-0
—	Avon	'Standard Goods'†	0-6-0
69	Avon	'River'	2-4-0
14	Avon	Taff Vale	0-6-0
7010	Avondale Castle	'Castle'	4-6-0
—	Avonside	'Hawthorn'†	2-4-0
6801	Aylburton Grange	'Grange'	4-6-0
—	Azalia	'Metro'†	2-4-0WT
—	Bacchus	'Unclassified'†	2-2-2
—	Bacchus	'Bacchus'†	0-6-0
3374	Baden Powell	'Atbara'	4-4-0
3292	Badminton	'Badminton'	4-4-0
6994	Baggrave Hall	'Hall'	4-6-0
4913	Baglan Hall	'Hall'	4-6-0
—	Balaklava	'Iron Duke'†	4-2-2
—	Balaklava	'Rover'†	4-2-2
3415	Baldwin	'Bulldog'	4-4-0
1	Balfour	Swansea Harbour Trust	0-4-0ST
6802	Bampton Grange	'Grange'	4-6-0
7011	Banbury Castle	'Castle'	4-6-0
—	Banshee	'Standard Goods'†	0-6-0
3466	Barbados	'Bulldog'	4-4-0
5043	Barbury Castle	'Castle'	4-6-0
5095	Barbury Castle	'Castle'	4-6-0
7803	Barcote Manor	'Manor'	4-6-0
6920	Barningham Hall	'Hall'	4-6-0
3293	Barrington	'Badminton'	4-4-0
7012	Barry Castle	'Castle'	4-6-0
174	Barrymore	'Saint'	4-6-0
4905	Barton Hall	'Hall'	4-6-0
—	Bath	'Swindon'†/Bristol & Exeter	0-6-0
4063	Bath Abbey	'Star'/'Castle'	4-6-0
7804	Baydon Manor	'Manor'	4-6-0
6934	Beachamwell Hall	'Hall'	4-6-0
19	Beacon	Brecon & Merthyr	0-6-0ST
1122	Beaconsfield	'Queen'	2-2-2
16	Beaconsfield	Cambrian	4-4-0
113	Bear	Brecon & Merthyr	0-4-0WT
6831	Bearley Grange	'Grange'	4-6-0
—	Beatrice	Llanelly	0-4-2
163	Beaufort	'157' ('Cobham')	2-2-2
3035*	Beaufort	'Achilles'	4-2-2
5078*	Beaufort	'Castle'	4-6-0
5977	Beckford Hall	'Hall'	4-6-0
—	Bee	'Metro'†	2-4-0WT
6808	Beenham Grange	'Grange'	4-6-0
4102	Begonia	'Flower'	4-4-0
—	Behemoth	'Pyracmon'†	0-6-0
3034	Behemoth	'Achilles'	4-2-2
4022*	Belgian Monarch	'Star'	4-6-0
—	Bellerophon	'Premier'†	0-6-0
3035	Bellerophon	'Achilles'	4-2-2
—	Bellona	'Fire Fly'†	2-2-2
6903	Belmont Hall	'Hall'†	4-6-0
52	Ben Jonson	West Midland (Oxford, Worcester & Wolverhampton)	2-2-2WT
6972	Beningbrough Hall	'Hall'	4-6-0
6995	Benthal Hall	'Hall'	4-6-0
—	Bergion	'Premier'†	0-6-0
4085	Berkeley Castle	'Castle'	4-6-0
4912	Berrington Hall	'Hall'	4-6-0
5012	Berry Pomeroy Castle	'Castle'	4-6-0
3295	Bessborough	'Badminton'	4-4-0
3022*	Bessemer	'3001'/'Achilles'	2-2-2
5044	Beverston Castle	'Castle'	4-6-0
5068	Beverston Castle	'Castle'	4-6-0
—	Bey	'Metro'†	2-4-0WT
—	Beyer	'Hawthorn'†	2-4-0
3416	Bibby	'Bulldog'	4-4-0
2933	Bibury Court	'Saint'	4-6-0
5967	Bickmarsh Hall	'Hall'	4-6-0
5921	Bingley Hall	'Hall'	4-6-0
4904	Binnegar Hall	'Hall'	4-6-0
6807	Birchwood Grange	'Grange'	4-6-0
8	Birkenhead	Birkenhead	2-2-2
11	Birkenhead	Birkenhead	0-6-0
25	Birkenhead	Birkenhead	2-4-0
3443	Birkenhead	'Bulldog'	4-4-0
—	Birmingham	'Swindon'†/Bristol & Exeter	0-6-0
6933	Birtles Hall	'Hall'	4-6-0
5053	Bishop's Castle	'Castle'	4-6-0
5064	Bishop's Castle	'Castle'	4-6-0
—	Bithon	'Banking'†	0-6-0ST
3004	Black Prince	'3001'/'Achilles'	2-2-2
3731	Blackbird	'Bulldog'	4-4-0
6806	Blackwell Grange	'Grange'	4-6-0
6996	Blackwell Hall	'Hall'	4-6-0
80	Blaendare	Taff Vale	0-6-0ST
4910	Blaisdon Hall	'Hall'	4-6-0
6810	Blakemere Grange	'Grange'	4-6-0
3	Blakeney	Cornwall Minerals	0-6-0T
4909	Blakesley Hall	'Hall'	4-6-0
17*	Blanche	Brecon & Merthyr	0-6-0ST
3353	Blasius	'Bulldog'	4-4-0
—11*	Blazer	Birkenhead	0-6-0
3294	Blenheim	'Badminton'	4-4-0
5073*	Blenheim	'Castle'	4-6-0
—	Blenkensop	'Hawthorn'†	2-4-0
6870	Bodicote Grange	'Grange'	4-6-0
5978	Bodinnick Hall	'Hall'	4-6-0
3470	Bombay	'Bulldog'	4-4-0
3354	Bonaventura	'Bulldog'	4-4-0
24	Borth	Cambrian	0-6-0ST
6921	Borwick Hall	'Hall'	4-6-0
3254	Boscawen	'Duke'	4-4-0
5988	Bostock Hall	'Hall'	4-6-0
6871	Bourton Grange	'Grange'	4-6-0
9	Bouverie	Alexandra (Newport & South Wales) Docks and Railway	2-6-2T
4911	Bowden Hall	'Hall'	4-6-0
—	Boyne	'Standard Goods'†	0-6-0
4096	Bradfield Hall	'Hall'†	4-6-0
7802	Bradley Manor	'Manor'	4-6-0
3333	Brasenose	'Bulldog'	4-4-0
6936	Breccles Hall	'Hall'	4-6-0
33(?)	Brecknock	Cambrian/Brecon & Merthyr	0-6-0
—	Brecon	Neath & Brecon	2-4-0
5023	Brecon Castle	'Castle'	4-6-0
—	Briareus	'Premier'†	0-6-0
6973	Bricklehampton Hall	'Hall'	4-6-0
187*	Bride of Lammermoor	'Saint'	4-6-0
5045	Bridgwater Castle	'Castle'	4-6-0
5096	Bridgwater Castle	'Castle'	4-6-0
—	Brigand	'Bogie'†	4-4-0ST
—	Brigand	South Wales Mineral	?
—	Bright Star	'Star'†	2-2-2
—	Brindley	'Victoria'†	2-4-0
3396	Brisbane	'Atbara'	4-4-0
—	Bristol	'Swindon'†/Bristol & Exeter	0-6-0
16	Bristol	'Taff Vale'	0-6-0
4082*	Bristol Castle	'Castle'	4-6-0
7013	Bristol Castle	'Castle'	4-6-0
3005	Britannia	'3001'/'Achilles'	2-2-2
3374	Britannia	'Atbara'	4-4-0
—	Britannia	Alexandra (Newport & South Wales) Docks and Railway	?
4021*	British Monarch	'Star'	4-6-0
5987	Brocket Hall	'Hall'	4-6-0
6804	Brockington Grange	'Grange'	4-6-0
4987	Brockley Hall	'Hall'	4-6-0
6832	Brockton Grange	'Grange'	4-6-0
14	Broneirion	Cambrian	0-6-0
—	Brontes	'Premier'†	0-6-0
4908	Broome Hall	'Hall'	4-6-0
7805	Broome Manor	'Manor'	4-6-0
5033	Broughton Castle	'Castle'	4-6-0
6805	Broughton Grange	'Grange'	4-6-0
4907	Broughton Hall	'Hall'	4-6-0
6935	Browsholme Hall	'Hall'	4-6-0
—	Brunel	'Victoria'†	2-4-0
14	Brunel	'Armstrong'	4-4-0
10	Brunlees	Alexandra (Newport & South Wales) Docks and Railway	2-6-2T
—	Brutus	'Standard Goods'†	0-6-0
—	Brutus	South Devon	0-6-0ST
6997	Bryn-Ivor Hall	'Hall'	4-6-0
6974	Bryngwyn Hall	'Hall'	4-6-0
6830	Buckenhill Grange	'Grange'	4-6-0
6803	Bucklebury Grange	'Grange'	4-6-0
—	Buckley (or Bulkeley)	Neath & Brecon	?
—	Buffalo	'Leo'†	2-4-0
—	Buffalo	South Devon	0-6-0ST
1134	Buffalo	'1076'	0-6-0ST
4086	Builth Castle	'Castle'	4-6-0
—	Bulkeley	'Rover'†	4-2-2
—	Bulkeley	'Sir Watkin'†/South Devon	0-6-0T
3072*	Bulkeley	'Achilles'	2-2-2
—	Bulldog	Golden Valley	2-4-0T
3312	Bulldog	'Duke'/'Bulldog'	4-4-0
3732	Bullfinch	'Bulldog'	4-4-0
4988	Bulwell Hall	'Hall'	4-6-0
25	Burcot	Alexandra (Newport & South Wales) Docks and Railway	2-6-2T
6809	Burghclere Grange	'Grange'	4-6-0
6829	Burmington Grange	'Grange'	4-6-0
—	Burntisland	Llanelly & Mynydd Mawr	0-4-0ST
—*	Burry Port	Burry Port & Gwendraeth Valley	0-6-0ST
3	Burry Port	Burry Port & Gwendraeth Valley	0-6-0ST
6998	Burton Agnes Hall	'Hall'	4-6-0
6922	Burton Hall	'Hall'	4-6-0
—	Burwarton	Cleobury Mortimer & Ditton Priors Light	0-6-0ST
6932	Burwarton Hall	'Hall'	4-6-0
—	Bury	'Hawthorn'†	2-4-0
—	Bute	Taff Vale	0-6-0
2934	Butleigh Court	'Saint'	4-6-0
6902	Butlers Hall	'Hall'	4-6-0
3417	C. G. Mott	'Bulldog'	4-4-0
7028	Cadbury Castle	'Castle'	4-6-0
6	Cader Idris	Manchester & Milford	2-4-2T
34*	Cader Idris	Cambrian	0-6-0
41	Cader Idris	Cambrian	2-4-0
—	Cadmus	Golden Valley	2-4-0T
7014	Caerhays Castle	'Castle'	4-6-0
49(?)	Caerleon	Cambrian/Brecon & Merthyr	0-6-0
10	Caerphilly	Alexandra (Newport & South Wales) Docks and Railway	0-6-0ST
50(?)	Caerphilly	Cambrian/Brecon & Merthyr	0-6-0
4073	Caerphilly Castle	'Castle'	4-6-0
—	Caersws	Cambrian	0-6-0ST
—	Caesar	'Caesar'†	0-6-0
4103	Calceolaria	'Flower'	4-4-0
6833	Calcot Grange	'Grange'	4-6-0
3468	Calcutta	'Bulldog'	4-4-0
4074	Caldicot Castle	'Castle'	4-6-0
4104	Calendula	'Flower'	4-4-0
—	Caliban	'Pyracmon'†	0-6-0
—	Caliph	'Standard Goods'†	0-6-0
6939	Calveley Hall	'Hall'	4-6-0
—	Camborne	West Cornwall	2-4-0T(?)
—	Camborne	West Cornwall	0-6-0
6	Cambria	Pembroke & Tenby	0-6-0
3296	Cambria	'Badminton'	4-4-0
27	Cambria	Cambrian	0-6-0
—	Cambrian	Taff Vale	0-6-0
10	Cambrian	Taff Vale	0-6-0
—	Cambyses	'Standard Goods'†	0-6-0
—	Camel	South Devon	0-6-0ST
3352	Camel	'Bulldog'	4-4-0
—	Camelia	'Metro'†	2-4-0WT
4105	Camellia	'Flower'	4-4-0
3355	Camelot	'Bulldog'	4-4-0
4106	Campanula	'Flower'	4-4-0
5941	Campion Hall	'Hall'	4-6-0
'C'	Canary	West Midland (Oxford, Worcester & Wolverhampton)	0-4-2
—	Cancer	'Leo'†	2-4-0
3397	Cape Town	'Atbara'	4-4-0
6999	Capel Dewi Hall	'Hall'	4-6-0
6975	Capesthorne Hall	'Hall'†	4-6-0
—	Capricornus	'Leo'†	2-4-0
6873	Caradoc Grange	'Grange'	4-6-0
—	Caradon	Liskeard & Looe and Liskeard & Caradon	0-6-0ST
3444	Cardiff	'Bulldog'	4-4-0
—	Cardiff	Taff Vale	0-4-2
37	Cardiff	Taff Vale	0-6-0
10	Cardiff	Swansea Harbour Trust	0-4-0ST
4075	Cardiff Castle	'Castle'	4-6-0
18	Cardigan	Cambrian	0-6-0ST
4087	Cardigan Castle	'Castle'	4-6-0
5024	Carew Castle	'Castle'	4-6-0
2	Carmarthen (or Caermarthen)	Manchester & Milford	2-4-0
4076	Carmarthen Castle	'Castle'	4-6-0
—	Carn Brea	West Cornwall	?
7015	Carn Brea Castle	'Castle'	4-6-0
4112	Carnation	'Flower'	4-4-0
35*	Castell Deudraeth	Cambrian	0-6-0
—	Castor	'Fire Fly'†	2-2-2
—	Castor	South Devon	4-4-0ST
?	Castor	West Midland (Oxford, Worcester & Wolverhampton)	0-6-0
—	Cato	'Standard Goods'†	0-6-0
—	Cato	South Devon	4-4-0ST
—	Cavendish	Taff Vale	2-4-0ST
5922	Caxton Hall	'Hall'	4-6-0
2935	Caynham Court	'Saint'	4-6-0
2936	Cefntilla Court	'Saint'	4-6-0

No	Name	Class	Wheel arrangement
—	*Centaur*	'Fire Fly'†	2-2-2
—	*Cerberus*	'Fire Fly'†	2-2-2
—	*Cerberus*	'Hawthorn'†	2-4-0
10	*Cerberus*	'Cambrian'†	4-4-0T
—	*Ceres*	'Standard Goods'†	0-6-0
—	*Ceres*	West Cornwall	?
3733	*Chaffinch*	'Bulldog'	4-4-0
—	*Champion*	'Standard Goods'†	0-6-0
154	*Chancellor*	'Chancellor'	2-4-0
38*	*Chandos*	Birkenhead	2-4-0
—	*Chanter*	West Cornwall	?
6904	*Charfield Hall*	'Hall'	4-6-0
3417*	*Charles Grey Mott*	'Bulldog'	4-4-0
178	*Charles J. Hambro*	'Saint'	4-6-0
3302*	*Charles Mortimer*	'Badminton'	4-4-0
—	*Charles Russell*	'Iron Duke'†	4-2-2
7	*Charles Saunders*	'Armstrong'	4-4-0
16	*Charles Saunders*	'Armstrong'	4-4-0
—	*Charon*	'Fire Fly'†	2-2-2
—	*Cheesewring*	Liskeard & Looe and Liskeard & Caradon	0-6-0ST
3282	*Chepstow Castle*	'Duke'	4-4-0
4077	*Chepstow Castle*	'Castle'	4-6-0
4989	*Cherwell Hall*	'Hall'	4-6-0
6812	*Chesford Grange*	'Grange'	4-6-0
—	*Chester*	'Swindon'†/Bristol & Exeter	0-6-0
12	*Chester*	Birkenhead	0-6-0
342	*Chester*	'342'	0-4-2ST
7016	*Chester Castle*	'Castle'	4-6-0
6906	*Chicheley Hall*	'Hall'	4-6-0
7809	*Childrey Manor*	'Manor'	4-6-0
5025	*Chirk Castle*	'Castle'	4-6-0
3275	*Chough*	'Duke'	4-4-0
—	*Chronos*	'Standard Goods'†	0-6-0
184	*Churchill*	'Saint'	4-6-0
—	*Cicero*	'Standard Goods'†	0-6-0
4107	*Cineraria*	'Flower'	4-4-0
3433	*City of Bath*	'City'	4-4-0
3434	*City of Birmingham*	'City'	4-4-0
3435	*City of Bristol*	'City'	4-4-0
3436	*City of Chester*	'City'	4-4-0
3442	*City of Exeter*	'City'	4-4-0
3437	*City of Gloucester*	'City'†	4-4-0
3438	*City of Hereford*	'City'	4-4-0
3439	*City of London*	'City'	4-4-0
3440	*City of Truro*	'City'	4-4-0
3441	*City of Winchester*	'City'	4-4-0
6905	*Claughton Hall*	'Hall'	4-6-0
4071	*Cleeve Abbey*	'Star'/'Castle'	4-6-0
6850	*Cleeve Grange*	'Grange'	4-6-0
—	*Cleobury*	Cleobury Mortimer & Ditton Priors Light	0-6-0ST
1*	*Clevedon*	Weston, Clevedon & Portishead	2-4-0T
—	*Clevedon*	Weston, Clevedon & Portishead	0-6-0T
—	*Clevedon*	Weston, Clevedon & Portishead	2-2-2
2937	*Clevedon Court*	'Saint'	4-6-0
5046	*Clifford Castle*	'Castle'	4-6-0
5071	*Clifford Castle*	'Castle'	4-6-0
5098	*Clifford Castle*	'Castle'	4-6-0
15	*Clifton*	Taff Vale	0-6-0
4990	*Clifton Hall*	'Hall'	4-6-0
7029	*Clun Castle*	'Castle'	4-6-0
—	*Clyde*	'Standard Goods'†	0-6-0
5951	*Clyffe Hall*	'Hall'	4-6-0
—	*Coalbrookvale*	Monmouthshire Railway and Canal Co	0-6-0ST
162	*Cobham*	'157' ('Cobham')	2-2-2
4991	*Cobham Hall*	'Hall'	4-6-0
7806	*Cockington Manor*	'Manor'	4-6-0
—	*Coeur de Lion*	'Waverley'†	4-4-0
180	*Coeur de Lion*	'Saint'	4-6-0
5952	*Cogan Hall*	'Hall'	4-6-0
5035	*Coity Castle*	'Castle'	4-6-0
3398	*Colombo*	'Atbara'	4-4-0
3375*	*Colonel Edgcumbe*	'Atbara'	4-4-0
5923	*Colston Hall*	'Hall'	4-6-0
3472	*Columbia*	'Bulldog'	4-4-0
—	*Columbia*	Taff Vale	4-2-0
—	*Comet*	'Sun'†	2-2-2
—	*Comet*	South Devon	4-4-0ST
3315	*Comet*	'Duke'	4-4-0
45	*Comet*	Taff Vale	0-6-0
4	*Commodore*	Birkenhead	2-2-2
5047	*Compton Castle*	'Castle'	4-6-0
5072	*Compton Castle*	'Castle'	4-6-0
5099	*Compton Castle*	'Castle'	4-6-0
7807	*Compton Manor*	'Manor'	4-6-0
4915	*Condover Hall*	'Hall'	4-6-0
7920	*Coney Hall*	'Hall'	4-6-0
3375	*Conqueror*	'Atbara'	4-4-0
6937	*Conyngham Hall*	'Hall'	4-6-0
7808	*Cookham Manor*	'Manor'	4-6-0
—*	*Copshaw*	Burry Port & Gwendraeth Valley	0-6-0ST
—	*Coquette*	'Standard Goods'†	0-6-0
5034	*Corfe Castle*	'Castle'	4-6-0
3734	*Cormorant*	'Bulldog'	4-4-0
6938	*Corndean Hall*	'Hall'	4-6-0
3274	*Cornishman*	'Duke'	4-4-0
—	*Cornubia*	West Cornwall	?
3255	*Cornubia*	'Duke'	4-4-0
—	*Cornwall*	Cornwall Minerals	?
—	*Corsair*	'Bogie'†	4-4-0ST
3037	*Corsair*	'Achilles'	4-2-2
2938	*Corsham Court*	'Saint'	4-6-0
5968	*Cory Hall*	'Hall'	4-6-0
—	*Coryndon*	West Cornwall	?
—*	*Coryndon*	West Cornwall	?
—	*Cossack*	'Standard Goods'†	0-6-0
3313	*Cotswold*	'Duke'	4-4-0
2*	*Countess*	Cambrian‡	0-6-0T
35*	*Countess Vane*	Cambrian	0-6-0
41*	*Countess Vane*	Cambrian	2-4-0
3801	*County Carlow*	'County'	4-4-0
3802	*County Clare*	'County'	4-4-0
3803	*County Cork*	'County'	4-4-0
3804	*County Dublin*	'County'	4-4-0
3805	*County Kerry*	'County'	4-4-0
3806	*County Kildare*	'County'	4-4-0
3807	*County Kilkenny*	'County'	4-4-0
3808	*County Limerick*	'County'	4-4-0
3821	*County of Bedford*	'County'	4-4-0
3474	*County of Berks*	'County'	4-4-0
1002	*County of Berks*	'County'	4-6-0
1007	*County of Brecknock*	'County'	4-6-0
3822	*County of Brecon*	'County'	4-4-0
3811	*County of Bucks*	'County'	4-4-0
1001	*County of Bucks*	'County'	4-6-0
1010*	*County of Caernarvon*	'County'	4-6-0
3812	*County of Cardigan*	'County'	4-4-0
1008	*County of Cardigan*	'County'	4-6-0
3813	*County of Carmarthen*	'County'	4-4-0
1009	*County of Carmarthen*	'County'	4-6-0
3823	*County of Carnarvon*	'County'	4-4-0
1010	*County of Carnarvon*	'County'	4-6-0
3814	*County of Cheshire*	'County'	4-4-0
3814*	*County of Chester*	'County'	4-4-0
1011	*County of Chester*	'County'	4-6-0
3824	*County of Cornwall*	'County'	4-4-0
1006	*County of Cornwall*	'County'	4-6-0
3825	*County of Denbigh*	'County'	4-4-0
1012	*County of Denbigh*	'County'	4-6-0
3478	*County of Devon*	'County'	4-4-0
1005	*County of Devon*	'County'	4-6-0
3476	*County of Dorset*	'County'	4-4-0
1013	*County of Dorset*	'County'	4-6-0
3826	*County of Flint*	'County'	4-4-0
3481	*County of Glamorgan*	'County'	4-4-0
1014	*County of Glamorgan*	'County'	4-6-0
3827	*County of Gloucester*	'County'	4-4-0
1015	*County of Gloucester*	'County'	4-6-0
3815	*County of Hants*	'County'	4-4-0
1016	*County of Hants*	'County'	4-6-0
3828	*County of Hereford*	'County'	4-4-0
1017	*County of Hereford*	'County'	4-6-0
3816	*County of Leicester*	'County'	4-4-0
1018	*County of Leicester*	'County'	4-6-0
3829	*County of Merioneth*	'County'	4-4-0
1019	*County of Merioneth*	'County'	4-6-0
3473	*County of Middlesex*	'County'	4-4-0
1000	*County of Middlesex*	'County'	4-6-0
3817	*County of Monmouth*	'County'	4-4-0
1020	*County of Monmouth*	'County'	4-6-0
1021	*County of Montgomery*	'County'	4-6-0
1022	*County of Northampton*	'County'	4-6-0
3830	*County of Oxford*	'County'	4-4-0
1023	*County of Oxford*	'County'	4-6-0
3482	*County of Pembroke*	'County'	4-4-0
1024	*County of Pembroke*	'County'	4-6-0
3818	*County of Radnor*	'County'	4-4-0
1025	*County of Radnor*	'County'	4-6-0
3819	*County of Salop*	'County'	4-4-0
1026	*County of Salop*	'County'	4-6-0
3477	*County of Somerset*	'County'	4-4-0
1004	*County of Somerset*	'County'	4-6-0
3480	*County of Stafford*	'County'	4-4-0
1027	*County of Stafford*	'County'	4-6-0
3479	*County of Warwick*	'County'	4-4-0
1028	*County of Warwick*	'County'	4-6-0
3475	*County of Wilts*	'County'	4-4-0
1003	*County of Wilts*	'County'	4-6-0
3820	*County of Worcester*	'County'	4-4-0
1029	*County of Worcester*	'County'	4-6-0
3809	*County Wexford*	'County'	4-4-0
3810	*County Wicklow*	'County'	4-4-0
—	*Courier*	'Iron Duke'†	4-2-2
—	*Courier*	'Rover'†	4-2-2
3006	*Courier*	'3001'/'Achilles'	2-2-2
6811	*Cranbourne Grange*	'Grange'	4-6-0
5048	*Cranbrook Castle*	'Castle'	4-6-0
5073	*Cranbrook Castle*	'Castle'	4-6-0
7030	*Cranbrook Castle*	'Castle'	4-6-0
4914	*Cranmore Hall*	'Hall'	4-6-0
5989	*Cransley Hall*	'Hall'	4-6-0
6872	*Crawley Grange*	'Grange'	4-6-0
—	*Creese*	'Sun'†	2-2-2
—	*Creon*	'Standard Goods'†	0-6-0
5026	*Criccieth Castle*	'Castle'	4-6-0
39	*Cricket*	Birkenhead	0-4-0ST
—	*Crimea*	'Iron Duke'†	4-2-2
—	*Crimea*	'Rover'†	4-2-2
7031	*Cromwell's Castle*	'Castle'	4-6-0
2939	*Croome Court*	'Saint'†	4-6-0
4992	*Crosby Hall*	'Hall'	4-6-0
4917	*Crosswood Hall*	'Hall'	4-6-0
—	*Crow*	South Devon/Powlesland & Mason	0-4-0T
6923	*Croxteth Hall*	'Hall'	4-6-0
5979	*Cruckton Hall*	'Hall'	4-6-0
4916	*Crumlin Hall*	'Hall'	4-6-0
3036	*Crusader*	'Achilles'	2-2-2
6861	*Crynant Grange*	'Grange'	4-6-0
—	*Cupid*	'Standard Goods'†	0-6-0
—	*Cwm Mawr*	Burry Port & Gwendraeth Valley/Weston, Clevedon & Portishead	0-6-0ST
5	*Cwm Mawr*	Burry Port & Gwendraeth Valley	0-6-0ST
30	*Cwmcarn*	Cardiff	0-6-2T
—	*Cyclops*	'Fire Fly'†	2-2-2
—	*Cyclops*	West Cornwall	0-6-0
—	*Cyclops*	Severn & Wye and Severn Bridge/Taff Vale	?
17	*Cyclops*	[Crane Tank]	0-6-4
30	*Cyclops*	Taff Vale	0-6-0
20	*Cyclops*	Brecon & Merthyr	0-6-0ST
12	*Cyclops*	Cambrian	4-4-0T
24	*Cyfarthfa*	Brecon & Merthyr	0-6-0ST
40	*Cyfronydd*	Cambrian/Brecon & Merthyr	0-6-0
21	*Cymbeline*	Brecon & Merthyr	0-6-0ST
—	*Cymmer*	Taff Vale	0-6-0
23	*Cymmer*	Taff Vale	0-6-0
26	*Cynon*	Taff Vale	2-4-0
—	*Cyprus*	'Standard Goods'†	0-6-0
—	*Czar*	'Metro'†	2-4-0WT
19	*Daisy*	Alexandra (Newport & South Wales) Docks and Railway	0-6-0ST
4993	*Dalton Hall*	'Hall'	4-6-0
—	*Damon*	'Fire Fly'†	2-2-2
—	*Damon*	South Devon	4-4-0ST
4023*	*Danish Monarch*	'Star'	4-6-0
13	*Daphne*	Cambrian	4-4-0T
25	*Dare*	Taff Vale	2-4-0
—	*Dart*	'Fire Fly'†	2-2-2
—	*Dart*	South Devon	4-4-0ST
70	*Dart*	'River'	2-4-0
—	*Dart*	Brecon & Merthyr	?
4918	*Dartington Hall*	'Hall'	4-6-0
3276	*Dartmoor*	'Duke'	4-4-0
3356	*Dartmouth*	'Bulldog'	4-4-0
4088	*Dartmouth Castle*	'Castle'	4-6-0
6907	*Davenham Hall*	'Hall'	4-6-0
3421*	*David Mac Iver*	'Bulldog'	4-4-0
5	*Davies*	Port Talbot Railway and Docks	0-6-0
16(?)	*De Winton*	Cambrian/Brecon & Merthyr	0-6-0

No	Name	Class	Wheel arrangement
100	*Dean*	'Saint'	4-6-0
14	*Dee*	'Birkenhead'	0-6-0
38	*Dee*	'Birkenhead'	2-4-0
71	*Dee*	'River'	2-4-0
5080	*Defiant*	'Castle'	4-6-0
5074	*Denbigh Castle*	'Castle'	4-6-0
7032*	*Denbigh Castle*	'Castle'	4-6-0
—	*Derby*	Port Talbot Railway and Docks/Swansea Harbour Trust	0-6-0ST
6862	*Derwent*	Grange	4-6-0
5050	*Devizes Castle*	'Castle'	4-6-0
5075*	*Devizes Castle*	'Castle'	4-6-0
7002*	*Devizes Castle*	'Castle'	4-6-0
3038	*Devonia*	'Achilles'	2-2-2
—	*Dewrance*	'Hawthorn'†	2-4-0
27	*Diamond*	Birkenhead	0-4-0ST
—	*Diana*	'Standard Goods'†	0-6-0
35	*Dickinson*	'1490'/Brecon & Merthyr	4-4-0PT
6940	*Didlington Hall*	'Hall'	4-6-0
—	*Dido*	'Caesar'†	0-6-0
—	*Dido*	South Devon	0-6-0ST
—	*Dinas*	Taff Vale	0-4-2
4	*Dinas*	Taff Vale	0-6-0
5980	*Dingley Hall*	'Hall'	4-6-0
7820	*Dinmore Manor*	'Manor'	4-6-0
5924	*Dinton Hall*	'Hall'	4-6-0
—	*Disraeli*	Cambrian	0-6-0ST
7821	*Ditcheat Manor*	'Manor'	4-6-0
—	*Djerid*	'Sun'†	2-2-2
7901	*Dodington Hall*	'Hall'	4-6-0
—	*Dog Star*	'Star'†	2-2-2
4001	*Dog Star*	'Star'	4-6-0
5942	*Doldowlod Hall*	'Hall'	4-6-0
6863	*Dolhywel Grange*	'Grange'	4-6-0
3253	*Dominion of Canada*	'Bulldog'	4-4-0
4089	*Donnington Castle*	'Castle'	4-6-0
4919	*Donnington Hall*	'Hall'	4-6-0
4090	*Dorchester Castle*	'Castle'	4-6-0
5990	*Dorford Hall*	'Hall'	4-6-0
2940	*Dorney Court*	'Saint'	4-6-0
5	*Dorothy*	Powlesland & Mason	0-4-0ST
—	*Dorothy*	Powlesland & Mason	0-4-0ST
—*	*Dot*	Cambrian	0-4-0ST
—	*Dove*	Cambrian	2-2-2(?)
—	*Dowlais*	Taff Vale	0-4-2
47	*Dowlais*	Taff Vale	0-6-0
6908	*Downham Hall*	'Hall'	4-6-0
4994	*Downton Hall*	'Hall'	4-6-0
—	*Dragon*	'Iron Duke'†	4-2-2
—	*Dragon*	'Rover'†	4-2-2
—	*Dragon*	South Devon	0-6-0ST
	Dragon	'3001'/'Achilles'	2-2-2
7810	*Draycott Manor*	'Manor'	4-6-0
—	*Dreadnought*	'Premier'†	0-6-0
40	*Dreadnought*	Birkenhead	0-6-0
3039	*Dreadnought*	'Achilles'	2-2-2
—	*Dromedary*	'Leo'†	2-4-0
—	*Dromedary*	South Devon	0-6-0ST
—	*Druid*	'Caesar'†	0-6-0
7	*Druid*	Birkenhead	2-2-2
—	*Dryslwyn*	Llanelly	0-6-0
5051	*Drysllwyn*	'Castle'	4-6-0
5076	*Drysllwyn*	'Castle'	4-6-0
7018	*Drysllwyn Castle*	'Castle'	4-6-0
3066	*Duchess of Albany*	'Achilles'	2-2-2
3067	*Duchess of Teck*	'Achilles'	2-2-2
4091	*Dudley Castle*	'Castle'	4-6-0
—	*Duffryn*	Taff Vale	0-6-0
3068	*Duke of Cambridge*	'Achilles'	2-2-2
3065	*Duke of Connaught*	'Achilles'	2-2-2
3252	*Duke of Cornwall*	'Duke'	4-4-0
3064	*Duke of Edinburgh*	'Achilles'	2-2-2
23	*Duke of Lancaster*	Alexandra (Newport & South Wales) Docks and Railway	0-6-4T
1128	*Duke of York*	'Queen'	2-2-2
3063	*Duke of York*	'Achilles'	2-2-2
4920	*Dumbleton Hall*	'Hall'	4-6-0
6834	*Dummer Grange*	'Grange'	4-6-0
3399	*Dunedin*	'Atbara'	4-4-0
5953	*Dunley Hall*	'Hall'	4-6-0
7811	*Dunley Manor*	'Manor'	4-6-0
48	*Dunraven*	Taff Vale	0-6-0
4092	*Dunraven Castle*	'Castle'	4-6-0
4093	*Dunster Castle*	'Castle'	4-6-0
—	*Dunvant*	Llanelly	0-6-0
3400	*Durban*	'Atbara'/'City'	4-4-0
2	*Dusty*	Bristol Port Railway and Pier	0-4-2T
4024*	*Dutch Monarch*	'Star'	4-6-0
25(?)	*Dwarf*	Cambrian	0-4-0ST
6864	*Dymock Grange*	'Grange'	4-6-0
4094	*Dynevor Castle*	'Castle'	4-6-0
—	*Dyvatty*	Burry Port & Gwendraeth Valley	0-6-0ST
—	*E. J. Robertson Grant*	Llanelly & Mynydd Mawr	0-6-0ST
—	*Eadweade*	Lambourn Valley/Cambrian	0-6-0T
—	*Eagle*	'Unclassified'†	2-2-2
—	*Eagle*	South Devon	4-4-0ST
—	*Ealhswith*	Lambourn Valley/Cambrian	0-6-0T
5063	*Earl Baldwin*	'Castle'	4-6-0
3028	*Earl Bathurst*	'Earl'	4-4-0
5051*	*Earl Bathurst*	'Castle'	4-6-0
3210	*Earl Cairns*	'Earl'	4-4-0
5053*	*Earl Cairns*	'Castle'	4-6-0
3203	*Earl Cawdor*	'Earl'	4-4-0
3297	*Earl Cawdor*	'Badminton'	4-4-0
5046*	*Earl Cawdor*	'Castle'	4-6-0
5060*	*Earl of Berkeley*	'Castle'	4-6-0
5061*	*Earl of Birkenhead*	'Castle'	4-6-0
3069	*Earl of Chester*	'Achilles'	4-2-2
24	*Earl of Chester*	Alexandra (Newport & South Wales) Docks and Railway	0-6-4T
5058*	*Earl of Clancarty*	'Castle'	4-6-0
3418	*Earl of Cork*	'Bulldog'	4-4-0
3204	*Earl of Dartmouth*	'Earl'	4-4-0
5047*	*Earl of Dartmouth*	'Castle'	4-6-0
3277	*Earl of Devon*	'Duke'	4-4-0
3205	*Earl of Devon*	'Earl'	4-4-0
5048*	*Earl of Devon*	'Castle'	4-6-0
3211	*Earl of Ducie*	'Earl'	4-4-0
5054*	*Earl of Ducie*	'Castle'	4-6-0
3202	*Earl of Dudley*	'Earl'	4-4-0
5045*	*Earl of Dudley*	'Castle'	4-6-0
3201*	*Earl of Dunraven*	'Earl'	4-4-0
5044*	*Earl of Dunraven*	'Castle'	4-6-0
3212	*Earl of Eldon*	'Earl'	4-4-0
5055*	*Earl of Eldon*	'Castle'	4-6-0
3200	*Earl of Mount Edgcumbe*	'Earl'	4-4-0
5043*	*Earl of Mount Edgcumbe*	'Castle'	4-6-0
3206	*Earl of Plymouth*	'Earl'	4-4-0
5049*	*Earl of Plymouth*	'Castle'	4-6-0
5056*	*Earl of Powis*	'Castle'	4-6-0
3208	*Earl of Radnor*	'Earl'	4-4-0
5052*	*Earl of Radnor*	'Castle'	4-6-0
5062*	*Earl of Shaftesbury*	'Castle'	4-6-0
3207	*Earl of St Germans*	'Earl'	4-4-0
5050*	*Earl of St Germans*	'Castle'	4-6-0
3070	*Earl of Warwick*	'Achilles'	2-2-2
5059*	*Earl St. Aldwyn*	'Castle'	4-6-0
5057*	*Earl Waldegrave*	'Castle'	4-6-0
6813	*Eastbury Grange*	'Grange'	4-6-0
5925	*Eastcote Hall*	'Hall'	4-6-0
6835	*Eastham Grange*	'Grange'	4-6-0
5052	*Eastnor Castle*	'Castle'	4-6-0
5077	*Eastnor Castle*	'Castle'	4-6-0
7004	*Eastnor Castle*	'Castle'	4-6-0
2941	*Easton Court*	'Saint'	4-6-0
4995	*Easton Hall*	'Hall'	4-6-0
4921	*Eaton Hall*	'Hall'	4-6-0
7902	*Eaton Mascot Hall*	'Hall'	4-6-0
3	*Ebor*	Barry	0-6-0T
—	*Eclipse*	'Sun'†	2-2-2
33334	*Eclipse*	'Bulldog'	4-4-0
3278	*Eddystone*	'Duke'	4-4-0
4996	*Eden Hall*	'Hall'	4-6-0
3375	*Edgcumbe*	'Atbara'	4-4-0
—	*Edinburgh*	Llanelly	0-6-0
—	*Edith Mary*	Burry Port & Gwendraeth Valley	0-6-0ST
7921	*Edstone Hall*	'Hall'	4-6-0
4	*Edward Thomas*	Corris‡	0-4-2ST
3413	*Edward VII*	'Bulldog'	4-4-0
1	*Edward VII*	Cambrian	2-6-2T
—	*Electra*	'Fire Fly'†	2-2-2
—	*Elephant*	'Leo'†	2-4-0
—	*Elephant*	South Devon	0-6-0ST
8	*Elephant*	Brecon & Merthyr	0-6-0
—	*Elfin*	Fishguard & Rosslare Railways and Harbours Co.	0-4-0ST
—	*Elk*	'Prince'†	2-2-2
—	*Elk*	South Devon	4-4-0ST
29(?)	*Elk*	West Midland (Newport, Abergavenny & Hereford)	2-4-0
5943	*Elmdon Hall*	'Hall'	4-6-0
7003	*Elmley Castle*	'Castle'	4-6-0
4997	*Elton Hall*	'Hall'	4-6-0
33	*Ely*	Taff Vale	2-4-0
3041	*Emlyn*	'Achilles'	2-2-2
3071	*Emlyn*	'Achilles'	2-2-2
—	*Emlyn*	Weston, Clevedon & Portishead	0-6-0ST
—	*Emperor*	'Iron Duke'†	4-2-2
—	*Emperor*	'Rover'†	4-2-2
—	*Emperor*	South Devon/South Wales Mineral	0-6-0ST
3008	*Emperor*	'3001'/'Achilles'	2-2-2
3467	*Empire of India*	'Bulldog'	4-4-0
3040	*Empress of India*	'Achilles'	4-2-2
6814	*Enborne Grange*	'Grange'	4-6-0
1	*Enterprise*	Cambrian	0-6-0ST(?)
4922	*Enville Hall*	'Hall'	4-6-0
—	*Erebus*	'Fire Fly'†	2-2-2
7812	*Erlestoke Manor*	'Manor'	4-6-0
—	*Ernest*	Llanelly	0-6-0
98*	*Ernest Cunard*	'Saint'	4-6-0
3420	*Ernest Palmer*	'Bulldog'	4-4-0
6942	*Eshton Hall*	'Hall'	4-6-0
—	*Esk*	'Standard Goods'†	0-6-0
—	*Estaffete*	'Iron Duke'†	4-2-2
6836	*Estevarney Grange*	'Grange'	4-6-0
—	*Ethon*	'Standard Goods'†	0-6-0
—	*Etna*	'Leo'†	2-4-0
—	*Etna*	South Devon/Carmarthen & Cardigan	4-4-0ST
23*	*Etna*	Birkenhead	2-4-0
3335	*Etona*	'Bulldog'	4-4-0
—	*Eupatoria*	'Iron Duke'†	4-2-2
—	*Eupatoria*	'Rover'†	4-2-2
3078*	*Eupatoria*	'Achilles'	2-2-2
—	*Euripides*	'Bogie'†	4-4-0ST
—	*Europa*	'Standard Goods'†	0-6-0
3419	*Evan Llewellyn*	'Bulldog'	4-4-0
—	*Evening Star*	'Star'†	2-2-2
4002	*Evening Star*	'Star'	4-6-0
4923	*Evenley Hall*	'Hall'	4-6-0
4065	*Evesham Abbey*	'Star'/'Castle'	4-6-0
3256	*Excalibur*	'Duke'	4-4-0
—*	*Exe*	'Unclassified'†	2-2-2
72	*Exe*	'River'	2-4-0
3357	*Exeter*	'Bulldog'	4-4-0
3279	*Exmoor*	'Duke'/'Bulldog'	4-4-0
4924	*Eydon Hall*	'Hall'	4-6-0
4925	*Eynsham Hall*	'Hall'	4-6-0
4998	*Eyton Hall*	'Hall'	4-6-0
5954	*Faendre Hall*	'Hall'	4-6-0
1473	*Fair Rosamund*	'517'	0-4-2T
5077*	*Fairey Battle*	'Castle'	4-6-0
29	*Fairfield*	Bristol & Exeter (Steam Railmotor)	–
4926	*Fairleigh Hall*	'Hall'	4-6-0
—	*Fairy*	Brecon & Merthyr	?
—	*Falcon*	'Fire Fly'†	2-2-2
—	*Falcon*	South Devon	4-4-0ST
—	*Falmouth*	West Cornwall	2-4-0
3280	*Falmouth*	'Duke'/'Bulldog'	4-4-0
5027	*Farleigh Castle*	'Castle'	4-6-0
4927	*Farnborough Hall*	'Hall'	4-6-0
6943	*Farnley Hall*	'Hall'	4-6-0
2942	*Fawley Court*	'Saint'	4-6-0
—	*Fenton*	'Hawthorn'†	2-4-0
6941	*Fillongley Hall*	'Hall'	4-6-0
—	*Fire Ball*	'Fire Fly'†	2-2-2
—	*Fire Brand*	'Fire Fly'†	2-2-2
—	*Fire Fly*	'Fire Fly'†	2-2-2
—	*Fire King*	'Fire Fly'†	2-2-2
3010	*Fire King*	'3001'/'Achilles'	2-2-2
42	*Firefly*	Birkenhead	0-4-2
3735	*Flamingo*	'Bulldog'	4-4-0
6944	*Fledborough Hall*	'Hall'	4-6-0
—	*Fleetwood*	Cleobury Mortimer & Ditton Priors Light	0-6-0ST
—	*Fleur-de-Lis*	'Metro'†	2-4-0WT
—	*Flirt*	'Standard Goods'†	0-6-0
—	*Flora*	'Standard Goods'†	0-6-0
—	*Florence*	'Caesar'†	0-6-0
3009	*Flying Dutchman*	'3001'/'Achilles'	2-2-2
7903	*Foremarke Hall*	'Hall'	4-6-0
13*	*Forerunner*	Birkenhead	0-6-0
5	*Forester*	Severn & Wye and Severn Bridge	0-6-0
—	*Forester*	Severn & Wye and Severn Bridge	0-6-0T
—	*Forth*	'Standard Goods'†	0-6-0
6837	*Forthampton Grange*	'Grange'	4-6-0
—	*Foster*	'Hawthorn'†	2-4-0
7904	*Fountains Hall*	'Hall'	4-6-0
3	*Fowey*	Cornwall Minerals	0-6-0T
3281	*Fowey*	'Duke'	4-4-0
7019	*Fowey Castle*	'Castle'	4-6-0
7905	*Fowey Hall*	'Hall'	4-6-0
—	*Fowler*	'Sir Watkin'†/South Devon	0-6-0T
—	*Fox*	West Cornwall	0-4-0ST
22	*Fox*	Alexandra (Newport & South Wales) Docks and Railway	0-6-4T
7822	*Foxcote Manor*	'Manor'	4-6-0
3707	*Francis Mildmay*	'Bulldog'	4-4-0
3416*	*Frank Bibby*	'Bulldog'	4-4-0
6816	*Frankton Grange*	'Grange'	4-6-0
3042	*Frederick Saunders*	'Achilles'	4-2-2
5981	*Frensham Hall*	'Hall'	4-6-0
7813	*Freshford Manor*	'Manor'	4-6-0
6909	*Frewin Hall*	'Hall'	4-6-0
—	*Friar Tuck*	Severn & Wye and Severn Bridge	0-6-0T
6815	*Frilford Grange*	'Grange'	4-6-0
7816	*Frilsham Manor*	'Manor'	4-6-0
7814	*Fringford Manor*	'Manor'	4-6-0
7815	*Fritwell Manor*	'Manor'	4-6-0
7906	*Fron Hall*	'Hall'	4-6-0
—	*Fulton*	'Victoria'†	2-4-0
—	*Fury*	'Premier'†	0-6-0

No	Name	Class	Wheel arrangement
7017	*G. J. Churchward*	'Castle'	4-6-0
—	*Gadlys*	Taff Vale	0-6-0
—	*Gallo*	Fishguard & Rosslare Railways and Harbours Co	0-4-0ST
—	*Ganymede*	'Fire Fly'†	2-2-2
4108	*Gardenia*	'Flower'	4-4-0
7817	*Garsington Manor*	'Manor'	4-6-0
5955	*Garth Hall*	'Hall'	4-6-0
4928	*Gatacre Hall*	'Hall'	4-6-0
—	*Gaveller*	Severn & Wye and Severn Bridge	0-6-0ST
—	*Gazelle*	'Sun'†	2-2-2
—	*Gazelle*	South Devon	4-4-0ST
30(?)	*Gazelle*	West Midland (Newport, Abergavenny & Hereford)	2-4-0
40	*Gazelle*	Taff Vale	0-6-0
50	*Gelly Gaer*	Taff Vale	0-6-0
—	*Gemini*	'Leo'†	2-4-0
1	*General Don*	Weston, Clevedon & Portishead	2-4-0T
1	*General Wood*	Manchester & Milford	0-6-0
3061*	*George A. Wills*	'Achilles'	4-2-2
3705	*George A. Wills*	'Bulldog'	4-4-0
—	*George Waddell*	Llanelly & Mynydd Mawr	0-6-0T
—	*Geryon*	'Standard Goods'†	0-6-0
14*	*Gheber*	Birkenhead	0-6-0
—	*Giant*	Golden Valley	2-4-0T
—	*Giaour*	'Standard Goods'†	0-6-0
3401	*Gibraltar*	'Atbara'/'City'	4-4-0
?	*Gipsy*	West Midland (Newport, Abergavenny & Hereford)	?
2	*Gipsy Hill*	Weston, Clevedon & Portishead	0-6-0T
—	*Giraffe*	'Sun'†	2-2-2
—	*Giraffe*	South Devon	4-4-0ST
—	*Gladiator*	'Standard Goods'†	0-6-0
5076*	*Gladiator*	'Castle'	4-6-0
53	*Gladstone*	Cambrian	2-4-0
58	*Gladys*	Cambrian	2-4-0T
42	*Glandovey*	Cambrian	2-4-0
1	*Glanmor*	Swansea Harbour Trust	0-4-0ST
6	*Glansevern*	Cambrian/Brecon & Merthyr	0-4-2
15	*Glansevern*	Cambrian	0-6-0
6945	*Glasfryn Hall*	'Hall'	4-6-0
3336	*Glastonbury*	'Bulldog'	4-4-0
4061	*Glastonbury Abbey*	'Star'	4-6-0
?	*Glendower*	Birkenhead	?
3018*	*Glenside*	'Achilles'	2-2-2
—	*Gloucester*	'Swindon'†/Bristol & Exeter	0-6-0
—	*Gloucester*	Taff Vale	4-2-0
7020	*Gloucester Castle*	'Castle'	4-6-0
—	*Glyn*	Golden Valley	2-4-0T
—	*Glyncorrwg*	South Wales Mineral/Bristol & Exeter	0-4-2ST
—	*Gnat*	'Metro'†	2-4-0WT
12	*Gnome*	Birkenhead	0-6-0
—	*Goat*	South Devon	0-4-0T
3358	*Godolphin*	'Bulldog'	4-4-0
3736	*Goldfinch*	'Bulldog'	4-4-0
—	*Goliah*	'Hercules'†	0-6-0
—	*Goliah*	South Devon	0-6-0ST
—	*Gooch*	'Hawthorn'†	2-4-0
1130	*Gooch*	'Queen'	2-2-2
8	*Gooch*	'Armstrong'	4-4-0
6838	*Goodmoor Grange*	'Grange'	4-6-0
5014	*Goodrich Castle*	'Castle'	4-6-0
—	*Goonbarrow*	Cornwall Minerals (Goonbarrow branch)	0-6-0ST
4999	*Gopsal Hall*	'Hall'	4-6-0
29	*Gordon*	Taff Vale	0-6-2T
—	*Gorgon*	'Fire Fly'†	2-2-2
—	*Gorgon*	South Devon	4-4-0ST
6910	*Gossington Hall*	'Hall'	4-6-0
4929	*Goytrey Hall*	'Hall'	4-6-0
6924	*Grantley Hall*	'Hall'	4-6-0
7818	*Granville Manor*	'Manor'	4-6-0
6	*Grasshopper*	Birkenhead	0-4-0ST
6976	*Graythwaite Hall*	'Hall'	4-6-0
—	*Great Britain*	'Iron Duke'†	4-2-2
—	*Great Britain*	'Rover'†	4-2-2
3013	*Great Britain*	'3001'/'Achilles'	2-2-2
—	*Great Mountain*	Llanelly & Mynydd Mawr	0-6-0T
—	*Great Western*	'Great Western'†	2-2-2
—	*Great Western*	'Rover'†	4-2-2
3012	*Great Western*	'3001'/'Achilles'	2-2-2
7007*	*Great Western*	'Castle'	4-6-0
—*	*Green Dragon*	Cambrian/Brecon & Merthyr	0-6-0ST
5991	*Gresham Hall*	'Hall'	4-6-0
—	*Greyhound*	'Fire Fly'†	2-2-2
3011	*Greyhound*	'3001'/'Achilles'	2-2-2
3058*	*Grierson*	'Achilles'	4-2-2
—	*Grongar*	Llanelly	0-6-0
3298	*Grosvenor*	'Badminton'	4-4-0
5926	*Grotrian Hall*	'Hall'	4-6-0
6977	*Grundisburgh Hall*	'Hall'	4-6-0
3316	*Guernsey*	'Duke'	4-4-0
5927	*Guild Hall*	'Hall'	4-6-0
3257	*Guinevere*	'Duke'	4-4-0
184*	*Guy Mannering*	'Saint'	4-6-0
6817	*Gwenddwr Grange*	'Grange'	4-6-0
—	*Gwendraeth*	Burry Port & Gwendraeth Valley	0-4-0ST
6	*Gwendraeth*	Burry Port & Gwendraeth Valley	0-6-0ST
—	*Gyfeillon*	'Standard Goods'†	0-6-0
22	*H.M.B.*	Port Talbot Railway and Docks	0-6-0ST
6949	*Haberfield Hall*	'Hall'	4-6-0
6925	*Hackness Hall*	'Hall'	4-6-0
—	*Hackworth*	'Hawthorn'†	2-4-0
5928	*Haddon Hall*	'Hall'	4-6-0
—	*Hades*	'Standard Goods'†	0-6-0
4930	*Hagley Hall*	'Hall'	4-6-0
3402	*Halifax*	'Atbara'/'City'	4-4-0
5074*	*Hampden*	'Castle'	4-6-0
2943	*Hampton Court*	'Saint'	4-6-0
4931	*Hanbury Hall*	'Hall'	4-6-0
5929	*Hanham Hall*	'Hall'	4-6-0
5930	*Hannington Hall*	'Hall'	4-6-0
6818	*Hardwick Grange*	'Grange'	4-6-0
—	*Hare*	West Midland (Oxford, Worcester & Wolverhampton)	2-2-2
52	*Harlech*	Cambrian	0-6-0
4095	*Harlech Castle*	'Castle'	4-6-0
—	*Harold*	Alexandra (Newport & South Wales) Docks & Railway/Weston, Clevedon & Portishead	0-6-0ST
6978	*Haroldstone Hall*	'Hall'	4-6-0
—	*Harpy*	'Fire Fly'†	2-2-2
—*	*Harriet*	Port Talbot Railway and Docks/Swansea Harbour Trust	0-6-0ST
5982	*Harrington Hall*	'Hall'	4-6-0
7907	*Hart Hall*	'Hall'	4-6-0
17	*Hartington*	Cambrian	4-4-0
7033	*Hartlebury Castle*	'Castle'	4-6-0
5931	*Hatherley Hall*	'Hall'	4-6-0
4932	*Hatherton Hall*	'Hall'	4-6-0
6874	*Haughton Grange*	'Grange'	4-6-0
7021	*Haverfordwest Castle*	'Castle'	4-6-0
—	*Haverhill*	Cornwall Minerals	0-6-0T
—	*Hawk*	'Fire Fly'†	2-2-2
—	*Hawk*	'Hawthorn'†	2-4-0
—	*Hawk*	South Devon	4-4-0ST
14*	*Hawkstone*	Birkenhead	0-6-0
—	*Hawthorn*	'Hawthorn'†	2-4-0
5932	*Haydon Hall*	'Hall'	4-6-0
—	*Hayle*	West Cornwall	?
5901	*Hazel Hall*	'Hall'	4-6-0
6840	*Hazeley Grange*	'Grange'	4-6-0
6852	*Headbourne Grange*	'Grange'	4-6-0
6946	*Heatherden Hall*	'Hall'	4-6-0
—	*Hebe*	'Standard Goods'†	0-6-0
—	*Hebe*	South Devon	0-6-0ST
—	*Hecate*	'Fire Fly'†	2-2-2
2*	*Hecate*	Bristol Port Railway and Pier	0-4-2T
—	*Hecla*	'Leo'†	2-4-0
—	*Hecla*	South Devon/Carmarthen & Cardigan	4-4-0ST
—	*Hector*	'Fire Fly'†	2-2-2
—	*Hector*	South Devon	4-4-0ST
—	*Hecuba*	'Standard Goods'†	0-6-0
—	*Hedley*	'Hawthorn'†	2-4-0
—*	*Helena*	Llanelly	0-4-0
6947	*Helmingham Hall*	'Hall'	4-6-0
6912	*Helmster Hall*	'Hall'	4-6-0
6979	*Helperly Hall*	'Hall'	4-6-0
—	*Helston*	Llynvi & Ogmore/West Cornwall	2-4-0
5970	*Hengrave Hall*	'Hall'	4-6-0
5983	*Henley Hall*	'Hall'	4-6-0
7908	*Henshall Hall*	'Hall'	4-6-0
—	*Hercules*	'Hercules'†	0-6-0
—	*Hercules*	South Devon	0-6-0ST
16	*Hercules*	(Crane tank)	0-6-4
3044	*Hercules*	'Achilles'	4-2-2
19	*Hercules*	Cambrian/Brecon & Merthyr	0-6-0
32	*Hercules*	Taff Vale	0-6-0
27	*Hercules*	Brecon & Merthyr	0-6-0ST
1	*Hercules*	British Railways	0-4-0ST
4	*Hercules*	Bristol Port Railway and Pier	0-4-2T
—	*Hercules No. 2*	Severn & Wye and Severn Bridge	?
—	*Hereford*	'Swindon'†/Bristol & Exeter	0-6-0
15(?)	*Hereford*	Cambrian/Brecon & Merthyr	?
7022	*Hereford Castle*	'Castle'	4-6-0
	Hero	'Caesar'†	0-6-0
—	*Hero*	South Devon	0-6-0ST
23	*Hero*	Bristol Port Railway and Pier	0-4-2T
—	*Heron*	South Devon/Carmarthen & Cardigan	4-4-0T
3376	*Herschell*	'Atbara'	4-4-0
—	*Hesiod*	'Bogie'†	4-4-0ST
—	*Hesperus*	'Sun'†	2-2-2
4	*Hesperus*	Watlington & Princes Risborough/Weston Clevedon & Portishead	2-4-0T
—*	*Hesperus*	North Pembrokeshire & Fishguard	0-6-0ST
7909	*Heveningham Hall*	'Hall'	4-6-0
6839	*Hewell Grange*	'Grange'	4-6-0
4096	*Highclere Castle*	'Castle'	4-6-0
2944	*Highnam Court*	'Saint'	4-6-0
6819	*Highnam Grange*	'Grange'	4-6-0
—	*Hilda*	Llanelly & Mynydd Mawr	0-6-0ST
15	*Hill*	(Steam Railmotor)	—
2945	*Hillingdon Court*	'Saint'	4-6-0
37(?)	*Himalaya*	West Midland (Oxford, Worcester & Wolverhampton)	0-6-0
4933	*Himley Hall*	'Hall'	4-6-0
5900	*Hinderton Hall*	'Hall'	4-6-0
6875	*Hindford Grange*	'Grange'	4-6-0
4934	*Hindlip Hall*	'Hall'	4-6-0
7819	*Hinton Manor*	'Manor'	4-6-0
—	*Hirondelle*	'Iron Duke'†	4-2-2
—	*Hirondelle*	'Rover'†	4-2-2
5	*Hirondelle*	Birkenhead	2-2-2
3045	*Hirondelle*	'Achilles'	4-2-2
3403	*Hobart*	'Atbara'/'City'	4-4-0
1	*Hodroyd*	Alexandra (Newport & South Wales) Docks and Railway	0-6-0ST
6948	*Holbrooke Hall*	'Hall'	4-6-0
6911	*Holker Hall*	'Hall'	4-6-0
6926	*Holkham Hall*	'Hall'	4-6-0
7	*Holmwood*	Pembroke & Tenby/'1813'	0-6-0T
—	*Homer*	'Bogie'†	4-4-0ST
5969	*Honington Hall*	'Hall'	4-6-0
—	*Hook Norton*	Hook Norton Ironstone Partnership Ltd/Fishguard & Rosslare Railways and Harbours Co	0-6-0ST
7823	*Hook Norton Manor*	'Manor'	4-6-0
6865	*Hopton Grange*	'Grange'	4-6-0
—	*Horace*	'Bogie'†	4-4-0ST
—	*Hornet*	'Metro'†	2-4-0WT
5956	*Horsley Hall*	'Hall'	4-6-0
5992	*Horton Hall*	'Hall'	4-6-0
3300	*Hotspur*	'Badminton'†	4-4-0
5902	*Howick Hall*	'Hall'	4-6-0
7910	*Hown Hall*	'Hall'	4-6-0
3299	*Hubbard*	'Badminton'	4-4-0
—	*Humber*	'Standard Goods'†	0-6-0
2	*Humber*	Midland & South Western Junction	0-6-0T
—	*Hurricane*	'Unclassified'†	2-2-2
3044	*Hurricane*	'Achilles'	2-2-2
5072*	*Hurricane*	'Castle'	4-6-0
6851	*Hurst Grange*	'Grange'	4-6-0
5957	*Hutton Hall*	'Hall'	4-6-0
4113*	*Hyacinth*	'Flower'	4-4-0
4113	*Hyacinthe*	'Flower'	4-4-0
—	*Hydra*	'Fire Fly'†	2-2-2
—	*Iago*	'Banking'†	0-6-0ST
5944	*Ickenham Hall*	'Hall'	4-6-0
7824	*Iford Manor*	'Manor'	4-6-0
3445	*Ilfracombe*	'Bulldog'	4-4-0
—	*Ilkeston*	Alexandra (Newport & South Wales) Docks and Railway	0-6-0T
6951	*Impney Hall*	'Hall'	4-6-0
7034	*Ince Castle*	'Castle'	4-6-0
3720	*Inchcape*	'Bulldog'	4-4-0
35	*Inkerman*	Taff Vale	0-6-0
—	*Inkermann*	'Iron Duke'†	4-2-2
—	*Inkermann*	'Rover'†	4-2-2
—	*Inveravon*	Llanelly & Mynydd Mawr	0-4-0ST
—	*Iris*	'Standard Goods'†	0-6-0
—	*Iron Duke*	'Iron Duke'†	4-2-2
—	*Iron Duke*	'Rover'†	4-2-2
3014	*Iron Duke*	'3001'/'Achilles'	2-2-2
—	*Ironsides*	West Cornwall	?
29	*Irthlingborough*	Cardiff	0-6-2T
5069	*Isambard Kingdom Brunel*	'Castle'	4-6-0
12	*Isebrook*	'Sentinel'	4whVBT
73	*Isis*	'River'	2-4-0
3316*	*Isle of Guernsey*	'Duke'/'Bulldog'	4-4-0
3317*	*Isle of Jersey*	'Duke'	4-4-0
3288*	*Isle of Tresco*	'Duke'	4-4-0
4025*	*Italian Monarch*	'Star'	4-6-0
—	*Ivanhoe*	'Waverley'†	4-4-0
181	*Ivanhoe*	'Saint'	4-6-0
—	*Ixion*	'Fire Fly'†	2-2-2
—	*Ixion*	South Devon	4-4-0ST
5	*J. C. Parkinson*	Alexandra (Newport & South Wales) Docks and Railway	0-6-0ST
3	*J. R. Maclean*	Alexandra (Newport & South Wales) Docks and Railway	0-6-0ST
3737	*Jackdaw*	'Bulldog'	4-4-0

No	Name	Class	Wheel arrangement
3464	*Jamaica*	'Bulldog'	4-4-0
3041*	*James Mason*	'Achilles'	4-2-2
3703	*James Mason*	'Bulldog'	4-4-0
1	*James Watt*	Cambrian	0-6-0
—	*Janus*	'Standard Goods'†	0-6-0
4026*	*Japanese Monarch*	'Star'	4-6-0
—	*Jason*	'Premier'†	0-6-0
—	*Javelin*	'Sun'†	2-2-2
—	*Jay*	South Devon/Powesland & Mason	0-4-0T
6	*Jean*	Swansea Harbour Trust	0-4-0ST
—	*Jeannie Waddell*	Llanelly & Mynydd Mawr	0-6-0ST
3317	*Jersey*	'Duke'	4-4-0
4	*Joan*	Swansea Harbour Trust	0-4-0ST
10*	*John*	Swansea Harbour Trust	0-4-0ST
3060*	*John G. Griffiths*	'Achilles'	4-2-2
3702	*John G. Griffiths*	'Bulldog'	4-4-0
—	*John Gray*	'Hawthorn'†	2-4-0
—	*John Owen*	Whitland & Cardigan	0-6-0ST
3059*	*John W. Wilson*	'Achilles'	4-2-2
3706	*John W. Wilson*	'Bulldog'	4-4-0
—	*John Waddell*	Llanelly & Mynydd Mawr	0-4-0T(?)
—	*John Waddell*	Llanelly & Mynydd Mawr	0-6-0ST
3724	*Joseph Shaw*	'Bulldog'	4-4-0
—	*Jumbo*	Swansea Harbour Trust	0-4-0ST
14*	*Jumbo*	Cambrian	0-6-0ST
—	*Juno*	'Banking'†	0-6-0ST
—	*Juno*	South Devon	0-6-0ST
—	*Jupiter*	'Fire Fly'†	2-2-2
—	*Jupiter*	South Devon	2-4-0T
3318	*Jupiter*	'Duke'/'Bulldog'	4-4-0
14	*Jupiter*	Brecon & Merthyr	0-6-0ST
—	*Juvenal*	'Bogie'†	4-4-0ST
—	*Kaiser*	'Metro'†	2-4-0WT
—*	*Kate*	Alexandra (Newport & South Wales) Docks and Railway	0-4-0ST
3319	*Katerfelto*	'Duke'	4-4-0
5903	*Keele Hall*	'Hall'	4-6-0
3383	*Kekewich*	'Atbara'	4-4-0
5904	*Kelham Hall*	'Hall'	4-6-0
3337	*Kenilworth*	'Bulldog'	4-4-0
4097	*Kenilworth Castle*	'Castle'	4-6-0
3015	*Kennet*	'3001'/'Achilles'	2-2-2
—	*Kertch*	'Iron Duke'†	4-2-2
4935	*Ketley Hall*	'Hall'	4-6-0
—	*Khan*	'Metro'†	2-4-0WT
3378	*Khartoum*	'Atbara'	4-4-0
—	*Kidwelly*	Burry Port & Gwendraeth Valley/Gwendraeth Valleys	0-6-0ST
4	*Kidwelly*	Burry Port & Gwendraeth Valley	0-6-0ST
	Kidwelly	Gwendraeth Valleys	0-6-0ST
4098	*Kidwelly Castle*	'Castle'	4-6-0
4099	*Kilgerran Castle*	'Castle'	4-6-0
3408*	*Killarney*	'City'	4-4-0
—	*Kilmar*	Liskeard & Looe and Liskeard & Caradon	0-6-0ST
3379	*Kimberley*	'Atbara'	4-4-0
6952	*Kimberley Hall*	'Hall'	4-6-0
—	*King*	South Devon	2-4-0T
3258	*King Arthur*	'Duke'	4-4-0
4025	*King Charles*	'Star'	4-6-0
6010	*King Charles I*	'King'	4-6-0
6009	*King Charles II*	'King'	4-6-0
4021	*King Edward*	'Star'	4-6-0
6024	*King Edward I*	'King'	4-6-0
6023	*King Edward II*	'King'	4-6-0
6022	*King Edward III*	'King'	4-6-0
6017	*King Edward IV*	'King'	4-6-0
6016	*King Edward V*	'King'	4-6-0
6012	*King Edward VI*	'King'	4-6-0
6001	*King Edward VII*	'King'	4-6-0
6029*	*King Edward VIII*	'King'	4-6-0
4023	*King George*	'Star'	4-6-0
6006	*King George I*	'King'	4-6-0
6005	*King George II*	'King'	4-6-0
6004	*King George III*	'King'	4-6-0
6003	*King George IV*	'King'	4-6-0
6000	*King George V*	'King'	4-6-0
6028*	*King George VI*	'King'	4-6-0
4030	*King Harold*	'Star'	4-6-0
4027	*King Henry*	'Star'	4-6-0
6028	*King Henry II*	'King'	4-6-0
6025	*King Henry III*	'King'	4-6-0
6020	*King Henry IV*	'King'	4-6-0
6019	*King Henry V*	'King'	4-6-0
6018	*King Henry VI*	'King'	4-6-0
6012	*King Henry VII*	'King'	4-6-0
6013	*King Henry VIII*	'King'	4-6-0
4024	*King James*	'Star'	4-6-0
6011	*King James I*	'King'	4-6-0
6008	*King James II*	'King'	4-6-0
4028	*King John*	'Star'	4-6-0
6026	*King John*	'King'	4-6-0
4026	*King Richard*	'Star'	4-6-0
6027	*King Richard I*	'King'	4-6-0
6021	*King Richard II*	'King'	4-6-0
6015	*King Richard III*	'King'	4-6-0

No	Name	Class	Wheel arrangement
4029	*King Stephen*	'Star'	4-6-0
6029	*King Stephen*	'King'	4-6-0
4022	*King William*	'Star'	4-6-0
6007	*King William III*	'King'	4-6-0
6002	*King William IV*	'King'	4-6-0
3738	*Kingfisher*	'Bulldog'	4-4-0
3359	*Kingsbridge*	'Bulldog'	4-4-0
6876	*Kingsland Grange*	'Grange'	4-6-0
6950	*Kingsthorpe Hall*	'Hall'	4-6-0
6820	*Kingstone Grange*	'Grange'	4-6-0
5933	*Kingsway Hall*	'Hall'	4-6-0
5015	*Kingswear Castle*	'Castle'	4-6-0
4936	*Kinlet Hall*	'Hall'	4-6-0
5993	*Kirby Hall*	'Hall'	4-6-0
3	*Kirkella*	Midland & South Western Junction	0-6-0T
178*	*Kirkland*	'Saint'	4-6-0
3374*	*Kitchener*	'Atbara'	4-4-0
3377	*Kitchener*	'Atbara'	4-4-0
168	*Kitchener*	Taff Vale	0-6-2T
5934	*Kneller Hall*	'Hall'	4-6-0
4020	*Knight Commander*	'Star'	4-6-0
4017*	*Knight of Liége*	'Star'	4-6-0
4017*	*Knight of Liège*	'Star'	4-6-0
4015	*Knight of St John*	'Star'	4-6-0
4013	*Knight of St Patrick*	'Star'	4-6-0
4014	*Knight of the Bath*	'Star'	4-6-0
4017	*Knight of the Black Eagle*	'Star'	4-6-0
4011	*Knight of the Garter*	'Star'	4-6-0
4016	*Knight of the Golden Fleece*	'Star'/'Castle'	4-6-0
4018	*Knight of the Grand Cross*	'Star'	4-6-0
4012	*Knight of the Thistle*	'Star'	4-6-0
4019	*Knight Templar*	'Star'	4-6-0
5958	*Knolton Hall*	'Hall'	4-6-0
5905	*Knowsley Hall*	'Hall'	4-6-0
102	*La France*	'De Glehn Compound'	4-4-2
25	*La Savoie*	Cardiff	0-6-0
16*	*Lady Cornelia*	Brecon & Merthyr	0-6-0ST
—	*Lady Cornewall*	Golden Valley	2-2-2T(?)
2907	*Lady Disdain*	'Saint'	4-6-0
3	*Lady Elizabeth*	Manchester & Milford	2-4-0
2904	*Lady Godiva*	'Saint'	4-6-0
2905	*Lady Macbeth*	'Saint'	4-6-0
—	*Lady Margaret*	Liskeard & Looe and Liskeard & Caradon	2-4-0T
7911	*Lady Margaret Hall*	'Hall'	4-6-0
2906	*Lady of Lynn*	'Saint'	4-6-0
2903	*Lady of Lyons*	'Saint'	4-6-0
2909	*Lady of Provence*	'Saint'	4-6-0
2908	*Lady of Quality*	'Saint'	4-6-0
2910	*Lady of Shalott*	'Saint'	4-6-0
2902	*Lady of the Lake*	'Saint'	4-6-0
2901	*Lady Superior*	'Saint'	4-6-0
6	*Lady Tredegar*	Alexandra (Newport & South Wales) Docks and Railway	0-6-0ST
3380	*Ladysmith*	'Atbara'	4-4-0
—	*Lagoon*	'Standard Goods'†	0-6-0
3338	*Laira*	'Bulldog'	4-4-0
—	*Lalla Rookh*	'Waverley'†	4-4-0
182	*Lalla Rookh*	'Saint'	4-6-0
3055*	*Lambert*	'Achilles'	2-2-2
4	*Lampeter*	Manchester & Milford	0-6-0ST
5054	*Lamphey Castle*	'Castle'	4-6-0
5078	*Lamphey Castle*	'Castle'	4-6-0
7005	*Lamphey Castle*	'Castle'	4-6-0
—	*Lance*	'Sun'†	2-2-2
—	*Lance*	South Devon	4-4-0ST
—	*Lance*	South Devon	4-4-0ST
4937	*Lanelay Hall*	'Hall'	4-6-0
2946	*Langford Court*	'Saint'	4-6-0
6914	*Langton Hall*	'Hall'	4-6-0
—	*Lark*	South Devon/Powesland & Mason	0-4-0T
15	*Latona*	Birkenhead	2-2-2
1	*Latona*	Cambrian	4-4-0T
3360	*Launceston*	'Bulldog'	4-4-0
5000	*Launceston Castle*	'Castle'	4-6-0
—	*Laurel*	'Metro'†	2-4-0WT
5906	*Lawton Hall*	'Hall'	4-6-0
—	*Leander*	'Standard Goods'†	0-6-0
6821	*Leaton Grange*	'Grange'	4-6-0
7825	*Lechlade Manor*	'Manor'	4-6-0
5945	*Leckhampton Hall*	'Hall'	4-6-0
30	*Leeds*	Birkenhead	2-2-2
8	*Leighton*	Cambrian/Brecon & Merthyr	0-4-2
6953	*Leighton Hall*	'Hall'	4-6-0
—	*Leo*	'Leo'†	2-4-0
—	*Leo*	Llanelly	0-6-0
—	*Leon*	Brecon & Merthyr	?
—	*Leonidas*	'Standard Goods'†	0-6-0

No	Name	Class	Wheel arrangement
—	*Leopard*	'Fire Fly'†	2-2-2
—	*Leopard*	South Devon	4-4-0ST
—	*Leopold*	'Victoria'†	2-4-0
—	*Lethe*	'Fire Fly'†	2-2-2
6913	*Levens Hall*	'Hall'	4-6-0
—	*Libra*	'Leo'†	2-4-0
4938	*Liddington Hall*	'Hall'	4-6-0
—	*Liffey*	'Standard Goods'†	0-6-0
—	*Lightning*	'Iron Duke'†	4-2-2
—	*Lightning*	'Rover'†	4-2-2
3016	*Lightning*	'3001'/'Achilles'	2-2-2
6927	*Lilford Hall*	'Hall'	4-6-0
21	*Lilleshall*	Cambrian	0-4-0ST
—	*Lily*	'Metro'†	2-4-0WT
5984	*Linden Hall*	'Hall'	4-6-0
—	*Lion*	'Unclassified'†	2-2-2
—	*Lion*	South Devon	4-4-0ST
—	*Liskeard*	Liskeard & Looe and Liskeard & Caradon	0-6-0T(?)
2	*Little John*	Severn & Wye and Severn Bridge	0-4-0
—	*Little John*	Severn & Wye and Severn Bridge	0-6-0T
7912	*Little Linford Hall*	'Hall'	4-6-0
7913	*Little Wyrley Hall*	'Hall'	4-6-0
4939	*Littleton Hall*	'Hall'	4-6-0
3446	*Liverpool*	'Bulldog'	4-4-0
3259	*Lizard*	'Duke'	4-4-0
—	*Lizzie*	Burry Port & Gwendraeth Valley	0-4-0ST
—	*Llancaiach*	Taff Vale	0-4-2
5	*Llancaiach*	Taff Vale	0-6-0
—	*Llandaff*	Taff Vale	0-6-0
11	*Llandaff*	Taff Vale	0-6-0
—	*Llandinam*	Pembroke & Tenby/Cambrian	0-6-0ST
5001	*Llandovery Castle*	'Castle'	4-6-0
7	*Llanerchydol*	Cambrian	0-4-2
6877	*Llanfair Grange*	'Grange'	4-6-0
6827	*Llanfrecha Grange*	'Grange'	4-6-0
4941	*Llangedwyn Hall*	'Hall'	4-6-0
—	*Llanidloes*	Cambrian	?
6980	*Llanrumney Hall*	'Hall'	4-6-0
5004	*Llanstephan Castle*	'Castle'	4-6-0
4068	*Llanthony Abbey*	'Star'/'Castle'	4-6-0
5028	*Llantilio Castle*	'Castle'	4-6-0
—	*Llantwit*	Taff Vale	0-4-2
8	*Llantwit*	Taff Vale	0-6-0
6825	*Llanvair Grange*	'Grange'	4-6-0
1(?)	*Llewelyn*	Cambrian	?
7914	*Lleweni Hall*	'Hall'	4-6-0
100(A1)	*Lloyd's*	'Castle'	4-6-0
8	*Llywelyn*	Cambrian	2-6-2T
—	*Load Star*	'Star'†	2-2-2
4109	*Lobelia*	'Flower'	4-4-0
—	*Locke*	'Victoria'†	2-4-0
20	*Locke*	Birkenhead	2-2-2
5081*	*Lockheed Hudson*	'Castle'	4-6-0
—	*Locust*	'Metro'†	2-4-0WT
4003	*Lode Star*	'Star'	4-6-0
—	*London*	'Swindon'†/Bristol & Exeter	0-6-0
6878	*Longford Grange*	'Grange'	4-6-0
34	*Longmoor*	'34 & 35'	0-4-2T
7826	*Longworth Manor*	'Manor'	4-6-0
—	*Looe*	Liskeard & Looe and Liskeard & Caradon	0-6-0ST
174*	*Lord Barrymore*	'Saint'	4-6-0
3707*	*Lord Mildmay of Flete*	'Bulldog'	4-4-0
3046	*Lord of the Isles*	'Achilles'	4-2-2
175*	*Lord Palmer*	'Saint'	4-6-0
—	*Lord Robartes*	Cornwall Minerals	0-6-0
2	*Lord Robartes*	Cornwall Minerals	0-6-0T
2	*Lord Tredegar*	Alexandra (Newport & South Wales) Docks and Railway	0-6-0ST
3047	*Lorna Doone*	'Achilles'	4-2-2
6954	*Lotherton Hall*	'Hall'	4-6-0
—	*Loughor*	Llanelly	2-4-0ST
—	*Louisa*	Llanelly	0-6-0
—	*Lucan*	'Bogie'†	4-4-0ST
—	*Lucifer*	'Fire Fly'†	2-2-2
—	*Lucretius*	'Bogie'†	4-4-0ST
4940	*Ludford Hall*	'Hall'	4-6-0
5002	*Ludlow Castle*	'Castle'	4-6-0
5003	*Lulworth Castle*	'Castle'	4-6-0
—	*Luna*	'Standard Goods'†	0-6-0
6	*Lupus*	Birkenhead	2-2-2
6955	*Lydcott Hall*	'Hall'	4-6-0
5055	*Lydford Castle*	'Castle'	4-6-0
5079	*Lydford Castle*	'Castle'	4-6-0
7006	*Lydford Castle*	'Castle'	4-6-0
7827	*Lydham Manor*	'Manor'	4-6-0
—	*Lynx*	'Fire Fly'†	2-2-2
—	*Lynx*	South Devon	4-4-0ST
3361	*Lyonesse*	'Bulldog'	4-4-0
5036	*Lyonshall Castle*	'Castle'	4-6-0
5079*	*Lysander*	'Castle'	4-6-0
3404*	*Lyttelton*	'City'	4-4-0

3404	*Lyttleton*	'Atbara'/'City'	4-4-0
3421	*Mac Iver*	'Bulldog'	4-4-0
3469	*Madras*	'Bulldog'	4-4-0
2947	*Madresfield Court*	'Saint'	4-6-0
3382	*Mafeking*	'Atbara'	4-4-0
—	*Magi*	'Standard Goods'†	0-6-0
57	*Maglona*	Cambrian	2-4-0T
179	*Magnet*	'Saint'	4-6-0
—	*Magpie*	South Devon/Carmarthen & Cardigan	4-4-0T
—	*Maid Marian*	Severn & Wye and Severn Bridge	0-6-0T
4942	*Maindy Hall*	'Hall'	4-6-0
3373*	*Maine*	'Atbara'	4-4-0
3381	*Maine*	'Atbara'	4-4-0
3048	*Majestic*	'Achilles'	4-2-2
24	*Majestic*	Birkenhead	2-4-0
4062	*Malmesbury Abbey*	'Star'	4-6-0
3407	*Malta*	'Atbara'/'City'	4-4-0
4066	*Malvern Abbey*	'Star'	4-6-0
—	*Mammoth*	'Pyracmon'†	0-6-0
5005	*Manorbier Castle*	'Castle'	4-6-0
6822	*Manton Grange*	'Grange'	4-6-0
3340	*Marazion*	'Bulldog'	4-4-0
5907	*Marble Hall*	'Hall'	4-6-0
6981	*Marbury Hall*	'Hall'	4-6-0
10	*Marchioness*	Cambrian	0-6-0
3339	*Marco Polo*	'Hall'	4-4-0
4069	*Margam Abbey*	'Star'	4-6-0
—	*Margaret*	North Pembrokeshire & Fishguard/Gwendraeth Valleys	0-6-0ST
4114	*Marguerite*	'Flower'	4-4-0
4115	*Marigold*	'Flower'	4-4-0
3282	*Maristow*	'Duke'/'Bulldog'	4-4-0
3309*	*Maristowe*	'Bulldog'	4-4-0
6841	*Marlas Grange*	'Grange'	4-6-0
3303	*Marlborough*	'Badminton'	4-4-0
6	*Marquis*	Cambrian	0-6-0
41	*Marquis Douro*	Birkenhead	0-4-2
4943	*Marrington Hall*	'Hall'	4-6-0
—	*Mars*	'Unclassified'†	2-2-2
—	*Mars*	'Fire Fly'†	2-2-2
—	*Mars*	'West Cornwall'	0-6-0ST
3341	*Mars*	'Bulldog'	4-4-0
27	*Mars*	Taff Vale	0-6-0
5946	*Marwell Hall*	'Hall'	4-6-0
3405	*Mauritius*	'Atbara'/City'	4-4-0
30*	*Mawddwy*	Cambrian	0-6-0ST
5959	*Mawley Hall*	'Hall'	4-6-0
—	*Mazeppa*	'Fire Fly'†	2-2-2
—	*Mazeppa*	South Devon	4-4-0ST
28	*Mazeppa*	Cambrian	2-4-0
—	*Medea*	'Fire Fly'†	2-2-2
—	*Medusa*	'Fire Fly'†	2-2-2
3406	*Melbourne*	'Atbara'/City'	4-4-0
—	*Melling*	'Hawthorn'†	2-4-0
6982	*Melmerby Hall*	'Hall'	4-6-0
1	*Melton Constable*	Cornwall Minerals	0-6-0T
27	*Memnon*	Birkenhead	0-4-0T
3323	*Mendip*	'Duke'	4-4-0
—	*Menton*	'Fire Fly'†	2-2-2
—	*Mercury*	'Unclassified'†	2-2-2
—	*Mercury*	'Fire Fly'†	2-2-2
—	*Mercury*	South Devon	2-4-0T
3323	*Mercury*	'Duke'	4-4-0
—	*Mercury*	Taff Vale	0-6-0
7915	*Mere Hall*	'Hall'	4-6-0
5971	*Merevale Hall*	'Hall'	4-6-0
—	*Meridian*	'Sun'†	2-2-2
17	*Merion*	Cambrian	0-6-0ST
—	*Merkland*	Llanelly & Mynydd Mawr	0-6-0T
3260	*Merlin*	'Duke'	4-4-0
—	*Mermaid*	Fishguard & Rosslare Railways and Harbours Co	0-4-0ST
—	*Mersey*	'Standard Goods'†	0-6-0
13	*Mersey*	Birkenhead	0-6-0
23	*Mersey*	Birkenhead	2-4-0
3322	*Mersey*	'Duke'/'Bulldog'	4-4-0
23	*Mersey*	Brecon & Merthyr	0-6-0ST
7	*Mersey*	Alexandra (Newport & South Wales) Docks and Railway	2-6-2T
—	*Merthyr*	Taff Vale	0-4-2
6	*Merthyr*	Taff Vale	0-6-0
—	*Meteor*	'Sun'†	2-2-2
—	*Meteor*	South Devon	4-4-0ST
3320	*Meteor*	'Duke'	4-4-0
—	*Metis*	'Standard Goods'†	0-6-0
—	*Midas*	'Standard Goods'†	0-6-0
4944	*Middleton Hall*	'Hall'	4-6-0
—*	*Miers*	Neath & Brecon	0-6-0WT
4116	*Mignonette*	'Flower'	4-4-0
—	*Miles*	'Sir Watkin'†	0-6-0T
2	*Milford*	Pembroke & Tenby	2-2-2T
3	*Milford*	Cambrian	0-4-2ST
4945	*Milligan Hall*	'Hall'	4-6-0
—	*Milo*	'Fire Fly'†	2-2-2
—	*Minerva*	'Standard Goods'†	0-6-0
31	*Minerva*	Cambrian	2-4-0
—	*Minos*	'Fire Fly'†	2-2-2

6916	*Misterton Hall*	'Hall'	4-6-0
7916	*Mobberley Hall*	'Hall'	4-6-0
—	*Mogul*	'Metro'†	2-4-0WT
—	*Monarch*	'Standard Goods'†	0-6-0
3301	*Monarch*	'Badminton'	4-4-0
8*	*Monk*	Birkenhead	2-2-2
5037	*Monmouth Castle*	'Castle'	4-6-0
5	*Montgomery*	Cambrian/Brecon & Merthyr	0-4-2
5016	*Montgomery Castle*	'Castle'	4-6-0
3460	*Montreal*	'Bulldog'	4-4-0
1956	*Monty*	'850'	0-6-0ST
—	*Moorsom*	Taff Vale	4-2-0
6853	*Morehampton Grange*	'Grange'	4-6-0
5908	*Moreton Hall*	'Hall'	4-6-0
6866	*Morfa Grange*	'Grange'	4-6-0
5038	*Morlais Castle*	'Castle'	4-6-0
—	*Morning Star*	'Star'†	2-2-2
381	*Morning Star*	'Sir Daniel'	2-2-2
4004	*Morning Star*	'Star'	4-6-0
3302	*Mortimer*	'Badminton'	4-4-0
4946	*Moseley Hall*	'Hall'	4-6-0
—	*Mosquito*	'Metro'†	2-4-0WT
5985	*Mostyn Hall*	'Hall'	4-6-0
6956	*Mottram Hall*	'Hall'	4-6-0
3261	*Mount Edgcumbe*	'Duke'	4-4-0
—	*Mount's Bay*	Llynvi & Ogmore/West Cornwall	2-4-0
37	*Mountaineer*	Cambrian/Brecon & Merthyr	0-4-0ST
—	*Mountaineer*	Rhymney/Taff Vale	0-6-0ST
—*	*Mountaineer*	Burry Port & Gwendraeth Valley	0-4-4-0
—	*Mountaineer*	Neath & Brecon	0-4-4-0
3283	*Mounts Bay*	'Duke'	4-4-0
'F'	*Mudlark*	West Midland (Oxford, Worcester & Wolverhampton)	?
—	*Murdock*	'Hawthorn'†	2-4-0
6915	*Mursley Hall*	'Hall'	4-6-0
—	*Myrtle*	'Metro'†	2-4-0WT
5996	*Mytton Hall*	'Hall'	4-6-0
4947	*Nanhoran Hall*	'Hall'	4-6-0
6826	*Nannerth Grange*	'Grange'†	4-6-0
14	*Nantclwyd*	Cambrian	0-6-0ST
—	*Napoleon*	'Victoria'†	2-4-0
—	*Napoleon III*	Llanelly	2-4-0
4117	*Narcissus*	'Flower'	4-4-0
3458	*Natal*	'Bulldog'	4-4-0
3458*	*Natal Colony*	'Bulldog'	4-4-0
—	*Neath*	Neath & Brecon	2-4-0
4070	*Neath Abbey*	'Star'/'Castle'†	4-6-0
—	*Neath Abbey*	Taff Vale	0-4-2
—	*Nelson*	'Standard Goods'†	0-6-0
—	*Nelson*	Severn & Wye and Severn Bridge	?
3017	*Nelson*	'3001'/'Achilles'	2-2-2
3049*	*Nelson*	'Achilles'	4-2-2
—	*Nemesis*	'Standard Goods'†	0-6-0
—	*Neptune*	'Unclassified '†	2-2-2
—	*Neptune*	'Standard Goods'†	0-6-0
—	*Nero*	'Standard Goods'†	0-6-0
—*	*Nestor*	West Cornwall	0-6-0
1	*Nestor*	Monmouthshire Railway and Canal Co	0-6-0
3454	*New Zealand*	'Bulldog'	4-4-0
—	*Newbridge*	Taff Vale	0-6-0
12	*Newbridge*	Taff Vale	0-6-0
3362	*Newlyn*	'Bulldog'	4-4-0
—	*Newport*	'Swindon'†/Bristol & Exeter	0-6-0
3447	*Newport*	'Bulldog'	4-4-0
5058	*Newport Castle*	'Castle'	4-6-0
5065	*Newport Castle*	'Castle'	4-6-0
—	*Newquay*	Cornwall Minerals/South Wales Mineral	0-4-2ST
—	*Newquay*	Cornwall Minerals	0-6-0T
3284	*Newquay*	'Duke'	4-4-0
32(?)	*Newton*	Shrewsbury & Chester	2-2-2(?)
5909	*Newton Hall*	'Hall'	4-6-0
3739	*Nightingdale*	'Bulldog'	4-4-0
—	*Nimrod*	'Standard Goods'†	0-6-0
—	*Nipper*	Fishguard & Rosslare Railways and Harbours Co	0-4-0ST
—	*Nora Creina*	'Caesar'†	0-6-0
6957	*Norcliffe Hall*	'Hall'	4-6-0
7917	*North Aston Hall*	'Hall'	4-6-0
—	*North Star*	'Star'†	2-2-2
380	*North Star*	'Sir Daniel'	2-2-2
3072	*North Star*	'Achilles'	4-2-2
40	*North Star*	'Star'/'Castle'	4-4-2
—	*Northiam*	Weston, Clevedon & Portishead	?
4948	*Northwick Hall*	'Grange'	4-6-0
5935	*Norton Hall*	'Hall'†	4-6-0
4027*	*Norwegian Monarch*	'Star'	4-6-0
6842	*Nunhold Grange*	'Grange'	4-6-0
5029	*Nunney Castle*	'Castle'	4-6-0
6823	*Oakley Grange*	'Grange'	4-6-0

5936	*Oakley Hall*	'Hall'	4-6-0
—	*Octavia*	'Standard Goods'†	0-6-0
7828	*Odney Manor*	'Manor'	4-6-0
5056	*Ogmore Castle*	'Castle'	4-6-0
5080	*Ogmore Castle*	'Castle'	4-6-0
7007	*Ogmore Castle*	'Castle'	4-6-0
7035	*Ogmore Castle*	'Castle'	4-6-0
6917	*Oldlands Hall*	'Hall'	4-6-0
5972	*Olton Hall*	'Hall'	4-6-0
—	*Olympus*	'Standard Goods'†	0-6-0
3384	*Omdurman*	'Atbara'	4-4-0
3363	*One and All*	'Bulldog'	4-4-0
3408	*Ophir*	'Atbara'/'City'	4-4-0
—	*Orion*	'Fire Fly'†	2-2-2
—	*Orion*	South Devon	4-4-0ST
3342	*Orion*	'Bulldog'	4-4-0
31	*Orion*	Taff Vale	0-6-0
18	*Orleton*	Cambrian	0-6-0
—	*Orpheus*	'Standard Goods'†	0-6-0
—	*Orson*	'Standard Goods'†	0-6-0
—	*Oscar*	'Victoria'†	2-4-0
—	*Osiris*	'Standard Goods'†	0-6-0
—	*Osiris*	South Devon	4-4-0ST
—	*Osiris*	South Devon	4-4-0ST
—	*Ostrich*	'Fire Fly'†	2-2-2
—	*Ostrich*	'Hawthorn'†	2–4–0
—	*Ostrich*	South Devon	4-4-0ST
—	*Otho*	'Victoria'†	2–4–0
3461	*Ottawa*	'Bulldog'	4–4–0
6983	*Otterington Hall*	'Hall'	4-6-0
6879	*Overton Grange*	'Grange'	4-6-0
—	*Ovid*	'Bogie'†	4-4-0ST
7	*Owain Glyndŵr*	Cambrian	2-6-2T
4	*Owen*	Powlesland & Mason	0-6-0
—	*Owl*	South Devon	0-4-0T
6984	*Owsden Hall*	'Hall'	4-6-0
6958	*Oxburgh Hall*	'Hall'	4-6-0
—	*Oxford*	'Swindon'†/Bristol & Exeter	0-6-0
3304	*Oxford*	'Badminton'	4-4-0
4949	*Packwood Hall*	'Hall'	4-6-0
3448	*Paddington*	'Bulldog'	4-4-0
—	*Pallas*	'Standard Goods'†	0-6-0
54	*Palmerston*	Cambrian	2-4-0
—	*Pandora*	'Standard Goods'†	0-6-0
13	*Pandora*	Brecon & Merthyr	0-6-0ST
—	*Panthea*	'Standard Goods'†	0-6-0
—	*Panther*	'Fire Fly'†	2-2-2
5910	*Park Hall*	'Hall'	4-6-0
2	*Parnassus*	Monmouthshire Railway and Canal Co	0-6-0
6985	*Parwick Hall*	'Hall'	4-6-0
—	*Pasha*	'Iron Duke'†	4-2-2
4950	*Patshull Hall*	'Hall'	4-6-0
6845	*Paviland Grange*	'Grange'	4-6-0
—	*Peacock*	'Hawthorn'†	2-4-0
3740	*Peacock*	'Bulldog'†	4-4-0
—	*Pearl*	'Standard Goods'†	0-6-0
6959	*Peating Hall*	'Hall'	4-6-0
—	*Pegasus*	'Fire Fly'†	2-2-2
3343	*Pegasus*	'Bulldog'	4-4-0
29	*Pegasus*	Cambrian	2-4-0
3741	*Pelican*	'Bulldog'	4-4-0
—	*Pelops*	'Standard Goods'†	0-6-0
7	*Pembrey*	Burry Port & Gwendraeth Valley	0-6-0ST
3	*Pembroke*	Pembroke & Tenby	2-4-0
3386	*Pembroke*	'Atbara'	4-4-0
4078	*Pembroke Castle*	'Castle'	4-6-0
46	*Penarth*	Taff Vale	0-6-0
—	*Pendarves*	West Cornwall	?
4951	*Pendeford Hall*	'Hall'	4-6-0
3300	*Pendennis Castle*	'Duke'/'Bulldog'	4-4-0
4079	*Pendennis Castle*	'Castle'	4-6-0
3364	*Pendragon*	'Bulldog'	4-4-0
3742	*Penguin*	'Bulldog'	4-4-0
6844	*Penhydd Grange*	'Grange'	4-6-0
—	*Penn*	'Hawthorn'†	2-4-0
6868	*Penrhos Grange*	'Grange'	4-6-0
5057	*Penrice Castle*	'Castle'	4-6-0
5081	*Penrice Castle*	'Castle'	4-6-0
7023	*Penrice Castle*	'Castle'	4-6-0
—	*Penwith*	South Devon/West Cornwall	2-4-0
?	*Penwyllt*	Neath & Brecon	?
—	*Penylan*	Port Talbot Railway and Docks/South Wales Mineral	0-6-0ST
—	*Penzance*	Llynvi & Ogmore/West Cornwall	2-4-0
—	*Penzance*	West Cornwall	?
3429	*Penzance*	'Bulldog'	4-4-0
4952	*Peplow Hall*	'Hall'	4-6-0
—	*Peri*	'Prince'†	2-2-2
—	*Perseus*	'Iron Duke'†	4-2-2
3345	*Perseus*	'Bulldog'	4-4-0
22	*Perseverance*	West Midland (Newport, Abergavenny & Hereford)	0-4-2T
–*	*Perseverance*	South Devon	2-4-0(?)
3365	*Pershore Plum*	'Bulldog'	4-4-0
2998*	*Persimmon*	'Saint'	4-6-0
6867	*Peterston Grange*	'Grange'	4-6-0
4110	*Petunia*	'Flower'	4-4-0
2985*	*Peveril of the*		

No	Name	Class	Wheel arrangement
	Peak	'Saint'	4-6-0
—	*Phlegethon*	'Fire Fly'†	2-2-2
—	*Phlegethon*	'Hawthorn'†	2-4-0
34	*Phoebus*	'Birkenhead'	2-4-0T
—	*Phoenix*	'Fire Fly'†	2-2-2
—	*Phoenix*	Cornwall Minerals	0-4-2
—	*Pioneer*	'Standard Goods'†	0-6-0
—	*Pioneer*	Fishguard & Rosslare Railways and Harbours Co	0-4-0ST
10(?)	*Pioneer*	Cambrian/Brecon & Merthyr	0-6-0ST
—	*Pioneer*	Burry Port & Gwendraeth Valley	0-4-4-0
8	*Pioneer*	Burry Port & Gwendraeth Valley	0-6-0T
—	*Pirate*	'Waverley'†	4-4-0
—	*Pisces*	'Leo'†	2-4-0
4953	*Pitchford Hall*	'Hall'	4-6-0
4954	*Plaish Hall*	'Hall'	4-6-0
—	*Planet*	'Unclassified'†	2-2-2
36	*Plasfynnon*	Cambrian	0-4-0ST
4955	*Plaspower Hall*	'Hall'	4-6-0
—	*Plato*	'Banking'†	0-6-0ST
4956	*Plowden Hall*	'Hall'	4-6-0
—	*Plutarch*	'Standard Goods'†	0-6-0
—	*Pluto*	'Fire Fly'†	2-2-2
—	*Pluto*	South Devon	4-4-0ST
3365	*Pluto*	'Bulldog'	4-4-0
44	*Pluto*	Taff Vale	0-6-0
—	*Plutus*	'Standard Goods'†	0-6-0
—	*Plym*	'Standard Goods'†	0-6-0
3365	*Plymouth*	'Bulldog'	4-4-0
—	*Plymouth*	Taff Vale	0-4-2
3	*Plymouth*	Taff Vale	0-6-0
2	*Plynlimmon*	Manchester & Milford	2-4-2T
43	*Plynlimon*	Cambrian	2-4-0
—	*Polar Star*	'Star'†	2-2-2
4005	*Polar Star*	'Star'†	4-6-0
—	*Pollux*	'Fire Fly'†	2-2-2
—	*Pollux*	'Hawthorn'†	2-4-0
—	*Pollux*	South Devon	4-4-0ST
39(?)	*Pollux*	West Midland (Oxford, Worcester & Wolverhampton)	0-6-0
4118	*Polyanthus*	'Flower'	4-4-0
2	*Pontyberem*	Burry Port & Gwendraeth Valley	0-6-0ST
7	*Pontypridd*	Alexandra (Newport & South Wales) Docks and Railway	0-6-2ST
9	*Pontypridd*	Alexandra (Newport & South Wales) Docks and Railway	0-6-0ST
9	*Porth*	Taff Vale	0-6-0
2*	*Portishead*	Weston, Clevedon & Portishead	0-6-0T
—	*Portishead*	Weston, Clevedon & Portishead	0-6-0T
2	*Portishead*	Weston, Clevedon & Portishead	0-6-0ST
4957	*Postlip Hall*	'Hall'	4-6-0
6843	*Poulton Grange*	'Grange'	4-6-0
3301	*Powderham*	'Duke'/'Bulldog'	4-4-0
4080	*Powderham Castle*	'Castle'	4-6-0
3385	*Powerful*	'Atbara'	4-4-0
3392*	*Powerful*	'Atbara'	4-4-0
5059	*Powis Castle*	'Castle'	4-6-0
5082	*Powis Castle*	'Castle'	4-6-0
7024	*Powis Castle*	'Castle'	4-6-0
—	*Precelly*	North Pembrokeshire & Fishguard	0-6-0ST
—	*Premier*	'Unclassified'†	2-2-2
—	*Premier*	'Premier'†	0-6-0
103	*President*	'De Glehn Compound'	4-4-2
190	*Preston*	Taff Vale	0-6-0ST
5911	*Preston Hall*	'Hall'	4-6-0
3374*	*Pretoria*	'Atbara'	4-4-0
3389*	*Pretoria*	'Atbara'	4-4-0
—	*Priam*	'Fire Fly'†	2-2-2
—	*Priam*	South Devon	4-4-0ST
4119	*Primrose*	'Flower'	4-4-0
—	*Prince*	'Prince'†	2-2-2
—	*Prince*	South Devon	2-4-0ST
4042	*Prince Albert*	'Star'	4-6-0
—	*Prince Alfred*	Llanelly	0-4-0
1118	*Prince Christian*	'Queen'	2-2-2
21	*Prince Eugene*	Birkenhead	2-2-2
4044	*Prince George*	'Star'	4-6-0
4043	*Prince Henry*	'Star'	4-6-0
4045	*Prince John*	'Star'	4-6-0
19	*Prince of Wales*	Shrewsbury & Chester	2-2-2
—	*Prince of Wales*	Llanelly	0-6-0
1132	*Prince of Wales*	'Queen'	2-2-2
4041	*Prince of Wales*	'Star'	4-6-0
12	*Prince of Wales*	Cambrian	0-6-0
9	*Prince of Wales*	Cambrian‡	2-6-2T
—	*Princess*	South Wales Mineral	0-4-0ST
4053	*Princess Alexandra*	'Star'	4-6-0
—	*Princess Alice*	Llanelly	0-4-0
4050	*Princess Alice*	'Star'	4-6-0
4058	*Princess Augusta*	'Star'	4-6-0
4052	*Princess Beatrice*	'Star'	4-6-0
4054	*Princess Charlotte*	'Star'	4-6-0
4057	*Princess Elizabeth*	'Star'	4-6-0
4060	*Princess Eugenie*	'Star'	4-6-0
—	*Princess Helena*	Llanelly	0-4-0
3074	*Princess Helena*	'Achilles'	4-2-2
4051	*Princess Helena*	'Star'	4-6-0
3075	*Princess Louise*	'Achilles'	4-2-2
4047	*Princess Louise*	'Star'	4-6-0
4056	*Princess Margaret*	'Star'	4-6-0
4046	*Princess Mary*	'Star'	4-6-0
4048*	*Princess Mary*	'Star'	4-6-0
4049	*Princess Maud*	'Star'	4-6-0
1129	*Princess May*	'Queen'	2-2-2
3077	*Princess May*	'Achilles'	4-2-2
1119	*Princess of Wales*	'Queen'	2-2-2
4059	*Princess Patricia*	'Star'	4-6-0
—	*Princess Royal*	Llanelly	0-6-0
3073	*Princess Royal*	'Achilles'	4-2-2
4055	*Princess Sophia*	'Star'	4-6-0
4048	*Princess Victoria*	'Star'	4-6-0
4958	*Priory Hall*	'Hall'	4-6-0
—	*Progress*	Monmouthshire Railway and Canal Co/Brecon & Merthyr/Neath & Brecon	0-4-4-0
6	*Progress*	Swansea Harbour Trust	0-6-0ST
—	*Prometheus*	'Iron Duke'†	4-2-2
—	*Prometheus*	'Rover'†	4-2-2
3017*	*Prometheus*	'3001'/'Achilles'	2-2-2
3049	*Prometheus*	'Achilles'	4-2-2
38	*Prometheus*	Cambrian	0-4-0ST
—	*Proserine*	'Fire Fly'†	2-2-2
—	*Psyche*	'Standard Goods'†	0-6-0
4959	*Purley Hall*	'Hall'	4-6-0
4960	*Pyle Hall*	'Hall'	4-6-0
—	*Pyracmon*	'Pyracmon'†	0-6-0
4961	*Pyrland Hall*	'Hall'	4-6-0
—	*Python*	South Devon	0-6-0ST
3324	*Quantock*	'Duke'/'Bulldog'†	4-4-0
3409	*Quebec*	'Atbara'/'City'	4-4-0
—	*Queen*	'Prince'†	2-2-2
—	*Queen*	Torbay & Brixham	0-4-0WT
3	*Queen*	Shrewsbury & Birmingham	2-2-2
—	*Queen*	Severn & Wye and Severn Bridge/Taff Vale	?
55	*Queen*	'Queen'	2-2-2
11	*Queen*	Cambrian	0-6-0
4034	*Queen Adelaide*	'Star'	4-6-0
4032	*Queen Alexandra*	'Star'/'Castle'	4-6-0
4038	*Queen Berengaria*	'Star'	4-6-0
4040	*Queen Boadicea*	'Star'	4-6-0
4035	*Queen Charlotte*	'Star'	4-6-0
4036	*Queen Elizabeth*	'Star'	4-6-0
4031	*Queen Mary*	'Star'	4-6-0
4039	*Queen Matilda*	'Star'	4-6-0
4037	*Queen Philippa*	'Star'/'Castle'	4-6-0
4033	*Queen Victoria*	'Star'	4-6-0
5912*	*Queen's Hall*	'Hall'	4-6-0
5912	*Queen's Hall*	'Hall'	4-6-0
3471	*Queensland*	'Bulldog'	4-4-0
179*	*Quentin Durward*	'Saint'	4-6-0
3025*	*Quicksilver*	'3001'/'Achilles'	2-2-2
172	*Quicksilver*	'Saint'	4-6-0
3018	*Racer*	'3001'/'Achilles'	2-2-2
190*	*Radcliffe*	Taff Vale	0-6-0ST
5008	*Raglan Castle*	'Castle'	4-6-0
4962	*Ragley Hall*	'Hall'	4-6-0
7829	*Ramsbury Manor*	'Manor'	4-6-0
—	*Ranger*	Severn & Wye and Severn Bridge	0-6-0
—	*Ravelston*	Llanelly & Mynydd Mawr	0-6-0T
—	*Raven*	South Devon/Torbay & Brixham	0-4-0T
—	*Raven*	Severn & Wye and Severn Bridge	0-6-0ST
6960	*Raveningham Hall*	'Hall'	4-6-0
—	*Reading*	'Swindon'†/Bristol & Exeter	0-6-0
3449	*Reading*	'Bulldog'	4-4-0
4064	*Reading Abbey*	'Star'/'Castle'	4-6-0
—	*Red Gauntlet*	'Waverley'†	
183	*Red Gauntlet*	'Saint'	4-6-0
—	*Red Star*	'Star'†	2-2-2
4006	*Red Star*	'Star'	4-6-0
2983*	*Redgauntlet*	'Saint'	4-6-0
—	*Redruth*	South Devon/West Cornwall	0-6-0
—	*Redruth*	West Cornwall	?
2	*Reepham*	Cornwall Minerals	0-6-0T
—	*Regulus*	'Standard Goods'†	0-6-0
28(?)	*Reindeer*	West Midland (Newport, Abergavenny & Hereford)	2-4-0
—	*Remus*	South Devon	0-6-0ST
—	*Remus*	'Standard Goods'†	0-6-0
—	*Rennie*	'Victoria'†	2-4-0
—	*Rescue*	Llynvi & Ogmore	?
—*	*Resolute*	Burry Port & Gwendraeth Valley	0-6-0ST
6869	*Resolven Grange*	'Grange'	4-6-0
3366	*Restormel*	'Bulldog'	4-4-0
5010	*Restormel Castle*	'Castle'	4-6-0
—	*Rhea*	'Standard Goods'†	0-6-0
44	*Rheidol*	Cambrian	2-4-0
3*	*Rheidol*	Cambrian	2-4-0T
45	*Rhiewport*	Cambrian	0-6-0
—	*Rhondda*	'Standard Goods'†	0-6-0
4	*Rhondda*	Alexandra (Newport & South Wales) Docks and Railway	0-6-0ST
—	*Rhondda*	Taff Vale	2-2-2
2	*Rhondda*	Taff Vale	2-4-0
7918	*Rhose Wood Hall*	'Hall'	4-6-0
5039	*Rhuddlan Castle*	'Castle'	4-6-0
34	*Rhymney*	Taff Vale	2-4-0
4963	*Rignall Hall*	'Hall'	4-6-0
—	*Ringing Rock*	North Pembrokeshire & Fishguard	0-6-0ST
5914	*Ripon Hall*	'Hall'	4-6-0
—	*Rising Star*	'Star'†	2-2-2
4007	*Rising Star*	'Star'	4-6-0
3431	*River Fal*	'Bulldog'	4-4-0
3428	*River Plym*	'Bulldog'	4-4-0
3268*	*River Tamar*	'Duke'/'Bulldog'†	4-4-0
3430	*River Tawe*	'Bulldog'†	4-4-0
3432	*River Yealm*	'Bulldog'†	4-4-0
—	*Rob Roy*	'Waverley'†	4-4-0
2988	*Rob Roy*	'Saint'	4-6-0
—	*Roberts*	'Hawthorn'†	2-4-0
3387	*Roberts*	'Atbara'	4-4-0
177	*Robertson*	'Saint'	4-6-0
187	*Robertson*	'Saint'	4-6-0
—	*Robin Hood*	'Waverley'†	4-4-0
—	*Robin Hood*	Severn & Wye and Severn Bridge	0-6-0T
186	*Robin Hood*	'Saint'†	4-6-0
173	*Robins Bolitho*	'Saint'†	4-6-0
—	*Rocket*	'Sun'†	2-2-2
—	*Rocket*	South Devon	4-4-0ST
4964	*Rodwell Hall*	'Hall'	4-6-0
?	*Roebuck*	Cornwall Minerals	?
5973	*Rolleston Hall*	'Hall'	4-6-0
—	*Romulus*	'Standard Goods'†	0-6-0
—	*Romulus*	South Devon	0-6-0ST
4965	*Rood Ashton Hall*	'Hall'	4-6-0
—	*Rook*	South Devon/Powesland & Mason	0-4-0T
—	*Rosa*	South Devon/Llynvi & Ogmore	4-4-0ST
—	*Rose*	'Metro'†	2-4-0WT
—	*Rougemont*	'Iron Duke'†	4-2-2
3022	*Rougemont*	'3001'/'Achilles'	2-2-2
5008	*Rougemont Castle*	'Castle'	4-6-0
4028*	*Roumanian Monarch*	'Star'	4-6-0
6854	*Roundhill Grange*	'Grange'	4-6-0
—	*Rover*	'Iron Duke'†	4-2-2
—	*Rover*	'Rover'†	4-2-2
3019	*Rover*	'3001'/'Achilles'	2-2-2
—	*Royal*	Llanelly	0-6-0
—*	*Royal*	Llanelly	0-6-0
10	*Royal Albert*	'9 & 10'	2-2-2
3050	*Royal Sovereign*	'Achilles'	2-2-2
3357*	*Royal Sovereign*	'Bulldog'	4-4-0
3373	*Royal Sovereign*	'Atbara'	4-4-0
—	*Royal Star*	'Star'†	2-2-2
4008	*Royal Star*	'Star'	4-6-0
5994	*Roydon Hall*	'Hall'	4-6-0
—	*Ruby*	'Standard Goods'†	0-6-0
6846	*Ruckley Grange*	'Grange'	4-6-0
28	*Rumney*	Brecon & Merthyr	0-6-0ST
7919	*Runter Hall*	'Hall'	4-6-0
5913	*Rushton Hall*	'Hall'	4-6-0
2	*Ruthin*	Cambrian	0-4-0
6986	*Rydal Hall*	'Hall'	4-6-0
—	*Sabrina*	Severn & Wye and Severn Bridge	0-6-0T
—	*Sagittarius*	'Leo'†	2-4-0
6855	*Saighton Grange*	'Grange'	4-6-0
2912	*Saint Ambrose*	'Saint'	4-6-0
2913	*Saint Andrew*	'Saint'	4-6-0
2911	*Saint Augusta*	'Saint'	4-6-0
2914	*Saint Augustine*	'Saint'	4-6-0
2915	*Saint Bartholomew*	'Saint'	4-6-0
2916	*Saint Benedict*	'Saint'	4-6-0
5947*	*Saint Benet's Hall*	'Hall'	4-6-0
5947	*Saint Benets Hall*	'Hall'	4-6-0
2917	*Saint Bernard*	'Saint'	4-6-0
4972*	*Saint Brides Hall*	'Hall'	4-6-0
2918	*Saint Catherine*	'Saint'	4-6-0
2919	*Saint Cecilia*	'Saint'	4-6-0
2929*	*Saint Cuthbert*	'Saint'	4-6-0
2920	*Saint David*	'Saint'	4-6-0
2921	*Saint Dunstan*	'Saint'	4-6-0
5960	*Saint Edmund Hall*	'Hall'	4-6-0
2922	*Saint Gabriel*	'Saint'	4-6-0
2923	*Saint George*	'Saint'	4-6-0
2924	*Saint Helena*	'Saint'	4-6-0
2925	*Saint Martin*	'Saint'/'Hall'	4-6-0

No	Name	Class	Wheel arrangement
2926	*Saint Nicholas*	'Saint'	4-6-0
2927	*Saint Patrick*	'Saint'	4-6-0
7900	*Saint Peter's Hall*	'Hall'	4-6-0
2928	*Saint Sebastian*	'Saint'	4-6-0
2929	*Saint Stephen*	'Saint'	4-6-0
2930	*Saint Vincent*	'Saint'	4-6-0
7922	*Salford Hall*	'Hall'	4-6-0
1123	*Salisbury*	'Queen'	2-2-2
11	*Salisbury*	Alexandra (Newport & South Wales) Docks and Railway	2-6-2T
21	*Salopian*	Shrewsbury & Birmingham	2-2-2
—	*Sampson*	'Hercules'†	0-6-0
—	*Sampson*	South Devon	0-6-0ST
3305	*Samson*	'Badminton'†	4-4-0
26	*Samson*	Brecon & Merthyr	0-6-0ST
6918	*Sandon Hall*	'Hall'	4-6-0
—	*Sappho*	'Bogie'†	4-4-0ST
5060	*Sarum Castle*	'Castle'	4-6-0
5097	*Sarum Castle*	'Castle'	4-6-0
—	*Saturn*	'Fire Fly'†	2-2-2
—	*Saturn*	South Devon	2-4-0T
—	*Saunders*	'Sir Watkin'†/South Devon	0-6-0T
—	*Saus*	'Standard Goods'†	0-6-0
3308	*Savernake*	'Badminton'†	4-4-0
—	*Scorpio*	'Leo'†	2-4-0
3743	*Seagull*	'Bulldog'†	4-4-0
59	*Seaham*	Cambrian	2-4-0T
—	*Sebastopol*	'Iron Duke'†	4-2-2
—	*Sebastopol*	'Rover'†	4-2-2
3351	*Sedgemoor*	'Bulldog'	4-4-0
—	*Sedley*	South Devon	4-4-0ST
22	*Sefton*	Birkenhead	2-2-2
—	*Seneca*	'Bogie'†	4-4-0ST
—	*Severn*	'Standard Goods'†	0-6-0
3328	*Severn*	'Duke'	4-4-0
13	*Severn*	Taff Vale	0-6-0
22	*Severn*	Brecon & Merthyr	0-6-0ST
2*	*Severn*	Bristol Port Railway and Pier	0-4-2T
—	*Severn Bridge*	Severn & Wye and Severn Bridge	0-4-0T
—	*Severn Bridge*	Severn & Wye and Severn Bridge	0-6-0T
—	*Severus*	'Standard Goods'†	0-6-0
—	*Seymour Clarke*	Llanelly & Mynydd Mawr	0-6-0ST
—	*Shah*	'Metro'†	2-4-0WT
4966	*Shakenhurst Hall*	'Hall'	4-6-0
3309	*Shakespeare*	'Badminton'	4-4-0
—	*Shamrock*	'Metro'†	2-4-0WT
—	*Shannon*	'Standard Goods'†	0-6-0
5	*Shannon*	Wantage Tramway	0-4-0WT
—	*Sharp*	'Hawthorn'†	2-4-0
—	*Sharpness*	Severn & Wye and Severn Bridge	0-6-0T
3306	*Shelburne*	'Badminton'	4-4-0
6987	*Shervington Hall*	'Hall'	4-6-0
5030	*Shirburn Castle*	'Castle'	4-6-0
4967	*Shirenewton Hall*	'Hall'	4-6-0
—	*Shooting Star*	'Star'†	2-2-2
3078	*Shooting Star*	'Achilles'	4-2-2
4009	*Shooting Star*	'Star'	4-6-0
4968	*Shotton Hall*	'Hall'	4-6-0
—	*Shrewsbury*	'Swindon'†/Bristol & Exeter	0-6-0
3307	*Shrewsbury*	'Badminton'	4-4-0
5009	*Shrewsbury Castle*	'Castle'	4-6-0
4969	*Shrugborough Hall*	'Hall'	4-6-0
—	*Sibyl*	'Standard Goods'†	0-6-0
5948	*Siddington Hall*	'Hall'	4-6-0
3412	*Singapore*	'Atbara'	4-4-0
999	*Sir Alexander*	'Queen'	2-2-2
3708	*Sir Arthur Yorke*	'Bulldog'	4-4-0
378	*Sir Daniel*	'Sir Daniel'	2-2-2
3389	*Sir Daniel*	'Atbara'	4-4-0
5070	*Sir Daniel Gooch*	'Castle'	4-6-0
3704*	*Sir Edward Elgar*	'Bulldog'	4-4-0
7005*	*Sir Edward Elgar*	'Castle'	4-6-0
3420*	*Sir Ernest Palmer*	'Bulldog'	4-4-0
175*	*Sir Ernest Palmer*	'Saint'	4-6-0
5066*	*Sir Felix Pole*	'Castle'	4-6-0
3053	*Sir Francis Drake*	'Achilles'	2-2-2
?	*Sir George*	Alexandra (Newport & South Wales) Docks and Railway	?
1	*Sir George Elliot*	Alexandra (Newport & South Wales) Docks and Railway	0-6-0ST
3	*Sir Haydn*	Corris‡	0-4-2ST
25	*Sir Ivor*	Brecon & Merthyr	0-6-0ST
7001*	*Sir James Milne*	'Castle'	4-6-0
3422	*Sir John Llewelyn*	'Bulldog'	4-4-0
3263	*Sir Lancelot*	'Duke'/'Bulldog'	4-4-0
3423	*Sir Massey*	'Bulldog'	4-4-0
3423*	*Sir Massey Lopes*	'Bulldog'	4-4-0
3424*	*Sir N. Kingscote*	'Bulldog'	4-4-0
3424	*Sir Nigel*	'Bulldog'	4-4-0
3388	*Sir Redvers*	'Atbara'	4-4-0
3054	*Sir Richard Grenville*	'Achilles'	4-2-2
4066*	*Sir Robert Horne*	'Star'	4-6-0
3368	*Sir Stafford*	'Bulldog'	4-4-0
3425	*Sir W. H. Wills*	'Bulldog'	4-4-0
3052	*Sir Walter Rayleigh*	'Achilles'	4-2-2

No	Name	Class	Wheel arrangement
—	*Sir Watkin*	'Sir Watkin'†	0-6-0T
471	*Sir Watkin*	'Sir Daniel'	2-2-2
39	*Sir Watkin*	Cambrian	0-6-0
3427	*Sir Watkin Wynn*	'Bulldog'	4-4-0
3425*	*Sir William Henry*	'Bulldog'	4-4-0
—	*Sirius*	'Standard Goods'†	0-6-0
4970	*Sketty Hall*	'Hall'	4-6-0
3744	*Skylark*	'Bulldog'	4-4-0
—	*Slaughter*	'Hawthorn'†	2-4-0
—	*Smeaton*	'Victoria'†	2-4-0
3357*	*Smeaton*	'Bulldog'	4-4-0
—	*Snake*	'Unclassified'†	2-2-2
51	*Snowdon*	Cambrian	0-6-0
—	*Sol*	South Devon	4-4-0ST
3327	*Somerset*	'Duke'/'Bulldog'	4-4-0
6962	*Soughton Hall*	'Hall'	4-6-0
4029*	*Spanish Monarch*	'Star'	4-6-0
5997	*Sparkford Hall*	'Hall'	4-6-0
7923	*Speke Hall*	'Hall'	4-6-0
—	*Sphinx*	'Standard Goods'†	0-6-0
—	*Spit Fire*	'Fire Fly'†	2-2-2
5071*	*Spitfire*	'Castle'	4-6-0
—	*Squirrel*	Cambrian	?
3287	*St Agnes*	'Duke'	4-4-0
3264	*St Anthony*	'Duke'/'Bulldog'	4-4-0
3367	*St Aubyn*	'Bulldog'	4-4-0
3326	*St Austell*	'Duke'	4-4-0
4972	*St Brides Hall*	'Hall'	4-6-0
3325	*St Columb*	'Duke'/'Bulldog'	4-4-0
5017	*St Donats Castle*	'Castle'	4-6-0
3285	*St Erth*	'Duke'	4-4-0
5067	*St Fagans Castle*	'Castle'	4-6-0
3025	*St George*	'3001'/'Achilles'	2-2-2
3265	*St Germans*	'Duke'	4-4-0
—	*St Ives*	Llynvi & Ogmore/West Cornwall	2-4-0
3266	*St Ives*	'Duke'	4-4-0
3411	*St Johns*	'Atbara'	4-4-0
—	*St Just*	West Cornwall	0-6-0
3286	*St Just*	'Duke'/'Bulldog'	4-4-0
5018	*St Mawes Castle*	'Castle'	4-6-0
3267	*St Michael*	'Duke'	4-4-0
3201	*St Michael*	'Earl'	4-4-0
2948	*Stackpole Court*	'Saint'	4-6-0
—	*Stag*	'Fire Fly'†	2-2-2
—	*Stag*	South Devon	4-4-0ST
39	*Stag*	Taff Vale	0-6-0
—	*Stag*	Brecon & Merthyr	?
2949	*Stanford Court*	'Saint'	4-6-0
5937	*Stanford Hall*	'Hall'	4-6-0
3701	*Stanley Baldwin*	'Bulldog'	4-4-0
5938	*Stanley Hall*	'Hall'	4-6-0
4971	*Stanway Hall*	'Hall'	4-6-0
3745	*Starling*	'Bulldog'	4-4-0
—	*Status*	'Bogie'†	4-4-0ST
6961	*Stedham Hall*	'Hall'	4-6-0
8	*Stella*	Pembroke & Tenby/'Stella'	2-4-0
—	*Stenton*	'Fire Fly'†	2-2-2
4120	*Stephanotis*	'Flower'	4-4-0
—	*Stephenson*	'Victoria'†	2-4-0
1	*Stephenson*	Port Talbot Railway and Docks	0-6-0ST
—	*Steropes*	'Pyracmon'†	0-6-0
18	*Steropes*	(Crane tank)	0-6-4
—	*Stewart*	'Hawthorn'†	2-4-0
—	*Stiletto*	'Sun'†	2-2-2
5040	*Stokesay Castle*	'Castle'	4-6-0
3024	*Storm King*	'3001'/'Achilles'	2-2-2
3051	*Stormy Petrel*	'Achilles'	4-2-2
74	*Stour*	'River'	2-4-0
6856	*Stowe Grange*	'Grange'	4-6-0
—	*Stradey*	Llanelly	0-6-0
—	*Stromboli*	'Leo'†	2-4-0
—*	*Stromboli*	South Devon	0-6-0ST
18	*Stuart*	Taff Vale	0-6-0
5061	*Sudeley Castle*	'Castle'	4-6-0
7025	*Sudeley Castle*	'Castle'	4-6-0
—	*Sultan*	'Iron Duke'†	4-2-2
—	*Sultan*	'Rover'†	4-2-2
3020	*Sultan*	'3001'/'Achilles'	2-2-2
—	*Sun*	'Sun'†	2-2-2
—	*Sunbeam*	'Sun'†	2-2-2
—*	*Susan*	Burry Port & Gwendraeth Valley	0-6-0ST
—	*Swallow*	'Iron Duke'†	4-2-2
—	*Swallow*	'Rover'†	4-2-2
3023	*Swallow*	'3001'/'Achilles'	2-2-2
4007*	*Swallowfield Park*	'Star'	4-6-0
3450	*Swansea*	'Bulldog'	4-4-0
—	*Swansea*	Swansea Harbour Trust	0-4-0ST
7008	*Swansea Castle*	'Castle'†	4-6-0
4030*	*Swedish Monarch*	'Star'	4-6-0
4973	*Sweeney Hall*	'Hall'	4-6-0
3350	*Swift*	'Bulldog'	4-4-0
—	*Swindon*	'Swindon'†/Bristol & Exeter	0-6-0
3446*	*Swindon*	'Bulldog'	4-4-0
7037	*Swindon*	'Castle'	4-6-0
6988	*Swithland Hall*	'Hall'	4-6-0
5082*	*Swordfish*	'Castle'	4-6-0
3410	*Sydney*	'Atbara'	4-4-0

No	Name	Class	Wheel arrangement
—	*Sylla*	'Standard Goods'†	0-6-0
—	*Sylph*	'Prince'†	2-2-2
—	*Taff*	Taff Vale	2-2-2
1	*Taff*	Taff Vale	2-4-0
29	*Taff*	Brecon & Merthyr	0-6-0ST
—	*Talbot*	'Standard Goods'†	0-6-0
34	*Talerddig*	Cambrian	0-6-0
13	*Talerddig*	Cambrian	0-6-0T
4974	*Talgarth Hall*	'Hall'	4-6-0
2989	*Talisman*	'Saint'	4-6-0
35	*Talisman*	Birkenhead	0-4-2
3	*Talybont*	Cambrian	2-4-0T
—	*Tamar*	'Standard Goods'†	0-6-0
3268	*Tamar*	'Duke'	4-4-0
5939	*Tangley Hall*	'Hall'	4-6-0
—	*Tantalus*	'Standard Goods'†	0-6-0
2950	*Taplow Court*	'Saint'	4-6-0
—	*Tarndune*	Llanelly & Mynydd Mawr	0-6-0T
—	*Tartar*	'Iron Duke'†	4-2-2
—	*Tartar*	'Rover'†	4-2-2
3057	*Tartar*	'Achilles'	2-2-2
3457	*Tasmania*	'Bulldog'	4-4-0
1	*Tattoo*	Corris‡	0-4-0ST
3451	*Taunton*	'Bulldog'	4-4-0
7036	*Taunton Castle*	'Castle'	4-6-0
—	*Taurus*	'Leo'†	2-4-0
—	*Taurus*	South Devon	0-6-0ST
3348	*Tavy*	'Bulldog'	4-4-0
2951	*Tawstock Court*	'Saint'	4-6-0
—	*Tay*	'Standard Goods'†	0-6-0
—	*Teifi*	Manchester & Milford	0-6-0ST
—	*Teign*	'Unclassified'†	2-2-2
75	*Teign*	'River'	2-4-0
—	*Teilo*	Llanelly	0-6-0
—	*Telford*	'Victoria'†	2-4-0
—	*Telica*	'Premier'†	0-6-0
1	*Tenby*	Pembroke & Tenby	2-2-2T
6*	*Tenby*	Pembroke & Tenby	0-6-0
5062	*Tenby Castle*	'Castle'	4-6-0
7026	*Tenby Castle*	'Castle'	4-6-0
3390	*Terrible*	'Atbara'	4-4-0
36	*Thalaba*	Birkenhead	0-4-2
—	*Thames*	'Standard Goods'†	0-6-0
3027	*Thames*	'3001'/'Achilles'	2-2-2
3329	*Thames*	'Duke'	4-4-0
172*	*The Abbot*	'Saint'	4-6-0
4022*	*The Belgian Monarch*	'Star'	4-6-0
4021*	*The British Monarch*	'Star'	4-6-0
2	*The Countess*	Cambrian‡	0-6-0T
4023*	*The Danish Monarch*	'Star'	4-6-0
4024*	*The Dutch Monarch*	'Star'	4-6-0
1	*The Earl*	Cambrian‡	0-6-0T
36	*The Earl of Dumfries*	Cardiff	2-4-2T
5017*	*The Gloucestershire Regiment 28th 61st*	'Castle'	4-6-0
111	*The Great Bear*	'111'	4-6-2
4026*	*The Japanese Monarch*	'Star'	4-6-0
3259*	*The Lizard*	'Duke'	4-4-0
4027*	*The Norwegian Monarch*	'Star'	4-6-0
171*	*The Pirate*	'Saint'	4-6-0
3041*	*The Queen*	*'Achilles'*	*2-2-2*
4028*	*The Roumanian Monarch*	'Star'	4-6-0
4016*	*The Somerset Light Infantry (Prince Albert's)*	'Castle'	4-6-0
4037*	*The South Wales Borderers*	'Castle'	4-6-0
4029*	*The Spanish Monarch*	'Star'	4-6-0
4030*	*The Swedish Monarch*	'Star'	4-6-0
3349	*The Wolf*	'Bulldog'	4-4-0
—	*Theocritus*	'Bogie'†	4-4-0ST
—	*Theseus*	'Standard Goods'†	0-6-0
6965	*Thirlestaine Hall*	'Hall'	4-6-0
—	*Thistle*	'Metro'†	2-4-0WT
6964	*Thornbridge Hall*	'Hall'	4-6-0
5063	*Thornbury Castle*	'Castle'	4-6-0
7027	*Thornbury Castle*	'Castle'	4-6-0
7924	*Thornycroft Hall*	'Hall'	4-6-0
6963	*Throwley Hall*	'Hall'	4-6-0
3079	*Thunderbolt*	'Achilles'	4-2-2
—	*Thunderer*	'Unclassified'†	0-4-0
—	*Thunderer*	'Caesar'†	0-6-0
37	*Thunderer*	Birkenhead	0-6-0
6847	*Tidmarsh Grange*	'Grange'	4-6-0
—	*Tiger*	'Fire Fly'†	2-2-2
—	*Tiger*	South Devon	4-4-0ST
—	*Timour*	'Iron Duke'†	4-2-2
—	*Timour*	'Rover'†	4-2-2
3056	*Timour*	'Achilles'	4-2-2
3269	*Tintagel*	'Duke'/'Bulldog	4-4-0

No	Name	Class	Wheel arrangement
5011	*Tintagel Castle*	'Castle'	4-6-0
—*	*Tintern*	Taff Vale	2-4-0
4067	*Tintern Abbey*	'Star'/'Castle'	4-6-0
—	*Tiny*	South Devon	0-4-0VBT
23(?)	*Tiny*	Cambrian/Brecon & Merthyr	0-4-0ST
—	*Titan*	South Devon	4-4-0ST
3348	*Titan*	'Bulldog'	4-4-0
2953	*Titley Court*	'Saint'	4-6-0
—	*Tityos*	'Hercules'†	0-6-0
5041	*Tiverton Castle*	'Castle'	4-6-0
2954	*Tockenham Court*	'Saint'	4-6-0
6848	*Toddington Grange*	'Grange'	4-6-0
8	*Tor*	Brecon & Merthyr/Neath & Brecon	0-6-0ST
3290*	*Tor Bay*	'Duke'	4-4-0
3290	*Torbay*	'Duke'	4-4-0
—	*Tornado*	'Iron Duke'†	4-2-2
—	*Tornado*	'Rover'†	4-2-2
—	*Tornado*	'South Devon'	0-6-0ST
3026	*Tornado*	'3001'/'Achilles'	2-2-2
3459	*Toronto*	'Bulldog'	4-4-0
3372	*Torquay*	'Bulldog'	4-4-0
7800	*Torquay Manor*	'Manor'	4-6-0
2955	*Tortworth Court*	'Saint'	4-6-0
5031	*Totnes Castle*	'Castle'	4-6-0
3	*Touchstone*	Birkenhead	2-2-2
?	*Towy*	Llanelly	?
—	*Towy*	Llanelly	0-6-0
46	*Towyn*	Cambrian	0-6-0
5961	*Toynbee Hall*	'Hall'	4-6-0
—	*Trafalgar*	'Standard Goods'†	0-6-0
3055	*Trafalgar*	'Achilles'	4-2-2
8	*Tranmere*	Alexandra (Newport & South Wales) Docks and Railway	2-6-2T
3271	*Tre Pol and Pen*	'Duke'/'Earl'	4-4-0
5019	*Treago Castle*	'Castle'	4-6-0
1	*Treffrey*	Cornwall Minerals	0-6-0T
1*	*Treffry*	Cornwall Minerals	0-6-0T
55	*Treflach*	Cambrian	2-4-0
—	*Treforest*	Taff Vale	0-6-0
21	*Treforest*	Taff Vale	0-6-0
3289	*Trefusis*	'Duke'	4-4-0
3371	*Tregeagle*	'Bulldog'	4-4-0
3291	*Tregenna*	'Duke'	4-4-0
5006	*Tregenna Castle*	'Castle'	4-6-0
3347	*Tregothnan*	'Bulldog'	4-4-0
3369	*Trelawny*	'Bulldog'	4-4-0
6828	*Trellech Grange*	'Grange'	4-6-0
5020	*Trematon Castle*	'Castle'	4-6-0
5949	*Trematon Hall*	'Hall'	4-6-0
3370	*Tremayne*	'Bulldog'	4-4-0
5915	*Trentham Hall*	'Hall'	4-6-0
3288	*Tresco*	'Duke'	4-4-0
4072	*Tresco Abbey*	'Star'/'Castle'	4-6-0
5064	*Tretower Castle*	'Castle'	4-6-0
5094	*Tretower Castle*	'Castle'	4-6-0
—	*Trevithick*	'Victoria'†	2-4-0
3270	*Trevithick*	'Duke'	4-4-0
5998	*Trevor Hall*	'Hall'	4-6-0
3465	*Trinidad*	'Bulldog'	4-4-0
5916	*Trinity Hall*	'Hall'	4-6-0
?	*Trio*	West Midland (Newport, Abergavenny & Hereford)	?
—	*Trojan*	Alexandra (Newport & South Wales) Docks and Railway	0-4-0ST
—	*Truro*	West Cornwall	0-4-2(?)
26	*Tubal Cain*	Cambrian	0-6-0
6857	*Tudor Grange*	'Grange'	4-6-0
—	*Tweed*	'Standard Goods'†	0-6-0
2952	*Twineham Court*	'Saint'	4-6-0
6919	*Tylney Hall*	'Hall'	4-6-0
—	*Tyne*	'Standard Goods'†	0-6-0
—	*Typhon*	'Standard Goods'†	0-6-0
—	*Ulysses*	'Standard Goods'†	0-6-0
3058	*Ulysses*	'Achilles'	4-2-2
4975	*Umberslade Hall*	'Hall'	4-6-0
—	*Una*	South Devon/Llynvi & Ogmore	0-6-0ST
6928	*Underley Hall*	'Hall'	4-6-0
6065	*Upton Castle*	'Castle'	4-6-0
5093	*Upton Castle*	'Castle'	4-6-0
—	*Usk*	Alexandra (Newport & South Wales) Docks and Railway	0-6-0ST
—	*Usk*	Cambrian/Brecon & Merthyr	2-4-0
5032	*Usk Castle*	'Castle'	4-6-0
3463	*Vancouver*	'Bulldog'	4-4-0
98	*Vanguard*	'Saint'	4-6-0
1*	*Velindre*	Gwendraeth Valleys	0-6-0ST
—	*Venus*	'Unclassified'†	2-2-2
—	*Venus*	'Fire Fly'†	2-2-2
41	*Venus*	Taff Vale	2-4-0
—	*Vesper*	'Standard Goods'†	0-6-0
—	*Vesta*	'Standard Goods'†	0-6-0
—	*Vesuvius*	'Premier'†	0-6-0
—	*Victor*	Llanelly/Carmarthen & Cardigan	0-6-0
—*	*Victor*	Severn & Wye and Severn Bridge	0-6-0T
—	*Victor Emanuel*	'Victoria'†	2-4-0
—	*Victoria*	'Victoria'†	2-4-0
9	*Victoria*	Birkenhead	2-2-2
—	*Victoria*	Llanelly	0-6-0
—	*Victoria*	Llanelly Railway & Dock Co	0-6-0
9	*Victoria*	'9 & 10'	2-4-2T
1	*Victoria*	Cambrian	0-6-0
29	*Victoria*	Burry Port & Gwendraeth Valley	0-6-6-0
6	*Victoria*	Alexandra (Newport & South Wales) Docks and Railway	2-6-2T
21	*Victoria & Albert*	Shrewsbury & Chester	2-2-2
—	*Victory*	Llanelly & Mynydd Mawr	0-6-0T
—	*Violet*	'Metro'†	2-4-0WT
—*	*Violet*	Birkenhead	2-2-2
—	*Viper*	'Unclassified'†	2-2-2
—	*Virgil*	'Bogie'†	4-4-0ST
—	*Virgo*	'Leo'†	2-4-0
111*	*Viscount Churchill*	'Castle'	4-6-0
175	*Viscount Churchill*	'Saint'	4-6-0
184*	*Viscount Churchill*	'Saint'	4-6-0
4066*	*Viscount Horne*	'Star'/'Castle'	4-6-0
7000	*Viscount Portal*	'Castle'	4-6-0
38(?)	*Viso*	West Midland (Oxford, Worcester & Wolverhampton)	0-6-0
—	*Vixen*	'Standard Goods'†	0-6-0
32	*Volante*	Birkenhead	2-4-0
—	*Volcano*	'Caesar'†	0-6-0
—	*Volcano*	South Devon	0-6-0ST
33	*Voltigeur*	Birkenhead	2-4-0T
3059	*Voltigeur*	'Achilles'	4-2-2
—	*Volunteer*	Cambrian	0-4-2
—	*Vulcan*	'Unclassified'†	2-2-2
—	*Vulcan*	South Devon	0-6-0ST
2	*Vulcan*	Shrewsbury & Birmingham	2-2-2
3330	*Vulcan*	'Duke'/'Bulldog'	4-4-0
20	*Vulcan*	Cambrian/Brecon & Merthyr	0-6-0
29	*Vulcan*	Taff Vale	0-6-0
—	*Vulture*	'Fire Fly'†	2-2-2
—*	*Wales*	Llanelly	0-6-0
—	*Wales*	Llanelly	0-6-0
5974	*Wallsworth Hall*	'Hall'	4-6-0
3426	*Walter Long*	'Bulldog'	4-4-0
3057*	*Walter Robinson*	'Achilles'	4-2-2
6849	*Walton Grange*	'Grange'	4-6-0
5918	*Walton Hall*	'Hall'	4-6-0
—	*Walton Park*	Weston, Clevedon & Portishead	0-6-0ST
5962	*Wantage Hall*	'Hall'	4-6-0
5950	*Wardley Hall*	'Hall'	4-6-0
5066	*Wardour Castle*	'Castle'	4-6-0
4976	*Warfield Hall*	'Hall'	4-6-0
—	*Warhawk*	'Standard Goods'†	0-6-0
—	*Warlock*	'Iron Duke'†	4-2-2
—	*Warlock*	'Rover'†	4-2-2
3060	*Warlock*	'Achilles'	4-2-2
—	*Warrior*	'Standard Goods'†	0-6-0
4081	*Warwick Castle*	'Castle'	4-6-0
—	*Wasp*	'Metro'†	2-4-0WT
4977	*Watcombe Hall*	'Hall'	4-6-0
3310	*Waterford*	'Badminton'	4-4-0
—	*Watt*	'Victoria'†	2-4-0
—	*Waverley*	'Waverley'†	4-4-0
2990	*Waverley*	'Saint'	4-6-0
—	*Wear*	'Standard Goods'†	0-6-0
—	*Weasel*	South Devon	0-4-0T
26	*Weaver*	Birkenhead	2-4-0
—	*Wellington*	'Standard Goods'†	0-6-0
3028	*Wellington*	'3001'/'Achilles'	2-2-2
5075*	*Wellington*	'Castle'	4-6-0
51*	*Wellington*	Taff Vale	0-6-2T
49	*Werfa*	Taff Vale	0-6-0
—	*Western Star*	'Star'†	2-2-2
4010	*Western Star*	'Star'	4-6-0
4069*	*Westminster Abbey*	'Star'/'Castle'	4-6-0
5917	*Westminster Hall*	'Hall'	4-6-0
7925	*Westol Hall*	'Hall'	4-6-0
—*	*Weston*	Burry Port & Gwendraeth Valley/ Weston, Clevedon & Portishead	0-6-0ST
—	*Weston*	Weston, Clevedon & Portishead	2-2-2
3729	*Weston-super-Mare*	'Bulldog'	4-4-0
3030	*Westward Ho*	'3001'/'Achilles'	2-2-2
4978	*Westwood Hall*	'Hall'	4-6-0
3331	*Weymouth*	'Duke'/'Bulldog'	4-4-0
6970	*Whaddon Hall*	'Hall'	4-6-0
—	*Whetham*	'Sir Watkin'†	0-6-0T
5940	*Whitbourne Hall*	'Hall'	4-6-0
3392	White	'Atbara'	4-4-0
3029	*White Horse*	'3001'/'Achilles'	2-2-2
56	*Whittington*	Cambrian	2-4-0
5021	*Whittington Castle*	'Castle'	4-6-0
13	*Whixall*	Cambrian	0-6-0ST
6929	*Whorlton Hall*	'Hall'	4-6-0
5995	*Wick Hall*	'Hall'	4-6-0
6989	*Wightwick Hall*	'Hall'	4-6-0
3021	*Wigmore Castle*	'3001'/'Achilles'	2-2-2
5022	*Wigmore Castle*	'Castle'	4-6-0
—	*Wild Fire*	'Fire Fly'†	2-2-2
3056*	*Wilkinson*	'Achilles'	4-2-2
—	*Will Scarlet*	Severn & Wye and Severn Bridge/Alexandra (Newport & South Wales) Docks and Railway	0-6-0T
51(?)	*Will Shakespeare*	West Midland (Oxford, Worcester & Wolverhampton)	2-2-2
6967	*Willesley Hall*	'Hall'	4-6-0
7926	*Willey Hall*	'Hall'	4-6-0
46	*William*	Barry	0-6-2T
100*	*William Dean*	'Saint'	4-6-0
7927	*Willington Hall*	'Hall'	4-6-0
2963	*Wimpole Hall*	'Hall'	4-6-0
5042	*Winchester Castle*	'Castle'	4-6-0
—	*Windsor*	'Swindon'†/Bristol & Exeter	0-6-0
4	*Windsor*	Swansea Harbour Trust	0-4-0ST
3080	*Windsor Castle*	'Achilles'	4-2-2
4082	*Windsor Castle*	'Castle'	4-6-0
7013*	*Windsor Castle*	'Castle'	4-6-0
3462	*Winnipeg*	'Bulldog'	4-4-0
5975	*Winslow Hall*	'Hall'	4-6-0
176	*Winterstoke*	'Saint'	4-6-0
185	*Winterstoke*	'Saint'	4-6-0
1	*Wirral*	Birkenhead	2-2-2
—	*Witch*	'Prince'†	2-2-2
6966	*Witchingham Hall*	'Hall'	4-6-0
6990	*Witherslack Hall*	'Hall'	4-6-0
—	*Wizard*	'Iron Duke'†	4-2-2
—	*Wolf*	'Sun'†	2-2-2
—	*Wolf*	South Devon	4-4-0ST
7928	*Wolf Hall*	'Hall'	4-6-0
5999	*Wollaton Hall*	'Hall'	4-6-0
3391	*Wolseley*	'Atbara'	4-4-0
5964	*Wolseley Hall*	'Hall'	4-6-0
—	*Wolverhampton*	'Swindon'†/Bristol & Exeter	0-6-0
3452	*Wolverhampton*	'Bulldog'	4-4-0
—	*Wood*	'Hawthorn'†	2-4-0
6968	*Woodcock Hall*	'Hall'	4-6-0
5965	*Woollas Hall*	'Hall'	4-6-0
6858	*Woolston Grange*	'Grange'	4-6-0
4979	*Wootton Hall*	'Hall'	4-6-0
158	*Worcester*	'157' ('Cobham')†	2-2-2
3027*	*Worcester*	'Achilles'	4-2-2
5919	*Worsley Hall*	'Hall'	4-6-0
6969	*Wraysbury Hall*	'Hall'	4-6-0
33	*Wrekin*	Shrewsbury & Chester	?
23	*Wrekin*	Shrewsbury & Birmingham	2-2-2
4980	*Wrottesley Hall*	'Hall'	4-6-0
5920	*Wycliffe Hall*	'Hall'	4-6-0
—	*Wye*	'Standard Goods'†	0-6-0
—*	*Wye*	Severn & Wye and Severn Bridge	0-4-0T
—	*Wye*	Golden Valley	0-4-0ST
76	*Wye*	'River'	2-4-0
—	*Wye*	Cambrian/Brecon & Merthyr	2-4-0
7929	*Wyke Hall*	'Hall'	4-6-0
—	*Wyncliffe*	Fishguard & Rosslare Railways and Harbours Co	0-4-0ST
3311	*Wynnstay*	'Badmington'	4-4-0
4	*Wynnstay*	Cambrian/Brecon & Merthyr	0-4-2
—	*Xerxes*	'Standard Goods'†	0-6-0
—	*Yataghan*	'Sun'†	2-2-2
6859	*Yiewsley Grange*	'Grange'	4-6-0
—	*Zebra*	'Sun'†	2-2-2
—	*Zebra*	South Devon	4-4-0ST
1	*Zeno*	Birkenhead	2-4-0T
—	*Zetes*	'Standard Goods'†	0-6-0
2	*Zillah*	Birkenhead	2-2-2
5	*Zillah*	Birkenhead	0-4-0
—	*Zina*	'Standard Goods'†	0-6-0
2	*Zopyrus*	Birkenhead	2-4-0T
4	*Zyglia*	Birkenhead	0-4-0

Absorbed railways' named locomotives

Alexandra (Newport & South Wales) Docks and Railway

No	Name	Wheel arrangement
—	*Active*	0–4–0ST
—	*Alexandra*	0–4–0ST
—	*Annie*	0–4–0ST(?)
—	*Britannia*	?
—	*Harold*	0–6–0ST
	(also Weston, Clevedon & Portishead Railway)	
—	*Ilkeston*	0–6–0T
—*	*Kate*	0–4–0ST
—	*Trojan*	0–4–0ST
—	*Usk*	0–6–0ST
—	*Will Scarlet*	0–6–0T
	(also Severn & Wye and Severn Bridge Railway	
1	*Hodroyd*	0–6–0ST
1	*Sir George Elliot*	0–6–0ST
2	*Lord Tredegar*	0–6–0ST
3	*J. R. Maclean*	0–6–0ST
4	*Rhondda*	0–6–0ST
5	*J. C. Parkinson*	0–6–0ST
6	*Lady Tredegar*	0–6–0ST
6	*Victoria*	2–6–2T
7	*Mersey*	2–6–2T
7	*Pontypridd*	0–6–2ST
8	*Aberdare Valley*	0–6–0ST
8	*Tranmere*	2–6–2T
9	*Bouverie*	2–6–2T
9	*Pontypridd*	0–6–0ST
10	*Brunlees*	2–6–2T
10	*Caerphilly*	0–6–0ST
11	*Alexandria*	0–6–0ST
11	*Salisbury*	2–6–2T
19	*Daisy*	0–6–0ST
22	*Fox*	0–6–4T
23	*Duke of Lancaster*	0–6–4T
24	*Earl of Chester*	0–6–4T
25	*Burcot*	2–6–2T
?	*Sir George*	?

Barry Railway

No	Name	Wheel arrangement
3	*Ebor*	0–6–0T
46	*William*	0–6–2T

Birkenhead Railway

No	Name	Wheel arrangement
—*	*Violet*	2–2–2
1	*Wirral*	2–2–2
1	*Zeno*	2–4–0T
2	*Zillah*	2–2–2
2	*Zopyrus*	2–4–0T
3	*Touchstone*	2–2–2
4	*Commodore*	2–2–2
4	*Zyglia*	0–4–0
5	*Hirondelle*	2–2–2
5	*Zillah*	0–4–0
6	*Grasshopper*	0–4–0ST
6	*Lupus*	2–2–2
7	*Druid*	2–2–2
8	*Birkenhead*	2–2–2
8*	*Monk*	2–2–2
9	*Victoria*	2–2–2
10	*Albert*	2–2–2
11	*Birkenhead*	0–6–0
11*	*Blazer*	0–6–0
12	*Chester*	0–6–0
12	*Gnome*	0–6–0
13	*Mersey*	0–6–0
13*	*Forerunner*	0–6–0
14	*Dee*	0–6–0
14*	*Gheber*	0–6–0
14*	*Hawkstone*	0–6–0
15	*Latona*	2–2–2
20	*Locke*	2–2–2
21	*Prince Eugene*	2–2–2
22	*Sefton*	2–2–2
23	*Mersey*	2–4–0
23*	*Etna*	2–4–0
24	*Majestic*	2–4–0
25	*Birkenhead*	2–4–0
26	*Weaver*	2–4–0
27	*Diamond*	0–4–0ST
27	*Memnon*	0–4–0T
27*	*Acton*	0–4–0T
30	*Leeds*	2–2–2
32	*Volante*	2–4–0
33	*Voltigeur*	2–4–0T
34	*Phoebus*	2–4–0T
35	*Talisman*	0–4–2
36	*Thalaba*	0–4–2
37	*Thunderer*	0–6–0
38	*Dee*	2–4–0
38*	*Chandos*	2–4–0
39	*Cricket*	0–4–0ST
40	*Dreadnought*	0–6–0
41	*Marquis Douro*	0–4–2
42	*Firefly*	0–4–2
?	*Glendower*	?

Brecon & Merthyr Railway

No	Name	Wheel arrangement
—	*Dart*	?
—	*Fairy*	?
—*	*Green Dragon*	0–6–0ST
	(also Cambrian Railways)	
—	*Leon*	?
—	*Progress*	0–4–4–0
	(also Monmouthshire Railway & Canal Co and Neath & Brecon Railway)	
—	*Stag*	?
—	*Usk*	2–4–0
	(also Cambrian Railways)	
—	*Wye*	2–4–0
	(also Cambrian Railways)	
4	*Wynnstay*	0–4–2
	(also Cambrian Railways)	
5	*Montgomery*	0–4–2
	(also Cambrian Railways)	
6	*Glansevern*	0–4–2
	(also Cambrian Railways)	
7	*Allt*	0–6–0ST
	(also Neath & Brecon Railway)	
7	*Antelope*	0–6–0
8	*Elephant*	0–6–0
8	*Leighton*	0–4–2
	(also Cambrian Railways)	
8	*Tor*	0–6–0ST
	(also Neath & Brecon Railway)	
10(?)	*Pioneer*	0–6–0ST
	(also Cambrian Railways)	
13	*Pandora*	0–6–0ST
14	*Jupiter*	0–6–0ST
15(?)	*Hereford*	?
	(also Cambrian Railways)	
16*	*Lady Cornelia*	0–6–0ST
16(?)	*De Winton*	0–6–0
	(also Cambrian Railways)	
17*	*Blanche*	0–6–0ST
18	*Atlas*	0–6–0ST
19	*Beacon*	0–6–0ST
19	*Hercules*	0–6–0
	(also Cambrian Railways)	
20	*Cyclops*	0–6–0ST
20	*Vulcan*	0–6–0
	(also Cambrian Railways)	
21	*Cymbeline*	0–6–0ST
22	*Severn*	0–6–0ST
23	*Mersey*	0–6–0ST
23(?)	*Tiny*	0–4–0ST
	(also Cambrian Railways)	
24	*Cyfarthfa*	0–6–0ST
25	*Sir Ivor*	0–6–0ST
26	*Samson*	0–6–0ST
27	*Hercules*	0–6–0ST
28	*Rumney*	0–6–0ST
29	*Taff*	0–6–0ST
32(?)	*Alexander*	0–6–0
	(also Cambrian Railways)	
33(?)	*Brecknock*	0–6–0
	(also Cambrian Railways)	
37	*Mountaineer*	0–4–0ST
	(also Cambrian Railways)	
40	*Cyfronydd*	0–6–0
	(also Cambrian Railways)	
49(?)	*Caerleon*	0–6–0
	(also Cambrian Railways)	
50(?)	*Caerphilly*	0–6–0
	(also Cambrian Railways)	
113	*Bear*	0–4–0WT

Bristol & Exeter Railway

No	Name	Wheel arrangement
—	*Bath*	0–6–0
	(also GWR 'Swindon' class)	
—	*Birmingham*	0–6–0
	(also GWR 'Swindon' class)	
—	*Bristol*	0–6–0
	(also GWR 'Swindon' class)	
—	*Chester*	0–6–0
	(also GWR 'Swindon' class)	
—	*Gloucester*	0–6–0
	(also GWR 'Swindon' class)	
—	*Glyncorrwg*	0–4–2ST
	(also South Wales Mineral Railway)	
—	*Hereford*	0–6–0
	(also GWR 'Swindon' class)	
—	*London*	0–6–0
	(also GWR 'Swindon' class)	
—	*Newport*	0–6–0
	(also GWR 'Swindon' class)	
—	*Oxford*	0–6–0
	(also GWR 'Swindon' class)	
—	*Reading*	0–6–0
	(also GWR 'Swindon' class)	
—	*Shrewsbury*	0–6–0
	(also GWR 'Swindon' class)	
—	*Swindon*	0–6–0
	(also GWR 'Swindon' class)	
—	*Windsor*	0–6–0
	(also GWR 'Swindon' class)	
—	*Wolverhampton*	0–6–0
	(also GWR 'Swindon' class)	
29	*Fairfield*	—
	(Steam Railmotor)	

Bristol Port Railway and Pier

No	Name	Wheel arrangement
2	*Dusty*	0–4–2T
2*	*Hecate*	0–4–2T
2*	*Severn*	0–4–2T
4	*Hercules*	0–4–2T
23	*Hero*	0–4–2T

British Railways

No	Name	Wheel arrangement
1	*Hercules*	0–4–0ST

Burry Port & Gwendraeth Valley Railway

No	Name	Wheel arrangement
—*	*Burry Port*	0–6–0ST
—*	*Copshaw*	0–6–0ST
—	*Cwm Mawr*	0–6–0ST
	(also Weston, Clevedon & Portishead Railway)	
—	*Dyvatty*	0–6–0ST
—	*Edith Mary*	0–6–0ST
—	*Gwendraeth*	0–4–0ST
—	*Kidwelly*	0–6–0ST
	(also Gwendraeth Valleys Railway)	
—	*Lizzie*	0–4–0ST
—*	*Mountaineer*	0–4–4–0
—	*Pioneer*	0–4–4–0
—*	*Resolute*	0–6–0ST
—*	*Susan*	0–6–0ST
—*	*Weston*	0–6–0ST
	(also Weston, Clevedon & Portishead Railway)	
1	*Ashburnham*	0–6–0ST
2	*Pontyberem*	0–6–0ST
3	*Burry Port*	0–6–0ST
4	*Kidwelly*	0–6–0ST
5	*Cwm Mawr*	0–6–0ST
6	*Gwendraeth*	0–6–0ST
7	*Pembrey*	0–6–0ST
8	*Pioneer*	0–6–0T
29	*Victoria*	0–6–6–0

Cambrian Railways

No	Name	Wheel arrangement
—	*Aelfred* (also Lambourn Valley Railway)	0–6–0T
—	*Alyn*	0–6–0ST
—	*Caersws*	0–6–0ST
—	*Disraeli*	0–6–0ST
—*	*Dot*	0–4–0ST
—	*Dove*	2–2–2(?)
—	*Eadweade* (also Lambourn Valley Railway)	0–6–0T
—	*Ealhswith* (also Lambourn Valley Railway)	0–6–0T
—*	*Green Dragon* (also Brecon & Merthyr Railway)	0–6–0ST
—	*Llandinam* (also Pembroke & Tenby Railway)	0–6–0ST
—	*Llanidloes*	?
—	*Squirrel*	?
—	*Usk* (also Brecon & Merthyr Railway)	2–4–0
—	*Volunteer*	0–4–2
—	*Wye* (also Brecon & Merthyr Railway)	2–4–0
1	*Enterprise*	0–6–0ST(?)
1	*James Watt*	0–6–0
1	*Latona*	4–4–0T
1(?)	*Llewelyn*	?
1	*Victoria*	0–6–0
1	*The Earl* (narrow gauge)	0–6–0T
1	*Edward VII* (narrow gauge)	2–6–2T
2	*Ruthin*	0–4–0
2	*The Countess* (narrow gauge)	0–6–0T
2*	*Countess* (narrow gauge)	0–6–0T
3	*Milford*	0–4–2ST
3	*Talybont*	2–4–0T
3*	*Rheidol* (narrow gauge)	2–4–0T
4	*Alexandra*	0–6–0
4	*Wynnstay* (also Brecon & Merthyr Railway)	0–4–2
5	*Montgomery* (also Brecon & Merthyr Railway)	0–4–2
6	*Marquis*	0–6–0
6	*Glansevern* (also Brecon & Merthyr Railway)	0–4–2
7	*Llanerchydol*	0–4–2
7	*Owain Glyndû* (narrow gauge)	2–6–2T
8	*Llywelyn* (narrow gauge)	2–6–2T
8	*Leighton* (also Brecon & Merthyr Railway)	0–4–2T
9	*Prince of Wales* (narrow gauge)	2–6–2T
10	*Cerberus*	4–4–0T
10	*Marchioness*	0–6–0
10(?)	*Pioneer* (also Brecon & Merthyr Railway)	0–6–0ST
11	*Queen*	0–6–0
12	*Cyclops*	4–4–0T
12	*Prince of Wales*	0–6–0
13	*Daphne*	4–4–0T
13	*Talerddig*	0–6–0T
13	*Whixall*	0–6–0ST
14	*Broneirion*	0–6–0
14	*Nantclwyd*	0–6–0ST
14*	*Jumbo*	0–6–0ST
15	*Aurora*	4–4–0T
15	*Glansevern*	0–6–0
15(?)	*Hereford* (also Brecon & Merthyr Railway)	?
16	*Beaconsfield*	4–4–0
16(?)	*De Winton* (also Brecon & Merthyr Railway)	0–6–0
17	*Hartington*	4–4–0
17	*Merion*	0–6–0ST
18	*Cardigan*	0–6–0ST
18	*Orleton*	0–6–0
19	*Hercules* (also Brecon & Merthyr Railway)	0–6–0
20	*Vulcan* (also Brecon & Merthyr Railway)	0–6–0
21	*Lilleshall*	0–4–0ST
23(?)	*Tiny* (also Brecon & Merthyr Railway)	0–4–0ST
24	*Borth*	0–6–0ST
25(?)	*Dwarf*	0–4–0ST
26	*Tubal Cain*	0–6–0
27	*Cambria*	0–6–0
28	*Mazeppa*	2–4–0
29	*Pegasus*	2–4–0
30	*Albion*	2–4–0
30*	*Mawddwy*	0–6–0ST
31	*Minerva*	2–4–0
32(?)	*Alexander* (also Brecon & Merthyr Railway)	0–6–0
33(?)	*Brecknock* (also Brecon & Merthyr Railway)	0–6–0
34*	*Cader Idris*	0–6–0
34	*Talerddig*	0–6–0
35*	*Castell Deudraeth*	0–6–0
35*	*Countess Vane*	0–6–0
36	*Plasfynnon*	0–4–0ST
37	*Mountaineer* (also Brecon & Merthyr Railway)	0–4–0ST
38	*Prometheus*	0–4–0ST
39	*Sir Watkin*	0–6–0
40	*Cyfronydd* (also Brecon & Merthyr Railway)	0–6–0
41	*Cader Idris*	2–4–0
41*	*Countess Vane*	2–4–0
42	*Glandovey*	2–4–0
43	*Plynlimon*	2–4–0
44	*Rheidol*	2–4–0
45	*Rhiewport*	0–6–0
46	*Towyn*	0–6–0
49(?)	*Caerleon* (also Brecon & Merthyr Railway)	0–6–0
50(?)	*Caerphilly* (also Brecon & Merthyr Railway)	0–6–0
51	*Snowdon*	0–6–0
52	*Harlech*	0–6–0
53	*Gladstone*	2–4–0
54	*Palmerston*	2–4–0
55	*Treflach*	2–4–0
56	*Whittington*	2–4–0
57	*Maglona*	2–4–0T
58	*Gladys*	2–4–0T
59	*Seaham*	2–4–0T

Cardiff Railway

No	Name	Wheel arrangement
25	*La Savoie*	0–6–0
29	*Irthlingborough*	0–6–2T
30	*Cwmcarn*	0–6–2T
36	*The Earl of Dumfries*	2–4–2T

Carmarthen & Cardigan Railway

No	Name	Wheel arrangement
—	*Etna* (also South Devon Railway)	4–4–0ST
—	*Hecla* (also South Devon Railway)	4–4–0ST
—	*Heron* (also South Devon Railway)	4–4–0T
—	*Magpie* (also South Devon Railway)	4–4–0T
—	*Victor* (also Llanelly Railway & Dock Co)	0–6–0

Cleobury Mortimer & Ditton Priors Light Railway

No	Name	Wheel arrangement
—	*Burwarton*	0–6–0ST
—	*Cleobury*	0–6–0ST
—	*Fleetwood*	0–6–0ST

Cornwall Minerals Railway

No	Name	Wheel arrangement
—	*Cornwall*	?
—	*Haverhill*	0–6–0T
—	*Lord Robartes*	0–6–0
—	*Newquay*	0–6–0T
—	*Newquay* (also South Wales Mineral Railway)	0–4–2ST
—	*Phoenix*	0–4–2
1	*Melton Constable*	0–6–0T
1	*Treffrey*	0–6–0T
1*	*Treffry*	0–6–0T
2	*Lord Robartes*	0–6–0T
2	*Reepham*	0–6–0T
3	*Blakeney*	0–6–0T
3	*Fowey*	0–6–0T
?	*Roebuck*	?

Cornwall Minerals Railway (Goonbarrow branch)

No	Name	Wheel arrangement
—	*Goonbarrow*	0–6–0ST

Corris Railway

No	Name	Wheel arrangement
1	*Tattoo* (narrow gauge)	0–4–0ST
3	*Sir Haydn* (narrow gauge)	0–4–2ST
4	*Edward Thomas* (narrow gauge)	0–4–2ST

Fishguard & Rosslare Railways and Harbours Co

No	Name	Wheel arrangement
—	*Elfin*	0–4–0ST
—	*Gallo*	0–4–0ST
—	*Hook Norton* (also Hook Norton Ironstone Partnership Ltd)	0–6–0ST
—	*Mermaid*	0–4–0ST
—	*Nipper*	0–4–0ST
—	*Pioneer*	0–4–0ST
—	*Wyncliffe*	0–4–0ST

Golden Valley Railway

No	Name	Wheel arrangement
—	*Bulldog*	2–4–0T
—	*Cadmus*	2–4–0T
—	*Giant*	2–4–0T
—	*Glyn*	2–4–0T
—	*Lady Cornewall*	2–2–2T(?)
—	*Wye*	0–4–0ST

Gwendraeth Valleys Railway

No	Name	Wheel arrangement
—	*Kidwelly*	0–6–0ST
—	*Kidwelly* (also Burry Port & Gwendraeth Valley Railway)	0–6–0ST
—	*Margaret* (also North Pembrokeshire & Fishguard Railway)	0–6–0ST
1*	*Velindre*	0–6–0ST

Hook Norton Ironstone Partnership Ltd

No	Name	Wheel arrangement
—	*Hook Norton* (also Fishguard & Rosslare Railways and Harbours Co)	0–6–0ST

Lambourn Valley Railway

No	Name	Wheel arrangement
—	*Aelfred* (also Cambrian Railways)	0–6–0T
—	*Eadweade* (also Cambrian Railways)	0–6–0T
—	*Ealhswith* (also Cambrian Railways)	0–6–0T

Liskeard & Looe and Liskeard & Caradon Railways

No	Name	Wheel arrangement
—	*Caradon*	0–6–0ST
—	*Cheesewring*	0–6–0ST
—	*Kilmar*	0–6–0ST
—	*Lady Margaret*	2–4–0T
—	*Liskeard*	0–6–0T(?)
—	*Looe*	0–6–0ST

Llanelly Railway & Dock Co

No	Name	Wheel arrangement
—	*Albert*	0–6–0
—	*Albert*	0–4–2
—	*Alexandra*	0–6–0
—*	*Alfred*	0–4–2
—*	*Alice*	0–4–2
—	*Amman*	2–4–0ST
—	*Arthur*	0–6–0
—	*Beatrice*	0–4–2
—	*Drysllwyn*	0–6–0
—	*Dunvant*	0–6–0
—	*Edinburgh*	0–6–0

No	Name	Wheel arrangement
—	*Ernest*	0–6–0
—	*Grongar*	0–6–0
—*	*Helena*	0–4–0
—	*Leo*	0–6–0
—	*Loughor*	2–4–0ST
—	*Louisa*	0–6–0
—	*Napoleon III*	2–4–0
—	*Prince Alfred*	0–4–0
—	*Prince of Wales*	0–6–0
—	*Princess Alice*	0–4–0
—	*Princess Helena*	0–4–0
—	*Princess Royal*	0–6–0
—	*Royal*	0–6–0
—*	*Royal*	0–6–0
—	*Stradey*	0–6–0
—	*Teilo*	0–6–0
—	*Towy*	0–6–0
—	*Victor*	0–6–0
	(also Carmarthen & Cardigan Railway)	
—	*Victoria*	0–6–0
—	*Victoria*	0–6–0
—*	*Wales*	0–6–0
—	*Wales*	0–6–0
?	*Towy*	

Llanelly & Mynydd Mawr Railway

No	Name	Wheel arrangement
—*	*Astley Green*	0–4–0T(?)
—	*Burntisland*	0–4–0ST
—	*E.J. Robertson Grant*	0–6–0ST
—	*George Waddell*	0–6–0T
—	*Great Mountain*	0–6–0T
—	*Hilda*	0–6–0ST
—	*Inveravon*	0–4–0ST
—	*Jeannie Waddell*	0–6–0ST
—	*John Waddell*	0–4–0T(?)
—	*John Waddell*	0–6–0ST
—	*Merkland*	0–6–0T
—	*Ravelston*	0–6–0T
—	*Seymour Clake*	0–6–0ST
—	*Tarndune*	0–6–0T
—	*Victory*	0–6–0T

Llynvi & Ogmore Railway

No	Name	Wheel arrangement
—	*Ada*	0–6–0ST
	(also South Devon Railway)	
—	*Rescue*	?
—	*Helston*	2–4–0
	(also West Cornwall Railway)	
—	*Mount's Bay*	2–4–0
	(also West Cornwall Railway)	
—	*Penzance*	2–4–0
	(also West Cornwall Railway)	
—	*Rosa*	4–4–0ST
	(also South Devon Railway)	
—	*St Ives*	2–4–0
	(also West Cornwall Railway)	
—	*Una*	0–6–0ST
	(also South Devon Railway)	

Manchester & Milford Railway

No	Name	Wheel arrangement
—	*Teifi*	0–6–0ST
1	*General Wood*	0–6–0
2	*Carmarthen*	
	(or Caermarthen)	2–4–0
2	*Plynlimmon*	2–4–2T
3	*Lady Elizabeth*	2–4–0
4	*Aberystwyth*	0–6–0
4	*Lampeter*	0–6–0ST
6	*Cader Idris*	2–4–2T

Midland & South Western Junction Railway

No	Name	Wheel arrangement
2	*Humber*	0–6–0T
3	*Kirkella*	0–6–0T

Monmouthshire Railway and Canal Co

No	Name	Wheel arrangement
—	*Coalbrookvale*	0–6–0ST
—	*Progress*	0–4–4–0
	(also Brecon & Merthyr Railway and Neath & Brecon Railway)	
1	*Nestor*	0–6–0
2	*Parnassus*	0–6–0
11	*Aegeon*	?

Neath & Brecon Railway

No	Name	Wheel arrangement
—	*Anglesea*	0–6–0WT
—	*Brecon*	2–4–0
—	*Buckley*	
	(or Bulkeley)	?
—*	*Miers*	0–6–0WT
—	*Mountaineer*	0–4–4–0
—	*Neath*	2–4–0
?	*Penwyllt*	?
—	*Progress*	0–4–4–0
	(also Monmouthshire Railway & Canal Co and Brecon & Merthyr)	
7	*Allt*	0–6–0ST
	(also Brecon & Merthyr Railway)	
8	*Tor*	0–6–0ST
	(also Brecon & Merthyr Railway)	

North Pembrokeshire & Fishguard Railway

No	Name	Wheel arrangement
—*	*Hesperus*	0–6–0ST
—	*Margaret*	0–6–0ST
	(also Gwendraeth Valleys Railway)	
—	*Precelly*	0–6–0ST
—	*Ringing Rock*	0–6–0ST

Pembroke & Tenby Railway

No	Name	Wheel arrangement
—	*Llandinam*	0–6–0ST
	(also Cambrian Railways)	
1	*Tenby*	2–2–2T
2	*Milford*	2–2–2T
3	*Pembroke*	2–4–0
6	*Cambria*	0–6–0
6*	*Tenby*	0–6–0
7	*Homlwood*	0–6–0T
	(also GWR '1813' class)	
8	*Stella*	2–4–0
	(also GWR 'Stella' class)	

Port Talbot Railway and Docks

No	Name	Wheel arrangement
—	*Derby*	0–6–0ST
	(also Swansea Harbour Trust)	
—*	*Harriet*	0–6–0ST
	(also Swansea Harbour Trust)	
—	*Penylan*	0–6–0ST
	(also South Wales Mineral Railway)	
1	*Stephenson*	0–6–0ST
5	*Davies*	0–6–0
22	*H.M.B*	0–6–0ST

Powlesland & Mason Railway

No	Name	Wheel arrangement
—	*Crow*	0–4–0T
	(also South Devon Railway)	
—	*Dorothy*	0–6–0ST
—	*Jay*	0–4–0T
	(also South Devon Railway)	
—	*Lark*	0–4–0T
	(also South Devon Railway)	
—	*Rook*	0–4–0T
	(also South Devon Railway)	
4	*Owen*	0–6–0
5	*Dorothy*	0–4–0ST

Rhymney Railway

No	Name	Wheel arrangement
—	*Mountaineer*	0–6–0ST
	(also Taff Vale Railway)	

Severn & Wye and Severn Bridge Railway

No	Name	Wheel arrangement
—	*Ajax*	0–6–0
—	*Alan-a-dale*	0–6–0T
—	*Cyclops*	?
	(also Taff Vale Railway)	
—	*Forester*	0–6–0T
—	*Friar Tuck*	0–6–0T
—	*Gaveller*	0–6–0ST
—	*Hercules No. 2*	?
—	*Little John*	0–6–0T
—	*Maid Marian*	0–6–0T
—	*Nelson*	?
—	*Queen*	?
	(also Taff Vale Railway)	
—	*Ranger*	0–6–0
—	*Raven*	0–6–0ST
—	*Robin Hood*	0–6–0T
—	*Sabrina*	0–6–0T
—	*Severn Bridge*	0–4–0T
—	*Severn Bridge*	0–6–0T
—	*Sharpness*	0–6–0T
—*	*Victor*	0–6–0T
—	*Will Scarlet*	0–6–0T
	(also Alexandra (Newport & South Wales) Docks and Railway)	
—*	*Wye*	0–4–0T
2	*Little John*	0–4–0
5	*Forester*	0–6–0

Shrewsbury & Birmingham Railway

No	Name	Wheel arrangement
2	*Vulcan*	2–2–2
3	*Queen*	2–2–2
21	*Salopian*	2–2–2
23	*Wrekin*	2–2–2

Shrewsbury & Chester Railway

No	Name	Wheel arrangement
19	*Prince of Wales*	2–2–2
21	*Victoria & Albert*	2–2–2
32(?)	*Newton*	2–2–2(?)
33	*Wrekin*	?

South Devon Railway

No	Name	Wheel arrangement
—	*Achilles*	0–6–0ST
	(also South Wales Mineral Railway)	
—	*Ada*	0–6–0ST
	(also Llynvi & Ogmore Railway)	
—	*Ajax*	0–6–0ST
—	*Antelope*	4–4–0ST
—	*Argo*	0–6–0
—	*Atlas*	0–6–0ST
—	*Aurora*	4–4–0ST
—	*Bulkeley*	0–6–0T
	(also GWR 'Sir Watkin' class)	
—	*Brutus*	0–6–0ST
—	*Buffalo*	0–6–0ST
—	*Camel*	0–6–0ST
—	*Castor*	4–4–0ST
—	*Cato*	4–4–0ST
—	*Comet*	4–4–0ST
—	*Crow*	0–4–0T
	(also Powlesland & Mason Railway)	
—	*Damon*	4–4–0ST
—	*Dart*	4–4–0ST
—	*Dido*	0–6–0ST
—	*Dragon*	0–6–0ST
—	*Dromedary*	0–6–0ST
—	*Eagle*	4–4–0ST
—	*Elephant*	0–6–0ST
—	*Elk*	4–4–0ST
—	*Emperor*	0–6–0ST
	(also South Wales Mineral Railway)	
—	*Etna*	4–4–0ST
	(also Carmarthen & Cardigan Railway)	
—	*Falcon*	4–4–0ST
—	*Fowler*	0–6–0T
	(also GWR 'Sir Watkin' class)	
—	*Gazelle*	4–4–0ST
—	*Giraffe*	4–4–0ST
—	*Goat*	0–4–0T
—	*Goliah*	0–6–0ST
—	*Gorgon*	4–4–0ST
—	*Hawk*	4–4–0ST
—	*Hebe*	0–6–0ST
—	*Hecla*	4–4–0ST
	(also Carmarthen & Cardigan Railway)	
—	*Hector*	4–4–0ST
—	*Hercules*	0–6–0ST
—	*Hero*	0–6–0ST
—	*Heron*	4–4–0T
	(also Carmarthen & Cardigan Railway)	
—	*Ixion*	4–4–0ST
—	*Jay*	4–4–0T
	(also Powlesland & Mason Railway)	
—	*Juno*	0–6–0ST
—	*Jupiter*	2–4–0T
—	*King*	2–4–0T
—	*Lance*	4–4–0ST
—	*Lance*	4–4–0ST
—	*Lark*	0–4–0T
	(also Powlesland & Mason Railway)	
—	*Leopard*	4–4–0ST
—	*Lion*	4–4–0ST
—	*Lynx*	4–4–0ST
—	*Magpie*	0–4–0T
	(also Carmarthen & Cardigan Railway)	

No	Name	Wheel arrangement
—	*Mazeppa*	4–4–0ST
—	*Mercury*	2–4–0T
—	*Meteor*	4–4–0ST
—	*Orion*	4–4–0ST
—	*Osiris*	4–4–0ST
—	*Ostrich*	4–4–0ST
—	*Owl*	0–4–0T
—	*Penwith* (also West Cornwall Railway)	2–4–0
—*	*Perseverance*	2–4–0(?)
—	*Pluto*	4–4–0ST
—	*Pollux*	4–4–0ST
—	*Priam*	4–4–0ST
—	*Prince*	2–4–0ST
—	*Python*	0–6–0ST
—	*Raven* (also Torbay & Brixham Railway)	4–4–0T
—	*Redruth* (also West Cornwall Railway)	0–6–0
—	*Remus*	0–6–0ST
—	*Rocket*	4–4–0ST
—	*Romulus*	0–6–0ST
—	*Rook* (also Powlesland & Mason Railway)	0–4–0T
—	*Rosa* (also Llynvi & Ogmore Railway)	4–4–0ST
—	*Sampson*	0–6–0ST
—	*Saunders* (also GWR 'Sir Watkin' class)	0–6–0T
—	*Saturn*	2–4–0T
—	*Sedley*	4–4–0ST
—	*Sol*	4–4–0ST
—	*Stag*	4–4–0ST
—	*Stromboli*	0–6–0ST
—	*Taurus*	0–6–0ST
—	*Tiger*	4–4–0ST
—	*Tiny*	0–4–0VBT
—	*Titan*	4–4–0ST
—	*Tornado*	0–6–0ST
—	*Una* (also Llynvi & Ogmore Railway)	0–6–0ST
—	*Volcano*	0–6–0ST
—	*Vulcan*	0–6–0ST
—	*Weasel*	4–4–0T
—	*Wolf*	4–4–0ST
—	*Zebra*	4–4–0ST

South Wales Mineral Railway

No	Name	Wheel arrangement
—	*Achilles* (also South Devon Railway)	0–6–0ST
—	*Brigand*	?
—	*Emperor* (also South Devon Railway)	0–6–0ST
—	*Glyncorrwg* (also Bristol & Exeter Railway)	0–4–2ST
—	*Newquay* (also Cornwall Minerals Railway)	0–4–2ST
—	*Penylan* (also Port Talbot Railway and Docks)	0–6–0ST
—	*Princess*	4–4–0ST

Swansea Harbour Trust

No	Name	Wheel arrangement
—	*Albert Edward*	4–4–0ST
—	*Derby* (also Port Talbot Railway and Docks)	0–6–0ST
—*	*Harriet* (also Port Talbot Railway and Docks)	0–6–0ST
—	*Jumbo*	4–4–0ST
—	*Swansea*	4–4–0ST
1	*Balfour*	4–4–0ST
1	*Glanmor*	4–4–0ST
4	*Joan*	4–4–0ST
4	*Windsor*	4–4–0ST
6	*Jean*	4–4–0ST
6	*Progress*	0–6–0ST
10	*Cardiff*	4–4–0ST
10*	*John*	4–4–0ST

Taff Vale Railway

No	Name	Wheel arrangement
—	*Aberaman*	0–6–0
—	*Aberdare*	0–4–2
—	*Abergwawr*	0–6–0
—	*Bute*	0–6–0
—	*Cambrian*	0–6–0
—	*Cardiff*	0–4–2
—	*Cavendish*	2–4–0ST
—	*Columbia*	4–2–0
—	*Cyclops* (also Severn & Wye and Severn Bridge Railway)	?
—	*Cymmer*	0–6–0
—	*Dinas*	0–4–2
—	*Dowlais*	0–4–2
—	*Duffryn*	0–6–0
—	*Gladlys*	0–6–0
—	*Gloucester*	4–2–0
—	*Llancaiach*	0–4–2
—	*Llandaff*	0–6–0
—	*Llantwit*	0–4–2
—	*Mercury*	0–6–0
—	*Merthyr*	0–4–2
—	*Moorsom*	4–2–0
—	*Mountaineer* (also Rhymney Railway)	0–6–0ST
—	*Neath Abbey*	0–4–2
—	*Newbridge*	0–6–0
—	*Plymouth*	0–4–2
—	*Queen* (also Severn & Wye and Severn Bridge Railway)	?
—	*Rhondda*	2–2–2
—	*Taff*	2–2–2
—*	*Tintern*	2–4–0
—	*Treforest*	0–6–0
1	*Taff*	2–4–0
2	*Rhondda*	2–4–0
3	*Plymouth*	0–6–0
4	*Dinas*	0–6–0
5	*Llancaiach*	0–6–0
6	*Merthyr*	0–6–0
7	*Aberdare*	0–6–0
8	*Llantwit*	0–6–0
9	*Porth*	0–6–0
10	*Cambrian*	0–6–0
11	*Llandaff*	0–6–0
12	*Newbridge*	0–6–0
13	*Severn*	0–6–0
14	*Avon*	0–6–0
15	*Clifton*	0–6–0
16	*Bristol*	0–6–0
17	*Aberaman*	0–6–0
18	*Stuart*	0–6–0
21	*Treforest*	0–6–0
23	*Cymmer*	0–6–0
25	*Dare*	2–4–0
26	*Cynon*	2–4–0
27	*Mars*	0–6–0
28	*Atlas*	0–6–0
29	*Gordon*	0–6–2T
29	*Vulcan*	0–6–0
30	*Cyclops*	0–6–0
31	*Orion*	0–6–0
32	*Hercules*	0–6–0
33	*Ely*	2–4–0
34	*Rhymney*	2–4–0
35	*Inkerman*	0–6–0
36	*Alma*	0–6–0
37	*Cardiff*	0–6–0
38	*Antelope*	0–6–0
39	*Stag*	0–6–0
40	*Gazelle*	0–6–0
41	*Venus*	2–4–0
43	*Apollo*	0–6–0
44	*Pluto*	0–6–0
45	*Comet*	0–6–0
46	*Penarth*	0–6–0
47	*Dowlais*	0–6–0
48	*Dunraven*	0–6–0
49	*Werfa*	0–6–0
50	*Gelly Gaer*	0–6–0
51*	*Wellington*	0–6–2T
80	*Blaendare*	0–6–0ST
168	*Kitchener*	0–6–2T
190	*Preston*	0–6–0ST
190*	*Radcliffe*	0–6–0ST

Torbay & Brixham Railway

No	Name	Wheel arrangement
—	*Queen*	0–4–0WT
—	*Raven* (also South Devon Railway)	0–4–0T

Wantage Tramway

No	Name	Wheel arrangement
5	*Shannon*	0–4–0WT

Watlington & Princes Risborough Railway

No	Name	Wheel arrangement
4	*Hesperus* (also Weston Clevedon & Portishead Railway)	2–4–0T

West Cornwall Railway

No	Name	Wheel arrangement
—	*Apollo*	0–6–0
—	*Camborne*	2–4–0T(?)
—	*Camborne*	?
—	*Carn Brea*	?
—	*Ceres*	?
—	*Chanter*	?
—	*Cornubia*	?
—	*Coryndon*	?
—*	*Coryndon*	?
—	*Cyclops*	0–6–0
—	*Falmouth*	2–4–0
—	*Fox*	0–4–0ST
—	*Hayle*	?
—	*Helston* (also Llynvi & Ogmore Railway)	2–4–0
—	*Ironsides*	?
—	*Mars*	0–6–0ST
—	*Mount's Bay* (also Llynvi & Ogmore Railway)	2–4–0
—*	*Nestor*	0–6–0
—	*Pendarves*	?
—	*Penwith* (also South Devon Railway)	2–4–0
—	*Penzance*	?
—	*Penzance* (also Llynvi & Ogmore Railway)	2–4–0
—	*Redruth* (also South Devon Railway)	0–6–0
—	*Redruth*	?
—	*St Ives* (also Llynvi & Ogmore Railway)	2–4–0
—	*St Just*	0–6–0
—	*Truro*	0–4–2(?)

West Midland Railway (Newport, Abergavenny & Hereford)

No	Name	Wheel arrangement
22	*Perseverance*	0–4–2T
27	*Antelope*	2–4–0
28(?)	*Reindeer*	2–4–0
29(?)	*Elk*	2–4–0
30(?)	*Gazelle*	2–4–0
?	*Gipsy*	?
?	*Trio*	?

West Midland Railway (Oxford, Worcester & Wolverhampton)

No	Name	Wheel arrangement
—	*Hare*	2–2–2
37(?)	*Himalaya*	0–6–0
38(?)	*Viso*	0–6–0
39(?)	*Pollux*	0–6–0
51(?)	*Will Shakespere*	2–2–2
52	*Ben Jonson*	2–2–2WT
'C'	*Canary*	0–4–2
?	*Castor*	0–6–0
'F'	*Mudlark*	?

Weston, Clevedon & Portishead (Light) Railway

No	Name	Wheel arrangement
—	*Clevedon*	0–6–0T
—	*Clevedon*	2–2–2
—	*Cwm Mawr* (also Burry Port & Gwendraeth Valley Railway)	0–6–0ST
—	*Emlyn*	0–6–0ST
—	*Harold* (also Alexandra (Newport & South Wales) Docks and Railway)	0–6–0ST
—	*Northiam*	?
—	*Portishead*	0–6–0T
—	*Walton Park*	0–6–0ST
—	*Weston*	2–2–2
—*	*Weston* (also Burry Port & Gwendraeth Valley Railway)	0–6–0ST
1	*General Don*	2–4–0T
—1*	*Clevedon*	2–4–0T
2	*Gipsy Hill*	0–6–0T

No	Name	Wheel arrangement
2*	*Portishead*	0–6–0T
2	*Portishead*	0–6–0ST
4	*Hesperus*	2–4–0T

(also Watlington & Princes Risborough Railway)

No	Name	Wheel arrangement
6	*Ashtead*	0–6–0T

Whitland & Cardigan Railway

No	Name	Wheel arrangement
1	*John Owen*	0–6–0ST

GWR broad gauge named locomotives, by class

No | Name | Notes

'Avalanche' 0–6–0(?) (built 1846)

— *Avalanche*

'Bacchus' 0–6–0 (built 1849)

— *Bacchus*

'Banking' 0–6–0ST (built 1852–54)

— *Bithon*
— *Iago*
— *Juno*
— *Plato*

'Bogie' 4–4–0ST (built 1854–55)

— *Brigand*
— *Corsair*
— *Euripides*
— *Hesiod*
— *Homer*
— *Horace*
— *Juvenal*
— *Lucan*
— *Lucretius*
— *Ovid*
— *Sappho*
— *Seneca*
— *Statius*
— *Theocritus*
— *Virgil*

'Caesar' 0–6–0ST (built 1851–52)

— *Caesar*
— *Dido*
— *Druid*
— *Florence*
— *Hero*
— *Nora Creina*
— *Thunderer*
— *Volcano*

'Fire Fly' 2-2-2 (built 1840–42)

— *Acheron*
— *Achilles*
— *Actaeon*
— *Arab*
— *Argus*
— *Arrow*
— *Bellona*
— *Castor*
— *Centaur*
— *Cerberus*
— *Charon*
— *Cyclops*
— *Damon*
— *Dart*
— *Electra*
— *Erebus*
— *Falcon*
— *Fire Ball*
— *Fire Brand*
— *Fire Fly*
— *Fire King*
— *Ganymede*
— *Gorgon*
— *Greyhound*
— *Harpy*
— *Hawk*
— *Hecate*
— *Hector*
— *Hydra*
— *Ixion*
— *Jupiter*
— *Leopard*

No | Name | Notes

— *Lethe*
— *Lucifer*
— *Lynx*
— *Mars*
— *Mazeppa*
— *Medea*
— *Medusa*
— *Menton*
— *Mercury*
— *Milo*
— *Minos*
— *Orion*
— *Ostrich*
— *Panther*
— *Pegasus*
— *Phlegethon*
— *Phoenix*
— *Pluto*
— *Pollux*
— *Priam*
— *Proserine*
— *Saturn*
— *Spit Fire*
— *Stag*
— *Stenton*
— *Tiger*
— *Venus*
— *Vulture*
— *Wild Fire*

'Great Western' 2-2-2 (built 1846)

— *Great Western*

'Hawthorn' 2-4-0 (built 1865–66)

— *Acheron*
— *Avonside*
— *Beyer*
— *Blenkensop*
— *Bury*
— *Cerberus*
— *Dewrance*
— *Fenton*
— *Foster*
— *Gooch*
— *Hackworth*
— *Hawk*
— *Hawthorn*
— *Hedley*
— *John Gray*
— *Melling*
— *Murdock*
— *Ostrich*
— *Peacock*
— *Penn*
— *Phlegethon*
— *Pollux*
— *Roberts*
— *Sharp*
— *Slaughter*
— *Stewart*
— *Wood*

'Hercules' 0-6-0 (built 1842)

— *Goliah*
— *Hercules*
— *Sampson*
— *Tityos*

'Iron Duke' 4-2-2 (built 1847–55)

— *Alma*
— *Amazon*
— *Balaklava*
— *Charles Russell*

No | Name | Notes

— *Courier*
— *Crimea*
— *Dragon*
— *Emperor*
— *Estaffete*
— *Eupatoria*
— *Great Britain*
— *Hirondelle*
— *Inkermann*
— *Iron Duke*
— *Kertch*
— *Lightning*
— *Pasha*
— *Perseus*
— *Prometheus*
— *Rougemont*
— *Rover*
— *Sebastopol*
— *Sultan*
— *Swallow*
— *Tartar*
— *Timour*
— *Tornado*
— *Warlock*
— *Wizard*

'Leo' 2-4-0 (built 1841–42)

— *Aquarius*
— *Aries*
— *Buffalo*
— *Cancer*
— *Capricornus*
— *Dromedary*
— *Elephant*
— *Etna*
— *Gemini*
— *Hecla*
— *Leo*
— *Libra*
— *Pisces*
— *Sagittarius*
— *Scorpio*
— *Stromboli*
— *Taurus*
— *Virgo*

'Metro' 2-4-0WT (built 1862–64)

— *Azalia*
— *Bee*
— *Bey*
— *Camelia*
— *Czar*
— *Fleur-de-Lis*
— *Gnat*
— *Hornet*
— *Kaiser*
— *Khan*
— *Laurel*
— *Lily*
— *Locust*
— *Mogul*
— *Mosquito*
— *Myrtle*
— *Rose*
— *Shah*
— *Shamrock*
— *Thistle*
— *Violet*
— *Wasp*

'Premier' 0-6-0 (built 1846–47)

— *Ajax*
— *Argo*
— *Bellerophon*

No	Name	Notes
—	*Bergion*	
—	*Briareus*	
—	*Brontes*	
—	*Dreadnought*	
—	*Fury*	
—	*Jason*	
—	*Premier*	
—	*Telica*	
—	*Vesuvius*	

'Prince' 2-2-2 (built 1846–47)

No	Name	Notes
—	*Elk*	
—	*Peri*	
—	*Prince*	
—	*Queen*	
—	*Sylph*	
—	*Witch*	

'Pyracmon' 0-6-0 (built 1847–48)

No	Name	Notes
—	*Alligator*	
—	*Bhemoth*	
—	*Caliban*	
—	*Mammoth*	
—	*Pyracmon*	
—	*Steropes*	

'Rover' 4-2-2 (built 1871–88)

No	Name	Notes
—	*Alma*	
—	*Amazon*	
—	*Balaklava*	
—	*Bulkeley*	
—	*Courier*	
—	*Crimea*	
—	*Dragon*	
—	*Emperor*	
—	*Eupatoria*	
—	*Great Britain*	
—	*Great Western*	
—	*Hirondelle*	
—	*Inkermann*	
—	*Iron Duke*	
—	*Lightning*	
—	*Prometheus*	
—	*Rover*	
—	*Sebastopol*	
—	*Sultan*	
—	*Swallow*	
—	*Tartar*	
—	*Timour*	
—	*Tornado*	
—	*Warlock*	

'Sir Watkin' 0-6-0T (built 1865–66)

No	Name	Notes
—	*Bulkeley*	*(also South Devon Railway)*
—	*Fowler*	*(Also South Devon Railway)*
—	*Miles*	
—	*Saunders*	*(also South Devon Railway*
—	*Sir Watkin*	
—	*Whetham*	

'Standard Goods' 0-6-0 (built 1852–63)

No	Name	Notes
—	*Amphion*	
—	*Ariadne*	
—	*Avon*	
—	*Banshee*	
—	*Boyne*	
—	*Brutus*	
—	*Caliph*	
—	*Cambyses*	
—	*Cato*	
—	*Ceres*	
—	*Champion*	
—	*Chronos*	
—	*Cicero*	
—	*Clyde*	
—	*Coquette*	
—	*Cossack*	
—	*Creon*	
—	*Cupid*	
—	*Cyprus*	
—	*Diana*	
—	*Esk*	
—	*Ethon*	
—	*Europa*	
—	*Flirt*	
—	*Flora*	
—	*Forth*	
—	*Geryon*	
—	*Giaour*	
—	*Gladiator*	
—	*Gyfeillon*	
—	*Hades*	
—	*Hebe*	
—	*Hecuba*	
—	*Humber*	
—	*Iris*	
—	*Janus*	
—	*Lagoon*	
—	*Leander*	
—	*Leonidas*	
—	*Liffey*	
—	*Luna*	
—	*Magi*	
—	*Mersey*	
—	*Metis*	
—	*Midas*	
—	*Minerva*	
—	*Monarch*	
—	*Nelson*	
—	*Nemesis*	
—	*Neptune*	
—	*Nero*	
—	*Nimrod*	
—	*Octavia*	
—	*Olympus*	
—	*Orpheus*	
—	*Orson*	
—	*Osiris*	
—	*Pallas*	
—	*Pandora*	
—	*Panthea*	
—	*Pearl*	
—	*Pelops*	
—	*Pioneer*	
—	*Plutarch*	
—	*Plutus*	
—	*Plym*	
—	*Psyche*	
—	*Regulus*	
—	*Remus*	
—	*Rhea*	
—	*Rhondda*	
—	*Romulus*	
—	*Ruby*	
—	*Saus*	
—	*Severn*	
—	*Severus*	
—	*Shannon*	
—	*Sibyl*	
—	*Sirius*	
—	*Sphinx*	
—	*Sylla*	
—	*Talbot*	
—	*Tamar*	
—	*Tantalus*	
—	*Tay*	
—	*Thames*	
—	*Theseus*	
—	*Trafalgar*	
—	*Tweed*	
—	*Tyne*	
—	*Typhon*	
—	*Ulysses*	
—	*Vesper*	
—	*Vesta*	
—	*Vixen*	
—	*Warhawk*	
—	*Warrior*	
—	*Wear*	
—	*Wellington*	
—	*Wye*	
—	*Xerxes*	
—	*Zetes*	
—	*Zina*	

'Star' 2-2-2 (built 1837–41)

No	Name	Notes
—	*Bright Star*	
—	*Dog Star*	
—	*Evening Star*	
—	*Load Star*	
—	*Morning Star*	
—	*North Star*	
—	*Polar Star*	
—	*Red Star*	
—	*Rising Star*	
—	*Royal Star*	
—	*Shooting Star*	
—	*Western Star*	

'Sun' 2-2-2 (built 1840–42)

No	Name	Notes
—	*Antelope*	
—	*Assagais*	
—	*Aurora*	
—	*Comet*	
—	*Creese*	
—	*Djerid*	
—	*Eclipse*	
—	*Gazelle*	
—	*Giraffe*	
—	*Hesperus*	
—	*Javelin*	
—	*Lance*	
—	*Meridian*	
—	*Meteor*	
—	*Rocket*	
—	*Stiletto*	
—	*Sun*	
—	*Sunbeam*	
—	*Wolf*	
—	*Yataghan*	
—	*Zebra*	

'Swindon' 0-6-0 (built 1865–66)

No	Name	Notes
—	*Bath*	*(also Bristol & Exeter Railway)*
—	*Birmingham*	*(also Bristol & Exeter Railway)*
—	*Bristol*	*(also Bristol & Exeter Railway)*
—	*Chester*	*(also Bristol & Exeter Railway)*
—	*Gloucester*	*(also Bristol & Exeter Railway)*
—	*Hereford*	*(also Bristol & Exeter Railway)*
—	*London*	*(also Bristol & Exeter Railway)*
—	*Newport*	*(also Bristol & Exeter Railway)*
—	*Oxford*	*(also Bristol & Exeter Railway)*
—	*Reading*	*(also Bristol & Exeter Railway)*
—	*Shrewsbury*	*(also Bristol & Exeter Railway)*
—	*Swindon*	*(also Bristol & Exeter Railway)*
—	*Windsor*	*(also Bristol & Exeter Railway)*
—	*Wolverhampton*	*(also Bristol & Exeter Railway)*

'Unclassified' 0-4-0 (built 1838)

No	Name	Notes
—	*Thunderer*	

'Unclassified' 2-2-2 (built 1837–40)

No	Name	Notes
—	*Aeolus*	
—	*Ajax*	
—	*Apollo*	
—	*Ariel*	
—	*Atlas*	
—	*Bacchus*	
—	*Eagle*	
—	*Exe*	
—	*Hurricane*	
—	*Lion*	
—	*Mars*	
—	*Mercury*	
—	*Neptune*	
—	*Planet*	

No	Name	Notes
—	*Premier*	
—	*Snake*	
—	*Teign*	
—	*Venus*	
—	*Viper*	
—	*Vulcan*	

'Victoria' 2-4-0 (built 1856–64)

No	Name	Notes
—	*Abdul Medjid*	
—	*Alexander*	
—	*Brindley*	
—	*Brunel*	
—	*Fulton*	
—	*Leopold*	
—	*Locke*	
—	*Napoleon*	
—	*Oscar*	
—	*Otho*	
—	*Rennie*	
—	*Smeaton*	
—	*Stephenson*	
—	*Telford*	
—	*Trevithick*	
—	*Victor Emanuel*	
—	*Victoria*	
—	*Watt*	

'Waverley' 4-4-0 (built 1855)

No	Name	Notes
—	*Abbot*	
—	*Antiquary*	
—	*Coeur de Lion*	
—	*Ivanhoe*	
—	*Lalla Rookh*	
—	*Pirate*	
—	*Red Gauntlet*	
—	*Robin Hood*	
—	*Rob Roy*	
—	*Waverley*	

GWR standard gauge named locomotives, by class

'9&10' 2–4–2T (built 1881–86)

No	Name	Notes
9	*Victoria*	
10	*Royal Albert*	

'34&35' 0–4–2T (built 1866)

No	Name	Notes
34	*Longmoor*	

'111' 4–6–2 (built 1908)

No	Name	Notes
111	*The Great Bear*	

'157' ('Cobham') 2–2–2 (built 1878–79)

No	Name	Notes
158	*Worcester*	
162	*Cobham*	
163	*Beaufort*	

'342' 0–4–2ST (built 1856)

No	Name	Notes
342	*Chester*	

'517' 0–4–2T (built 1868–85)

No	Name	Notes
1473	*Fair Rosamund*	

'850' 0–6–0ST (built 1874–95)

No	Name	Notes
1956	*Monty*	

'1076' 0–6–0ST (built 1870–81)

No	Name	Notes
1134	*Buffalo*	

'1490' 4–4–0PT (built 1898)

No	Name	Notes
35	*Dickinson*	*(also Brecon & Merthyr Railway)*

'1813' 0–6–0T (built 1882–84)

No	Name	Notes
7	*Holmwood*	*(also Pembroke & Tenby Railway)*

'3001'/'Achilles' 2–2–2 (built 1891–92)

No	Name	Notes
3001	*Amazon*	
3002	*Atlanta*	
3003	*Avalanche*	
3004	*Black Prince*	
3005	*Britannia*	
3006	*Courier*	
3007	*Dragon*	
3008	*Emperor*	
3009	*Flying Dutchman*	
3010	*Fire King*	
3011	*Greyhound*	
3012	*Great Western*	
3013	*Great Britain*	
3014	*Iron Duke*	
3015	*Kennet*	
3016	*Lightning*	
3017	*Nelson*	
3017*	*Prometheus*	
3018	*Racer*	
3019	*Rover*	
3020	*Sultan*	
3021	*Wigmore Castle*	
3022	*Rougemont*	
3022*	*Bessemer*	
3023	*Swallow*	
3024	*Storm King*	
3025	*St George*	
3025*	*Quicksilver*	
3026	*Tornado*	
3027	*Thames*	
3028	*Wellington*	
3029	*White Horse*	
3030	*Westward Ho*	

'Achilles' 2–2–2 (built 1892–99)

No	Name	Notes
3018*	*Glenside*	
3027*	*Worcester*	
3031	*Achilles*	
3032	*Agememnon*	
3033	*Albatross*	
3034	*Behemoth*	
3035	*Bellerophon*	
3035*	*Beaufort*	
3036	*Crusader*	
3037	*Corsair*	
3038	*Devonia*	
3039	*Dreadnought*	
3040	*Empress of India*	
3041	*Emlyn*	
3041*	*James Mason*	
3041*	*The Queen*	
3042	*Frederick Saunders*	
3044	*Hercules*	
3044	*Hurricane*	
3045	*Hirondelle*	
3046	*Lord of the Isles*	
3047	*Lorna Doone*	
3048	*Majestic*	
3049	*Prometheus*	
3049*	*Nelson*	
3050	*Royal Sovereign*	
3051	*Stormy Petrel*	
3052	*Sir Walter Rayleigh*	
3053	*Sir Francis Drake*	
3054	*Sir Richard Grenville*	
3055	*Trafalgar*	
3055*	*Lambert*	
3056	*Timour*	
3056*	*Wilkinson*	
3057	*Tartar*	
3057*	*Walter Robinson*	
3058	*Ulysses*	
3058*	*Grierson*	
3059	*Voltigeur*	
3059*	*John W. Wilson*	
3060	*Warlock*	
3060*	*John G. Griffiths*	
3061	*Alexandra*	
3061*	*George A. Wills*	
3062	*Albert Edward*	
3063	*Duke of York*	
3064	*Duke of Edinburgh*	
3065	*Duke of Connaught*	
3066	*Duchess of Albany*	
3067	*Duchess of Teck*	
3068	*Duke of Cambridge*	
3069	*Earl of Chester*	
3070	*Earl of Warwick*	
3071	*Emlyn*	
3072	*North Star*	
3072*	*Bulkeley*	
3073	*Princess Royal*	
3074	*Princess Helena*	
3075	*Princess Louise*	
3077	*Princess May*	
3078	*Shooting Star*	
3078*	*Eupatoria*	
3079	*Thunderbolt*	
3080	*Windsor Castle*	

'Armstrong' 4–4–0 (built 1894)

No	Name	Notes
7	*Charles Saunders*	
7*	*Armstrong*	
8	*Gooch*	
14	*Brunel*	
15	*Charles Saunders*	

'Atbara' 4–4–0 (built 1900–01)

No	Name	Notes
3373	*Atbara*	
3373*	*Maine*	
3373*	*Royal Sovereign*	
3374	*Baden Powell*	
3374*	*Britannia*	
3374*	*Kitchener*	
3374*	*Pretoria*	
3375	*Conqueror*	
3375*	*Colonel Edgcumbe*	
3375*	*Edgcumbe*	
3376	*Herschell*	
3377	*Kitchener*	
3378	*Khartoum*	
3379	*Kimberley*	
3380	*Ladysmith*	
3381	*Maine*	
3382	*Mafeking*	
3383	*Kekewich*	
3384	*Omdurman*	
3385	*Powerful*	
3386	*Pembroke*	
3387	*Roberts*	
3388	*Sir Redvers*	
3389	*Sir Daniel*	
3389*	*Pretoria*	
3390	*Terrible*	
3391	*Wolseley*	
3392	*White*	
3392*	*Powerful*	
3393	*Auckland*	
3394	*Adelaide*	
3395	*Aden*	
3396	*Brisbane*	
3397	*Cape Town*	
3398	*Columbo*	
3399	*Dunedin*	
3410	*Sydney*	
3411	*St Johns*	
3412	*Singapore*	

'Atbara'/'City' 4–4–0 (rebuilt 1902–09)

No	Name	Notes
3400	*Durban*	
3401	*Gibraltar*	
3402	*Halifax*	
3403	*Hobart*	
3404	*Lyttleton*	
3405	*Mauritius*	
3406	*Melbourne*	

No	Name	Notes
3407	*Malta*	
3408	*Ophir*	
3409	*Quebec*	

'Badminton' 4–4–0 (built 1897–99)

No	Name	Notes
3292	*Badminton*	
3293	*Barrington*	
3294	*Blenheim*	
3295	*Bessborough*	
3296	*Cambria*	
3297	*Earl Cawdor*	
3298	*Grosvenor*	
3299	*Hubbard*	
3299*	*Alexander Hubbard*	
3300	*Hotspur*	
3301	*Monarch*	
3302	*Mortimer*	
3302*	*Charles Mortimer*	
3303	*Marlborough*	
3304	*Oxford*	
3305	*Samson*	
3306	*Shelburne*	
3307	*Shrewsbury*	
3308	*Savernake*	
3309	*Shakespeare*	
3310	*Waterford*	
3311	*Wynnstay*	

'Bulldog' 4–4–0 (built 1899–1910)

No	Name	Notes
3253	*Dominion of Canada*	
3309*	*Maristowe*	
3332	*Avalon*	
3333	*Brasenose*	
3334	*Eclipse*	
3335	*Etona*	
3336	*Glastonbury*	
3337	*Kenilworth*	
3338	*Laira*	
3339	*Marco Polo*	
3340	*Marazion*	
3341	*Mars*	
3342	*Orion*	
3343	*Pegasus*	
3345	*Perseus*	
3347	*Tregothnan*	
3348	*Tavy*	
3348	*Titan*	
3349	*The Wolf*	
3350	*Swift*	
3351	*Sedgemoor*	
3352	*Camel*	
3353	*Blasius*	
3354	*Bonaventura*	
3355	*Camelot*	
3356	*Dartmouth*	
3357	*Exeter*	
3357*	*Royal Sovereign*	
3357*	*Smeaton*	
3358	*Godolphin*	
3359	*Kingsbridge*	
3360	*Launceston*	
3361	*Lyonesse*	
3362	*Newlyn*	
3363	*One and All*	
3364	*Pendragon*	
3365	*Pershore Plum*	
3365	*Pluto*	
3365	*Plymouth*	
3366	*Restormel*	
3367	*St Aubyn*	
3368	*Sir Stafford*	
3369	*Trelawny*	
3370	*Tremayne*	
3371	*Tregeagle*	
3372	*Torquay*	
3413	*Edward VII*	
3414	*Albert Brassey*	
3415	*Baldwin*	
3415*	*Alfred Baldwin*	
3416	*Bibby*	
3416*	*Frank Bibby*	
3417	*C. G. Mott*	
3417*	*Charles Grey Mott*	
3418	*Earl of Cork*	
3419	*Evan Llewellyn*	
3420	*Ernest Palmer*	

No	Name	Notes
3420*	*Sir Ernest Palmer*	
3421	*Mac Iver*	
3421*	*David Mac Iver*	
3422	*Sir John Llewelyn*	
3423	*Sir Massey*	
3423*	*Sir Massey Lopes*	
3424	*Sir Nigel*	
3424*	*Sir N. Kingscote*	
3425	*Sir W. H. Wills*	
3425*	*Sir William Henry*	
3426	*Walter Long*	
3427	*Sir Watkin Wynn*	
3428	*River Plym*	
3429	*Penzance*	
3430	*River Tawe*	
3431	*River Fal*	
3432	*River Yealm*	
3443	*Birkenhead*	
3444	*Cardiff*	
3445	*Ilfracombe*	
3446	*Liverpool*	
3446*	*Swindon*	
3447	*Newport*	
3448	*Paddington*	
3449	*Reading*	
3450	*Swansea*	
3451	*Taunton*	
3452	*Wolverhampton*	
3454	*New Zealand*	
3455	*Australia*	
3456	*Albany*	
3457	*Tasmania*	
3458	*Natal*	
3458*	*Natal Colony*	
3459	*Toronto*	
3460	*Montreal*	
3461	*Ottawa*	
3462	*Winnipeg*	
3463	*Vancouver*	
3464	*Jamaica*	
3465	*Trinidad*	
3466	*Barbados*	
3467	*Empire of India*	
3468	*Calcutta*	
3469	*Madras*	
3470	*Bombay*	
3471	*Queensland*	
3472	*Columbia*	
3701	*Stanley Baldwin*	
3702	*John G. Griffiths*	
3703	*James Mason*	
3704	*A. H. Mills*	
3704*	*Sir Edward Elgar*	
3705	*George A. Wills*	
3706	*John W. Wilson*	
3707	*Francis Mildmay*	
3707*	*Lord Mildmay of Flete*	
3708	*Sir Arthur Yorke*	
3712	*Aberystwyth*	
3720	*Inchcape*	
3724	*Joseph Shaw*	
3729	*Weston-super-Mare*	
3731	*Blackbird*	
3732	*Bullfinch*	
3733	*Chaffinch*	
3734	*Cormorant*	
3735	*Flamingo*	
3736	*Goldfinch*	
3737	*Jackdaw*	
3738	*Kingfisher*	
3739	*Nightingale*	
3740	*Peacock*	
3741	*Pelican*	
3742	*Penguin*	
3743	*Seagull*	
3744	*Skylark*	
3745	*Starling*	

'Castle' 4–6–0 (built 1923–50)

No	Name	Notes
100(*A1*)	*Lloyd's*	
111*	*Viscount Churchill*	
4016*	*The Somerset Light Infantry (Prince Albert's)*	
4037*	*The South Wales Borderers*	
4073	*Caerphilly Castle*	
4074	*Caldicot Castle*	

No	Name	Notes
4075	*Cardiff Castle*	
4076	*Carmarthen Castle*	
4077	*Chepstow Castle*	
4078	*Pembroke Castle*	
4079	*Pendennis Castle*	
4080	*Powderham Castle*	
4081	*Warwick Castle*	
4082	*Windsor Castle*	
4082*	*Bristol Castle*	
4083	*Abbotsbury Castle*	
4084	*Aberystwyth Castle*	
4085	*Berkeley Castle*	
4086	*Builth Castle*	
4087	*Cardigan Castle*	
4088	*Dartmouth Castle*	
4089	*Donnington Castle*	
4090	*Dorchester Castle*	
4091	*Dudley Castle*	
4092	*Dunraven Castle*	
4093	*Dunster Castle*	
4094	*Dynevor Castle*	
4095	*Harlech Castle*	
4096	*Highclere Castle*	
4097	*Kenilworth Castle*	
4098	*Kidwelly Castle*	
4099	*Kilgerran Castle*	
5000	*Launceston Castle*	
5001	*Llandovery Castle*	
5002	*Ludlow Castle*	
5003	*Lulworth Castle*	
5004	*Llanstephan Castle*	
5005	*Manorbier Castle*	
5006	*Tregenna Castle*	
5008	*Raglan Castle*	
5008	*Rougemont Castle*	
5009	*Shrewsbury Castle*	
5010	*Restormel Castle*	
5011	*Tintagel Castle*	
5012	*Berry Pomeroy Castle*	
5013	*Abergavenny Castle*	
5014	*Goodrich Castle*	
5015	*Kingswear Castle*	
5016	*Montgomery Castle*	
5017	*St Donats Castle*	
5017*	*The Gloucestershire Regiment 28th 61st*	
5018	*St Mawes Castle*	
5019	*Treago Castle*	
5020	*Tremanton Castle*	
5021	*Whittington Castle*	
5022	*Wigmore Castle*	
5023	*Brecon Castle*	
5024	*Carew Castle*	
5025	*Chirk Castle*	
5026	*Criccieth Castle*	
5027	*Farleigh Castle*	
5028	*Llantilio Castle*	
5029	*Nunney Castle*	
5030	*Shirburn Castle*	
5031	*Totnes Castle*	
5032	*Usk Castle*	
5033	*Broughton Castle*	
5034	*Corfe Castle*	
5035	*Coity Castle*	
5036	*Lyonshall Castle*	
5037	*Monmouth Castle*	
5038	*Morlais Castle*	
5039	*Rhuddlan Castle*	
5040	*Stokesay Castle*	
5041	*Tiverton Castle*	
5042	*Winchester Castle*	
5043	*Barbury Castle*	
5043*	*Earl of Mount Edgcumbe*	
5044	*Beverston Castle*	
5044*	*Earl of Dunraven*	
5045	*Bridgwater Castle*	
5045*	*Earl of Dudley*	
5046	*Clifford Castle*	
5046*	*Earl Cawdor*	
5047	*Compton Castle*	
5047*	*Earl of Dartmouth*	
5048	*Cranbrook Castle*	
5048*	*Earl of Devon*	
5049	*Denbigh Castle*	
5049*	*Earl of Plymouth*	
5050	*Devizes Castle*	
5050*	*Earl of St Germans*	

No	Name	Notes
5051	*Drysllwyn Castle*	
5051*	*Earl Bathurst*	
5052	*Eastnor Castle*	
5052*	*Earl of Radnor*	
5053	*Bishop's Castle*	
5053*	*Earl Cairns*	
5054	*Lamphey Castle*	
5054*	*Earl of Ducie*	
5055	*Lydford Castle*	
5055*	*Earl of Eldon*	
5056	*Ogmore Castle*	
5056*	*Earl of Powis*	
5057	*Penrice Castle*	
5057*	*Earl Waldegrave*	
5058	*Newport Castle*	
5058*	*Earl of Clancarty*	
5059	*Powis Castle*	
5059*	*Earl St Aldwyn*	
5060	*Sarum Castle*	
5060*	*Earl of Berkeley*	
5061	*Sudeley Castle*	
5061*	*Earl of Birkenhead*	
5062	*Tenby Castle*	
5062*	*Earl of Shaftesbury*	
5063	*Thornbury Castle*	
5063*	*Earl Baldwin*	
5064	*Tretower Castle*	
5064*	*Bishop's Castle*	
5065	*Newport Castle*	
5066	*Wardour Castle*	
5066*	*Sir Felix Pole*	
5067	*St. Fagans Castle*	
5068	*Beverston Castle*	
5069	*Isambard Kingdom Brunel*	
5070	*Sir Daniel Gooch*	
5071	*Clifford Castle*	
5071*	*Spitfire*	
5072	*Compton Castle*	
5072*	*Hurricane*	
5073	*Cranbrook Castle*	
5073*	*Blenheim*	
5074	*Denbigh Castle*	
5074*	*Hampden*	
5075	*Devizes Castle*	
5075*	*Wellington*	
5076	*Drysllwyn Castle*	
5076*	*Gladiator*	
5077	*Eastnor Castle*	
5077*	*Fairey Battle*	
5078	*Lamphey Castle*	
5078*	*Beaufort*	
5079	*Lydford Castle*	
5079*	*Lysander*	
5080	*Ogmore Castle*	
5080*	*Defiant*	
5081	*Penrice Castle*	
5081*	*Lockheed Hudson*	
5082	*Powis Castle*	
5082*	*Swordfish*	
5093	*Upton Castle*	
5094	*Tretower Castle*	
5095	*Barbury Castle*	
5096	*Bridgwater Castle*	
5097	*Sarum Castle*	
5098	*Clifford Castle*	
5099	*Compton Castle*	
6065	*Upton Castle*	
7000	*Viscount Portal*	
7001	*Denbigh Castle*	
7001*	*Sir James Milne*	
7002	*Devizes Castle*	
7003	*Elmley Castle*	
7004	*Eastnor Castle*	
7005	*Lamphey Castle*	
7005*	*Sir Edward Elgar*	
7006	*Lydford Castle*	
7007	*Ogmore Castle*	
7007*	*Great Western*	
7008	*Swansea Castle*	
7009	*Athelney Castle*	
7010	*Avondale Castle*	
7011	*Banbury Castle*	
7012	*Barry Castle*	
7013	*Bristol Castle*	
7013*	*Windsor Castle*	
7014	*Caerhays Castle*	

No	Name	Notes
7015	*Carn Brea Castle*	
7016	*Chester Castle*	
7017	*G. J. Churchward*	
7018	*Drysllwyn Castle*	
7019	*Fowey Castle*	
7020	*Gloucester Castle*	
7021	*Haverfordwest Castle*	
7022	*Hereford Castle*	
7023	*Penrice Castle*	
7024	*Powis Castle*	
7025	*Sudeley Castle*	
7026	*Tenby Castle*	
7027	*Thornbury Castle*	
7028	*Cadbury Castle*	
7029	*Clun Castle*	
7030	*Cranbrook Castle*	
7031	*Cromwell's Castle*	
7032	*Denbigh Castle*	
7033	*Hartlebury Castle*	
7034	*Ince Castle*	
7035	*Ogmore Castle*	
7036	*Taunton Castle*	
7037	*Swindon*	

'Chancellor' 2–4–0 (built 1862)

No	Name
154	*Chancellor*

'City' 4–4–0 (built 1901–03)

No	Name
3404*	*Lyttelton*
3408*	*Killarney*
3433	*City of Bath*
3434	*City of Birmingham*
3435	*City of Bristol*
3436	*City of Chester*
3437	*City of Gloucester*
3438	*City of Hereford*
3439	*City of London*
3440	*City of Truro*
3441	*City of Winchester*
3442	*City of Exeter*

'County' 4–4–0 (built 1904–12)

No	Name
3473	*County of Middlesex*
3474	*County of Berks*
3475	*County of Wilts*
3476	*County of Dorset*
3477	*County of Somerset*
3478	*County of Devon*
3479	*County of Warwick*
3480	*County of Stafford*
3481	*County of Glamorgan*
3482	*County of Pembroke*
3801	*County Carlow*
3802	*County Clare*
3803	*County Cork*
3804	*County Dublin*
3805	*County Kerry*
3806	*County Kildare*
3807	*County Kilkenny*
3808	*County Limerick*
3809	*County Wexford*
3810	*County Wicklow*
3811	*County of Bucks*
3812	*County of Cardigan*
3813	*County of Carmarthen*
3814	*County of Cheshire*
3814*	*County of Chester*
3815	*County of Hants*
3816	*County of Leicester*
3817	*County of Monmouth*
3818	*County of Radnor*
3819	*County of Salop*
3820	*County of Worcester*
3821	*County of Bedford*
3822	*County of Brecon*
3823	*County of Carnarvon*
3824	*County of Cornwall*
3825	*County of Denbigh*
3826	*County of Flint*
3827	*County of Gloucester*
3828	*County of Hereford*
3829	*County of Merioneth*
3830	*County of Oxford*

'County' 4–6–0 (built 1945–47)

No	Name	Notes
1000	*County of Middlesex*	
1001	*County of Bucks*	
1002	*County of Berks*	
1003	*County of Wilts*	
1004	*County of Somerset*	
1005	*County of Devon*	
1006	*County of Cornwall*	
1007	*County of Brecknock*	
1008	*County of Cardigan*	
1009	*County of Carmarthen*	
1010	*County of Carnarvon*	
1010*	*County of Caernarvon*	
1011	*County of Chester*	
1012	*County of Denbigh*	
1013	*County of Dorset*	
1014	*County of Glamorgan*	
1015	*County of Gloucester*	
1016	*County of Hants*	
1017	*County of Hereford*	
1018	*County of Leicester*	
1019	*County of Merioneth*	
1020	*County of Monmouth*	
1021	*County of Montgomery*	
1022	*County of Northampton*	
1023	*County of Oxford*	
1024	*County of Pembroke*	
1025	*County of Radnor*	
1026	*County of Salop*	
1027	*County of Stafford*	
1028	*County of Warwick*	
1029	*County of Worcester*	

'De Glehn Compound' 4–4–2 (built 1903–05)

No	Name
102	*La France*
103	*President*
104	*Alliance*

'Duke' 4–4–0 (built 1895–99)

No	Name
3252	*Duke of Cornwall*
3254	*Boscawen*
3255	*Cornurbia*
3256	*Exalibur*
3257	*Guinevere*
3258	*King Arthur*
3259	*Lizard*
3259*	*The Lizard*
3260	*Merlin*
3261	*Mount Edgcumbe*
3265	*St Germans*
3266	*St Ives*
3267	*St Michael*
3268	*Tamar*
3270	*Trevithick*
3272	*Amyas*
3274	*Cornishman*
3275	*Chough*
3276	*Dartmoor*
3277	*Earl of Devon*
3278	*Eddystone*
3281	*Fowey*
3282	*Chepstow Castle*
3283	*Mounts Bay*
3284	*Newquay*
3285	*St Erth*
3287	*St Agnes*
3288	*Tresco*
3288*	*Isle of Tresco*
3289	*Trefusis*
3290	*Torbay*
3290*	*Tor Bay*
3291	*Tregenna*
3313	*Cotswold*
3315	*Comet*
3316	*Guernsey*
3317	*Jersey*
3317*	*Isle of Jersey*
3319	*Katerfelto*
3320	*Meteor*
3323	*Mendip*
3323	*Mercury*
3326	*St Austell*
3328	*Severn*
3329	*Thames*

'Duke'/'Bulldog' 4–4–0 (rebuilt 1906)

No	Name
3263	*Sir Lancelot*
3264	*St Anthony*

No	Name	Notes
3268*	River Tamar	
3269	Tintagel	
3273	Armorel	
3280	Falmouth	
3282	Maristow	
3286	St Just	
3300	Pendennis Castle	
3301	Powderham	
3312	Bulldog	
3316*	Isle of Guernsey	
3318	Jupiter	
3322	Mersey	
3324	Quantock	
3325	St Columb	
3327	Somerset	
3330	Vulcan	
3331	Weymouth	

'Duke'/'Earl' 4–4–0 (rebuilt 1929)

No	Name	Notes
3265	Tre Pol and Pen	

'Earl' 4–4–0 (rebuilt 1936–39)

No	Name	Notes
3200	Earl of Mount Edgcumbe	
3201	St Michael	
3201*	Earl of Dunraven	
3202	Earl of Dudley	
3203	Earl Cawdor	
3204	Earl of Dartmouth	
3205	Earl of Devon	
3206	Earl of Plymouth	
3207	Earl of St Germans	
3208	Earl Bathurst	
3209	Earl of Radnor	
3210	Earl Cairns	
3211	Earl of Ducie	
3212	Earl of Eldon	

'Flower' 4–4–0 (built 1908)

No	Name	Notes
4101	Auricula	
4102	Begonia	
4103	Calceolaria	
4104	Calendula	
4105	Camellia	
4106	Campanula	
4107	Cineraria	
4108	Gardenia	
4109	Lobelia	
4110	Petunia	
4111	Anemone	
4112	Carnation	
4113	Hyacinthe	
4113*	Hyacinth	
4114	Marguerite	
4115	Marigold	
4116	Mignonette	
4117	Narcissus	
4118	Polyanthus	
4119	Primose	
4120	Stephanotis	

'Grange' 4–6–0 (built 1936–39)

No	Name	Notes
6800	Arlington Grange	
6801	Aylburton Grange	
6802	Bampton Grange	
6803	Bucklebury Grange	
6804	Brockinton Grange	
6805	Broughton Grange	
6806	Blackwell Grange	
6807	Birchwood Grange	
6808	Beenham Grange	
6809	Burghclere Grange	
6810	Blakemere Grange	
6811	Cranbourne Grange	
6812	Chesford Grange	
6813	Eastbury Grange	
6814	Enborne Grange	
6815	Frilford Grange	
6816	Frankton Grange	
6817	Gwenddwr Grange	
6818	Hardwick Grange	
6819	Highnam Grange	
6820	Kingstone Grange	
6821	Leaton Grange	
6822	Manton Grange	
6823	Oakley Grange	
6824	Ashley Grange	
6825	Llanvair Grange	
6826	Nannerth Grange	
6827	Llanfrecha Grange	
6828	Trellech Grange	
6829	Burmington Grange	
6830	Buckenhill Grange	
6831	Bearley Grange	
6832	Brockton Grange	
6833	Calcot Grange	
6834	Dummer Grange	
6835	Eastham Grange	
6836	Estevarney Grange	
6837	Forthampton Grange	
6838	Goodmoor Grange	
6839	Hewell Grange	
6840	Hazeley Grange	
6841	Marlas Grange	
6842	Nunhold Grange	
6843	Poulton Grange	
6844	Penhydd Grange	
6845	Paviland Grange	
6846	Ruckley Grange	
6847	Tidmarsh Grange	
6848	Toddington Grange	
6849	Walton Grange	
6850	Cleeve Grange	
6851	Hurst Grange	
6852	Headbourne Grange	
6853	Morehampton Grange	
6854	Roundhill Grange	
6855	Saighton Grange	
6856	Stowe Grange	
6857	Tudor Grange	
6858	Woolston Grange	
6859	Yiewsley Grange	
6860	Aberporth Grange	
6861	Cryant Grange	
6862	Derwent Grange	
6863	Dolhywel Grange	
6864	Dymock Grange	
6865	Hopton Grange	
6866	Morfa Grange	
6867	Peterston Grange	
6868	Penrhos Grange	
6869	Resolven Grange	
6870	Bodicote Grange	
6871	Bourton Grange	
6872	Crawley Grange	
6873	Caradoc Grange	
6874	Haughton Grange	
6875	Hindford Grange	
6876	Kingsland Grange	
6877	Llanfair Grange	
6878	Longford Grange	
6879	Overton Grange	

'Hall' 4–6–0 (built 1924–50)

No	Name	Notes
4901	Adderley Hall	
4902	Aldenham Hall	
4903	Astley Hall	
4904	Binnegar Hall	
4905	Barton Hall	
4906	Bradfield Hall	
4907	Broughton Hall	
4908	Broome Hall	
4909	Blakesley Hall	
4910	Blaisdon Hall	
4911	Bowden Hall	
4912	Berrington Hall	
4913	Baglan Hall	
4914	Cranmore Hall	
4915	Condover Hall	
4916	Crumlin Hall	
4917	Crosswood Hall	
4918	Dartington Hall	
4919	Donnington Hall	
4920	Dumbleton Hall	
4921	Eaton Hall	
4922	Enville Hall	
4923	Evenley Hall	
4924	Eydon Hall	
4925	Eynsham Hall	
4926	Fairleigh Hall	
4927	Farnborough Hall	
4928	Gatacre Hall	
4929	Goytrey Hall	
4930	Hagley Hall	
4931	Hanbury Hall	
4932	Hatherton Hall	
4933	Himley Hall	
4934	Hindlip Hall	
4935	Ketley Hall	
4936	Kinlet Hall	
4937	Lanelay Hall	
4938	Liddington Hall	
4939	Littleton Hall	
4940	Ludford Hall	
4941	Llangedwyn Hall	
4942	Maindy Hall	
4943	Marrington Hall	
4944	Middleton Hall	
4945	Milligan Hall	
4946	Moseley Hall	
4947	Nanhoran Hall	
4948	Northwick Hall	
4949	Packwood Hall	
4950	Patshull Hall	
4951	Pendeford Hall	
4952	Peplow Hall	
4953	Pitchford Hall	
4954	Plaish Hall	
4955	Plaspower Hall	
4956	Plowden Hall	
4957	Postlip Hall	
4958	Priory Hall	
4959	Purley Hall	
4960	Pyle Hall	
4961	Pyrland Hall	
4962	Ragley Hall	
4963	Rignall Hall	
4964	Rodwell Hall	
4965	Rood Ashton Hall	
4966	Shakenhurst Hall	
4967	Shirenewton Hall	
4968	Shotton Hall	
4969	Shrugborough Hall	
4970	Sketty Hall	
4971	Stanway Hall	
4972	St. Brides Hall	
4972*	Saint Brides Hall	
4973	Sweeney Hall	
4974	Talgarth Hall	
4975	Umberslade Hall	
4976	Warfield Hall	
4977	Watcombe Hall	
4978	Westwood Hall	
4979	Wootton Hall	
4980	Wrottesley Hall	
4981	Abberley Hall	
4982	Acton Hall	
4983	Albert Hall	
4984	Albrighton Hall	
4985	Allersley Hall	
4985*	Allesley Hall	
4986	Aston Hall	
4987	Brockley Hall	
4988	Bulwell Hall	
4989	Cherwell Hall	
4990	Clifton Hall	
4991	Cobham Hall	
4992	Crosby Hall	
4993	Dalton Hall	
4994	Downton Hall	
4995	Easton Hall	
4996	Eden Hall	
4997	Elton Hall	
4998	Eyton Hall	
4999	Gopsal Hall	
5900	Hinderton Hall	
5901	Hazel Hall	
5902	Howick Hall	
5903	Keele Hall	
5904	Kelham Hall	
5905	Knowsley Hall	
5906	Lawton Hall	
5907	Marble Hall	
5908	Moreton Hall	
5909	Newton Hall	
5910	Park Hall	
5911	Preston Hall	
5912	Queens Hall	

No	Name	Notes
5912*	*Queen's Hall*	
5913	*Rushton Hall*	
5914	*Ripon Hall*	
5915	*Trentham Hall*	
5916	*Trinity Hall*	
5917	*Westminster Hall*	
5918	*Walton Hall*	
5919	*Worsley Hall*	
5920	*Wycliffe Hall*	
5921	*Bingley Hall*	
5922	*Caxton Hall*	
5923	*Colston Hall*	
5924	*Dinton Hall*	
5925	*Eastcote Hall*	
5926	*Grotrian Hall*	
5927	*Guild Hall*	
5928	*Haddon Hall*	
5929	*Hanham Hall*	
5930	*Hannington Hall*	
5931	*Hatherley Hall*	
5932	*Haydon Hall*	
5933	*Kingsway Hall*	
5934	*Kneller Hall*	
5935	*Norton Hall*	
5936	*Oakley Hall*	
5937	*Stanford Hall*	
5938	*Stanley Hall*	
5939	*Tangley Hall*	
5940	*Whitbourne Hall*	
5941	*Campion Hall*	
5942	*Doldowlod Hall*	
5943	*Elmdon Hall*	
5944	*Ickenham Hall*	
5945	*Leckhampton Hall*	
5946	*Marwell Hall*	
5947	*Saint Benets Hall*	
5947*	*Saint Benet's Hall*	
5948	*Siddington Hall*	
5949	*Tremanton Hall*	
5950	*Wardley Hall*	
5951	*Clyffe Hall*	
5952	*Cogan Hall*	
5953	*Dunley Hall*	
5954	*Faendre Hall*	
5955	*Garth Hall*	
5956	*Horsley Hall*	
5957	*Hutton Hall*	
5958	*Knolton Hall*	
5959	*Mawley Hall*	
5960	*Saint Edmund Hall*	
5961	*Toynbee Hall*	
5962	*Wantage Hall*	
5963	*Wimpole Hall*	
5964	*Wolseley Hall*	
5965	*Woollas Hall*	
5966	*Ashford Hall*	
5967	*Bickmarsh Hall*	
5968	*Cory Hall*	
5969	*Honington Hall*	
5970	*Hengrave Hall*	
5971	*Merevale Hall*	
5972	*Olton Hall*	
5973	*Rolleston Hall*	
5974	*Wallsworth Hall*	
5975	*Winslow Hall*	
5976	*Ashwicke Hall*	
5977	*Beckford Hall*	
5978	*Bodinnick Hall*	
5979	*Cruckton Hall*	
5980	*Dingley Hall*	
5981	*Frensham Hall*	
5982	*Harrington Hall*	
5983	*Henley Hall*	
5984	*Linden Hall*	
5985	*Mostyn Hall*	
5986	*Arbury Hall*	
5987	*Brocket Hall*	
5988	*Bostock Hall*	
5989	*Cransley Hall*	
5990	*Dorford Hall*	
5991	*Gresham Hall*	
5992	*Horton Hall*	
5993	*Kirby Hall*	
5994	*Roydon Hall*	
5995	*Wick Hall*	
5996	*Mytton Hall*	
5997	*Sparkford Hall*	
5998	*Trevor Hall*	
5999	*Wollaton Hall*	
6900	*Abney Hall*	
6901	*Arley Hall*	
6902	*Butlers Hall*	
6903	*Belmont Hall*	
6904	*Charfield Hall*	
6905	*Claughton Hall*	
6906	*Chicheley Hall*	
6907	*Davenham Hall*	
6908	*Downham Hall*	
6909	*Frewin Hall*	
6910	*Gossington Hall*	
6911	*Holker Hall*	
6912	*Helmster Hall*	
6913	*Levens Hall*	
6914	*Langton Hall*	
6915	*Mursley Hall*	
6916	*Misterton Hall*	
6917	*Oldlands Hall*	
6918	*Sandon Hall*	
6919	*Tylney Hall*	
6920	*Barningham Hall*	
6921	*Borwick Hall*	
6922	*Burton Hall*	
6923	*Croxteth Hall*	
6924	*Grantley Hall*	
6925	*Hackness Hall*	
6926	*Holkham Hall*	
6927	*Lilford Hall*	
6928	*Underley Hall*	
6929	*Whorlton Hall*	
6930	*Aldersey Hall*	
6931	*Aldborough Hall*	
6932	*Burwarton Hall*	
6933	*Birtles Hall*	
6934	*Beachamwell Hall*	
6935	*Browsholme Hall*	
6936	*Breccles Hall*	
6937	*Conyngham Hall*	
6938	*Corndean Hall*	
6939	*Calveley Hall*	
6940	*Didlington Hall*	
6941	*Fillongley Hall*	
6942	*Eshton Hall*	
6943	*Farnley Hall*	
6944	*Fledborough Hall*	
6945	*Glasfryn Hall*	
6946	*Heatherden Hall*	
6947	*Helmingham Hall*	
6948	*Holbrooke Hall*	
6949	*Haberfield Hall*	
6950	*Kingsthorpe Hall*	
6951	*Impney Hall*	
6952	*Kimberley Hall*	
6953	*Leighton Hall*	
6954	*Lotherton Hall*	
6955	*Lydcott Hall*	
6956	*Mottram Hall*	
6957	*Norcliffe Hall*	
6958	*Oxburgh Hall*	
6959	*Peatling Hall*	
6960	*Raveningham Hall*	
6961	*Stedham Hall*	
6962	*Soughton Hall*	
6963	*Throwley Hall*	
6964	*Thornbridge Hall*	
6965	*Thirlestaine Hall*	
6966	*Witchingham Hall*	
6967	*Willesley Hall*	
6968	*Woodcock Hall*	
6969	*Wraysbury Hall*	
6970	*Whaddon Hall*	
6971	*Athelhampton Hall*	
6972	*Beningbrough Hall*	
6973	*Bricklehampton Hall*	
6974	*Bryngwyn Hall*	
6975	*Capesthorne Hall*	
6976	*Graythwaite Hall*	
6977	*Grundisburgh Hall*	
6978	*Haroldstone Hall*	
6979	*Helperly Hall*	
6980	*Llanrumney Hall*	
6981	*Marbury Hall*	
6982	*Melmerby Hall*	
6983	*Otterington Hall*	
6984	*Owsden Hall*	
6985	*Parwick Hall*	
6986	*Rydal Hall*	
6987	*Shervington Hall*	
6988	*Swithland Hall*	
6989	*Wightwick Hall*	
6990	*Witherslack Hall*	
6991	*Acton Burnell Hall*	
6992	*Arborfield Hall*	
6993	*Arthog Hall*	
6994	*Baggrave Hall*	
6995	*Benthal Hall*	
6996	*Blackwell Hall*	
6997	*Bryn-Ivor Hall*	
6998	*Burton Agnes Hall*	
6999	*Capel Dewi Hall*	
7900	*Saint Peter's Hall*	
7901	*Dodington Hall*	
7902	*Eaton Mascot Hall*	
7903	*Foremarke Hall*	
7904	*Fountains Hall*	
7905	*Fowey Hall*	
7906	*Fron Hall*	
7907	*Hart Hall*	
7908	*Henshall Hall*	
7909	*Heveningham Hall*	
7910	*Hown Hall*	
7911	*Lady Margaret Hall*	
7912	*Little Linford Hall*	
7913	*Little Wyrley Hall*	
7914	*Lleweni Hall*	
7915	*Mere Hall*	
7916	*Mobberley Hall*	
7917	*North Aston Hall*	
7918	*Rhose Wood Hall*	
7919	*Runter Hall*	
7920	*Coney Hall*	
7921	*Edstone Hall*	
7922	*Salford Hall*	
7923	*Speke Hall*	
7924	*Thornycroft Hall*	
7925	*Westol Hall*	
7926	*Willey Hall*	
7927	*Willington Hall*	
7928	*Wolf Hall*	
7929	*Wyke Hall*	

'King' 4–6–0 (built 1927–36)

No	Name
6000	*King George V*
6001	*King Edward VII*
6002	*King William IV*
6003	*King George IV*
6004	*King George III*
6005	*King George II*
6006	*King George I*
6007	*King William III*
6008	*King James II*
6009	*King Charles II*
6010	*King Charles I*
6011	*King James I*
6012	*King Edward VI*
6013	*King Henry VIII*
6014	*King Henry VII*
6015	*King Richard III*
6016	*King Edward V*
6017	*King Edwrd IV*
6018	*King Henry VI*
6019	*King Henry V*
6020	*King Henry IV*
6021	*King Richard II*
6022	*King Edward III*
6023	*King Edward II*
6024	*King Edward I*
6025	*King Henry III*
6026	*King John*
6027	*King Richard I*
6028	*King Henry II*
6028*	*King George VI*
6029	*King Stephen*
6029*	*King Edward VIII*

'Manor' 4–6–0 (built 1938–50)

No	Name
7800	*Torquay Manor*
7801	*Anthony Manor*

No	Name	Notes
7802	*Bradley Manor*	
7803	*Barcote Manor*	
7804	*Baydon Manor*	
7805	*Broome Manor*	
7806	*Cockington Manor*	
7807	*Compton Manor*	
7808	*Cookham Manor*	
7809	*Childrey Manor*	
7810	*Draycott Manor*	
7811	*Dunley Manor*	
7812	*Erlestoke Manor*	
7813	*Freshford Manor*	
7814	*Fringford Manor*	
7815	*Fritwell Manor*	
7816	*Frilsham Manor*	
7817	*Garsington Manor*	
7818	*Granville Manor*	
7819	*Hinton Manor*	
7820	*Dinmore Manor*	
7821	*Ditcheat Manor*	
7822	*Foxcote Manor*	
7823	*Hook Norton Manor*	
7824	*Iford Manor*	
7825	*Lechlade Manor*	
7826	*Longworth Manor*	
7827	*Lydham Manor*	
7828	*Odney Manor*	
7829	*Ramsbury Manor*	

'Queen' 2–2–2 (built 1873–75)

No	Name	Notes
55	*Queen*	
999	*Sir Alexander*	
1118	*Prince Christian*	
1119	*Princess of Wales*	
1122	*Beaconsfield*	
1123	*Salisbury*	
1128	*Duke of York*	
1129	*Princess May*	
1130	*Gooch*	
1132	*Prince of Wales*	

'River' 2–4–0 (built 1895–97)

No	Name	Notes
69	*Avon*	
70	*Dart*	
71	*Dee*	
72	*Exe*	
73	*Isis*	
74	*Stour*	
75	*Teign*	
76	*Wye*	

'Saint' 4–6–0 (built 1902–13)

No	Name	Notes
98	*Vanguard*	
98*	*Ernest Cunard*	
100	*Dean*	
100*	*William Dean*	
171	*Albion*	
171*	*The Pirate*	
172	*Quicksilver*	
172*	*The Abbot*	
173	*Robins Bolitho*	
174	*Barrymore*	
174*	*Lord Barrymore*	
175	*Viscount Churchill*	
175*	*Lord Palmer*	
175*	*Sir Ernest Palmer*	
176	*Winterstoke*	
177	*Robertson*	
178	*Charles J. Hambro*	
178*	*Kirkland*	
179	*Magnet*	
179*	*Quentin Durward*	
180	*Coeur de Lion*	
181	*Ivanhoe*	
182	*Lalla Rookh*	
183	*Red Gauntlet*	
184	*Churchill*	
184*	*Guy Mannering*	
184*	*Viscount Churchill*	
185	*Winterstoke*	
186	*Robin Hood*	
187	*Robertson*	
187*	*Bride of Lammermoor*	
2901	*Lady Superior*	
2902	*Lady of the Lake*	
2903	*Lady of Lyons*	
2904	*Lady Godiva*	
2905	*Lady Macbeth*	
2906	*Lady of Lynn*	
2907	*Lady Disdain*	
2908	*Lady of Quality*	
2909	*Lady of Provence*	
2910	*Lady of Shalott*	
2911	*Saint Augusta*	
2912	*Saint Ambrose*	
2913	*Saint Andrew*	
2914	*Saint Augustine*	
2915	*Saint Bartholomew*	
2916	*Saint Benedict*	
2917	*Saint Bernard*	
2918	*Saint Catherine*	
2919	*Saint Cecilia*	
2920	*Saint David*	
2921	*Saint Dunstan*	
2922	*Saint Gabriel*	
2923	*Saint George*	
2924	*Saint Helena*	
2926	*Saint Nicholas*	
2927	*Saint Patrick*	
2928	*Saint Sebastian*	
2929	*Saint Stephen*	
2929*	*Saint Cuthbert*	
2930	*Saint Vincent*	
2931	*Arlington Court*	
2932	*Ashton Court*	
2933	*Bibury Court*	
2934	*Butleigh Court*	
2935	*Caynham Court*	
2936	*Cefntilla Court*	
2937	*Clevedon Court*	
2938	*Corsham Court*	
2939	*Croome Court*	
2940	*Dorney Court*	
2941	*Easton Court*	
2942	*Fawley Court*	
2943	*Hampton Court*	
2944	*Highnam Court*	
2945	*Hillingdon Court*	
2946	*Langford Court*	
2947	*Madresfield Court*	
2948	*Stackpole Court*	
2949	*Stanford Court*	
2950	*Taplow Court*	
2951	*Tawstock Court*	
2952	*Twineham Court*	
2953	*Titley Court*	
2954	*Tockenham Court*	
2955	*Tortworth Court*	
2983*	*Redgauntlet*	
2985*	*Peveril of the Peak*	
2988	*Rob Roy*	
2989	*Talisman*	
2990	*Waverley*	
2998*	*Persimmon*	

'Saint'/'Hall' 4–6–0 (rebuilt 1924)

No	Name	Notes
2925	*Saint Martin*	

'Sir Daniel' 2–2–2 (built 1866–69)

No	Name	Notes
378	*Sir Daniel*	
380	*North Star*	
381	*Morning Star*	
471	*Sir Watkin*	

'Star' 4–6–0 (built 1906–23)

No	Name	Notes
4001	*Dog Star*	
4002	*Evening Star*	
4003	*Lode Star*	
4004	*Morning Star*	
4005	*Polar Star*	
4006	*Red Star*	
4007	*Rising Star*	
4007*	*Swallowfield Park*	
4008	*Royal Star*	
4009	*Shooting Star*	
4010	*Western Star*	
4011	*Knight of the Garter*	
4012	*Knight of the Thistle*	
4013	*Knight of St Patrick*	
4014	*Knight of the Bath*	
4015	*Knight of St John*	
4017	*Knight of the Black Eagle*	
4017*	*Knight of Liège*	
4017*	*Knight of Liége*	
4018	*Knight of the Grand Cross*	
4019	*Knight Templar*	
4020	*Knight Commander*	
4021	*King Edward*	
4021*	*The British Monarch*	
4021*	*British Monarch*	
4022	*King William*	
4022*	*Belgian Monarch*	
4022*	*The Belgian Monarch*	
4023	*King George*	
4023*	*Danish Monarch*	
4023*	*The Danish Monarch*	
4024	*King James*	
4024*	*Dutch Monarch*	
4024*	*The Dutch Monarch*	
4025	*King Charles*	
4025*	*Italian Monarch*	
4026	*King Richard*	
4026*	*Japanese Monarch*	
4026*	*The Japanese Monarch*	
4027	*King Henry*	
4027*	*Norwegian Monarch*	
4027*	*The Norwegian Monarch*	
4028	*King John*	
4028*	*Roumanian Monarch*	
4028*	*The Roumanian Monarch*	
4029	*King Stephen*	
4029*	*Spanish Monarch*	
4029*	*The Spanish Monarch*	
4030	*King Harold*	
4030*	*Swedish Monarch*	
4030*	*The Swedish Monarch*	
4031	*Queen Mary*	
4033	*Queen Victoria*	
4034	*Queen Adelaide*	
4035	*Queen Charlotte*	
4036	*Queen Elizabeth*	
4038	*Queen Berengaria*	
4039	*Queen Matilda*	
4040	*Queen Boadicea*	
4041	*Prince of Wales*	
4042	*Prince Albert*	
4043	*Prince Henry*	
4044	*Prince George*	
4045	*Prince John*	
4046	*Princess Mary*	
4047	*Princess Louise*	
4048	*Princess Victoria*	
4048*	*Princess Mary*	
4049	*Princess Maud*	
4050	*Princess Alice*	
4051	*Princess Helena*	
4052	*Princess Beatrice*	
4053	*Princess Alexandra*	
4054	*Princess Charlotte*	
4055	*Princess Sophia*	
4056	*Princess Margaret*	
4057	*Princess Elizabeth*	
4058	*Princess Augusta*	
4059	*Princess Patricia*	
4060	*Princess Eugenie*	
4061	*Glastonbury Abbey*	
4062	*Malmesbury Abbey*	
4066	*Malvern Abbey*	
4066*	*Sir Robert Horne*	
4069	*Margam Abbey*	

'Star'/'Castle' 4–6–0 (rebuilt 1924–29)

No	Name	Notes
40	*North Star*	
4016	*Knight of the Golden Fleece*	
4032	*Queen Alexandra*	
4037	*Queen Philippa*	
4063	*Bath Abbey*	
4064	*Reading Abbey*	
4065	*Evesham Abbey*	
4066*	*Viscount Horne*	
4067	*Tintern Abbey*	
4068	*Llanthony Abbey*	
4069*	*Westminster Abbey*	
4070	*Neath Abbey*	
4071	*Cleeve Abbey*	
4072	*Tresco Abbey*	

'Stella' 2–4–0 (built 1884–85)

No	Name	Notes
8	*Stella (also Pembroke & Tenby Railway)*	

No	Name	Notes

Miscellaneous

Crane tank 0–6–4PT (built 1901–21)

No	Name	Notes
16	*Hercules*	
17	*Cyclops*	
18	*Steropes*	

Steam Railmotor (built 1905)

No	Name	Notes
15	*Hill*	

Sentinel 4-wheel VBT (built 1926)

No	Name	Notes
12	*Isebrook*	

APPENDIX D

The GWR preserved (including stocklist of preserved locomotives)

Although much smaller than either the LMS or LNER, there are far more preserved GWR locomotives, carriages and wagons than those of the other 'Big Four' companies. Also, the GWR is the only one which has a society devoted solely to preserving as wide a spectrum as possible of its artefacts from working locomotives to tickets.

In 1981 one writer listed 107 preserved GWR steam locomotives, 69 LMS, 52 SR, 32 LNER and 29 BR. In 1983 the RCTS recorded 153 GWR steam locomotives still in existence. One can argue about the total and whether various replica 'singles', such as *North Star* built for the 1935 Centenary, Madame Tussaud's *Queen* of 1983, *Iron Duke* built by the NRM in 1985 and *Fire Fly* currently building at Didcot, should be included, but not, surely, the 14 GWR-design engines turned out by British Railways. Nor can we include the Nord 4-4-2 at Mulhouse, or the Robinson 2-8-0 in the National Collection, although examples of both types were owned by the GWR. It is perhaps safest to say that there are in excess of 150 GWR-design steam locomotives preserved, although by no means all are in working order.

The first GWR engine to be preserved was Gooch's *North Star* of 1837, the second his *Lord of the Isles* of 1851. Both were inexplicably scrapped in 1906, though parts of the former reappeared in the 1935 replica. The sole Broad Gauge survivor was No 2180 *Tiny*, a vertical boiler 0-4-0T built by Sara & Co of Plymouth in January 1868 for the South Devon Railway. It stood from 1927 until 1980 on Newton Abbot station; it is now at Buckfastleigh.

The Dean/Churchward record breaking 4-4-0 No 3440 *City of Truro* was the first standard gauge GWR engine to be preserved, entering the old LNER York Museum in March 1931. Next came 'Star' Class 4-6-0 No 4003 *Lode Star*. Withdrawn in July 1951 and later restored at Swindon to its original 1907 condition, it was not put on public display until the GWR Museum, Faringdon Road, Swindon, opened in June 1962. In 1961 the Consultative Panel on railway historical relics scheduled 71 locomotives for preservation, a mere eight from the GWR. Apart from the *North Star* replica, *City of Truro* and *Lode Star*, these were a Dean Goods 0-6-0, a '28xx' 2-8-0, a '94xx' pannier tank, *Caerphilly Castle* and *King George V*.

Amongst those horrified at such meagre recognition of 'God's Wonderful Railway' were four 16-year-old West London schoolboys, Jon Barlow, Angus Davis, Mike Peart and Graham Perry. Jon wrote a letter which was published in the August 1961 *Railway Magazine* appealing for funds to preserve a '14xx' 0-4-2T and an auto-trailer. On 18 March 1964, No 1466 was duly bought and later in the year auto-trailer No 231 joined it. Thus the Great Western Society, as the group had become in May 1962, was formed. Today at its base at Didcot Railway Centre there are presently 21 GWR-designed steam locomotives ranging from pannier tanks to 'Kings', 42 GWR-designed carriages, a GWR diesel railcar, 33 GWR-designed wagons and vans, a complete GWR engine shed, a transfer shed built for transferring freight from broad to standard gauge wagons, two signal boxes (from Frome and Radstock, the latter in full working order), a complex network of standard and broad gauge track, a branch-line halt, another station under construction, a Small Relics Museum housing a priceless collection of GWR memorabilia ranging from sports club colours through tickets and waybills to a complete office, and much else.

No railway, probably anywhere in the world, has had its history so faithfully recorded and brought to life. The Severn Valley Railway Society was founded in July 1965 and on 23 May 1970 its first train, consisting of Collett 0-6-0 No 3205 and four GWR carriages, ran the 4½ miles from Bridgnorth to Hampton Loade. Now Severn Valley trains run 15 miles from Bridgnorth to Kidderminster, and in 1989 the railway had a turnover in excess of £2 million, a milestone in the railway preservation movement. The majority of its steam engines are of GWR origin: there are two 'Halls', three 'Manors', a 2-8-0, a 2-6-0, four 2-6-2Ts, and four 0-6-0Ts. The majority of its 27 GWR-design carriages are in everyday use and many of its 29 wagons are run in demonstration goods trains. Its wonderfully restored stations have won many awards.

Equally fine are the B&ER-built stations of the West Somerset Railway. Stretching 19¾ miles from Taunton to Minehead, it is the longest preserved railway in Britain. It has three working GWR engines, including the pioneer Severn Valley No 3205, now permanently transferred, and a number of former 'Toplight' camping carriages in departmental service.

The Dart Valley Railway began operations between Buckfastleigh and Totnes in May 1969 and was able to acquire a number of GWR engines and carriages straight from BR service. Three years later the company took over the Paignton to Kingswear branch, its steam trains replacing BR diesel ones without the line actually closing, a unique situation. A 'Manor', a '52xx' 2-8-0T, two '45xx' 2-6-2Ts, three pannier tanks and two '14xx' 0-4-2Ts have worked at various times, the larger engines usually on the Torbay line. The Dart Valley also possesses some fine GWR carriages, but seldom uses them in ordinary service.

The Dean Forest Railway, which is based at Norchard, near Lydney, has a number of former GWR engines and carriages some in working order, whilst the Gloucester Warwickshire Railway on the former Birmingham to Cheltenham main line, and the Swindon & Cricklade Railway on a portion of the former M&SWJR, both have GWR locomotives undergoing restoration, together with some carriages formerly in BR departmental use.

The long-established Birmingham

Railway Museum is based at the former GWR Tyseley shed. It regularly sends out the only restored double-chimney Castle, No 7029 *Clun Castle*, and the single-chimney No 5080 *Defiant* on main-line runs. It also has a working pannier tank, one or two GWR-design carriages and other GWR engines awaiting restoration. It is hoped that the now closed Moor Street station in Birmingham, into which Tyseley-based engines have occasionally worked, may be restored and be used in conjunction with the Birmingham Railway Museum. Further north, a 'Manor' 4-6-0 works on the picturesque Llangollen Railway, once part of the GWR's route to Barmouth.

Former GWR engines, some in working order, some not yet restored, can also be seen on the Great Central Railway at Loughborough, on the North Yorkshire Moors Railway, on the East Lancashire Railway and at Bodmin, Southall, Quainton Road, Wallingford, Cranmore, Tiverton, Caerphilly, Blaenavon, Hereford, Telford, Southport, Carnforth, the Science Museum in London, and the National Railway Museum at York. 'King', 'Castle', 'Hall' and 'Manor' 4-6-0s once again hauled expresses on the West of England main line in 1985 during the 150th anniversary celebrations, and GWR-designed engines can regularly be seen on enthusiasts' specials working over BR tracks out of Didcot and elsewhere. The Vale of Rheidol Railway operates three 1 ft 11½ in gauge locomotives built or rebuilt at Swindon plus rakes of GWR-built carriages, whilst there are other narrow gauge concerns in Wales with GWR connections, notably the Welshpool & Llanfair. Finally, abroad there is *Pendennis Castle* in Australia.

List compiled by Michael H.C. Baker, updated to February 1993 by Peter Nicholson.

Stocklist of surviving GWR locomotives, and their locations as at February 1993.

Named locomotives

Class No	Name	Location
'Castle' 4–6–0		
4073	*Caerphilly Castle*	Science Museum, London
4079	*Pendennis Castle*	Hammersley Iron Mine, Australia
5029	*Nunney Castle*	Didcot
5043	*Earl of Mount Edgcumbe*	Tyseley
5051	*Drysllwyn Castle*	Didcot
5080	*Defiant*	Tyseley
7027	*Thornbury Castle*	Tyseley
7029	*Clun Castle*	Tyseley
'City' 4–4–0		
3440	*City of Truro*	NRM, York
'Hall' 4–6–0		
4920	*Dumbleton Hall*	Paignton & Dartmouth Steam Railway
4930	*Hagley Hall*	Severn Valley Railway
4936	*Kinlet Hall*	Llangollen
4942	*Maindy Hall*	Didcot
4953	*Pitchford Hall*	Crewe
4979	*Wootton Hall*	Fleetwood
4983	*Albert Hall*	Tyseley
5900	*Hinderton Hall*	Didcot
5952	*Cogan Hall*	Llangollen
5967	*Bickmarsh Hall*	Blaenavon
5972	*Olton Hall*	Procor (UK) Ltd, Wakefield
'Modified Hall' 4–6–0		
6960	*Raveningham Hall*	Severn Valley Railway
6984	*Owsden Hall*	Bicester
6989	*Wightwick Hall*	Quainton Road
6990	*Witherslack Hall*	Great Central Railway
6998	*Burton Agnes Hall*	Didcot
7903	*Foremark Hall*	Swindon & Cricklade Railway
7927	*Willington Hall*	Cardiff Bute Road
'King' 4–6–0		
6000	*King George V*	Swindon
6023	*Kind Edward II*	Didcot
6024	*King Edward I*	Didcot
'Manor' 4–6–0		
7802	*Bradley Manor*	Severn Valley Railway
7808	*Cookham Manor*	Didcot
7812	*Erlestoke Manor*	Severn Valley Railway
7819	*Hinton Manor*	Severn Valley Railway
7820	*Dinmore Manor*	Tyseley
7821	*Ditcheat Manor*	Llangollen
7822	*Foxcote Manor*	Llangollen
7827	*Lydham Manor*	Paignton & Dartmouth Steam Railway
7828	*Odney Manor*	East Lancashire Railway
'Star' 4–6–0		
4003	*Lode Star*	NRM, York
'32xx' 4–4–0		
3217	*Earl of Berkeley*	Bluebell Railway

Unnamed locomotives

Class/No	Location
'1361' 0–6–0ST	
1363	Didcot
'1366' 0–6–0PT	
1369	South Devon Railway
'14xx' 0–4–2T	
1420	South Devon Railway
1442	Tiverton Museum
1450	South Devon Railway
1466	Didcot
'15xx' 0–6–0PT	
1501	Severn Valley Railway
'16xx' 0–6–0PT	
1501	Kent & East Sussex Railway
'2251' 0–6–0	
3205	West Somerset Railway
'2301' 0–6–0	
2516	Swindon
'28xx' 2–8–0	
2807	Gloucestershire Warwickshire Railway
2818	NRM, York
2857	Severn Valley Railway
2859	Llangollen
2861	Cardiff Bute Road
2873	Tyseley (dismantled for spares)
2874	Blaenavon
2885	Southall
3802	Bodmin
3803	Tyseley
3814	Grosmont
3822	Didcot
3845	Brighton
3850	West Somerset Railway
3855	Blaenavon
3862	Pitsford
'42xx' 2–8–0T	
4247	Cholsey & Wallingford Railway
4248	Brightlingsea
4253	Blaenavon
4270	Llansamlet
4277	Private site
'5205' 2–8–0T	
5224	Great Central Railway
5227	Cardiff Bute Road
5239	Paignton & Dartmouth Steam Railway
'43xx' 2–6–0	
5322	Didcot
'45xx' 2–6–2T	
4555	Paignton & Dartmouth Steam Railway
4561	West Somerset Railway
4566	Severn Valley Railway
4588	Paignton & Dartmouth Steam Railway
5521	Swindon
5526	Swindon
5532	Llangollen
5538	Barry
5539	Cardiff Bute Road
5541	Dean Forest Railway
5542	West Somerset Railway
5552	Bodmin
5553	Private site (Midlands)
5572	Didcot
'51xx' 2–6–2T	
4110	Southall
4115	Cardiff Bute Road
4121	Crewe
4141	Crewe
4144	Didcot
4150	Severn Valley Railway

4160	West Somerset Railway
5164	Severn Valley Railway
5193	Southport
5199	Long Marston

'56xx' 0–6–2T

5619	Gloucestershire Warwickshire Railway
5637	Swindon & Cricklade Railway
5643	Lakeside & Haverthwaite Railway
5668	Blaenavon
6619	North York Moors Railway
6634	East Somerset Railway
6686	Cardiff Bute Road
6695	Swanage Railway
6697	Didcot

'57xx' 0–6–0PT

3650	Didcot
3738	Didcot
4612	Swindon
5764	Severn Valley Railway
5775	Keighley & Worth Valley Railway
5786	Hereford
7714	Severn Valley Railway
7715	Quainton Road
7752	Tyseley
7754	Llangollen
7760	Tyseley

'8750' 0–6–0PT

9600	Tyseley
9629	Cardiff
9642	Llansamlet
9681	Dean Forest Railway
9682	Southall

'61xx' 2–6–2T

6106	Didcot

'64xx' 0–6–0PT

6412	West Somerset Railway
6430	Long Marston
6435	Paignton & Dartmouth Steam Railway

'72xx' 2–8–2T

7200	Quainton Road
7202	Didcot
7229	East Lancashire Railway

'93xx' 2–6–0

9303	Severn Valley Railway

'94xx' 0–6–0PT

9400	Swindon
9466	Quainton Road

Absorbed companies' locomotives

Cardiff Railway 0–4–0ST

1338	Didcot

Alexandra Docks & Railway 0-4-0ST

1340 *Trojan*	Didcot

Powlesland & Mason 0-4-0ST

921	Coalville

Taff Vale Railway '01' Class 0-6-2T

450	Caerphilly

Taff Vale Railway '02' Class 0-6-2T

426	Keighley & Worth Valley Railway

Port Talbot Railway & Docks 0-6-0ST

813	Severn Valley Railway

North Pembrokeshire & Fishguard Railways 0-6-0ST

1378 Margaret	Haverfordwest

Wantage Tramway 0-4-0WT

5 *Shannon*	Didcot

Broad gauge locomotives

South Devon Railway 0-4-0WT

2180 *Tiny*	South Devon Railway

Narrow gauge locomotives

Vale of Rheidol 2-6-2T

7 *Owain Glyndwr*	Vale of Rheidol Railway
8 *Llywelyn*	"
9 *Prince of Wales*	"

Corris Railway 0-4-2T

3 *Sir Haydn*	Talyllyn Railway
4 *Edward Thomas*	"

Welshpool & Llanfair Railway 0-6-0T

822 *The Earl*	Welshpool
823 *The Countess*	"

Diesel railcars

4	Swindon
20	Kent & East Sussex Railway
22	Didcot

Full-size replicas

Broad gauge 4-2-2

Iron Duke	NRM, York

Broad gauge 2-2-2

Fire Fly	Didcot
North Star	Swindon

'3001' 4-2-2

3041 *The Queen*	Windsor

No 5080 Defiant *making a guest appearance on the Gloucester Warwickshire Railway, October 1990.* (W. Adams)

APPENDIX E

Bibliography

The following bibliography contains a selection of the most important of the many books dealing with the Great Western Railway and its constituents. For a fuller bibliography, readers are referred to *A Bibliography of British Railway History* by George Ottley (HMSO, 2nd ed 1983, Supplement 1988) which lists a huge number of books and other contemporary reference sources. The following list has been divided, sometimes rather arbitrarily, into subject headings.

History

Allen, C. J. *Great Western* (Ian Allan, 1962)

Awdry, Christopher *Brunel's Broad Gauge Railway* (OPC, 1992)

Barman, C. *The Great Western Railway's Last Look Forward* (David & Charles, 1972)—a reprint of *Next Station* (Allen & Unwin, 1947)

Behrend, G. *Gone With Regret* (Lambarde Press, 1964; 3rd ed rev by N. Spearman for Jersey Artists, 1969)

Booker, F. *Great Western Railway: a New History* (David & Charles, 1977)

Bryan, T. *The Golden Age of the Great Western Railway: 1895-1914* (Patrick Stephens Ltd, 1991)

Clinker, C.R. *New Light on the Gauge Conversion* (Avon-Anglia, 1978)

Cooke, R.A. *Atlas of the Great Western Railway as at 1947* (Wild Swan, 1988)

Gale, P.R. *GWR: Routes, Statutes, Opening Dates and Other Particulars* (Avon-Anglia, 1986)

Gibbs, G.H. (ed Jack Simmons) *The Birth of the Great Western Railway* (pub 1910, new ed Adams & Dart, 1971) —extracts from Gibbs's diary and correspondence

GWR *Great Western Progress, 1835-1935* (London, 1935, reprinted David & Charles, 1972)

Kingdom, A.R. *The Great Western at the Turn of the Century* (OPC, 1976)

MacDermot, E.T. and Clinker, C.R. *History of the Great Western Railway,* Vol 1 *1833-1863,* Vol 2 *1863-1921* (Ian Allan, rev ed 1964)—see also Vol 3 by O.S. Nock below

Nock, O.S. *History of the Great Western Railway,* Vol 3 *1923-1947* (Ian Allan, 1967)

The Great Western Railway in the Nineteenth Century (Ian Allan, 1962)

The Great Western Railway in the Twentieth Century (Ian Allan, 1964)

Sekon, G.A. *A History of the Great Western Railway: being the story of the broad gauge* (Digby Long, 1895)

Semmens, P.W.B. *History of the Great Western Railway,* Vol 1 *Consolidation,* Vol 2 *The Thirties,* Vol 3 *Wartime and the Final years* (George Allen & Unwin, 1985)

Vaughan, A. *The Great Western at Work 1921-1939* (OPC, 1993)

Great Western Junction Stations (Ian Allan, 1988).

Lines, locations and constituent companies

Anthony, G.H. *The Tavistock, Launceston and Princetown Railways* (Oakwood, 1971—Library of Rly History No 29)

Atkinson, J.B. *The West London Joint Railways* (Ian Allan, 1984)

Barrie, D.S.M. *The Barry Railway* (Oakwood 1962, Library of Rly History No 57)

South Wales (Vol 12, Regional History of the Railways of Great Britain) (David & Charles, 1980)

The Taff Vale Railway (Oakwood, 2nd ed 1950—Library of Rly History No 2)

The Rhymney Railway (Oakwood, 1952—Library of Rly History No 9)

Baughan, P.E. *North and Mid Wales* (Vol 11, Regional History of the Railways of Great Britain) (David & Charles, 1980)

Beck, K.M. *Great Western North of Wolverhampton* (Ian Allan, 1986)

Bick, D.E. *The Gloucester and Cheltenham Railway and the Leckhampton Quarry Tramroads* (Oakwood, 1968—Locomotion Papers No 43)

Body, G. *The Cornwall Railway* (BR(W) and Avon–Anglia, 1984)

PSL Field Guide to the Railways of the Western Region (Patrick Stephens Ltd, 1983)

Borley, H.V. and Kidner, R.W. *The West London Railway and the WLER* (Oakwood, 1969—Library of Rly History No 22)

Chapman, C. *The Cowbridge Railway* (OPC, 1984)

Christiansen, R. *Forgotten Railways: The West Midlands* (David & Charles, 1985)

Thames and Severn (Vol 13, Regional History of the Railways of Great Britain) (David & Charles, 1981)

The West Midlands (Vol 7, Regional History of the Railways of Great Britain) (David & Charles, 1973)

Clinker, C.R. *The West Somerset Railway: A History in Pictures* (Exmoor Press, 1980)

Coles, C.R.L. *On the North and West Route* (Ian Allan, 1984)

Railways Through the Chilterns (Ian Allan, 1980)

Corris Railway Society *A Return to Corris* (Avon–Anglia, 1988)

Crombleholme, R., Stuckey, D. and Whetmath, C.F.D. *The Culm Valley Light Railway (The Hemyock Branch)* (Branch Line Handbooks, 1964)

Davies, R. and Grant, M.D. *Forgotten Railways: Chilterns and Cotswolds* (David & Charles, 1975)

Farr, M. and others *The Wrington Vale Light Railway* (Avon–Anglia, 1978)

Fenton, D.M. *The Malmesbury Railway* (Oakwood, 1977–Library of Rly History No 41)

Fraser, D., Green, D. and Scott, B. *The Midland and South Western Junction Railway* (Kingfisher, 1985)

Goode, C.T. *The North Warwickshire Railway* (Oakwood, 1978–Locomotion Papers No 114)

Gregory, R.H. *The South Devon Railway* (Oakwood, 1982)

GWR Museum, Swindon *Swindon and the GWR* (GWR Museum, Swindon)

Hale, M. *Twixt London and Bristol* (OPC, 1985)

Holden, J.S. *The Watlington Branch* (OPC, 1974)

The Manchester & Milford Railway (Oakwood, 1979—Library of Rly History No 50)

Hutton, J. *Taff Vale Railway Miscellany* (OPC)

Jackson, B.L. and Tattershall, M.S. *The Bridport Branch* (OPC, 1976)

Jenkins, S.C. *The Fairford Branch* (Oakwood, 1975—Locomotion Papers No 86)

The Great Western & Great Central Joint Railway (Oakwood, 1978—Library of Rly History No 46)

Jenkins, S.C. and Quayle, H.I. *The Oxford, Worcester & Wolverhampton Railway* (Oakwood, 1977—Library of Rly History No 40)

Karau, P. *Great Western Branch Line Termini,* Vols 1 & 2 (OPC, 1977 and 1978)

Kendall, H.G. *The Plymouth & Dartmoor Railway and its forerunners* (Oakwood, 1968—Library of Rly History No 23)

Kidner, R.W. *The Cambrian Railways* (Oakwood, 1954—Library of Rly History No 55)

Kingdom, A.R. *The Ashburton Branch and the Totnes Quay line* (OPC, 1077)

The Princetown Branch (OPC, 1979)

The Yealmpton Branch (S Hams Light Railway) (OPC, 1974)

Krause, I. *Great Western Branch Line Album* (Ian Allan, 1969)

Leigh, C. *Rail Routes in Devon and Cornwall* (Ian Allan, 1982)

Lingard, R. *The Princes Risborough-Thame-Oxford Railway* (OPC, 1979)

The Woodstock Branch (OPC, 1973)

Lucking, J.H. *The Great Western at Weymouth—a railway and shipping history* (David & Charles, 1971)

Madge, R. *Railways Round Exmoor* (Exmoor Press, 1971)

Maggs, C. *The Bath to Weymouth Line* (Oakwood, 1982)

The Bristol Port and Pier and the Clifton Extension Railway (Oakwood, 1975—Library of Rly History No 37)

The East Somerset Railway 1858–1972 (ESR/Avon–Anglia, 1977)

Rail Centres: Bristol (Ian Allan)

Rail Centres: Exeter (Ian Allan, 1985)

Rail Centres: Swindon (Ian Allan, 1983)

The Taunton to Barnstaple Line (Oakwood)

Maggs, C. and Nicholson, P. *The Honeybourne Line* (Line One, 1985)

Messenger, M.J. *Caradon and Looe: The Canal, Railways and Mines* (Twelveheads Press, 1978)

Morgan, H. *South Wales Branch Lines* (Ian Allan, 1984)

Morris, J.P. *The North Pembrokeshire & Fishguard Railway* (Oakwood, 1969—Library of Rly History No 24)

Oakley, M. *Railways in Avon* (Avon–Anglia, 1986)

The Oxford–Hereford Line (BR(W)/Avon–Anglia, 1985)

Paar, H.W. *A History of the Railways of the Forest of Dean,* Part 2: *The Great Western Railway in Dean* (David & Charles, 1965)

Page, J. *Rails in the Valleys* (David & Charles, 1989)

Pearse, M. & J. *Twyford's Railway Heritage* (Twyford & Ruscombe Local History Society, 1985)

Pomroy, L.W. *The Teign Valley Line* (OPC, 1984)

Pope, I., How, Bob and Karau, P. *The Severn & Wye Railway* Vols 1 & 2 (Wild Swan, 1983 and 1985)

Price, M.R.C. *The Lambourn Valley Railway* (Oakwood, 1964—Locomotion Papers No 32)

The Whitland & Cardigan Railway (Oakwood, 1976—Library of Rly History No 39)

Railways of Central and West Wales (BR(W)/Avon–Anglia, 1987)

Robertson, K. and Abbott, D. *GWR: The Badminton Line* (Alan Sutton, 1988)

Roche, T.W.E. *Plymouth & Launceston* (Branch Line Handbooks (No 15), 1965)

Rocksborough-Smith, S. *Main Lines to the West* (Ian Allan, 1981)

Russell, J.H. *The Banbury & Cheltenham Railway 1887–1962* (OPC, 1977)

Sands, T.B. *The Didcot, Newbury & Southampton Railway* (Oakwood, 1971—Library of Rly History No 28)

The Midland & South Western Junction Railway (Oakwood, 1959—Library of Rly History No 16)

Smith, D. J. *The Severn Valley Railway* (Town & Country Press, for the SVR Soc, 1968)

Smith, P. *Forest of Dean Railways* (OPC, 1983)

Smith, T.M. and Heathcliffe, G. *An Illustrated History of the Highworth Branch* (Wild Swan, 1979)

Smith, W. and Beddoes, K. *The Cleobury Mortimer & Ditton Priors Light Railway* (OPC, 1980)

Sprinks, N. and Body, G. *The Heart of Wales Line* (BR(W)/Avon–Anglia, 1981)

Tanner, G.H.J. *The Calne Branch* (OPC, 1972)

Thomas, D.St J. *The Great Way West: the history and romance of the Great Western Railway's route from Paddington to Penzance* (David & Charles, 1975)

The West Country (Vol 1, The Regional History of the Railways of Great Britain) (David & Charles, 1960)

Vaughan, A. *A History of the Faringdon Branch and Uffington Station* (OPC, 1979)

Vaughan, J. *The Newquay Branch and its Branches* (OPC, 1991)

Vincent, M. *Lines to Avonmouth* (OPC, 1979)

Reflections of the Portishead Branch (OPC, 1983)

Through Countryside and Coalfield: the GWR's Bristol & North Somerset Railway (OPC)

Walker, C. *Twixt Hatton & Harbury* (Oxford Illus'd Press, 1973—Steam Railway Scenes No 8)

Warnock, D.W. *The Bristol & North Somerset Railway* 1863–1884 (Temple Cloud, 1978)

Warnock, D.W. and Parsons, R.G. *The Bristol & North Somerset Railway since 1884* (Avon–Anglia, 1979)

White, H.P. *Greater London* (Vol 3, The Regional History of the Railways of Great Britain) (David & Charles, 1963)

Whitehouse, P.B. *Pre-Grouping in the West Midlands* (OPC, 1984)

Wilkinson, R. *The Wantage Tramway* (Oakwood, 1974—Locomotion Papers No 92)

Williams, K. and Reynolds, D. *The Kingsbridge Branch (The Primrose Line)* (OPC, 1977)

Wren, W.J. *The Tanat Valley: its railways and industrial archaeology* (David & Charles, 1968)

Tanat Valley Light Railway (Oakwood, 1979—Library of Rly History No 48)

Wright, I.L. *Branch Line Railways,* Vol 3: *South Wales* (Atlantic, 1988)

Architecture, stations and civil engineering

Body, G. *The Severn Tunnel* (BR(W)/Avon–Anglia, 1986)

BR *The Severn Tunnel and its Pumping Station, Sudbrook* (BR, 1968)

Chapman, W.G. *Track Topics: a book of railway engineering for boys of all ages* (GWR, 1935—various reprints available)

Clark, R.H. *A Historical Survey of Selected Great Western Stations: layouts and illustrations,* Vols 1, 2 & 3 (OPC, 1976, 1979 and 1981) (See also Potts, C.R., for Vol 4)

Clinker, C.R. *Great Western Railway: a register of halts and platforms 1903–1979* (2nd ed, Avon–Anglia, 1979)

New Light on the Gauge Conversion (Avon–Anglia, 1978)

Day, L. Broad Gauge (HMSO)

Karau, P. *Great Western Branch Line Termini,* Vols 1 & 2 (OPC, 1977 and 1978)

Leigh, C. *GWR Country Stations* (Ian Allan, 1981)

Potts, C.R. *A Historical Survey of Selected Great Western Stations: layouts and illustrations,* Vol 4 (OPC, 1985)

Rhodes, M. *British Marshalling Yards* (OPC, 1988)

Rolt, L.T.C. *Isambard Kingdom Brunel* (Longmans, 1957; Pelican, 1970)
Vaughan, A. *A Pictorial Record of Great Western Architecture* (OPC, 1977)
Great Western Railway Junction Stations (Ian Allan, 1989)
Isambard Kingdom Brunel: engineering knight errant (John Murray, 1991)
Walker, T.A. *The Severn Tunnel: its construction and difficulties 1872–1887* (Kingsmead, 1990)

Signalling

Vaughan, A. *A Pictorial Record of Great Western Signalling* (OPC, 1973)

Services

Allen, C.J. *Titled Trains of the Western* (Ian Allan, 1974)
Body, G. *Riviera Express: the train and its route* (BR(W)/Avon–Anglia, 1979)
Chapman, W.G. *Cheltenham Flyer* (GWR, 1934; Patrick Stephens Ltd 1971)
The 10.30 Limited (GWR, 1923; Patrick Stephens Ltd, 1970)
Great Western Railway Timetables of 1865 (GWR, 1865; OPC 1971)
Timetables of the Great Western Railway (GWR, 1902; Ian Allan, 1967)
Timetables: July 18th to September 11th 1932 (GWR, 1932; OPC, 1973)
Timetables, October 6th 1947 and until further notice (GWR, 1947; OPC, 1976)
Locomotive Publishing Co *Great Western Expresses* 1901 (Loco Pub Co 1901; OPC)
Nock, O.S. *Fifty Years of Western Running* (Everard, 1954)
The Limited: the story of the Cornish Riviera Express (Allen & Unwin, 1979)
Peacock, T.B. *Great Western London Suburban Services* (Oakwood, 1978—Locomotion Papers No 48)
Roche, T.W.E. *The Cornish Riviera Limited: a review of the life of a famous train* (Town & Country Press, 1969)
Semmens, P.W.B. *The Heyday of GWR Train Services* (David & Charles, 1991)
Wilson, R.B. *Go Great Western; a history of GWR publicity* (David & Charles, 1970)

Locomotives, sheds and Locomotive Engineers

Bloom, A. *Locomotives of the Great Western Railway* (Jarrold, 1979)
Casserley, H.C. *British Locomotive Names of the Twentieth Century* (Ian Allan, 1963)
Casserley, H.C. and Johnston, S.W. *Locomotives at the Grouping, 4: Great Western Railway* (Ian Allan, 1966)
Castles and Kings: a pictorial tribute (Roundhouse, 1964)
Chapman, W.G. *Caerphilly Castle* (GWR, 1924)
Locos of the Royal Road (GWR, 1936; Patrick Stephens Ltd, 1971)
Coffin, R.O. *Kings of the Great Western* (6000 Loco Assoc, 1977)
Cook, K.J. *Swindon Steam 1921–1951* (Ian Allan, 1974)
Freezer, C.J. *Locomotives in Outline: GWR* (Peco, 1977)
Gasson, H. *Firing Days: reminiscences of a Great Western fireman* (OPC, 1973)
Footplate Days: more reminiscences of a Great Western fireman (OPC, 1976)
Nostalgic Days: further reminiscences of a Great Western fireman (OPC, 1980)
Griffiths, D. *Locomotive Engineers of the GWR* (Patrick Stephens Ltd, 1987)
Griffiths, R. *Locomotive Sheds in Camera* (OPC)
Haresnape, B. *Collett and Hawksworth Locomotives* (Ian Allan, 1978)
Haresnape, B. and Swain, A. *Churchward Locomotives: a pictorial history* (Ian Allan, 1976)
Haswell, E.G.F. and Shepperd, K. *Great Western Shed Diagrams* (Ian Allan, 1969)
Holden, B. and Leech, K.H. *Portraits of 'Kings'* (Moorland 1979)
Judge, C. *Great Western AEC Diesel Railcars* (OPC)
Leech, K.H. *The Great Western Railway 'Kings'* (Stephenson Locomotive Soc, 1962)
Leech, K.H. and Higson, M.F. *Pendennis Castle* (Roundhouse, 1965)
Lyons, E.T. *An Historical Survey of Great Western Engine Sheds, 1947* (OPC 1972; 2nd ed OPC and GW Soc, 1974)
Lyons, E.T. and Mountford, E.R. *A Historical Survey of Great Western Engine Sheds 1837–1947* (OPC, 1979)
Morgan, B. and Meyrick, B. *Behind the Steam* (Hutchinson, 1973)
Mountford, E. *Caerphilly Works 1901–1964* (Roundhouse, 1965)
Nock, O.S. *Great Locomotives of the GWR* (Patrick Stephens Ltd, 1991)
GWR Steam (David & Charles, 1972)
The GWR Stars, Castles and Kings, Parts 1 & 2 (David & Charles, 1967 and 1970)
Engine 6000: the saga of a locomotive (David & Charles, 1972)
Standard Gauge *Great Western 4-4-0s,* Parts 1 & 2 (David & Charles, 1977 and 1978)
The GWR Mixed Traffic 4-6-0 Classes (Ian Allan, 1978)
Railway Correspondence and Travel Society *The Locomotives of the Great Western Railway,* 13 vols (RCTS, 1951–)
Rogers, H.C.B. *G.J. Churchward: a locomotive biography* (Allen & Unwin, 1975)
Rowledge, J.W.P. *GWR Locomotive Allocations 1932–1967* (David & Charles, 1986)
Russell, J.H. *A Pictorial Record of Great Western Engines,* Vols 1 & 2 (OPC, 1975)
A Pictorial Record of Great Western Absorbed Engines (OPC, 1978)
Steele, A.K. *Great Western Broad Gauge Album* (OPC, 1972)
Tuplin, W.A. *Great Western Steam* (Allen & Unwin, 1958)
Great Western Saints and Sinners (Allen & Unwin, 1971)
Great Western Power (Allen & Unwin, 1975)
Veal, C. and Goodman, J. *Heavy Freight: 28XX and 38XX Consolidations of the Great Western* (Great Western Soc, 1980)
Webb, B. *Locomotive Engineers of the GWR* (Ian Allan, 1946)
Whitehurst, B. *Great Western Engines: names, numbers, types, classes: 1940 to preservation* (OPC, 1973)
Wilson, R.B. (ed) *Sir Daniel Gooch: memoirs and diary* (David & Charles, 1972)

Rolling-stock

Atkins, A.G. and others *A History of GWR Goods Wagons,* Vols 1 & 2 (David & Charles, 1975 and 1976)
Harris, M. *Great Western Coaches, 1890–1954* (David & Charles, 1966; 2nd ed 1972)
Mountford, E.R. *A Register of GWR Absorbed Coaching Stock, 1922–3* (Oakwood, 1978)
Russell, J.H. *GWR Freight Wagons and Loads* (OPC)
A Pictorial Record of Great Western Wagons (OPC, 1971; Appendix, 1974)
A Pictorial Record of Great Western Coaches, Part 1 *1838–1903,* Part 2 *1903–1948* and Appendix (OPC, 1972 and 1973)
Great Western Wagon Plans (OPC, 1976)

Modelling

Booth, T.J. *Modellers' Guide to the GWR* (Patrick Stephens Ltd, 1990)
Freezer, C.J. *Locomotives in Outline: GWR* (Peco, 1977)

General

Allen, C.J. *Salute to the Great Western* (Ian Allan, 1970)
Alsop, J. *The Official Railway Postcard Book* (Author, 1987)
Railway Postcard Checklist No 7 (GWR & constituent companies) (Author, 1990)
Arlett, M. and Lockett D. *Great Western Steam in the West Country* (OPC)

Awdry, C. *Encyclopaedia of British Railway Companies* (Patrick Stephens Ltd, 1990)

Beck, K. and Harris, N. *GWR Reflections: a collection of photographs from the Hulton Picture Library* (Silver Link, 1987)

Biddle, G. and Nock, O.S. *The Railway Heritage of Britain* (Michael Joseph, 1983)

Blenkinsop, R.J. *Shadows of the Great Western* (OPC, 1972)

Echoes of the Great Western (OPC, 1973)

Reflections of the Great Western (OPC, 1974)

Silhouettes of the Great Western (OPC, 1976)

D. Bradford Barton—a large number of picture albums—too numerous to list here—have been published by this company, dealing with ex-GWR steam in various locations

Clinker, C.R. *Register of Closed Passenger Stations and Goods Depots, 1830–1980* (Avon-Anglia, 1988)

Cooke, R.A. *Atlas of the Great Western Railway as at 1947* (Wild Swan, 1988)

Earley, M.W. *The Great Western Scene* (OPC, 1970)

Truly the Great Western (OPC, 1975)

England, G. and Blenkinsop, R.J. *Great Western Steam Album* (OPC)

Esau, M. *Spirit of the Great Western* (OPC, 1980)

Gammell, C.J. *Great Western Branch Lines 1955–1965* (OPC, 1975)

Hamilton, J.A.B. *Britain's Railways in World War One* (Allen & Unwin, 1967)

Jowett, A. *Jowett's Railway Atlas of Great Britain and Ireland* (Patrick Stephens Ltd, 1989)

Judge, C.W. *The Great Western Era* (OPC, 1976)

Measom, G. *Illustrated Guide to the Great Western Railway* (Marshall, 1852; facsimile reprint, Berkshire County Library and Countryside Books, 1985)

Montague, K. *Great Western* (OPC, Pocket Railway Books No 2, 1976)

Nock, O.S. and Meadway, C. & W. *Great Western in Colour* (Blandford, 1978)

Nock, O.S. *The Great Western Railway: an appreciation* (Heffer, 1951)

Great Western (Ian Allan, 1975)

Riley, R.C. *Great Western Album Nos 1 & 2* (Ian Allan, 1966 and 1970)

Russell, J. H. *A Great Western Miscellany*, Vols 1 & 2 (OPC, 1978 and 1979)

Terry, T.H. *Great Western Reflections* (OPC, 1984)

Vaughan, A. *Great Western Portrait 1913–21* (OPC, 1971)

Grub, Water & Relief: Tales of the Great Western 1835-1892 (John Murray, 1985)

Grime & Glory: Tales of the Great Western 1892-1947 (John Murray, 1985)

Whitehouse, P. and Thomas, D.StJ. *Great Western Railway: 150 glorious years* (David & Charles, 1984)

Whiteley, J.S. *Great Western Remembered* (OPC, 1985)

INDEX

This Index contains subjects that occur in the Encyclopaedia elsewhere than just under a main heading; subjects that only appear under the appropriate alphabetical main heading are not indexed. Page numbers in **bold** refer to the main entry for that subject.

The letters 'a', 'b' and 'c' following the page number refer to the column on that page. If a subject is mentioned in more than one column of a single entry, only one reference may be given to cover the whole entry, depending on its length. The letter 't' indicates inclusion of the subject in a table.

Page numbers in *italics* refer to illustrations. The letter 'm' signifies that the illustration is a map or plan.

(The Appendices are not included in this Index.)

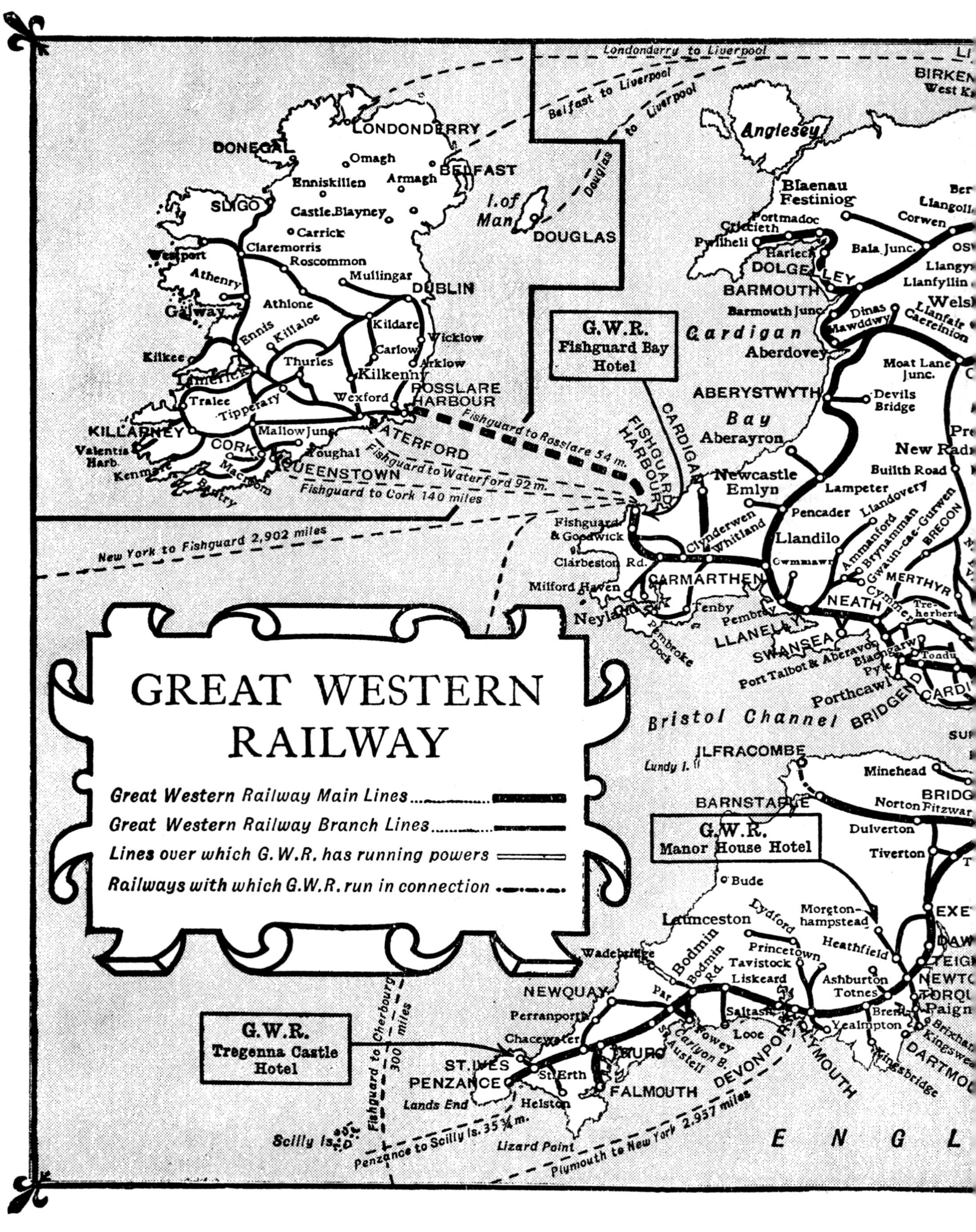

GREAT WESTERN RAILWAY
Great Western Railway Main Lines
Great Western Railway Branch Lines
Lines over which G.W.R. has running powers
Railways with which G.W.R. run in connection
G.W.R. Fishguard Bay Hotel
G.W.R. Manor House Hotel
G.W.R. Tregenna Castle Hotel
Londonderry to Liverpool
Belfast to Liverpool
Douglas to Liverpool
Fishguard to Rosslare 54 m.
Fishguard to Waterford 92 m.
Fishguard to Cork 140 miles
New York to Fishguard 2,902 miles
Fishguard to Cherbourg 300 miles
Penzance to Scilly Is. 35 ¾ m.
Plymouth to New York 2,957 miles
LONDONDERRY
DONEGAL
BELFAST
SLIGO
DUBLIN
I. of Man
DOUGLAS
KILLARNEY
CORK
QUEENSTOWN
WATERFORD
ROSSLARE HARBOUR
Anglesey
Cardigan Bay
Bristol Channel
FISHGUARD HARBOUR
CARMARTHEN
SWANSEA
NEATH
ABERYSTWYTH
BARMOUTH
ILFRACOMBE
BARNSTAPLE
NEWQUAY
PENZANCE
ST. IVES
FALMOUTH
PLYMOUTH
DEVONPORT
Lands End
Lizard Point
Scilly Is.
Lundy I.
E N G L